Real estate and urban development

Real estate and urban development

HALBERT C. SMITH, D.B.A., S.R.P.A.
Professor of Real Estate and Urban Analysis
University of Florida

CARL J. TSCHAPPAT, Ph.D., S.R.E.A., A.I.P.
President
Land Development Analysts, Inc.

RONALD L. RACSTER, Ph.D.
Professor of Real Estate and Urban Analysis
The Ohio State University

Revised edition

1977

RICHARD D. IRWIN, INC. Homewood, Illinois 60430
Irwin-Dorsey Limited Georgetown, Ontario L7G 4B3

Revised Edition

4 5 6 7 8 9 0   5 4 3 2 1 0 9

ISBN 0-256-01931-2

Library of Congress Catalog Card No. 76–49307

Printed in the United States of America

To Ruth, Barbara, and Janie

PREFACE

THE REVIVAL of academic interest in real estate, about which we commented in the Preface to the First Edition of *Real Estate and Urban Development*, appears to have developed into a significant expansion of real estate education in colleges and universities. Courses and programs of real estate education now are offered at many of the leading universities in the United States and Canada. The growth in the number of students majoring in real estate in a number of collegiate business schools has exceeded the growth rate of other, better established disciplines. Furthermore, real estate instruction has expanded dramatically in industry-sponsored and community college programs.

Research in the field of real estate and urban analysis has also continued to increase. Additional centers for research in real estate and urban studies have been established and at least one major new academic journal (*Journal of the American Real Estate and Urban Economics Association*) has been established since 1973 to serve the communication needs of the field. Graduate programs have continued to expand in recognition of the growing sophistication required for real estate analysis. The supply of Ph.D.'s in the field has also increased significantly, yet the demand for college and university teachers and researchers has not been satisfied.

Whether academic interest both by students and faculty will continue to expand or will moderate can only be known with the passage of time. Further expansion, however, will require the discipline to be interesting and relevant to important problems of individuals and society. To this end, we believe that beginning courses in real estate and urban analysis should rely upon basic disciplines such as economics, accounting, psychology, and sociology, and that the teaching-learning process should seek to develop an understanding of the interrelationships among land resources and other productive factors. Further, we believe strongly that a beginning course in real estate should be equally as rigorous as beginning courses in such fields as accounting, economics, and finance. The course should go beyond definitions and current practice; its focus should be real estate, not real estate brokerage. A general approach recognizing the principles and relationships among investment decision-making, urban development, and social problems, determined by the framework of legal, social, and economic systems should be the goal for real estate education.

We were pleased by the acceptance of the First Edition of *Real Estate and Urban Development*. It was used in real estate courses in a number of leading universities. We believe it was recognized as an attempt to bring an integrative, theory-based learning aid to the field of real estate education. This edition, we hope, retains the basic attributes of the First Edition while providing new and updated materials, greater organizational cohesiveness, and improved clarity of style and content.

The Revised Edition retains the same basic organization structure. It is divided into four sections: Framework for Analysis, Investment Opportunity and Constraint, Real Estate Functions, and Real Estate Administration in the Public Sector. New chapters have been added on Real Estate Taxation, Real Estate Planning, and Environmental Issues. The chapter on Federal Income Taxes has been completely rewritten, as have substantial portions of other chapters.

As did the First Edition, this edition attempts to focus upon real estate investment decision-making and execution of those decisions within the urban environment. It further attempts to provide insight into the role of the investment decision-making process both in contributing to and in alleviating social problems of cities. In so doing, much of the material that is traditionally taught in real estate principles courses is included. To comply with the new approach, however, some traditional material is inevitably omitted, while other such materials are reorganized or de-emphasized.

We continue to acknowledge our many debts to numerous people. Our obligations begin with our parents, families, teachers, and friends who have encouraged us along the road of academic pursuit. Economists of the past have developed our field and provided the base upon which a professional approach to real estate analysis can be built. And contemporary scholars such as Raleigh Barlow, Byrl N. Boyce, James R. Cooper, Karl L. Guntermann, Robert O. Harvey, William N. Kinnard, Jr., Stephen P. Messner, Hugh Nourse, Richard U. Ratcliff, Arthur M. Weimer, and Paul F. Wendt have contributed immeasurably to our thinking. We also wish to acknowledge the constructive comments of Robert H. Zerbst, Arthur Warner, James A. Graaskamp, Lester L. Hoover, Bill W. West, and Leonard Vidger whose reviews of the previous edition provided important inputs to this edition. Also, our thanks are extended to our colleagues—Wayne R. Archer, William B. Brueggeman, Clayton C. Curtis, Louis A. Gaitanis, and Herman Kelting—who have provided us with valuable feedback concerning the book's use as a classroom aid.

Our primary goal for the book is that it serve the needs of students beginning their study of real estate in colleges and universities, either at the advanced undergraduate or graduate level. It may also be useful in the growing number of courses and programs required both for the licensing of a new breed of professional real estate business people and for entrance to and maintenance of standing in professional organizations.

February 1977   HALBERT C. SMITH
                                                   CARL J. TSCHAPPAT
                                                   RONALD L. RACSTER

CONTENTS

PART I   Framework for analysis

1. Real estate administration   **3**

Economic importance of real estate. Nature of real estate. Real
estate administration: *Functional activities for administration. The
investment process.* Constraints upon real estate decisions: *Police
power. Taxation. Eminent domain. Doctrine of escheat.*

2. The investment approach   **19**

Premises. Objectives. Investment criteria. Patterns of development:
*Land-use patterns. Theories of urban growth. Proportionality. Ap-
plicability of the investment approach.*

3. Value: The central idea   **39**

Value as a market concept: *Value in a perfectly competitive market.
Real estate market characteristics.* Market value. Investment value.
Market value, price, and cost. The concept of highest and best use:
Vacant site. Improved sites.

4. The measurement of value   **57**

Value estimation by income capitalization: *Nature of the income
approach. The capitalization process. Valuation inputs. Examples
of the income approach. Several techniques, but only one estimated
market value.* Value estimation by direct sales comparison. Value
estimation by cost analysis: *Relation of cost to value. Reproduction
cost. Accrued depreciation—penalties. Cost approach example.*

5. The investment calculation **91**

Investment value and investment profitability. Investment value calculation: *Income flows. Investment value from appraisal methodologies. Investment value from aftertax cash flow. Determinants of the required return on equity.* Investment criteria: *Multipliers. Financial ratios. Profitability ratios.* Varying the assumptions: *Role of computers.* Motivation of investors.

PART II   Investment opportunity and constraint

6. Productivity analysis **115**

Nature of productivity: *Elements of productivity. Significance of the distinction between transfer characteristics and physical characteristics. Implications of the distinction between transfer characteristics and physical characteristics.* Physical characteristics: *Analysis of physical characteristics—the site. Analysis of physical characteristics—the major improvement. Use of checklists.* Transfer characteristics: *The use assumption. Analysis procedure.*

7. Market analysis **130**

Market functions. Market models: *Implications of theory.* Determinants of demand: *Need for housing and other types of real estate. Societal trends. Values and attitudes. National income. Regional income. Community income. Price structure.* Determinants of supply: *Anticipations of demand. Utilization of existing real estate resources. Availability and prices of land and utilities. Availability and price of financing. Availability and prices of materials and labor. Taxes.* Conceptualizing the local housing market: *Filtering.* Market and feasibility analyses: *Market analysis. Feasibility analysis.*

8. Property ownership rights **167**

Working definition of real estate and real property. Real estate descriptions: *Street and number. Metes and bounds. Monuments. Government or rectangular survey. Recorded plat.* Personal property and fixtures. Real property ownership rights: *Freehold estates of inheritance. Freehold estates not of inheritance. Less than freehold estates. Incorporeal property rights.* Ownership by more than one person. Property ownership strategy.

9. Conveying ownership rights **190**

Conveyancing functions: *Making an offer. Reaching agreement. Closing the sale. Transferring ownership. The deed. Searching title. Securing funds. Transferring partial ownership rights. Minimizing equity investment: The land contract. Selling the property. Other functions.*

10. Income taxation and real estate decisions   228

Investment real estate: *Depreciation. Deduction of operating expenses and interest expense. Capital gains. Tax preference items and the minimum tax.* Tax deferral: *Exchanges. Installment sale.* Tax factors affecting the homeowner.

PART III Real estate functions

11. Real estate marketing   261

The marketing mix. Marketing strategy: *Unimproved acreage sales. Predeveloped land sales. Developed land sales. Improved land sales. Resale property sales. Leasing as a marketing specialty. Marketing specialized services. Buyer market segmentation.* The buying process: *Stages in the buying process. Buying process roles. Benefits of buying process analysis.* Marketing properties or service? *Firms as monopolistic competitors. Firms as oligopolists. Price-fixing.* Developing monopolistic advantage. Legal framework of real estate marketing.

12. Real estate production   285

Economic significance. Implications of theory. Land development: *Activities in land development. Significance to urban development. Role of the developer-investor. Role of the development lender. Role of the secondary financing market.* Construction: *Structure of the industry. The construction process. Functions. Role of the builder. Administrative problems and considerations.*

13. Real estate financing   315

Flow of funds to finance real estate: *Savings and loan associations. Life insurance companies. Commercial banks. Mutual savings banks. Real estate investment trusts. Mortgage bankers. Summary of the flow of funds into real estate finance.* Lending and borrowing decisions: *Types of real estate loans. Financial analysis.* Instruments of real estate finance. Specialized types of real estate finance: *Condominiums. Cooperatives. Real estate syndicates.* Risk in real estate financing. Government influence on real estate finance: *Regulation of the supply of funds and interest rates. Secondary market activities. Supervision and insurance. Mortgage loan insurance and guarantee. Special aid for low-income housing and urban renewal. Taxation.*

14. Real estate planning   354

Public planning: *Comprehensive planning. Zoning. Social and economic issues.* Private planning. Trends and the future.

PART IV   Real estate administration in the public sector

15.   Government involvement in real estate decisions   371

The role of government: *How much government? Public sector decision makers.* The decision-making process in the public sector. Economic analysis in the decision-making process.

16.   Real estate taxation   385

Nature of the property tax. Establishing the tax rate. Special assessments. Economic and social issues.

17.   Government in housing and community development   394

Reasons for government involvement. Housing: *Unsubsidized. Subsidized.* Community development: *Urban renewal. Rehabilitation and conservation. Direct block grants.* Impact of federal housing programs: *Policy for the provision of adequate housing. Income redistribution effects.*

18.   Environmental issues and real estate development   412

Rise of environmental concern: *Underlying factors of environmental concern.* Responses to environmental concern: *Federal response. U.S. Army Corps of Engineers. State response.* Economic aspects of environmental issues: *Externalities. Marginal cost pricing. Economies of scale. Cost-benefit analysis.* Trends and the future.

19.   Urban transportation and real estate development   437

Urban transportation system: *User benefits. Transportation and the value of urban sites. Regional effects. Transportation and urban land use. The traffic artery as an urban land use.* Urban transportation problem: *Alleviation of the urban transportation problem.*

20.   Overview   460

Prognosis

Appendixes   467

Glossary of terms   537

Index   553

PART I

Framework
for analysis

chapter 1

REAL ESTATE
ADMINISTRATION

ALL PEOPLE USE REAL ESTATE. Upon it and within it we eat, sleep, walk, ride, sit, and perform every other activity of human endeavor. Businesses use real estate to support and protect employees, machines, and capital goods. Private and public institutions and governments similarly use real estate to house and protect employees, to protect equipment and other valuable items, to provide areas of recreation and training, and to create monumental symbols of prestige and status. Even spacecraft depend upon guidance and sustenance from the earth, and the space travelers of tomorrow will regard a certain area of the earth's surface as their home base. The preamble to the Code of Ethics of the National Association of Realtors emphasizes the all-pervasive influence of real estate on human affairs in stating the truism, "Under all is the land."

Because of the extent to which real estate must be used by human beings, it has received much attention by economists, lawyers, agronomists, geologists, archeologists, architects, and home gardeners. Our concern is primarily one of economic utilization of land resources, recognizing that within this viewpoint we must consider the privileges and limitations provided by the law and the utility characteristics imparted by factors such as fertility, mineral composition, and building design. The importance of economic theory is recognized throughout the book as the basis for real estate analysis.

The use of economic principles in controlling the use of real estate is manifested in decisions regarding the size of a parcel of land to be utilized for a particular purpose, the size and type of structure to be constructed, the legal rights to be obtained in a transaction, and many other kinds of decisions, such as whether to buy, sell, or improve a given

3

parcel of real estate or let it deteriorate. The rationale upon which such decisions are based, the process by which the decisions are made, and the considerations that enter into the decision-making process for real estate are all parts of the subject matter of this book. We attempt to provide an integrated study of real estate from the viewpoint of a decision-maker who considers real estate to be an investment.

Hoagland has aptly chided the American public for its lack of knowledge about real estate and the decision-making processes affecting it by pointing out, "All Americans 'know' real estate.... At least most of us think we do."[1] The implication of this observation is, of course, that while usage of the physical commodity brings a feeling of familiarity, this is not sufficient for acquiring an understanding of the economic, social, and legal processes affecting land usage. Yet this knowledge is the key to maximizing successfully the usefulness of real estate. It is the source of understanding about how people explicitly or implicitly strive to obtain maximum benefit from the resources available.

Economic importance of real estate

Perhaps the first step in gaining an understanding of real estate is to obtain a feel for its relative importance and magnitude in the national economy. To grasp the importance of land resources, we may note that privately owned urban real estate constitutes approximately $1,600 billion (about 50 percent) of the national wealth.[2] New construction annually contributes almost 10 percent to the gross national product. The construction industry is the largest single industry classified and employs approximately 3.5 million people directly and millions more in related activities. Credit for real estate, which enables people to buy and build homes, offices, schools, apartments, churches, stores, and factories, is the largest single component of debt in the country and has expanded from 46.8 percent of private long-term debt in 1920 to approximately 60 percent in 1973. In actual amounts, mortgage debt increased from $25.5 billion to more than $635 billion during this period. The purchase of a home is often a family's single largest investment, and about 64 percent of the occupied housing units in the United States are owned by the occupants.[3]

Nature of real estate

Real estate is not simply the earth's surface. Rather, it is a term com-

---

[1] Henry E. Hoagland, *Real Estate Principles* (New York: McGraw-Hill, 1955), p. 1.

[2] U.S. Bureau of the Census, *Statistical Abstract of the United States: 1975*, 96th ed. (Washington, D.C.: U.S. Government Printing Office, 1975), p. 411.

[3] Ibid., p. 718.

monly used to denote the physical "good" involved in the legal concept of real property. Although the term *property* connotes legal rights in the use or the exclusive right to control an economic good—in this case a parcel of real estate—the terms *real estate* and *real property* are often used interchangeably in everyday affairs.

In addition to the earth's surface the concept of real property includes the air space above the earth's surface and the earth beneath the surface, extending theoretically to the center of the earth. Since this planet is a spheroid, the resulting shape of a square or rectangular parcel of surface land is an inverted pyramid, with the apex at the earth's center. The pyramid is not closed at the base because no limit is known in space.

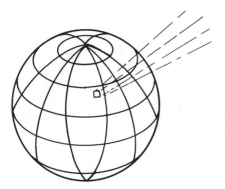

One may ask several interesting questions concerning this concept of real estate: Must property owners allow airplanes, spacecraft, or rockets to fly through their real property? Does one theoretically own areas of other planets or stars when these space bodies are in the path of the outer fringes of the inverted pyramid? Although interesting, such questions have no practical significance. Public rights for the operation of aircraft have been decreed to exist a reasonable height above the earth's surface, and the concept of land would undoubtedly end at the outer limit of the earth's atmosphere. Also, the earth orbits and rotates in such a manner that no other heavenly body would remain in the inverted pyramid's path for more than an instant.

More practical questions arise concerning exactly what physical items within the inverted pyramid are considered to be real estate. The law makes a major distinction between real property and personal property. Usually real property consists of ownership rights in land, buildings permanently attached to the land, growing crops, trees, and other vegetation gaining its sustenance from the earth, minerals below the earth's surface, and the air space. Problems and disagreements often come about with respect to whether given items, such as carpet, drapes, television antennas, and so on, are part of the real estate when it is being sold.[4] However, if an item is considered a permanent part of a building, it is legally considered to be real estate.

Finally, we may point out that there are many interests in real estate other than complete ownership. Life estates, reversions, remainders, and leaseholds are examples of real property interests that may have value and are governed by real property law.[5]

REAL ESTATE ADMINISTRATION

Real estate resources are allocated among various economic units in the economy. Individuals, businesses, governments, and institutions acquire, hold, and dispose of real estate as the need arises and they are financially able to do so. The processes of making a decision as to the proper course of action and the carrying out of a decision once it has been made comprise the framework of microadministration. An understanding of these processes is necessary for one to be assured that intelligent decisions are made and that they are properly carried out. Only when most individual investors understand this process will effective competition result in efficient utilization of land resources. Needless to say, when unintelligent decisions are made or proper decisions regarding real estate utilization are ineffectively executed, the overall (or macro) result is a loss of benefit to society.

Microadministration. As suggested above, administration can be viewed from two perspectives—"micro" and "macro." In the "micro" sense, administration involves the decision-making phase and the execution phase. As shown in Figure 1–1, these phases are further divided into

FIGURE 1–1

Microadministration

Decision-Making	*Execution*
1. Determine objectives.	1. Plan the operation.
2. Develop hypotheses.	2. Organize the factors of production
3. Collect and analyze data.	(land, labor, capital, and
4. Specify alternatives.	management).
5. Formulate conclusions.	3. Direct the operation.
6. Make a decision.	4. Control the operation.

the functions that must be performed in each process. The steps in formulating a decision are essentially an application of the scientific method,

---

[4] The tests that courts apply to such disagreements are discussed more fully in Chapter 8.

[5] These interests are discussed more fully in Chapter 8.

while the execution process utilizes the management functions of planning, organizing, directing, and controlling. Although management theorists would undoubtedly prefer the entire decision-making process to be included as a part of the planning function, we feel that separating decision-making from execution more accurately describes the concept of administration. The decision-making process employs microeconomic analysis and is quite different from the action implied in the management functions of the executive process. Microadministration basically involves accomplishment of a given objective by working with people. Weimer, Hoyt, and Bloom emphasize that it involves action.[6] Individuals, business firms, and government agencies make decisions and carry them out by seeing that the necessary tasks are accomplished by employees or professional agents.

Further, we should note that the activities concerning real estate of producing, marketing, financing, appraising, counseling, managing, and consulting are the functions to which the process of microadministration is applied. In accomplishing these functions, individual business firms and government agencies perform the administrative process. Decisions that arise in the performance of real estate functions are made by people in these economic units and are executed through people employed temporarily or permanently.

Although the administrative process implies rational behavior both in the decision-making phase and in the management phase, human emotions often result in irrational decisions and behavior. Psychological and sociological theories and research have provided much insight into how people react in certain situations; certainly synthesis of current knowledge and continuation of research in these two fields could be of great value to real estate businesses. For example, answers to such questions as which features attract homebuyers and why, how various kinds of living arrangements in apartment buildings influence the behavior patterns of groups, and what factors business executives consider to be most important in deciding where to locate offices and plants would provide better bases for decisions by sales people, planners, architects, and investors. We should hope for and expect much more of this type of investigation in the future. However, knowledge of individual and social actions does not negate the primary value of approaching the study of real estate within a functional, decision-making, and managerial framework. We assume that rational behavior in the solution of investment problems is always to be preferred to irrational, seat-of-the-pants decisions.

This viewpoint does not deny the value of using research results produced by the application of behavioral tools; indeed, we have incorporated

[6] Arthur M. Weimer, Homer Hoyt, and George F. Bloom, *Real Estate*, 6th ed. (New York: Ronald Press, 1972), p. 14.

such knowledge in various sections of the book, particularly in the chapter on real estate marketing.[7] Rather, a behaviorist framework constitutes another way of viewing the *same* problem or process, and it attempts to provide better data for the functional process. To state our position another way, psychological and social factors may determine the nature of the inputs to the various steps in the administrative process, but these steps or functions are still present.

Steps two through five of the decision-making phase depicted in Figure 1–1 involve applied economic analysis. This analysis is often the least understood and the most infrequently used portion of the administrative process, particularly for decisions made by small-scale, individual investors. Nevertheless, it is essential, and its misuse or nonuse renders the remaining portion of the process meaningless. Thus, a major effort of this book is to present a logical framework for the economic analysis and to integrate the determinants of economic objectives into the framework.

Macroadministration. In the "macro" point of view we are concerned with the total effect of all the individual decisions. The *process* of *administering* is not the focus as in the "micro" viewpoint; rather, the organization for and the results of microadministration are the topics considered in macroadministration. Under organization we study and analyze the units into which the economy is organized for accomplishing real estate functions or activities. Thus, the nature, organization structures, interrelationships, and effects on resource allocation of business firms, government agencies, and private investors, together with the laws, regulations, and policies affecting them are the topics of macroadministration.

Particularly important in the macroadministration of real estate is the role of the federal government. It is the country's largest property owner, and decisions regarding the purchase, disposition, or use of such property often affect many persons. For example, the decision to close a military base can have dire economic effects upon a community, region, or state. More importantly, however, several governmental (or quasi-governmental) agencies, such as the Federal Home Loan Bank Board, Federal Home Loan Mortgage Corporation, Department of Housing and Urban Development, Federal Reserve Board, Environmental Protection Agency, Federal National Mortgage Association, and the Government National Mortgage Association, play crucial roles in real estate administration. They regulate the flow of funds to real estate, administer programs for housing and community development, control the general economic climate, regulate environmental matters, and channel funds into real estate uses. *In short, microadministration concerns the decision-making and managerial process, while macroadministration concerns the manner in which economic functions are performed.*

---

[7] See Chapter 11.

Functional activities for administration

Activities regarding real estate are performed by individuals, private businesses, and governmental agencies. In carrying out their activities or functions, these persons, businesses, or government agencies engage in the process of administration—they make decisions and execute them. Individuals purchase residential real estate for the purpose of consuming its services, and they invest in income-producing real estate for the purpose of earning a profit or return on their investment. They also must decide whether to sell, improve, expand, modify, or allow their properties to deteriorate. In making and carrying out such decisions, individuals may perform most or all of the activities to which real estate administration is applied. For example, an individual might appraise, finance, purchase, and improve a parcel of real estate. Usually, however, many of the functions are carried out by specialists or specialized firms, whose activities cause them to be considered part of the real estate business.

As with all businesses in a private enterprise economy, a real estate business will exist only so long as it performs a useful service for which members of society are willing to pay an amount sufficient to enable the business to earn a long-run profit. The various types of real estate businesses are discussed under the activities they are organized to accomplish.

Governmental agencies perform activities concerning real estate in carrying out the decisions and programs formulated by the legislative branches of government. Since the state legislatures and Congress are elected by the voting public, the nature and direction of these programs over the long run must be approved by society.

Producing. The production of physical real estate resources involves the construction of buildings, the modification of existing buildings, the application to land of nonbuilding improvements (such as blacktopping for a parking lot or landscaping for a public park), and the development of raw land so that additional capital improvements may be applied. These activities are usually performed by firms that specialize in development and construction—remodeling, demolishing, landscaping, and paving. Construction firms usually specialize by type of structures erected; for example, some firms build only single-family residences, while others specialize in erecting the steel framework for skyscrapers.

Marketing. Marketing activities are performed by real estate brokerage firms, speculative construction and development firms, individuals, government agencies, and businesses that wish to sell real estate without engaging a broker. Most real estate marketing activity is carried on by subdivision development and construction firms and by brokerage firms. Development and construction firms often build entire subdivisions and market each house on a speculative basis (that is, no buyer has agreed to purchase the house before construction). Brokerage firms enter into a contract, usually with the owner of real estate, agreeing to attempt to find a buyer for the property. If the firm is successful, it will earn a commission percentage on the property's sale price. The Realtors National Marketing Institute (an affiliate of the National Association of Realtors) is the principal professional organization in this field.

Financing. The financing of real estate is performed primarily by private financial institutions. Commercial banks, mutual savings banks, savings and loan associations, and life insurance companies provide approximately 75 percent of the dollar value of all mortgage financing. The remaining portion is furnished by trust funds, pension funds, endowment funds, government agencies, individuals, and nonfinancial businesses. When obtaining financing, the borrower (mortgagor) usually signs a note evidencing the debt to the lender (mortgagee) and also executes a mortgage. The mortgage pledges the property for possible sale in case the mortgagor defaults on the debt to the mortgagee. The decision-making phase of financing concerns whether or not a loan will be made, while the management (or execution) phase involves the actual lending and supervision processes (see Figure 1–1).

Appraising. Real estate appraisal has as its objective the estimation of value of specific parcels of real estate. The activity is performed primarily by professional appraisers and real estate brokers. Brokers are usually knowledgeable about markets and the factors which create value, but they frequently cut short most of the appraisal function in order to arrive quickly at a *listing price.* Professional appraising involves rigorous analysis of various types of market data.[8] Normally brokers have not been adequately trained in appraisal methodology nor do they usually maintain the files of market information required to perform the appraisal function. The appraiser is a specialized consultant and in recent years has gained much prominence in the shaping of real estate decisions. Three professional organizations—the Society of Real Estate Appraisers, the American Institute of Real Estate Appraisers, and the American Society of Appraisers—have been instrumental in upgrading the standards and educational requirements for those wishing to enter the appraisal field in the United States. In Canada, the Appraisal Institute of Canada, as well as the Society of Real Estate Appraisers, has performed this function.

Consulting and counseling. Various types of consultants are often required in matters concerning real estate. With the complexity of real property law, the lawyer is often required. Architects may be employed to design functional and aesthetically desirable buildings. Engineers may be required to design and oversee the construction of factories, bridges, roads, and other land improvements. Economists and business analysts may be needed to search out and analyze locations and to provide analysis, suggestions, and a continual review of microadministrative procedures.

---

[8] Professional appraising is explained more fully in Chapter 4.

Counseling is usually regarded as a more narrow term than consulting in the real estate field. The American Society of Real Estate Counselors (an affiliate of the National Association of Realtors) has popularized the term in regard to the type of service offered by its members, although the counseling function is not limited to those who are members of the organization. Counseling entails the rendering of investment advice to a client. An estimate of the value of a parcel of real estate may be one of the major considerations in the decision process of investors, but it is not the only important factor. The investors' financing requirements, their income tax situation, their portfolio of other investments, and their personal preferences should be considered by the counselor-consultant in advising clients about investment decisions.

Managing. The function of managing a property is often performed by a hired property management firm. For smaller investment properties the owner sometimes performs the management function. Whether a hired manager or the owner does it, however, management involves expense in terms of the manager's fees or the owner's time. Hired managers have become increasingly important since World War II because of the great mobility of the population which has led to increasing absentee ownership of real estate. It is not uncommon for the owner of a small parcel of investment real estate in the North to vacation in Florida during the winter months, leaving property in the hands of a professional manager. The Institute of Real Estate Management (also an affiliate of the National Association of Realtors), which awards the CPM (Certified Property Manager) designation to highly trained and qualified property managers, is the main professional organization in this field.

The investment process

It cannot be emphasized too strongly that the analysis and decisions concerning real estate are similar to the analysis and decisions concerning other factors of production and other investments which represent combinations of resources. Because real estate is often studied independently from other factors of production, the similarities between the various investments are obscured. Obviously, real estate, with its fixity of location and high-unit value, can be differentiated from other resources, and the law affecting real property is in many ways different from that affecting personal property. However, of primary importance is not the differences, but rather an understanding of the total investment process and how the *process is applied to real estate.*

The central theme of this book is that the theory of investment is relevant to the decision-making process involving real estate. The theory may be defined as the identification of factors causing people and firms to make decisions about income-producing assets and the description and measurement of the relationships among those factors. Investment theory boils down to the fundamental proposition that investors give up or pay a certain amount of valuable asset (often money) for the right to receive income or other valuable benefits in return. Algebraically, this proposition may be expressed in the following way:

$$P = (f)B$$

where P equals price or value, (f) is the functional relationship, and B equals the benefits to be derived, perhaps over a period of years. An understanding of investment theory allows one to analyze and predict how decisions will be made and thus how parcels of real estate will be developed. Analyzing patterns of decisions allows one to understand and predict city growth and development.

CONSTRAINTS UPON REAL ESTATE DECISIONS

Although real estate decisions are made within the framework of private enterprise, four major types of constraints limit an investor's scope of decision-making authority. These limitations represent the government's residual, but inherent, powers to legislate and regulate on behalf of the general welfare and to claim unowned property. While real estate is subject to many indirect influences (such as economic and social trends) all direct limitations in the form of laws and regulations emanate from one or more of the following four categories: police power, right of taxation, right of eminent domain, and doctrine of escheat.

Police power

The police power represents the right of governmental units to limit the rights that individual property owners have in their property. The justification of the police power is for the protection of the general welfare of all people in the regulation of public health, morals, and safety. McQuillan has noted that this power concerns "the inherent right of people through organized government to protect their health, life, limb, individual liberty of action, property, and to provide for public order, peace, safety, and welfare."[9] Examples of uses of the police power with respect to real estate are in the areas of zoning, building codes, open housing laws, and the licensing of real estate brokers.

Zoning. Zoning involves the division of a city or other area into districts for various types of land uses. The zones or districts are usually delineated within a pattern established by a city plan. Within a zone

---

[9] Eugene McQuillan, *The Law of Municipal Corporations,* 3d ed. (Chicago: Callaghan and Co., 1949), vol. 6, p. 464.

such aspects as the height of buildings, the proportion of land covered by the building, and the uses to which the building may be put are regulated. In zoning residential areas, density may also be controlled by requiring a specified number of square feet of area or a given number of lineal feet of frontage per structure. Most zoning laws will not allow the invasion into one zone of a use from another zone. Thus, industrial uses are not allowed to enter a residential district.

Although zoning necessarily places limitations upon the rights of individual property owners, most experts as well as the general population seem to feel that zoning accomplishes worthwhile objectives such as raising land values, reducing traffic problems and nuisances, and improving the allocation of public utilities and recreational facilities. In order for zoning to be successful, however, the right amount of land must be set aside for each type of use. If an oversupply of land is zoned for commercial use while insufficient land is zoned for industrial use, the prices of the latter will be bid up relatively out of proportion to the former. Thus, zoning authorities must be cognizant of the economic needs of the city both now and in the future. Furthermore, the zoning ordinance must not be a straitjacket of inflexibility. Exceptions are usually needed to allow the overall plan to be realistically workable; nevertheless, indiscriminate and unnecessary deviation should not be allowed. As with most restrictions, therefore, zoning must combine inflexibility with a tempering degree of flexibility so that legitimate exceptions to the rule may be made.[10]

Building codes. Building codes regulate the quality and strength of materials for the purposes of controlling safety, fire prevention, and sanitation. The thickness and height of walls, spacing of beams and girders, and allowable stresses are usually governed, as well as the control over plumbing, vents, ventilation, height and size of rooms, and strength of materials that go into the building.

Building codes are established by local government agencies, usually the municipal governments. As with zoning ordinances, we should note that the regulations should stress a tempering rigidity with a degree of flexibility. In this case the flexibility refers to the ability of obtaining changes in building codes as new materials and construction processes replace older methods and materials. In too many cases in the past, building codes have not measured up to this requirement. A result has been in some cases a lack of progress. A good example is St. Louis, Missouri, which for many years enforced very restrictive, archaic building codes. In 1961 a change in the building code allowing utilization of newer materials resulted in a downtown building boom which continued for several years after the change.[11]

---

[10] Appendix B describes some typical zoning requirements and procedures.

[11] Robert L. Bartley, "Business Helps St. Louis Fight Decay," *Wall Street Journal* 46, no. 159 (May 26, 1966): 14.

Although building codes by their nature must deal with some details, the amount of detail should be limited to an absolute minimum, while the emphasis is placed upon the objectives to be accomplished. The modern approach is to state standards in terms of *capacity to perform* rather than in terms of the *amounts* and *kinds* of materials going into the structure. Such criteria would encourage the introduction of improved building methods and materials.

A major problem with building codes has been that they differ among communities within the same metropolitan area. This situation forces construction firms to know several different code requirements, unnecessarily complicating their work. In many cities it also has resulted in special interest groups having a great deal of influence over the code. Dealers of presently approved products and craft unions understandably fight code changes which could weaken their market positions. Such groups can form strong lobbies against major improvements, such as the acceptance of prefabricated units or more efficient new products. Recommendations for the improvement of building codes have included the placement of code formulation and enforcement at the state government level. The codes would be uniform for an entire state and would be less subject to pressures from local, special interest groups.[12]

Licensing of brokers. Licensing is required in practically every state before one may perform the functions of a real estate broker or sales representative. Although this limitation is not directly concerned with an individual parcel of real estate, it does have considerable influence upon the total market activity for real estate resources. The license laws are designed to set a minimum standard of competence and honesty for real estate brokers. As is the case with respect to the licensing of physicians, attorneys, dentists, and other professional and business activities deemed to be in the public welfare, the licensing of real estate brokers has as its objective the protection of the public in an area where special, technical knowledge is required. It should be noted that the license laws presently do not contain standards that would elevate the real estate brokerage business to that of a profession. However, many states require varying amounts of basic education in real estate either prior or subsequent to licensing. While some licensed brokers and sales personnel pursue more advanced education, advancement of the field is limited by the vast numbers of licensees who achieve only the required, minimum levels of education and training.

Open housing laws. Statutes and court decisions outlaw discrimination in real estate transactions on the basis of race, religion, sex, or national origin. Although the federal fair housing law, some state fair housing laws,

---

[12] Carl J. Tschappat, "The Modernization of Building Codes" (unpublished paper, September 1965).

and the U.S. Supreme Court decision outlawing discrimination occurred in the late 1960s, a number of laws had been enacted in the early and mid-1960s by a few cities and states to forbid housing discrimination. These early efforts were sporadic and some suffered setbacks. For example, a state fair housing law enacted by the legislature in California was over-turned by referendum. However, a 1966 decision of the California Supreme Court declared the referendum to be unconstitutional. Also in 1966, a federal fair housing law was introduced in Congress as part of civil rights legislation. And, in 1963 an order barring discrimination in transactions involving government underwritten loans was issued by President Kennedy.

On April 11, 1968, Title VIII of the Civil Rights Act of 1968 was signed into law by President Johnson. This law bans discrimination in the sale, rental, and leasing of housing *except* in the rental of apartments up to four units in size if the owner occupies one of the units, by religious organizations or private clubs, and by homeowners not using the services of an agent. These exemptions were negated by a decision of the U.S. Supreme Court in 1968 that the federal Civil Rights Act of 1866 outlawed *all* racial discrimination in housing. Additionally, some states also passed laws closing all avenues of discrimination in housing. For example, the Ohio fair housing law (House Bill 432) which took effect on November 12, 1969, outlaws discrimination in the sale, rental, or leasing of housing on the basis of race, color, religion, national origin, or ancestry.[13]

Taxation

Although the right of taxation has been said to be the right to stifle or kill worthwhile projects, the lack of the right of taxation would be even more disastrous. Collective action through governments is a necessity for the operation of modern societies. Therefore, governments (other than the federal government) have the right to impose taxes upon the property within their jurisdictions. Much of the burden of providing needed services and facilities by local governments is incurred by the tax on real property. As with other liens, when tax payments are not made the property may be sold to satisfy the debt.[14]

Although the federal government is prohibited from taxing property directly, the earnings produced by property are taxable in the form of federal income taxes. The federal income tax has an important bearing upon the decision-making process and will be considered in those investment calculations.[15] Suffice it to note here that the income tax is in reality merely an *indirect* tax upon property of all types, real and personal.

---

[13] See Appendix A for the provisions of these major antidiscrimination housing laws.

[14] Real estate taxation is discussed in Chapter 16.

[15] This is discussed more fully in Chapter 10.

Eminent domain

The right of eminent domain is the right of governments and other designated agencies to take private property for public use. When relinquishing private property for public use, the owners must be compensated for the value of the property taken. Although they have the right to be paid, title holders do not have the option of refusing to give up their property. The right of eminent domain is one which can force owners to sell for just compensation even if owners do not wish to sell.

Often the governmental agencies cannot agree with the owner of the property as to what just compensation for the property is. When agreement cannot be reached, the governmental agency will condemn the property, and the court will determine the amount of just compensation. The right of eminent domain is vested in the federal government, the various state governments, municipal governments, and other public corporations such as public utilities whose function is regarded as essential to the public welfare.

Doctrine of escheat

The doctrine of escheat, although much less onerous than other limitations, nevertheless restricts the absolute control of property by private individuals. This doctrine is of common law origin and states, in effect, that when there are no longer any identifiable owners of a particular parcel of real estate, ownership or title to the real estate will vest in the state. This doctrine has greater influence upon private personal property such as bank accounts, savings and loan accounts, and so on, which many times go unclaimed by owners. With respect to real estate this type of occurrence is much less frequent, but nevertheless it does occur.

SUMMARY

If this brief overview of the real estate field seems to describe a large, multifaceted, complex sphere of activities, the impression is correct. In the segment of microadministration, decisions are made and actions are taken in a number of different types of business firms. Construction firms, real estate marketing firms, management firms, appraisal firms, consulting firms, land development firms, and financial institutions all play important roles in the field of real estate.

Many decisions involving real estate are also made by public or government agencies. Local governments pass zoning ordinances, and building and housing codes. They also levy real estate taxes. State governments build highways and decide who can and cannot be in the real estate business. The federal government owns and leases much real estate and occasionally buys and sells property. More importantly, however, several government agencies, such as the Department of Housing and Urban Development, the Federal Home Loan Bank Board, the Federal Reserve System, the Federal National Mortgage Association, the Federal Housing Administration, the Government National Mortgage Association, the Federal Home Loan Mortgage Corporation, and the Environmental Protection Agency, regulate many aspects of real estate activity and help channel funds into the mortgage market.

The results of all these decisions and influences within a framework of legal constraints produce patterns of types of institutions, funds flows, and land uses which can be studied in the area of macroadministration. Basic mechanisms contributing to these patterns are commonalities in laws, economic behavior, psychological makeup, and social mores. The legal framework results from the four types of public limitations on property rights—police power, taxation, eminent domain, and the doctrine of escheat. The decision-making or investment process is the means by which these commonalities are translated into patterns of behavior. This process, the legal framework, functions performed, and the influences of public decision-makers are the general topics for consideration in this book.

QUESTIONS FOR REVIEW

1. Why is the term *administration* important to an understanding of real estate?
2. How would you distinguish between administration and decision-making?
3. What kinds of organizations serve mainly a macroadministrative function?
4. What control do you have of activities that may occur in the air space above your land?
5. Can you identify real estate firms in your community engaged in each of the functional activities of producing, marketing, financing, appraising, counseling, managing, and consulting?
6. Why is investment theory important in understanding real estate?
7. Would you pay more or less than $2,000 for the right to receive $1,000 per year for the next two years? Would you pay more or less than $10,000 for the right to receive $1,000 per year for the next ten years? Why?
8. What are the reasons for limiting private property rights of real estate owners? Do you believe additional limitations will be placed on ownership rights? If so, what types of additional limitations do you foresee?
9. The real estate tax is often cited as being an unfair and regressive tax. Can you think of reasons that it could be regarded in this way?

REFERENCES

Calkins, Robert D. "The Decision-Making Process in Administration." *Business Horizons* 2, no. 3 (Fall 1959): 19–25.

Hoagland, Henry E.   *Real Estate Principles.* New York: McGraw-Hill, 1955, chap. 1.

Kinnard, William N., Jr.   "Reducing Uncertainty in Real Estate Decisions." Beyer-Nelson Distinguished Lecture at Ohio State University, 1968. Published in *Real Estate Appraiser* 34, no. 7 (November–December 1968): 10–16.

Ratcliff, Richard U.   *Real Estate Analysis.* New York: McGraw-Hill, 1961, chap. 1.

Simon, Herbert A.   *The New Science of Management Decision.* New York: Harper & Row, 1960.

Weimer, Arthur M.   "Real Estate Decisions Are Different." *Harvard Business Review* 44, no. 6 (November–December 1966): 105–12.

Weimer, Arthur M.; Hoyt, Homer; and Bloom, George F.   *Real Estate.* 6th ed. New York: Ronald Press, 1972, chaps. 1 and 2 and pp. 266–98.

chapter 2

THE INVESTMENT APPROACH

DECISIONS MUST BE MADE regarding almost every aspect of existence—what time to get up in the morning, what to eat for breakfast, where to go for a vacation, what person to marry, and what investments to purchase at what price and at what time. These are a few examples of choices that must be made by most people. Some decisions, after having been repeated often enough, become routine or habit and actually lose the characteristics of a decision. Some people become so accustomed to awakening at a particular time, for example, that they automatically wake up even though they might have decided to sleep another hour.

Other decisions are usually recognized as having a much greater potential influence on one's life and are given greater consideration and analysis. When one takes a job or purchases a home the alternatives are usually considered quite carefully, and the position or parcel of real estate believed to be in the long run best interest is chosen. The same can be noted for a business firm. Its officers will carefully consider the alternatives before hiring important personnel, purchasing a new machine, or building a new factory. A certain price must be paid to obtain such items, and the firm or individual wants to receive the maximum benefit from that price.

Premises

The investment approach to decision-making in real estate is based upon the premise that many alternatives are available to the investor. Individual investors have a choice of purchasing stocks, bonds, real estate, a private business, or many other items. If the decision is made to purchase stock they have an endless variety of companies and industries from which to choose equity investments. If the investors decide to purchase bonds, an almost infinite variety of legal provisions and features are available from many firms in different industries. Similarly, real estate investments are as varied as all the individual properties and legal provisions compounded. Investors have almost an infinite variety of investment alternatives from which to choose.

A second premise is that market imperfections may cause the price of an investment property to be higher or lower than the property's value. If perfect competition reigned, the market price would by definition equal value, and the price the purchaser paid would be justified. Markets, however, are not perfectly competitive. For example, real estate prices may fluctuate during the year if the market is more active in some seasons than others. Sellers may harbor an inflated opinion as to their property's worth. Or owners may be under pressure to sell because they need their capital quickly or because they are moving out of town. If investors pay too high a price, their return on investment (ROI) will be lower than necessary. But if investors pay a price lower than the property's market value, their ROI will be higher than market returns on properties of comparable risk. Smart investors should continually be watching for "good buys"—properties whose prices are less than their long-term values. Successful investment strategy usually requires the ability to exploit market imperfections.

A third premise—and a corollary of the first two—is that the investors (or their advisers) must collect, assimilate, analyze, and draw conclusions from a large quantity of market data. To make choices among the almost infinite variety of investments and to identify good buys or bad buys, information must be available concerning the types of available properties, income and expense characteristics of the properties, rates of return being obtained in the market by other investors, and rates of return obtainable from other types of competing investments. Investors who do not rely upon analyses of market data to guide their investment decisions are really not investors; they are gamblers.

Objectives

With the great diversity of people, motives, and criteria applied by investors, one might expect chaos to reign without public planning and dictated decisions. Such is not the case. Even with the diversity of criteria and weights applied to these criteria, investors, as well as business enterprises, have certain ultimate objectives in common. These have been termed the profit, service, and social objectives.[1]

---

[1] See John F. Mee, "Management Philosophy for Professional Executives," *Business Horizons,* Bureau of Business Research, School of Business, Indiana University (December 1956): 5–11.

Although there may be disagreement as to the relative importance of the three objectives, most people in the real estate market, as in other markets, attempt to fulfill these objectives in a variety of ways. We do not contend that one thinks explicitly about the objectives; rather, these objectives are in the nature of economic and social norms, the fulfillment of which determines in the eyes of contemporaries whether one has been successful or not.

Profit objective. Economic science is based upon the premise that people attempt to maximize their welfare by acquiring an optimal mix of valuable commodities and services. The extent to which one purchases any one commodity or service depends upon the benefit—financial or psychological—to be obtained from the item relative to the price that must be paid for it. Income is one of the primary benefits to be obtained from owning a productive commodity such as real estate. Income is desirable because with it one can purchase other commodities and services for ultimate consumption; the rental income to many landlords buys their groceries.

Another major type of benefit to be obtained from owning real estate is the psychological benefit (or amenities) buyers expect when they purchase residential real estate for self-occupancy. As in the case of the purchasers of income-producing properties, home purchasers are investors in the sense that they attempt to buy the type of house at the lowest price which will give them the greatest psychological "profit" or satisfaction.

At times, business real estate is purchased for the prestige and status that may be attached to an impressive building. Business firms often construct buildings that are much more elaborate than would be necessary to carry on the firm's functions adequately and efficiently. The Seagram Building on Park Avenue in New York City, for example, is constructed of bronze, which is artistically more striking, but it is also much more expensive than functionally comparable steel. In such cases it is doubtful whether the increased prestige will result in income that is sufficient to justify the increased cost of the building in a purely financial sense. Thus, profit must be measured in both financial and psychological terms.

Service objective. The service objective can be described from two points of view—both relative to the profit objective. First, service may be regarded as the ultimate objective. In this view each economic unit—a person or business—should strive to provide a service. If a needed service is provided at a reasonable price, the business or investor will indeed make a profit.

The second viewpoint regards profit as the ultimate objective. If business firms or investors obtain a profit in the long run, a service has been provided.

Since debating which of the two viewpoints is correct is a little like arguing which came first, the chicken or the egg, it may be well to regard profit and service as equally important. Certainly the two go hand in hand, and the accomplishment of both is necessary for the continued existence of an economic unit.

Social objective. If the profit and service objectives are regarded as having equal importance, they must share the glory with yet another motivating force. The social objective recognizes an investor's or a business' responsibility to society. This responsibility stems from the fact that no business executive or investor is truly "self-made." As Samuelson points out:

> If ever a person becomes arrogantly proud of *his* economic productivity and *his* level of real earnings, let him pause and reflect. If he were transported with all his skills and energies intact to a primitive desert island, how much would his money earnings buy? Indeed, without capital machinery, without rich resources, without other labor, and above all without the technological knowledge which each generation inherits from society's past, how much could he produce? It is only too clear that all of us reap the benefits of an economic world we never made.[2]

How does the investor-business executive pursue the social objective? By engaging in an economically and socially useful activity which is both legal and ethical. The danger of engaging in illegal activities is evident. The danger of engaging in unethical activities is not so clear. Consider the case of a landlord who creates or maintains an unsafe, unhealthful, slum tenement. In most cases, refusal to improve undesirable conditions has been defended by landlords on the grounds that the additional rent cannot be sufficiently charged to justify the added expenditure of maintaining or improving property. In some cases this contention is valid. Particularly where government-imposed barriers exist—such as the long-standing rent control in New York City or confiscatory levels of the property tax—proper maintenance of existing units, as well as the construction of new units, is inhibited. Public policy should effect a more viable economic framework that will justify maintenance expenditures. However, in other cases slumlords have condoned unacceptable living conditions in their rental units when the income produced by the units would have justified greater maintenance expenditures. Such practices may be extremely profitable in the short run, and for individuals the short run may be a sufficiently long period of time to enable them to acquire desired wealth. Over a longer period of time, however, such activities will be limited or precluded by society.

In attempting to accomplish the three objectives, investors often arrive at similar conclusions about how best to go about the task. For example, in striving to maximize the benefits of home ownership within their capacities, many people have similar ideas of what type, size, and location

---

[2] Paul A. Samuelson, *Economics*, 6th ed. (New York: McGraw-Hill, 1964), p. 435.

of a house best fulfills their wants. Thus, we find districts and neighborhoods having homes with similar characteristics. Further, the residents of those homes would likely have similar income levels, educational attainment, and social status in the community.

Investment criteria

The real estate decision-maker needs to consider certain criteria in judging alternative investments. In effect the following questions are asked: "What is a good investment for my particular purpose? What purchase price should be paid?" The following criteria provide the standards by which to answer these questions.

Return on investment. Return on investment, or yield, is a percentage relationship between the price investors must pay and the stream of income dollars they obtain from the investment. For example, if $1,000 was paid for a piece of land from which investors expected to receive net $100 per year for as long as they hold the land, their return on investment would be 10 percent.

In the case of land, investors assume it does not wear out or lose value during the life of the investment; therefore, the investors could recover their capital at any time simply by selling the land, which should bring about $1,000. The ROI calculation becomes more complicated for investments such as buildings which wear out and lose value during the life of the investment. In addition to receiving a return *on* their invested capital, the investors must plan for the return *of* their capital from the income stream. For example, if investors pay $10,000 for a building and the building loses value (depreciates) over the next 20 years, the investors must obtain, in addition to their 10 percent on the outstanding balance of the investment, 5 percent of $10,000 ($500) so that at the end of the 20th year they will have recovered the $10,000 invested capital.[3]

Business risk. Two types of risk enter into a determination of whether an expected return for a specific investment is sufficiently high—business risk and financial risk. Business risk concerns the probability that the income-producing ability of the investment (or business) will not be as great as expected. Although a return on the investment has been estimated, there is some probability that this expectation will not be realized. Any cause of such a loss that has its source in the investment itself would constitute a part of the business risk. For example, if an apartment building cannot be rented at the rates anticipated by an investor, the property may have to be sold to pay the investor's obligations. Manifestation of business risk will have resulted in loss of the investment.

---

[3] Note: Compare this with the purchase of a corporate bond.

Business risk stems from two sources—internal operating difficulties (or inefficiencies) and external factors. The ROI calculation may assume that revenues and expenses will be kept at a particular level. Perhaps, however, poor management does not achieve a high tenant occupancy or does not take advantage of discounts in purchasing supplies. Because of such internal operating inefficiencies the return will be lower than expected.

Externally the demand for a particular product or the services provided by real estate may diminish. New apartment buildings may be erected, causing the relative attractiveness of older buildings to decline; or general economic conditions may force business tenants to get by with less office space, thus affecting the ability of management to lease space designed for this purpose.

The uncertainties associated with investment ventures of this kind can be compared to relatively riskless investments such as government bonds. With the latter type of investment there is virtually no business risk. The investor can be confident of receiving interest as scheduled and return of principal at the bonds' maturity. Obviously, the increased risk associated with real estate investments causes the investor to demand a greater return expectation before investing. The greater the business risk, the higher must be the expected return over and above the available rate on relatively riskless government bonds.

Financial risk. Most real estate investors use borrowed funds in the purchase of real estate. Although business risk is present even when no borrowed funds are used, financial risk is strictly dependent upon the amount of and legal provisions concerning borrowed funds. If the income produced by an investment falls below the payment which was specified in the debt agreement, the owner will have to either sell the property to satisfy the debt or make the payments from other resources. For most investments, of course, the property's income-producing ability is expected to cover all expenses including debt service.

In deciding upon an acceptable rate of return investors should consider financial risk. They should not accept a return that barely compensates them for the burden of losing the property if debt payments cannot be made. On the other hand, if investors have adequate personal resources to cover any such deficiency, the financial risk is lower.

Cost of capital. An investor's cost of capital determines whether the expected return on investment is sufficiently high. Investors should not purchase any investment which does not provide a return equal to the price they must pay for borrowed funds and the return they could obtain on competing investments. In calculating their cost of capital, investors should weight the cost from each source by the percentage of funds obtained from that source. For example, if a $100,000 investment property were financed by 60 percent debt funds and 40 percent equity (the investor's own funds), the cost rates of each would be weighted accordingly. Suppose the debt funds cost 8 percent interest on a mortgage and other equity investments with a comparable risk yield 12 percent. If the proportion of debt and equity funds employed by investors are expected to remain constant, the cost of capital calculation would be as follows:

Mortgage debt (.60 × 8%) 4.8%
Equity (.40 × 12%) 4.8%
Weighted average cost of capital 9.6%

The investment should not be purchased unless its expected return is at least 9.6 percent.

Stability of income. The stability of income can be of importance in an investment situation. Particularly with respect to the financial expenses, the income pattern can be crucial. If the income should fall below the debt service requirement for any period, the owner would either have to use other resources to make the payment, allow the property to be sold, or make special arrangements with the lender. Over a longer period the income might be adequate to provide the desired return; in the short run it could mean loss of the property.

This graph depicts a dangerous situation for investors. During two months of the year the income is less than the debt service requirement. The difference of $250 per month will have to be paid out of investors' personal funds, or they must be prepared to lose the property.

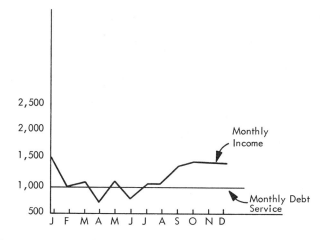

Liquidity. While the aforementioned criteria may be favorable, investors might not find the investment desirable. They may realize that at any time they might have to sell the investment to meet a specific need. Real estate is sometimes vulnerable to a lack of liquidity, which is defined as the ability to sell the property quickly for at least as much as the amount invested. Therefore, in most such investments there should be a high probability that neither the equity funds nor the borrowed funds will be needed on short notice.

Investments providing high liquidity typically yield a lower return than less liquid investments. In other words, investors must be willing to pay for liquidity, and if they need a high degree of liquidity, they would probably resort to lower-yielding, high-grade corporate or government bonds.

The degree of liquidity for real estate is often a function of the type of property under consideration. Special purpose properties of relatively high value are less liquid than general use properties. Houses of medium-price range (say $40,000 to $60,000) are more liquid than very large or small houses. The wider the market for any investment, the greater is usually the chance for recovering the capital invested.

PATTERNS OF DEVELOPMENT

Decision-makers, whether they be private investors, government agencies, or business firms, apply different weights to the various criteria upon which they base their decisions. For example, some homebuyers demand five bedrooms, while others want three bedrooms; some buyers prefer a brick house, while others want frame or stone. Even when the same criteria are used, different weights are assigned to them by the various buyers in the market. For example, while the availability of water is important to all industrial firms in choosing a location, it is of relatively greater importance to a brewery than to most other types of firms.

We have pointed out, however, that even with the great diversity of investors, there are common objectives and investment criteria operating within the private enterprise framework. In pursuing common objectives, investors rank the various criteria and produce patterns of similar decisions. Groups of similar decisions, in turn, result in discernible patterns of land use and types of structures. We now consider these patterns and the tendencies toward proportionality that result from the actions of a myriad of individual real estate decision-makers.

Land-use patterns

If the types of land use are categorized and a map made showing the categories, it would show for all cities definite areas devoted predominantly to a particular use. Figures 2–1 and 2–2 show two views (one, a close-up view) of a land-use map of Columbus, Ohio. The uses shown on the map are categorized into various degrees of residential density and other land uses, such as industrial, commercial and offices, and public and quasi-public facilities. One can notice that commercial usage predominates at the center of the city, while high density residential areas surround the core.

Relatively independent residential areas develop outward from the older residential, commercial, and light manufacturing areas. These may be communities within the major city or they may be suburban

FIGURE 2–1
Land-use map of Columbus, Ohio

communities having separate governments. They are satellites to the major city, however, in that many of their residents work in the major city. In short, there is usually economic integration of the major city and outlying suburban communities, but there is also segregation of economic classes, races, and social structure. The satellite communities, whether within the major city or politically separate, are served by stores selling primarily convenience goods, but with some stores having shopping goods. From an everyday living standpoint the satellite communities are independent; from the point of view of the breadwinner's source of income, location of major shopping purchases, and location of entertainment and cultural activities, the satellite communities are part of the major city.

FIGURE 2–2
Close-up view of land-use map of Columbus, Ohio

Industrial areas are scattered somewhat sporadically around the city, although heavy manufacturing is usually located on the periphery of the densely occupied area or along railroad tracks or river fronts.

Theories of urban growth

In looking at land-use patterns that have developed in the expansion of urban areas, one may begin to wonder what forces brought about the quiltwork of uses that at the same time seems to have both chaos and order. The identification and description of these forces would be an important step in the prediction of the future growth patterns of cities. Growth theory would also help to decide what is an optimal distribution or quantity of various land-use types and at least provide some clues about how to cope with the social problems of poverty, crime, and juvenile delinquency which occur in overpopulated areas. If some of the expansionary forces that breed these conditions could be controlled and regulated, both privately and through action of city governments, perhaps these problems could be attacked more intelligently.

Concentric circle theory. Several theories of urban growth have been advanced. These are the concentric circle theory, the axial theory, the sector theory, and the multiple nuclei theory. The first of these, the concentric circle theory, was proposed by Ernest W. Burgess in 1925.[4] It states that cities grow in circular areas emanating from the central business district. Thus, at the center of the city the central business district contains the large office buildings, retail establishments, and governmental buildings.

The second circular area is called the zone of transition. Within this zone reside primarily immigrants and members of low socioeconomic classes. Although luxurious apartment buildings, night clubs, theaters, and restaurants also are located here, the living conditions constitute the slums of the city. Also within the zone are light manufacturing industries.

Zone 3 contains primarily the workers who work in zone 2. The housing tends to be typically large mansions converted into apartments, physically acceptable, but it is functionally out of date.

Zone 4 is composed of high-class apartments and single-family houses, along with entertainment and commercial establishments. Zone 5 is the commuters' zone, consisting of suburbs, or semirural areas. It would take from 30 to 60 minutes to ride the commuter train to the central business district from zone 5.

The axial theory. This theory is not traceable to one particular author. It has been recognized by several early authors in the field of urban analysis, and the implications of axial growth have been discussed by land-value theorists. Basically, the theory says that an urban area tends to grow along its lines of transportation. This is due to the desire for the economic advantage of accessibility. Transportation time to the center of the urban area will tend to be equal from every point on the periphery. Therefore, the periphery will extend further out along the transportation lines and move in toward the center in areas not on major lines of transport to the central city.

The sector theory. This theory, developed by Homer Hoyt in the 1930s, is concerned primarily with the growth of residential neighborhoods. In the sector theory residential neighborhoods are viewed as wedge-shaped sectors surrounding the central business district. Over time, the original high-rent and high-price areas near the center of the city deteriorate, inducing the wealthy and high-income population to move into new areas. Usually, the new, high-class residential areas are developed along highways and other fast transportation facilities. Lower-

---

[4] Ernest W. Burgess, "The Growth of the City," in *The City*. Edited by Robert E. Park, Ernest W. Burgess, and Roderick D. McKenzie. (Chicago: The University of Chicago Press, 1925), pp. 47–62.

class areas remain in the deteriorated sections of the city and in other low-priced housing developments, often near places of employment. Intermediate-class neighborhoods usually surround or adjoin the high-class neighborhoods.

The sector theory is based on the following general tendencies or premises:

1. The various groups in the social order tend to be segregated into rather definite areas according to their incomes and social positions. While there are exceptions to this rule, it appears to have fairly general validity.
2. The highest-income groups live in the houses which command highest prices and rents, while the lower-income groups live in houses which are offered for the lower prices and rents. Generally the low-rent areas are located near the business and industrial center of the city and then tend to expand outward on one side or sector of the city, occupying the land which is not preempted by higher-rent residential areas or by business and industrial districts.
3. The principal growth of American cities has taken place by new building at the periphery rather than by the rebuilding of older areas. This means that some of our cities are beginning to resemble a hollow shell, with the major demands for land uses by-passing many of the "near-in" areas. In other cases these "near-in" areas become slums with little possibility of being rehabilitated through ordinary market processes.[5]

The multiple nuclei theory.   The multiple nuclei theory is essentially a modification of the sector theory and describes urban development in terms of various districts or areas which form around nuclei, or centralized activities. The theory, developed by Harris and Ullman,[6] advances four reasons why urban areas tend to develop in clusters around nuclei:

1. Certain activities require specialized facilities.
2. Certain like activities group together because they profit from cohesion.
3. Certain unlike activities are detrimental to each other.
4. Certain activities are unable to afford the high rents of the most desirable sites.

Why a nucleus and cluster will develop in a particular location is determined by factors such as transportation, relative prices, communication possibilities, socioeconomic classes, and ethnic groups residing nearby. Thus, heavy industry locates at the edge of cities on transportation facilities; principal business activities are located in the central business

---

[5] Weimer, Hoyt, and Bloom, *Real Estate*, p. 276.

[6] Chauncey D. Harris and Edward L. Ullman, "The Nature of Cities," in *Building the Future City, Annals of the American Academy of Political and Social Sciences*, no. 242, November 1945, pp. 7–17.

district; and financial, legal, and administrative offices congregate in close proximity just beyond the central business district.

FIGURE 2–3
Theories of urban growth

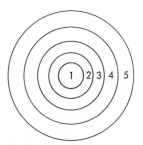

Concentric Circle Theory

Sector Theory

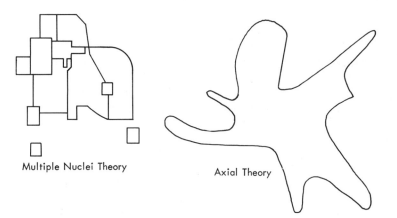

Multiple Nuclei Theory

Axial Theory

In forming conclusions about the adequacy of the so-called theories or hypotheses of urban growth, one may think of many exceptions to the ideas expressed in each. As Ratcliff points out:

Certain modern tendencies conspire to make the foregoing generalization less and less useful as a basis for forecasting coming urban patterns. The decline of public mass transportation is breaking down the structure of residential areas as it is described by Hoyt. The industrial worker neither depends on public transportation nor is his home necessarily near his place of employment. The executive drives to work, save in the largest metropolises, and lives where he will. This freedom of choice is leading to a greater diffusion, more mixture of neighborhoods, and less structuring of the metropolis.

Industrial development is no longer tied closely to rail lines, with the result that a greater scatter of industry characterizes recent development. Driven from central locations by the need for large acreage and by the congestion which hampers operations and employee movements, industrial plants are seeking suburban locations.

Retail conformations are changing to a lesser degree, but the change is significant. The central core of retail services remains dominant but is not growing in extent. New major suburban shopping centers are absorbing the added purchasing power of the growing metropolis. Suffering decline are the small neighborhood service centers, the older inlying retail sub-centers, and the string-street retail developments.[7]

To these trends we would point out that the increased emphasis that today is placed upon zoning, city planning, urban renewal, and public housing is additional cause why the theories of city growth developed 25 to 50 years ago cannot be expected to predict city growth in the future. To the extent that these arrangements modify the patterns people would otherwise develop in their real estate decisions, they lessen the value of theories which do not take them into account.

Although the theories may be inadequate for many predictive purposes, one may call to mind many instances in which the theories appear to have had some validity in describing the growth process. To the extent that each theory or combination of theories lends understanding to the urbanizing process, the decision-maker should be able to analyze current developments more effectively. Whether more adequate theories will be developed remains to be seen; however, it seems doubtful.

Proportionality

Land uses. The city is composed of a variety of different land uses. Important uses typically are single-family residential, multifamily residential, commercial, and industrial. Subcategories of each are usually provided in zoning codes. In certain areas single-family residential housing predominates, while in other areas industrial or multifamily residential uses predominate.

When the city is viewed in its entirety, however, the amount of land devoted to each type of use bears some percentage relation to other uses. For example, residential uses may account for 70 percent; commercial, 15 percent; industrial, 10 percent; and other uses, 5 percent of the total land

---

[7] Richard U. Ratcliff, *Real Estate Analysis* (New York: McGraw-Hill, 1961), p. 41.

area. These relationships reflect the economic needs of the population and result in the macroeffect of proportionality; economic forces tend to allocate approximately the right amount of land for each major use.

Proportionality and real estate markets. To most of us it seems only logical that there should be a variety and proportionality of types of land uses. Yet consider the system and the decision-making process which results in this diversity or proportionality of land-use types. Proportionality of land uses results from many individual private decisions which have little or no external compulsion. The only force that in most cases dictates the decision for a particular use to be made of a parcel of land is the motive resulting from the market system of private choice. Each decision, therefore, was thought at the time it was made to be in the best economic interests of the investor-owner in competition with other investors and with the knowledge that other competing uses could also be applied to the land.

Although markets are discussed in considerably greater detail later in this book, it is well to note here two particular characteristics of the market system. First, a market, although not necessarily confined to one location, must consist of a number of buyers and sellers bidding against each other. How many buyers and sellers are necessary to constitute a market is not an answerable question; however, as the number of buyers and sellers in a market increases, the efficiency of the market increases. Conversely, as the number of buyers and sellers decreases, the efficiency of a market economy can be presumed to decline. It seems obvious, then, that individuals and groups of individuals should not be excluded from any market for noneconomic reasons. The exclusion of racial, ethnic, or religious groups from a market weakens the market and thus weakens the private enterprise system.

Second, to constitute a market, freedom must be present. Freedom implies that there is no external compulsion in the decision-making process. Individuals are free to choose that course of action which they believe will be in their own best interest. This requirement would exclude direct governmental intervention in the setting of market prices and would demand a minimum of social, racial, religious, ethnic, and class pressures and the elimination of any other noneconomic external forces. Obviously these requirements are not met in the real-world real estate market. They do, however, represent market characteristics which would be desirable, even though unobtainable.

Structures. In addition to the proportionality of types of land uses that are observable in any land area, a proportionality exists with respect to the types and characteristics of structures within each use category. Within the residential category, for example, we find many styles of houses, different sizes, and different heights. In the commercial use category we find small single-story buildings, multifloor department stores, and office buildings. In the industrial category we would find small light-industrial manufacturing uses and a range therefrom all the way up to vast industrial complexes occupying thousands of acres of land. In the office building category are small single offices and a range all the way up to 100-story skyscrapers. In the office building use category, however, we do not find nearly as many 100-story skyscrapers as we would find 40- or 50-story skyscrapers. Nor do we find as many 50-story skyscrapers as we would find 10- to 20-story buildings, and we would not find nearly as many 10- to 20-story buildings as 1- to 5-story buildings.

The location of buildings having similar heights is another manifestation of proportionality. If the typical city which is large enough to have skyscrapers is viewed, it can be noted that the buildings at the outskirts are quite limited in height, usually being one, two, three, or four stories. Looking toward the center of the city, a few buildings of somewhat greater height can be found, and, as the downtown area is looked at, there is a number of tall buildings. A cross-section side view of a city would show something of the nature of a low-rising tent effect with the apex of the tent occurring near the center of the city in the highly commercialized downtown area. Of course, there are many modifications of this pattern, as seen from the sector theory and multiple nuclei theory.

Centers other than the downtown area may develop, and within these centers taller buildings may be constructed. However, the principles are the same in that the higher concentration of activity within the nucleus of the sector provides economic rationale for the construction of taller buildings. A good example of this latter effect is Houston, Texas, where many subnucleus areas with very tall buildings have developed in outlying areas from the downtown. The cross-section effect is something like a multicenter pole tent. The fact that in some cities, such as Los Angeles, Indianapolis, and Topeka, buildings are not so tall as in New York and Chicago does not negate the principle. Land has not sold at such premium prices to encourage more intensive use. The higher the land values at the center of the city, which result from the supply and demand conditions for land, the taller will be the buildings at the center of the city.

Applicability of the investment approach

In this book we include our entire study of real estate within the framework of the investment approach. We feel that this approach is superior to others because it facilitates the important aspect of decision-making. Decision-making was shown in Chapter 1 to be the key element in the administration of real estate resources, and it is through the investment approach that decision-making is understood.

Nonincome-producing properties. The investment approach might be regarded as inappropriate for the analysis of properties that do not produce dollar income such as single-family residences, public parks, school buildings, or libraries. The benefits from properties of this type may not accrue in the form of monetary income and may be indirect or even immeasurable. Coons and Glaze have shown that in buying a home most people are concerned with consumption motives, such as the services the home will provide and the prestige and status to be obtained, rather than financial advantage.[8] A "good address" or an impressive architectural design for a home or the beauty of a park or attractiveness of a school are intangible benefits. Decisions are made whether to develop or purchase these types of properties. Upon what basis are these decisions made? What type of analysis goes into these decisions? We submit that the investment approach, which recognizes that the outlay must be justified by the expected returns—whether these returns be monetary or psychic—provides the best approach for understanding the ubiquitous decision-making requirement.

The expected future stream of psychic benefits (amenities) can be considered analogous to financial benefits in a dollar-income-producing investment. For dollar-income-producing investments a percentage relationship (or ROI) is calculated between these benefits and the price that must be paid. For psychic-income-producing investments we cannot make such a calculation because the benefits themselves are not directly measurable in dollar terms. This does not negate the theory or analytical approach, however. Rather, it means that we must compare prices of alternative properties, as these prices are related to the benefits and to the other criteria discussed in this chapter.

The home purchaser should recognize that the business risk associated with a home purchase concerns the probability that the production of amenities by the home will not be as great as anticipated. Will the location continue to provide the expected benefits? What is the probability the neighborhood will decline more rapidly than anticipated?

As with income properties, financial risk associated with amenity-producing properties concerns the probability that the mortgage payment cannot be met. To assess this probability purchasers must weigh their expected future incomes against personal expenses, housing expenses, and the periodic mortgage payments. Two rough rules of thumb are that purchasers having no abnormal personal expenses can pay up to two and one-half times their annual gross incomes for a home, and that they can afford to pay up to 25 percent of their monthly income in housing expense.

Homebuyers should also consider the liquidity of their investments. Can they sell the home in a reasonable time if they should so desire? What is the probability they will need to sell within two, three, five, or ten years?

---

[8] Alvin E. Coons and Bert T. Glaze, *Housing Market Analysis and the Increase in House Ownership* (Columbus: Bureau of Business Research, Ohio State University, 1964).

Lastly, stability of benefits should be considered. Will the home provide satisfactory benefits in winter as well as summer? Is it sufficiently well decorated that a family will enjoy the benefits of homeownership as soon as they move in, or will they have to wait some period of time until the home can be redecorated?

The investment approach to homeownership thus involves a weighing of costs against returns. The principal returns are the psychic benefits or amenities produced by the property and the right not to pay rent. Costs include the interest that must be paid for borrowed money and the alternative monetary or psychic benefits that could be obtained from an alternative investment. These burdens comprise the home investor's cost of capital.

Social problems.   One last question about the applicability of the investment approach concerns its role in social analysis: How does the macroapproach to real estate problems fit within this microlevel framework? What justification would we have for including in this book a discussion of urban decay and redevelopment, mass transit, city planning, low-income housing, and so forth? A clue to our answer may have been noted earlier in this chapter when we discussed the *patterns* that develop from many individual land-use decisions. We described zoning ordinances and other regulations that attempt to control such patterns. We recognized that market imperfections and inadequate regulation and enforcement may contribute to the continuance of socially unhealthful consequences such as slums and racial ghettos. Understanding of the investment process may reveal ways the decision-making process can be altered to effect more desirable social results.

Additionally, however, knowledge of the investment approach can help identify those areas where social action must be taken to remedy patterns that cannot be changed efficiently through the private decision-making process. One such area is urban renewal. The housing market is generally considered an inadequate device to renew and rehabilitate slum areas of our cities. Several owners of slum properties cannot fix up their properties while the rest of the area remains deteriorated; rents cannot be increased to justify the expenditure. Furthermore, no one developer is large enough to accumulate all the properties in a slum area so as to be able to rehabilitate the entire area of blight. Clearly the market is inadequate, and governmental assistance is needed. The investment in such a rehabilitation project must be justified from a social standpoint rather than from a private investor's potential return.

SUMMARY

The investment approach can be regarded as a philosophy of making decisions and solving problems. It entails identifying and measuring the benefits to be derived from a course of action and the costs that must be incurred to achieve that action. The costs are weighed against the benefits for alternative courses of action in order to decide which way to proceed.

Real estate analysis is particularly appropriate for the investment approach because benefits in the form of income or amenities are usually present and, at least for income-producing properties, are measurable. Similarly, the costs of purchase and maintenance can usually be identified and estimated. Relationships between costs and benefits for several properties or projects can then be calculated and evaluated.

Several motivating and constraining forces serve to channel real estate investment decisions into observable patterns. Common objectives of profit, service, and social function stimulate investors to seek the same rewards. Common expectations about future growth and development tend to cause investors to evaluate similarly the various ways of achieving their objectives.

Investment criteria relevant to real estate are return on investment, the amount of cash generated after the payment of expenses, the liquidity of the property, and the business risk and financial risk associated with the property. The cost of obtaining funds for investment is determined by a weighted average cost of equity and debt funds and is a major determinant of the rate of return on investment that is demanded by investors.

Decisions by many individual real estate investors result in identifiable patterns of market behavior. These patterns are reflected in types of land use, intensity of land use, growth characteristics of cities, and characteristics of structures within any given land use and intensity level. Growth patterns of cities have been observed and classified into several theories— the concentric circle theory, the sector theory, the axial theory, and the multiple nuclei theory. Each of these, either separately or in combination with others, can help in understanding where and why growth has occurred in a city and where future growth may be expected.

QUESTIONS FOR REVIEW

1. What is the role of the three objectives of profit, service, and social in producing patterns of land use?
2. Why are the service and social objectives given equal weight with the profit objective?
3. What is meant by *liquidity?* Look up in a book on finance a definition of *marketability.* How do the two terms differ? Which is more important in real estate analysis? Why?
4. What are some of the considerations that should be taken into account when deciding what an appropriate ROI should be?
5. What would you say are the costs and the benefits of obtaining a college

education? Can the question of whether to pursue a college education be regarded as an investment decision? Why or why not? Would everyone come to the same conclusion regarding the relationship between costs and benefits associated with four years spent at a college or university? Why or why not?

6. How would you measure business risk? In what way is business risk reflected in ROI?

7. Why are investment criteria in addition to ROI important? Can you think of a situation in which the expected ROI might be acceptable but another criterion would cause a proposed investment to be unfavorable?

8. Can you think of examples in a city or cities of the growth patterns suggested by each of the theories of urban growth?

9. How could a real estate developer use each of the theories of urban growth to identify desirable areas for residential development?

10. Visualize a side-section profile through the center of a large city. How does the height of buildings illustrate the principle of proportionality? How is the principle of proportionality related to the economic principle of increasing and decreasing returns?

REFERENCES

Brown, Robert K. *Real Estate Economics.* Boston: Houghton Mifflin Co., 1965, pp. 27–37.

Harvey, Robert O., and Clark, W. A. V. "The Nature and Economics of Urban Sprawl," *Land Economics* 41, no. 1 (February 1965): 1–9.

Hoyt, Homer. "The Growth of Cities from 1800 to 1960 and Forecasts to Year 2000," *Land Economics* 39, no. 2 (May 1963).

Lynch, Kevin. "The Pattern of the Metropolis," in *Metropolis: Values in Conflict.* Edited by C. E. Elias, Jr., James Gillies, and Svend Riemer. Belmont, Calif.: Wadsworth Publishing Co., 1964.

Ratcliff, Richard U. *Real Estate Analysis.* New York: McGraw-Hill, 1961, pp. 306–31.

Ricks, R. Bruce. "New Town Development and the Theory of Location." *Land Economics* 46, no. 1 (February 1970): 5–11.

Sauvain, Harry C. *Investment Management.* 3d ed. Englewood Cliffs, N.J.: Prentice-Hall, 1967, pp. 3–20.

Seldin, Maury, and Swesnik, Richard H. *Real Estate Investment Strategy.* New York: Wiley-Interscience, 1970, pp. 3–39.

Wendt, Paul F., and Cerf, Alan R. *Real Estate Investment and Taxation.* New York: McGraw-Hill, 1969, pp. 1–12.

chapter 3

VALUE: THE
CENTRAL IDEA

DECISION MAKING IN REAL ESTATE centers around the investment calculation. Potential investors wish to pay a price which is sufficiently low to allow them to obtain a future return on their investments. Sellers of real estate wish to obtain a price high enough to allow them to have obtained a return on their investment in the past. Each transaction affecting ownership or use of real estate involves such basic investment calculations whether the real estate is an owner-occupied, single-family residence, an investment property, a lease arrangement, a share in a syndicate, or some other form of joint ownership. The investment calculation may involve income and expenses in dollars or, in the case of the owner-occupied home, it must be conceptualized in terms of amenities—housing services provided by the unit—and net satisfaction.

Investment calculations reoccur during the period of ownership of real estate. Owners must repeatedly determine whether or not to spend for maintenance and repair. Less frequently, decisions must be made about rehabilitation, modernization, expansion, property conversion to another use, or demolition of the existing improvements and reuse of the site. Even the decision to abandon the real estate involves an investment calculation.

The investment process consists of two phases. Phase 1 is the estimation of market value or the most probable selling price of the property. Phase 2 is the investment calculation.[1] The concepts of market value and investment value and the procedures by which the value of real estate is measured are discussed in this chapter.[2]

---

[1] A discussion of the investment calculation is reserved for Chapter 5.

[2] See also Chapter 4.

VALUE AS A MARKET CONCEPT

The concept of value is a market concept. It is the result of interacting forces of supply and demand. It rests upon the presence of willing buyers and sellers freely bidding in competition with one another. The modern concept of value was synthesized by Alfred Marshall whose famous book, *Principles of Economics,* became the world's leading economics textbook.[3] In this book Marshall introduced the famous scissors analogy of supply and demand operating in the market. As each blade of a pair of scissors is necessary for the unit to function, so is supply and demand necessary for the economic unit—a market—to function. The interaction of both of these forces is important in determination of price.

Value in a perfectly competitive market

Value is a phenomenon of a competitive market. If real estate markets were perfectly competitive, supply and demand would *determine* value, which would be identical with price. The criteria of a perfect market are the following items:

1. Homogeneity of products.
2. A product divisible into small economic units.
3. A transportable product enabling supply to flow to areas of high demand.
4. Many buyers and sellers.
5. No buyer or seller large enough to influence the market.
6. No external influence.
7. Complete knowledge as to possible uses.
8. Agreement as to expectations.

If the requirements of this model were met, there would be no need for value estimates to be made. In analyzing any market, however, it soon becomes clear that the requirements are impossible to attain. For example, the wheat market is often cited as the market closely approaching the idea of a perfect market; yet, even in this market the product is not homogeneous (there are different grades of wheat). Additionally, the market is influenced by governmental activities and has within it buyers and sellers who do not have complete knowledge and are not in agreement as to the future. If the characteristics of the real estate market are compared with the requirements in this same way, the extreme imperfections become apparent. Because real estate markets are far from perfect, real estate analysts look at many indications of market activity, including transaction prices, in an effort to *estimate* value.

---

[3] Alfred Marshall, *Principles of Economics,* 8th ed. (London: Macmillan & Co., 1920).

Real estate market characteristics

Real estate markets are imperfect in part because real estate is different from other economic goods. The differences between real estate and other economic goods concern its physical immobility, its length of economic life, and its economic size. Real estate markets may also have relatively few buyers or sellers at any given time.

Physical immobility. The physical immobility of real estate, although an obvious characteristic, leads to several important economic considerations discussed in this section.[4]

Because of the physical immobility of real estate, the market for each parcel is largely determined by those who demand and supply properties in a localized area. Although the demand side of the market may contain buyers from outside the local area, in many instances prospective purchasers of real estate come from the local area. The supply side is, of course, local. To the extent, however, that a parcel in one locality may substitute for one in another locality, the supply side becomes broader in scope. The fact remains, however, that each parcel of real estate is imperfectly substitutable for other parcels.

The physical immobility of real estate has an important implication for the valuation of real estate. Since the parcel of real property cannot be moved from its location, its value is subject to the effects of economic, social, or political developments emanating from the national, regional, community, and neighborhood levels. With respect to moveable economic goods, such as a refrigerator or rug, purely local economic forces have much less effect on their values. Why? Simply because they can be moved to escape such influences.

Social, political, and economic developments at all levels require subjective assessment and often are tenuous in their relationship to value. Nevertheless, value estimates should be based upon some assumptions about future conditions in the society, although quantification of their effects is difficult. The appraiser or investment analyst considers these influences by beginning with the broadest influence and working down to more and more localized influences, that is, from national to regional to city to district or neighborhood factors. Favorable trends tend to increase estimates of the gross income to be derived from a property or to increase one's confidence in a predicted level of income. Trends supporting demand have the effect of reducing vacancy expectations, reducing the risk factor in capitalization rates, or lowering one's expectation of future depreciation or obsolescence. Unfavorable trends would have opposite effects.

Examples of some of the large-scale social trends that might be con-

---

[4] These economic considerations in turn provide the reasoning and justification for the valuation procedures discussed in Chapter 4.

sidered in evaluating the worth of a property are those toward the formation of smaller families, delayed marriages, urban living, and long-term apartment tenancy. These trends may be accentuated or mitigated within any one region or community, although social conditions in local communities are usually reflective of national trends.

Political trends are even more difficult to assess. The emphasis upon housing programs by Congress; the status of zoning laws, housing and building codes, open occupancy laws, and programs; and school integration efforts are but some of the current political conditions that may affect property values.

Although it is fairly obvious that national economic conditions can influence a property's value (during the recession of 1973–74, many parcels of real estate declined in value), the more localized types of influences may be more obscure. Examples: the decline in coal mining in southern Illinois from 1945 to 1960 caused the entire region to suffer economically and produced a commensurate loss in real estate values. Several cities, such as Evansville, Indiana, and Pittsburgh, experienced economic declines during the 1950s and early 1960s for a variety of reasons which were accompanied by sluggishness and value decreases in real estate markets.[5] Probably every reader can think of several examples of district and neighborhood developments that have adversely affected real estate values in an area.

Economic trends generally are more amenable to quantifiable analysis. Such considerations would include an analysis of income levels, availability of financing and interest rates, outlook for monetary policy, levels of savings, prices of housing relative to other economic goods, expected investment in housing and other kinds of real estate, and various demographic data, such as numbers of population and mobility trends.

Short-term analysis of the national economy is particularly helpful in determining an appropriate capitalization rate. As we shall see in the income approach to value, capitalization rates are simply interest rates added to capital recovery rates. Since capitalization rates are used to convert a parcel of real estate's earning expectancy to value, a property's value would tend to be inversely correlated with interest rates in the economy.

At the local level economic trends become more directly translated into market analyses for a particular type of property being considered. In assessing economic trends affecting housing, social and demographic factors are combined with income projections to estimate housing requirements and their predicted effects on rents, vacancy rates, and transaction prices. Similar types of analyses are important in the valuation and

---

[5] In the case of Evansville, the decline was caused by several large industries leaving the town following labor difficulties and mergers. The Pittsburgh decline was largely attributed to increasing automation in steel plants.

investment analyses of offices, commercial property (including shopping centers), and industrial property.[6]

In addition to an analysis of social, economic, and political factors at the national, regional, and local levels, a thorough examination and analysis of the physical and legal characteristics of the property must be made. The physical immobility of real estate means that every parcel is different from every other parcel. If similar in every other respect, it differs in its location relative to other parcels; it is either closer to or farther from the corner than the adjacent parcel. Similarly the legal rights and obligations may vary between two otherwise similar parcels. One seller may be contemplating the sale of an estate for life, another the sale of a leasehold, and still another a fee simple estate. The appraiser or investor must be aware of the exact physical items to be included in a purchase and of the legal rights and obligations accompanying the physical items.

Long length of economic life. Another major atypical characteristic of real estate is its relatively long economic life. Land, or more specifically location, lasts forever, and buildings usually are built to last from 25 to several hundred years. In contrast are other economic goods which last much shorter periods of time. For example, automobiles may last five to ten years, clothing two to five years, and groceries one day to a month. What is the implication of this characteristic for the economics of real estate? It is that the purchase of real property represents a long-term commitment. The purchaser's viewpoint should be long range, and he or she should be convinced of the ability of the property to provide the services desired over its entire economic life. The purchase of real estate thus requires a thorough analysis aimed at predicting the type, amount, and quantity of future benefits to be obtained from the property. It also requires a prediction of the *expected* expenses to be incurred by the property, for the resultant of the two—net operating income (NOI)—is the generating engine of value.

Economic size. Another major atypical characteristic of most parcels of real estate is its relatively large economic size. To purchase a parcel of real estate one usually must pay a price of anywhere from several thousand dollars on up. It is not unusual for a family to spend $40,000 to $80,000 for its home or for purchasers of investment properties to pay $500,000 or more. Contrast this with the price of groceries, clothes, or even automobiles. Thus, the single largest purchase of most families throughout their lives is for a home.

The relative size of most real estate transactions has two implications from an economics standpoint for real estate investors. The first of these

---

[6] Market analysis is discussed more fully in Chapter 7, and an outline of market analyses conducted by the Federal Housing Administration is contained in Appendix D.

is that the purchase of real estate must be viewed as an important, long-term commitment, and the second is that financing considerations are important determinants of the investment feasibility. Although one can trade in real estate—as one trades in stock, bonds, or other investments—traders in real estate, even to a greater extent than with respect to other types of investments, should be convinced of the long-term soundness of their purchases. A real estate investment may be less liquid and less marketable than other types of investments. Even traders in real estate may have to hold property one or perhaps even five years to expect to profit from their purchases. Investors, as contrasted with traders or speculators, are concerned with the income-producing potential of the property. Thus, in purchasing property for trading, the basic question is simply whether the price for which the property can be purchased is less than the price warranted by a long-term investment analysis.

The second implication of the large economic size of real estate transactions impels the investor to consider the present state of financing conditions and the impact of the specific financing arrangement on each transaction. A complex structure of financing institutions has evolved for the purpose of financing real estate transactions. Savings and loan associations, commercial banks, mutual savings banks, real estate investment trusts, and life insurance companies are all important institutions in this area. The cost of borrowing funds and the terms demanded by these institutions are obviously important considerations to the real estate investor.

Because of the large amount of money that must usually be borrowed for a family to purchase its home, long-term amortized loan arrangements have been developed. It is not unusual for a family to agree to repay a large loan over a period of 25 years in monthly installments which include both interest and repayment of the principal amount of the loan. Real estate investors, whether they are home purchasers or commercial property purchasers, should attempt to obtain the most favorable terms and interest rate possible from a reliable institution. But more important they must analyze the effect this will have upon their total income position. Will the income from the real estate or the amenities derived from home ownership be sufficient to more than offset the financing expense? What income will be left over after paying the financing expense? How does this amount compare with the income to be obtained from other investments?

The individual terms and interest rates that investors can obtain from various institutions vary from time to time in relation to the fiscal and monetary policies of the U.S. government. Investors should be aware of the basic determinants of interest rates and financing terms and should understand the relationship between fiscal and monetary policies and loan arrangements for real estate investment. One study of the cyclical effect of these policies showed a close relation between restrictive monetary and fiscal policies of the government and significantly decreased levels of real estate construction and investment.[7] In such times marginal buyers are excluded from the market because of the high cost and their inability to obtain financing.

Few buyers and sellers. Real estate markets may have relatively large numbers of potential buyers and sellers, but not all of these buyers and sellers are active in the market at any one time. A community may have 1,000 single-family residences similar enough to be in the same submarket. Only 50 residences may be offered for sale and fewer than 50 families may be shopping the market for a home. The going price for this type of housing will be determined by the forces of supply and demand, and the prices will indicate the value of all properties of this type in the submarket. Markets for shopping centers, warehouses, and office buildings may be even thinner, that is, have fewer buyers or sellers. The real estate analyst often must estimate the market value of properties competing in thin markets. In these instances, the transaction price negotiated in the open market may vary from estimated market value within a wider range than when the appraiser is working with a property that competes in an active market where buyers and sellers of similar properties are numerous.

Money and the value concept. An addendum to our explanation of the value concept is now necessary to clarify the role of money in economic (value) decisions. The role of money is often misunderstood because of its own characteristic ability to change in value. Although money serves both as a medium of exchange and a standard of value, the standard itself can change from year to year, day to day, or hour to hour. Some currencies, in fact, have experienced such rapid devaluation (for example, the German mark following World War I) that the change was noticeable almost minute by minute.

Since the values of economic goods are cited and compared in money terms, the value of an economic good may not have changed, even though the number of dollars measuring its value is different from one time to another. Thus, in order to compare dollar measurements of value over a time period during which the value of the dollar has changed, it is necessary to adjust the dollar measurements to conform to each other. This is done by the familiar method of inflating or deflating one of the dollar measurements to the level represented at the time of the other dollar measurement.

---

[7] Halbert C. Smith and Carl J. Tschappat, "Monetary Policy and Real Estate Values," *Appraisal Journal* 34, no. 1 (January 1966): 18–26.

Value is a real concept. As expressed by Adam Smith, it is "the power of a good to command other goods or labor services in exchange."

An illustration of this definition of value and the clouding role of money is provided by two appraisals that were performed on the same downtown commercial building four years apart. The first appraisal estimated the building's value at approximately $200,000, while the second appraisal estimated the value at $220,000. As measured by the consumer and wholesale price indexes, there had been about a 10 percent decline in the value of the dollar during that four-year period. Thus, it is clear that the real (constant dollar) value of the building was about the same four years after the first appraisal, even though the dollar measurement increased by $20,000. Stated differently, the real estate would command about the same goods in exchange as it did four years previously.

MARKET VALUE

Real estate appraisers have definitions of value which provide workable, measurable concepts in an imperfect market and which are recognized by the courts. One such definition of *market value* formulated by the Society of Real Estate Appraisers and the American Institute of Real Estate Appraisers is the following:

The highest price in terms of money which a property will bring in a competitive and open market under all conditions requisite to a fair sale, the buyer and seller, each acting prudently, knowledgeably and assuming the price is not affected by undue stimulus.

Implicit in this definition is the consummation of a sale as of a specified date and the passing of title from seller to buyer under conditions whereby:

1. Buyer and seller are typically motivated.
2. Both parties are well informed or well advised, and each acts in what he or she considers his or her own best interest.
3. A reasonable time is allowed for exposure in the open market.
4. Payment is made in cash or its equivalent.
5. Financing, if any, is on terms generally available in the community at the specified date and typical for the property type in its locale.
6. The price represents a normal consideration for the property sold unaffected by special financing amounts and/or terms, services, fees, costs, or credits incurred in the transaction.[8]

Although the definition is somewhat similar to the definition of value under perfect competition, some of the perfect competition requirements are missing and some are less stringent. The real world thus dictates a

---

[8] Byrl N. Boyce, *Real Estate Appraisal Terminology* (Cambridge, Mass.: Ballinger Publishing Co., 1975), p. 137; this publication is jointly sponsored by the American Institute of Real Estate Appraisers and the Society of Real Estate Appraisers.

compromise between the theoretically pure concept of a market and the necessity to make decisions and settle disputes.

Market value is but one kind of value of concern to the real estate analyst. Other values that sometimes must be estimated are included in the following list:

Assessed value: A dollar amount assigned to taxable property by an assessor for the purpose of taxation; frequently a statutorily determined percentage of market value.

Condemnation value: Value sought in condemnation proceedings is market value. In the instance of a partial taking, adjustments to the value of the part taken may be made for damages and/or special benefits to the remainder property.

Excess value: Value over and above market value which is ascribable to a lease that guarantees contract rental income in excess of market rental at the time of the appraisal.

Fair market value; fair cash value: Market value.

Forced "value"; liquidation "value": The price paid in a forced sale or purchase when time is not sufficient to permit negotiations resulting in market value being paid; should be called forced price or liquidation price, rather than value.

Going concern value: The value of the business enterprise and the real estate it occupied, includes goodwill.

Insurable value: Value of the destructible portions of a property.

Intangible value: A value not imputable to any part of the physical property, such as the excess value attributable to a favorable lease, or the value attributable to goodwill.

Investment value: Value to a particular investor based upon individual investment requirements, as distinguished from the concept of market value, which is impersonal and detached.

Leasehold value: The value of a leasehold interest; the right to the use, enjoyment, and profit existing by virtue of the rights granted under a lease instrument.

Mortgage value: Value for mortgage lending purposes.

Stabilized value: A value estimate which excludes from consideration an abnormal relation of supply and demand . . . a long-term value; or which excludes from consideration any transitory condition which may cause excessive cost of construction . . . and which may cause an excessive sale price.[9]

Many of these value concepts are basically market value, as previously defined, to which certain adjustments have been made to reflect the purpose or use to which the value estimate will be put. Assessed value, condemnation value, insurable value, leasehold value, and mortgage value are examples.

---

[9] Ibid.

INVESTMENT VALUE

Investment value is the basis of phase 2 of the two-phase investment process in real estate. Investment value can be defined for the buyer and for the seller. In both instances, investment value is the "value in use," that is, what the property is worth to that particular individual. A buyer's investment value is the *maximum* that he or she would be willing to pay for a particular property. The seller's investment value is the *minimum* he or she would be willing to accept. Both the buyer and seller have their respective investment values determined by the same factors. The individual's assessment of risk and future productivity of the property is reflected in the investment value, in addition to the financing arrangements, tax situation, and other personal investment requirements. Investment value also depends upon how well matched the real estate is to the individual's needs and preferences.

Example

Fifty potential buyers may be shopping the local market for a small apartment property of eight units. Each of these buyers could have a different investment value for the various properties offered for sale. For seller X's property, buyer A may be willing to pay $160,000; buyer B, $145,000; buyer C, $165,000; and so on. Buyer C may foresee productivity that A and B do not; C may be misinformed. Buyer C may be willing to accept a lower return on investment than A or B, perhaps because of a lower opportunity cost; C may have more favorable financing or may be more creative in the financial arrangements; C could be in a higher tax bracket; the property may be more suited to C's needs. All of these factors, and the list is not intended to be inclusive, could cause C to have a higher investment value for this property than A or B. The seller of the property, X, has an investment value of $150,000 for the property. If this price cannot be obtained for the property, it will not be sold.

In a competitive, although imperfect, real estate market, competition among buyers interested in similar properties and among sellers offering these properties results in transaction prices. These transaction prices array themselves in a distribution. The real estate analyst observes this distribution of prices and uses it as factual evidence in the estimation of market value for a property of that type. The more active the market (the larger the number of buyers and sellers), the more similar the properties and the buyers and sellers, and the more knowledgeable the buyers and sellers about the uses to which the property can be put, the narrower will be the range within which transaction prices are negotiated and the more reliable will be the estimate of market value as an indication of probable transaction price.

Each transaction price in this market will be equal to or below the investment value of the buyer involved and equal to or above the investment value of the seller of that property. In a competitive market, properties are sold without buyers or sellers having to pay or accept their investment value. Competition among sellers of similar properties, who are aware of alternatives available to potential buyers, prevents a seller from differentiating among buyers—from singling out a buyer and extracting the maximum investment value. On the other side of the market, competition among buyers prevents a buyer from forcing a particular seller to accept the minimum reservation price for the property. Competition among sellers sets the ceiling on transaction prices in the market; competition among buyers sets the floor under price. Between this floor and ceiling, individual transaction prices are negotiated for properties of this type.

Example

In the above example, a transaction could only occur between seller X and buyer A or C. Buyer B had an investment value below that of seller X. Suppose that buyer A paid $159,000 for the property. If the seller had been more aware of the demand for the property and had been a better negotiator or had been willing to engage in a longer bargaining process, a transaction might have been consummated with buyer C, who would be willing and able to outbid A. Buyer A is a satisfied purchaser in an imperfect market. A is pleased to have obtained the property for $1,000 less than the maximum investment value, for this means A will attain a greater ROI than A was willing to accept if A had paid $160,000 investment value. The return which A will earn on the $159,000 investment has been market-determined, that is, determined by the competition of buyers and sellers for properties of this type. Seller X is satisfied because the price of $150,000 would have been accepted, if competition had forced X to the minimum reservation price. The seller has received a windfall profit—a profit greater than that which would have induced X to supply the property. Other owners of similar properties who are not now part of the active supply can be viewed as having investment values greater than the going price for properties of that type.

In summary, market value is an estimate of most probable selling price in a competitive market. Market value is estimated from observed transaction prices of similar properties. These transaction prices are negotiated in an imperfect market between buyers and sellers, each having his or her own investment value for the property. Awareness of alternatives and the need to compete cause these transaction prices to exhibit some central tendency. Investment value and market value thus are linked through the competitive market process that determines transaction prices.

MARKET VALUE, PRICE, AND COST

The preceding discussion of the determination of transaction prices and the use of these prices as indications of market value clearly demonstrate that the price paid for real estate can vary from its estimated market value. Price is dollar amount actually paid; market value is the estimate of what should have been paid given conditions described by the definition of market value.

Cost is a historical fact; market value is dependent upon future productivity, either income or amenities. A building may have cost $100,000 to produce ready for occupancy and use. The improvements may be on a site which "cost" the investor $30,000 (the price paid for the site). The price paid for the site, which is viewed by the investor as part of the total investment in the property, can differ from its market value. The cost to create the improvements also may have been more or less than their market value. A favorable lease, creative financing, a change in the character of the neighborhood, or a strong demand for that type of property can result in value for the improvements in excess of their cost. Conversely, a building which cost $100,000 to create may have a market value upon completion of only $90,000. This circumstance could occur when the site is improved with the wrong type of improvement or when the site is over- or underimproved. An overimprovement results when too much has been invested in improvements on a given site; an underimprovement results from too little investment in improvements.

The discrepancy between the costs of production of real estate improvements, including a normal profit as part of cost, and the value of these improvements can result from actions of misinformed individuals and from the necessity that value estimates be made at a point in time. The real estate analyst is always providing value estimates in the market time period in which supply, demand, and price may not be in long-run equilibrium. Market disequilibrium in the form of a rising demand not yet met by the supply can result in market value greater than cost. The cost to create improvements does not necessarily set the upper limit on improvement value. In the long run, of course, competition and supply adjustments would result in no unit's being supplied unless price (value) covered the costs of production. Market disequilibrium in the form of excess supply can result in market values lower than cost. The real estate analyst provides value estimates at all points on the cycle of real estate starts and values, both at the peak of a cycle and in the trough; in times of inflation and recession. The value estimate is made using current market data and reflects existing supply and demand conditions. Only if "stabilized value" is estimated are the existing market data adjusted to reflect long-run "normal" conditions.[10]

---

[10] Defined on p. 47.

THE CONCEPT OF HIGHEST AND BEST USE

Highest and best use is a profit maximization concept which provides an explanation for the type and intensity of improvements initially developed and now in place on urban sites. The developer-investor is assumed to be a rational, knowledgeable individual who strives to maximize profitability, that is, to achieve the greatest dollar ROI. Sites are assumed to sell in a competitive market under conditions inherent in the definition of market value (buyers and sellers are knowledgeable about possible uses to which the site can be put, no coercion, normal offering time, and so on). In such circumstances, sites would sell at a price (value) reflecting their productivity under the improvements constituting their highest and best use. A knowledgeable seller would accept no less than this price; the buyer would pay no more. The concept of highest and best use attempts to show how development decisions are made in the private sector only. Decision-making in the public sector may result in the site's being developed for a public purpose such as a park or school. In this instance, social benefits and costs become the determinants of land use.

The real estate analyst always values the site under its highest and best use. To make this concept workable in "real world" situations, the analyst visualizes highest and best use in two separate circumstances. One situation involves a vacant site; the second is a site with existing improvements.

Vacant site

Highest and best use of a vacant site is that use of the site which will provide the greatest income to the site after deducting the capital and labor expenses of the improvements. The highest and best use is the most profitable use of the vacant site. The program of use to which the land is put must be long term in nature. If the site is vacant, all of the logical, feasible, alternative uses can be analyzed to decide which use would provide the greatest income residual to the site. This analysis involves estimating total NOI under each proposed use and subtracting from it the portion of income allocable to the improvement. The improvement's required income is calculated by multiplying the capitalization rate times the improvement cost.

The highest and best use decision may be simplified by constraining conditions. For example, in an area zoned for single-family residential structures, the analysis is limited to considering alternative homes. Commercial, industrial, or multifamily uses need not be considered; they are illegal. Although it is often easy to eliminate many potential uses, a decision about what is the highest and best use may require a considerable amount of comparative analysis of several properties. For single-family residential properties, the highest and best use decision usually requires analysis of such factors as location, style, design, quality of construction, relation to lot, and size. All such factors must be considered in terms of the surrounding properties. Does the style, size, design, and so on blend in with neighboring uses? Too great a deviation in these factors would signify an over- or underimprovement.

For income properties the decision as to whether a particular improvement is the highest and best use requires comparative analysis of income streams and economic lives. Where there is a wide variety of possible income-producing uses, the return provided to the land by each use must be calculated and compared with other possible returns. The following example should clarify how this determination is made.

Suppose that you have the opportunity to buy a vacant corner lot on a well-traveled, commercial "strip" street. The location is zoned for commercial usage, but it is adjacent to residential areas.

In the preliminary analysis it is noted that the most apparent needs are for a supermarket or a dry cleaner. A demand-analysis survey is favorable for both types of stores and the following cost and expected rental figures are indicated for two sizes of supermarkets and a dry cleaner store and processing unit:

Supermarket: $10/square foot
   10,000-square-foot supermarket: $100,000 cost
      Expected revenue: 1 percent of gross sales of $1,000,000: $10,000
   8,000-square-foot supermarket: $80,000 cost
      Expected revenue: 1 percent of gross sales of $900,000: $9,000
Dry cleaner: $10/square foot
   7,000-square-feet: $70,000 cost
      Expected revenue: flat $600/month or $7,200/year

All leases would provide net income to the owner. The market-determined rate of ROI in the alternative capital improvements must be obtained. For simplicity, let us assume that each of the three alternative improvements would yield an 8 percent return in the market. Combining the 8 percent ROI with a 2 percent straight-line recapture rate (each improvement has a 50-year economic life expectancy) gives a 10 percent capitalization rate for investment in the alternative improvements. For the 10,000-square-foot supermarket, a $10,000 income would be required to support the $100,000 investment in improvements. The 8,000-square-foot supermarket would require an $8,000 income; the dry cleaning establishment, $7,000. Subtracting the "building income" from the expected NOI of each property leaves $–0–, $1,000, and $200 residual income to the site. The conclusion is that the $8,000-square-foot supermarket is the highest and best use. In a competitive market of knowledgeable buyers and sellers, this site would be expected to sell for $12,500 ($1,000 ÷ 0.08), its value under the highest and best use.

If the $12,500 market value were paid for the site and the 8,000-square-foot supermarket were constructed, the investor would receive 8 percent on investment in the site and improvement and recapture an $80,000 improvement cost out of the stream of future NOI over the economic life of the improvement. Construction of either the 10,000-square-foot supermarket or the 7,000-square-foot dry cleaner would result in the investor's making less than 8 percent on investment or, viewed in another way, the value of the improvements in either instance would be less than their cost to create.

Assuming the site to be purchased at $12,500 (its value under highest and best use), $1,000 would be required to provide an 8 percent return on site value. The 100,000-square-foot supermarket would have $9,000 income remaining to support the investment of $100,000 in improvements. The $9,000 of income capitalized at 10 percent provides a value of $90,000 for improvements costing $100,000 to create. The dry cleaner improvement costing $70,000 would be valued at $62,000. The 10,000-square-foot supermarket is an overimprovement; the dry cleaner is an underimprovement. *When the proper type and intensity of land use has been achieved (the highest and best use), improvement value equals its cost to create.*

Improved sites

Existing improvements may be the highest and best use of the site, if they continue to produce income or amenities and thus have value in their own right. In fact, existing improvements remain the highest and best use until it becomes economically feasible to reuse the site for a more profitable purpose. At this time, the existing improvements are said to contribute nothing to the value of the site. The value of the site under the new program of use is great enough to permit purchase of the property (existing improvements and site), demolition of the existing structure, and preparation of the site for reuse. Until this point in time is reached, the existing improvements remain the highest and best use, and the site is valued under that type of use.

Suppose that the site in the preceding illustration is improved with an older single-family residence, rather than being vacant. The market value of the house and lot is $25,000 and is estimated by comparison with similar residences that have sold recently. In this instance, the analyst would conclude that the existing single-family residence is the highest and best use of the site. The value of this site would be $5,000, which is the value of a single-family residential lot in this location; the structure is appraised at $20,000. The site in this instance is valued under a single-family residential use, not a commercial use.

As time passes, the house may suffer further loss of value because of physical wear and a deterioration of its location for residential purposes. At the same time, the value of a vacant site under the highest and best commercial use may rise. At some future date, this site will have "ripened" for reuse. Site value under the new commercial highest and best use might reach $20,000; the market value of the site improved with the deteriorating single-family residence would fall to $18,000, since $2,000 is required to demolish the existing improvements and to prepare the site for reuse. At this point, the highest and best use becomes the commercial structure, and the site would be valued as though vacant and put to commercial use. The existing single-family residence would add nothing to the value of the site. Until this point in time, the residential improvements remain the highest and best use of the site. In either instance, whether valued under an existing residence or under a commercial use, the site's value is determined by its highest and best use.

SUMMARY

Investment decisions are based upon an appraisal of a property's value. Although investment analysis requires consideration of other factors in addition to value (such as financing requirements and income taxes), the primary criterion is value. The process of estimating value can thus be regarded as a major portion of investment analysis.

Value is a market phenomenon which is the resultant of the interaction of supply and demand. In turn, supply and demand are the market effects of the relative scarcity and utility associated with an economic good. Under perfect competition value would equal the price paid for the good. There would be no necessity to measure value independently; it would be automatically measured by the price of each transaction. However, since markets (particularly the real estate market) are less than perfectly competitive, value must be estimated independently by competent appraisers or analysts.

Real estate appraisers have a definition of market value that accommodates some market imperfections. Other "values" are defined according to the purpose or use to which the value estimate will be put. Investment value is one of these other value concepts. Investment value and market value are shown to be linked through the negotiations that produce transaction prices in imperfect real estate markets.

Market value, price, and cost can differ at any point in time. Market value can be regarded as the consensus of knowledgeable buyers and sellers about the price that should be paid for the real estate; price is the number of dollars actually paid in an imperfect market. The cost to create the improvements may be greater or lesser than their market value at the date of the market value estimate. Special considerations affecting the particular property under appraisal, such as a favorable lease, could result in a value for the improvements greater than their cost. Shifting market demand and supply conditions, which may not be in long-run equilibrium at the date of an appraisal, can produce a value that varies from the cost to create the improvement.

The concept of highest and best use provides an explanation of why land is developed in the private sector with a particular type and intensity of land use. A site is developed to its highest and best use when improvements are constructed that maximize profitability (overall return on investment) and, at the same time, produce the highest land value. A vacant site would sell under conditions of perfect competition at a price (value) determined by its highest and best use. A knowledgeable seller would not accept less; a knowledgeable buyer would be willing to pay the price, knowing that a use exists that will produce sufficient income to provide the required return on investment. Although real estate markets are less than perfect, the analyst estimates the value of the vacant site under its highest and best use. When the site under appraisal is improved with an existing building, the analyst concludes that the present improvements are the highest and best use unless a new improvement would generate sufficient site value to enable the present improvements to be demolished. As long as the present improvement remains the highest and best use, the site is valued under that type of land use.

QUESTIONS FOR REVIEW

1. What role does money play in the identification and measurement of value? How does money both help and hinder the measurement of value?
2. Discuss the contention that "Value is the basic criterion of all decision-making."
3. What are the characteristics of real estate and real estate markets that result in a definition of real property value different from value under perfect competition?
4. How does *market value* differ from a *normal* or *stabilized* value?
5. How does *investment value* differ from *market value*?
6. What are the two concepts of highest and best use?
7. Why would the cost to create improvements differ from the market value of the improvements when either an overimprovement or an underimprovement has been constructed?

PROBLEMS

1. A large home on the crest of a hill commanding a beautiful view of the river below was offered for sale at $250,000. The home had been built 15 years earlier by a wealthy business tycoon near the small town of his birth in Southern Missouri. Although no one in the town could afford such an expensive property, all of the town's people agreed the home was probably

worth at least $250,000. A local businessman offered $100,000 but the offer was rejected. Finally, the property was sold for $150,000 to a Chicago family as a summer vacation home.

    a. Did an effective market exist for the property?

    b. In your opinion, what was the value of the property?

    c. Does sale price necessarily equal value?

    d. Would you have paid $150,000 for the property?

    e. Would you have sold for $150,000?

2. Assume that you own a parcel of land for which you paid $10,000 three years ago. The annual real estate tax amounts to $175. You now need your money and want to sell. If inflation has been averaging 5 percent per year, would you accept $11,576 ($10,000 plus 5 percent compounded annually)? Why or why not? What additional costs might you want to cover in your asking price?

REFERENCES

American Institute of Real Estate Appraisers.   *The Appraisal of Real Estate.* 6th ed. Chicago, 1973.

Boyce, Byrl N.   *Real Estate Appraisal Terminology.* Cambridge, Mass.: Ballinger Publishing Co., 1975.

Featherston, J. B.   "Historic Influences on the Development of the Theory of Value," *Appraisal Journal* 43, no. 2 (April 1975): 165–82.

Ring, Alfred A.   *The Valuation of Real Estate.* 2d ed. Englewood Cliffs, N.J.: Prentice-Hall, 1970.

Smith, Halbert C.   *Real Estate Appraisal.* Columbus, Ohio: Grid Publishing Co., 1976.

Society of Real Estate Appraisers.   *An Introduction to Appraising Real Property.* Chicago, 1975.

Turvey, Ralph.   *The Economics of Real Property.* London: George Allen and Unwin, 1957.

Wendt, Paul F.   *Real Estate Appraisal Review and Outlook.* Athens: University of Georgia Press, 1974.

chapter 4

THE MEASUREMENT
OF VALUE

THE PROBLEM OF VALUE MEASUREMENT arises because of the existence of market imperfections. Price may or may not equal value in any less-than-perfect market; therefore, an independent measurement is required to arrive at a value figure. And even after a value figure is obtained by an independent process, it is not certain the figure is the price that will occur in an active, viable market. Thus, the best that one can do is to estimate the value of an economic good.

Obviously, since real estate is an economic good, these general statements are applicable—even more so than for most economic goods—to the estimation of real property values. Real estate markets are fraught with hazardous variances from the concept of an ideal market; therefore, the estimate of value of a parcel of real estate requires a wider range of possible error than value estimates for other economic goods. The price obtained for a special purpose, income-producing property valued at $300,000 might vary by as much as 25 percent in either direction from the appraised value. In contrast, the price of a bushel of wheat is probably so close to its value that there would be little discernible difference between value and price. These differences among markets in the efficiency and accuracy of the price-setting process largely result from the economic nature of the products themselves.

In Chapter 3, the features of real estate that lead to its economic uniqueness were discussed, and the economic implication of each characteristic was related to its influence on value. The following methods and procedures of value measurement should incorporate the effects of economic characteristics into estimates of income, capitalization rates, costs, and market prices.

There are three classical approaches, or frameworks of analysis, by which the value of a parcel of real estate is estimated. These are the income approach, the direct sales comparison approach, and the cost approach. Occasionally appraisal literature contains reports of newly developed approaches to real estate valuation; however, upon close examination it can be seen that many so-called new approaches have their roots in one or more of the three classical approaches.

Although we discuss each of the three approaches separately from the others, each approach is closely related to the other two. Since all roads lead to the final objective—the concept of value—the three approaches can be regarded as being different ways of looking at the same problem. The analyst needs to understand clearly the relationships among the three approaches and to be able to discern which approach is appropriate in a given situation.

VALUE ESTIMATION BY INCOME CAPITALIZATION

Nature of the income approach

The income approach focuses attention upon the value to investors of an expected future stream of net income to be derived from a parcel of real estate.[1] The right to receive the income in future years is the right associated with property ownership. This legal right has value, and it is this value which the income approach measures. In carrying out the income approach several variables must be considered, all of which constitute inputs to the basic value formula that:

$$V = (f) I$$

where

V = Value
I = Income
(f) = Relationship between value and income.

In estimating value, we attempt to predict total income (I) and to estimate the appropriate, current (f) or capitalization rate. Income is net operating income (NOI). The capitalization rate is a composite of the discount rate and recapture rate. The latter rate is a function of the remaining economic life of the depreciating portion of the asset and the pattern of capital recapture.

---

[1] A thorough treatment of the income capitalization approach to estimating market value is contained in William N. Kinnard, Jr., *Income Property Valuation* (Lexington, Mass.: D. C. Heath & Co., 1971), and Halbert C. Smith, *Real Estate Appraisal* (Columbus, Ohio: Grid Publishing Co., 1976), chaps. 5 and 6.

4 / The measurement of value

The capitalization process

The process of capitalization involves conversion of a forecasted stream of future income into its present value. This conversion process is termed capitalization and is based upon the principles of discounting.[2] The present value of any economic good is an amount less than the sum total of all of the future income payments to be derived from that economic good. There are basically two reasons for this. The first is that if investors already had all of the payments to be derived in the future from the property, they could put these in a perfectly safe government or institutional investment and receive a return. Investors presumably would be incurring no risk of not obtaining their money at the end of the time. The second reason is that on top of the pure payment for the use of money, the investors must be compensated for added risk—the risk that they will not obtain their capital back. The percentage amounts for each of these two reasons, the pure interest rate and the risk rate, are the two components that make up the rate of return on investment (ROI). The ROI plus the straight-line or sinking fund recapture rate make up the capitalization rate. The sinking fund recapture rate for estimating the value of an annuity is the amount necessary to be obtained each period, compounding at the discount rate, to accumulate to one dollar.[3] The ROI is also often termed the discount rate.

$$ROI + ROC = R$$

where

$$ROI = \text{Return on total investment}$$
$$ROC = \text{Rate of recapture of capital}$$
$$R = \text{Capitalization rate}$$

Valuation inputs

The income capitalization process requires that decisions be made regarding a property's expected net operating income, its remaining economic life, the expected pattern of the income stream, and the appropriate capitalization rate. When the decisions have been made, the valuation process is reduced to arithmetic calculation.

Net operating income. In attempting to predict future net income the most useful type of information is the historical experience of the

---

[2] The mathematics of discounting and the use of the compound interest tables are explained in Appendix F. The reader who requires further explanation of the derivation and use of these tables should carefully read this Appendix.

[3] Column 3 in Appendix G is a table of sinking fund factors.

property itself. In the case of a commercial, industrial, or apartment property, the first step is to analyze past years' income figures. How far back should one go? There is no definite answer, but preferably the record for at least five years should be examined. In analyzing past revenues the following two questions should be answered:

1. *Is each source of revenue appropriate and reasonable?*

Sometimes certain revenues should be discounted or eliminated. For example, some income statements show revenue from tenants for janitorial service. The offsetting expense will, of course, reduce or eliminate this item. But in some cases, even when the revenue is currently larger than the commensurate expense, it is unreasonable to project this situation into the future.

Whether each amount of revenue is reasonable can be ascertained only in relation to other comparable sources. If an apartment rental is either too low or too high it should be adjusted to the proper or reasonable rent. This is termed the *market rent* and is distinguished from *contract rent* which is the amount actually paid. Market rent is what should be paid and, therefore, is the amount that can be expected in the future.

2. *What is the trend of revenues for the time being analyzed?*

If the trend is either upward or downward, there may be some reason for the trend that the analyst has not discerned. Before proceeding it should be decided whether the trend is expected to continue or to change. This, of course, is the reason for analyzing a period of several years. Whether the past is an accurate predictor of the future can never be known for certain at the prediction stage of any analysis, but this makes it all the more important for analysts to utilize available data, their analytic powers, and their judgment derived from experience.

In analyzing past expenses, four questions should be considered:

1. *Is each item of expense appropriate and reasonable?*

The same comments that were made with respect to revenues are appropriate here. Additionally, however, we should mention that the problem of discerning and eliminating inappropriate expense figures from an owner's statement is usually greater than with respect to revenues. Most owners' income statements include expense items that are not appropriate to the property's value. Typical of such items are financing expense and income tax expense. These expenses are not allocable to the real estate. They do not necessarily have to be incurred by the real estate for it to produce income. Some owners would not need to bear such expenses, but all owners would have to expect janitorial or fuel expense. The former are thus personal or business expenses of the owner and should be eliminated from a statement of property expenses.

2. *What is the trend for each expense?*

As with the analysis for the trend of revenues, the trend of each expense should be noted and analyzed if necessary. If the trend of an expense is either upward or downward (and most expenses will be upward), there may be some reason for predicting higher or lower expenses in the future. On the other hand, analysts may uncover an upward trend of some expenses that effective and efficient management could correct. If so, analysts would then adjust the predicted expense downward under the assumption that effective and efficient management will be available for the property. The point to be emphasized with respect to analysis of the expense trend is that the trend should not be extrapolated blindly into the future. Often trends can be changed with proper management, and these possibilities will be detected by analysts when they look at the causes for basic factors underlying the trends.

3. *Should any expenses not included in the owner's statement be included?*

Often an owner's statement has been compiled for tax purposes or for other accounting reasons and not for the purpose of estimating the property's value. In these cases only the actual expenses incurred should be included. However, since the objective is to predict all the *future* expenses necessary for the property to have value—regardless of who owns the property—certain expenses should be added. Two good examples of such expenses typically are vacancy and collection losses and management expense.

Vacancy losses and often collection losses involve little or no out-of-pocket expense. Yet, in predicting the future net income for a parcel of real estate, analysts would be remiss in not recognizing the high probability that reductions from total possible gross income will result because of these reasons. Keep in mind that the objective is to predict future net income, and that particularly as buildings become older, their owners should expect to experience some periods between lessees when their property will not be drawing income and some tenants who for various reasons will not pay their rent. Thus analysts should include this expense as one expected for the future.

Particularly with respect to a small, owner-managed investment property the expense of managing the property is often not included in an owner's statement of income and expenses. The owner in such a case manages the property, and management does not represent an out-of-pocket expense. Management is thus not entered as a specific and identified expense. The function of property management, however, will have to be performed in the future for the property to obtain income for the owner. This reasoning provides the justification for including management as an expense that will be incurred by a property in the future—whether accomplished by the owner or by a hired manager. In cases where the owner has hired a manager and this expense is identified in the operating statement, and provided the expense is reasonable both with respect to amount and trend, this figure could be entered as the analyst's best estimate of the future expense. In those cases where the owner has not hired a manager and no management expense is indicated in the statement, the analyst should impute a future management expense to the property. The owner's time is worth money, since he or she could be earning money during the time spent managing the property. The amount imputed usually varies between 2 and 10 percent of effective gross income, which is the difference between total possible gross income and vacancy and collection losses.

4. *Are large replacement item expenses amortized over the expected life of the replacements?*

Some large components of a building such as its heating system, air-conditioning system, water heater, or roof can be expected to wear out faster than the building itself. A roof, for example, may have to be replaced every 15 years, while the building can be expected to last perhaps 50 to 100 years. Over its total life, then, the building will undoubtedly have several roofs. Many times analysts will find that the owners have not amortized these large expenditures over their expected lives. Rather, as the large expense is incurred for replacing a roof or heating system, this expense will be included as a deduction from that year's income. This is not the proper procedure, however, for forecasting stabilized income. It must be recognized that the roof wears out each hour each day and each year, rather than all at once. It is fallacious to assign the entire expense of a new roof to one earning period only. Therefore, in predicting future expenses to the real estate, analysts typically include an amount allocable each period for major repairs and replacements of components of the building that last a shorter time than the building itself. These items are not included in depreciation assignable to the basic building.

In predicting future revenues and expenses for a parcel of real property through the procedure of analyzing past operating statements of the owner, the analyst obtains a new statement of expected revenues and expenses which is called a reconstructed operating statement.[4]

Remaining economic life.   Another variable to be considered is the length of economic life of the property. All material things wear out over some period of time, and buildings are no exception. Buildings wear out, meaning that expenses will increase over the life of the building, while revenues at some point will begin to decline and will decline

---

[4] Examples of the owner's operating statement and of the appraiser's reconstructed operating statement are shown in Figures 4–2 and 4–3.

more and more as time goes along. Eventually, the expenses will become equal to and possibly greater than the revenues being produced by the property. The point at which expenses exactly equal revenues is the end of the economic life of the property; at this point the property no longer has value. Figure 4–1 depicts the determinants of remaining economic life.

FIGURE 4–1
Determinants of economic life

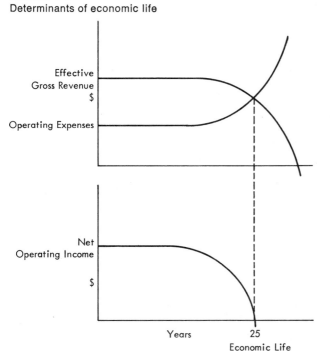

Certain income capitalization procedures (land residual, building residual, and property residual techniques) require that the remaining economic life of the improvements be estimated, because it is the period during which an owner can expect to obtain net income from an investment. Typically the economic life for buildings runs from 25 to 75 years, although exceptions can be found at both ends of the range. The actual measurement of this variable can only come from knowledge of construction techniques and judgment associated with long experience in dealing with buildings and estimating their economic lives. Other income capitalization techniques, such as the Ellwood technique, use an assumed investment holding period and project net operating income over, say, ten years rather than over the entire economic life of the improvements.

Pattern of income. Another input in the income approach is the pattern of the income to be received over the remaining economic life of the building (or over an assumed investment holding period). The forecasted pattern is reflected in the process by which future income is discounted to a present value. An income stream's pattern will usually take one of the following two basic forms.

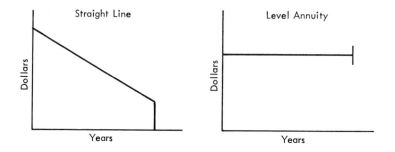

The straight-line pattern assumes that the net income will decrease by the same percentage every year to the end of the building's economic life, while the level annuity assumes the net income will remain constant.

The decision as to which pattern will be most realistic for a property being appraised must be based upon the analyst's assumption about the method of capital recapture. The straight-line pattern assumes that an equal percentage of the capital investment in the building (an equal yearly dollar amount) is recaptured every year.

If the remaining economic life of a building were estimated to be 25 years, a $100,000 investment cost would be recaptured by drawing equal annual amounts of $4,000 from the income stream each year for the 25-year period. The first year's income that would be produced would be the $4,000 plus the expected rate of return on the $100,000. If this rate were 8 percent the income would be $12,000 during the first year. For the second year the income would be $4,000 plus 8 percent of the remaining capital balance of $96,000, or $7,680, for a total income payment of $11,680. Each year the dollar return would be reduced because of the capital recapture assumption, as shown below. The value of the income stream would be estimated by dividing the capitalization rate of 8 percent plus 4 percent (12 percent) into the first year's income of $12,000. The resulting value is $100,000.

The crucial assumption contained in the use of the straight-line method is that the amounts of recapture drawn from the income stream ($4,000 in the above example) are *not* reinvested and thus do not earn interest. These amounts presumably are deposited by the owners in their checking accounts, hidden in their mattresses, or used in some

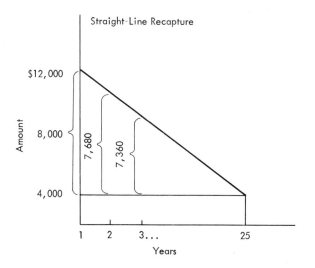

Straight-Line Recapture

other way in which no return is earned. Since this assumption is considered unrealistic by many real estate analysts, the straight-line method of capitalization has lost favor in recent years.

The level annuity method of capitalization contains a more realistic assumption about the capital recapture portion of the income stream. In this method the capital recaptured each period is assumed to be reinvested in another property or investment yielding the same rate of return as the property being appraised. Thus, the amount of capital recapture before reinvestment is less than in the straight-line method.

In level annuity capitalization, a sinking fund factor is added to the ROI rate to obtain the total capitalization rate. If the same income used in the above example of straight-line capitalization were capitalized by the level annuity method of capitalization, the capitalization rate would be 0.08 plus 0.01368 (annual sinking fund factor at 0.08, 25 years), or 0.09368. Note that the capitalization rate is lower than in the straight-line method and produces a higher value of about $128,000 ($12,000 ÷ 0.09368). The higher value results because the income stream is level, rather than declining. It is level because additional income is produced through reinvestment.

When deciding whether to use straight-line or level annuity capitalization, it is apparent that the net income pattern produced by the recapture assumption should be the basis for the decision. Do investors more typically place recapture dollars in nonincome-producing places for safekeeping? Or do they typically buy additional investments of a similar type? Most analysts of real estate, as well as of securities, believe investors do reinvest and thus choose level annuity capitalization. When analysts use the property residual technique of income capitalization, or the investment holding period concept, they typically choose the level annuity assumption. In these techniques, the property's total NOI is capitalized to a present value. The property's discounted reversion value is then added to the capitalized value of the income stream.

One additional point about the pattern of the net income stream is that although the actual amount of net income that will be received in any particular year may vary considerably from the amount forecasted under either the straight-line or level annuity pattern, the deviations on either side are likely to cancel out—leaving the basic pattern. In other words, the estimate may turn out to be too low in some years but in other years the estimate will turn out to be too high. These theoretical income streams are thus estimates of the pattern and not of the actual amounts to be received in any particular year.

Estimation of capitalization rates. We now return to a determination of the capitalization rate to be used in discounting the future income stream. The two components of the discount rate are (a) the pure cost for the use of money and (b) the additional business risk involved in a real estate investment. The addition of the discount rate and the recapture rate (straight-line or level annuity) provides the capitalization rate. The reciprocal of the capitalization rate is a factor obtainable from a table.[5] Discount rate determination, then, involves the question of what rate investors demand and can obtain for a given level of risk in a particular real estate investment.

At any point in time the pure interest for long-term investments is determined by the yield on long-term government bonds. If this latter rate is, say, 5 percent, a real estate investor would demand an additional return to compensate for the added risk. Rather than trying to determine the rate to be added to the pure rate of interest, however, the analyst or investor can usually more easily look at the overall rate of discount for similar real estate investments. If similar parcels were purchased for yields of 10 percent, the analyst would impute a 10 percent discount rate to the property in question. Similarly, if the going rate for the comparable parcels were 12 percent, this would be the return imputed to the parcel and used in the analysis. The idea is simple; only implementation is difficult.[6]

Site or property reversion. The only remaining variable to be determined in estimating the value of a property by the property residual technique is the value of the site. With an income capitalization method using an investment holding period assumption (Ellwood), the value of the property (site and improvements) at the end of the holding period must be estimated.

---

[5] Column 5 of the compound interest tables in Appendix G contains these factors.

[6] Other methods for determining capitalization rates are given in books on real estate appraising cited at the end of this chapter; in specialized valuation problems these methods may be appropriate and useful.

The site reversion value is necessary in the property residual technique, since the investor would be entitled to the continued use of the land after the building is worn out and no longer has value. For analysts to estimate the value of the total property, therefore, they must estimate the value of the reversionary right to use the land after the building is gone.

Since no analyst has a crystal ball and can say what the value of the site will be, say, 25 or 50 years into the future, most real estate analysts, unless they have better information, assume that the value of the site at the end of the life of the building will be the same as the value of the site today. The problem, therefore, becomes one of estimating the value of the site today and discounting that value for the remaining economic life of the building. The valuation procedures for the site are (a) by direct sales comparison with comparable vacant parcels of land and (b) by hypothetical highest and best use computation.[7] The direct sales comparison approach is discussed later in this chapter.

Site value can be estimated by capitalizing the difference between (a) the total net operating income available to the real estate if it were improved with the most profitable, long-term use and (b) the part of the income stream attributable to the building. The portion of the income stream remaining after building income is subtracted from total income is attributed to the site, and this income stream is capitalized to provide a present value for the land. In capitalizing an income stream to land, however, it must be recognized that this income stream theoretically can continue forever. That is, the legal right cannot be terminated so long as the owner lives up to the basic requirements of society. The income stream to a parcel of land, therefore, is capitalized to perpetuity. This process involves dividing the site's annual income by the discount rate (ROI) used in capitalizing the building's income.

In income capitalization methods that project NOI over an investment holding period, rather than over the economic life of the improvements, a judgment must be made about the dollar amount of property reversion at the end of the typical or average holding period. This property reversion includes both site value and improvement value, assuming that the improvements will have remaining economic life after the holding period. These techniques avoid assigning an absolute dollar amount to this property reversion. Instead, the analyst assumes that the present market value of the property will increase by some percentage (appreciate), decrease by a percentage (depreciate), or remain level. Factors causing an expected increase include inflation or long-run demand forces pressing against a limited supply. A percentage decrease in the property reversion could result from physical deteriora-

---

[7] The second procedure of estimating the value of a site was discussed in Chapter 3 as the highest and best use decision.

tion, functional obsolescence, and locational obsolescence (the site becomes less well suited for the existing improvements). Often appraisers do not attempt to forecast either increases or decreases in property value over a holding period that may be as long as ten years. Instead, the assumption is made that the property will sell for today's market value at the end of the investment holding period.

Examples of the income approach

Estimating the value of the ABC Building (described in the next section) illustrates many aspects of various income capitalization approaches. The reader is cautioned to remember that a real estate analyst would typically use only one of the following approaches in obtaining an indication of market value for a client.

Estimation of net operating income. The first step in a valuation problem is to estimate the future net operating income in the format of a reconstructed operating statement.

Assume that you are asked to estimate the value of the ABC Building, a two-story commercial structure on a major artery near downtown. Other commercial buildings of fairly high quality occupy the area, and this usage is expected to continue. Typical tenants in the area are service or specialty establishments, such as office machine firms, sporting goods stores, music stores, and carpet companies.

Four suites of rooms occupy the first floor and are rented on long-term leases for $200 per month. The second floor also contains four suites, two of which are leased for $150 per month. The remaining two suites are rented for $200 per month. One of these monthly rented suites tends to be vacant about 25 percent of the time.

The owner's operating statement is shown in Figure 4–2. The real estate analyst critically examines the owner's statement as well as cur-

FIGURE 4–2

ABC Commercial Building owner's operating statement

Gross rents collected (1975)		$17,600
Expenses:		
Power	$1,800	
Real estate tax	1,600	
Garbage removal	100	
Supplies	400	
Mortgage payments	2,500	
Insurance	1,500	
Decorating	600	
Repairs	1,700	
Depreciation	2,000	
Janitor	1,500	13,700
Net Income before Taxes		$ 3,900

rent and foreseeable market conditions for properties of this type. The reader is referred back to the discussion of net operating income for the factors to be considered in estimating NOI. The analyst's reconstructed operating statement is shown in Figure 4–3.

FIGURE 4–3

ABC Commercial Building reconstructed operating statement

Potential gross income		$18,000
Vacancy and collection losses		600
Effective gross income		$17,400
Expenses:		
Power	$1,800	
Real estate tax	1,600	
Garbage removal	100	
Supplies	400	
Insurance	1,500	
Decorating and repairs	600	
Reserve for replacements	1,700	
Management	800	
Janitor	1,500	10,000
Net Operating Income		$ 7,400

Property residual technique. Estimating the market value of this commercial property using the property residual technique requires an estimate of (a) the remaining economic life, (b) the value of the site reversion, and (c) the market-determined overall rate of return on investment (discount rate). The analyst knows that the building is 15 years old and that it has been well maintained. The property is in an attractive, well-located commercial district that serves a prosperous and stable residential area. In the judgment of the analyst, the building has 40 years of remaining economic life.

The site measures 80 by 120 feet. Recent sales of comparable vacant sites indicate a market value for the subject property's site of $2.60 per square foot, or $24,960.[8] Today's market value is assumed to be the value of the site at the end of the 40-year economic life of the building. Investors in properties of this type are requiring a 10 percent return on their total investment. A higher rate of discount (return on investment) would produce a lower value, while a lower rate would result

---

[8] Alternatively, site value might be estimated by hypothesizing the highest and best use of the site, as though vacant, and capitalizing the income residual to the land.

The highest and best use of the site, if vacant, would be a new, more modern commercial structure costing $80,000 and having a 50-year economic life. The building would have the same number of units, but all rents could be increased by $50 per month. Operating expenses would increase $1,500 per year. Investors in the market are able to obtain a 10 percent rate of return on an investment in this type of real

in a higher value. When market value is to be estimated, the rate of return should be justified from market experience.

The property residual technique produces a present value of $72,900 for the property (see Figure 4–4). The level annuity premise was used in capitalizing future income into present value. The site's value at the end of the building's economic life is assumed to be equal to its current market value. The discounted value of the site reversion was added to the present worth of the NOI to obtain total property value. Final value estimates are rounded to avoid spurious accuracy.

FIGURE 4–4

Valuation of ABC Commercial Building: Property residual technique

Value of NOI for 40 years:
  $7,400 × 9.779 (PV of Annuity of $1, 10%, 40 years) $72,365
Value of site reversion:
  $24,960 (by market comparison) × 0.022
  (PV of $1, 10%, 40 years)   549
Value of property ....$72,914, say $72,900

Building residual technique. Estimating the market value of the ABC commercial property using the building residual technique requires that the analyst estimate the remaining economic life of the building (40 years) and the value of site ($24,960). The market-determined rate of return on properties of this type also must be ascertained (say 10 percent).

The building residual technique produces a present value of $72,900 for the property (see Figure 4–5). The income necessary to give the investor a 10 percent return on the market value of the site was subtracted from NOI to find the income residual to the building. The

---

estate as demonstrated below. The indicated value for the site under its highest and best use is $24,820.

Site value under highest and best use

Potential gross income $22,800
  Vacancy and collection losses   750

Effective gross income $22,050
  Less: Expenses   11,500

Net operating income (highest and best use) $10,550

Value of site:
  Net operating income $10,550
    Less: Building income: $80,000 ÷ 9.915
    (PV of annuity of $1, 10%, 50 years)   8,068

  Site income .... $ 2,482
Site value ($2,482 ÷ 0.10) $24,820

building's income is capitalized into present value using the level annuity factor at 10 percent.[9]

FIGURE 4–5

Valuation of ABC Commercial Building: Building residual technique

NOI	$ 7,400
Income required to support site value:	
Site value ($24,960 × 0.10 site capitalization rate)	2,496
Income residual to building	$ 4,904
Value of building:	
$4,904 × 9.779 (PV of annuity of $1, 10%, 40 years)	$47,956
Value of site:	
$24,960 (by market comparison)	24,960
Property value	$72,916, say $72,900

Site residual technique. The analyst assumes that the cost to create the building equals its market value when working with the site residual technique. The site residual technique would *not be* used to appraise the ABC commercial property, which is improved with a 15-year-old structure. The assumption that the cost to create this building is equal to its market value would not be realistic, since the structure undoubtedly suffers from varying amounts of deterioration and obsolescence. The site residual technique is used only when new or almost new improvements exist—improvements which have yet to suffer loss of value

---

[9] The examples in Figures 4–4, 4–5, and 4–6, demonstrate that identical answers are obtained when the same data are used to work each of the three residual techniques. The property residual technique typically is worked using the level annuity tables. The building and site residual techniques, however, are sometimes worked using straight-line capitalization. If the preceding problem is worked by the building residual technique using straight-line capitalization of income, the answer would be $64,192. The discrepancy between answers obtained by the property residual and building residual techniques is caused by the assumptions in the two different capitalization methods used. The level annuity premise assumes the annual recapture is reinvested at the rate of discount, and straight-line capitalization assumes the initial investment is recaptured in equal annual amounts that earn no return.

Valuation of ABC Commercial Building: Building residual technique using straight-line capitalization

NOI	$ 7,400
Income required to support site value:	
Site value ($24,960 × 0.10 land capitalization rate)	2,496
Income residual to building	$ 4,904
Value of building:	
$4,904 ÷ 0.125 (0.10 percent return on investment plus 0.025 percent recapture of investment assuming 40-year economic life)	$39,232
Value of site	$24,960
Property value	$64,192

because of deterioration or obsolescence and which can be said to be the highest and best use of the site, if it were vacant.

The example in Figure 4–6 demonstrates that the site residual technique provides the same value estimate as the building and property residual techniques, when building cost (value) is assumed to be $47,956. The income necessary to provide the investor a market-determined 10 percent return on investment, and to return the initial investment of $47,956 over the economic life of the building, is deducted from NOI to give the income residual to the site. The income residual to the site is then capitalized as a perpetuity at 10 percent to obtain site value. Site value is added to building cost (assumed to equal building value) to give property value.

FIGURE 4–6

Valuation of the ABC Commercial Building: Site residual technique

NOI	$ 7,400
Income required to support building value (cost to create):	
Building cost (value) assumed to be $47,956 ÷ 9.779	
(PV of annuity of $1, 10%, 40 years)	4,904
Income residual to the site	$ 2,496
Value of site:	
($2,496 ÷ 0.10 land capitalization rate)	$24,960
Value (cost) of building	47,956
Property value	$72,916, say $72,900

Direct capitalization with an overall rate. Direct capitalization is accomplished simply by dividing the property's NOI by an overall capitalization rate. The overall capitalization rate is derived from market evidence by dividing the NOIs of comparable properties by their verified sales prices. Each comparable sale provides an indication of the appropriate overall capitalization rate (reciprocal of the net income multiplier). Analysts use a number of comparable sales to provide evidence in support of their selection of this market-determined rate. These comparable properties must have sold recently under conditions that permitted their market values to be realized, that is, arms-length negotiation among knowledgeable buyers and sellers, no coercion, and a normal offering time.

Direct capitalization is demonstrated in Figure 4–7, where the overall capitalization rate of .1025 is divided into the $7,400 NOI of the ABC commercial property to obtain a value estimate of $72,200. Only three comparables are used in Figure 4–7 to derive the overall capitalization rate; additional sales would be desirable when available.

Mortgage-equity and Ellwood techniques. Mortgage-equity appraisal

FIGURE 4–7

Valuation of the ABC Commercial Building: Direct capitalization

Selection of overall capitalization rate:
    $8,100 NOI ÷ $82,200 sale price of comparable A: 0.0985 indicated overall rate
    $7,800 NOI ÷ $76,100 sale price of comparable B: 0.1025 indicated overall rate
    $6,600 NOI ÷ $62,900 sale price of comparable C: 0.1049 indicated overall rate

Overall capitalization rate: 0.1025
    This rate was selected by the analyst because comparable B most closely resembles the ABC commercial property, and .1025 approximates the mean OAR from all three comparables.

Value of ABC Commercial Property
    $7,400 NOI ÷ 0.1025 overall capitalization rate ....$72,195, say $72,200

methods, of which the Ellwood technique is an example, divide the NOI into that part required to pay the installments on the mortgage debt (typically, these payments are for principal and interest on a level payment, fully-amortized mortgage) and into the cash flow to the equity position. In contrast to the income capitalization techniques described above, mortgage-equity appraisal explicitly incorporates financing in the appraisal methodology. A complete explanation of the derivation of the Ellwood overall capitalization rate is beyond the intent of this basic text.[10] The example in Figure 4–8 computes Ellwood's overall capitalization rate (R) and defines the components of the formula. The Ellwood overall capitalization rate is divided into NOI to obtain property value.

The assumptions incorporated into the Ellwood overall capitalization rate are summarized below.

1. A level NOI is projected over a typical or average investment holding period. Investors usually do not hold a property over the entire economic life of the improvements; 7 to 12 years is a more common holding period. Ellwood's tables are calculated for holding periods of 5, 10, 15, 20 and 25 years.
2. The NOI is divided between the income necessary to service the mortgage and the income flowing to the ownership position. The analyst builds into the Ellwood capitalization rate the typical financing terms available for the property at the time of appraisement. It is assumed that potential purchasers of the property would shop the market for the most favorable financing and that market value will reflect those terms.

---

[10] The interested reader is referred to L. W. Ellwood, *Ellwood Tables for Real Estate Appraising and Financing*, 2d ed. (Chicago: American Institute of Real Estate Appraisers, 1967). The Ellwood technique of mortgage-equity appraisal is, of course, named for its originator.

FIGURE 4–8

Valuation of the ABC Commercial Building: Ellwood (mortgage-equity) technique

Ellwood overall capitalization rate (R):

$$R = Y - M \left[[Y + (\frac{f}{i} - 1)(Sp - 1) \, 1/S_n] - f \right] + [\text{depreciation} \times 1/S_n] \text{ or}$$

$$- [\text{appreciation} \times 1/S_n]$$

Where

Y = Equity yield rate (0.12)
M = Loan to value ratio (0.70)
f = Annual mortgage constant for a monthly payment mortgage. A 9.5 percent, 20-year mortgage has a monthly mortgage constant of 0.009321 (Column 6 in 9.5 percent Monthly Compound Interest Table, Appendix G) × 12 months = 0.111852.
i = Mortgage interest rate (0.095)
Sp = Monthly future worth of 1 (Column 1 in Appendix G) at the mortgage interest rate for the assumed investment holding period (10 years), or 2.5760.
$1/S_n$ = Annual sinking fund factor (Column 3 in Appendix G) at the equity yield rate (0.12) for the assumed investment holding period (10 years), or 0.056984.
Depreciation or Appreciation = Percent depreciation or appreciation assumed in the value of the property over the investment holding period. In this calculation 2 percent appreciation (0.02) in the property's reversion value is forecast.

Substituting

$$R = 0.12 - .70 \left[[0.12 + (0.111852/0.095 - 1)(2.5760 - 1) \ 0.056984] - 0.111852 \right.$$
$$\left. - [0.02(0.056984)] \right.$$

$R = 0.102$

Value of ABC commercial property
$7,400 NOI ÷ 0.102 Ellwood overall capitalization rate ....$72,549, say $72,500

3. The property is assumed to be sold at the end of the investment holding period. The outstanding balance of the mortgage debt is retired at that time, and the remainder of the reversion price is available to the equity position.
4. Provision is made for anticipated appreciation or depreciation in the market value of the property over the investment holding period. In contrast to the property residual technique in which the projection of NOI over the economic life of the improvements results in a reversion of site value only, the assumption of an investment holding period produces a reversionary value that contains both site and improvement value.
5. The market value of the equity investment is the discounted value of the stream of income to the equity over the investment holding period, plus the discounted cash reversion to the equity when the property is sold. The appropriate rate of discount is the market

rate necessary to attract equity funds to this type of investment.[11]
6. The present value of the equity can be added to the initial amount of the mortgage to give property value. In effect, the initial amount of the mortgage represents the present value of the level debt service plus the present value of the mortgage reversion at the end of the holding period discounted at the mortgage rate of interest. Ellwood's method splits NOI into cash flow and a cash reversion to the equity and a flow of debt service and reversion to the lender, each of which is discounted at its respective rate to obtain present value.

Several techniques, but only one estimated market value

Proper application by the analyst of each of the several income capitalization techniques appropriate for the ABC commercial property would, in theory, produce identical estimates of market value. Market value is determined by demand and supply conditions and not by the methodology chosen by the appraiser to measure it. In practice, of course, we would be surprised if the answers obtained by use of two or more methods were identical. The realities of the imperfect markets that provide the valuation inputs such as discount rates, sales prices, loan terms, and so on, will result in discrepancies among market value estimates.

If each of these techniques is capable of providing the "correct" estimate of market value, why do we need more than one? Why not use only the simplest method—direct capitalization with an overall rate derived from verified transaction prices? The answer comes in part from history and in part from practical considerations. The various techniques did not appear simultaneously; the land and building residual methodologies preceded the property residual technique, with Ellwood's method being the most recent. The newer methodologies have never completely replaced older techniques. Instead they have been added. Analysts and academicians vary in their support of the methods. Kahn, Case, and Schimmel, for instance, contend that "The property residual technique is sufficiently elastic to meet any given appraisal problem.

---

[11] This equity rate is an after-financing, before-tax internal rate of return on equity value.

Although circuitous reasoning seems inherent in this conceptualization of Ellwood's mortgage-equity technique, his formulation of an overall capitalization rate avoids assuming that the absolute dollar value of the mortgage is known at the time of appraisal (only the loan-to-value ratio, the interest rate, and the maturity need to be specified), or that the absolute dollar sale price for the property reversion must be specified (only the percentage of expected appreciation or depreciation in property value over the holding period needs to be predicted).

It is the preferred technique."[12] The basic appraisal textbook published by the American Institute of Real Estate Appraisers is less conclusive in recommending one or the other income capitalization technique.

Therefore, the basis for the appraiser's choice of method is his belief that the subject property has characteristics that conform to those inherent in the method selected. Accordingly, *each method cannot always be applied correctly to the same property.* Usually, one method appears to be more consistent with the appraiser's conclusions concerning the characteristics of a particular property, and probable future trend and income behavior, interest (risk rate) and recapture requirements.[13]

In applying these techniques in the "real world," the real estate analyst is continuously faced with imprecision and uncertainties in the data. The lack of perfect information results in advocacy of the more complex techniques. For instance, an overall capitalization rate obtained directly from the market evidence by dividing the NOIs of comparable properties by their sale prices can produce a relatively wide dispersion of indicated overall rates. On the other hand, explicitly incorporating value-creating factors such as financing, the investment holding period, and potential appreciation or depreciation in property value over the holding period, raises these components in the valuation process to the level of consciousness. Here the appraiser can determine the value of the variables, rather than permitting them to remain buried in a relatively imprecise overall capitalization rate derived from the sale of comparable properties.

If increasing the variables that require conscious analysis and judgment on the part of the analyst improves the value estimate, why stop with the explicit introduction of financing into valuation methodology? Why not include income taxes as well and capitalize an aftertax cash flow and aftertax cash reversion to the equity? This approach is developed in the next chapter as a technique for determining investment value. Investment value, it may be recalled, is defined as a personal value that depends upon the particular financing that an individual investor can secure, the individual's required return on investment, and the individual's needs and investment goals. These investment goals cause an investor to select a particular tax depreciation schedule which, given his or her income tax bracket, will determine the amount of tax that must be paid, or the tax savings that will be obtained, as well as the magnitude of any aftertax cash reversion to the equity. The concept of investment value differs from market value in that the latter repre-

---

[12] Sanders A. Kahn, Frederick E. Case, and Alfred Schimmel, *Real Estate Appraisal and Investment* (New York: Ronald Press, 1963), p. 153.

[13] American Institute of Real Estate Appraisers, *The Appraisal of Real Estate*, 6th ed. (Chicago, 1973), p. 410.

sents a consensus of opinion among knowledgeable buyers and sellers concerning the price for which the property should sell under defined conditions. Market-derived data are used in the various appraisal methods that estimate market value. Even the financing arrangement in the mortgage-equity technique is assumed to be typical for that type of property—even when the financing is defined as the best obtainable. Rational and knowledgeable buyers are expected to shop to obtain these terms and nothing less would be acceptable. On the other hand, income tax considerations vary among buyers and sellers to the extent that generalization about "typical" tax factors for the type of property under appraisal becomes tenuous.

VALUE ESTIMATION BY DIRECT SALES COMPARISON

The idea of the direct sales comparison approach is straightforward: by comparing prices for similar properties the analyst can judge the price (and thus the value) of the property under consideration. The properties for which these prices are compared must be similar; it would be fallacious to compare prices of dissimilar properties. But how similar to each other must the properties be? Although a quantitative answer is not possible, the general rule is that the properties must be sufficiently similar so that all the differences among the properties can be identified and dollar values assigned to these differences. For example, a comparison between two houses which have as their only difference the lack of a basement in one would be quite feasible. A value difference could easily be assigned to the basement and the resulting market price imputed as one evidence of value.

In making comparisons it should be recognized that the determinants of supply and demand are operating to produce market prices, and that the analyst is looking at the end results of the market process. The actions of the market produce a price which can be viewed as a discounted value of the benefits that are expected from the property in the future. Thus, if buyers discount a property's expected benefits to a certain price they will tend to discount similar benefits available from other properties to similar prices.

This basic assumption of the direct sales comparison approach clearly shows its relation to the income approach. In the income approach the future net operating income to a property must, of course, be estimated while this step is not necessary in the direct sales comparison approach. The benefits or income to a property are expected when the analyst employs the direct sales comparison approach, just as in the income approach. The fact that they are not estimated does not mean that a buyer will agree to forego these benefits.

By the same reasoning, the income approach must contain a measure-

ment from the market to determine the value that should be placed
upon the expected income. This measurement comes through the capitalization rate. In effect, there is a market of capitalization rates just
as there is a market of prices. In the direct sales comparison approach,
analysts go to the market to determine prices; in the income approach
analysts go to the market to determine capitalization rates. They compare the capitalization rates for properties having similar risk and make
adjustments to the rate for any differences that are perceived.

In carrying out the direct sales comparison approach, probably the
most useful technique is to construct a grid, showing on one axis each
comparison property and on the other axis each item by which the
properties are different. Such a grid is shown in Figure 4–9. Values are
assigned to each difference and either added to or subtracted from the
known price of the comparable to derive a price for the property under
appraisal.

FIGURE 4–9
Grid analysis, direct sales comparison

	A	*B*	*C*	*D*	*Subject*
Price	24,300	17,200	20,600	20,500	?
Market conditions	this year	3 years ago +18% +$3,096	2 years ago +12% +$2,472	1 year ago +6% +$1,230	now
Location	equal	equal	poorer +$1,000	equal	—
Architecture	better −$400	poorer +$400	equal	equal	—
Rooms	6½ −$500	6	7 −$800	6	6
Baths	1½	1 +$800	1½	1 +$800	1½
Condition of property	better −$600	poorer +$500	equal	equal	—
Indicated value	$22,800	$21,996	$23,272	$22,530	

Adjustments that must be made reflect differences among physical
characteristics (such as number of rooms and baths, lot size, physical
condition, and architectural desirability), location, and market conditions.
Dollar or percentage adjustments are assigned to each differential in

the comparables, based upon how much more or less the property would be expected to bring in the market with or without the feature. For example, lack of a second bath in a property being appraised results in a subtraction from the price of a comparable property having a second bath. Similarly, better architecture or design of the subject property over a comparable property results in an addition to the price of a comparable property having inferior characteristics. Location of a single-family residential subject property in a less desirable neighborhood, or its exposure to a high-volume traffic artery, can result in a subtraction from the verified sale price of the comparable.

If the time of sale of a comparison property is over four to six months in the past, an adjustment often must be made to reflect changed market conditions. The adjustment takes account of any change in the value of the dollar and the real estate market that may have occurred. With the value of the dollar having decreased an average of about 5 percent per year for the last five years and many real estate markets experiencing even greater price increases, an adjustment of at least 6 percent will often be required. This adjustment was made to the comparable properties in Figure 4–9.

Additional adjustments to the comparable's sale price for terms and conditions of sale are sometimes attempted. An adjustment for terms of sale might reflect the amount, timing, type of repayment, and other obligations assumed by the buyer. The most stringent terms would be all cash at the time of sale. In a real estate transaction the seller may take a mortgage from the buyer as part payment, sell on installment contract, require no payment for a period of time, or lend the buyer funds at an attractive interest rate. The analyst may compensate for such terms by adjusting all transactions to a figure the analyst believes would be appropriate for a normal or typical transaction.

Adjustments for conditions of sale concerns the relationship between buyer and seller. Was each acting under undue pressure? Did each have knowledge of market conditions? Was the property on the market for a reasonable time? Was the transaction at arm's length, that is, is there a personal relationship between buyer and seller? *Although adjustments for terms and conditions of sale may be attempted, it is believed to be better practice not to use these properties as comparables.*

In conclusion, the direct sales comparison approach is appropriate for value estimation when there are active, viable markets for which sale prices are known and in which properties are truly comparable. Usually such markets exist for single-family residential properties and for some general purpose commercial and industrial properties. For more specialized types of properties, direct comparison of sales is impossible or implausible, and the appraiser must rely upon the income or cost approach.

VALUE ESTIMATION BY COST ANALYSIS

The cost approach to value estimation attempts to measure value by adding all the costs necessary to reproduce a building, subtracting therefrom any losses in value, and adding to this figure the site value. Because of its reliance on historical cost figures, the approach can be used when both market and income data are unavailable or unreliable. The main assumption upon which the cost approach is based, however, constitutes a theoretical weakness, and the task of measuring reductions in value on older buildings becomes its Achilles' heel in practicality.

Relation of cost to value

The principal assumption of the approach is that the cost of creating an economic good equals its value. However, since value of improvements is determined by the forces of supply and demand in the market, the equality of cost and value only rarely exists. Investors pay only scant attention to the historical cost of the good. Differences between value and reproduction cost can be identified and measured, but only with uncertainty.

As discussed in our previous analysis of highest and best use,[14] a vacant site is improved with its highest and best use when a building or other improvement provides to the owner of the land the highest percentage return. In this situation the cost of the improvement equals its value, and no further adjustments are required to estimate value. If too much capital is sunk into the building, the percentage return to land is lowered, and this condition is termed an overimprovement. If too little capital is invested in the improvement, which also would lower the land's return, an underimprovement results.

To repeat, the value of the building equals cost when the improvement is the highest and best use of a vacant site. It is important that this relationship be understood—specifically why value equals cost at the highest and best use. The answer most simply is that when the improvement is the highest and best use the cost incurred is justified. Intelligent, well-informed investors will gladly incur this cost so as to obtain the highest possible return.

Therefore, the cost approach is quite properly used whenever the analyst believes a new, or almost new, improvement to be the highest and best use of a vacant site. In this instance, no accrued depreciation need be deducted from the building's reproduction cost new to estimate its value. The value of the land is determined either by direct sales comparison or by assuming a hypothetical highest and best use of the site and capitalizing the site's residual income (as demonstrated in the

---

[14] See Chapter 3.

income capitalization section of this chapter). Older buildings and some new buildings suffer loss of value from various deficiencies. For these improvements, reproduction cost new less accrued depreciation provides a measure of value. Site value obtained independently and added to the value of the improvements equals property value through the cost approach.

Reproduction cost

Estimation of reproduction costs can be accomplished in several different ways. These are by (*a*) quantity survey, (*b*) unit-in-place costs, and (*c*) comparison.

The quantity survey method of estimating costs refers to the costing of each item and service going into the building. All the nails, lumber, bricks, concrete, plaster, and services of laborers, plasterers, carpenters, electricians, and others would be added up. The total cost of all such items and services would be the final reproduction cost. The quantity survey method is a lengthy and onerous procedure that would be used by a contractor or architect to determine a bid price for a new building. For value estimation the additional accuracy is not usually great enough to warrant its use over more concise methods.

The unit-in-place cost method is a shortcut of the quantity survey method. It usually involves the use of a cost service—a manual that is updated periodically and shows cost figures for various components of a structure. Examples of cost services appropriate for a variety of types of buildings are the Marshall-Swift *Valuation Quarterly* and the Boeckh *Building Valuation Manual;* Means' *Construction Costs* specializes in large buildings.

Basically, the method involves estimating cost of a unit of a major component or assembly of a structure and multiplying the cost of the unit by the number of units. For example, the cost of a square yard of roof would be multiplied by the number of square yards; the cost of a square foot of brick wall would be multiplied by the number of square feet; and the cost of a lineal foot of foundation would be multiplied by the number of lineal feet. The cost services provide such unit costs. They are kept current and are adjusted for regional cost differences.

The third method, the comparison method, requires the appraiser to keep personally up to date on construction costs and to keep current a set of "benchmark" buildings about which the costs are known. A surprisingly small number—usually 10 to 15—of benchmarks will provide the bases for estimating the costs of a fairly large number of types of buildings. The appraiser does this by applying the square foot or cubic foot cost of a benchmark structure to the structure under appraisal and making adjustments for differences between them. For example, if a subject house had a downstairs bath while the benchmark did not, an adjustment would have to be made.

Cost estimating is a crucial part of the cost approach; however, this discussion can do no more than acquaint the reader with the fundamental ideas of cost estimating. The important point to remember is that costs are prices and prices occur in markets; therefore, it is imperative for the cost estimator to keep up to date on the current market prices of materials, labor, and services. The use of published cost services can help the process, but they should be used with caution. Costs vary from locality to locality, and costs that are not current or that have not been determined for a specific city are likely to be inaccurate.

Accrued depreciation—penalities

Deductions from the reproduction cost new of a building in order to estimate the value of an existing structure are of three types and are perhaps most appropriately termed penalties.[15] These are penalties for physical deterioration, functional obsolescence, and locational obsolescence. The analyst measures each penalty and deducts them from the reproduction cost.

Physical deterioration. The first penalty, physical deterioration, reflects the fact that all material things wear out. Every physical thing is on the road to the junk yard, and buildings are no exception. Therefore, in valuing a building over two or three years old, one must deduct accrued depreciation for both the building's structure and for its replaceable parts.

First, analysts make a schedule of replacement items such as water heaters, roofs, and bathroom fixtures that are worn out. They would obtain cost figures for these items. Second, they would make a schedule of items and conditions that are partially worn out (depreciated). Such things as the furnace, water heater, roof, and paint job again would constitute candidates for this schedule. Again, they would be costed out (new), but the amount of remaining useful life deducted from the penalty. This is usually done by prorating the cost over the total expected life of the item. For example, a three-year-old paint job that should last five years and, costing $500, would have an indicated penalty of $300. Next, analysts would recognize the physical deterioration in the building itself (sometimes termed the bone structure). This penalty would be measured by multiplying the ratio of the building's effective age to total economic life by its reproduction cost.

Functional obsolescence. Functional obsolescence is the loss of relative ability by a building to perform its function. The development of

---

15 Robert O. Harvey, "Observations on the Cost Approach," *Appraisal Journal* 21, no. 4 (October 1953): 514–18.

new materials and processes and the acceptance of different styles and designs causes older buildings to become less desirable. The second penalty in the cost approach recognizes those differences between modern buildings and the existing building.

Possible sources of functional obsolescence are lack of air conditioning and elevators, out-of-date kitchens, old designs, rooms too small, ceilings too high, and so on. In some instances such deficiencies can be corrected, and the value increase will be equal to or greater than the cost incurred. In other instances the cost incurred to remedy a functional obsolescence deficiency will be greater than the value produced by incurring the cost. The former is termed a *curable* penalty, while the latter is known as an *incurable* penalty. Obviously, these terms do not apply to the physical ability to make the change; any building can be completely changed. Rather, the terms curable and incurable refer to the financial justification for making a change.

The distinction between curable and incurable penalties is an important one for deciding how to measure functional penalties. The procedure is simple for curable penalties; the cost of correcting the deficiency is used, since this cost equals the value loss of the deficiency. For incurable penalties, however, the matter is a bit more complex. Since the cost of correcting the deficiency is greater than the value, some other method must be employed to estimate the value. Either the lost income can be capitalized, or direct sales comparisons can be made with properties that are similar but do not have the deficiency.

Measurement of the value loss by the income approach rests on the fact that many deficiencies will cause various types of expenses to be larger. For example, ceilings that are too high require larger fuel and maintenance expense; unattractive architecture and design results in vacancy losses; out-of-date kitchens result in lower sale prices, and inconvenient arrangements produce a need to hire additional, part-time help. These negative income (or loss) streams can be estimated and capitalized, and the resultant penalties subtracted from the reproduction cost of the building.

The direct sales comparison approach can also be utilized to estimate incurable penalties. Ideally this would be accomplished by comparing transaction prices of properties that are similar in every respect except the deficiency. If, for example, houses similar to a house having an incurable kitchen deficiency sell for $2,000 more than other like houses having out-of-date kitchens, the penalty would be $2,000 (while the cost of putting in a new kitchen might be $3,000).

Locational obsolescence. The third penalty, locational obsolescence, is defined as a loss in value of the building because the site is no longer as desirable for the purpose served by the building. It represents, in other words, a relationship between the land and the building that is less ideal than it once was. It does not, however, connote a value loss for the land. In fact the land has in many such cases increased in value due to its increased desirability for commercial or industrial uses. Keep in mind that the building suffers the penalties; the land value is estimated separately.

How then is the locational obsolescence penalty measured? Answer: *By deducting the present value of the income stream lost because of the lack of adoption to its site or by the increased value of similar buildings on sites more suitable.* When a dollar rent can be imputed to the property, a loss of rent due to the deterioration of the site for that purpose can be capitalized and taken as the penalty. However, when a special purpose property that does not generate dollar income is under valuation, the penalty for locational deterioration can be taken by shortening the remaining economic life of the improvement (as in the following example). The theory is that the deteriorated relation between land and building will cause the building to be profitable a shorter time. (Physically, the building would be torn down sooner than would otherwise occur.) The percentage relationship of the present value of the income stream lost to the value of the income stream without the penalty can then be applied to the replacement cost less the first two penalties.[16] An example should clarify this complex description, as well as the entire cost approach.

Cost approach example

Assume that we wish to estimate the value of a 10-year-old school building (see Figure 4–10). Although in good physical condition, the

---

[16] Several other methods for estimating accrued depreciation are available to the analyst. For instance, the market value of the improvements (obtained by some other method, such as the building residual technique of income capitalization or by direct sales comparison) might be subtracted from the cost new of the improvements with the difference representing accrued depreciation (cost new, $100,000, less market value of improvements, $60,000, gives total accrued depreciation of $40,000). Or, straight-line depreciation may be used, with the rate of depreciation depending upon the economic life of new improvements of that type ($\frac{1}{50}$ years economic life = 2.0 percent). The rate of depreciation times the chronological age of the improvements provides an estimate of the percentage loss in value due to accrued depreciation from physical deterioration and functional obsolescence, but not loss of value due to locational obsolescence (0.02 × 20 years chronological age = 40 percent loss of value × $100,000 cost new = $40,000 depreciation from physical and functional causes; locational obsolescence would be measured separately). In the observed condition method, the analyst may break the total cost new of the building into the cost of its component parts (footings, walls, roof, heating system, and so on) and by observation (judgment) assign a total depreciation rate to each component (roof is 20 percent depreciated; heating system is 30 percent depreciated; and so on). The cost new of each component part times the percent depreciated, when aggregated, provides an estimate of accrued depreciation from physical deterioration. Loss of value resulting from functional obsolescence and locational deterioration must be derived separately. These alternative methods for taking accrued depreciation in the cost approach are illustrative only; other methods are available. See AIREA, *Appraisal of Real Estate*, pp. 237–61.

building is located in an area that has become ripe for industrial development. The school board has decided to determine whether the value of the building and land justifies abandonment of the school in favor of construction of a new building in a more desirable location.

FIGURE 4–10
Valuation of school property: Cost approach

Cost new for building		$239,520
Less accrued depreciation (penalties)		
1. Physical deterioration:		
Curable		
Repainting ....$	2,000	
Roof leaks	1,000	
Incurable		
Structural decay 1 percent per year—10 percent	23,950	$ 26,950
2. Functional obsolescence:		
Curable		
Poorly fitting windows ....$	3,000	
Needs acoustical tile in classrooms	5,000	
Incurable		
Inefficient heating system requires an extra		
part-time janitor—$1,000/year at 6 percent for		
15 years—life of heating system	9,712	$ 17,712
3. Locational obsolescence:		
Life of new school at appropriate site 100 years:		
6 percent PV factor	16.62	
Life of new school at present site 40 years:		
6 percent PV factor	15.05	
	1.57	

$$\frac{1.57}{16.62} = 9.4\%$$

Reproduction cost $239,520		
Less: Total physical and functional		
obsolescence penalties	44,662	
	$194,858	
9.4% × $194,858		$ 18,317
Value of building		$176,541
Value of site (by market comparison)		$ 50,000
Value of school property		$226,541

By use of the Marshall-Swift *Valuation Quarterly* we have classified the building as "Class B" in "good" condition. Class B construction has reinforced concrete frame in which the columns and frames can be either formed or precast concrete. "Good" quality refers to the second from best, out of four, quality classes. Such a building is designed for good appearance, comfort, and convenience. The cost cited of $19.96 per square foot totals $239,520 for the 12,000 square feet.

The penalties for accrued depreciation are subtracted from the cost new of the building. The penalty for physical deterioration contains both curable and incurable elements. The painting and roof repair can be accomplished readily and relatively inexpensively. The structural decay cannot be remedied without complete reconstruction of the building. Such a task would not add as much value to the building as it would cost. With the total economic life of the building, if new, estimated at 100 years, approximately 10 percent deterioration is estimated to have occurred.

The functional penalty is also divided between curable and incurable components. The windows and acoustical problems can be remedied by spending $8,000, and such cost would be justified. The heating system requires supervision that a newer system would not require; nevertheless, the cost of installation would be greater than the value lost by the present system.

The locational penalty is estimated by the percentage of the present value of the economic life lost to the total economic life of the building at an ideal location. This percentage is applied to the building in its existing condition—that is, after deducting the first two penalties from reproduction cost.

To the building value of $176,541 would be added the site value. If the site value were $50,000, total property value would be $226,541. The school board should not sell the property unless it could obtain at least that amount and construct a new school of comparable quality on a different site for a total cost (including land) not to exceed the price obtained for the old school. If the land value has appreciated sufficiently, this proposal could be feasible.

SUMMARY

This chapter describes the methods and techniques of value estimation. Emphasis is placed upon the valuation function because all decisions regarding real estate involve a consideration of value (price) or rate of return. Rates of return are a function of prices paid and received, and transaction prices in a market determine values. The central concept and beginning point for understanding investment analysis is that of market-determined prices—or value. The estimate of value is an important criterion in the investment decision-making process. Presumably, investors would not want to pay more than the market value for a property, even though their financing arrangements and income tax situation would permit them to pay a higher price.

The valuation process requires a consideration of all factors believed to influence income expectancy and capitalization rates. These factors are complex and play an exceedingly important role in the valuation of real estate because of its physical nature. Immobility, long life, and large size make real estate particularly vulnerable to economic, social, and political-legal developments. Trends in each of these areas must be considered at the national, regional, community, and neighborhood levels. Since real estate investment decisions require a long-term, future-oriented viewpoint and great reliance is placed upon financing, a real estate investor's success or failure is in large measure dependent upon perceptive analysis and prediction of such value-determining trends.

The steps required in each of the three approaches to value are shown in Figure 4–11. Theoretically, if each approach were equally applicable to a valuation problem and if equally complete and reliable data were available, all three approaches would produce the same estimate of market value. Depending upon the nature of the property and the market in which it would be bought and sold, one approach is usually more appropriate than the other two. Before embarking on the appraisal procedures, the legal rights being valued must be identified.

FIGURE 4–11

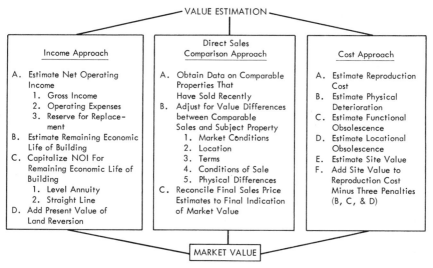

QUESTIONS FOR REVIEW

1. Why does the cost approach produce an estimate of market value? In other words, what market data are used in the cost approach?
2. Why does the income approach produce an estimate of market value? What market data are used in the income approach?
3. How does level annuity capitalization differ from straight-line capitalization in its assumption about recapture of capital? Which is more realistic?

4. What is meant by *functional obsolescence?* Could a new building contain functional obsolescence? Why?

5. How is business risk reflected in a capitalization rate? Would a higher level of business risk result in a higher or lower value for a property, other factors remaining unchanged?

6. How does an analyst know whether expenses are reasonable or unreasonable?

7. What main difficulty would you foresee in attempting to estimate the value of a 30-year-old property via the cost approach?

PROBLEMS

1. Calculate the value of an income stream of $12,000 for the first year with a discount rate of 8 percent and capital recapture required over 25 years under straight-line capitalization. What would be the value under level annuity? Can you explain the reason for the difference?

2. Estimate the value of the following property.

"... the building is a frame five-apartment structure which was constructed in 1950, with additions in 1962 and 1967. The structure is in excellent physical condition, but the neighborhood is in rapid transition from residential to light-industrial usage. Four of the apartments rent for $100 a month each, with the owner paying all of the expenses. The owner, who functions as both janitor and manager, lives in one of the apartments. If vacant, his apartment would rent for $75 a month. The demand for apartments has been strong in the community and should continue at high levels."

Other interesting data:

Expenses:
Fuel, water, power, and telephone	$ 300
Building supplies	100
Mortgage payments	500
Decorating and painting	200
Repairs and maintenance	300
Reserve for wasting parts	200
Insurance	100
Real estate tax	400
Land value (by market comparison)	$5,000
Estimated economic life of building	40 years
Rate of return derived from market	8%

a. Convert the given information into a reconstructed operating statement.

b. Identify the assumptions involved in your calculations.

c. What is your final value estimate?

3. You have been asked to appraise a vacant site on the north side of town. The neighborhood is zoned C-2 (allowing small commercial uses), but it is predominantly residential in character. The residences are mostly around 40 years old; doubles and some small apartment buildings (up to eight units) are also in the neighborhood. The site is a double residential lot, 120 feet

wide by 160 feet deep. After surveying the neighborhood and other comparable neighborhoods, you find the following sales that you believe can be used for comparison purposes. Assume a current date of January 1978.

	1	2	3	4
Size	60 × 160	60 × 160	60 × 175	120 × 160
Terrain	Equal	Equal	Equal	10% better
Market conditions	1/76	11/76	9/76	1/77
Location	10% better	Equal	Equal	15% worse
°Condition of sale	Arm's length	Forced purchase	Arm's length	Seller required to sell
Surroundings	5% better	Equal	5% worse	Equal
Price	$8,000	$7,500	$7,000	$14,000

° Forced conditions of sale are believed to result in sale prices 5 percent higher or lower than would have otherwise occurred.

The market has been rising about 5 percent per year; however, you believe no market adjustment is necessary for less than three months. Make any indicated adjustments and estimate the value of the site.

4. You are appraising the city hall of a town with a population of about 50,000. The building measures 100 ft. by 100 ft. and is one story in height (10 ft.). It was constructed in 1955, and the city is now considering selling the present city hall and erecting a new one in another location. You are unable to find any sales of buildings you feel would be sufficiently comparable to justify use of the direct sales comparison approach. Future economic life of the building is estimated at 25 years. The date on which you are making the appraisal is December 1974.

The highest and best use of the land, were it vacant, would be a 16-unit apartment building which would gross $24,480 per year and would net before depreciation about $9,800 per year. Such a building would have an expected economic life of 50 years. From comparable sales you feel that investors today must be able to foresee an 8 percent return on such an investment. You obtain cost estimates that indicate the 16-unit building could be constructed for $4,375 per unit.

The present building was built in 1955 at a cost of $89,500, and several contractors have told you the building could be replaced today for approximately $1.45 per cubic foot. Although the building has been well maintained, some wear and tear has occurred, and you believe physical deterioration of about 1.5 percent per year should be counted. Also, because of the inefficient room arrangement, not all of the city employees have been housed in the city hall, and five rooms in other locations have been rented to house some employees. The rental on these rooms has run $350 per year, and (according to the employees) about $100 per year has been consumed in gasoline in going back and forth so that the outlying employees could use the candy and coke machines at city hall. The building needs decorating at a cost of $800.

You believe that the new city hall more centrally located will have an expected economic life of about 60 years, while the same building at the subject site would serve for only 30 years.

a. Estimate the value of the property.

b. How do you account for the difference between your value and original cost? Do you believe the property will increase in value in the future?

c. How do you account for the difference between the cost of a highest and best use structure and value of the existing property?

d. Would you recommend demolishing the existing structure in order to erect the 16-unit apartment building?

e. Should the cost of demolishment be deducted from the value of the land? Why or why not?

REFERENCES

American Institute of Real Estate Appraisers. *The Appraisal of Real Estate.* 6th ed. Chicago, 1973.

Beaton, William R., and Bond, Robert J. *Real Estate.* Pacific Palisades, Calif.: Goodyear Publishing Co., 1976, chaps. 10 and 11.

Brown, Robert K. *Real Estate Economics.* Boston: Houghton Mifflin Co., 1965, pp. 78–111.

Kahn, S. A.; Case, F. E.; and Schimmel, A. *Real Estate Appraisal and Investment.* New York: Ronald Press, 1964.

Kinnard, William N., and Boyce, Byrl N. *An Introduction to Appraising Real Property.* Chicago: Society of Real Estate Appraisers, 1975.

Ring, Alfred A. *The Valuation of Real Estate.* 2d ed. Englewood Cliffs, N.J.: Prentice-Hall, 1970.

Smith, Halbert C. *Real Estate Appraisal.* Columbus, Ohio: Grid Publishing, 1976.

Smith, Halbert C., and Racster, Ronald L. "Should the Traditional Appraisal Process Be Restructured?" *Real Estate Appraiser* 36, no. 7 (November–December 1970): 6–11.

chapter 5

THE INVESTMENT CALCULATION

THE TWO PRECEDING CHAPTERS deal with the concept of market value and its measurement. We emphasized that value is an opinion; transaction price is a fact. Professional appraisers are often called upon to estimate the market value of parcels of real estate because the market value figure is the basis for economic transactions. A buyer does not usually wish to pay more, nor the seller to take less, than the market value of the property.

Nevertheless, for many purposes the market value estimate is not the whole story. It is only phase 1 of the calculation for decisions having an investment motive, that is, a conscious consideration of the expected returns in relation to the capital required. Since most decisions that determine the role of real estate resources in shaping the future of cities are made with the investment motive, it is our contention that the professional approach to the study of real estate and the making of intelligent decisions must employ the investment calculation as its base. These investment calculations are made whenever a property transaction is contemplated; when a maintenance or repair decision is made; when a structure is modernized, renovated, converted, abandoned, or demolished; and when a site is developed with a new set of improvements. Richard Ratcliff, a strong proponent of the investment approach, has stated: "Most of the critical real estate decisions which confront families, professional real estate operators, bankers, and businesses are, broadly speaking, investment decisions which call for predictions of productivity or value."[1]

The investment calculation begins where the value calculation ends. We can regard the valuation calculation as phase 1 and the investment

---

[1] Ratcliff, *Real Estate Analysis*, p. 4.

calculation as phase 2. Actually both phases may be viewed as the investment process, with phase 2 taking into account the personal and business considerations peculiar to the investor. Phase 1 will already have taken into account the general or average investment conditions in the market. To the extent that a particular investor's situation is different, the price one is willing to pay will differ from market value. However, the fact that investors may be willing to pay a price higher than market value does not necessarily mean that they will do so. They may pay a higher price if the seller is an astute negotiator and our investor is eager to buy and uncertain of the bids from other purchasers. The less competitive the market, the greater the likelihood that a transaction price will vary from market value. As we have seen in previous chapters, estimation of market value in these circumstances becomes more difficult. The range of observed transaction prices may be quite broad, and the market consensus is difficult to ascertain.

INVESTMENT VALUE AND INVESTMENT PROFITABILITY

Investment value was defined as the maximum the buyer would be willing to pay and the minimum the seller would be willing to accept.[2] Investment value in this manner can be expressed as an absolute dollar amount. Often, however, buyers find it more useful to analyze the profitability of an investment assuming that they purchase the property for a given price. This type of investment calculation permits buyers to compare alternative investments in terms of relative profitability and risk. These alternative investments may be real estate or other investments generating a calculable yield, such as securities, orange groves, cattle, or business ventures.

In the following sections, we first develop a calculation of investment value in terms of a dollar amount and then examine various returns on investment and other profitability measures.

INVESTMENT VALUE CALCULATION

Income flows

The basic figure with which phase 2 begins is net operating income as determined in the valuation phase. This figure, you will recall from Chapter 4, is the resultant of the analyst's estimate of future gross income less future expenses attributable to the real estate. For income-producing real estate, this figure is a measure of its productivity. The sources and analysis of real estate productivity are examined in Chapter 6. Our purpose in this chapter is to complete the framework of analysis so that the

---

[2] See Chapter 3.

role of productivity in the investment approach may be clearly understood.

Although NOI is the one best estimate of the future income to a parcel of real estate and would be the same under competent management (no matter who the owner), no such agreement may be reached with respect to the price each potential owner would pay. Personal considerations, such as the financing required for a potential investor to purchase the property, its expected effect on the investor's income tax position, and other immeasurable influences, such as the disposition of the investor's spouse, may enter into the bid price and the acceptable return. It is the function of phase 2 of the investment calculation to take into account the measurable personal and business influences (such as financing and income taxes) on the price investors are willing to pay, or to determine their possible returns given a price they must pay to acquire the property.

The injection of financing and income tax into the investment calculation produces several measures of income or flow in addition to NOI. These measures in turn can be related to appropriate investment amounts in order to measure profitability. These items are defined as follows:

1. *Cash throw-off and cash flow*
   Net operating income (NOI)
       Less: Annual mortgage payment (debt service)
   Cash throw-off (before-tax cash flow)
       Less: Annual income tax liability
   Cash flow (aftertax cash flow)

2. *Taxable income and tax liability*
   Net operating income (NOI)
       Less: Depreciation for tax computation
       Less: Annual interest on mortgage debt
   Annual taxable income (or loss) from the investment times investor's tax rate
   Annual income tax liability

3. *Tax shelter*
   Tax shelter is usually defined as a net loss for income tax purposes. That is, if NOI minus tax depreciation and mortgage interest is negative, the negative income is a loss for calculating income tax liability. The loss can be deducted from other income before computing the tax. Thus, if a tax loss of $1,000 occurs and the investor's tax bracket is 50 percent, $500 less in tax would be paid on other income than would be paid without the tax loss. This deduction from other taxable income is the tax shelter.

Of course, no investor wants a real loss. The tax loss occurs because investors can deduct interest and higher levels of depreciation and possibly other expenses than they actually incur. Thus, a tax loss may be claimed even though positive net income is being produced by the property at more realistic depreciation charges and even though the property may actually be increasing in value.

In a broader sense, tax shelter occurs whenever an expense deducted for income tax is larger than the actual expense. Although, such an expense may not be great enough to produce a tax loss, the investor's tax liability is lower than it otherwise would have been.

Investment value from appraisal methodologies

The income capitalization methods for estimation of market value would each produce an investment value if the requirements of an investor were substituted for market-determined variables. Instead of a market-determined rate of discount, the rate of return required by an investor can be substituted. Instead of a typical or average investment holding period, the anticipated holding period of the investor would be used. The particular financing arrangements would replace the most typical arrangements for the property. The absolute dollar investment value would be computed using the property's NOI (before financing and before tax) if the property residual, building residual, land residual, or Ellwood techniques are used. If the Ellwood methodology or other mortgage-equity techniques are employed, investment value would be determined by capitalizing cash throw-off. None of the appraisal methodologies gives explicit consideration to income taxes and the potential influence of tax factors on investment value.

Investment value from aftertax cash flow

An absolute dollar investment value can be obtained by discounting the projected aftertax cash flow and aftertax cash reversion to the equity position at the investor's required rate of return on the equity investment. An investor must determine the financing arrangements, the most probable investment holding period, the tax depreciation schedule, the desired equity rate of return, and any anticipated appreciation or depreciation in the market value of the property over the holding period.

In Figure 5–1, investment value is computed for an investor who is considering the purchase of a new apartment building having a market value (phase 1) of $170,000. This property has an NOI of $19,000 (see Figure 5–1). The investor, after shopping for the best financing terms available, discovers that a mortgage for $130,000 at 7 percent for 25 years can be obtained. The annual debt service on this mortgage will be

$11,154. The investor is in the 50 percent income tax bracket (50 percent of taxable income will be paid in taxes) and wishes to minimize taxable income. Consequently, 200 percent declining balance depreciation is elected. Allocation of the assumed $170,000 market value between building value and site value indicates that the depreciable basis is $120,000 (building value). The investment holding period is four years. The property is assumed to be sold for $170,000 at the end of the holding period (no appreciation or depreciation in market value is projected). A 12 percent aftertax return on equity investment in this property is required by the investor.

The property's investment value for this prospective purchaser is the sum of (a) the present value of equity position and (b) the amount of the mortgage. The present value of the equity is the sum of (a) the aftertax cash flow to the equity for four years discounted at 12 percent and (b) the aftertax cash reversion at the end of the holding period discounted at 12 percent. In Figure 5–1, the value of the equity position is shown to be $43,071, and the total investment value is $173,071. Thus, the maximum amount that the investor can pay, given all assumptions, and earn a 12 percent aftertax return on equity is about $173,000.

If an investor could purchase the property for less than $173,000, the return on equity would increase. Purchasing the property for its market value of $170,000 produces an aftertax return on equity of about 14.4 percent. If the amount of the mortgage can be increased or more favorable terms can be obtained, the return on equity would increase. The student will note later in this chapter that the 12 percent used in Figure 5–1 as the investor's required aftertax return on equity is also the "internal rate of return" on equity, if the price of $173,000 is paid for the property. If the property is purchased at its market value of $170,000, the aftertax internal rate of return on equity is 14.4 percent as shown in Figure 5–2.

Determinants of the required return on equity

In the problem example of Figure 5–1 a discount rate of 12 percent was used with no explanation as to why. This rate is the aftertax return required by a specific investor. The magnitude of this rate reflects the characteristics of the investment and investor. Some real estate investments generate more cash throw-off than others, which may offer greater tax shelter. An individual investor, perhaps a widow, may require cash income; tax shelters have little value to her. The physician, on the other hand, can often afford to hold for appreciation in market value and is interested in investments that generate tax shelters rather than cash income. Real estate investments also vary in the amount of personal attention required, which must either be hired from professionals or be

FIGURE 5–1

Calculation for determining investment value

	Year			
	1	*2*	*3*	*4*
NOI	.$19,000	$19,000	$19,000	$19,000
Less: Interest	9,100	8,956	8,802	8,638
Less: Depreciation (200% declin-				
ing balance, 40 years)	6,000	5,700	5,415	5,144
Taxable income	.$ 3,900	$ 4,344	$ 4,783	$ 5,218
NOI	.$19,000	$19,000	$19,000	$19,000
Less: Mortgage payment	11,154	11,154	11,154	11,154
Less: Taxes (50%)	1,950	2,172	2,392	2,609
Aftertax cash flow	.$ 5,896	$ 5,674	$ 5,454	$ 5,237

Sale price $170,000
Less: Outstanding mortgage balance 120,880

Equity .... $ 49,120
Less: Capital gain tax .... 8,129°

Aftertax cash reversion .... $ 40,991

° Calculated as follows:
Total depreciation charged $22,259
Less: Straight-line depreciation 12,000
Excess depreciation .... $10,259 × 50% = $5,129
Plus straight-line depreciation at 25% 3,000

Capital gain tax $8,129

Solution:

	PV of $1		
Payment	*at 12%*		
$ 5,896 × 0.893	=	$ 5,265	
5,674 × 0.797	=	4,522	
5,454 × 0.712	=	3,883	
5,237 × 0.636	=	3,331	
40,991 × 0.636	=	26,070	

Value of equity .... $ 43,071
Plus: Mortgage 130,000

Investment value $173,071

done by the investor. Investors with a high opportunity cost for their time might require a larger return on their equity than the investors who are able to handle profitably the chores of managing the property.

Real estate investments vary in the level of business risk associated with the property. Business risk reflects the stability of income, potential loss of future income and capital value, and the marketability of the investment (ability to cash out of the investment at market value without an unreasonable delay). Much of this text is concerned with the determinants of business risk. The physical characteristics of the property, its location, the character of the neighborhood and community, and real estate and financial market conditions are all determinants of business risk. Investors vary in the amount of risk they are willing or able to tolerate. The widow may require stability of income and value and can be expected to worry if the vacancy rate is greater than 5 percent. Another investor may be better able to tolerate fluctuating income and value, particularly if potential exists for long-run appreciation in market value.

The 12 percent return on equity used in the preceding example is a discount rate composed of two parts—the pure rate for the use of riskless capital and an additional premium required to compensate the investor for business risk. Further, the investor must consider financial risk.

Financial risk concerns the level and stability of income in relation to financing requirements. Mortgage payments are a contractual obligation upon the mortgagor, and any lack of income to meet these obligations, could cause the investment project to fail. Obviously, then, the investor should be able to foresee an income stream that provides a considerable margin of safety above operating expenses, reserves, taxes, and financing charges. Since most real estate investors utilize credit and thus incur fixed charges when purchasing real estate, the capitalization rate would usually contain a "normal" level of financial risk. But when an individual investor's financial risk level becomes greater than some minimum level acceptable to the market, an additional percentage must be added in determining the necessary return rate. For example, if the analyst believes the aftertax market discount rate is 14 percent, but a particular investor would have to incur a greater-than-average financial obligation to purchase the property, the desired rate of return should be increased proportionately to reflect the additional risk.

An investor's particularly strong financial situation and the ability to meet financial obligations out of personal funds can also be considered in determining return rate. Since the discount rate includes a normal rate for financial risk, a lower-than-normal financial risk for a particular investor could serve to reduce the desired return below the market discount rate. The investor would then be in a position to bid a somewhat higher price for the property than could the "average" investor who would have to incur a normal level of financing.

INVESTMENT CRITERIA

In addition to calculating an absolute dollar investment value, an investor may find it desirable to determine the attractiveness of the investment by analyzing a number of ratios and by assuming a seller's required minimum price. These ratios can be grouped into three categories

—multipliers, financial ratios, and profitability ratios. The ratios below are calculated using the data from the apartment property for which an investment value was calculated previously. The calculations assume the following facts:

Purchase price $170,000
Mortgage 130,000
Equity 40,000
Gross income 27,500
    Less: Vacancy and collection loss 1,375
    Less: Operating expenses 7,125

Net operating income ....$ 19,000
    Mortgage payment 11,154
Cash throw-off ....$ 7,846

Multipliers

Two kinds of multipliers can be used. The net income multiplier is not often used since its reciprocal, the capitalization rate, is commonly employed in real estate analysis. The gross income multiplier is used more frequently; however, it must be used with great care. To compare gross income multipliers, the properties should be traded in the same market and should be equivalent in expense patterns, risk, location, physical attributes, time, and terms of sale.

$$\begin{array}{c} \text{Gross income} \\ \text{multiplier (GIM)} \end{array} = \frac{\text{Value or price}}{\text{Gross income}} = \frac{\$170,000}{\$\ 27,500} = 6.2$$

$$\text{Net income multiplier} = \frac{\text{Value or price}}{\text{NOI}} = \frac{\$170,000}{\$\ 19,000} = 8.9$$

The multipliers can be used to obtain a quick estimate as to whether a property is priced reasonably in relation to its gross or net income. The gross income multiplier is usually regarded as less relevant for larger more complex properties, as their expense levels may vary greatly. However, one recent study showed that the use of the GIM produces value estimates almost as accurate as more sophisticated techniques.[3] If expense patterns among a class of properties vary significantly, however, use of the GIM as other than a rough guide to value is hazardous.

The multipliers are within the realm of reasonable expectation for an apartment property. While multipliers vary greatly, the range for annual gross income multipliers is normally between 4 and 10. Net income multipliers for apartment properties usually range between 5 and 12. Ap-

---

[3] Richard U. Ratcliff, "Don't Underrate the Gross Income Multiplier," *Appraisal Journal* 39, no. 2 (April 1971): 264–71.

propriate multipliers for a specific property would be estimated from actual transactions of comparable properties in the same market area.

Financial ratios

These ratios deal with the income-producing capacity of the property to meet operating and financial obligations.

$$\text{Operating ratio} = \frac{\text{Operating expenses}}{\text{Gross income}} = \frac{\$ 7{,}125}{\$27{,}500} = 25.9\%$$

$$\text{Break-even cash throw-off} =$$
$$\frac{\text{Operating expenses} + \text{Mortgage payment}}{\text{Gross income}} = \frac{\$18{,}279}{\$27{,}500} = 66.5\%$$

$$\text{Loan to value ratio} = \frac{\text{Loan}}{\text{Price or value}} = \frac{\$130{,}000}{\$170{,}000} = 76.5\%$$

$$\text{Debt service coverage} = \frac{\text{NOI}}{\text{Mortgage payment}} = \frac{\$19{,}000}{\$11{,}154} = 1.7$$

The operating ratio and break-even cash throw-off ratios should be computed for all properties under investment analysis that will require the investor to incur operating expenses and financing charges. A relatively efficient property will exhibit a low operating ratio. Similarly, the break-even cash throw-off ratio provides an indication of the magnitude of all cash charges relative to gross income. The margin of safety between cash inflows and cash outflows is the difference between 100 percent and the break-even cash throw-off ratio. For our apartments both ratios are low, primarily because of the low operating expenses. Operating ratios typically range from 25 to 50 percent, while the break-even cash throw-off ratio typically varies between 60 and 80 percent.

The loan to value ratio and the debt service coverage ratio are measures of the financial risk associated with the investment and should be computed for every investment using borrowed funds. The loan to value ratio on a newly financed property normally runs from 60 to 90 percent, while the debt service coverage ratio should normally be at least 1.3.[4] Legal requirements are usually imposed on the maximum loan to value ratios that institutional lenders can incur; the debt service coverage ratio provides an indication of safety from legal default in the event revenues would fall and the mortgage payment would be in jeopardy.

---

[4] When borrowers obtain loans of 100 percent of value or price paid, they are said to have "mortgaged out." A loan in excess of 100 percent produces a "windfall."

Profitability ratios

The ultimate determination of an investment's desirability is its capacity to produce income in relation to the capital required to obtain that income. Measures of relationship between income and capital for investment properties result in the following ratios:

$$\text{Payback period} = \frac{\text{Equity capital}}{\text{Cash throw-off}} = \frac{\$40,000}{\$\ 7,846} = 5.1 \text{ years}$$

$$\begin{array}{l}\text{Equity dividend rate}\\ \text{(before-tax return on} \\ \text{equity)}\end{array} = \frac{\text{Cash throw-off}}{\text{Equity}} = \frac{\$\ 7,846}{\$40,000} = 19.6\%$$

$$\begin{array}{l}\text{Overall capitalization}\\ \text{rate}\end{array} = \frac{\text{NOI}}{\text{Total investment}} = \frac{\$\ 19,000}{\$170,000} = 11.2\%$$

$$\begin{array}{l}\text{Aftertax equity dividend}\\ \text{rate (aftertax return}\\ \text{on equity)}\end{array} = \frac{\begin{array}{c}\text{Aftertax cash}\\ \text{flow}\end{array}}{\text{Equity}} = \frac{\$\ 5,896}{\$40,000} = 14.7\%$$

Calculation of tax and aftertax cash flow

NOI		$19,000
Less: Average mortgage interest	$ 9,100	
Less: Tax depreciation (5% double-declining balance, 40 years × $120,000 improvements)	6,000	15,100
Taxable income		$ 3,900
NOI		$19,000
Less: Debt service	$11,154	
Less: Tax (50% marginal tax rate × $3,900)	1,950	13,104
Aftertax cash flow		$ 5,896

$$\text{Gross yield on equity} = \frac{\text{Cash flow + mortgage principal repayment}}{\text{Equity}}$$

$$= \frac{\$\ 7,950}{\$40,000} = 19.9\%$$

Average aftertax return on equity =

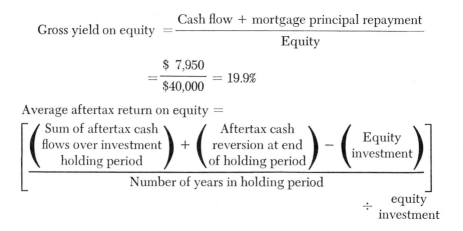

Example

Sum of aftertax cash flows[*]
Year 1 ....$	5,896
Year 2	5,674
Year 3	5,454
Year 4	5,237
Total ....$	22,261
Aftertax cash reversion (year 4)	40,991
Total aftertax income to equity ....$	63,252
Less: Equity investment	40,000
Return on equity investment ....$	23,252

$$\frac{\$23,252}{4 \text{ years}} \div \$40,000 \text{ equity} = \frac{\$ 5,813}{\$40,000} = 14.53\%$$

[*] Figure 5–2.

While most investors do not usually calculate all six of the above ratios in evaluating an investment, they are useful indexes of a project's profitability for a given year. We recommend that when the necessary data are available, at least five of the six ratios be calculated—and preferably for each of several years. The payback period is less important, since it is the reciprocal measure of the equity dividend rate. It also has the theoretical weakness, of course, of not discounting future years' earnings.

The equity dividend rate shows investors what percentage of their equity investment will be returned to them in cash before income taxes for one year. Although the noncash expense of depreciation is not deducted, the amount of mortgage repayment is deducted in arriving at cash throw-off. Thus, if mortgage principal repayment approximates actual depreciation, the ratio is a good approximation of the true before-tax yield on equity. The aftertax equity dividend rate provides a comparable yield on an aftertax basis, while the gross yield adds back the mortgage principal repayment. The latter ratio would be a more accurate aftertax yield *if* the property were believed not to be depreciating in value.

The overall capitalization rate measures the profitability of the entire property. It is produced by both the equity and debt portions of the investment and thus falls between the mortgage interest rate and the equity yield. This ratio is often used by appraisers in estimating the market value of an entire property—not just the equity portion.

The average aftertax return on equity provides a single measure of profitability that recognizes aftertax cash flow over an assumed investment holding period, as well as the aftertax cash reversion at the end of the holding period.[5] The average rate of return, of course, does not utilize

---

[5] A variety of average return calculations are possible. The average return on equity can be computed by using before-tax cash throw-off over the holding period; by using before-tax cash throw-off plus equity buildup resulting from paydown of the mortgage over the holding period; and by using only aftertax cash flow.

the time value of money. Two properties, each of which generate the same total aftertax income over an investment holding period, could have an identical average return on equity even though the income from one property was concentrated early in the holding period, while the investor would have to wait until the other property was sold to obtain the bulk of its total income. This absence of discounting future years' earnings can be partially overcome by using the payback period in conjunction with the average return on equity. The payback period reveals the pattern of the future income stream; the average rate of return measures the magnitude of future income relative to the investment required to produce it. In the example, the apartments yield an average aftertax return of 14.53 percent. Another apartment property, having the same financing, requiring a $40,000 equity investment, and producing a $2,000 per year aftertax cash flow over a four-year holding period and a $55,252 aftertax cash reversion, also would have a 14.53 percent average aftertax return on equity. Investors, of course, would prefer the property which returned their equity investment in the shortest period of time. Their investment value would be greater for the property in the above example ($173,071 at a 12 percent required return on equity), than for the second property, which returns $2,000 per year aftertax cash flow for four years and a $55,252 aftertax cash reversion (this property would have an investment value of $171,216 at a 12 percent return on equity). If the same price were paid for each property (perhaps $170,000), the internal rate of return (or true yield) earned would be greater for the property that returned the equity investment over the shortest period of time.

It should be recognized that each of these ratios has been calculated for one year only. The changing mortgage balance, depreciation, and income tax would cause some of the ratios to change each year. It is often advisable to calculate them for each of several years, as demonstrated in Appendix C.

Internal rate of return. The internal rate of return is defined as the interest rate which discounts a stream of future earnings equal to cost of the investment outlay. To compute an internal rate of return, the following data must be known or projected: equity investment outlay, aftertax cash flow, holding period, and selling price of the property at the end of the holding period. The calculations in Figure 5–2 produce an internal rate of return for the apartments over a holding period of four years. It is assumed that the property can be sold for the price paid, or $170,000.

The internal rate of return differs from previous measures of profitability in that it discounts the stream of earnings to be obtained over several future years. The internal rate of return is the most defensible of all profitability ratios. Unfortunately, as reported on pages 107–08, it has not received widespread usage among real estate investors. We recommend the internal rate of return measure of profitability whenever adequate data are available and the necessary predictions about the holding period and selling price can be made realistically.

FIGURE 5–2
Internal rate of return

	Year			
	1	2	3	4
NOI	$19,000	$19,000	$19,000	$19,000
Less: Interest	9,100	8,956	8,802	8,638
Less: Depreciation (200% declining balance, 40 years)	6,000	5,700	5,415	5,144
Taxable Income	3,900	4,344	4,783	5,218
NOI	19,000	19,000	19,000	19,000
Less: Mortgage payment	11,154	11,154	11,154	11,154
Less: Taxes (50%)	1,950	2,172	2,392	2,609
Aftertax Cash Flow	5,896	5,674	5,454	5,237

Sale price	$170,000
Less: Outstanding mortgage balance	120,880
Equity	$ 49,120
Less: Capital gain tax	8,129*
Aftertax Cash Reversion	$ 40,991

* Calculated as follows:

Total depreciation charged	$22,259
Less straight-line depreciation	12,000
Excess depreciation	$10,259 × 50% = $5,129
Plus straight-line depreciation at 25%	3,000
Capital Gain Tax	$8,129

Solution:

$$\$40,000 \text{ equity} = \frac{5,896}{(1+r)^1} + \frac{5,674}{(1+r)^2} + \frac{5,454}{(1+r)^3} + \frac{5,237}{(1+r)^4} + \frac{40,991}{(1+r)^4}$$

15%	14%			15%	14%	
5,130	5,130 =	5,896 ×	.87		.87	(PV of 1, 1 year)
4,312	4,369 =	5,674 ×	.76		.77	(PV of 1, 2 years)
3,600	3,654 =	5,454 ×	.66		.67	(PV of 1, 3 years)
2,985	3,090 =	5,237 ×	.57		.59	(PV of 1, 4 years)
23,365	24,185 =	40,991 ×	.57		.59	(PV of 1, 4 years)
39,392	40,428 ≈	almost 14.5%				

r = Aftertax internal rate of return
= Approximately 14.4%

VARYING THE ASSUMPTIONS

Although the estimates of gross income and operating expenses are presumably based upon market experiences of comparable properties (as well as the subject property) the assumptions involved in calculating mortgage payments and income taxes may be variable. These *investment expenses* are usually dependent upon the investor's financial position and capacity, not just the project or property being considered for purchase. Furthermore, given a certain financial capacity, loan terms and depreciation expense may be variable within limits. For example, investors may have the option of obtaining a 70 percent, 25-year, 7.5 percent face rate loan or a 75 percent, 20-year, 8 percent face rate loan. They may be able to calculate depreciation for tax purposes over 25, 30, or 40 years or to use accelerated methods.

Role of computers

Differences among the variable assumptions will cause the value of the investor's equity position to change. Or, given a certain price or cost to obtain a property, the rate of return on the investor's equity will change with differing loan terms or tax requirements. When considering a proposed investment, investors (or their advisers) should usually calculate several equity values or rates of return, using different assumptions about items such as loan terms and taxes. It is normally desirable to project the calculations over several years, so that the expected rate of return can be seen separately each year.

Although investment values and rates of return can be determined by hand calculation, the computations are greatly facilitated by the use of electronic computers, especially when a variety of inputs are considered for each of several years. Among the inputs that might be varied, in addition to loan terms and income taxes, are gross income, expected vacancy rate, type of depreciation expense (straight-line, declining balance, and so on), and individual expense items such as real estate taxes or maintenance expense. The estimated remaining economic life or expected holding period and the expected selling price of the property at the end of the holding period (reversion value) can also be varied. Investors or investment counselors can then see return rates (or investment values, given capitalization rates) within a range of most favorable to least favorable expected experiences.

A large firm may have its own computer and investment analysis programs. Medium- and smaller-sized firms can more efficiently either (*a*) utilize their own programs on a time-sharing computer service or (*b*) subscribe to a computerized investment analysis service. Perhaps the most widely used of the latter type of arrangement is provided by Realtron Corporation. Realtron offers to subscribers who pay a monthly fee an investment analysis service in the format shown in Figure 5–3. (Output definitions for Realtron are shown in Figure 5–4.) The subscriber telephones the input data to a central computer and receives the output back within

FIGURE 5–3

Realtron investment analysis

		Input		
MKT. VALUE 300,000			TAX BRKT. 22%	
TTL. LOANS 220,000			IMPRVMNT. 70%	
NET OP. INC. 25,000			DEPREC. ....S/L	
INT. RATE 8.50%			YRS. LIFE 30	
ANNL. P. & I 22,900			GRTH. RTE. 00%	

Analysis

	Year 1	Year 5	Year 10	Year 15	Year 20
MKT. VALUE 300,000		300,000	300,000	300,000	300,000
TTL. LOANS 220,000		200,073	163,510	107,668	22,381
EQUITY 80,000		99,927	136,490	192,332	277,619
CAP. RATE 8.33		8.33	8.33	8.33	8.33
NET OP. INC. 25,000		25,000	25,000	25,000	25,000
INT. PAY. 18,532		16,770	13,539	8,603	1,064
DEPREC. 7,000		7,000	7,000	7,000	7,000
TAXABLE IN. 532–		1,230	4,461	9,397	16,936
GR. SPEND. 2,100		2,100	2,100	2,100	2,100
INCOME TAX 117–		270	981	2,067	3,725
NET SPEND. 2,217		1,830	1,119	33	1,625–
EQUITY INC. 6,585		7,959	10,480	14,330	20,211
EQUITY RTE. 8.23		7.96	7.67	7.45	7.28
ADJ. COST B 293,000		265,000	230,000	195,000	160,000

Cumulative Totals

TAXABLE IN.	532–	1,558	16,855	53,135	121,464
GR. SPEND.	2,100	10,500	21,000	31,500	42,000
NET SPEND.	2,217	10,158	17,295	19,816	15,287
NET EQ. INC.	6,585	36,214	83,146	146,445	234,742

FIGURE 5–4

Realtron output definitions

Market value

This is the estimated value of the property and should be the list (sale) price of the property.

Total loans

The sum total of all encumbrances of record.

Equity

Determined by subtracting the total loans of record from the market value. (Note: The above figures are as of the first of the year.)

Capitalization rate

Expresses the percentage of the return the property will produce when it is free and clear. Capitalization rate, from the appraiser's viewpoint, consists of the return on and the return of the investment.

FIGURE 5–4 (continued)

Net operating income
That income which the property produces after proper deductions have been made for vacancy and credit losses and all operating expenses. Another method for arriving at net operating income is to multiply the market value and/or sale price by the capitalization rate. The result will be the net operating income.

Interest payments
All those interest costs for the loans that are of record.

Depreciation
The amount that the Internal Revenue Service will allow the taxpayer to deduct for the cost of the improvement over a given number of years as determined by the taxpayer. However, it should be noted that the government spells out specific guide lines with reference to the methods of depreciation and/or the economic life selected by the property owner.

Taxable income
That income that the property produces which will be subject to ordinary income tax. This often is expressed as a credit figure when the depreciation plus the interest exceeds that of the net operating income.

Gross spendable
The amount of income that remains after the property owner has deducted the principal and interest payments from the net operating income. This gross spendable is often referred to by many investors as "cash flow before income tax."

Income tax
As expressed in the analysis of an investment property, this is that tax liability which is created by the taxable income that the property produced. The amount of income tax to be payed will be determined by the income tax bracket or rate of the property owner.

Net spendable
What property owners have to spend after they have deducted the income tax liability and/or credit from the gross spendable income. Sometimes called "cash flow aftertax."

Equity income
This is (a) the amount of principal reduction in the loans, plus (b) the net spendable received, and (c) the increase in value because of appreciation.

Equity income rate
The net equity income divided by the equity in the property.

Adjusted cost basis
The book value of the property. (Initial cost basis less depreciation taken.)

Cumulative totals
The sum totals of the result of ownership. (a) Taxable income, (b) gross spendable income (c) net spendable income, and (d) net equity income are accumulated each year for that year and all previous years of ownership.

a few minutes. The example shown in Figure 5–3 shows the changing amounts and equity income rate given a property having a current market value of $300,000, total loans at time of purchase of $220,000, net operating income of $25,000, a mortgage interest rate of 8.50 percent, and annual principal and interest totaling $22,900. The investor is in the 22 percent tax bracket, improvements constitute 70 percent of the property's value, straight-line depreciation is used for tax purposes, the property's remaining economic life is 30 years, and no change is expected in the property's value over the next 20 years (00 percent growth).

Some investment analysis computer programs such as those developed by the Educational Foundation for Computer Applications in Real Estate (EDUCARE), a number of universities, and some business firms are more complex and provide greater sophistication in their output analyses. They require more input data and compute a greater variety of ratios and return rates, while allowing more variables in the input data.

A case example projecting various rates of return under different sets of assumptions is presented in Appendix C, Queensworth Apartments.[6] An investor's rates of return under three sets of assumptions are projected for the first year. The most logical and defensible of the three investment structures is then calculated for each of ten years—a normal holding period for such an investment.

MOTIVATION OF INVESTORS

A recent survey of apartment investors by the U.S. Department of Housing and Urban Development shows that cash flow is the most important criterion considered by all types of investors.[7] Individuals ranked tax shelter as the second most important motive, while real estate groups and investment trusts ranked this consideration third in importance.

The study indicated that the aftertax return for a 50 percent tax bracket investor on a property five years old or less amounted to 17.5 percent. This figure consisted of 14 percent return on cash equity plus a tax saving of 3.5 percent on other income. For properties between 11- and 20-years old the average aftertax annual return given as a percentage of cash equity came to 7 percent. Cash distribution was 9 percent, but there was a 2 percent tax liability instead of tax loss.

Other important reasons for investing were financial leverage, capital appreciation, and low risk. Location, demand for housing, the housing

---

[6] Although some of the concepts used in the case are not covered until Chapters 10 and 13, Appendix C should be studied in conjunction with this chapter as well as Chapters 10 and 13.

[7] Arnold H. Diamond, "Tax Considerations Affecting Multi-Family Housing Investments," Paper presented at the Annual Meeting of American Real Estate and Urban Economics Association, New Orleans, Louisiana, December 28, 1971.

supply, and mortgage financing opportunities influenced active investors, while passive investors rated location and builder reputation high among nonfinancial criteria for investment.

With respect to earnings, over two thirds of the active investors spoke in terms of the average annual rate of return. Thirteen percent used total dollar return, and 11 percent used payback period. Only 4 percent used the discounted rate of return, which gives less weight to earnings in future years and more weight to early earnings. This result is surprising in view of the emphasis given to present value concepts in real estate and financial investment courses.

About one third of the apartment investors believed that apartments yield more tax shelter than other real estate investments, 25 percent thought apartments yield a higher return, and 20 percent believed apartments provide a better hedge against inflation than other real estate investments.

A previous study by Ricks showed that equity investors and other participants in the real estate investment process regard the rate of return on equity investment as the most important measure of profitability and the rate of return on cost as the second most important measure.[8] The after-financing, before-tax return on equity was listed as the most important decision guide. Second and third in importance were the before-financing, before-tax return and the after-financing, aftertax return.

Among the factors considered in making a decision to commit funds to a real estate investment, Ricks found that investors and other participants regard market value appreciation, safety of investment funds, and a high rate of return on equity as first, second, and third in importance. Loan terms were generally more important than characteristics of the property in decisions to commit funds.

SUMMARY

The valuation process, as described in Chapter 4, may be regarded as phase 1 of the investment calculation. Phase 2, discussed in this chapter, extends phase 1 to include personal or business expenses that would be incurred with an investment, but which are omitted in the valuation process. Income taxes and financing charges are the two most important investment-related expenses which are often not directly associated with real estate for valuation purposes.

Phase 2 may also involve a different discount rate from the rate which is appropriate in estimating market value. The market rate includes risk levels applicable to the average or typical buyer; any individual investor's

[8] R. Bruce Ricks, *Real Estate Investment Process, Investment Performance and Federal Tax Policy,* Report of the Real Estate Investment Project for the U.S. Treasury Department (Los Angeles: University of California Press, 1969).

risk situation or return requirements may justify a higher or lower discount rate. Financial risk, to the extent that it is greater or less than the normal market level, is also reflected in the investor's discount rate.

Assumptions about financing terms, depreciation expense, and income taxes can be varied; investment value and rates of return can be calculated under several different combinations of assumptions. The calculations can be carried out for several years to show trends. Electronic computers greatly aid the calculation process and are a necessity if several investments are to be analyzed.

Other investment criteria, in addition to investment value, include multipliers, financial ratios, and profitability ratios. Given a selling price, a limited holding period, and aftertax cash flow, an internal rate of return can be computed for an equity investment.

Finally, we have noted some attitudes that investors claim to hold with respect to investment criteria. Cash flow and tax shelter are the two most important factors. Rate of return on equity is the most important profitability measure, while there would seem to be little attention paid to discounting processes that weigh future earnings less heavily than immediate earnings.

QUESTIONS FOR REVIEW

1. Why might an investor be willing to pay more for a property than its market value?
2. Why might an investor not be willing to pay as much as market value for a property?
3. Why might an investor not be willing to purchase a property at any price?
4. What is *financial risk?* How is it accounted for in investment analysis?
5. What is *business risk?* How is it accounted for in investment analysis?
6. How do you explain the results of investor surveys that show that little reliance is placed upon discounted cash flows in evaluating investments?
7. Do you believe that the Queensworth Apartments case contained in Appendix C describes a realistic investment situation? Why or why not? What types of investment calculations are presented in the case?
8. What is a *tax shelter?* Would you purchase a parcel of real estate to obtain a tax shelter? Why or why not?
9. Distinguish between depreciation for tax purposes and capital recovery for valuation or investment analysis purposes.
10. What is *profitability?* Upon which profitability ratios would you place primary reliance in evaluating an investment?
11. What is an *internal rate of return?*
12. What is *investment value?* How does it differ from market value?
13. Why is the face value of the mortgage loan added to the value of the equity benefits in arriving at investment value?

PROBLEMS

1. An investment is expected to produce $10,000 per year to perpetuity. If a 12 percent annual rate of return is required, how much is the investment worth?

2. If the life of the investment in problem 1 was expected to be 20 years, how much would the investment be worth?

3. A purchaser paid $80,000 for an investment property. How much annual income must the property produce to yield an 11 percent rate of return?

4. A couple purchases a home and obtains a $40,000 mortgage loan at 7 percent for 20 years to finance the deal. How much would their total mortgage payments be, including both principal and interest (annual debt service), if payments are made annually? If payments are made monthly?

5. In problem 4, how much of the first year's payment would be interest? How much interest would be paid in the second and third years? Approximately how much total interest would be paid over the 20 years? What would be the amount of *average* annual interest paid?

6. Look in a Federal Tax Rate Schedule and determine the tax liability of a married taxpayer having a $20,000 taxable income, filing a joint return, and having one dependent. What amount of tax would the same individual pay in the succeeding year if the income were increased to $25,000? How much is the difference in tax on the two amounts (or incremental tax)?

7. A property produces $10,000 annual NOI. The owner charges $2,000 per year depreciation and pays $5,000 in interest on an outstanding loan. Total annual debt service on the loan is $7,500. The owner is in the 34 percent tax bracket.
   a. How much is the cash throw-off?
   b. How much income tax must the owner pay on the income generated by the property?
   c. How much is the owner's aftertax cash flow?
   d. If the owner has $20,000 equity funds invested in the property, what is the equity dividend rate?

8. An individual has been willed a remainder estate in a parcel of land which allows her to obtain possession at the termination of a lease ten years from now. If the land is forecast to be worth $25,000 at that time, how much could the estate be sold for today to an investor demanding a 10 percent rate of return?

9. A property is expected to generate NOI of $10,000. Debt service will amount to $6,000 per year. If the investor contributes $25,000 in equity, how long is the payback period?

10. Calculate the internal rate of return for an investment property which is expected to yield $30,000 per year NOI and which can be purchased for $225,000. The investor plans to sell the property after five years for $250,000. The investor will pay all cash, use straight-line depreciation, a 25 year useful life, and is in the 40 percent tax bracket.

11. Calculate an investment value for projection 1 in the Queensworth Apartments case (see Appendix C).

REFERENCES

Beaton, William R. *Real Estate Investment.* Englewood Cliffs, N.J.: Prentice-Hall, 1971.

Kinnard, William N. *Income Property Valuation.* Lexington, Mass.: D.C. Heath & Co., 1971.

Ring, Alfred A. *Real Estate Principles and Practices.* 7th ed. Englewood Cliffs, N.J.: Prentice-Hall, 1972, pp. 231–44.

Seldin, Maury, and Swesnik, Richard H. *Real Estate Investment Strategy.* New York: Wiley-Interscience, 1970.

Smith, Halbert C. "Investment Analysis in Appraising," *Real Estate Appraiser* 32, no. 9 (September 1967): 19–25.

Wendt, Paul F., and Cerf, Alan R. *Real Estate Investment Analysis and Taxation.* New York: McGraw-Hill, 1969.

PART II
Investment opportunity and constraint

chapter 6

PRODUCTIVITY ANALYSIS

THE MEASUREMENT OF MARKET VALUE in Chapter 4 and the investment calculation in Chapter 5 naturally lead to the question of what factors are responsible for producing market value and investment value.

Modern value theory discussed in Chapter 3 emphasizes the role of productivity in relation to scarcity as the essential cause of real estate's ability to produce income. In this chapter, we are concerned with identifying and understanding the elements of real estate productivity. This understanding is essential if the investor is to attain insight into all the important factors that may affect a property's income-producing ability.

NATURE OF PRODUCTIVITY

The concept of productivity involves obtaining a greater output than the inputs which produced the output. Usually this phenomenon is accomplished by a rearranging of the inputs into a final product or service that has greater value than the sum total of the inputs. For example, various materials (such as steel, glass, and rubber), machines, labor, and managerial talent go into the production of automobiles. The materials are purchased, machines are depreciated, and workers' wages and managers' salaries are paid. Yet the automobile company may end up with a surplus above the payment of all costs. This surplus is a profit, and over the long run it represents the productivity of the firm.

Elements of productivity

Real estate can have value because it too enters into the productive process. It is combined with other factors of production to yield services and other goods, the sum total of which have a greater value than that of the factors added together. In the automobile example real estate should also be listed as one of the input factors. The land provides a location for assembling the automobiles, and a building provides shelter for the employees and a base for the machines used in the production process.

Location is an important element in the productivity of real estate because of the transportation and communication necessary between a parcel and other parcels of real estate. In the manufacturing of automobiles the factory's access to raw materials and labor inputs and to consumer markets partially determines whether the manufacturer makes a profit. Similarly, the ability of a parcel of real estate to fulfill certain physical requirements is a determinant of its income-producing ability. If the automobile factory had been built on marshy land, or if the building were too small, the company's profit position would be impaired.

Thus real estate can be productive in two general ways: first, in a parcel's convenience or location relative to other parcels of real estate and second, in a parcel's physical capacity to provide desirable materials or services. We shall term these two types of factors *transfer characteristics* and *physical characteristics*.[1] Hoover has called them transfer costs and processing costs and has described them as follows:

> In some uses the value of a site depends primarily on the access the site affords to other parties with whom the occupant may want to trade. A good site in this sense is one entailing low *transfer costs*. For downtown urban land uses in general, transfer costs are the important locational factor, and land is rented, bought, and sold on the basis of its positional advantages alone.
>
> At the other extreme are types of land use for which transfer costs are unimportant compared with differences in *processing costs* at good and bad sites. The more valuable the product in relation to its distribution costs per mile the greater is the significance of resource quality as against access to markets.[2]

Significance of the distinction between transfer characteristics and physical characteristics

Too often in current real estate administration a less-than-incisive analysis of a parcel's productivity results from an unclear distinction be-

---

[1] Other authors have also used two basic categories for analysis of productivity but have named them differently. For example, Ratcliff calls them location and physical characteristics. This seems to lead to some confusion in Ratcliff's classification of productivity factors. He includes exposure to view, sun, breeze, and offensive influences under location factors. Hoover labels such factors more correctly, we believe, as processing costs—which is analogous to our physical characteristics. Therefore, because of the confusion engendered by the everyday meaning of the word *location* and because the term *processing costs* is not such a meaningful term for improved urban real estate, we prefer to label these categories "transfer characteristics" and "physical characteristics."

[2] Edgar M. Hoover, *The Location of Economic Activity*, paperback ed. (New York: McGraw-Hill, 1963), pp. 90–91.

tween physical factors involving processing costs and location factors involving transfer costs. As pointed out in the passage by Hoover, the relative importance of these types of factors to each other depends upon the purpose for which the real estate is used. For mining, processing advantages are much more important than transfer advantages. But to attach the same importance to processing advantages in analyzing a site for a parking lot is obviously absurd. In less obvious situations, however, how many small retail establishments have been opened in a particular place simply because a suitable building was available? How many substandard dwellings are occupied by persons who could obtain better accommodations at the same rental in a different location? How many industries are operated in the founder's hometown, incurring higher than required transfer costs? All such situations are examples of uneconomic weighting being applied to the relative importance of physical and locational factors.

Implications of the distinction between transfer characteristics and physical characteristics

The ability of each parcel of real estate to enter the productive process can differ according to the favorable or unfavorable geographic relationship it has with other parcels of real estate. Differences in future productivity expectations—whether due to physical or transfer factors—usually result in different values among properties.

Another implication, however, which we hasten to emphasize, is that similarities in transfer characteristics in urbanized areas where physical factor differentials are unimportant result in land-use patterns that are both discernible and predictable. Similarities in the transfer advantages of a number of sites cause supply competition to take place, thus refuting the idea that land income is more of a monopolistic rent than is the income to other factors of production.[3] Certainly elements of monopoly may be motivating factors in producing land income, but no more so than for the return to labor or capital. When any commodity or service is in short supply, the owners thereof have some monopolistic control over it. A general theory of factor income would impute no difference between land and other production factors with respect to whether the income was caused by monopoly.

---

[3] See Edward Chamberlain, *Monopolistic Competition* (Cambridge: Harvard University Press, 1939), Appendix D, "Urban Rent as a Monopoly Income," pp. 214–17, for the viewpoint that income to real estate represents a monopoly return. This viewpoint derives from the contention that each parcel of land is unique in its locational characteristics and, therefore, cannot be considered as in direct competition with other parcels of real estate in supplying specific locational needs. According to Chamberlain, the locational characteristics of urban land are different from that of agricultural land. Urban land carries its market with it, and the rent paid represents the value of the monopoly privilege of providing retail services *at that particular place.*

PHYSICAL CHARACTERISTICS

The processing advantages specified by Hoover are the chemical and physical makeup of the site (for example, ore mining), availability of water, suitability of the soil and climate for agriculture, the natural flora and fauna (for trapping, fishing, hunting, forestry, or grazing), the amenities of the site (climate, view, and terrain), and those features of the site which determine construction and maintenance cost (primarily terrain, soil structure, and climate).[4]

Although Hoover's definition of processing advantages concerns only land, we extend this concept to include any and all improvements. Rather than dealing in sites alone, the real estate analyst deals with parcels of land which have been greatly modified. The site itself may have been leveled and graded, had storm and sanitary sewers installed, drives and walks paved, and the entire lot landscaped. In addition, a building may have been erected on the land which is several times as valuable as the land itself.

Even when no detectable improvements have been made to the site itself, public improvements (off-site improvements or improvements in common) serve to make the land more valuable. Streets, the lighting system, public sewers, parks, and sidewalks are all important value-determining characteristics. All such improvements, as well as on-site improvements, represent applications of labor, capital, and managerial talent to the parcel of land. They become wedded in an inseparable marriage in which the contribution of one factor cannot be separated from the others. In almost every instance of urban land analysis, it must be recognized that much more is involved than simply the original and indestructible qualities of land only. In this sense, then, real estate is, as Ratcliff has emphasized, a manufactured product.[5]

All such characteristics and modifications of urban land may be thought of as imparting processing advantages. They determine the efficiency and capacity with which real estate can perform services and provide benefits. They determine how well a parcel of real estate provides the amenities of homeownership, how much corn another parcel can produce, how well an office building performs its function, how many cattle can be supported on a range, how many automobiles can be produced in a factory, and how many lobsters can be caught in a particular oceanic area. The real estate analyst must examine and consider each characteristic or feature of a given parcel that would have a bearing on its future processing advantage. Poor construction, inadequate utilities, inappropriate style, and insufficient lighting would be examples of unfavorable factors that would influence the processing advantage of a par-

---

[4] Hoover, *Location of Economic Activity,* p. 91.

[5] Ratcliff, *Real Estate Analysis,* pp. 1, 43, 54–55.

cel of real estate relative to other, competing parcels. Such characteristics obviously would tend to reduce future net income or services in relation to other properties and thus to reduce its value.

Analysis of physical characteristics—the site

The physical characteristics of a parcel of real estate determine the property's processing costs. Characteristics of the site are usually analyzed separately from those of major on-site improvements. The major improvement will often dictate the type of analysis performed for the site, although this distinction would be unrealistic for some types of improvements. For example, an intensive analysis of the agricultural fertility of a parcel of real estate that is already improved with an appropriate, costly commercial structure would be inappropriate. Beginning with the site, then, analysis of the processing characteristics includes the following possible categories of factors: (*a*) geological characteristics, (*b*) agricultural fertility, (*c*) surface characteristics, and (*d*) facilitating improvements.

Geological characteristics. Subsurface characteristics of the soil are important in determining support which can be provided to buildings, drainage and seepage, and the possibility of mineral extraction. The degree to which the latter would be profitable can be analyzed only by competent specialists.

Subsurface soil characteristics also may impose strict limitations to the type of improvement that can be erected on the surface. Marshy, swampy areas or areas subject to volcanic activity require more costly construction techniques to support buildings, although in most cases suitable structures can be built if costly, specialized techniques are used. The Imperial Hotel in Tokyo, designed by Frank Lloyd Wright, is a foremost example of how potential damage from earthquakes can be overcome. It was erected in the years 1916 to 1922, using a revolutionary, floating cantilever construction to provide the required flexibility to absorb shocks. A tremendous earthquake shortly after the construction left the structure standing unaffected, while almost every other building in Tokyo was destroyed.

In Chicago, where land is marshy, huge piers must be sunk to bedrock to support tall buildings. The costs of this additional construction requirement limited the height of Chicago's skyscrapers to fewer than 45 stories until the mid-1960s when newer construction techniques allowed the 100-story John Hancock Center and the 60-story First National Bank Building to be constructed. Since then the Sears Tower, which is the world's tallest office building, has been constructed. Sometimes the culprit is quicksand. An adequate number of borings to test for the presence of quicksand and other geological characteristics should always be made before construction contracts are signed.

Where rock is close to the surface of the land additional costs for excavation are encountered. Basements are much costlier, and subsurface sewage, electrical, and telephone placements are more difficult and costly. Also, impervious soils and subsurface rock may affect the drainage and seepage of the land. The area may be subject to flooding, precluding the proper drainage of storm and sanitary sewage. The elevation of the surface in relation to surrounding land can also be a determinant of drainage.

Agricultural fertility. This factor should obviously be considered when a prospective real estate investment will involve agronomic endeavors. Appropriate agricultural experts should be employed to perform such analysis. A resort to do-it-yourself analysis, opinion by the owner or neighbors, or other nonscientific approaches will usually yield unreliable results.

Surface characteristics. The terrain, size, shape, vegetation, and exposure are characteristics of the surface of a parcel of real estate which may possibly influence value. Hilly terrain and woods require costly modifications for commercial, industrial, or low-cost residential uses. Long, narrow lots are not suitable in today's market for single-family residences. Extreme irregularity in shape of a residential lot is undesirable, while pleasant views and attractive neighborhood structures are important advantages. Additionally, the freedom from obnoxious odors and noises is a virtual necessity for middle- and upper-class residential neighborhoods. Having adequate foot traffic and exposure to appropriate clientele is necessary for commercial uses.

Sometimes a lot is of insufficient size to accommodate a desired use, and two or more parcels are combined to produce the desired size. When the several parcels together have a greater value than the sum of the individual parcels before being combined, the difference is called *plottage value.*

Facilitating improvements. These represent capital expenditures on *and* off the site for such improvements as utilities, paving, subsidiary buildings (for example, a garage), and landscaping. The analyst should identify all such improvements and consider their adequacy or the cost of installing adequate facilities. For well-established uses the amount of analysis may be relatively small; facilitating improvements would have been needed and installed already. New uses, however, may require significant attention to such items. For example, before Anheuser Busch located a new brewery near Columbus, Ohio, a great deal of analysis was required to determine whether the water supply would be adequate to meet the great needs of a large brewery.

Analysis of physical characteristics—the major improvement

Analysis of the major improvement must be tailored to the specific type of structure. Often experts are required to judge the quality and condition of the construction of large, steel-frame buildings or of special-purpose structures, such as a grain elevator or refinery. For any building the following items should be examined relative to their physical characteristics: (a) construction, (b) functional capability, and (c) subsidiary systems.

Construction. Quality and condition of the structural components are the criteria to be considered in evaluating construction. Studs, rafters, joists, subflooring, foundations, footings, and the roof are examples of such components. Quality of the physical components should be judged relative to their original character and workmanship, while condition should indicate how much physical deterioration has occurred. A ten-year-old bathtub that was of high quality when installed and is in good condition may contribute more to a home than a new tub of lesser quality. If the ten-year-old tub is functionally less desirable than a new tub, that penalty should be reflected under the following category.

Functional capability. The degree to which the size, shape, arrangement, lighting, and general appropriateness of the building and its component rooms are adequate determines functional capability. Such considerations can be of overriding importance to the financial success of a real estate venture. For example, a large, high-rise, luxury apartment building in a Midwestern city experienced financial difficulty because of the small size of the rooms and apartments. Persons seeking that type of housing were unwilling to accept the small quarters even at reduced rents. The investors lost their shirts, and the Federal Housing Administration, which insured the mortgage, was forced to take over the building.

Subsidiary systems. Heating, air-conditioning, electrical, plumbing, and elevator systems contribute to the overall productivity of the property. These systems should be examined with respect to their *future* capacity and efficiency. Usually the analyst must estimate the age of these components, their condition, and their capacity to continue to perform their intended functions. These systems will normally have to be replaced one or more times over the life of a building.

Use of checklists

To lessen the likelihood of omitting small but important details, the analyst should develop a checklist for use in analyzing a major improvement. In single-family residential buildings, for example, one should begin in the basement, examining such items as the floor, walls, foundation, plumbing, furnace, water heater, laundry facilities, subflooring, windows, and stairs. Upper floors should be examined in respect to room size, layout, shape, decorating, condition of walls, floors, and ceilings, electrical outlets, heating ducts, and for condition and adequacy of fixtures such as the kitchen sink, disposal, and bath appliances. The attic should be examined with respect to rafters, sheathing, insulation, ventilation, and general condition. Obviously, an analysis of larger commercial, industrial, and apartment buildings would be more complex.

Lastly, the exterior of a building should be examined. The siding, foundation, chimneys, porches, and windows should be noted for quality and condition. Aspects of the site, such as landscaping and paving, will have been considered under site processing advantages or costs discussed above.

TRANSFER CHARACTERISTICS

The second category of factors influencing the productivity of real estate involves the costs of transferring people, information, goods, and services from one site to other locations. Transfer characteristics are concerned with a property's geographic relationship to other parcels of real estate. As Ratcliff puts it:

The essence of location derives from one of the elemental physical facts of life, the reality of space. We cannot conceive of existence without space; if there were no such thing, all objects and all life would have to be at one spot. If this happened to be the case real estate would have no such quality as location; all real estate would be in the same place, equally convenient to every other piece of real estate and to every human activity and establishment. But under the physical laws of the universe, each bit of matter—each atom, molecule, stone, dog, house, and man—takes up space at or near the surface of the earth. As a result no two objects can be at the same place at the same time. Necessarily, then, all people, animals, and objects are distributed in a spatial pattern.[6]

From this explanation we can realize that transfer costs arise because the user of a parcel of real estate is not in immediate proximity to users of other parcels of real estate. The conveyance of people, information, goods, and services is hindered by the geographic barrier or *friction of space*. An analysis of transfer advantages is thus concerned with the cost associated with a parcel of real estate in overcoming this friction relative to such costs associated with competing parcels.

The use assumption

The use to which real estate is put is an important determinant of its transfer costs. For example, the transfer costs of a single-family residence will differ greatly from that of a retail store. Therefore, an assumption must be made as to the future use of a parcel of real estate. In some cases the future use is already determined. The zoning ordinance, for example, may limit the usage to single-family residential or to light industrial. Also, many parcels of real estate include a costly improvement component. A building that is several times as valuable as the land will

---

[6] Ratcliff, *Real Estate Analysis*, p. 62.

ordinarily not be torn down even if some other improvement would be a better use of the land; the costs of demolition and erection of a new structure usually outweigh the benefits to be gained. The analyst has little choice but to assume that the existing land use will be continued into the foreseeable future.

In cases where land-use determination has considerable leeway—for example, vacant, unzoned land or land improved with structures having relatively low value and not subject to stringent zoning regulations—the analyst cannot necessarily assume that the current usage will continue. Instead, it must be decided what use will provide the greatest return on investment after both processing and transfer costs have been deducted. Conceptually this is done by holding constant the income and processing costs of several potential uses to see how the transfer costs vary among them. When one finds several uses having low transfer costs, the total income expected less anticipated expenses or processing costs is examined. The combination yielding lowest transfer costs and highest income after process costs is the financially justified use to which the land should be put.

Analysis procedure

Transfer costs can be regarded as linkages with other parcels of real estate. The term *linkage* implies that there is a need or desire for communication or conveyance of goods, services, or persons between the subject parcel and other parcels of real estate. To the extent that one parcel of real estate is more favorably located with respect to the linkages for the use to which it is likely to be put than other parcels having similar use expectations, the subject parcel enjoys transfer advantages.

Several examples of the relationship between location and linkages can be cited. In the retailing business, location in terms of other compatible or incompatible businesses within the same trading center will affect the level of business volume. A drugstore located near a supermarket, bakery, or hardware store in a large shopping center would likely attract 10 to 20 percent more customers than if the surrounding businesses were gardening or household repair shops; its location near auto repair services or eating drive-ins would have a negative effect.[7] Trade and professional organizations and unions frequently locate near state capitals or in Washington, D.C., to conduct lobbying activities with state legislators, members of Congress, and senators. They also may require ready access to state and federal agencies, such as a state banking regulatory authority (by a state banker's association) or the U.S. Department of Labor (by

---

[7] Richard Lawrence Nelson, *The Selection of Retail Locations* New York: McGraw-Hill, 1958), pp. 70–77, lists tables predicting the degree of compatibility, or interchange between various types of stores in rural trading centers, neighborhood convenience centers, large shopping centers, and the central business district.

a national labor union). Fire departments locate along major arteries close to the center of the area to be served.

An identification of expected linkages, judgment as to their relative importance to each other, and comparison between the expected linkages of the subject parcel and linkages of other parcels having the same use potential are the steps necessary to carry out an analysis of transfer advantages.

Identification of expected linkages. Linkages arise because of the need for persons, goods, services, or information to come to the subject parcel or to go from the subject parcel to other locations. When the people, goods, services, or information come to the subject parcel they are termed *inputs;* when they go from the property they can be regarded as *outputs.* Thus, a manufacturing plant receives people (managers and laborers), goods (raw materials), capital (buildings and machines), and information as inputs. It processes all these factors and puts out manufactured products.

A residential property typically has inputs of capital (the structure and other improvements), people (the occupants), goods (groceries, clothes, furniture, and so on), and information; its outputs are people who have been sheltered, clothed, maintained, and pleasantly comforted. The output of residential services, as well as the produce of the manufacturing plant, must be transferred to (have linkages with) schools, stores, place of work, churches, and so forth. In a like way commercial establishments, public service facilities, and other land uses have inputs and outputs. Both types of transfer needs must be analyzed.

The significance of the input-output distinction lies in the determination of the most desirable location and physical situation for a particular function. If we think of input markets on one side and output markets on the other, we may graph the relative desirability of potential sites in terms of their total transfer costs, as shown in Figure 6–1.

There is an optimal location, assuming equal physical facilities, between the two markets. This optimal location is usually much closer to one market or the other, depending on whether the product is weight-gaining or weight-losing. A weight-gaining product is one such as beer or soft drinks which by the addition of material (water) gain weight in their processing. Obviously the transportation of water is very expensive relative to the value of the product; therefore, the choice between locating a brewery at the source of raw materials and at the consumption market should be made in favor of the latter.

Some products, iron for example, lose weight in processing. When relatively valuable material must be separated from other, heavy waste material, as in the case of separating iron ore from the earth, the location dictated is near the source of raw materials. Sometimes such a decision is determined by the presence of a vital input, such as cheap labor, in one

FIGURE 6-1

Input, output, and total transfer costs

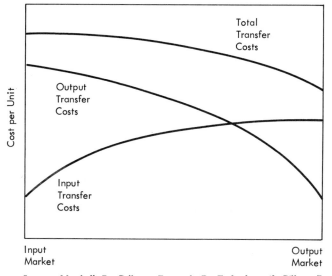

Source: Marshall R. Colberg, Dascomb R. Forbush, and Gilbert R. Whitaker, Jr., *Business Economics: Principles and Cases* (3d ed.: Homewood, Ill., Richard D. Irwin, Inc., 1964), p. 451; and Edgar M. Hoover, *The Location of Economic Activity,* paperback ed. (New York: McGraw-Hill, 1963), p. 39.

location but not in others. This factor, however, is a physical factor involving processing costs and does not properly fall under the category of transfer costs.

When identifying linkages which are believed to be important in the expected future use of a particular location, the analyst can often usefully employ a mapping technique such as that shown in Figure 6–2 for a residential property. The advantages of visualizing expected linkages are twofold: the analyst is less likely to omit important linkages, and in viewing the total linkage situation, their relative importances can be assessed. Only the important linkages need be shown. Minor linkage requirements will tend to even out in terms of relative advantage among prospective sites.

Judging relative importance of expected linkages. The importance of the various linkages must often be judged for the average or typical user of the real estate. For example, in deciding whether to invest in an apartment project, the investor must consider the places to which the typical occupant will desire to commute. If adequate facilities are not available for some necessary linkages, such as shopping centers and schools, the project should be rejected, or means should be found to provide these services in nearby locations. Similarly, in analyzing linkages

FIGURE 6–2

Linkages with single-family residence

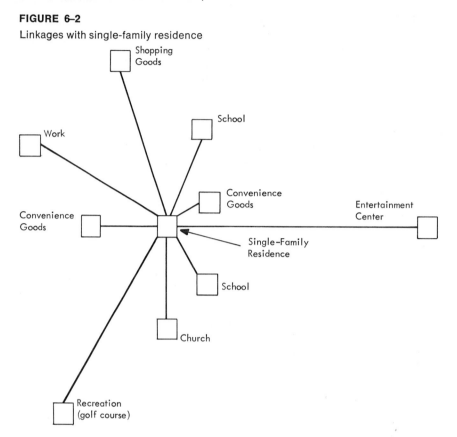

Note: The linkage lines are effective distances; that is, they account for difficulty as well as distance between the site and linked establishments.

for a speculative housing development, the analyst must consider what linkages most people in the market the developer hopes to serve will find desirable.

The prospective buyer-occupants also can analyze the linkages with respect to their own specific requirements. Unless definite plans can be made to stay permanently, however, the linkages other possible purchasers would find desirable should also be considered.

Comparison of transfer costs. Advantages of transfer provided by competing sites should be analyzed for the obvious reason that another site may have lower total transfer costs for the desired linkages. If the other important variables (income or benefits, processing costs, and price) are equally favorable, a decision to reject the subject site in favor of the competing site is required by financial sanity. The real estate specialist (broker, sales representative, investor, appraiser, or consultant) who works in a fairly small market area usually knows the relative advantages of all or most sites for fulfilling various functional requirements. Although the analysis may not be written or specified in the above manner, it is performed nonetheless. The person less familiar with the site and its surroundings would do well to perform the steps prescribed here in a definite, detailed manner.

SUMMARY

Productivity of real estate consists of two elements—physical characteristics and location (transfer characteristics). The physical characteristics of a property determine how well the property can be used for its intended purpose. Transfer characteristics determine how conveniently a property is situated in relation to other properties. The criterion for deciding whether some aspect (such as building design, convenience to a bus stop, or view) is a physical characteristic or a locational factor is whether the transfer of people, goods, or messages is involved. If transfer is involved, the factor under consideration is location; if not, it is a physical characteristic.

The distinction between transfer and physical characteristics facilitates analysis of the productivity of a parcel of real estate. Although the physical characteristics of a property might be quite attractive, its location could be detrimental to the property's intended use. Conversely, a well-located property might be much less valuable than other equally well-located properties because of an unattractive, poorly constructed, or disfunctional building.

The analysis procedure for physical characteristics requires identification and evaluation of each principal physical aspect of a property. In analyzing transfer characteristics all important linkages must be identified and their time-distances compared with competing properties.

QUESTIONS FOR REVIEW

1. What is meant by *location?*
2. What is meant by *processing costs?* Why is the term *physical characteristics* more applicable for improved real estate?
3. Is the view from an apartment overlooking San Francisco Bay a physical characteristic or location? What about an attractive neighborhood in relation to a single-family residence? Why?
4. Why is the financial center of the United States concentrated around Wall Street at the southern tip of Manhattan?
5. Why did Pittsburgh and Gary develop into steel-producing centers?
6. Several older, tall hotel buildings have been torn down in recent years (the

Park Plaza in New York, the LaSalle in Chicago). Why? Did your answer concern physical characteristics or location?

7. The authors know of a small, attractive shopping plaza containing a dinner-type restaurant, a beer and wine carryout, a barber shop, and a pizza parlor that was constructed a few years ago along a four-lane highway leading to the center of a large Midwestern city. Although traffic counts along the highway were high, a real estate consultant counseled against the project. The sketch shows the relationships between the plaza and surrounding land uses.

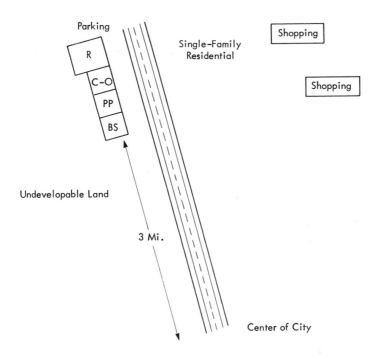

The experience of the plaza confirmed the consultant's advice. Although the restaurant's volume was sufficient to remain in business, the other three establishments went out of business within a year after opening. The turnover of tenants has continued to be high, and the developer sold out for less than the investment cost.

a. Why did the consultant recommend against the project? What factors do you believe were considered?

b. Might the recommendation have been different for an office building? Why?

c. Was the failure of the shopping plaza the result of locational factors or physical characteristics?

REFERENCES

Haggett, Peter. *Locational Analysis in Human Geography.* New York: St. Martin's Press, 1966.

Hoover, Edgar M. *The Location of Economic Activity.* New York: McGraw-Hill, 1963.

Lawrence, Richard L. *The Selection of Retail Locations.* New York: McGraw-Hill, 1958.

Ratcliff, Richard U. *Real Estate Analysis.* New York: McGraw-Hill, 1961, pp. 62–80.

chapter 7

MARKET ANALYSIS

THE EXTENT to which any parcel of real estate is productive and thus has value is determined by the market within which it is bought and sold. Any decision about a property's most productive use or its most likely use, whether to buy, sell, improve, let deteriorate, what type of building to construct, how many stories a building should have, internal features of a building, and the timing of all of these decisions, can only be determined within a market framework. This chapter thus deals with the nature of real estate markets, the many types of forces influencing decision-makers within a market, and the methods of analysis for estimating and predicting market decisions and trends.

A market may be conceptualized as including all of the people, both potential buyers and potential sellers, and all of the influences which tend to determine the price for which a property will be transacted. Beckman and Davidson define the term *market* as

a sphere within which price-making forces operate and in which exchanges of title tend to be accompanied by the actual movement of the goods affected. . . . On a more general plane, the market is the mechanism by which the valuable resources of our society are allocated among the various alternative ends that compete for their use.[1]

In analyzing a market, one must at least conceptually consider the types and characteristics of people on both the buying and selling side of the market and all of the activities, actions, and opinions occurring within society that may play a role in influencing the decisions of potential

---

[1] Theodore N. Beckman and William R. Davidson, *Marketing*, 8th ed. (New York: Ronald Press, 1967), pp. 3–6.

buyers and sellers. Obviously, there are so many potential influences on the motivations of human beings that all considerations can never be completely identified and measured. The reactions of people in the market to some new government policy or to a decision on land-use control by a city council can never be known with certainty. The influence on a community of the plans of a major industry to expand can never be predicted with complete accuracy. Nor can the actions of a foreign government or an institution, such as a bank, be translated into some precise effect upon the value of an individual parcel of real estate. Nevertheless, the analyst's job is to attempt to discern which influences are important and what approximate effect such influences may have upon real estate productivity, decisions, and value.

Also, it must be pointed out that although important influences may be correctly identified, the quantification of these influences may be extremely difficult and their translation into value changes extremely hazardous and qualitative. Social trends occurring in our society are some of the most important considerations that will influence long-run real estate values. The trend toward industrialization and urbanization, for example, has been one of the most important conditioners of life in our society. Industrial growth indicates new development of industrial real estate resources, which in turn leads to increased needs for commercial and residential resources. The effects of the trend toward industrialization, however, can be shown only in the most general terms, such as a general determination of which areas will grow, which areas will grow faster than others, and what type of growth to expect.

Social or behavioral trends may be of interest and value by themselves; however, real estate analysts attempt to relate them to the market with which they are dealing. A behavioral approach to the analysis of real estate would place primary reliance upon social and psychological variables. Only incidentally would social trends and psychological analysis result in economic measures of productivity. Since the purpose of this book, however, concerns the investment decision-making process, social and psychological variables discussed in this chapter are placed within an economic framework. They are regarded as constituting some of the determinants of market prices. One of the most fertile areas for further research in real estate is the relation of behavioral (social and psychological) variables to real estate values and trends.

This chapter first examines some economic models of market behavior. The purpose of this section is to allow the reader to understand the alternative models that are available and to build a case for one model, that of monopolistic competition, as being the most relevant for the economic good of real estate. Identification of a relevant market model allows the analyst to gain insight into the types of influences that may prevail in a market and what implication these influences may have upon potential buyers and sellers. Next, the chapter deals with the important types of influences on market behavior. These are divided into forces influencing demand and those influencing supply. A systematic identification and analysis of these forces is necessary in any market analysis. Then, the local housing market is conceptualized as interrelated submarkets. The filtering process is examined within the context of the conceptual model. Finally, the chapter deals with market analysis and feasibility analysis. The steps in each of these types of analysis are presented, and a step-by-step procedure is outlined for completing a market study.

MARKET FUNCTIONS

All markets perform the basic task of allocating resources among various uses in the economy. This allocation process involves the accomplishment of several functions by a market. Weimer, Hoyt, and Bloom identify three such functions: (*a*) apportioning existing quarters among those who need them, (*b*) contracting or expanding the space available in order to meet changed conditions, and (*c*) determining land use.[2] Ratcliff adds a fourth market function—price establishment[3] which could be included in Weimer, Hoyt, and Bloom's first function. The market conditions associated with the first function can be illustrated with a graph of short-run supply-demand relationships as shown in Figure 7–1.[4]

In the short-run the supply of housing space is shown to be price inelastic. Over a period of one to six months, or even a year, rents and prices may advance because of an increased demand. Such an increase may have been caused by a new employment source locating in the city or an expansion in an existing one. Although the demand may increase, as shown in Figure 7–1, from D_1 to D_2, the supply of housing available cannot increase proportionately. The market thus serves to allocate the available space among those who need it. Such a lag in housing construction usually lasts six months to a year, partly because the construction process will take in many cases at least six months or longer. Additionally, however, it should be recognized that potential investors in new housing to be made available for sale or rental must be convinced that the increased demand will be a long-term rather than a temporary phenomenon.

Sometimes builder-investors produce additional housing units in anticipation of future increases in demand. Sometimes builder-investors continue to add new units after demand has slackened. For example, in a speech to the Biennial Congress of the International Fraternity of Lambda

---

2 Weimer, Hoyt, and Bloom, *Real Estate,* p. 126.

3 Ratcliff, *Real Estate Analysis,* p. 229.

4 Weimer, Hoyt, and Bloom, *Real Estate,* p. 128.

FIGURE 7–1

Short-run supply-demand relationships

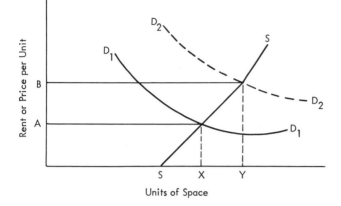

Units of Space

Alpha and the Land Economic Foundation on October 7, 1971, James Downs, chairman of the board of Real Estate Research Corporation, stated that "the effective demand is not there to absorb units at today's construction costs. . . . residential vacancy in the effective market is going up very rapidly and is going to continue to go up very rapidly until we cut the amount of building which we're doing next year."[5] Most desirably, however, increases in supply will occur when builder-investors correctly forecast additional demand for the immediate future. Ideally, the builder wants to be Johnny-on-the-spot with available housing when new long-term demand appears. This is the *raison d'être* for market analysis by suppliers of housing units.

The production of new units of housing space involves longer run adjustments in the quantity and quality of space—function 2 of the real estate market. This function operates during a time period long enough to allow new units to be created (usually six months and longer). Conceptually, the time period is not so long as to allow a shift in the usage to which the land can most profitably be put.

The third market function—land-use determination—operates over a sufficiently long time period for all factors to vary. Buildings can be torn down, and new ones constructed in their place. Although the market forces of competition must operate within the constraints of the zoning law, the market determines over a long period of time what land use is the most profitable. Presumably the most profitable land use (highest

---

[5] *Appraisal Briefs* (Chicago: Society of Real Estate Appraisers, October 1971).

and best use) will provide the greatest service to the community, since people will pay more for that usage than for alternative uses.

MARKET MODELS

As we discussed in Chapter 4, the concept of a perfect market contains several assumptions about participant behavior and the character of the goods exchanged. The perfect market has homogeneity of products; the product is divisible into small units and is transportable; there are many buyers and sellers with no single buyer or seller able to influence price; entry into the market is not hindered; and buyers and sellers have complete knowledge about possible uses for the product and are in agreement about expectations.

The wheat market might be visualized as an example of the most nearly competitive market. Each kernel of wheat is nearly like every other kernel (at least within a grade), most sellers must accept the going market price when they sell their wheat, and there are many buyers and sellers who actively bid in a well-organized market. Even here, however, the imperfections are evident. The product is not homogeneous; there are several grades of wheat. Some buyers and sellers are large enough to affect market price by withholding from or bringing to the market their wheat or bids. Entry to the market is not free or easy; considerable capital is required. And knowledge about the potential worth of the wheat is subject to disagreement. In fact, an active futures market for grain has developed. In this market, buyers bid to purchase grain which will be delivered at a future date. If the price goes up in the meantime, they will profit; if the price goes down, they will lose. On the other side, sellers are betting that the price of wheat will go down and thus agree to sell wheat they will obtain later at the present price, which they believe to be high.

In contrast with the wheat market, the real estate market is one of the least perfect markets we could identify. The product (a parcel of real estate) is highly differentiated. Large owners or buyers can sometimes affect market price. Entry to the market usually requires a sizable amount of capital, and knowledge about the potential productivity and value of real estate is subject to a lack of information as well as disagreement. Because of these market imperfections, some economists have stressed the monopolistic characteristics of urban real estate. According to this view, each parcel of real estate is a monopoly for its particular group of characteristics; no other parcel will substitute equally well. Greater profits will accrue more to some parcels than to others because the elements of productivity (transfer and physical characteristics) are superior in some parcels and inferior in others. Thus, a well-located office building will produce more income than an equally attractive poorly located one. A dime store located on a "100 percent" site will do better than one located a block away. And a residential property having desirable architectural and design qualities will tend to sell for a higher price than another property that is equally well located, but which has less desirable physical characteristics.

If each parcel of real estate were a true monopoly, we know from economic theory that the monopolist-owner would be assured of a profit —at least in the long run. In pure monopoly where there is only one producer or seller, that level of output that will maximize total profit can be chosen given market demand conditions. Although the monopolist may lose money or do no better than break even in the short run, the fact that the level of output may be chosen is assumed to insure in the long run that the monopolist will operate at a level that will provide a profit.

It should be evident that the case for urban real estate's falling under the classification of pure monopoly is no stronger than its falling under the model of pure competition. To refute the long-standing emphasis on the monopolistic aspects of urban land, Ratcliff has emphasized the "economic mobility" of urban land.[6] In this view, perfect substitutability is not required for effective competition. Woolworth or Kresge *can* accept a 98 percent location, particularly when obtainable at a disproportionately lower price than a 100 percent location. Thus, the fact that many parcels of urban land are to some extent in competition with each other for a given usage would seem to refute the idea of monopolistic control of urban land. As pointed out in Chapter 6, Chamberlain includes this product within the vast majority of commodities whose markets contain aspects of both competition and monopoly.[7] Since the real estate market is far from being a perfect market, we could conclude, by definition, that it contains elements of monopoly. Whether these are greater or less than the monopoly elements in other markets makes little difference. But the concept of monopolistic competition does seem appropriate in describing the operation of real estate markets.

In monopolistic competition, the firm decides at what level of output to operate in the same way as does the monopolist. However, monopolistic competition differs from pure monopoly because there is no true market demand for a product. Every firm or entity differentiates its product or service by producing a different brand or type of the economic good. Nevertheless, each brand or type is related to the other brands and types of the same commodity. That is, each is a close substitute (not perfect substitute) for the others. For example, Gleem toothpaste is a close sub-

---

[6] Richard U. Ratcliff, *Urban Land Economics* (New York: McGraw-Hill, 1949), chap. 12.

[7] Chamberlain, *Monopolistic Competition*, Appendix D.

stitute for Crest or Colgate. Thus, the level of output each firm can sell depends upon the prices and types of close substitutes, as well as its own price. Similarly, the prices of urban sites depend upon the prices and types of close substitutes.

There is another important difference between pure monopoly and monopolistic competition. The firm in monopolistic competition does not have a monopoly over the ability to satisfy the market, as does the pure monopolist. In pure monopoly, firm equilibrium is the same situation as market equilibrium. In monopolistic competition, however, the presence of profits will lead to new firms coming into the market with closely substitutable products. Assuming that market demand remains unchanged, profit levels in the industry shrink as new firms continue to enter the industry. Thus, in long-run equilibrium, profit levels of monopolistically competitive firms shrink toward zero.

Implications of theory

The real estate market's lack of qualification for being a perfect market implies justification for the role of intermediaries in the market. The existence of relatively few buyers and sellers at any one time for a given type of real estate, the incomplete knowledge and lack of agreement about future market conditions, the potential for any one buyer or seller to influence the market, and the lack of mobility into and out of the market necessitate the facilitating function of the real estate broker.

Nevertheless, the competitive aspects of real estate imply that investors must realize that, with a few possible exceptions, there are always substitutable parcels of real estate for any other parcel. If there is an active, viable market, an owner cannot expect to extract an unreasonable price from informed, intelligent potential buyers. At the same time, potential buyers can take comfort from the knowledge that there are normally a number of parcels of real estate that will serve a given need equally well. Some may be better than others, however, and a buyer must expect to pay a premium for those parcels having the greatest productivity potential. The point is that true monopoly profits are almost never attainable in real estate. Large profits will attract competitors, who will tend to drive prices and profits down.

On the other hand, it should be recognized that each parcel of real estate holds some—be it ever so small—degree of monopoly advantage. One parcel of residential real estate is located nearer the corner than other similar parcels. One house has a more desirable floor plan than another house in a comparable location. One commercial property is located at the center of pedestrian traffic patterns, while another is not. One industrial property has more complete docking and storage facilities than other comparably located properties. Prices reflecting these monopolistic advantages can be expected to be paid—but only in proportion to the degree of advantage perceived by the market. True monopoly prices reflecting total market demand will not be attainable.

DETERMINANTS OF DEMAND

The various types of influences on market behavior and prices can for convenience and for purposes of analysis be divided between the demand and supply sides of the market. The determinants of demand are all of those forces or influences that tend to cause real estate to be needed or desired plus the conditions making it possible for people to purchase and own property. Influences tending to cause real estate to be produced or supplied are all of those forces and conditions which motivate the suppliers of real properties to create and construct new real estate resources. Thus, this section of the chapter deals with the demand side of the market, and the next section deals with the supply side.

Although we make the distinction between demand and supply determinants, in reality it may be very difficult to separate the two. The fact that the population is growing is usually considered to be a demand factor, although realistically the growing population is a major determinant of supply as well. Similarly, the availability and relative prices of materials and labor are usually regarded as supply factors. They also influence demand, however, because of the competition of real estate with other economic goods. If the prices of real estate rise relative to other goods, demand will tend to be decreased, while if the prices of real estate decrease relative to other goods, the demand for real estate will tend to increase. We recognize the difficulties of arbitrarily assigning the various forces to the demand or the supply side of the market; however, it must be recognized that this classification is for convenience and analysis, and others are welcome to change the classification to fit their own needs.

Need for housing and other types of real estate

The productivity and the value of real estate are derived from its ability to be used beneficially by human beings. Many types of real estate are needed or desired to satisfy and fulfill the human condition. A broad classification of types of properties consists of residential, commercial, and industrial properties. The value of all of these types of properties is dependent upon the presence of people to utilize them effectively. Thus, housing is needed to provide shelter and a measure of privacy for individuals and groups. Commercial properties are needed and desired because they provide the means by which other economic goods are made available to people. Industrial real estate is needed and desired because it provides shelter and a base for the production of other economic goods. The demand for commercial and industrial real estate is a derived demand and is dependent upon the need for the goods and services produced or sold by firms requiring such real estate.

In considering the demand for residential real estate, the need for shelter must be regarded as basic. Protection from the elements, however, is only one of the functions which most housing in the United States provides today. Housing is much more than shelter; it involves emotional needs and desires, as well. Most housing today is a luxury good which attempts to fulfill the psychological and sociological, as well as physical, needs of people. Housing, as distinguished from shelter, includes architecturally pleasing designs, divided interior space, attractive wall and floor coverings, indoor plumbing, attractive kitchen and bathrooms, air-conditioning systems, space that may go unused for substantial periods of time, and many appliances and gadgets that make living more comfortable and more socially fulfilling.

People make a market and, therefore, the first determinant of demand must be people, or population. Population is important not only in terms of sheer size, but also in terms of characteristics (or subgroupings) of the total population, such as age groupings, educational levels, race, and occupation. Migratory patterns, indicating where people are moving to and where they came from, are a further dimension of population trends that determine the need or demand for real estate.

Marketing analysis begins with identifying broad characteristics and movements, including studying and analyzing national trends in population growth, movements of people to and from different regions, and identifying the characteristics of the people moving, as well as hypothesizing reasons for such movements. Regional population changes can then be more accurately predicted and the impact of population mobility translated to the community and neighborhood levels. The prime source of demographic information is the U.S. Bureau of the Census.

Data from the "100 percent coverage" portion of the 1970 Census reveal some of the current trends which are potentially useful to real estate market analysts. These trends include the following ones:

1. Internal migration—shifts of the population:
   a. From rural to urban areas.
   b. From central cities to suburbs.
   c. Into white and nonwhite concentrations in large central cities.
   d. From central geographic divisions of the nation to the coasts.
   e. From South to North in the case of blacks.
   f. Among the states resulting in changes in size-rankings of the states.
2. Differing decade-rates of growth among racial groups, including:

a. Reduced fertility and total growth rate of white populations.
b. Greater fertility and total growth rate of black populations.
c. Extremely high total growth rates of other nonwhite populations.
3. Younger population.
4. Smaller family size and reduced importance of male family heads.[8]

Shifts in population among states and regions may have dramatic effects for real estate marketers operating in those states experiencing significant shifts. Figure 7–2 shows the shifts among states between 1970 and 1974. As a general pattern, the South, Southwest, and West have

FIGURE 7–2
Net outmigration and inmigration by states, 1970–1974

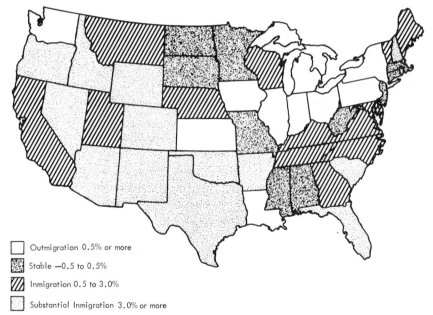

☐ Outmigration 0.5% or more
▨ Stable —0.5 to 0.5%
▨ Inmigration 0.5 to 3.0%
☐ Substantial Inmigration 3.0% or more

Source: The Urban Institute, Washington, D.C.

been gaining population by net inmigration, while the Northeast Central states have been experiencing population outflows. As can be seen in Figure 7–2, there are exceptions to the general trend—particularly New Hampshire, Washington, and Louisiana.

Within the state and regional patterns, however, population changes of cities can either accentuate or mitigate the general trend. As can be seen in Figure 7–3, the largest, older cities have been losing population

---

[8] James C. Yocum, "Population Changes in Two Decades," *Bulletin of Business Research* (Ohio State University) 46, no. 9 (September 1971): 1.

FIGURE 7–3

Growth and decline among all U.S. cities with population of half a million or more, 1960–1973

GROWING	% Population Gain	DECLINING[‡]	% Population Loss	NEW YORK CITY
Jacksonville*	172.6	St. Louis	-25.6	
Indianapolis*	66.3	Cleveland	-22.5	%
Phoenix	45.1	Pittsburgh	-20.7	Population
Houston	40.9	Buffalo	-20.2	Gain,
Honolulu	37.2	Detroit	-16.9	1960-70:
Memphis[†]	32.3	Cincinnati	-15.3	1.5
San Diego	32.1	Boston	-11.3	
San Antonio	28.6	Chicago	-10.6	%
Dallas [†]	20.0	Seattle	-9.7	Population
Columbus, Ohio	14.9	New Orleans	-8.8	Loss,
Los Angeles[†]	10.8	San Francisco	-7.2	1970-73:
Kansas City[†]	8.4	Philadelphia	-7.0	-1.8
Denver	4.5	Milwaukee	-6.9	
		Baltimore	-6.5	

* City-county consolidations.
† Since 1970, population has begun to decline.
‡ Excluding Washington, D.C.
Source: The Urban Institute, Washington, D.C.

while the smaller, younger large cities have been gaining. Certainly the demand for most types of real estate will remain stronger in those regions, states and urban areas experiencing population growth than in those areas experiencing declines. The types of real estate needs will also likely differ between growth and nongrowth areas.

As can be seen in Table 7–1, the total percentage of nonwhites increased substantially during the 20-year period, 1950–70, a reflection of the higher-than-average rate of increase in the birthrate for nonwhite as compared with the white population. Blacks and other minorities migrated from the South to the more industrialized states of the North. (There is evidence that the trend has not held during more recent years.)

The age composition of the United States during the 20 years shifted to a lower average age. Although the higher-age groups also increased proportionately, the lower average age is attributable to the even higher proportions of the population in the young age categories. The age composition of the U.S. population will remain low relative to former years for several years into the future; however, the long-term prospect is for an increasing average age of the population. The rate of population growth is already decreasing, and the number of children below the age of five has dropped dramatically. As the rate of increase of the population slows, the average age of the population will increase. As the

TABLE 7-1

Resident population of United States and geographic divisions, 1970, 1960, and 1950*

| Area | (Number of states) | Number 1970 | Percent increase | | Total population | | | | | | | | | Black population: Percent of U.S. | |
| | | | 1970 from 1960 | 1960 from 1950 | Percent of U.S. total | | | Percent urban | | | Percent nonwhite | | | | |
					1970	1960	1950	1970	1960	1950	1970	1960	1950	1970	1960
Divisions:															
E. North Central	(5)	40,252,678	11.1	19.3	19.8	20.2	20.1	74.8	73.0	69.7	10.2	8.2	6.1	17.1	12.0
Middle Atlantic	(3)	37,152,813	8.7	13.3	18.3	19.0	19.9	81.7	81.4	80.5	11.5	8.5	6.4	17.4	12.5
South Atlantic	(9)	30,671,337	18.1	22.6	15.1	14.5	14.0	63.7	57.2	49.1	21.5	22.8	24.3	28.3	33.9
Pacific†	(5)	26,525,774	25.1	40.2	13.1	11.8	10.0	86.0	81.1	74.4	11.1	8.9	5.2	6.7	3.4
W. South Central	(4)	19,322,458	14.0	16.6	9.5	9.5	9.6	72.6	67.7	55.6	16.3	16.9	17.2	13.4	16.2
W. North Central	(7)	16,324,389	6.0	9.5	8.0	8.6	9.3	63.7	58.8	52.0	5.1	4.2	3.4	3.1	2.8
E. South Central	(4)	12,804,552	6.3	5.0	6.7	6.7	7.6	54.6	48.4	39.1	20.5	22.5	23.6	11.5	17.9
New England	(6)	11,847,186	12.7	12.8	5.8	5.9	6.2	76.4	76.4	76.2	3.8	2.5	1.6	1.7	0.9
Mountain	(8)	8,283,585	20.8	35.1	4.1	3.8	3.3	73.1	67.1	44.9	5.8	5.0	4.5	0.8	0.4
U.S. Total†	(51)	203,184,772	13.3	18.5	100.0	100.0	100.0	73.5	69.9	64.3	12.6	11.4	10.7	100.0	100.0

* Total U.S. population, 1970, including U.S. citizens stationed abroad (U.S. armed forces and federal employees, and their dependents), 204,765,770.
† All 1950 figures derived from totals including Alaska and Hawaii.
Source: James C. Yocum, "Population Changes in Two Decades," *Bulletin of Business Research* (Ohio State University) 46, no. 9 (September 1971).

relatively large numbers of younger people in the 10 to 20 age category become older, they will tend to cause the average age to increase also.

The effects of these trends can already be noted in the real estate market, particularly in the larger cities. The increased percentages of apartments being constructed in almost every large city attests to the growing numbers of young people entering the housing market at this time. It reflects the trend of younger people waiting longer to get married and of married couples waiting longer to have children and having fewer of them. The advent of apartments for singles only or for young married couples without children is simply a manifestation of these population changes. In fast-growing regions of the country, such as Florida, the Southwest, and the West, complete new communities are being developed with increased emphasis on apartments and condominiums which provide smaller sized units with more complete services and facilities for the occupants.

Societal trends

Many changes occur in society which result in changing living patterns, changes in class structure, changes in work conditions and lifestyles, and changes in the way that people use their time. Most of these changes are a result of the increasing capabilities of technology. In the area of transportation and communication, improved technology has resulted in the beginnings of mass transit systems in some cities that formerly did not have them, new road systems allowing people to live farther from their work, and better communications among all parts of the country. As new transportation systems or additions to old systems are made, real estate values in the areas affected are changed, often dramatically. As many people have made the move to suburbia, their entire lifestyle has changed or at least it has been different from what it would have been had they lived in an apartment close to the center of a city. This trend, while much maligned, would seem to offer advantages in the minds of many people, or they would not have made the decisions to live in the outlying areas. It is not surprising that many people desire to have green space, trees, and desirable surroundings for their children when they can afford it. Without the ability to transfer themselves to and from important destinations, such as work, schools, and cultural centers, few people would have had the opportunity for these types of advantages.

Improved technology has also resulted in the greater use of machines and correspondingly increasing levels of efficiency. The requirement of fewer man-hours to produce the same amount of output as previously has led to more and more people obtaining greater amounts of time free from work. Greater emphasis upon leisure living and informality has created entire new markets for outdoor recreational equipment. Color televisions, picnic tables, and charcoal grills are but a few of the products demanded to satisfy this type of living pattern. Similarly, new houses are expected to contain patios, sliding glass doors, attractive yards and recreational areas, and often a pleasant view with green areas for recreation and relaxation. Bowling alleys, golf courses, and other recreational facilities have proliferated.

The new technology has made available for many homemakers such gadgets as self-cleaning ovens, dishwashers, built-in vacuum systems, automatic ice makers, electronic ranges, and many others. In short, changes in technology have shifted the society from an agricultural one to an industrialized one. An industrialized society has produced an urban society, where even rural residents have adopted and pursued the goals of their urban counterparts.

Values and attitudes

The values and attitudes adopted by a society change over time, and these changes, as well as the values and attitudes themselves, can have an important bearing upon the types of commodities, goods, and housing that people demand. Some values are associated with the entire society, while some are characteristic of subgroups or subcultures within a society. Religious groups, racial groups, members of social classes, and ethnic groups are some of these subcultures that may form their own values which vary somewhat from the overall society's values.

From the standpoint of society as a whole, some of the more important values and attitudes that seem to prevail are that leisure time is important in obtaining the benefits of the good life. Peoples' homes, and possibly their offices, are important measures of their social status. Informality in daily life and a willingness to make change are more characteristic of families today than was the case before World War II. These attitudes and values are interrelated, of course, since the importance of leisure time is reflected in the type of home that one purchases. Greater informality is reflected in smaller living rooms, larger family rooms, and patios. Also, as people are willing to make changes—to move from one section of the country to another, to change houses within the same city, and to change sources of employment—these trends are reflected in the emphasis placed upon new housing and new office buildings of every type. Only the new structures can adequately reflect the new tastes and preferences.

One of the most important types of subgroups that is important in determining demand is social class. Lloyd Warner's work in identifying social classes in U.S. cities showed that four characteristics are important in explaining class differences.[9] These variables are income, occupation,

---

[9] W. Lloyd Warner, *Social Class in America* (New York: Harper and Brothers, 1960).

house type, and area of residence; they produce a class structure as follows:

1. Upper class (0.9 percent of the population).
   a. Upper upper—old line, wealthy families.
   b. Lower upper—socially prominent, newly rich families.
2. Upper-middle class (7.2 percent of the population).
   Professionals and highly successful business executives.
3. Lower-middle class (28.4 percent of the population).
   Teachers, technicians, most sales representatives, white-collar workers.
4. Upper-lower class (44.0 percent of the population).
   Skilled workers, production workers, service workers, local politicians, and labor leaders.
5. Lower-lower class (19.5 percent of the population).
   Unskilled laborers, racial immigrants, and people in unrespectable occupations.

Social class, as any other subgrouping, holds significance for the real estate market analyst because people within one group have different needs and desires than people in the other groups. Studies have shown that people in different social classes respond differently to advertising media, have differing levels of interest in products and brands, and want to be treated differently by sales personnel. Given the same number of dollars to spend, they will spend the money differently.

Implications for real estate market analysts and real estate marketers are that as the size and composition of social classes in the society and within a community change, the types of housing and other real estate demanded will change.

Values attributed to different social classes are translated into different housing needs. Upper-middle class families, for example, place high value on privacy whereas upper-lower class families value friendliness and openness to the community. In the first instance, high fences around yards are acceptable, while in a lower-class community such physical barriers will be rejected and, in cases where erected, would be interpreted as an act of snobbishness. Dobriner illustrates in *Class in Suburbia* how hostilities arose in a new community as a result of value clashes (and in particular how values were interpreted into everyday living patterns) between two differing social classes moving into the same neighborhood.[10] Friction between the two classes ultimately led to members of one social class moving from the community.

While suburbia typically has been portrayed as an upper-middle class phenomenon, in actuality the metropolis is a network of suburbs of the

---

[10] William M. Dobriner, *Class in Suburbia* (Englewood Cliffs, N.J.: Prentice-Hall, 1963).

several class groups, with the exception of the lower-lower class. Suburbs exist which are identical economically, in terms of property values and income levels of the residents, but which differ in class structure and mode of living. In the Dobriner study cited above the intermixture of two classes residing in the same community was temporary. The community, a new development, was the first Levittown constructed at the end of World War II, a time when demand for housing was exceptionally great. The houses appealed to two diverse groups, one the young middle-class families who traditionally were homeowners and found that Levittown was what they could afford at that stage of their life cycle and second the working-class families who had accumulated enough savings during the war years to escape the crowded city and achieve for the first time the all-American dream of homeownership. While studies indicate class differences do exist, assessing their effects upon real estate development is difficult, offering a potentially fertile area for investigation.

National income

Along with people, who are the ultimate source of demand for real estate, must be income. Income turns potential demand into effective demand. If the people are there and they have the income to purchase real estate, properties will be sold and purchased in the market. As with population, at least three levels of income must be considered and analyzed. Income trends at the national, regional, and local levels ultimately determine the effective demand for an individual parcel of real estate. To analyze income trends at the national level, one may refer to three types of accounting systems. Each of these systems is designed to provide a different type of information and is useful for different purposes. It is likely that the greatest weight in analyzing market demand will be placed upon the first system to be discussed—the gross national product/national income accounts—since the other two systems do not deal directly with income. Nevertheless, the other two systems can be useful for specialized types of analyses. As discussed in the real estate financing chapter,[11] the flow of funds system is particularly useful in analyzing financial transactions. Similarly, the input-output accounts can be useful to an industrial real estate broker in analyzing industry trends.

Gross national product/national income accounting system. The gross national product/national income accounts provide a broad picture of national production and income. Predictions about the economic health of the country are made in terms of the gross national product (GNP). Trends in the components of GNP and national income can be analyzed to detect changing patterns of production and income. While

---

[11] See Chapter 13.

it is not consistent with the purpose of this book to describe in detail the GNP and income accounts, several trends illustrating the use of this accounting system can be cited. Within the GNP accounts, the services category of personal consumption expenditures has been the fastest growing component. This trend is in part a result of the growing affluence of a large part of the population, combined with the relatively mature characteristic of the economy in being able to produce and provide physical goods. Investment in residential structures has been growing comparatively slowly with other categories of private investment. State and local government purchases of goods and services have been growing rapidly. While national defense and other federal government expenditures have held fairly level in recent years, the state and local category has increased dramatically.

Flow of funds. The flow of funds accounting system describes how funds or assets have been used in the economy and the sources from which they came. This system is particularly useful in analyzing financial changes in the economy.[12] Some interesting trends that could be discerned from the flow of funds accounts, however, can be cited. The first of these is that the greatest percentage of funds in the economy have been used by real estate mortgages, during the decade of the 1960s. During the latter five years of the decade, however, this percentage dropped significantly. Corporate bonds and stocks increased in the percentage of funds used. Nevertheless, real estate mortgages continue to be the single most important use of funds, although the decline in importance is one that needs to be watched and analyzed by real estate market analysts. On the supply side, commercial banks have furnished the greatest proportion of funds. Savings and loan associations, while for several years being the fastest growing suppliers of funds, leveled out in the percentage of funds being supplied and then resumed the increase during the mid-1970s.

Input-output analysis. Input-output analysis involves the use of a table which quantifies the use of goods and services among major sectors or industries in the economy. For example, the amount of manufactured goods being used in agriculture and the amount of agricultural goods being utilized in manufacturing would show up in an input-output table. One can then trace through the amount and types of goods being used in each industry and from where they came.

Input-output tables are not available in series at the present time. However, there is increasing interest in this type of analysis, and when federal agencies are able to accumulate the type of data needed on a continuing basis, input-output tables may become available on a regular basis.

---

[12] These financial changes in the economy are analyzed more fully in Chapter 13.

Regional income

Real estate productivity and values also depend upon the level of income within a region. The regional income and economic prospects may differ significantly from national trends. Low per capita incomes in the Appalachian region, the demise of coal mining as a major industry in southern Illinois and the consequent depression of economic activity in that area, and the great growth and prosperity in southern California during the 1960s are but a few examples of regional trends that have varied substantially from the national experience. Real estate values in depressed regions have suffered commensurately with the decline in economic activity, while values in areas experiencing greater than average growth and prosperity have increased faster than the national average.

Although it is important for the real estate market analyst to keep abreast of regional economic trends, measures of these trends are less readily attainable than for trends either at the national or local levels. Two reasons for this lack of data can be cited. First, there is no standard delineation of regions. A region may vary in size from a group of states to a section of a city. A regional breakdown for one analyst or for one government agency would not be functionally useful for another analyst or another agency. Thus, there has not been agreement on how to divide up the country for the collection of regional data.

The second reason is that the boundaries of regions are much less meaningful as determinants of economic activity. It is much easier to identify the production of goods and services within the United States and to keep track of products and services flowing into and out of the country than it is to keep track of these same flows among regions. The federal government has shown much more interest in data collection for the entire country than for regions of the country. In recent years, however, many groups have become concerned about regional analysis, and government agencies, as well as academic and professional groups, have devoted more attention to the understanding and collection of regional data.

Input-output analysis. Input-output analysis would seem to hold some of the greatest potential as a tool for analyzing regions. While no regional input-output analysis is done on a series basis, the idea has been advocated, and indeed input-output analysis has been performed for a state. Hopefully, this tool may become operative and useful for states, and the state data could then be combined into regional groupings.

Other measures. Without a regular system of measuring regional income and production, a market analyst must keep track of other indicators of economic activity. Personal income and buying income are estimated for states. Personal income measures can be found in *Business Week* magazine, while *Sales Management* magazine publishes estimates of buying income for states and other geographic areas in its annual "buying power" issue. The bureaus of business research of many state universities are also valuable sources of data on regional economic trends and prospects. State departments of development and chambers of commerce are other potential sources of statewide information.

Community income

The principal tool or method for analyzing community income and economic prospects is economic base analysis. In its original concept, economic base analysis was designed as a tool to predict future population for a community. This prediction was accomplished by identifying all sources of employment in a community and dividing the number of employees between two categories—basic and service (or primary and secondary). Basic employment is recognized as the type for which products and services are exported beyond the community's borders. Service employment redistributes the income within the community. Examples of the former type are the automobile industry in Detroit, wherefrom the community derives much of its income by the shipment of automobiles out of the city, and a large university within a city which brings income from students who come from beyond the borders of a city. Examples of the second category, or service employment, are barber shops, beauty shops, real estate and insurance offices, and other types of service businesses that do not draw customers primarily from outside of the community. Figure 7–4 shows the various components of total community income.

A ratio is obtained between the number of basic and service employees, and then the basic sources of employment are surveyed to attempt to determine whether increases in this type of employment will be taking place in the future. Increases in service employment are then predicted in relation to the ratio between service and basic employment existing previously in the community. The total increase in population deriving from the increase in basic employment can then be projected on the basis of the ratio of total employment to total population existing in the community. For example, each new job of both basic and service types may result in an increased population of three persons. If total employment increases were estimated to be 5,000 persons for the coming year in a given community, the total population increase would be projected as 15,000 persons.

The process of surveying basic employment sources to determine planned increases in employment has proven to be an unreliable predicting method for determining future basic employment. Therefore, in carrying out economic base analyses, usually several techniques are em-

FIGURE 7–4

How the community earns its living

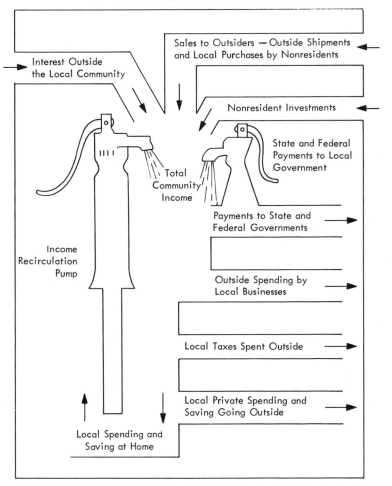

Source: Bank of America, Area Development Service, San Francisco.

ployed to project employment in various industry classifications. In a mammoth study of the Columbus, Ohio, economic base performed during the 1960s, the Ohio State University Bureau of Business Research utilized three projection techniques. County share of U.S. total value added per employee was determined for each industry classification, and ratios were projected into the future on the basis of projected total U.S. industry projections. Secondly, manufacturers were surveyed to determine future employment expectations according to the amount of sales expected outside the community and within the community. Thirdly, input-output tables were constructed to show the interrelationships among the various industries in metropolitan Columbus. Projected sales of each industry were then computed from the coefficients developed in the input-output matrix. Projected sales were then converted to projected employment. This large study of the Columbus economic base projected employment at various intervals 20 years into the future to 1985. A summary of the study is contained in Appendix E.

Other measures. Buying income is estimated by *Sales Management* for metropolitan areas. The magazine also estimates the number of people in various income categories. The analyst can use these data both in comparing a community with other similar communities and in developing trends for the community under analysis. Chambers of commerce also usually maintain data on incomes and numbers of households in a community, as well as information on the number and types of industries, the number and types of commercial establishments, current and expected development in the community, and other economic measures.

The Federal Housing Administration periodically performs market analyses for metropolitan areas. These studies can be extremely useful in analyzing a real estate market. Trade and professional organizations within a community, such as a home builders association or an apartment owners and managers association, may also maintain useful data and perform market studies.

Price structure

The prices of real estate in a community also help determine the demand for real estate. The price structure refers to the relationships among prices of properties within the community and to the relationship between prices of real estate and other economic goods. If real estate prices rise relative to other goods, people who would otherwise be in the market may refrain from buying until prices seem to be more reasonable. By the same token, if people expect the prices of real estate to increase in the future relative to other goods, they may decide to purchase now rather than later.

In addition to total price, other elements of price must be considered also. The downpayments required on real estate may become more liberal or more rigorous. As money conditions tighten in the overall economy, for example, lenders often require larger downpayments than during periods of relatively easy money. Also, sometimes institutional regulations are adjusted to allow smaller downpayments. When these happenings occur, the demand for real estate is likely to be affected.

The monthly housing expense can be regarded as part of the price mechanism for residential real estate. Families must budget their housing expense, and the extent to which monthly housing expense is expected to increase can affect the willingness of families to purchase homes.

DETERMINANTS OF SUPPLY

Anticipations of demand

Perhaps the single most important determinant of supply of new real estate resources is the expectation that suppliers have of demand. If developers and builders are optimistic about the future demand, they will tend to bring forth newly created resources. If, however, they are relatively pessimistic about the coming year's demand, they will tend to hold back the level of development and construction activity. These anticipations result from forecasts of national economic activity, regional changes, and community income and economic activity.

Utilization of existing real estate resources

If the existing stock of real estate resources is not being utilized at close to its capacity, the suppliers of new real estate resources will be hesitant to bring new properties onto the market. The degree of utilization of existing resources is usually measured by the vacancy rate in residential property, the vacancy rate in office buildings, the number of square feet utilized per employee in office buildings and other commercial buildings, the sales per square foot in commercial property, and the number of employees per square foot or the income generated per square foot of floor space for industrial property. If these ratios indicate an unusually high level of unused or underused space, developers and builders will tend not to supply new properties. For residential property, the normal or average vacancy rate may run around 5 percent; this rate may go as low as 2 percent, and it may go considerably higher than 5 percent. When the rate is much above 5 percent, however, suppliers tend to reduce the amount of new development and construction.

Availability and prices of land and utilities

Suitable land must be available for development; furthermore, land must be available at reasonable prices or development will be impeded. Land by itself, however, is not sufficient. Sewage facilities, storm drains, water mains, and power sources must be available. Some of the stickiest problems of real estate development today revolve around the obtaining of proper and adequate facilities of all types. Many communities have resisted the further provision of utilities without the payment of higher fees by developers. At the same time, communities have become cognizant of the ecological damage that can potentially be done by septic tanks, the use of private water systems, and the unregulated development of new projects. Suppliers of new real estate resources today must work carefully with city planning commissions, zoning boards, city councils, other administrative bodies of local governments, and private groups of interested citizens.

Availability and price of financing

The importance of financing in real estate markets is indicated by its position as both a determinant of demand and of supply. On the supply side of the market, financing for land development and construction are at least of equal importance with the availability and relative prices of financing for long-term mortgage commitments. Most developers and contractors operate with relatively small amounts of their own capital. If development and construction financing are not available, or are available only at relatively high prices, new development and construction will be unresponsive to any needs that exist.

Availability and prices of materials and labor

In normal times, materials and labor are available to real estate developers and contractors. During times of war, however, materials may be in short supply because they are diverted to a war effort. Very little building of nonstrategic resources took place in this country during World War II and the Korean War. The Vietnam War saw little constriction of the supply of materials because this war was less of a drain on our national economic resources. Undoubtedly, however, this war helped to inflate the prices of building materials above what they would have been otherwise.

The prices of labor, or wages, in the construction industry have been one of the country's severe unresolved economic problems. As discussed in the chapter on real estate production,[13] the structure for bargaining between the construction industry and the labor unions is not ideal. Unions have not received the assurances of security that their members want and need. As a substitute for security, unions have demanded wage rate increases consistently above the national average. Thus, the prices for labor in the construction industry have been inordinately high, helping to push prices of housing and other types of real estate beyond the reach of many people. Only wholesale reform in the relationships between unions and industry and in the provision of adequate security for construction workers

---

[13] See Chapter 12.

will resolve this problem and serve to make real estate more realistically priced relative to other economic goods.

Taxes

The real estate tax and the federal income tax play an important role in influencing both the demand and supply of real estate resources. The real estate tax serves as the principal means of financing for local communities, and faced with increasing demands, these communities have continually increased the levels of real estate taxation. In recent years there has been a revolt against the payment of higher and higher real estate taxes. Furthermore, the tax has served to discourage improvements in existing properties and desirable changes in land uses.

The federal income tax has an influence on both the form and financing of capital investment. Rules governing the deductions of various expenses applicable to real estate may produce favorable or unfavorable conditions for real estate investment. Deductions for interest on a mortgage loan and for depreciation of the improvements in a real estate investment and for other legitimate expenses may make some properties relatively desirable and others less desirable. Changes in the income tax laws[14] have changed the relative attractiveness of various types of real estate projects. No properties other than new apartments today receive the benefits of the most rapid form of depreciation allowed for computing income tax—200 percent declining balance. Before the Tax Reform Act of 1969, however, other properties received this advantage.

CONCEPTUALIZING THE LOCAL HOUSING MARKET

The basic determinants of demand and supply come into play in the process of allocating households among available housing units in the local housing market.[15] Households are diverse in their incomes, number of persons, stage in the family cycle, location of their places of employment, tastes, and preferences. Somehow, these heterogeneous households obtain shelter in a wide variety of housing units that differ in size, type (single-family detached, rowhouse, apartment), physical condition, architectural features, and locational attributes. In this allocation process, each household apportions its income between expenditures for

---

[14] See the discussion in Chapter 10.

[15] Antecedents of this conceptualization of a local housing market include the following: Wallace F. Smith, "An Outline Theory of the Housing Market with Special Reference to Low-Income Housing and Urban Renewal," Ph.D. dissertation, Seattle University of Washington, 1958; Chester Rapkin, Louis Winnick, and David M. Blank, *Housing Market Analysis* (Washington, D.C.: Housing and Home Finance Agency, 1953); and William G. Grigsby, *Housing Markets and Public Policy* (Philadelphia: University of Pennsylvania Press, 1963).

housing and expenditures for all other goods and services and, simultaneously, decides how much of the housing budget will be spent on quality and how much on quantity. The quantity attribute of housing is the size of the housing unit that will be occupied; the quality attribute is multidimensional and accounts for all other characteristics of the standing stock, including locational attributes. The quantity and quality dimensions of housing combine in a myriad of physical forms, resulting in the diversity of the standing stock of housing units. Each household locates in the housing unit that maximizes the total satisfaction of that household, given the price and amount of housing services provided by that unit and the prices of other goods and services.

This household joins other households as demanders of housing units in a local housing submarket. A housing submarket results from a group of households who, influenced by their incomes, needs, tastes and other factors, consider the housing units in the submarket to be closer substitutes, one for another, than they are for other units in the market. From the supply aspect, housing units in a submarket are similar in prices, in physical characteristics, and in locational attributes, although units in a submarket can be widely dispersed in the community or grouped in more than one geographic area. For instance, households may consider single-family homes in the $50,000 price range to be satisfactory substitutes for each other although the neighborhoods containing such homes are on opposite ends of the community. Such housing units may, on balance, produce linkages providing the same amounts of satisfaction to households in the submarket.[16]

Housing submarkets are generally more homogeneous with respect to supply characteristics than with respect to the characteristics of demanders in the submarket. Households demanding units in a submarket will display differences in income and other factors affecting their housing choices. It is the combined effect of these factors that allocates the households to units in the submarket, even though one household has an annual income of $30,000 and another, $20,000; and one household is an elderly couple and another, a young family of five persons.

Figure 7–5 depicts a local housing market composed of interrelated submarkets. Each submarket has its demand and suppy functions, price, and vacancy rate. Submarket A consists of dilapidated one-bedroom, walk-up apartments in the inner city, renting for $50 per month. Households in these units have a median income of $6,000 a year; a large proportion of the units are occupied by minority families with schoolage children. The supply of housing units in submarket A is fixed in the market time period (highly inelastic supply) and the demand for such units determines price, the number of available units occupied, and the

---

[16] See Chapter 6 for discussion of these locational attributes.

FIGURE 7–5

Interrelated housing submarkets

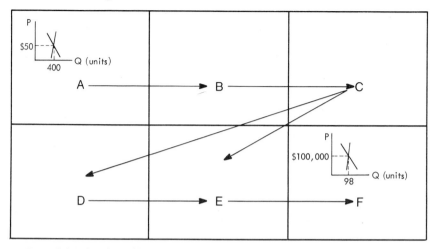

Key: Submarket A is 500 units of dilapidated one-bedroom apartments in inner city and submarket F is 100 units of luxurious single-family residences in preferred locations. Submarkets B, C, D, and E are intermediately linked with A and F.

vacancy rate. In submarket A, 400 of the 500 available units are occupied at $50 per month rent; the vacancy rate is 20 percent.

In a time period too short to adjust supply, vacancy rates can vary substantially among submarkets. The vacancy rate in submarket A may be 20 percent while in submarket F only 2 percent of the available units are vacant. Submarket F contains high-priced, single-family homes that perhaps are currently in great demand because of a recent inmigration of high-income households into the community. The housing units in submarket F are selling for around $100,000, which is a premium price in the market at this point in time. Suppliers of such units are earning an above average profit, as price exceeds long-run production costs.

The arrows in Figure 7–5 indicate linkages among submarkets. Linkages are an expression of the degree to which households in a submarket consider the housing units in a linked submarket to be acceptable (preferred) substitutes. Households in submarket E would prefer living in F, but were outbid by households occupying units in F. If the price of units in F falls sufficiently in the future, households in E will move from E to F. A linkage, then, expresses the cross-elasticity of demand in one submarket given a change in price on the linked submarket. The strength of a linkage (responsiveness of demand to a change in price in the linked submarket) depends upon the degree of substitutability of units in the two submarkets. A submarket can be linked to more than one other submarket (for example, submarket C is linked to both D and E); all submarkets are either directly or indirectly linked to each other. In reality, the local housing market is composed of many more sub-markets and linkages than are depicted in Figure 7–5. Discrimination preventing the free movement of minority households, the lack of knowl-edge about available alternatives, simple inertia, and other factors con-tributing to market imperfection weaken linkages and mitigate adjust-ments of demand to changing supply conditions in the various submarkets.

Premium rents and prices and abnormally low vacancy rates could not be maintained in the long run in a competitive market. In long-run equilibrium, each household would be occupying the housing unit that maximizes the household's total satisfaction; no household would have an incentive to move (given the prices of housing and of other goods and services, and all other supply and demand factors operating to affect housing choice). Supply adjustments would have produced "normal" vacancy rates in each submarket and an array of rents and prices equal to the costs of producing the volume of housing services comprising the various housing units (production costs include a normal profit to the supplier). A uniform risk-adjusted rate of return on capital investment would tend to be earned by suppliers across submarkets. The nominal return earned on investment would vary among submarkets in long-run equilibrium. Submarket A may have a 20 percent aftertax return and submarket C a 12 percent aftertax return on investment. However, when these returns are adjusted for the relative risk of investing in properties in the two submarkets, a uniform return on investment of, say, 10 percent is obtained. This risk-adjusted rate is earned by suppliers of housing services in all submarkets.

Suppliers in long-run equilibrium would have no incentive to increase investment by modernization, rehabilitation or conversion, nor would they desire to disinvest by foregoing repairs and maintenance. Capital improvements to the housing unit would increase the quantity of services provided by the unit. The costs associated with a capital improvement must be compensated by added value. Value is increased by generating a larger net operating income due to higher rents, by a reduction in vacancy losses, or by a lower operating ratio, or all three combined. The capital improvement also could extend the economic life of the improve-ment, or it might shift the property to a different submarket in which risk and the required return on investment are less; either result would increase the value of the property. Capital improvements made to shift the property to another submarket may be in response to persistent abnormal profits in the other submarket.

Disinvestment can occur in response to persistently high-vacancy losses; in response to rents and net operating income continuing below the costs of producing the level of services provided by the unit; or by permitting the housing unit to fall into another, lower-valued submarket that is experiencing continued above normal profits. In long-run equilibrium, these abnormal profits would disappear, and supply and demand in the several submarkets would be in equilibrium.

Filtering

The literature of housing economics contains several concepts of filtering.[17] Some authors have used the term synonymously with the turnover of housing resulting from movement of households among units. Grigsby defines filtering as occurring "only when value declines more rapidly than quality so that families can obtain either higher quality and more space at the same price or the same quality and space at a lower price than formerly."[18] Ratcliff conceptualizes filtering by assuming demand factors constant and introducing additional housing units (new construction) into the market. The process referred to as filtering down "... is described most simply as the changing of occupancy as the housing that is occupied by one income group becomes available to the next lower income group as a result of decline in market price, that is, in sales price or rent value."[19]

Cast in our housing submarket framework, an increase in housing units supplied in submarket E will depress price (given demand) and permit lower-income families to move from linked submarkets into submarket E. The vacancies created in linked submarkets (such as D and C) exert a downward influence on rents or prices in those submarkets, permitting still lower-income families to improve their housing condition at the same or less expense. Ultimately, through the linkages among submarkets, units are vacated in submarket A, which contains the lowest quality, least desirable housing in the community. No demand exists for units in submarket A, and they are abandoned.

Filtering as described above is a slow, uncertain process. The multiplicity of linkages among submarkets can diffuse the impact on prices or rents. The filtering process can be impeded or halted by discrimination, lack of knowledge about available housing alternatives, undoubling (an existing household forms two separate households leaving no vacancy behind), and inmigration of households who absorb vacancies.

Has filtering improved the housing condition of American households over time? Our answer would be "No, it has not." This reply is not dependent upon market imperfections that slow or stop the filter-

---

[17] The interested reader will find a discussion of several of these concepts in Grigsby, *Housing Markets and Public Policy*, pp. 84–130. Also see William B. Brueggeman, "An Analysis of the Filtering Process with Special Reference to Housing Subsidies," in *National Housing Policy Study Papers*, November 5, 1973.

[18] Grigsby, *Housing Markets and Public Policy*, p. 97.

[19] Ratcliff, *Urban Land Economics*, pp. 321–22.

ing process. Rather, it is based upon the contention that the housing market is reasonably competitive. Suppliers of housing seize opportunities to achieve abnormal profits; households consume housing in a manner to maximize their net satisfaction. The "benefits" view of filtering, where households by moving are able to improve their housing condition at the same or less expense, will not be sustained in the long run.[20] Households obtain only the quality and quantity of housing for which they are willing and able to pay. Any supply-induced reduction in price or rent in the market will result in disinvestment by suppliers until the equilibrium return on investment is again attained and until price again covers the cost of production of the housing services provided.

Our nation over time has indeed become better housed. This overall improvement in housing condition has resulted from numerous factors affecting housing demand and supply. Among these factors are the rising standard of living enjoyed by American households; technological innovations in construction and materials; tax advantages provided homeowners and investors in housing; and various institutional arrangements that reduce the cost and increase the availability of mortgage financing. Such basic determinants of supply and demand either increase the total expenditure for housing, make it possible to buy more housing per dollar spent, or increase the supply of housing made available at a given price. Collectively, these factors contribute to the overall improvement in the housing condition of American households. The movements of households among units and housing submarkets are observable adjustments in a market continually affected by changing supply and demand conditions.

MARKET AND FEASIBILITY ANALYSES

Market and feasibility analyses are the end results of the consideration of all the factors discussed heretofore in this chapter.[21] These studies attempt to relate all of the determinants of supply and demand to the problem of anticipating future real estate needs in a community. As such, they represent the practical application of the theory of market behavior. Whether market studies and feasibility analyses are reliable and useful is thus a function of two considerations—validity of the theory and ability to attach accurate measures to the elements and relationships of the theory.

---

[20] Brueggeman, "Analysis of the Filtering Process."

[21] Although we discuss only market studies and feasibility studies, other types of economic studies are sometimes useful. For a discussion of a number of different types of studies, including highest and best use studies, land use studies, land utilization studies, marketability studies, reuse appraisals, and cost-benefit studies, see Anthony Downs, "Characteristics of Various Economic Studies," *Appraisal Journal,* July 1966, pp. 329–38.

To be reliable, market and feasibility analyses must be painstaking and thorough. Past trends and relationships may not hold for the future. The analyst may have to dig beneath the surface to find qualitative indicators of future quantitative changes. Household size may not remain steady but may decline because of a declining birthrate, greater financial independence of older and younger persons (leading to undoubling), older marriage ages, and an increasing divorce rate. To predict such a change, the market analyst must understand social trends and changes in values and attitudes, as well as economic conditions and trends.

Market analysis

A market analysis is a study designed to determine the types and quantities of additional real estate resources which can be absorbed by the market over a reasonable period of time. Typically, market studies are limited to an analysis of a particular type of real estate, such as housing, industrial, or commercial real estate. The predominant type of study concerns housing.

Individual businesses; industry trade groups; and governmental agencies at local, state, and federal levels have interest in market studies. Businesses with markets of national scope, such as lumber and hardware suppliers, appliance manufacturers, and home furnishers, base their budgeting procedures on the estimated aggregate demand for new real estate for the coming year. Home builders' associations usually engage in market research to help their members plan the types, styles, and price ranges of new homes to produce during the coming year. And governmental agencies need to understand the economic and social needs of their constituencies in order to formulate policies that will encourage the proper amounts and types of housing and other real estate to be produced. In short, market analysis is a planning or budgeting tool. As one well-known analyst has said, "Market analysis is a study of the reasons why prices are being paid. It has far more to do with the future than with either the present or the past."[22]

Perhaps the organization most concerned with housing market analysis is the Federal Housing Administration (FHA) of the U.S. Department of Housing and Urban Development. The FHA has developed comprehensive techniques and instructions for the undertaking of market analyses in local communities across the country.[23] The purpose of an FHA market study is to identify and measure the housing needs in a

---

[22] W. A. Bowes, "What Is Market Analysis?" *Real Estate Appraiser,* July–August 1968, p. 11.

[23] Federal Housing Administration, U.S. Department of Housing and Urban Development, *FHA Techniques of Housing Market Analysis* (Washington, D.C.: U.S. Government Printing Office, 1970).

community. The FHA then uses the market study in determining which projects that it has been requested to underwrite can be absorbed by the market. Each FHA market analysis is concerned with the following broad subject areas:[24]

1. *Delineation of the market area*—the area within which dwelling units are competitive with one another.
2. *The area's economy*—principal economic activities, basic resources, economic trends.
3. *Demand factors*—employment, incomes, population, households, family size.
4. *Supply factors*—residential construction activity, housing inventory, conversions, demolitions.
5. *Current market conditions*—vacancies, unsold inventory, marketability

TABLE 7–2

Estimated annual demand for nonsubsidized housing
Gainesville, Florida, housing market area (April 1, 1971–April 1, 1973)

A. Single-family

Sales price	Number of units	Percent of total
Under $22,499	85	17
$22,500–24,499	85	17
25,000–29,999	145	29
30,000–34,999	100	20
35,000 and over	85	17
Total	500	100

B. Multifamily

Gross monthly rent*	Unit size			
	Efficiency	One bedroom	Two bedrooms	Three bedrooms
Under $130	15	—	—	—
$130–149	5	85	—	—
150–169	—	40	50	—
170–189	—	15	60	5
190–209	—	5	35	10
210–229	—	5	20	5
230–249	—	—	10	5
250–269	—	—	5	5
270–290	—	—	5	5
290 and over	—	—	5	5
Total	20	150	190	40

* Gross rent is shelter rent plus the cost of utilities.
Source: FHA Housing Market Analysis of Gainesville, Florida.

[24] Ibid., p. 5. (Note: A detailed outline for FHA housing market analyses is shown in Appendix D, this volume.)

of sales and rental units, prices, rents, building costs, mortgage defaults and foreclosures, disposition of acquired properties.

6. *Quantitative and qualitative demand*—prospective number of dwelling units that can be absorbed economically at various price and rent levels under conditions existing on the "as of" date.

Some of the end results of a housing market analysis can be seen in Tables 7–2 and 7–3. They were compiled in a 1971 FHA housing market analysis of the Gainesville, Florida, housing market.

TABLE 7–3
Estimated annual occupancy for subsidized rental housing
Gainesville, Florida, housing market area (April 1, 1971–April 1, 1973)

A. Families

	Section 236° exclusively	Eligible for both programs	Public housing exclusively	Total for both programs
1 bedroom	30	0	60	90
2 bedrooms	90	20	120	230
3 bedrooms	70	0	90	160
4+bedrooms	40	0	50	90
Total	230	20†	320†	570

B. Elderly

Efficiency	20	30	25	75
1 bedroom	20	10	15	45
Total	40	40‡	40‡	120

° Estimates are based upon exception income limits.
† Forty-seven percent of these families also are eligible under the rent supplement program.
‡ All of the elderly couples and individuals also are eligible for rent supplement payments.
Source: FHA Housing Market Analysis of Gainesville, Florida.

As can be seen from the tables, housing demand is broken down between nonsubsidized and subsidized housing needs, between single-family and multifamily needs and the price classes of each, and between programs and among unit sizes for subsidized housing. By keeping track of any changes in the conditions upon which these forecasts were made and the numbers and types of units supplied during the two-year period, the FHA, local builders, lending institutions, and local government agencies can determine whether housing demand is being fulfilled, whether shortages continue to exist, or whether overbuilding is occurring.

In the above example an apparent oversupply of some types of housing was being constructed. Compared with the predicted annual housing demand of 1,590 units (nonsubsidized and subsidized), 3,484 housing units were constructed during the first 50 weeks of 1971. The FHA analysis indicated an annual need for 500 single-family units and 400 multifamily units. By contrast, building permit data for 1971 showed projected construction of 760 single-family units and 2,769 multifamily units. In 1970, only 555 single-family and 105 multifamily unit building permits were issued. Certainly the evidence suggests that (a) the conditions upon which the FHA analysis was based had changed, (b) the FHA analysis was incorrect, or (c) an oversupply was developing. The FHA, local builders, and other interested organizations would want to determine which of these alternative reasons (or combination) explain the situation and to identify more precisely any submarkets that were experiencing overbuilding.

Feasibility analysis

While closely related to market analysis, feasibility analysis differs in that it deals with the acceptability and desirability of a particular real estate project. Market analysis may establish the need for more apartments of a particular type and price class in a community; whether a specific apartment project is sufficiently desirable to be absorbed by the market is another question. This question can be answered only by an intensive examination of the property's ability to meet various requirements and its relative desirability to prospective consumers.

A feasibility study involves one of three basic types of problems:[25]

1. A site or building in search of a user.
2. A user in search of a site or certain improvements.
3. An investor looking for an opportunity.

A specific hypothesis is usually advanced as to how each type of problem may be solved. A site may be analyzed to determine whether an apartment project would be a desirable type of use; an oil company may analyze an available site to determine whether a service station would be a profitable investment for the company; or analysts may study the desirability of a shopping center investment for clients wishing to liquidate their stock holdings in favor of a real estate venture. In short, a feasibility study attempts to forecast whether a particular course of action regarding a parcel of real estate fulfills the objectives of an owner-investor and meets externally or internally imposed conditions or requirements.

One of the most common objectives of an investor is that a project must produce a specified or desired rate of return. If the specified rate is the market rate of return, the capitalized value of the project will be its market value. And, as G. I. M. Young points out if this value equals or

---

[25] James A. Graaskamp, *A Guide to Feasibility Analysis* (Chicago: Society of Real Estate Appraisers, 1970), p. 11.

exceeds cost, the project is *prima facie* justified.[26] However, *prima facie* justification of feasibility is not the end of a feasibility study. Other conditions and objectives may have to be met, and income may be further maximized.

The requirements which must be met by a real estate use are economic, political, legal, physical, and ethical in nature. A proposed use must be consistent with market needs; may depend on convincing community officials to provide water or sewer service; and must be within the realm of permissible uses and conform to space, site planning, and design standards imposed by zoning and planning commissions. Furthermore, the site must be capable of supporting the proposed improvements; and the proposed use must meet the ethical requirements of environmental concerns, the requirements of prospective tenants and employees, and the self-imposed standards of conduct of investors themselves in providing resources that will be used usually for many years. Failure on any one of the counts is sufficient to render a proposed project "unfeasible."

The following examples illustrate how each of these types of conditions or requirements may affect a project's feasibility:

1. A proposed 60-story office building in Cincinnati was nixed before design work was begun because a market study showed that the projected demand for high-quality office space was amply supplied for the next five years.

2. An apartment project on the outskirts of Orlando, Florida, was stymied because sewer facilities were not available to the project, and the city commission had ruled that septic tanks were unacceptable.

3. A low-rent housing project to be constructed in a section of $40,000 to $50,000 homes in a medium-sized southern city was unacceptable because the number of square feet of living space in each unit was less than required by the zoning ordinance.

4. Before the 1960s the height of Chicago's skyscrapers was limited to about 50 stories because the subsoil conditions would not support taller buildings. Newer technology developed after World War II allowed caissons to be sunk to bedrock economically so that taller buildings could be supported. Today several buildings, including the John Hancock Center, First National Bank Building, Standard Oil Building, Lakepoint Tower Apartments, Marina Towers, and the Sears Tower all exceed 60 stories.

5. An oil refinery which was thought to be of great economic benefit to Maine was nixed by the state because of the potential for ecological damage that would occur from oil spills and leaks.

6. A high-rise public housing building for families in Columbus, Ohio, was converted to other uses because of social and physical problems that

---

[26] G. I. M. Young, "Feasibility Studies," *Appraisal Journal*, July 1970, p. 379.

tenants experienced by being grouped into small areas with only one elevator for access to the entire building.

In addition to meeting certain conditions and requirements, a project must be feasible in meeting other objectives, in addition to a desired rate of return. A project that does not produce tax shelter for high-income investors would not be feasible from their standpoints. Cash flow may be important to another investor, while maximizing return on total investment may be important to another investor. Generally, the investor's objective for an overall rate of return on the total investment can be incorporated into an appraisal of the property. As one well-known real estate analyst puts it, "An apartment project is economically feasible when its projected future net income affords an investor an appropriate rate of earnings on capital and provides for its recapture."[27]

The necessity of identifying objectives of the potential owner-investor suggests that criteria need to be established to judge whether the objective will be attained. Minimum requirements should be established for tax shelter, cash flow, return on equity, or return on total investment. Sometimes, however, the objective may be less definable and the criteria less specific. One firm was willing to spend up to $1 million for a relatively small office building if the building would enhance the firm's image. It is difficult enough to define image, let alone to measure its enhancement. Nevertheless, criteria were established calling for an "air of quality" about the building, its access to view by many passing motorists, aesthetically enriching landscaping, hidden parking, and proximity to a body or stream of water. In this instance cash flow, tax shelter, and return on investment were relatively unimportant.

Sometimes it may be desirable to develop a mathematical model to measure the returns produced by alternative uses or by differing intensities of development. Singer has developed such a model for identifying that intensity which provides the maximum rate of return on overall investment.[28] The model is built around the relationships between profit, value, and costs; rentable building area, gross building area, and building efficiency; and development costs, developer's profit, and investment profit.

In any type of feasibility study, analysts should understand that their clients have a problem for which they need help in solving. A feasibility analysis that does not identify the client's objectives or establish meaningful decision criteria will produce meaningless results. A study that has not analyzed in depth the relevant variables for measuring the criteria may produce erroneous results. And a study that is undertaken with a prior

[27] James E. Gibbons, "Apartment Feasibility Studies," *Appraisal Journal,* July 1968, p. 326. Gibbons further develops the point that a carefully prepared appraisal constitutes a feasibility study—a viewpoint that would be contested by some others.

[28] Bruce Singer, "Determining Optimum Developmental Intensity," *Appraisal Journal,* July 1970, pp. 406–17.

positive conclusion helps neither the client nor the analyst's reputation for objectivity. Unfortunately, many feasibility studies that the authors have seen could be accused of one or all of these defects.

If the situation warrants, one of the most valuable types of advice an analyst can give a client is *not* to undertake a project—or at least how to modify a project to render it feasible. Any positive bias should be toward helping the client, not toward a proposed project. In turn, the client should grant analysts complete freedom of objectivity. Without this freedom, the investor will likely be misled, and analysts will find that their professional integrity is undermined.

SUMMARY

The analysis of real estate markets is facilitated by a concept or model of the way in which the market functions. An examination of the models of pure competition and pure monopoly shows that neither is applicable to real estate markets. Rather, the model of monopolistic competition, we contend, best explains how the forces of price determination operate.

Market activity can be analyzed and forecast through the determinants of demand and supply. Market analyses can be carried out that are national, regional, community, or district in scope. Markets can also be divided into submarkets on the basis of various characteristics, such as price class of property, income class of buyers, ethnic and racial composition, legal tenure of occupants (owners versus renters), and geographic location. Although a direct relationship between national economic and social trends and the value of an individual parcel of real estate is often difficult to demonstrate, careful evaluation of these factors can often provide clues about broad patterns of demand that may be developing.

Market and feasibility studies are the most commonly useful types of economic studies requiring market analysis. While market studies attempt to analyze and predict the future demand for various types of real estate and to relate the demand to existing supply, feasibility studies attempt to determine whether a particular use will fulfill the objectives of a potential investor. Additionally, a project must meet externally and internally imposed physical, legal, political, ethical, and financial conditions or requirements. One of the requirements normally is that a project be absorbable by the market.

QUESTIONS FOR REVIEW

1. What is a *market?* How many potential buyers and sellers must there be before a market can exist?

2. What is the role of social class in real estate markets? Can you think of some examples of the way social class affects housing patterns?
3. Are real estate markets efficient? Why or why not? How do you measure and judge efficiency?
4. Consider the population mobility trends cited in the chapter. What implications for real estate values do these trends have? What changes in the mobility trends do you anticipate in the coming ten years?
5. How has the change from a rural to an urban society affected real estate markets and values? What do you see as the future trend of urbanization?
6. What is the relationship between a market analysis and a feasibility study? What is the viewpoint of each?
7. How is economic base analysis used in analyzing communities? What possible weaknesses do you see in using this technique?
8. What is the "benefits" view of filtering? Describe the filtering process in a housing market comprised of interrelated submarkets.
9. Has filtering improved the housing condition of families in the United States? Why or why not?

REFERENCES

Beaton, William R., and Bond, Robert J.   *Real Estate*. Pacific Palisades, Calif.: Goodyear Publishing Co., 1976, chap. 2.

Beckman, Theodore N., and Davidson, William R.   *Marketing*. 8th ed. New York: Ronald Press, 1967.

Dobriner, William M.   *Class in Suburbia*. Englewood Cliffs, N.J.: Prentice-Hall, 1963.

Federal Housing Administration, U.S. Department of Housing and Urban Development.   *FHA Techniques of Housing Market Analysis*. Washington, D.C.: U.S. Government Printing Office, 1970.

Graaskamp, James A.   *A Guide to Feasibility Analysis*. Chicago: Society of Real Estate Appraisers, 1970.

McCarthy, E. Jerome.   *Basic Marketing*. 4th ed. Homewood, Ill.: Richard D. Irwin, 1971, pp. 89–164.

chapter 8

PROPERTY OWNERSHIP RIGHTS

IN MOST INSTANCES, real estate investors are in the fortunate position of being able to choose consciously the precise legal form of ownership they are to employ. Investors have the prerogative to make decisions about leasing or owning outright and can elect to own individually or jointly with others. Investors are able to specify the fixtures which are to be acquired with land and are in a position to adjudge the impact that various easements, private deed restrictions, and zoning ordinances will have on the use of the land. Ownership can involve establishing a corporation or entering a partnership, syndicate, or investment trust which owns property. Such forms offer tax benefits and limited liability which could be critical to the fulfillment of the investor's objectives, although the magnitude and quality of property ownership rights are not affected by the interjection of the separate holding entity.

For the investor to make sound decisions concerning ownership, an awareness is necessary of the types of situations which might arise when potential investment properties are considered. The investor cannot acquire a greater ownership right than that of the existing owner, so complete information about those rights must be obtained before the venture is undertaken. This requires a familiarity with the types of ownership rights which exist and the means available for transferring them.

Several ownership rights such as fee tail and qualified fee estates rarely appear and are generally in disfavor with courts of law and with investors in general. However, the individual investor must analyze the minimum ownership rights required to make use of a given property before condemning a particular right. A determinable fee estate or a lease from period to period may be adequate. In any event, the investor should be cognizant of all possible types of rights in deciding whether or not to enter a specific transaction.

The investor's option to join with others in an investment situation also requires careful attention to ownership form. Ownership with others can be effected in a manner that the various owners can freely deed or will their individual rights to others, or ownership can be established with a right of survivorship where the surviving owners acquire the share of any owner who dies. The first form, *tenancy in common,* is by far the more frequently used. It grants investors more freedom of action, and it permits them to use the property ownership to provide for their heirs in the event of their death. The second form, *joint tenancy,* leads to continuity of the ownership venture by preventing the heirs of a deceased owner from interfering with the plans of the surviving owners. Here again, the specific plans of the individual investors dictate the ownership form to be used.

The development of a proper group ownership form is one of the most important decisions that must be made in any real estate investment. The corporation and the trust permit the loss liability of investors to be limited to their cash or property investment in the project. The partnership, tenancy in common, and joint tenancy forms fail to limit liability, but they permit individual investors to obtain personal income tax deductions. The limited partnership form allows liability limitation for one category of partners while retaining the full tax deduction status for all partners. The strategy implications of selecting a group ownership form are considered in this chapter.

A different type of multiple ownership situation arises through special legislation providing for married couples. Some states recognize a special form known as *tenancy by the entireties* wherein the right of survivorship exists between the married partners. Upon the death of one partner, title to all properties held in tenancy by the entireties automatically passes to the other, a situation which is true even if one of the partners sells his or her share to a third party (without the signature of the other partner). State laws vary considerably in this area; tenancy by the entireties and other forms such as community property and condominium require state enabling laws. For investors this means two things: (a) they must be familiar with the possible forms of ownership in each state where they consider investments and (b) they must decide which forms they prefer when an option is available.

WORKING DEFINITION OF REAL ESTATE AND REAL PROPERTY

An awareness of the distinction between the terms *real estate* and *real property* is essential to an understanding of property ownership rights. As mentioned in Chapter 1, *real estate can usually be defined as land and anything permanently attached to land*. A parcel of real estate is tangible; it is described in terms of size, shape, and location, and it extends from a point at the center of the earth outward to the outermost layer of the earth's atmosphere. Mineral, oil, and water contained in the land and air rights above the land are included. Anyone standing upon the parcel or on an adjoining parcel can physically view it. *Real property, on the other hand, is an embodiment of intangible ownership rights*. These ownership rights are available to individuals in a free enterprise economy such as that of the United States, and they are retained by sovereign government in directed economies such as the USSR. They are described in terms of extent of ownership, considering factors of possession, control, enjoyment, and disposition.[1]

Given a society in which private property prevails, ownership rights can range from virtually absolute to highly limited. An individual is entitled to own a parcel of real estate "outright," with complete rights to possession, control, enjoyment, or disposition in whole or in part. The government which permits private ownership imposes only one restriction—to refrain from creating conditions which could be harmful to public health and/or welfare. Limited ownership usually occurs by contract, where one individual acquires part of the ownership rights of the outright owner. Examples are leasing agreements, public utility easements, and mineral rights purchases.

REAL ESTATE DESCRIPTIONS

Legal documents involved in real estate transactions should describe the property as precisely as possible. Such documents include sales contracts, deeds, mortgages, and long-term leases. Precise descriptions of real estate also are necessary in subdividing, building, and financing activities. Generally, there are five ways of describing real estate— one method of general, everyday usage and four that are more precise.

Street and number

A description by street and number is sufficiently precise for most nonlegal purposes, such as providing general locations and postal delivery. It is also legally acceptable in contracts for the sale of real estate and other legal documents, provided the street and number can be found. However, for taxation, conveyancing, and other purposes where the real estate must be described precisely, one of the legal methods

---

[1] Alfred A. Ring, *Real Estate Principles and Practices* (Englewood Cliffs, N.J.: Prentice-Hall, 1972), p. 46.

should be used. If one of these methods is used properly, no misunderstanding about the size of the parcel or the location of its boundaries should occur. Disagreements and law suits will be avoided.

Metes and bounds

A metes and bounds description utilizes instructions as to direction and distance (metes) between the boundaries, or corners (bounds), of a parcel of land. The description begins at a point on the site's boundary and proceeds around the outer limits of the property until the point of beginning is reached and the entire parcel has been circumscribed. An example of a metes and bounds description is as follows:

Beginning at a point in the east line of Goddard Avenue 50 feet north of the north line of 22d Street 200 feet to the center of Hogtown Creek; thence northwesterly along the center line of Hogtown Creek 175 feet; thence west on a line parallel to the north line of 22d Street, 182 feet to the east line of Goddard Avenue; thence south along the east line of Goddard Avenue, 180.5 feet to the place of beginning.

Metes and bounds descriptions are used in those parts of the country where the government has not surveyed the land. Figure 8–1 shows the extent of the government survey system. It can be seen that New England, the Middle Atlantic States, and Texas are the principal areas not surveyed and thus are the most likely areas in which one could expect to find metes and bounds descriptions. Nevertheless, they can be used in any part of the country and are often used in combination with the rectangular survey system when a tract has not been platted.

Monuments

Description by monuments is similar to metes and bounds; however, the measurements along the boundaries are not given. The corners of the property are indicated by permanent monuments, such as trees, rocks, streams, or street intersections, concrete markers, or steel stakes. One corner of the property is described by its monument, and the directions are then prescribed to the succeeding circumferential monuments, until the point of beginning is reached.

A difficulty in describing real estate by monuments is that the monuments may not be so permanent as originally believed. Trees can die, rocks can be moved, stream and street intersections can change, and manmade monuments can deteriorate or be lost. Thus, the use of this method is not recommended.

IGURE 8–1

rincipal meridians of the federal system of rectangular surveys

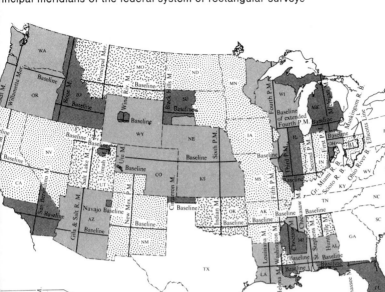

Note: The shading shows the area governed by each principal meridian and its base line.
Source: U.S. Department of the Interior, Bureau of Land Management.

Government or rectangular survey

As shown in Figure 8–1, much of the country has been surveyed by the federal government. The survey consists of a system of grid lines on a map of the earth's surface running north and south, and east and west. The origin for an area of description is the intersection of a principal meridian (running north and south) and base line (running east and west). Secondary meridians and parallels are established at 24-mile intervals. The area contained within such a 24-mile square is termed a *check*, which is subdivided into 16 six-mile squares called *townships*.

A township is the largest subdivision identified in land descriptions and is identified by the number of tiers (rows) of townships north or south of the base line and the number of ranges (columns) of townships east or west of the principal meridian. Thus, in Figure 8–2, the subdivided townships would be described as Township 2 North, Range

FIGURE 8–2

Rectangular survey system

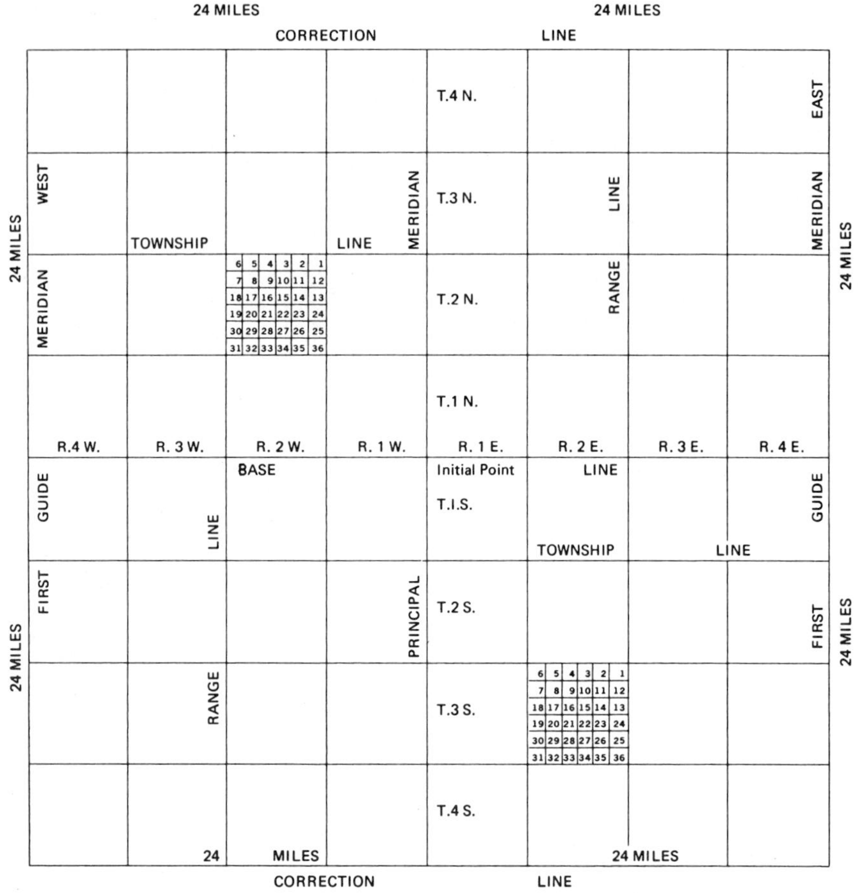

Source: William Atterberry, Karl Pearson, and Michael Litka, *Real Estate Law* (Columbus, Ohio: Grid Publishing Co., 1974), p. 62.

2 West and Township 3 South, Range 2 East of the specified principal meridian and base line.

Since a township consists of a six-mile square area, it obviously contains 36 square miles. This area is further divided into 36 one-mile square units, called *sections*. The sections are numbered beginning with the northeastern corner, as shown in Figure 8–2. A section contains 640 acres and is identified by its number within the specified township.

A section can be further subdivided into halves, quarters, subhalves, and subquarters. Each quarter of a section contains 160 acres, each half of a quarter section contains 80 acres, and each quarter of a quarter section contains 40 acres. Additional subdivisions can be made, if necessary. The description of the crosshatched area in Figure 8–3 would be the NW ¼ of the SE ¼ of the SW ¼ of Section 17 of Township 2 North, Range 2 West.

Recorded plat

Usually when areas of 40 acres or less (and often when larger areas) are developed or subdivided, a map, or *plat,* must be filed with the county clerk or recorder. Each street or block must be named or num-

FIGURE 8–3

A divided section

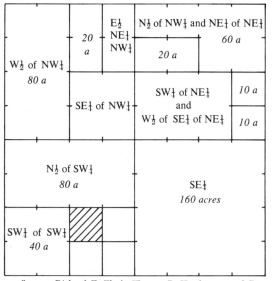

Source: Richard F. Fleck, Thomas P. Henderson, and Ross H. Johnson, *Real Estate Principles and Practices* (Columbus, Ohio: Charles E. Merrill Publishing Co., 1976), p. 24.

bered, and each lot assigned a number. Sometimes only a subdivision name and lot numbers are required. Upon acceptance and recording of the plat by the appropriate county official, the lot and block numbers of the named subdivision constitute an exact legal description. The exact size, dimensions, and boundary locations may be obtained by referring to the recorded plat. For example, a lot in a plat recorded under the name "STR Acres" might be identified as

Lot No. 7, Block 16 of STR Acres,
as recorded on page 31 of Book 27
in the Tippecanoe County Recorder's Office.

Of course, the recorded plat would often be contained in an area originally surveyed by the government. The recorded plat would therefore refer to the section and township identified by government survey.

PERSONAL PROPERTY AND FIXTURES

Our definition of real estate in terms of land and its permanent attachments is very vague insofar as the word *permanent* is involved. Items not permanently attached to land are considered to be personal property, personalty, or movables. They are not real estate, and they can be removed from the real estate at any time by the holder of the personal property rights.

A *fixture* is an item that was once personal property but later attached to real estate in a permanent manner. Fixtures go to the buyer in a sale of real property, and they cannot be removed from the real estate without the permission of the real estate owner. The law of fixtures is one of the most complex areas in the study of real estate law, with every case having unique considerations. In general, the courts apply four tests to determine whether or not an article is permanently attached to real estate.[2]

Intention of the parties. The most important test is whether or not the article was intended to be permanently attached at the time of attachment. This is a commonsense approach which attempts to determine whether or not a reasonable person would consider an item to be a fixture.

Manner of attachment. In general, an item is permanently attached if its removal damages the real estate.

Character of the article and its adaptation to the real estate. Articles built especially for a particular building are normally considered fixtures.

Relation of the parties. Courts tend to favor certain parties in disputes, primarily on the grounds that their adversaries should know better than to permit fixture disputes to arise. For example, buyers tend to be favored over sellers where sales agreements are indefinite, and tenants are normally favored over landlords in gaining permission to remove personal property they may have inadvertently attached to the landlord's property.

Residential property transactions create many problems of defining personal property and fixtures. Buyers sometimes assume that they are buying houses completely equipped with storm windows, carpets, elaborate light fixtures, special plumbing attachments, and so on, which the

---

[2] Robert Kratovil, *Real Estate Law*, 6th ed. (Englewood Cliffs, N.J.: Prentice-Hall, 1974), Chapter 3.

sellers do not wish to sell. A deal is closed, and the buyers learn to their dismay that the items which were so instrumental in their decision to buy are gone when they prepare to take possession. Thus, investors must question all fixtures and personal property items to determine whether or not they are part of the sales agreement. When they are in doubt as to the permanence of any item, they should state in the offer to buy that they plan to acquire it. Sellers then have an opportunity to reject the offer, but no confusion or misunderstanding is likely to arise. The two parties agree as to the items included in the price, and the sale is either consummated or cancelled.

REAL PROPERTY OWNERSHIP RIGHTS

The interest that an individual holds in real estate is referred to as an estate. Estates are of two types: estates in possession and estates not in possession. Estates in possession are by the far the more common, being divided into freehold estates and estates of less than freehold. Freeholds represent substantial ownership rights and are treated as real property by the law; estates of less than freehold, that is, leaseholds, are considered personal property. Estates not in possession represent future interests in property which convert to estates in possession upon the occurrence of a specified event. The relationship between types of estates is presented in Figure 8–4.

Freehold estates of inheritance

The most complete forms of ownership are those which can be enjoyed by the owners during their lifetimes and then passed on to designated heirs or lineal descendants. Fee simple absolute and fee tail estates endure throughout the lifetimes of the owners. The owners can change the form of the estate by grant or by will, such as the establishment of a life estate for their daughter with the property to go to specified heirs upon her death, but the estate remains fee simple or fee tail in absence of such actions. Qualified fee estates endure either indefinitely or until a specified event occurs—this event not normally being the death of the estate holder.

Fee simple estates. The fee simple owner is entitled to freedom of action with regard to the property as long as the actions are lawful and do not conflict with public interest. It may be improved in any manner, leased to anyone, given away, sold; trees may be removed or planted; and soil and minerals may be removed or added. Fee simple ownership can be restricted by law through zoning, where only specified uses of the land are permitted, or by voluntary deed restrictions

FIGURE 8–4

Estates in land

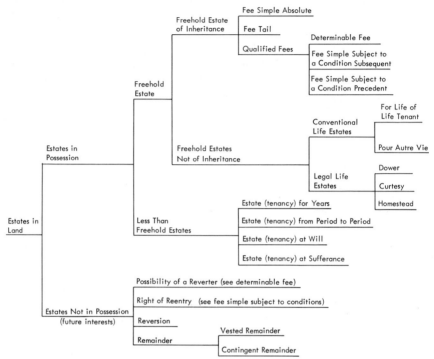

Source: William Velman, Ohio State University lecture handout, 1963.

which specify permitted uses. Nuisances cannot be maintained, such as a deep hole which could endanger children; the public welfare is harmed by jeopardizing the health and safety of others.

Fee tail estates. The concept of fee tail is a carryover from feudal times where the ownership of property was granted to individuals and their heirs. Early common law held that the property reverted back to the original grantor when the blood line of the grantee terminated, but modern (U.S.) statutory law either refuses to recognize a fee tail or limits it to lives in being at the time of the original grant. Fee tail estates are rarely encountered today, but investors must be aware of what they are and be certain that they can derive a fee simple ownership from the seller's fee tail.

Qualified fee estates. A qualified, determinable, or base fee estate is one which terminates upon the occurrence of a specified event. Words such as "as long as" or "during" are used in its creation. An example of a determinable fee estate is where an individual grants property to a peace-promoting charity for as long as the United States remains a member of the United Nations. If the United States later withdraws from the United Nations, ownership reverts back to the grantors or their heirs. The grantors' right in the property between the time of grant and the time of U.S. withdrawal is called a *possibility of a reverter* rather than a *reversion*, since the United States might never withdraw from the United Nations. If an event had been stated which is reasonably certain to occur, such as granting the property until January 1, 2000, the grantor would possess an outright reversion. The charity's right to the property prior to U.S. withdrawal is a fee simple right, since ownership could possibly continue forever. The charity can sell the property, but the buyer obtains only the determinable fee subject to the possibility of a reverter.

Two other forms of qualified fee estates, fee simple subject to a condition subsequent and fee simple subject to a condition precedent, work the same way as a determinable fee, except that a condition must be fulfilled by the grantee. In the U.S.–U.N. situation, ownership reverts back to the grantor following an action taken by the U.S. government. The grantee has no control over this action, and the reversion occurs automatically at the time of U.S. withdrawal. The fee simple subject to a condition subsequent requires action (or lack of action) on the part of the grantee, such as where grantors grant their property to a school as long as it is used for school purposes. If the school sells the property or converts it to a nonschool use, the grant becomes void and the grantors or their heirs have the right to reenter the property and assume absolute ownership. However, in recent years courts have held that sale of land owned under qualified fee is permitted if the proceeds are put to a use which fulfills the conditions of the agreement with the grantors. This would be where the school sells land held under qualified fee and uses the proceeds to buy a parcel of land better suited for school business.

The fee simple subject to a condition precedent is identical to the fee simple subject to a condition subsequent except for the timing of the condition. To use the above example, a condition precedent would arise if the property owners were to grant their property to the charity *as of* the date the United States withdraws from the United Nations. If the United States withdraws, fee simple absolute passes to the charity. The grantor retains ownership as long as the United States remains a member. Obviously, the condition precedent fits few practical situations. Most states have abolished estates on condition precedent.

The qualified fee estate has been in disfavor with courts for many years. It provides a vehicle for unusual situations which inevitably require court action before the rightful owner of a property can gain possession. An individual might grant property to a distant nephew so long as the nephew refrains from drinking alcoholic beverages, while another individual might devise a grant in which the grantee must follow a specified religious faith. The extent to which conditions of this type are upheld is impossible to measure, and the courts tend to interpret the law in a manner that the fee simple character of the grantee's right outweighs the conditions imposed. However, the investor must be very careful whenever a deed contains peculiarities of this type. An attorney should be consulted to ascertain whether or not fee simple absolute could be achieved in the purchase.

Freehold estates not of inheritance

A life estate is an interest in real property granted to an individual for the duration of his, her, or someone else's lifetime. At the time of death of the designated person, the property reverts back to the original owner or heirs.

Life estates are of two types: conventional and legal.[3] Conventional life estates are created by the grantor and grantee(s) involved in the estate. In most cases life tenants receive the property right for the duration of their own lifetime. If they retain their right for the lifetime of another person, such as would be the case where a man grants his son the rights to a property for the lifetime of his (the grantor's) wife, the estate is known as a life estate *pour autre vie.*

A life estate can be sold or leased, but the buyers or lessees must realize that they might have to surrender the property on short notice after the death of the life estate holder. Thus, the economic value of a life estate is normally based on personal utilization or a composite of short-term leases.

Legal life estates are created by operation of law. They are of three types:

Dower. This refers to the ownership rights of a wife in her husband's property during her lifetime. As long as the husband is alive, dower is said to be "inchoate," which means that the wife has only the possibility of a right rather than the right itself. Upon the husband's death, the dower right becomes consummate. Under the laws of many states, the dower ripens into a life estate in one third of the real property owned by the husband during the marriage. All real property owned by the husband during the marriage is included, even though part or all might have been sold prior to his death.

Dower right, in those states which recognize it, is an important consideration for purchasers of real property. To obtain an unencum-

---

[3] Harold F. Lusk and William B. French, *Law of the Real Estate Business,* 3d ed. (Homewood, Ill.: Richard D. Irwin, 1975), p. 30.

bered title, they must be certain that the seller's wife relinquishes her dower right to the subject property in writing. Otherwise, she is entitled to a life estate upon her husband's death, although the property is not a part of his estate.

As in any life estate, property acquired by a wife through her dower right is hers to use in any manner she pleases during her lifetime. Upon her death, the property passes on to a party named by the husband in his will, or to his natural heirs of succession, if he dies intestate (without a will). The party named by the husband or his heirs holds the *right of remainder*. This right is normally vested (that is, absolute and definite; cannot be taken from them), but it is contingent in situations where a remainderman cannot be ascertained at the time of transfer. Some people still retain the practice in wills of naming "my oldest son" or "my first-born child" where no such son or child had been born at the time the life estate is created. A remainder exists in either the vested or contingent situation, however, and the property eventually passes on to the remainderman. Even in those rare cases when a man dies with no heirs or assigns, the government is a contingent remainderman through the power of escheat.

Dower provides the wife a claim to real property superior to claims of the husband's debtors. Dower is terminated by divorce in nearly all states; however, a few states terminate dower only where the wife is at fault in the divorce proceedings.

Curtesy. Curtesy is a man's right in real property owned by his wife during their marriage. Very few states recognize curtesy today, and where it exists it is usually treated the same as dower. The laws of some states grant the husband dower rather than curtesy. Other states grant curtesy only where the wife is survived by a child of the marriage to the surviving husband. Regardless of the requirements imposed on curtesy, a buyer of real property should obtain a release of curtesy in the same manner as dower to be certain of obtaining an unencumbered title.

Homestead. The laws of a few states permit a family to declare either a specified amount of land or a specified dollar value of property as a homestead.[4] A properly declared and recorded homestead is exempt from foreclosure by creditors to the extent of the legal maximum amount of area or dollar value. The family cannot be evicted from the land during the husband's lifetime, and his widow is protected after his death. The states' laws which provide for homestead generally require that a family exists, that the homestead be used as the family's residence, and that the head of the family possesses an ownership interest

---

[4] No choice is involved; each state determines how the homestead is to be established.

in the property.[5] Most states also require that the family file for homestead and have it recorded in the county records.

The right of homestead is actually a protection of other ownership rights rather than an independent estate in land. Homesteads are owned either in fee simple or fee tail, with the homestead right granting protection of ownership. The homesteader's widow receives substantial protection through this right; the husband cannot convey clear title during his lifetime without the wife's permission, and the wife's right to the homestead is prior to the claims of the husband's creditors upon his death.

Less than freehold estates

Earlier in this chapter, we noted that an individual does not have to be absolute owner of a parcel of real estate in order to derive valuable benefits. Many business firms have found that they can create extra profits by selling their business realty and obtaining long-term leases. Physical use of the property is not disturbed by this financing arrangement, but fee simple ownership is transferred into the hands of an absentee landlord. The former owners no longer have capital tied up in realty and they can deduct all rents for tax purposes. The new owners acquire an investment which should yield a satisfactory return.

A leasehold can be defined very simply as the right to use the property of another. Complete utilization with no restrictions is rarely granted; the most common situation is one in which the use to which the land can be put by the lessee and the manner in which the use is carried out are regulated by contract between lessor and lessee. Leases generally can be classified by duration of lease. Four types of estates can be created by varying the length of time for which the property is leased:

Estate for years—beginning and ending point of lease specified. Leases of this type are usually measured in periods extending over several years, but they can be for any specified period—even less than a year. The key distinguishing factor is that the exact duration of the lease must be specified.

Tenancy from year to year. As in the estate for years, the period of measurement can be something other than a year. A tenancy from year to year (actually period to period) is automatically renewed every period until one of the parties gives sufficient notice of termination.

Tenancy at will. In most states, a tenancy at will exists without a definite agreement among parties. It can be terminated at any time (without notice) by either party. A tenancy at will frequently arises

---

[5] Lusk and French, *Law of the Real Estate Business,* p. 41.

where the tenant holds over without objection by the landlord after the expiration of the lease.

Tenancy at sufferance. This final form of tenancy arises when a tenant continues to use property after the agreement with the landlord has completely expired. It is a wrongful tenancy, and it cannot exist if the owner exercises the right of repossession. Tenancy at sufferance also arises where a person moves onto a property owned by someone else without the owner's knowledge or consent.

The differences in the four types of leasehold described here are significant to both lessors and lessees. Lessees must beware of the last two forms if a fairly permanent lease is contemplated. Where termination without notice is possible, unscrupulous landlords can let a tenant build up a successful business and then cancel the lease in order to take over the business. Lessees of homes can find themselves evicted if they fail to comply with unreasonable rent demands. From the lessor's standpoint, some degree of certainty of income is required for sound planning. The "midnight movers" who leave under the cover of darkness on the day the rent is due create significant management problems for the landlord. For either party, a temporary arrangement may be desired for a test period. However, the benefits of a lease of known duration outweigh the disadvantages, and a test arrangement should be replaced in a reasonable time if trouble is to be avoided.

Incorporeal property rights

The owners of an estate in land can, if they wish, grant the privilege of using their land to others without surrendering any of their property ownership rights. Such privileges do limit freedom of use, however, and they normally must be included in the definition of ownership. They are of three types: (*a*) easement, (*b*) license, and (*c*) profit.

Easements. An easement is a nonpossessory interest one person holds in the real estate of another. It is not considered to be an estate in land, although it cannot be revoked by the landowner. The most common form of easement is the *commercial easement in gross,* such as a right-of-way for a pipeline, electric line, telephone line, or railroad. An easement in gross also exists as an individual's personal right. The commercial form can be assigned, conveyed, or inherited, but the individual form is granted to a single individual for his or her lifetime only. Few courts recognize the individual, noncommercial easement in gross today, since the easement appurtenant and the license are defined broadly enough to include nearly every situation which may arise.

The easement appurtenant is a grant made by the owners of one parcel of property, the *servient tenement,* to permit their land to be used in some manner by the owners of an adjoining parcel, the *dominant tenement*. The most common easement appurtenant is a right-of-way granted to a neighbor for ingress and egress. Once granted, the benefits attach to the dominant tenement and the obligation to permit use attaches to the servient tenement. Both dominant and servient tenements exist in an easement appurtenant, while only the servient land is involved in an easement in gross.

Most easements are formed through express grants in writing, although they can arise by will, by implication, or by prescription. Easements established by grant are normally part of a conveyance by deed, although they can be created by written contract. Implied easements arise where landowners sell a portion of their parcel which is completely surrounded by other land that they own. The buyers can safely imply that they are entitled to establish a right-of-way across the sellers' land, although the sellers are entitled to select a reasonable location for the right-of-way. An easement by prescription arises where a person's land is used by another on an adverse, visible, open, notorious, and continuous basis under claim of right by the user for an uninterrupted period of time as prescribed by law. The owner of the property in question can stop the running of the prescribed period by interrupting use of the easement for a short time, thereby making the prescribed easement exceptionally difficult to obtain. Permission may also be granted for the use at one point in time, thereby eliminating the essential requirement of adverse use. Easements by prescription arise almost exclusively in the case of vehicular rights-of-way, although courts tend to include nonadverse party driveways under this procedure.

License. A license is a privilege granted to a single individual permitting him or her to go upon the servient land. Permission to hunt or fish is one example; another is the sale of admission tickets for theatrical or sporting performances. Licenses can be made orally, and they are revocable by the owner of the servient land.

Profit. A profit, or *profit a pendre,* is the right to remove soil or minerals from the servient tenement. Profits are personal rights which can be assigned, conveyed, or inherited, although they can be established in favor of a single dominant tenement.

OWNERSHIP BY MORE THAN ONE PERSON

Many parcels of real estate are owned by more than one individual. The total parcel is usually owned in fee simple, so the problems of multiple owners arise in determining how to divide interests among the various owners. The following types of multiple ownership are prevalent in the United States.

Tenancy in common. Ownership in the form of tenancy in common works like a common stock corporation. A single parcel of real property, undivided in the sense that each owner exercises the rights of ownership of the entire parcel rather than a staked-off portion, is operated by the owners exactly as though it were a business firm. The individual owners have a say in making decisions about the parcel and can sell their interest, give it away, or grant it to their heirs as they wish.

Joint tenancy. A tenancy in common is created automatically whenever two or more people acquire concurrent ownership of a parcel of real estate. Joint tenancy, on the other hand, requires a formal written instrument evidencing the desire to create an ownership situation different from that of tenancy in common. In a joint tenancy, all owners have equal ownership rights. The ownership rights of individual owners pass upon their deaths to the other owners—again being split equally among them.

A joint tenancy between two or more persons is enforced by the courts only where four "unities" exist. These unities, or common bonds, are these:

1. *Unity of interest.* The ownership rights of each of the parties must be equal and endure for the same length of time.
2. *Unity of time.* The interests of each of the parties must be acquired at the same time.
3. *Unity of title.* All joint tenants must receive their interest through a single conveyance of title.
4. *Unity of possession.* All joint tenants must have equal rights of possession, although these rights do not have to be exercised by any of the parties.

The unique characteristic of joint tenancy is that it can exist for either the entire parcel or part of the parcel. For example, a group of five men pool their money to buy an investment property. Each man supplies 20 percent of the money for an undivided 20 percent ownership right. A tenancy in common is formed among the five men. Three of the men wish to form a joint tenancy as to their 60 percent combined interest, so they prepare a binding legal agreement to that effect. They have their wives sign the agreement in order to avoid any claim of dower right, and they make use of the property with their two partners by tenancy in common. If one of the three men dies, his two joint tenant partners each receives 10 percent additional ownership—the property now being owned 30 percent by each of the two joint tenants and 20 percent by each of two tenants in common.

If one of the three joint tenants does not die, but grants his 20 percent interest to an outside party, the joint tenancy is upset as far as his share is concerned. His 20 percent falls back into the tenancy in common status. However, the other two joint tenants can continue the joint tenancy on the 40 percent.

Joint tenancies have created many problems over the years and are currently in disfavor with the courts. An ironclad agreement must exist for the joint tenancy to be recognized over the rights of the surviving spouse of a joint tenant.

Tenancy by the entireties. Tenancy by the entireties is a special form of joint tenancy in some states which can be employed only by husband and wife. Any real property acquired by them during their marriage can be established as a tenancy by the entireties, thereby guaranteeing each partner a right of survivorship to the other's share. The right of survivorship continues even when one of the partners conveys his or her share to a third party. Like joint tenancies, tenancy by the entireties is held in disfavor by many states, and they require a binding written agreement for the tenancy to be enforced.

Community property. The concept of community property is of Spanish origin, and it is prevalent in several western states. It holds that husband and wife each own 50 percent of all real property purchased after their marriage. The only property excluded is that which is purchased with funds which are clearly owned by only one of the married partners. Both owners must sign transfer papers on community property.

Condominium. Many state laws have been passed in recent years to permit the development of condominium apartment units. Each owner holds a fee simple interest in an apartment and a tenancy in common in halls, elevators, lawns, and so on. The separate ownership forms have been discussed previously, but the condominium combination is unique.[6]

Corporation, trust, and partnership. A parcel of real estate can be owned by a single legal entity that is in itself an aggregation of individual owners. The legal framework that unites the owners also defines the manner in which ownership interests are divided. The use of corporations, trusts, and partnerships is considered here in terms of property ownership strategy.

PROPERTY OWNERSHIP STRATEGY

The goals of investors and the risks associated with individual properties determine the proper form of ownership structure in each investment situation. In general, high-risk projects are more properly structured as corporations or trusts. These two forms are also excellent

---

[6] Condominiums are discussed further in Chapter 13.

choices for situations in which large numbers of investors are called upon to provide equity capital.

Partnerships and tenant in common structures are well suited for tax shelter investments and other investments that involve small numbers of investors. The limited partnership is particularly popular as a vehicle for syndicators to use in assembling equity money from small numbers of investors who seek limited liability and freedom from management decisions.

The major consideration in selecting an ownership form is the objectives of investor groups. Small-scale investors frequently fear the partnership form in which the ownership shares have no active market and cannot be sold easily. Larger investors at times find the corporation and trust forms useful for those projects that are to be subdivided and sold at ordinary income rates or for those projects that are to be operated to yield tax-sheltered cash income. The same investors might prefer the partnership form for projects yielding tax deductions via depreciation or those yielding capital gains through sale.

The variables in the ownership decision are (*a*) avoidance of double taxation when using a corporation; (*b*) avoidance of personal liability for investors; (*c*) marketability of shares; and (*d*) acquisition of maximum income tax deduction benefits. These variables are reflected in the four basic ownership forms as follows.

Corporation. The corporate form is designed for easy transfer of small portions of ownership, and it offers total limitation of liability for investors. However, it creates a taxable entity that pays tax in addition to that which must be paid by investors individually. Also, the corporate form fails to permit investors to deduct net taxable losses from their personal income tax returns.

The corporate form is of maximum value to investors who place a much higher priority upon easy transferability of ownership and liability limitation than on income tax minimization. However, careful tax planning can lead to a need for one or more corporations in achieving desired salaries, pension plans, medical plans, deductibility of automobiles and other expenditures, and so on. These issues go beyond the basic real estate planning and are not considered in this text.

Tax-free real estate investment trust. The tax-free real estate investment trust (REIT) became popular in the 1960s and early 1970s as a vehicle for achieving a single tax on income plus the desired liability limitation. However, tax losses cannot be passed through to investors. To retain its tax-free status, the trust must pay 90 percent of its income to investors, and it must follow numerous rules regarding the percentage of investments that must be in real estate and the length of time that investments must be held. Virtually all income must be passive in nature rather than the result of direct project operation by a trust's management. Substantial losses caused REIT's to lose popularity during the mid-1970s.

Partnership.   The partnership form avoids double taxation and allows tax losses to be deducted by individual investors. Liability is unlimited for all investors in the general partnership, but it can be limited in the limited partnership for partners who are not involved in project management. Broadly based markets for partnership shares rarely exist, but shares are easily transferred and purchasers can usually be found for shares in a quality offering.

Most states have securities registration laws that affect partnership interests (as well as trusts and tenancies in common). When out-of-state investors are involved, the Securities and Exchange Commission (SEC) requires registration of partnerships. These laws frequently have exemptions for those entities that stay intrastate and maintain small ownership groups. Registration is time consuming and expensive, and the form of ownership and size of share is often kept small to achieve exemption from registration laws.

Tenancy in common.   The tenancy in common shares most of the features of the partnership. Liability is more difficult to limit, but an agreement among tenants in common can be devised in which one owner assumes all liability incurred by the owners. If the other owners pay off a partnership debt to an outside party, they can secure reimbursement from the managing (liable) owner.

Summary regarding strategy.   The proper ownership form for a group of individuals or for a combination of individuals, trusts, partnerships, and corporations is a function of investor objectives and project characteristics. Tax implications, transferability of shares, and liability limitations must be considered. Compromise solutions can lead to an optimal ownership structure. These compromises must be minor in nature; investors with widely divergent objectives usually should not invest together. Individuals structuring a real estate ownership arrangement should learn everything possible about the objectives of their investors and carefully place each investor in a project that best meets his or her objectives.

Sophisticated real estate syndicators frequently attempt to construct large files of investors in which those investors having a common interest are brought together. This has been an exceptionally effective approach for Realty Research Corporation in Atlanta, Georgia.

Large-scale developers tend to develop a successful joint-venture arrangement with one or more financial institutions that can be used repeatedly on different projects. Cousins Properties, Inc., of Atlanta, Georgia, has followed this pattern in several major developments with Fidelity Mutual Life Insurance Company. U.S. Steel Realty Company has joint ventured projects with Connecticut Mutual Life Insurance

Company, and John Hancock Life Insurance Company has devised a successful joint-venture format that has been used in conjunction with many developers throughout the nation. The limited partnership tends to be the most popular form for these joint ventures, but any of the other forms could meet investor objectives.

SUMMARY

Real estate is land and everything permanently attached to the land. Four legal methods of describing real estate are available for use in any situation or document where the exact boundaries and dimensions of a parcel of land may be required. These are (*a*) metes and bounds, (*b*) monuments, (*c*) government or rectangular survey, and (*d*) recorded plat. The last method, recorded plat, is usually available for residential subdivisions. The first three are normally applied to larger tracts. In most sections of the country that have been surveyed by the government, the government or rectangular survey system is the preferred method for describing land. Metes and bounds or monuments are used predominately in areas not so surveyed, although they can also be used in surveyed areas. Description by street address is satisfactory for everyday usage—situations in which disputes are not likely to arise.

Real property is a legal concept that refers to the right to own, use, or occupy real estate. Fixtures are items of personal property which have become real property, often because of permanent attachment to the real estate. Property rights can take several forms, called *estates* in real property, such as the fee simple, fee tail, determinable fee, fee subject to condition subsequent or precedent, life estate, estate for years or from period to period, reversion, remainder, dower, and community property. The market value and investment value of real property are dependent upon the legal interest under valuation, which should always be carefully defined by the analyst.

The ownership form selected for a real estate investment situation determines the relationship among investors, between investors and lenders, and between investors and their officers or partners. Many forms of legal protection for all parties involved can be created in corporate charters, trust agreements, partnership agreements, or agreements among tenants in common.

When real estate is owned by only one person, fee simple ownership is the most desirable form. It provides the maximum ownership rights. However, some property titles are encumbered with conditional titles, life estates, and other limitations which prevent the investor from gaining the maximum bundle of ownership rights.

At times, an investor might prefer to lease, rather than own outright, a parcel of property. Leases can be established for any period of time and on several renewal bases, and most state laws are quite articulate about what constitutes an enforceable clause or an act of renewing a lease.

Given many alternatives of ownership form and structure, investors must plan workable strategies for their projects that optimize their protection from liability, their income tax deduction status, and their protection against lenders, officers, and other investors. The corporate and trust forms offer excellent liability protection, but they limit opportunities for investors to obtain income tax deductions. A tenancy in common form offers excellent income tax liability deductibility, but unlimited liability for debts of all types. The limited partnership form provides liability limitation, tax deductions, and protections among limited partners, but it requires that the limited partners refrain from making managerial decisions, thereby causing them to lose ownership control. Thus, investors must devise the optimal structure for each project based upon their goals and a project's risks.

QUESTIONS FOR REVIEW

1. What is *real estate?* How does this term differ from *real property?*
2. How does one determine whether an asset is a fixture or an item of realty?
3. Distinguish between estates in possession and estates not in possession.
4. Distinguish between freehold estates of inheritance and freehold estates not of inheritance.
5. What are the three types of incorporeal rights to real property?
6. What are the four unities of a joint tenancy?
7. Indicate the ownership form that appears to be most practical for a joint venture. Defend your choice.
8. Why must legal descriptions, rather than street and number, often be used to describe real estate?
9. What are the four methods of legal description?
10. How many sections are in a township? How many acres are in a section? How many square feet are in an acre?
11. What is the principal difficulty in describing real estate by monuments?
12. When describing a parcel of real estate by rectangular survey, why must the principal meridian and base line be cited?
13. Make a rough sketch of Section 3 of Township 1 North, Range 2 East of the Tallahassee Principal Meridian and Base Line and indicate the S ½ of the NW ¼ of the NE ¼.

REFERENCES

Curtis, Clayton C. *Real Estate for the New Practitioner.* 4th ed. Gainesville, Fla.: B. J. Publishing, 1975, chap. 2.

Kratovil, Robert. *Real Estate Law.* 6th ed. Englewood Cliffs, N.J.: Prentice-Hall, 1974.

Lusk, Harold F., and French, William B. *Law of the Real Estate Business.* 3d ed. Homewood, Ill.: Richard D. Irwin, 1975.

Ring, Alfred A. *Real Estate Principles and Practices.* 7th ed. Englewood Cliffs, N.J.: Prentice-Hall, 1972, chaps. 5 and 12.

Semenow, Robert W. *Questions and Answers on Real Estate.* 7th ed. Englewood Cliffs, N.J.: Prentice-Hall, 1972.

Unger, Maurice A. *Real Estate Principles and Practices.* 5th ed. Cincinnati: South-Western Publishing Co., 1974.

chapter 9

CONVEYING
OWNERSHIP RIGHTS

THE LAWS pertaining to real estate conveyancing require that formal procedures be followed in all types of transactions. Offers, contracts, closings, title transfers, rentals, and many other activities are framed in legal terms with precisely worded documents evidencing them. Many of these documents appear to be cumbersome, but less precise terminology leads to ambiguity, and failure to insert the many clauses can easily cause disagreement among the parties at a later date.

Nearly all real property transactions are governed by state Statutes of Frauds, laws requiring that all transactions other than short-term leases must be in writing. Oral clauses or oral agreements pertaining to the writings are not enforceable until they have been set down in writing and incorporated properly into the document. This is a reasonable statute; many disagreements are avoided where oral testimony is not permitted, and people tend to plan more carefully when all provisions are stated in writing.

Investors who enter written agreements concerning real property should have all pertinent documents examined by an attorney to be certain that agreement is reached on all essential points and to provide a measure of protection against undesirable provisions. However, the attorney cannot do the entire job. The investor is the person who will be bound by the agreement and is in a position to know exactly what the objectives are and what clauses can meet them best. For example, a land contract containing a forfeiture clause (which states that failure to make a payment causes the land to revert back to the seller) might be advantageous for a speculator who would like to withdraw from the investment if it were not profitable. The same clause would be disadvantageous for a couple having a low income who are buying their home under land contract to avoid making a large downpayment. Speculators know that the decision to forfeit or not forfeit is their own; the person who could not afford the downpayment is at the mercy of the seller, if illness or other problems cause one or more payments to be missed.

The frequent investor in real estate must learn to read documents thoroughly in a short period of time. The investor must be able to determine whether or not all pertinent items are included, and investment objectives must be analyzed to determine which clauses should or should not be inserted. Other clauses are subject to negotiation, and investors must know enough about them to determine that an agreement is equitable, given their particular objectives.

The first step in preparing a document for a real estate transaction is to determine whether or not it is proper for the purpose. Warranty deeds, deeds of bargain and sale, and quitclaim deeds all transfer ownership rights, but only the warranty deed employs wording that calls for the seller to guarantee the quality of the ownership right which is transferred. A quitclaim deed conveys only the seller's interest, no matter how encumbered. The use of these and other documents varies among the states, and the investor must become familiar with all practices within the investor's realm of operation.

Many of the documents involved in real property transactions are preprinted in standard form. Offers to purchase, deeds, closing statements, mortgages, liens, leases, trading agreements, trust agreements, escrow agreements, and brokers' listing contracts are examples of documents that are typically prepared *en masse* by trade groups and individual firms. Local boards of Realtors usually prescribe a certain set of forms for their members, but each board can prescribe a different form, and not all members of a particular board adhere to the entire package of prescribed forms. Also, many brokers do not have access to Realtor-approved forms. Lenders normally develop their own forms, as do escrow agents, trustees, and landlords.

Many functions must be performed in even the least complicated conveyancing transaction. The most frequently encountered activities are considered here, presented in chronological order from the initial purchase offer to the listing agreement employed in selling.

CONVEYANCING FUNCTIONS

Making an offer

Upon finding a desirable property, investors normally prepare a formal, written offer to submit to the owner. This offer ripens into a contract for sale if it is accepted by the owner, and it permits the owner to make a counteroffer if a change in terms is desired. As a practical matter, investors usually learn of the property's availability through a broker who holds a listing contract with the seller. The investor thus has a statement of the owner's desired terms as a guide in preparing the offer.

Two points are worth noting about the offer to purchase: (*a*) The buyer should be specific as to exactly what is being offered to buy. Storm windows and screens, light fixtures, carpets, and so on to be included or excluded from the sale should be specified. Anything the buyer wishes to receive which might be considered personal property should be listed. (*b*) The seller might wish to state the terms of the listing contract in a general enough manner that offers to buy may be rejected because of certain specific items they contain. On the other hand, the seller might wish to make the listing extremely specific and hold that the listing must be agreed upon exactly by a buyer. Either way, the seller may accept any offer, even if the terms deviate widely from the listing.

Once an offer to buy is tendered to the seller, the potential buyer and the seller can negotiate as to the price and what the sale includes until they make a satisfactory arrangement or terminate negotiations. The offer to buy is merely an offer; many counteroffers and counter-counter-offers might be necessary to effect a sale.

The offer must state formally that an offer is being made, and it must indicate clearly each of the following items:

1. Name of offeror, offeree, and broker.
2. Detailed description of property and fixtures, including a listing of all items that are to be made part of the transaction.
3. Amount to be paid and terms of payment. The offer can be worded to make it contingent upon obtaining a specific financing arrangement.
4. Type of deed to be received and specific ownership restrictions and encumbrances that will be permitted.
5. Manner in which expenses, taxes, rentals, and so on are to be prorated between buyer and seller.
6. Options available to the offeror if the property is damaged or destroyed before the final closing and statements evidencing the insurable interests of the parties.
7. Duration of offer.
8. Time and place of closing and length of time permitted for title search and removal of objections to title.
9. Manner in which earnest money deposits are to be handled and provision for the broker's commission.
10. Statement of how the broker's commission is to be computed.

11. A complete agreement clause that excludes all facts and material items not considered in the writing. This clause requires that oral agreements be incorporated in the document.
12. Offeror's witnessed signature, owner's acceptance of the offer, and receipt for deposit.

A standard offer form approved by the Atlanta Real Estate Board is presented as Figure 9–1 to indicate the manner in which these factors are commonly considered. The offer to purchase is designed to meet the needs of the offeror. The standard clauses contained in Figure 9–1 avoid most of the problems that could arise in the event of damage to the property, failure to obtain clear title or proper financing at closing, failure to pay the broker's commission, and so forth. Other clauses can be inserted to meet any type of need, such as those regarding an exchange of properties, a sale of previously owned properties, or the establishment of a corporation or syndicate to hold the real estate assets. The standard form is a logical and desirable instrument for most transactions, but specialized activities call for individualized provisions. The wording of these provisions must be precise, and an attorney should normally be consulted in preparing them.

Reaching agreement

When a buyer and seller agree as to the exact terms of a real property transaction, a written contract is prepared that describes the property and all extras, states the price to be paid, and indicates the time at which title is to pass. A contract of sale does not have to be a formal document to be legally enforceable. It is frequently represented as an accepted offer to purchase. Kratovil provides an example of a contract similar to the following that was enforced by one court, indicating that the contract does not even have to state the specific details of transfer:[1]

> New York, February 29, 1908
> Received of John Smith $200 on said purchase of property 2293 Jones Avenue, New York, New York at a price of $18,000.
> T. Wilson

Obviously, this is not good practice. The contract should identify clearly the parties, the property to be transferred, including personal property, if any, and the type of deed to be granted. It should specify that a merchantable title is to pass, and should contain the signatures of both parties.

One of the most important functions of the contract of sale is to stipulate the time for title to be passed from seller to buyer. If the

---

[1] Kratovil, *Real Estate Law*, p. 110.

FIGURE 9–1

ATLANTA REAL ESTATE BOARD
Residential Sales Contract
September, 1972

(YOUR FIRM NAME)
REALTORS
Atlanta, Georgia

As a result of the efforts of   YOUR FIRM NAME _____ ,
a licensed Broker, the undersigned Purchaser agrees to buy, and the undersigned Seller agrees to sell, all that tract or parcel of land,
with such improvements as are located thereon, described as follows:

together with all electrical, mechanical, plumbing, air-conditioning, and any other systems or fixtures as are attached thereto and all
plants, trees, and shrubbery now on the premises.
    The purchase price of said property shall be:
_____ DOLLARS, $ _____
to be paid as follows:

Purchaser has paid to the undersigned _____ , Broker,
$ _____ (____) cash (____) check, receipt whereof is hereby acknowledged by Broker, as earnest money, which earnest
money is to be promptly deposited in Broker's escrow account and is to be applied as part payment of purchase price of said
property at the time sale is consummated.
    Seller warrants that he presently has title to said property, and at the time the sale is consummated, he agrees to convey good
and marketable title to said property to Purchaser by general warranty deed subject only to (1) zoning ordinances affecting said
property, (2) general utility easements of record serving said property, (3) subdivision restrictions of record, and (4) leases, other
easements, other restrictions and encumbrances specified in this contract. In the event leases are specified in this contract, the
Purchaser agrees to assume the Seller's responsibilities thereunder to the tenant and to the Broker who negotiated such leases.
    The Purchaser shall move promptly and in good faith after acceptance of this contract to examine title and to furnish Seller with
a written statement of objections affecting the marketability of said title. Seller shall have reasonable time after receipt of such
objections to satisfy all valid objections and if Seller fails to satisfy such valid objections within a reasonable time, then at the option
of the Purchaser, evidenced by written notice to Seller, this contract shall be null and void. Marketable title as used herein shall mean
title which a title insurance company licensed to do business in the State of Georgia will insure at its regular rates, subject only to
standard exceptions unless otherwise specified herein.
    Seller and Purchaser agree that such papers as may be necessary to carry out the terms of this contract shall be executed and
delivered by such parties at time the sale is consummated.
    Purchaser, its agents, or representatives, at Purchaser's expense and at reasonable times during normal business hours, shall have
the right to enter upon the property for the purpose of inspecting, examining, testing, and surveying the property. Purchaser assumes
all responsibility for the acts of itself, its agents, or representatives in exercising its rights under this paragraph and agrees to hold
Seller harmless for any damages resulting therefrom.
    Seller warrants that when the sale is consummated the improvements on the property will be in the same condition as they are
on the date this contract is signed by the Seller, natural wear and tear excepted. However, should the premises be destroyed or
substantially damaged before the contract is consummated, then at the election of the Purchaser: (a) the contract may be cancelled,
or (b) Purchaser may consummate the contract and receive such insurance as is paid on the claim of loss. This election is to be
exercised within ten (10) days after the Purchaser has been notified in writing by Seller of the amount of the insurance proceeds, if
any, Seller will receive on the claim of loan; if Purchaser has not been notified within forty-five (45) days subsequent to the
occurance of such damage or destruction, Purchaser may, at its option, cancel the contract.
    In negotiating this contract, Broker has rendered a valuable service for which reason Broker is made a party to enable Broker to
enforce his commission rights hereunder against the parties hereto on the following basis: Seller agrees to pay Broker the full
commission when the sale is consummated and in the event the sale is not consummated because of Seller's inability, failure or
refusal to perform any of the Seller's covenants herein, then the Seller shall pay the full commission to Broker, and Broker, at the
option of Purchaser, shall return the earnest money to Purchaser. Purchaser agrees that if Purchaser fails or refuses to perform any of
Purchaser's covenants herein, Purchaser shall forthwith pay Broker the full commission; provided that Broker may first apply
one-half of the earnest money toward payment of, but not to exceed, the full commission and may pay the balance thereof to seller
as liquidated damages of Seller, if Seller claims balance as Seller's liquidated damages in full settlement of any claim for damages,
whereupon Broker shall be released from any and all liability for return of earnest money to Purchaser. If this transaction involves
exchange of real estate, the full commission shall be paid in respect to the property conveyed by each party to the other and notice
of the dual agency is hereby given and accepted by Seller and Purchaser. The commission on an exchange shall be calculated on the
amount on the basis of which each property is taken in such exchange, according to the contract between the parties, and if no value
is placed on any property exchange, then according to the reasonable value thereof. In the event of an exchange, each party shall be
regarded as Seller as to the property conveyed by each party.
    Commission to be paid in connection with this transaction has been negotiated between Seller and Broker and shall be
_____

    Time is of essence of this contract.
    This contract shall inure to the benefit of, and be binding upon, the parties hereto, their heirs, successors, administrators,
executors and assigns.
    The interest of the Purchaser in this contract shall not be transferred or assigned without the written consent of Seller.
    This contract constitutes the sole and entire agreement between the parties hereto and no modification of this contract shall be
binding unless attached hereto and signed by all parties to this agreement. No representation, promise, or inducement not included in
this contract shall be binding upon any party hereto.
    The following stipulations shall, if conflicting with printed matter, control:

FIGURE 9–1 (continued)

SPECIAL STIPULATIONS

1. Real Estate taxes on said property shall be prorated as of the date of closing.
2. Seller shall pay State of Georgia property transfer tax.
3. Sale shall be closed on or before _____ .
4. Possession of presmises shall be granted by Seller to Purchaser no later than _____

    This instrument shall be regarded as an offer by the Purchaser or Seller who first signs to the other and is open for acceptance by the other until _____O'clock ___ M., on the ____ day of _____,19___ ,by which time written acceptance of such offer must have been actually received by Broker, who shall promptly notify other party, in writing of such acceptance.

The above proposition is hereby accepted
this _____ day of _____ , 19 ____.

_____
(Purchaser)

_____
(Purchaser)

_____
(Seller)

_____
(Seller)

_____
(Broker)

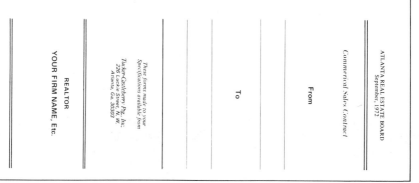

time is not specified, the law holds that title must be conveyed within a reasonable time after the signing of the sale contract. Adequate time is allowed to permit the buyer to ascertain the seller's ownership rights and determine whether or not any encumbrances exist that could prevent a clear title from passing. Both parties must work out their financial arrangements within this time.

Closing the sale

The contract for sale is a binding legal contract that states the manner in which ownership rights are to be transferred. At the time of transfer, a statement is prepared indicating the manner in which expenses are to be prorated, the costs to be paid by the buyer, and the costs to be paid by the seller. All expenses are subject to negotiation, but the purchaser normally is required to pay (a) appraisal fees, survey fees, and photograph costs, (b) title search charges or title insurance premiums, (c) recording and transfer fees, (d) attorney fees, and (e) costs incidental to obtaining a new mortgage such as a credit report, mortgage origination fees, and the cost of special title insurance fees to protect the lender. The seller typically pays (a) broker's commission, (b) repair costs needed to improve the property to the condition specified in the contract for sale, (c) state revenue stamps, (d) attorney fees, and (e) discounts charged the buyer by lenders on Federal Housing Administration (FHA) and Veterans Administration (VA) mortgages. The most important items to be prorated are property taxes, prepaid homeowner's insurance premiums, and prepaid tenant rent. Utility bills can be prorated when it is not convenient to obtain a special billing at the date of closing.

Closing costs vary widely among transactions, as would be indicated by the nature of the charges. A small, single-family home in an established subdivision typically requires much less work in preparing an appraisal, a title search, a survey, or a cost proration than would a farm property or a high-rise apartment building. Nearly every service performed does have a minimum charge, however, making the minimum total cost several hundred dollars in most cases. Certain services such as the appraisal can be eliminated at times, but the title search and attorney fee are almost inescapable. Thus, closing costs must be anticipated in nearly every real estate transaction.

The closing statement is the final accounting in a real property conveyance. All costs, services, and prorated expenses are listed in the closing statement so that all parties understand their responsibilities and the flow of funds that results from these responsibilities (see Figures 9–2, 9–3, and 9–4 for examples of closing documents).

Closing documents similar to those shown in Figures 9–2, 9–3, and

FIGURE 9–2

CLOSING STATEMENT

Property   Broker   C. A. BAKER REAL ESTATE

Seller   Purchaser

Date of Contract _____   Date of Closing _____

	Credit Purchaser	Credit Seller
PURCHASE PRICE		
EARNEST MONEY		
FIRST MORTGAGE		
INTEREST		
SECOND MORTGAGE		
INTEREST		
GENERAL TAXES		
GENERAL TAXES — Pro Rated		
SPECIAL ASSESSMENTS		
INSURANCE PREMIUMS (Unearned — Pro Rated)		
RENTS		
COAL OR OIL		
SERVICES		
WATER		
GAS AND LIGHT		
REVENUE STAMPS		
. . . .		
CHECK OR CASH TO BALANCE		
TOTAL . . .		

Buyer Acceptance	Seller Acceptance
_____	_____
_____	_____

SETTLEMENT	Debit	Credit
BALANCE FROM ABOVE		
EARNEST MONEY		
ABSTRACT OR GUARANTY POLICY		
RECORDING FEES		
COMMISSION		
BALANCE		
TOTAL . . .		

FIGURE 9–3

Form 10-1-1

Escrow Agent

SETTLEMENT STATEMENT

Closed by No._____   (As of:_____.)   Title or Escrow No._____
                                              Date

_____   _____
        Seller   Purchaser

                                          _____(Location of Property)

	Credit to Purchaser	Due to Seller
1. Purchase Price:_____	• • • • • • •	
2. Earnest Money (Paid to_____):		• • • • • •
3. Outstanding Liens assumed by purchaser:		
(a) First Loan: Prin. $_____Int. $_____: Total		• • • • • •
(b) Second Loan: Prin. $_____Int. $_____: Total		• • • • • •
4. Purchase money notes executed by purchaser to seller_____		• • • • • •
5. Adjusted (Pro-rated) Items:		
(a) City taxes for present year: Assmt. $_____Amt. $_____		
(b) S.&C. taxes for present year: Assmt. $_____Amt. $		
(c) Insurance Premiums (Paid to_____)____		
Amount $_____Agent_____		
(d) Rent: (Paid to_____at $_____per month)____		
(e) Water Bill: (Paid to_____)____		
(f) Reserves for taxes, Ins., etc., in escrow with mortgagee_____	• • • • • • •	
(g) F. H. A. Insurance paid in advance (Paid to_____).	• • • • • • •	
6. Miscellaneous Items:_____		
7. Balance due seller as per statement on back hereof:_____		• • • • • •
TOTALS		

READ AND APPROVED:

_____   _____
        Seller   Purchaser
                      (over)

FIGURE 9–4

ESCROW MEMORANDUM

Received of the PURCHASER the following amounts for the following purposes:

1. Balance due the seller as per statement on reverse side (Item 7) _____ $_____

2. Title fee and Escrow fee (Includes "Lawyers Title" Insurance) _____ $_____

3. Clerk's fee for recording Warranty Deed_____ $_____

4. _____ $_____

                              Total   _____ $_____

Received of the SELLER the total amount as shown below,
    for the following purposes:

1. Internal Revenue Stamps on Warranty Deed_____ $_____

2. Recording fees and cancellations_____ $_____

3. Agent's Commission: To:_____ $_____

4. Taxes: _____ $_____

5. Payment of loans on property not assumed by purchaser:

    To:_____ $_____

    _____ $_____

6. Payment of other items as follows:_____ $_____

    _____ $_____

    _____ $_____

                              Total   _____ $_____

Check to seller for balance of purchase price_____ $_____

                              Total $_____

Date_____   _____   **Escrow Agent**
                               By

REMARKS AND EXPLANATIONS:

9–4 may remain in use to accomplish the final settlement. In addition to these forms, most lenders must complete a Uniform Settlement Statement, to be given to the borrower when title to a one-to-four family property is transferred.[2] A Uniform Settlement Statement is provided in Figure 9–5.[3] This requirement was imposed by the Real Estate Settlement Procedures Act of 1974 (RESPA). RESPA resulted from the lack of uniformity in settlement procedures, from observed inadequate legal protection for the buyer in the settlement process, and from the belief that settlement costs were sometimes excessive.[4]

RESPA applies when title to one-to-four family units is transferred. Exempted from the act are refinancings, construction loans, junior mortgages, transfers with the existing loan being assumed or taken subject to (unless the loan terms are modified or the lender imposes charges of more than $50), real estate purchased with intent to resell in the ordinary course of business, vacant lot sales (unless the loan will be used in part to finance construction of a dwelling), sales involving properties of 25 acres or more, and mobile home purchases (unless both the mobile home and lot are purchased jointly).

A lender gives the homebuyer a booklet describing RESPA when the prospective buyer makes written application for a loan. At this time, the lender also provides a "good faith" estimate of the amount or range of specific closing costs the borrower is likely to incur. Points or discounts associated with the loan, however, need not be estimated at this time. The Uniform Settlement Statement itself (see Figure 9–5) is to be made available to the borrower one business day prior to closing at the borrower's request. At this time all closing costs are specified including points and discounts. The borrower is given a completed Uniform Settlement Statement within a reasonable period after closing, unless the borrower has waived this right.

Transferring ownership

The term *estate* defines the characteristics of an interest in land.[5] Formal government recognition of an estate is expressed in terms of *title*. Individuals may hold title to both personal and real property,

---

[2] Not all lenders must comply with the Real Estate Settlement Procedures Act. For instance, individuals are exempted from compliance if they are not lending on the security of a "federally assisted" mortgage. Most home mortgage loans, however, are subject to the act.

[3] The final form of this settlement statement had not been determined at the time of this writing. However, the form in Figure 9–5 is believed to be a reasonable facsimile of the final document.

[4] Paul Barron, *Federal Regulation in Real Estate: The Real Estate Settlement Procedures Act* (Boston: Warren, Gorham and Lamont, 1975).

[5] See the discussion in Chapter 8 for more detail.

FIGURE 9–5

Form Approved
OMB No. 63–R1501

A.		B. TYPE OF LOAN:

A. U.S. DEPARTMENT OF HOUSING AND URBAN DEVELOPMENT

DISCLOSURE/SETTLEMENT STATEMENT

B. TYPE OF LOAN:
1. ☐ FHA   2. ☐ FMHA   3. ☐ CONV. UNINS.
4. ☐ VA   5. ☐ CONV. INS.
6. FILE NUMBER   7. LOAN NUMBER

If the Truth-in-Lending Act applies to this transaction, a Truth-in-Lending statement is attached as page 3 of this form.
8. MORTG. INS. CASE NO.

C. NOTE: This form is furnished to you prior to settlement to give you information about your settlement costs, and again after settlement to show the actual costs you have paid. The present copy of the form is:

☐ ADVANCE DISCLOSURE OF COSTS. Some items are estimated, and are marked "(e)". Some amounts may change if the settlement is held on a date other than the date estimated below. The preparer of this form is not responsible for errors or changes in amounts furnished by others.

☐ STATEMENT OF ACTUAL COSTS. Amounts paid to and by the settlement agent are shown. Items marked "(p.o.c.)" were paid outside the closing; they are shown here for informational purposes and are not included in totals.

D. NAME OF BORROWER	E. SELLER	F. LENDER

G. PROPERTY LOCATION	H. SETTLEMENT AGENT	I. DATES	
		LOAN COMMITMENT	ADVANCE DISCLOSURE
	PLACE OF SETTLEMENT	SETTLEMENT	DATE OF PRORATIONS IF DIFFERENT FROM SETTLEMENT

J. SUMMARY OF BORROWER'S TRANSACTION

100. GROSS AMOUNT DUE FROM BORROWER:	
101. Contract sales price	
102. Personal property	
103. Settlement charges to borrower *(from line 1400, Section L)*	
104.	
105.	
Adjustments for items paid by seller in advance:	
106. City/town taxes to	
107. County taxes to	
108. Assessments to	
109. to	
110. to	
111. to	
112. to	
120. GROSS AMOUNT DUE FROM BORROWER:	
200. AMOUNTS PAID BY OR IN BEHALF OF BORROWER:	
201. Deposit or earnest money	
202. Principal amount of new loan(s)	
203. Existing loan(s) taken subject to	
204.	
205.	
Credits to borrower for items unpaid by seller:	
206. City/town taxes to	
207. County taxes to	
208. Assessments to	
209. to	
210. to	
211. to	
212. to	
220. TOTAL AMOUNTS PAID BY OR IN BEHALF OF BORROWER	
300. CASH AT SETTLEMENT REQUIRED FROM OR PAYABLE TO BORROWER:	
301. Gross amount due from borrower *(from line 120)*	
302. Less amounts paid by or in behalf of borrower *(from line 220)*	( )
303. CASH (☐ REQUIRED FROM/ OR (☐ PAYABLE TO/ BORROWER:	

K. SUMMARY OF SELLER'S TRANSACTION

400. GROSS AMOUNT DUE TO SELLER:	
401. Contract sales price	
402. Personal property	
403.	
404.	
Adjustments for items paid by seller in advance:	
405. City/town taxes to	
406. County taxes to	
407. Assessments to	
408. to	
409. to	
410. to	
411. to	
420. GROSS AMOUNT DUE TO SELLER:	
NOTE: The following 500 and 600 series sections are not required to be completed when this form is used for advance disclosure of settlement costs prior to settlement.	
500. REDUCTIONS IN AMOUNT DUE TO SELLER:	
501. Payoff of first mortgage loan	
502. Payoff of second mortgage loan	
503. Settlement charges to seller *(from line 1400, Section L)*	
504. Existing loan(s) taken subject to	
505.	
506.	
507.	
508.	
509.	
Credits to borrower for items unpaid by seller:	
510. City/town taxes to	
511. County taxes to	
512. Assessments to	
513. to	
514. to	
515. to	
520. TOTAL REDUCTIONS IN AMOUNT DUE TO SELLER:	
600. CASH TO SELLER FROM SETTLEMENT:	
601. Gross amount due to seller *(from line 420)*	
602. Less total reductions in amount due to seller *(from line 520)*	( )
603. CASH TO SELLER FROM SETTLEMENT	

HUD–1 (5–75)

FIGURE 9–5 *(continued)*

Page 2

L. SETTLEMENT CHARGES	PAID FROM BORROWER'S FUNDS	PAID FROM SELLER'S FUNDS
700. SALES/BROKER'S COMMISSION based on price $ @ %		
701. Total commission paid by seller		
Division of commission as follows:		
702. $ to		
703. $ to		
704.		
800. ITEMS PAYABLE IN CONNECTION WITH LOAN.		
801. Loan Origination fee %		
802. Loan Discount %		
803. Appraisal Fee to		
804. Credit Report to		
805. Lender's inspection fee		
806. Mortgage Insurance application fee to		
807. Assumption/refinancing fee		
808.		
809.		
810.		
811.		
900. ITEMS REQUIRED BY LENDER TO BE PAID IN ADVANCE.		
901. Interest from to @ $ /day		
902. Mortgage insurance premium for mo. to		
903. Hazard insurance premium for yrs. to		
904. yrs. to		
905.		
1000. RESERVES DEPOSITED WITH LENDER FOR:		
1001. Hazard insurance mo. @$ /mo.		
1002 Mortgage insurance mo. @$ /mo.		
1003. City property taxes mo. @$ /mo.		
1004. County property taxes mo. @$ /mo.		
1005. Annual assessments mo. @$ /mo.		
1006. mo. @$ /mo.		
1007. mo. @$ /mo.		
1008. mo. @$ /mo.		
1100. TITLE CHARGES:		
1101. Settlement or closing fee to		
1102. Abstract or title search to		
1103. Title examination to		
1104. Title insurance binder to		
1105. Document preparation to		
1106. Notary fees to		
1107. Attorney's Fees to		
(includes above items No.:)		
1108. Title insurance to		
(includes above items No.:)		
1109. Lender's coverage $		
1110. Owner's coverage $		
1111.		
1112.		
1113.		
1200. GOVERNMENT RECORDING AND TRANSFER CHARGES		
1201. Recording fees: Deed $; Mortgage $ Releases $		
1202. City/county tax/stamps: Deed $; Mortgage $		
1203. State tax/stamps: Deed $; Mortgage $		
1204.		
1300. ADDITIONAL SETTLEMENT CHARGES		
1301. Survey to		
1302. Pest inspection to		
1303.		
1304.		
1305.		
1400. TOTAL SETTLEMENT CHARGES (entered on lines 103 and 503, Sections J and K)		

NOTE: *Under certain circumstances the borrower and seller may be permitted to waive the 12-day period which must normally occur between advance disclosure and settlement. In the event such a waiver is made, copies of the statements of waiver, executed as provided in the regulations of the Department of Housing and Urban Development, shall be attached to and made a part of this form when the form is used as a settlement statement.*

HUD-1 (5-75)

given that their government holds claim of original title through discovery, conquest, occupancy, or cession. The government has the power to cancel the title for the following reasons: (*a*) condemnation—the land is needed for public purposes; (*b*) forfeiture—the owners failed to pay taxes or committed treason; (*c*) confiscation—the owners were enemies during time of war; or (*d*) escheat—the owners died without heirs or assigns.

Obviously, government cancellation of real estate titles rarely occurs. Individuals are free to enjoy their property, and they can transfer it to others in a number of ways. The most common means of transferring property are discussed here.

Private grant. A voluntary transfer of real property during the grantor's lifetime is known as a private grant. Grantors *deed* their property rights to another party, the grantee, either by sale or by gift. The property deeded can represent anything from the right to enter the property and fish in its waters to complete fee simple ownership.

Devise or descent. The second most common means of transferring title is by will (devise) or, in the absence of a will, by legal statute specifying the manner in which property passes to descendants (descent).

Foreclosure. The holder of a valid lien on real property is entitled to request that the property be sold at public sale when the fee simple owner defaults in satisfying the claim which caused the lien to arise. The fee simple owner's rights of ownership are cut off at the time of sale by a court-appointed official, and the buyer at the sale receives a fee simple title. The court does not guarantee the quality of this title; the buyer takes it subject to any defects that existed in the hands of the former owner.

Adverse possession. Individuals can take away the title of another person if they use that person's property on an actual, continuous, hostile, visible, and exclusive basis for a period of time prescribed by law. This change of title is based upon the concept that land should be used rather than left idle. In other words, anyone who owns property for the prescribed period—usually 7 to 21 years—and fails to use the property or assert a claim of ownership against the adverse possessor should lose the property when the adverse possessor did make profitable use of the land.

Prescription. When an individual uses the land of another for a period of time stated by law, such as using a roadway across a neighbor's land, the user obtains a right of easement in the neighbor's land. This use must have most of the attributes of adverse possession, except that it need not be exclusive.

Title from nature (riparian rights). As discussed in the following section, recorded deeds contain a legal description of the owner's parcel of property. Many descriptions are expressed in terms of monuments or natural boundaries, and these can change. Where a body of water washes land into the described area, title is obtained through *accretion*. Where boundary water recedes and leaves dry land, *reliction* adds to the title holder's land. The only case in which such changes do not convey title is when a boundary river or stream changes course (avulsion). The dry bed is still the boundary.

The deed

A deed is a written instrument that evidences transfer of ownership (see Figure 9–6). Whether property rights are sold outright, given away, or sold at public auction to satisfy a lien, every exchange requires a properly prepared and properly recorded deed in order for a legally recognized exchange to occur. There are numerous types of deeds, including these: (*a*) general warranty deed, (*b*) quitclaim deed, (*c*) deed of bargain and sale, (*d*) special warranty deed, and (*e*) officer's deed.

The most desirable type of deed from the buyer's viewpoint is the general warranty deed. In such a deed, the seller normally makes the following three guarantees or covenants:

1. The seller possesses a legally recognizable title to the property conveyed. This is known as the covenant of seizin.
2. There are no encumbrances against the title other than those stated therein. This is the covenant against encumbrances.
3. The seller will protect the grantee against persons claiming to have superior title to the conveyed property. This is the covenant for quiet enjoyment.

The buyer must keep in mind that the seller's guarantees are worthless when the seller is financially irresponsible, but they do provide grounds for legal action when the buyer finds that a good title did not pass, when unknown encumbrances arise, or when claims are made against the property. Aside from this margin of protection, the guarantees in a warranty deed give the buyer a feeling of security in the transaction.

A quitclaim deed passes the seller's ownership rights to the buyer without guarantees. Buyers are, and should be, suspect of such deeds. They are definitely meant to be advantageous to sellers. However, they are used frequently in situations where partial ownership rights are involved. A woman who possesses dower right in a parcel of real estate sold by her husband might be willing to sign a quitclaim deed after the sale in order that the buyer can pass unencumbered title to other parties. Heirs of former owners of property who might wish to bring

FIGURE 9–6

Form 10–8

——————————————————————
——————————————————————

===== BRANCH OFFICE

WARRANTY DEED

STATE OF   COUNTY OF

THIS INDENTURE, Made the   day of   , in the year
one thousand nine hundred   , between

of the County of   , and State of Georgia, as party or parties of the
first part, hereinafter called Grantor, and

as party or parties of the second part, hereinafter called Grantee (the words "Grantor" and
"Grantee" to include their respective heirs, successors and assigns where the context requires or
permits).

WITNESSETH that: Grantor, for and in consideration of the sum of
(   ) DOLLARS
in hand paid at and before the sealing and delivery of these presents, the receipt whereof is hereby
acknowledged, has granted, bargained, sold, aliened, conveyed and confirmed, and by these presents
does grant, bargain, sell, alien, convey and confirm unto the said Grantee,

TO HAVE AND TO HOLD the said tract or parcel of land, with all and singular the rights,
members and appurtenances thereof, to the same being, belonging, or in anywise appertaining, to the
only proper use, benefit and behoof of the said Grantee forever in FEE SIMPLE.

AND THE SAID Grantor will warrant and forever defend the right and title to the above
described property unto the said Grantee against the claims of all persons whomsoever.

IN WITNESS WHEREOF, the Grantor has signed and sealed this deed, the day and year above
written.

Signed, sealed and delivered in presence of:

_____   _____(Seal)

_____   _____(Seal)

_____   _____(Seal)

claims against the property due to slight legal technicalities in title transfer will often sign a quitclaim deed for a price. Many nuisance situations of this type arise, and the quitclaim deed is an effective means of handling them.

A third type of deed, the deed of bargain and sale, is worded in a manner that the land itself is said to be conveyed rather than the ownership interest therein. A fine line of distinction exists between the deed of bargain and sale and the other two forms, but there are times when a seller wishes to convey ownership without warranties but also without using the quitclaim deed which a buyer might not accept. Corporations frequently use the deed of bargain and sale to effect such an arrangement.

The special warranty deed is one in which grantors covenant only against claims arising from the time during which they owned the property. It is typically used when title has an old encumbrance that cannot be cured but is not expected to create a difficulty for subsequent purchasers.

Officer's deeds are used in conjunction with mortgage foreclosure sales and to convey tax titles. They record transfers from a public official to an auction purchaser, with the ownership rights of the foreclosed owner being cut off after a stated redemption period. No warranties are made.

Regardless of which type of deed is employed, the following requirements must be met.

1. There must be a grantor, and the grantor's legal name must appear in the body of the deed. The grantor must be of full age and sound mind and must be acting without duress.
2. There must be a grantee. The deed must state to whom the property is to be conveyed.
3. Words of conveyance must be included from grantor to grantee.
4. A description of the conveyed property that is adequate to permit identification is needed.
5. There must be a statement of consideration—that is, something to be paid in exchange for the real estate. The amount paid for the property may not need to be stated, the usual consideration being "one dollar plus other valuable consideration." Some states, for example, Nebraska, require the exact amount to be stipulated.
6. The grantor must sign the deed, and in some states must affix a seal. The grantee is not required to sign or seal, although it is usually customary to do so.
7. The deed must be delivered to the grantee. Further, delivery must be accomplished in a manner that the grantor and grantee have a

meeting of minds that the transaction is consummated. Improper delivery, such as when the grantee picks up the deed from the grantor's secretary without the grantor's knowledge, does not result in a valid transaction.

The above list represents the absolute minimum requirements for a valid deed. Some states also require that the deed be dated, witnessed, and acknowledged, and the parties involved may agree that it should contain warranties of title and statements of encumbrances. The investor should note that the law offers only partial protection in deed transactions; the investor must make an individual effort to bring out the warranties and statement of debts or liens.

A final requirement to have a deed recorded is that it must contain an adequate number of state (or county) revenue stamps where required. A federal tax formerly was imposed on all deeds conveying real estate, except in the case of gifts or other transactions where there was no monetary consideration. Federal revenue stamps are not required on deeds recorded after December 31, 1967, but a number of state governments require state revenue stamps. Georgia, for example, requires stamps at the rate of 10 cents per $100 valuation on all deeds recorded after January 1, 1968.

A few essentials on deeds can save the investor many legal problems.

1. The investor should always sign his or her full legal name (middle initial is satisfactory). The other party to the contract should do the same.
2. Words, phrases, or clauses that are uncertain, unneeded, or ambiguous should not be used. Many phrases which sound very legal and impressive do not further the purpose of the deed and can raise legal questions.
3. A deed form that is recognized by the state in which the real estate is located must be used. Ownership rests in the state containing the property, rather than the owner's state of residence (where different), and variations in state laws can affect the validity of the deed.

Searching title

A deed conveys title, but it can convey a bad title as well as a good one. The investor seeks a good title in every transaction, as evidenced by one of the following: (a) abstract or certificate of title; (b) title insurance policy; (c) Torrens certificate.

Abstract and attorney's opinion. The most common evidence of title in the United States is the *abstract* and *attorney's opinion.* An abstract is a summary of all deeds, liens, land contracts, or any other recorded instruments that may affect ownership. If lost or destroyed, it can be replaced by a new abstract or a title insurance policy. Many abstracts are lengthy when a property has changed hands frequently, but fortunately, the attorney who traces title can update it from the last transfer and review earlier documents effectively in a short period of time. An opinion is then expressed as to the probability that the buyer will encounter claims against the property. This opinion is not legally binding against the attorney unless the research was negligent. However, an expert researcher's opinion is usually quite reliable, especially when the property has changed hands infrequently and is purchased from a person who has owned it for a long period of time.

Title insurance. Investors will usually find that lending institutions require that they be provided with a title insurance policy which protects their interests against most possible claims. The mortgagee policy does not protect the investors' equity in the property, but the owners can obtain a separate equity policy at a cost lower than that of the mortgagee's policy. The title insurance company searches the title through the abstract and the public records, granting a policy only when the probability is low that the company will have to pay a claim. If a policy is issued, a single premium is charged to the property buyer at the initiation of coverage. After that time, the insurance company handles any claims or lawsuits relating to title.

Torrens certificate. The Torrens certificate involves a formal land registration approach to title verification. A list of persons can be developed from the abstract who could have an interest in the property. This list is submitted to a county registrar of Torrens certificates with an application for a certificate. The application serves as a lawsuit against those named on the list, requiring them to contest any claims they might have to prevent issuance of the certificate. The registrar also publishes the application in local newspapers, advertising for claims against the property. If no claims arise, a certificate is issued declaring the applicant to be the owner of the land. Declared owners need have little worry about future claims after this procedure has been followed, but the owner must defend him or herself if one should arise. Indemnity funds are provided by counties for paying claims, but these accumulated funds are often insufficient to provide complete indemnity.

The Torrens certificate is an inexpensive means of obtaining freedom from fear as to title claims, but it is a time-consuming and complicated procedure. Future transfers require both a deed passage and a certificate transfer, thereby adding further complications. For these reasons, and because (a) covered property cannot be removed from the system without court permission and (b) the system has not been tested for constitutional validity, Torrens certificates are not widely employed.

Securing funds

Owners of real estate can normally earn a higher return on invested dollars by borrowing a high percentage of value from professional lenders at a fixed interest rate than they can by providing 100 percent financing. Thus, most transactions involve debt financing. Two closely related agreements are typically involved in this process: one in which the owner borrows the needed funds, while the other pledges the real estate as collateral for the obligation. The first is evidenced by a note, the latter by a mortgage.

The note. The promissory note is a formal, written acknowledgment of a debt. Matters relating to the amount of the debt, the rate of interest to be paid, manner of repayment, and the conditions which constitute default are considered in the note. An example of a promissory note is shown in Figure 9–7. The mortgaged property is usually referred to in the note to cross-reference the note and the mortgage.

Mortgage loans can be classified by manner of repayment. The "norm" today is the *fully amortized loan* in which payments are made each month and interest computed on the outstanding balance at the end of the month. This is an alternative to a *straight-term loan,* in which no payments are made until the due date, or to the *partially amortized loan,* in which some payments are made periodically and a large payment is made at the end of the term. The partial amortization form has been abused substantially. Unscrupulous lenders in the past would establish a low monthly payment level with an unexpected "balloon" payment at the end. This practice is not permitted to most lenders today on long-term mortgage loans.

Investors should familiarize themselves with four clauses that are frequently found in the mortgage indenture. First, lenders normally insist upon an *acceleration clause* which makes the entire debt due and payable upon default (default being defined in the agreement). Without the acceleration feature, the lender would have to bring a separate lawsuit for each payment missed during the life of the debt. This is a reasonable feature that should not be objectionable to the investor.

The second common clause is the *prepayment clause.* Unless a statement is made in the note that the debtors are entitled to pay more than the scheduled payment in any period, they are not entitled to prepay. Prepayment is a matter of contract—not an inherent right. The prepayment clause states the manner in which prepayment is permitted, usually specifying (*a*) whether a penalty is to be charged by the lender, (*b*) whether extra payments directly reduce the principal upon which interest is computed or serve to eliminate the final payment, and (*c*) whether the size of extra payments or the number of extra payments per

FIGURE 9-7
Promissory note

The Citizens & Southern National Bank

ATLANTA, GA., _____ 19____ $ _____

_____ AFTER DATE, THE UNDERSIGNED PROMISES TO PAY TO THE ORDER OF

The Citizens & Southern National Bank (HEREAFTER, TOGETHER WITH ANY HOLDER HEREOF, CALLED "HOLDER"), AT ATLANTA, GEORGIA, OR AT SUCH OTHER PLACE AS THE HOLDER MAY DESIGNATE AND NOTIFY UNDERSIGNED.

_____ **DOLLARS**

with interest from date until maturity at _____ per cent per annum, and with interest after maturity until paid at eight per cent (8%) per annum, together with all costs of collection, including fifteen per cent (15%) of the principal and interest as attorney's fees if collected by law or through an attorney at law. To secure the payment of this Note and all other indebtedness or liability of the undersigned to Holder, however and whenever incurred or evidenced, whether direct or indirect, absolute or contingent, or due or to become due (hereafter with this Note, collectively called "Liabilities"), undersigned transfers and conveys to Holder any and all balances, credits, deposits, accounts, items and monies of the undersigned now or hereafter with the Holder, and the undersigned agrees that the Holder shall have a lien upon, security title to and a security interest in all property of the undersigned of every kind and description now or hereafter in the possession or control of the Holder for any reason, including all dividends and distributions on or other rights in connection therewith.

In the event of nonpayment when due of any amount payable on any of Liabilities, or if the Holder shall feel insecure for any reason whatsoever (1) any and all of Liabilities may, at the option of Holder and without demand or notice of any kind, be declared and thereupon immediately shall become due and payable, (2) the Holder may exercise from time to time any of the rights and remedies available to Holder under the Uniform Commercial Code as in effect at that time in Georgia, or otherwise available to Holder and (3) the Holder may, at any time, without demand or notice of any kind, appropriate and apply toward the payment of such of Liabilities, and in such order of application as the Holder may from time to time elect, any balances, credits, deposits, accounts, items or monies of the undersigned with the Holder.

Undersigned transfers, assigns and conveys to the Holder a sufficient amount of homestead and exemption which undersigned or undersigned's family may have under or by virtue of the Constitution or laws of Georgia or any other State of the United States as against Liabilities and to pay them. In case of bankruptcy, undersigned authorizes and directs the Trustee to deliver to the Holder a sufficient amount of property or money claimed as exempt to pay Liabilities and the Holder is appointed attorney in fact for undersigned to claim any and all homestead exemptions allowed by law.

If more than one party shall execute this Note, the term undersigned as used herein shall mean all parties signing this Note and each of them, who shall be jointly and severally obligated hereunder.

Given under the hand and seal of each of the undersigned.

DUE _____ NO. _____

ADDRESS _____

TELEPHONE NO. _____

_____ (SEAL)

_____ (SEAL)

CREDIT LIFE INSURANCE

DATE OF BIRTH OF
PERSON TO BE INSURED

15-542 NOTE REV. 1-64

year are restricted. Some lenders, such as life insurance companies, wish to place their funds for the maximum length of time possible, and they frequently impose a penalty for higher-than-agreed-upon payments during the first few years. Savings and loan associations and commercial banks, on the other hand, encourage prepayment by subtracting all principal payments from the outstanding balance upon which they compute interest. Thus, the policies of lending institutions vary with regard to prepayment. Investors should select that lender whose prepayment policy agrees with the investors' most optimistic repayment schedule.

The third clause to be considered is the *cognovit*, or confession of judgment, clause. This clause authorizes any attorney at law to obtain from the court a judgment lien against the debtor. The debtor gives up a "day in court," even in situations when he or she might have valid grounds for contesting the creditor's claims. The cognovit clause can be abused easily by unscrupulous lenders, and few states uphold it. However, in those states that consider it valid, it is used widely and the investor may be forced to accept it if financing is to be obtained.

Notes may also contain an *escalator clause* that permits the lender to vary the interest rate as money market conditions change. If the rate of interest in the current market increases, the rate charged on the specific loan would increase. If the going rate falls, the rate on the specific loan falls. This arrangement is rarely employed today. A similar plan that is used when rates must be fixed calls for the establishment of a high stated rate, representing the maximum the lender expects to charge under adverse conditions. The going rate is then charged as long as it is lower than the stated rate.

Another variant of the escalator clause is the variable rate mortgage. It *requires* the interest rate to vary according to a previously specified index of interest rates. The rate is adjusted upward or downward by (*a*) increasing or decreasing the loan's maturity and/or (*b*) increasing or decreasing the monthly payment.

The mortgage. A mortgage is written evidence of the right of a creditor to have property of a debtor sold upon default of the debt. This right, or lien, is exercised through the judicial system under modern law, with the creditor requesting that a court foreclose the property, sell it at sheriff's auction sale, and apply the proceeds toward repayment of the debt. A deed to secure debt is shown in Figure 9–8. The debtor is permitted to correct a default prior to the sheriff's sale, a privilege known as the right or equity of redemption. In some states, an additional period after the sale is permitted, known as the statutory redemption period.

The various states are classified as *title theory* or *lien theory* states in the format of mortgages, a distinction which years ago determined

FIGURE 9–8

BRANCH OFFICE

DEED TO SECURE DEBT

STATE OF

County.

THIS INDENTURE, Made the   day of   ,in the year
one thousand nine hundred   , between

of the County of   , and State of   , as party or parties of
the first part, hereinafter called Grantor, and

as party of the second part, hereinafter called Grantee
WITNESSETH, That Grantor, for the consideration hereinafter set forth, in hand paid at and
before the sealing and delivery of these presents, the receipt whereof is hereby acknowledged, has
granted, bargained, sold, aliened, conveyed and confirmed, and by these presents does grant, bargain, sell, alien, convey and confirm unto the said Grantee, all that tract or parcel of land lying and
being in

THIS CONVEYANCE is made under the provisions of the existing Code of the State of Georgia
to secure a debt (and interest thereon and other indebtedness as described herein) evidenced by
                    note   dated   made by Grantor to order of Grantee, for
the principal sum of   ($) Dollars

FIGURE 9–8 (*continued*)

The title, interest, rights and powers granted herein by Grantor to Grantee, particularly the power of sale granted herein, shall inure to the benefit of anyone to whom Grantee shall assign the indebtedness herein secured, and/or convey the property herein described, as well as to the successors and legal representatives of Grantee.

In case the debt hereby secured shall not be paid when it becomes due by maturity in due course, or by reason of a default as herein provided, Grantor hereby grants to Grantee, the following irrevocable power of attorney: To sell all or any part of the said property at auction, at the usual place for conducting sales at the Court House in the County where the land or any part thereof lies, in said State, to the highest bidder for cash, after advertising the time, terms and place of such sale once a week for four weeks immediately preceding such sale (but without regard to the number of days) in a newspaper published in the County where the land or any part thereof lies, or in the paper in which the Sheriff's advertisements for such County are published, all other notice being hereby waived by Grantor, and Grantee (or any person on behalf of Grantee) may bid and purchase at such sale and thereupon execute and deliver to the purchaser or purchasers at such sale a sufficient conveyance of said property in fee simple, which conveyance may contain recitals as to the happening of the default upon which the execution of the power of sale herein granted depends, and Grantor hereby constitutes and appoints Grantee the agent and attorney in fact of Grantor to make such recitals, and hereby covenants and agrees that the recitals so made by Grantee shall be binding and conclusive upon Grantor, and that the conveyance to be made by Grantee shall be effectual to bar equity of redemption of Grantor in and to said property, and Grantee shall collect the proceeds of such sale, and after reserving therefrom the entire amount of principal and interest due, together with the amount of taxes, assessments and premiums of insurance or other payments theretofore paid by Grantee, with eight per centum per annum thereon from date of payment, together with all costs and expenses of sale and ten per centum of the aggregate amount due for attorney's fees, shall pay any over-plus to Grantor as provided by law.

AND Grantor further covenants that in case of a sale as hereinbefore provided, Grantor, or any person in possession under Grantor, shall then become and be tenants holding over and shall forthwith deliver possession to the purchaser at such sale, or be summarily dispossessed, in accordance with the provisions of law applicable to tenants holding over.

The power and agency hereby granted are coupled with an interest and are irrevocable by death or otherwise and are granted as cumulative to the remedies for collection of said indebtedness provided by law.

It is agreed that the Grantee shall be subrogated to the claims and liens of all parties whose claims or liens are discharged or paid with the proceeds of the loan secured hereby.

Whenever the terms "Grantor" or "Grantee" are used in this deed such terms shall be deemed to include the heirs, administrators, executors, successors and assigns of said parties. All rights and powers herein granted to the Grantee shall inure to and include his, her or its heirs, administrators, executors, successors and assigns, and all obligations herein imposed on the Grantor shall extend to and include Grantor's heirs, administrators, executors, successors and assigns.

IN WITNESS WHEREOF, Grantor has caused this instrument to be executed and sealed the day and year first above written.

Signed, sealed and delivered in the presence of

(L. S.)

(UNOFFICIAL WITNESS)

(L. S.)

NOTARY PUBLIC

(L. S.)

FORM L2 5M

whether or not the creditor, or mortgagee, could assume possession of the mortgaged property without formal foreclosure proceedings. Title theory states held that the mortgage is an actual passage of title to the mortgagee, and that the mortgagee, as actual owner, could assume possession whenever a default occurred. Lien theory states reasoned that the mortgage passes only equitable title, requiring proper foreclosure. Obviously, a strict interpretation of the title theory can create unjust situations. Property owners who mortgage their property do not intend to transfer ownership for any purpose other than to secure a debt, and the owners should not be subject to ejectment from the premises when a minor default occurs.

One of three approaches has been taken by nearly every title theory state (for example, Alabama, Maine, Maryland, and Tennessee) to eliminate inequities. A few states have adopted an intermediate title theory (Illinois, New Jersey, North Carolina, and Ohio, for example) which requires foreclosure proceedings, but which permits the mortgagee to assume possession of the property between the time of the debtor's default and the time of the sheriff's sale. This protects mortgagees against waste that might be committed by the mortgagors who know that foreclosure is in process and that they are to be removed soon, and it protects the mortgagors from removal without due process of law. A similar alternative used mainly in California (not a title theory state) is to employ a *trust deed in the nature of a mortgage*. The owner conveys a contingent title to a trustee who holds it as security for the lender. The trustee is empowered to sell the property if the debtor defaults.

The third means of tempering the effects of the title theory is for the courts of the title theory states to hold that foreclosure proceedings must be followed in the same manner as the lien theory states. This equates the title theory and the lien theory except for the formal wording on documents. Currently, fewer than 20 states follow the title theory, with all others following the lien theory.

Regardless of which theory is followed, a mortgage is terminated when the debt which created it is satisfied. In addition nearly all mortgages contain a provision known as a *defeasance clause* stating that the mortgagee cannot foreclose so long as the debtor upholds the conditions of the mortgage.

A mortgage conveys an interest in real estate, so it must be in writing to be enforceable. This writing must meet most of the requirements of a valid deed,[6] except that the statement of consideration might be a reference to a separate document, the note, that evidences the debt which caused the mortgage lien to arise. The mortgage itself is a *lien*— not evidence of a debt.

---

[6] Deed requirements are discussed on pp. 206–7 of this chapter.

The owners or buyers of a parcel of real estate might find that one lender will not provide as great a sum of money as is needed to acquire or retain ownership. The major lender demands a first lien on the property, that is, the right to be paid before others if foreclosure becomes necessary, but the owners may be able to obtain additional funds from others on a second or third lien basis if their credit rating is favorable. These lower level liens are called "junior mortgages." A junior mortgage is usually a second mortgage having only one senior lien existing at the time it is created. However, tax liens, mechanics liens, or other liens can demand priority over existing senior or junior mortgages, thereby reducing the second mortgage to third or fourth lien priority. If the first mortgage is paid off, the second mortgage automatically achieves top priority.

The only time priority of liens becomes important is when the mortgagor is in financial difficulty. The importance of priority cannot be overemphasized at that time because the debt may have to be satisfied by selling the property. There are several instances where priority planning is important to the investor.

1. One instance is when investors own land and are asked by a developer to accept a purchase money mortgage that is subordinated in lien to future construction loans. The investors are more concerned about their roles as investors than as creditors in this case, since they are willing to grant a first priority lien to the lenders who supply cash for improvements even though they are entitled to the first lien themselves.

2. Another instance might be when investors are buying on land contract and the seller wishes to borrow against the property deed. Investors must agree (in writing) to subordinate their equitable title to the claims of the new lender if the seller is to succeed in getting the money desired.

3. When borrowers have a second mortgage and they wish to renegotiate with the first mortgage lender for a larger sum is another instance. The first mortgage lender wishes to retain a first lien basis on all sums loaned, yet the existing second mortgagee would have rights that are prior to additional loans. To avoid this situation, some lenders have promoted the "open-end" mortgage that permits several sums to be loaned at different times on a first lien basis.

Second mortgages can be employed profitably by investors in two ways. First, these mortgages can often be purchased at a price that provides an attractive yield. Extreme caution must be exercised by an investor in selecting lenders and properties, but the rates of interest can run as high as three times the first mortgage rate. Second, an investor might wish to become a second mortgage debtor in periods of tight mortgage money to provide a large downpayment that would secure the best possible interest rates. A second mortgage obtained from family or friends can provide this downpayment, usually at rates low enough to make that dual borrowing operation worthwhile. Second mortgage borrowing from most professional second mortgage lenders should be avoided whenever possible, however, due to its prohibitively high cost.

Mortgages are usually liens against fee ownership interests, but many interests are mortgageable. Long-term leaseholds are frequently mortgaged in commercial properties. Mineral rights, air rights, and life estate interests also may have mortgaging possibilities. If the owner can establish a verifiable value in ownership, he or she likely would be able to borrow against it.

Mortgage by purpose. Mortgage forms have been devised to accomplish many purposes. Subdividers of large tracts employ a "blanket" mortgage on the entire tract which permits small portions of the land to be paid off, released from the mortgage, and sold. The lender usually requires that an amount greater than the pro rata share be paid to secure the release, but the ability to retain financing until lots are sold makes the blanket mortgage ideal.

Financial institutions offer homeowners a "package" mortgage secured both by real estate and certain home equipment items such as a range, refrigerator, dishwasher, and air conditioner. Low real estate mortgage interest rates apply to the appliances as well as the real estate, and lenders are able to increase the sum of money invested profitably with no additional lending costs and little additional risk.

As mentioned above, lenders also offer an open-end mortgage which permits additional sums to be lent on a single mortgage. This insures a safe priority position for the lender, and it permits the homeowner to obtain low-cost financing for improvements and replacements.

Participation mortgage. During periods of high interest rates, a conflict sometimes occurs between returns required by lenders and state usury laws, which state the ceiling interest rate that an individual may legally pay. Constant annual loan payments as high as 11.5 percent of the original loan balance are not uncommon, and many borrowers compete for funds regardless of the high interest rates. However, few investors could afford to pay fixed mortgage cost at these high levels, and lenders have devised plans wherein a lower fixed rate of interest is charged on money advanced, accompanied by a percentage of gross or net income. This is a participation mortgage arrangement.

In the most widely used form of participation mortgage the lenders receive their normal loan amortization payment plus a small percentage of gross income in excess of a stated amount. The stated amount is usually the current gross income level, and the excess represents inflation in rents after the loan is made. This permits the lenders to realize a satisfactory return on current rentals and an increasing return as rents go up.

Mortgage loans that call for a percentage of net income offer the lenders the highest possible return potential. However, this provision is unpopular with borrowers, and it is used only in periods of tight money.

Conventional, insured, and guaranteed mortgages. The majority of mortgages today are conventional, that is, they are agreements between borrower and lender in which only the borrower's credit worthiness and property as collateral support the obligation to pay. Lenders prefer conventional mortgages for these reasons: (*a*) they can impose their own individual requirements upon borrowers and properties, thereby permitting individualized programs that best meet the needs of both parties; (*b*) they are not required to submit reports to insuring or guaranteeing institutions that increase costs of administration; and (*c*) they do not have to charge discount points, that is, charges necessary to increase yields from rates fixed by insuring and guaranteeing institutions to competitive market rates. Discount points are required for conventional mortgages only in those states such as New York, Delaware, and Maryland in which state usury rates are so low that competitive market rates may exceed them. Georgia, for example, does not permit mortgage lenders to charge more than 9 percent interest, thereby requiring lenders to "discount" loans when competitive rates exceed that figure.

The Federal Housing Administration insures mortgage loans against lender default by agreeing to compensate lenders against losses resulting from forced foreclosure sales. A charge of 0.5 percent per annum is made against the borrower for the privilege of obtaining FHA insurance. Property values covered by this insurance vary between $15,000 and $45,000, depending upon money market conditions. The FHA exercises substantial control over both borrowers and properties, maintaining strict loan-to-income restrictions and construction requirements. These restrictions and requirements vary slightly as market conditions change, but they are enforced strictly at all times.

The borrower derives one basic advantage from FHA insurance; lenders will loan a higher percentage of appraised value with the insurance than under conventional terms, running as high as 97 percent for some properties. It is true that the lender cannot charge more than the maximum interest permitted by the FHA, which varies with market conditions, and the borrower is not permitted to pay the discount points that arise in periods of high conventional interest rates. However, sellers of properties that qualify for FHA financing normally increase their selling price to include these charges.

The Veterans Administration offers qualified veterans a guarantee program that is, in effect, a loan cosigned by the government. No premium charge is made, however, and requirements imposed upon borrowers and properties are less severe. Upon default, the VA will pay up to $17,500 of any loss incurred by the lender. Many VA loans are 100 percent of the selling prices, with the borrowers paying only the loan closing costs. An eligible veteran is normally entitled to only one VA loan, although in some cases the loan may be transferred to another eligible veteran in a manner that the original borrower's VA right is restored.

Transferring partial ownership rights

The investor might arrange with the owner of a selected parcel of real estate to obtain only partial ownership rights. Those who desire mineral rights, air rights, or surface-use rights might find leasing arrangements more advantageous than fee simple ownership. Leases permit minimal capital investment and tax deductibility of the rental payments. Leases can be established in any manner desired by the parties. Short-term oral leases are enforced by law in most states.

Typical lease contents. Long-term leases must be in writing to be enforced, and agreement must normally be reached on all the following matters to protect the parties against unforeseen contingencies:

1. Repairs and landlord's right to enter. Any obligation imposed upon the landlord to repair and maintain the property must be accompanied by a statement of his or her right to enter. Landlords normally would like to be able to inspect the property for damage or excess wear and would designate certain times that they may be permitted to do so.
2. Use and care of the premises.
3. Payment of taxes, utilities, and insurance premiums. Related to this is a statement of insurable interests of the parties.
4. Construction of buildings and changes of improvements.
5. Assignments of the lease or subletting by the lessee-tenant.
6. Subordination of the lessee's lien rights to subsequent mortgages obtained by the fee owner or lessor. The lessee jeopardizes his or her rights upon mortgage default, but this clause may be required by the lessor. Otherwise, it is disadvantageous to the lessee.
7. Right of the lessee to mortgage his or her leasehold interest.
8. Restrictions prohibiting objectionable occupancy or illegal activities.
9. Requirement that municipal ordinances be obeyed.
10. Rights of the parties in the event that one of them enters bankruptcy or that the property is condemned.
11. Rights and penalties if liens arise or waste is incurred.
12. Rights of the parties regarding termination, public use condemnation, renewal, or purchase by lessee. Arbitration procedures should be established to protect against disagreements regarding renewals.

These requirements are representative of the many different problems that may be considered. Most lease situations are unique; therefore, each lease is usually a highly individualized document.

Lease payment plans. Lease payment plans are generally one of three types:

1. *Flat lease.* Constant monthly, quarterly, or annual payments are made during the life of the lease.
2. *Graduated lease, graded lease, or step-up lease.* A formula is established regarding the rental to be paid during the first five years, the second five years, and so on.
3. *Reappraisal lease.* A procedure is stated for reviewing and adjusting rentals at fixed intervals.

A lease may also be gross, in which the lessor, or fee owner, pays taxes, insurance premiums, and upkeep, or net, in which the lessee, or tenant, pays these costs.

Specialized leasing arrangements. Leases are frequently designed to accommodate sale-and-leaseback arrangements, large land purchases through lease and release, and long-term ground leases when sales cannot be effected by law. Sale-and-leaseback arrangements permit property owners to sell without sacrificing possession, thereby releasing funds for other purposes. Lease rentals are fully tax deductible on income-producing property when the property is transferred irrevocably, while building depreciation is expensable when the property is owned.

Land developers normally find that many thousands of dollars are needed to acquire a tract of land and make the minimum improvements necessary to sell or build upon the land. One means of minimizing the land investment employed by residential subdividers is to lease a large parcel of land with a provision in the lease that individual lots will be released from the lease and sold as buyers are found. Subdividers act as intermediaries insofar as transfers go, but they pay more than 100 percent of the agreed-upon price for lots until they pay off the entire parcel. Their leases establish the price of both the entire parcel and the individual lots, and they make a profit on all revenues in excess of their original cost.

Long-term ground leases are employed in lieu of land sales in many Eastern states and in Indian lands that by law cannot be sold. Ground leases must be extremely precise and irrevocable when they are used to acquire land upon which expensive improvements are to be placed. They are usually drawn for 21 or 99 years with a "renewable forever" clause being common. State laws vary the form of these leases, the "Baltimore" and "Pennsylvania" systems being most common, but the long-term and irrevocability features are contained in all.

Minimizing equity investment: The land contract

Many real estate transactions are consummated in a manner that the sellers are called upon to wait for their money for a substantial period of time. The sellers might accept a second mortgage, or they might prefer a land contract for deed. Under the latter plan, the sellers retain title until a substantial portion of the purchase price, frequently 50 percent to 75 percent, is paid by the buyers. The price paid under land contract is usually higher than the cash price. In addition, the sellers can often obtain an installment sale[7] arrangement in which taxable profits are recognized in small amounts over many years.

The land contract must incorporate all of the provisions of a mortgage-note combination. In addition, the seller and buyer must work out agreements regarding:

1. Time of passing of title.

2. Whether or not the land contract is to be recorded. The seller would prefer not to record the contract, but the buyer's interest is protected by doing so.

3. Whether or not the deed is to be placed in escrow during the land contract period. The seller cannot dispose of the property easily when the deed is in escrow; an additional measure of protection is thereby added for the buyer.

4. The extent to which the seller may mortgage the property during the land contract period. The buyer can be in a dilemma if the contract is paid off, but the seller has a large mortgage against the property that cannot be retired. As a general rule, the land contract agreement should not permit the mortgage debt to exceed the amount owed by the buyer to the seller. The buyer should also retain the right to approve any new loans against the property.

5. Buyers' and sellers' rights in the event of rescision or forfeiture of the contract. Sellers would wish to retain payments made by buyers in the event of default and rescind the buyers' interest. Conversely, buyers would like to be able to forfeit their rights at will and walk away from the project if it should turn out to be unproductive. A mutually satisfactory balance of the two forces should be developed.

The land contract is an expert land speculator's tool. It requires a high degree of specialized knowledge, and investors who use this tool must feel that every agreement must be strongly in their favor. Investors will usually have to negotiate with sellers on such items as interest rates, recording, escrows, and mortgages, and they must be able to hold firm to forfeiture rights and other essential clauses while convincing sellers of the desirability of some other aspects of the contract —usually the interest rate and selling price.

---

[7] See Chapter 10 for installment sale rule.

Selling the property

One who wishes to sell a real estate holding frequently lists the property with a real estate broker. A listing contract is an agreement between a real estate broker and individuals who plan to sell a property stipulating the price to be asked for the property, the amount (usually a percentage of the selling price) the broker is to receive for finding a buyer, and the length of duration of the agreement. There are three basic types of listing contracts: (*a*) open listing, (*b*) exclusive listing, and (*c*) exclusive right to sell. A fourth type, net listing, is mentioned frequently in the literature but is frowned upon in practice, and a fifth, multiple listing, is a subtype of the exclusive right to sell contract.

Open listing. The open listing contract is one which permits the seller to grant a similar contract to all brokers who will accept. No broker has an exclusive right to sell, and the first broker to produce an acceptable offer for the property is entitled to the commission. All others get nothing. If the owner sells the property without the help of a broker, no commission is paid.

Open listings require a minimum commitment by the seller, but they rarely occur because few brokers will accept them. In most cases, the broker must cultivate potential buyers for days or even weeks to convince them to buy. With an open listing, the broker might find the buyer just after another broker effected the sale. One might say that open listings "keep brokers honest," but the rationale for brokers not accepting such contracts is strong.

Exclusive agency listing. In an exclusive listing, the seller hires only one broker but retains the right to sell the property through his or her own efforts without paying a commission. Even if another broker sells the property, the broker holding the exclusive listing is entitled to a commission. This type of contract is more common than an open listing, but brokers are somewhat reluctant to accept a contract when they must compete with the seller.

Exclusive right to sell. The contract type which grants the major legal advantage to the broker is the exclusive right to sell. Regardless of who sells the property—owner included—the broker with an exclusive right to sell listing is entitled to receive the commission (see Figure 9–9). Obviously, brokers prefer the exclusive right to sell listing arrangement, and sellers are frequently satisfied to accept it, particularly after they have failed to sell their properties through their own efforts. Under this contract type, the broker can proceed in obtaining contacts without fear of being too late to make the sale.

Net listing. The net listing contract is one in which the seller specifies a price desired from the sale, and the broker keeps everything in excess of that amount. Obviously, this would encourage brokers to at-

FIGURE 9–9

Address	Rooms	Bdrms	Baths	Suburb	Price

C. A. BAKER
REAL ESTATE

PHONE SY 8-8000
CHICAGO PHONE PU 5-0760
18661 DIXIE HIGHWAY
HOMEWOOD, ILLINOIS

				REMARKS
Type property		Carpeting		
Construction		Draperies		
Lot size		Ven. blinds		
Taxes		Fireplace		
Age-Condition		Tiled bath		
Why selling		Tiled kitchen		
Possession		Dishwasher		
Foundation		Disposal		
Basement		Softener		
Utility Rm.		Exhaust	**ROOMS**	**SIZE-1st FLOOR**
Floors		Built in	Living room	
Walls		Air cond.	Dining room	
Heat		Storm win.	Kitchen	
Water Heater		Screens	Cabinet	
Garage		TV antenna	Family room	
Rec. Rm.		Fenced yard	Baths	
Patio		Storm sewer	Bedroom	
Porch		San. sewer	Bedroom	
Catholic school		Septic tank	Bedroom	
Churches		Gas		**SIZE-2nd FLOOR**
Public school		Water	Bedroom	
Title		Well	Bedroom	
Sign		Paved street	Bedroom	
Owner		Driveway	Bedroom	
Tenant		No. of closets	Baths	

Information herein is not warranted and subject to change without notice. We assume no liability for errors

FIGURE 9–9 *(continued)*

EXCLUSIVE SALES CONTRACT   PREPARED BY   **NO. 4-S**   MAXIM HIRSCH

COPYRIGHT 1949
UNIVERSITY PRINTING COMPANY
1410 EAST 62ND ST.   CHICAGO

_____, 19____

TO____ _____

     In consideration of your promise to list as of this date and exhibit the realty of the address noted below and in further consideration of your promise to advertise it at your expense for sale ____ ____hereby give you the sole and exclusive right to sell through your efforts or with any brokers cooperating with you the property located at and known as_____

in the City of_____, County of_____,

State of_____, for the period of

_____from the date hereof at a price of $_____

or any less sum that_____may hereafter accept, subject to the incumbrances of record this date in the

amount of $_____, due_____. Terms to be

_____cash and balance payable_____.

    Thereafter this agreement shall automatically renew itself for a like term but may be terminated by either party by personally notifying the other party in writing of such intention 30 days in advance of such intended termination date.

    In the event said property is sold or title conveyed while this agreement is in force by you or the undersigned or anyone else, _____hereby agree to pay you_____% commission in such sale price. In the event said property is sold or title conveyed within 90 days after termination date to any prospective purchaser previously procured through or by you, you shall likewise have earned your commission hereunder.

    You have the privilege of purchasing this property, if you so desire, title to said realty to be conveyed to the name of anyone you may designate.

    _____agree to furnish upon demand, as quickly as possible, satisfactory evidence of title brought down to date of contract with purchaser, and convey title by warranty deed with release of dower and homestead rights, and pay all unpaid installments of special assessments for improvement completed, and pro-rate, on customary basis, taxes, interest and all other items of income and expense to date of delivery of deed.

    _____further agree to protect you by quoting a selling price of $_____and referring all inquiries to you during the time covered hereby.

    It is understood that this agreement is irrevocable during above stated period and that you make no guarantee of sale. You are hereby authorized to advertise the said property "For Sale" and to place a "For Sale" sign on the same.

Accepted:

    C. A. BAKER REAL ESTATE   _____(SEAL)

By_____   _____(SEAL)

---

tempt to establish low net prices for sellers, and it would encourage them to inflate prices. Thus, sellers would tend to become dissatisfied with the arrangement, and a few unscrupulous brokers would give the brokerage profession a bad name.

    Multiple listing. One arrangement that has been very satisfactory for sellers, buyers, and brokers is the multiple listing in which the seller grants an exclusive right to sell listing to a broker who agrees to put the property in a pool operated by an organized group of brokers. All of the brokers work to sell the property, and all or part of the commission is shared by the participating members of the group. Sellers find the multiple listing advantageous because the prospective buyers being serviced by several brokers become potential buyers for the subject property. Brokers find that a rapid turnover of properties brings in more business and promotes greater profit and greater efficiency than is possible through individual operation. However, the multiple listing concept does have two problems which keep it from being used more widely: (*a*) some brokers tend to rely upon their coparticipants to bring in most or all of the listings and (*b*) some brokers withhold choice listings for their individual sale. The latter problem can be quite serious; "vest-pocket" listings can dissolve a multiple listing arrangement very quickly. The first problem can also cause serious difficulties with the multiple listing service and particularly in small organizations may ultimately cause its downfall.

Establishing a reasonable duration for listing contracts is an important problem faced by brokers. Many legal actions have been brought by brokers who introduced a buyer to seller only to find that the two of them conspired to wait until the listing contract terminated so that they could transact a sale without paying a commission. Today, the courts generally hold that a broker is entitled to a commission when one of the following occurs.[8]

1. The deal falls through because owners change their minds and refuse to sign the deed to the purchaser or a contract to sell. The rule is the same when the land has increased in value and the owner rejects the broker's buyer for this reason. If the seller refuses to sign, giving as the reason the fact that the seller has changed his or her mind, the seller cannot thereafter shift ground and claim that the buyer's offer was not in compliance with the listing. *Russell* v. *Ramm*, 200 Cal. 348, 254 Pac. 532.

2. The deal falls through because the owner's wife refuses to sign the contract or deed. *Pliler* v. *Thompson*, 84 Okla. 200, 202 Pac. 1016.

3. The deal falls through because of defects in the owner's title. *Triplett* v. *Feasal*, 105 Kan. 179, 182 Pac. 551.

4. The deal falls through because of the owner's fraud. *Hathaway* v. *Smith*, 187 Ill. App. 128.

5. The deal falls through because the owner is unable to deliver possession within a reasonable time.

6. The deal falls through because seller insists on terms and provisions not mentioned in the listing contract, as where the seller insists on the right to remain in possession after the deal has been closed. *Brown* v. *Ogle* 75 Ind. App. 90, 130 N.E. 147.

7. After the contract of sale has been signed, the seller and buyer get together and cancel the contract. *Steward* v. *Brock* 60 N.M. 216, 290 P. 2d. 682.

Even when there is no reluctance on the part of the seller to pay the broker's commission, a question arises as to the point in time when the commission is earned. In general, the broker has earned a commission

---

[8] Kratovil, *Real Estate Law*, pp. 82–83.

when he or she introduces the seller to a buyer who is ready, willing, and able to buy the property according to the terms specified in the listing. *Ready* and *willing* mean that the buyer wishes to purchase immediately; *able* indicates that the buyer has financial means to acquire the property. A sale need not result from this union of seller and buyer in order for the commission to be earned; the seller must pay the commission even though he or she refuses to consummate the deal (unless the refusal is due to the buyer being other than ready, willing, and able). If the seller and potential buyer both sign a contract of sale but later cancel for any reason, the commission must be paid. This is true even if the *buyer* fails to fulfill the contract, the seller's remedy being to sue the buyer for damages because of breach of contract—the damages being primarily the commission.

To avoid the possibility of paying a commission without the property's being sold, a seller may specify in the listing contract that the broker is entitled to a commission only if the property is sold to a buyer introduced by the broker.[9]

Other functions

Purchasing an option.   An *option* is an agreement between buyer and seller in which the seller agrees to hold an offer open for a specified time and the buyer agrees to pay a sum of money as consideration. No real property ownership rights pass at the time the option is granted. The buyer is merely purchasing the right to buy at a fixed price within a stated period. If the offer is accepted, a purchase contract results. The consideration paid for the option is kept by the seller regardless of the buyer's decision.

Employing an escrow agent.   An escrow operation is one in which a person is asked to serve as a neutral third party to a business transaction. The usual situation is when a banker or other lending institution official is employed to hold a seller's property deed and a buyer's purchase money until the property title is cleared. The third party, referred to as an escrow agent, escrow company, or escrow holder, requires a detailed set of instructions regarding provisions such as when title is to pass, how delivery is to occur, and actions to be taken if impediments of title or other complications arise. Both parties to the business transaction can work together to terminate the escrow arrangement, but neither party can terminate it alone. Since the agreement is legally binding, it should be composed in a manner that little or nothing is subject to interpreta-

---

[9] Under such a provision the buyer may be introduced *indirectly* by the broker, such as when a newspaper advertisement leads to a sale; the broker is still entitled to a commission. Such a provision cannot be specified in an exclusive right to sell listing, however, since the broker gets a commission regardless of who sells the property.

tion by the escrow holder. The instructions should be complete and thorough, and provisions should be made for both parties to reach agreement upon any item of uncertainty.

Exchanging properties. Current tax laws concerning capital gains frequently make it desirable to trade one parcel of real estate for another rather than to effect separate sale and repurchase transactions. Most Realtors have a contract form for this that specifies the exact nature of each property and the manner in which the commission is to be paid. The exchange contract contains most of the aspects of the contract for sale discussed previously in this chapter.

The commission on an exchange is agreed to by all parties to the transaction. The amount is often determined by charging a flat percentage of the exchange value of each property (actually two commissions), although wide variations in practice are found. Most brokers who specialize in selling homes do not operate as intermediaries between two trading parties. In the residential real estate market very few cases arise in which a person wishing to trade a home would desire to trade the home for the exact home which another person wishes to trade. Therefore, the broker acts as a principal for both parties, buying their old homes and selling them new ones. The "pure" exchange arrangement in which the broker does not acquire title to either property is more commonly used in business and investment real estate.

Income tax issues. Income taxes are an especially important consideration in disposing of property ownership. Depreciation methodology, timing of disposition, and manner of disposition (for example, cash sale, installment sale, tax-free exchange, or credit sale) should all be planned with the help of an income tax expert.[10]

SUMMARY

Basic conveyancing functions examined in this chapter include (a) making offers, (b) settlement of property transactions, (c) securing funds, and (d) transferring partial ownership rights. Legal documents are presented, and the important elements of each are discussed. The important point to be made in the chapter is that planning for investment return, income taxation, and liability protection can be the most productive use of time only when the investor achieves skill at conveyancing. He or she must learn to minimize time in activities that facilitate the basic task, and developing skills in conveyancing is the only way to avoid losing a great deal of time in working with deeds, mortgages, contracts, and other documents.

Attorneys can relieve the investor of much of the conveyancing

---

[10] The basic income tax issues of conveyancing are presented in Chapter 10.

burden, but only the investor can evaluate documents in terms of varied objectives. A carefully drawn statement of objectives, coupled with sound ownership and tax planning, should help the investor develop a sound pattern of action to follow in conveyancing.

QUESTIONS FOR REVIEW

1. What is the Statute of Frauds?
2. Identify ten provisions normally covered in an offer for sale.
3. What costs are to be paid by the buyer and the seller in a normal closing statement?
4. What are the basic deed forms?
5. How are titles searched? What evidence of a good title can one obtain?
6. Distinguish clearly between a note and a mortgage.
7. What is a participation mortgage?
8. What is the difference between a VA and an FHA mortgage?
9. Indicate three types of lease payment plans.
10. What is a land contract?
11. What is an option on real estate?
12. Describe the various forms of listing contracts used by real estate brokers.

REFERENCES

Beaton, William R., and Bond, Robert J.   *Real Estate.* Pacific Palisades, Calif.: Goodyear Publishing Co., 1976, chaps. 5, 6, and 7.

Curtis, Clayton C.   *Real Estate for the New Practitioner.* 4th ed. Gainesville, Fla.: B. J. Publishing, 1975, chaps. 3, 4, and 5.

Friedman, Milton R.   *Contracts and Conveyances of Real Property.* New York: Practicing Law Institute, 1972.

Gray, Charles D., and Steinberg, Joseph L.   *Real Estate Sales Contracts: From Preparation Through Closing.* Englewood Cliffs, N.J.: Prentice-Hall, 1970.

Harvey, David C. B.   *Harvey Law of Real Property Title and Closing.* New York: Clark Boardman Co., 1972, 3 vols. ·

Kratovil, Robert.   *Real Estate Law.* 6th ed. Englewood Cliffs, N.J.: Prentice-Hall, 1974.

Lusk, Harold F., and French, William B.   *Law of the Real Estate Business.* 3d ed. Homewood, Ill.: Richard D. Irwin, 1975.

Ring, Alfred A.   *Real Estate Principles and Practices.* 7th ed. Englewood Cliffs, N.J.: Prentice-Hall, 1972, chaps. 5, 8, 9, 10, and 11.

chapter 10

INCOME TAXATION AND
REAL ESTATE DECISIONS

The profitability of real estate investment decisions often depends upon the amount and timing of the federal income tax. As demonstrated in Chapter 5, the federal income tax, as well as the annual debt service, is deducted from NOI in deriving cash flow from a property or project. The greater the amount of tax that must be paid, the lower will be an investor's cash flow. And, even if the same total amount of taxes would be paid over a property's useful life, lower taxes in earlier years would make the project more profitable than either a level annual tax liability or higher taxes followed by lower taxes.

Two important types of considerations have guided Congress in the formulation of tax policy and laws. The first consideration is equity. Since the federal income tax is levied on the general populace, relatively equal and fair treatment of all taxpayers is a desirable, if perhaps unattainable, goal. In this regard, economists and other tax experts generally agree that the taxpayer's burden should reflect the ability to pay. Thus, a taxpayer who earns $10,000 per year should pay less in taxes than one who earns $50,000 per year. Furthermore, Congress has decided that equity and fairness require the $50,000-per-year taxpayer to pay a higher *percentage* of income in taxes than a lower-income taxpayer. This concept of equity is the basis for our graduated income tax system.

The second major consideration concerns the social and economic needs of the country. The tax burden can be imposed in such a way to favor certain taxpayers over others. Taxpayers who make favored types of investments, or those who hold assets for long-term gains (rather than short-term speculative profits) have been awarded relatively favorable tax treatment. For example, the tax factors affecting real estate in part reflect the felt need to provide adequate housing and sufficient amounts of other real estate resources such as factories, warehouses, shopping centers, and office buildings. The employment generated directly and indirectly by construction activity has been a continuing concern.

Income tax advantages promote the social goal of homeownership. When the federal government instituted supply-oriented housing programs, investors were given tax advantages in addition to subsidy dollars to induce the desired investment in housing for the disadvantaged. As the emphasis switched in federal housing programs from the provision of new low- and moderate-income housing to use of the existing housing stock, renovation was encouraged by permitting rehabilitation expenditures to be amortized over a five-year period.

Most recently, a tax credit was provided to homebuyers who purchased and occupied eligible residences between May 12, 1975 and January 1, 1976. The tax credit was intended to reduce a surplus of units which was hampering new starts. These examples illustrate that our federal tax policy has been formulated in part to provide incentives to real estate investors and consumers. These incentives tend to be called "tax shelters" by persons benefited and "tax loopholes" by others.

Taxes affecting real estate are a function of statutes, and the administrative regulations and court decisions interpreting these statutes. Federal tax statutes underwent major revisions in the Tax Reform Acts of 1969 and 1976. These reforms generally reduce the favorable tax treatment accorded real estate investors. This trend can be detected by a brief review of recent changes.

Among recent restrictive changes in taxes affecting real estate are (a) limitations on the use of accelerated depreciation; (b) recapture of excess depreciation; (c) limitations on the amount of investment interest which noncorporate investors can use to offset ordinary taxable income; (d) elimination of the shelter afforded by prepaid interest; (e) imputation of interest on installment contracts when no interest or an abnormally low rate of interest has been stated; (f) classifying certain items as tax preferences on which a surtax may be levied; and (g) capitalization of construction period interest and taxes. Although changes have occurred that have been favorable for the real estate investor, the tendency has been an overall reduction in the tax advantages from real estate investment.

Basic income tax factors affecting the noncorporate investor and the homeowner are presented in this chapter.[1] In adopting the view-

---

[1] The history of real estate tax advantages are omitted in this discussion. The 1969 and 1976 Tax Reform Acts established various transitional periods before full imple-

point of the noncorporate taxpayer, we are identifying a group of investors who are motivated to maximize their aftertax return on investment. Income taxes are an important variable in the determination of investment value for the real estate investor and, through negotiation in the market, the determination of market value.

Tax factors, however, are not a uniform concern among various categories of investors. Prospective purchasers of a shopping center, for instance, might include a partnership syndicate, a real estate corporation, an insurance company, a real estate investment trust, and Harvard University. These organizations receive different treatment under the federal tax laws. One investor among this group may be better able to take advantage of tax shelters and, *all else equal,* have a higher investment value for the shopping center.

In reality, of course, the factors affecting investment value (maximum price that can be paid and earn the desired return on investment) are never equal among investors. Tax factors are but one variable determining the investment values of potential purchasers, who may differ in their opportunity costs, willingness to accept risk, financing arrangements and other factors. The value-creating factors for investors combine to qualify them as bidders on the demand side of the market. These demanders interact with suppliers in the imperfect real estate markets to negotiate transaction prices and to determine market value.

INVESTMENT REAL ESTATE

Tax shelters available to real estate investors include the ability to elect accelerated depreciation for certain properties; the ability to deduct operating expenses and mortgage interest in calculating ordinary taxable income; potentially favorable capital gains treatment of proceeds received at time of sale; and methods of tax deferral such as the installment sale or exchange of properties of "like kind." Factors moderating these tax advantages include restrictions on the use of accelerated depreciation; recapture of excess depreciation; an investment interest limitation imposed on the noncorporate investor; and tax preference items and a potential tax surcharge. The following discussion of these basic tax factors, using simple examples, indicates that an individual should seek expert tax counsel before undertaking real estate investment.

Depreciation

Real estate on which depreciation can be taken must meet the following criteria:

---

mentation of many of the provisions in the act. The tax treatment of properties acquired before, during, and after these transitional periods can differ and is beyond the scope of this introductory chapter.

1. Improvements (structures and other improvements on the site) and furnishings are depreciable. Neither land nor one's personal residence is depreciable.

2. The real estate must be held for the production of income or used in one's trade or business. Real estate considered to be one's stock-in-trade is not depreciable.

3. The person or entity holding the property must be classified as an investor with respect to that property. Dealers in real estate cannot depreciate their stock-in-trade. Brokers, builders, and developers are dealers with respect to properties that they hold for sale to customers; these same individuals may be classified as investors with respect to properties held for the production of income. Investor versus dealer status remains a gray area in the tax laws and regulations. Investors may avoid dealer status if they remain passive by not improving their property for sale; if they refrain from continuous advertising of the property "for sale" and do not often sell property; or if they receive only a small portion of their total annual income from the sale of property.

Original tax basis and depreciable basis. The original tax basis is the cost of acquisition of the real estate, which is the price paid plus any acquisition expenses paid by the buyer or, in the case of improvements constructed by the investor, the cost of construction plus the acquisition cost of the site.[2] The tax basis is not affected by mortgage financing. The buyer giving a purchase money mortgage to the seller or assuming or taking subject to an existing mortgage will not alter the original tax basis, which remains the cost of acquisition. Similarly, a mortgage placed upon the property after acquisition or after construction of improvements does not affect the original tax basis. Thus, the real estate investor is able to depreciate both the equity investment in improvements and the portion of the improvements' value financed with borrowed money.

The original tax basis must be allocated between depreciable improvement value and land value which cannot be depreciated. In performing this allocation, evidence is presented to indicate the market value of land and improvements at time of acquisition. Appraisals and the assessed valuations of land and improvements have been accepted as evidence of proper allocation. When the investor has constructed the improvements on an acquired site, the cost of construction becomes improvement value and the acquisition cost of the land is taken as land value.

The portion of the original tax basis allocated to improvements becomes the depreciable basis. The depreciable basis may be altered

---

[2] The tax bases for properties acquired by gift, will, exchange, foreclosure, or involuntary conversion are each defined by special provisions beyond the scope of this chapter.

over the investment holding period by capital improvements to the property. Capital improvements add to the value of the real estate, extend its useful life, or adapt the property to a different use. Capital improvements are distinguished from expenditures for ordinary repair and maintenance, which are expensed annually as made. Capital improvements may be a new roof, new wiring, remodeling, or modernization expenditures.

Salvage value technically must be considered in establishing the depreciable basis. Salvage value is the estimated market value of the improvements (or other depreciable assets such as furniture and furnishings) at the end of their useful life. The salvage value of improvements can be reduced by the cost of their removal, which typically exceeds the salvage value at the end of their useful life. Investors intending to hold the property over the useful life of the improvements therefore can use a zero net salvage value in establishing their depreciable basis.

The depreciation expense taken each year depends in part upon the useful life of the improvements. A guideline to useful lives has been provided by the Internal Revenue Service for various broad categories of improvements and short-lived furnishings, equipment, and fixtures. Examples of these guidelines include the following:

	Years
Apartments	40
Hotels	40
Office buildings	45
Warehouses	60
Dwellings	45
Stores	50
Factories	45

The taxpayer, of course, usually prefers the shortest possible useful life when maximization of aftertax cash flow is an important consideration. The investor may be able to justify a useful life shorter than the guideline provides if circumstances warrant. In Los Angeles, an investor constructed a retail store on a site to be taken for a freeway within seven or eight years. He obtained a ten-year useful life for depreciation of the improvements, with the resulting tax losses creating substantial deductions from other income. The deductions made the property particularly desirable (and thus valuable) to investors having high incomes.

Allowable depreciation methods. Allowable methods of depreciation depend upon whether the improvement is residential or nonresidential and whether the investor takes a new property as a "first user" or purchases used real estate. Residential real estate is defined as having 80 percent of gross income from dwelling units. In accumulating the 80 percent, rent can be imputed for an owner-occupied unit. Taking as "first user" means that no other investor has taken depreciation on the property. Allowable depreciation methods are summarized below for new (first user) and used residential improvements, and for nonresidential improvements.

New residential improvements (taken as first user)

1. Straight-line depreciation—taken at a constant rate of the original depreciable basis.

Example

40-year useful life = $\frac{1}{40}$ or 0.025 annual rate × $100,000 depreciable basis (cost of improvements; no salvage value is assumed) = $2,500 annual depreciation.

2. Double-declining balance—taken at no more than 200 percent of the straight-line rate and calculated on the outstanding balance of the depreciable basis. A rate less than 200 percent of the straight-line rate can be used. Salvage value is never considered with this method.

Example

40-year useful life = 0.025 straight-line rate × 2.0 = 0.05 double-declining balance rate × $100,000 depreciable basis = $5,000 depreciation in the first year. Depreciation in the second year: 0.05 × $95,000 = $4,750; in the third year: 0.05 × $90,250 = $4,512; and so on.

3. Sum-of-the-years' digits—another rapid write-off depreciation method in which the annual rate of depreciation changes and is applied each year to the original depreciable basis. Salvage value is assumed to be zero.

Example

40-year useful life. The formula for determining the rate of depreciation in the first year is to sum the digits for each year of useful life and to divide 40 by this sum; in the second year, 39 is divided by the sum; and so on.

Year	
	1
	2
	3
	. . .
	40
Total	820

A formula, $n(n + 1)/2$, can be used to obtain this total, where n = useful life.

Depreciation in the first year is 40/820 × $100,000 = $4,878. Depreciation in the second year is 39/820 × $100,000 = $4,756; in the third year, 38/820 × $100,000 = $4,634; and so on.

4. Component depreciation—the component parts of the structure are depreciated separately over their respective useful lives. Rapid write-off methods may be used providing the useful life of the component is longer than three years. Component depreciation is available only for new improvements (construction cost is the depreciable basis).

Example

Building cost—$100,000

Components	Depreciable basis	Life	Straight-line first year	Double declining first year
Shell	$ 55,000	60	$ 935	$1,870
Roof	7,000	15	469	938
Electricity	6,000	20	300	600
Plumbing	7,000	20	350	700
Elevator	15,000	10	1,500	3,000
Air conditioner	10,000	10	1,000	2,000
Total	$100,000		$4,554	$9,108

Used residential improvements (not taken as first user)

1. Straight-line depreciation.
2. A 125 percent declining balance—the depreciation rate is no greater than 125 percent of the straight-line rate. This method is allowed only if the useful life of the improvement is 20 or more years, otherwise, only straight-line depreciation is permitted. The allowable rate is taken times the outstanding balance.

Example

40-year useful life = 0.025 straight-line rate × 1.25 = 0.03125 × $100,000 depreciable basis = $3,125 depreciation in the first year; 0.03125 × $96,875 = $3,025 in the second year; 0.03125 × $93,850 = $2,933 in the third year; and so on.

New nonresidential improvements (taken as first user)

1. Straight-line depreciation.
2. A 150 percent declining balance—the depreciation rate is no greater than 150 percent of the straight-line rate. Annual depreciation is calculated on the outstanding balance of the depreciable basis.

Example

40-year useful life = 0.025 straight-line rate × 1.50 = 0.0375 × $100,000 depreciable basis (no salvage value) = $3,750 depreciation in the first year; 0.0375 × $96,250 = $3,609 in the second year; 0.0375 × $92,641 = $3,474 in the third year; and so on.

3. Component depreciation—maximum depreciation rate allowable is 150 percent of the straight-line rate.

Used nonresidential improvements (not taken as first user)

Straight-line depreciation only.

Furniture and furnishings

Furniture and furnishings may be depreciated separately from the improvements provided the item has a useful life of three or more years. Allowable methods are the following:

New
1. Straight-line depreciation.
2. Double-declining balance.
3. Sum-of-the-years' digits.

Used
1. Straight-line depreciation.
2. 150 percent straight-line.

Additional depreciation on furniture and furnishings

Additional depreciation is allowed on furniture and furnishings in the first year, provided the useful life of the item is six years or longer. Up to 20 percent of the cost of new or used personal property is allowed, with taxpayers filing a joint return limited to a maximum of $20,000 of such depreciation.

Rehabilitation expenditures for low-income housing

Investors rehabilitating existing housing units to be made available to lower income families under a subsidized housing program, such as Section 8, may elect to amortize rehabilitation expenditures totaling $20,000 per dwelling unit over a five-year period.[3] Amortization must use the straight-line rate, permitting 20 percent of the rehabilitation cost to be deducted in each of the five years in addition to depreciation of the remainder of the depreciable basis. The 1976 Tax Reform Act extended this benefit until January 1, 1978.

---

[3] The Section 8 housing program is discussed in Chapter 17.

Election of method. An investor electing to use an allowable rapid write-off depreciation method is permitted to switch to straight-line depreciation during the investment holding period in order to depreciate fully the remaining balance of the depreciable basis. This election is in a year of the taxpayer's choosing and can be done only once in an investment holding period. The year in which the switch should be made to minimize the tax liability can be computed at the beginning of the holding period, given the depreciable basis, useful life, and depreciation method chosen. As the example below shows, allowable depreciation under the rapid write-off method will be less in year 22 than if the investor had switched to straight-line depreciation in year 21.

Example

40-year useful life; $100,000 depreciable basis. Double-declining balance depreciation is used initially.

		Straight-line depreciation	
Year	Double-declining balance depreciation	Rate	End-of-year balance
1	$ 5,000		$ 95,000
2	4,750		90,250
3	4,512		85,738
4	4,287		81,451
5	4,072		77,379
6	3,869		73,510
7	3,676		69,834
8	3,492		66,342
9	3,317		63,025
10	3,151		59,874
11	2,994		56,880
12	2,844		54,036
13	2,702		51,334
14	2,567		48,767
15	2,438		46,329
16	2,316		44,013
17	2,201		41,812
18	2,091		39,721
19	1,986		37,735
20	1,887		35,848
21°	1,792		34,056
22	1,702	$ 1,792	
23		1,792	
. . .		. . .	
40		1,792	
	$65,944†	$34,048†	$ 0

° The taxpayer would switch to straight-line depreciation in year 21. Depreciation of the remaining outstanding depreciable basis at the beginning of year 22 ($34,056) at the straight-line rate for the remaining years of useful life (19 years) provides greater depreciation than if he or she had remained with the double-declining balance method. The more rapid the method of taking depreciation, the more quickly the switch will occur.

† Discrepancy of total depreciation taken from $100,000 caused by rounding.

Leasehold improvements.   An investor who leases land and improves the site can depreciate the cost of improvement over its useful life, if the useful life is less than the term of the lease.

Example

An investor leases a site for 49 years and constructs an office building with a 45-year useful life. The investor can depreciate the improvement cost using 150 percent declining balance or straight-line depreciation.

If the term of the lease is shorter than the useful life of the improvements, the investor-lessee is permitted to amortize the cost of improvements over the term of the lease using straight-line amortization. If the intention of the investor is to amortize improvement cost over the term of the lease, care must be taken that any renewal options are not construed by the Internal Revenue Service to be part of the lease term.

Rapid write-off depreciation and the return on investment.   The use of an allowable method of rapid write-off depreciation permits a larger portion of the cash throw-off from investment real estate to be sheltered from taxation. If the total of depreciation expense, operating expenses, and interest expense exceed the property's effective gross income, a negative taxable income (tax loss) is realized. The investor is permitted to use this "paper" loss as an offset against taxable income from other sources such as wages, salaries, and other investment income. The consequent reduction in the investor's total income tax bill represents a tax savings imputable to the property which produced the tax loss. The aftertax return on the equity investment in that property is increased because of the tax savings. Even if the total of tax deductions do not exceed the property's realized gross income, a portion of the cash throw-off comes "tax free" to the investor as long as the depreciation expense exceeds the principal retirement portion of the annual debt service. This truism can be shown by comparing the deductions determining cash throw-off and taxable income.

Items (1) and (2) below are identities in the computation of cash flow and taxable income. To the extent that depreciation exceeds the principal retirement on the mortgage, taxable income will be less than cash throw-off and a portion of the cash throw-off comes tax free to the investor.

Cash throw-off	*Taxable income*
(1) Net operating income	(1) Net operating income
Less: Debt service	Less:
(2) Mortgage interest	(2) Mortgage interest
(3) Mortgage principal repayment	(3) Depreciation
Equals: Cash throw-off	Equals: Taxable income

Deduction of operating expenses and interest expense

Real estate investors are permitted to deduct from their taxable in- comes all operating expenses associated with the property and the interest expense on money borrowed to finance the investment. Operating expenses are actual cash expenditures made to operate the property, including keeping it in good repair; they are not capital expenditures.

Investment interest limitation. Noncorporate investors are permitted to deduct interest expense on investment real estate. Currently, however, these taxpayers are subject to an "investment interest limitation." The total interest deduction allowed is determined by the sum of these items:

1. The amount of $10,000 on a joint return.
2. Net investment income.

Interest expense in excess of that permitted as a deduction under the above formula can be carried forward under restrictive rules. Corporations are not affected by the investment interest limitation; there are no limitations on the amount of "business" interest expense that is deductible. Interestingly, rental real estate (apartments, shopping centers, office buildings, and so on) has been classified as business property by the Internal Revenue Service. The interest expense associated with such property is not subject to the investment interest limitation.

Real estate investors affected by the limitation are speculators in land, property owners who have a net lease arrangement where the tenant pays practically all of the operating expenses, or property owners who are guaranteed a rate of return on their investment. The investment interest limitation is designed to prevent the high-bracket noncorporate taxpayer from excessive use of interest expense to shelter other income from taxes while holding the investment for appreciation in market value that will be given favorable capital gain treatment at the end of the investment holding period.

Points and discounts. Under certain conditions, points charged by the lender may be treated as additional interest expense by the taxpayer. The 1976 Tax Reform Act requires points considered to be interest to be prorated and deducted over the term of the loan. However, points charged on a mortgage used to purchase or to improve a taxpayer's personal residence are deductible when paid, if it is the local custom to charge points when making such a loan.

Discounts are sometimes used by lenders to increase their effective interest yield on the mortgage. A discount is considered to be mortgage interest and is therefore deductible. However, accrual basis taxpayers must amortize the discount over the term of the loan; they deduct only the prorated amount as interest expense in any one taxable year. Cash basis taxpayers have an interest expense deduction annually when they pay their mortgage payment to the extent that a portion of the payment represents a prorata portion of the discount.[4]

Prepaid interest. Prior to the 1976 Tax Reform Act, investors might have found it advantageous to induce the sellers to accept a portion of the initial equity payment as prepaid interest on a purchase money mortgage. The maximum amount of prepaid interest allowable was limited to the current year's interest expense plus the interest expense for the following year. A further limitation was imposed in that the amount of prepaid interest could not materially distort income. The prepaid interest would be taxable to the seller as ordinary income. If the seller were a nonprofit organization, an individual with a loss in that taxable year, or a dealer who could not realize a capital gain from the sale of the property, the seller might have been indifferent about receipt of the proceeds as interest. Prepaid interest provided investors reporting on a cash basis with additional first-year tax deductions.

The 1976 Tax Reform Act requires that any interest which is prepaid by the borrower must be allocated and deducted over the term of the loan. The interest deduction taken annually must represent the charge for the use of funds borrowed for that period. Consequently, prepaid interest has been effectively removed as a tax shelter for the cash basis investor, who now receives the same treatment as a taxpayer using the accrual method.

Construction period interest and real estate taxes. The 1976 Tax Reform Act requires individuals and Subchapter S corporations to capitalize and amortize interest and property taxes paid during the construction period. The construction period begins when construction or reconstruction of the building begins, and ends when the improvement is ready for use or for sale. Prior to the 1976 Act, these expenditures could be deducted when paid or capitalized and depreciated.

This provision becomes effective over time depending upon the type of property. Nonresidential properties on which construction began in 1976 are subject to the provision, residential properties are affected beginning in 1978, and low-income housing in 1981. The amortization period will be progressively lengthened over time for each class of property until the permanent 10-year amortization period is reached in 1982 for nonresidential property, 1984 for residential, and 1988 for low-income housing.

---

[4] Investors can report income and expenses on either a cash or accrual basis. The cash method recognizes income in the taxable year received; deductions are allowed in the year paid. The accrual method recognizes income and expenses in the year in which the right to receive the income or the liability for the expense occurs.

Capital gains

The taxable gain realized upon disposition of real estate may be treated as a long-term capital gain if the following criteria are met:

1. The property is held for longer than nine months, beginning in 1977, and for twelve months for properties purchased in 1978 and thereafter. Property purchased in 1976 remains under the six-month holding period for a long-term capital gain. Properties sold within shorter periods of time result in a short-term capital gain, which is taxed as ordinary income.
2. The property must be held as an investment, for the production of income, or used in one's trade or business. Dealers in real estate cannot take a capital gain upon sale of their stock in trade.

Capital gains defined. A capital gain is defined as the net sale price less the adjusted basis. Net sale price is the sum of (*a*) cash received; (*b*) other consideration received (notes, market value of other property, and so on); and (*c*) any mortgages assumed or taken subject to by the buyer, *less:* (*a*) the broker's commission and (*b*) other expenses of sale (legal fees, recording fees, but not the state or local transfer tax). The adjusted tax basis is the original tax basis (plus any capital additions) less depreciation taken during the holding period.

Example

Mr. and Mrs. A sold their apartment property for $50,000. They had invested $10,000 in capital improvements during the ten years they owned the property. Their original tax basis was $30,000, $23,000 of which was allocated to improvements and $7,000 to land. They have taken $7,250 depreciation during the holding period. Their capital gain . . .

Proceeds from sale (cash)		$50,000
Less: Broker's commission	$3,500	
Attorney's fee	200	3,700
Net sale price		$46,300
Original tax basis		$30,000
Plus: Capital additions		10,000
		$40,000
Less: Depreciation taken		7,250
Adjusted tax basis		$32,750
Net sale price		$46,300
Less: Adjusted basis		32,750
Capital gain		$13,550

Capital gain tax bill. The tax rates applicable to a long-term capital gain realized by noncorporate taxpayers are 25 percent on the first $50,000 of gain and 35 percent on all of the long-term capital gain over $50,000.[5] The amount of tax owed upon sale of real estate held as an investment by noncorporate taxpayers can be computed by either (*a*) adding one half of the long-term capital gain to their other ordinary taxable income and paying according to the ordinary income tax rate applicable or (*b*) if the above alternative results in a larger tax bill, electing to pay the maximum 25 percent capital gain rate on the first $50,000 of capital gain and then paying at 35 percent or at their ordinary tax rate on all gain above $50,000. If the second alternative is chosen, the long-term capital gain is not halved in calculating taxes owed.

Example

Mr. and Mrs. A sold land for a $10,000 long-term capital gain. Taxable income from other sources is $50,000. Mr. and Mrs. A file a joint return.

Alternative 1

Ordinary taxable income	$50,000
Plus: One-half of the long-term capital gain	5,000
Total taxable income	$55,000
Effective ordinary rate	× 0.3572
Taxes due	$19,650

Alternative 2

Tax on first $50,000 of long-term capital gain at 25% ($10,000 × 0.25)	$ 2,500
Balance of capital gain	0
Plus: Other taxable income	50,000
Effective ordinary rate	× 0.3412
Taxes	$17,060
Plus: Tax on $10,000 gain	2,500
Total taxes due	$19,560

Example

Mr. and Mrs. A realize a $60,000 long-term capital gain with all other factors the same as the above example. (In situations where a large capital gain results in an abnormally large income for the taxpayer, income averaging would be explored.)

---

[5] The corporate taxpayer pays 30 percent on long-term capital gain or the regular corporate rate if it is lower. Corporations can carry a long-term capital loss back three years and forward five years. However, the loss carried back or forward can be used only to offset long- or short-term capital gains.

Alternative 1

Ordinary taxable income....	$50,000
Plus: One-half of long-term capital gain	30,000
Total taxable income	$80,000
Effective ordinary rate	× 0.4168
Taxes due	$33,340

Alternative 2

Tax on first $50,000 of long-term capital gain at 25%		$12,500
Tax on balance of gain at 35%, which is lower than the 37.17% tax rate that would result if the balance of the gain had been added to other taxable income	$10,000	
	× 0.35	3,500
Other ordinary taxable income	$50,000	
Effective ordinary rate .... × 0.3412		17,060
Taxes		$33,060

Long-term capital loss. Treatment of a long-term capital loss varies depending upon whether the property qualifies as a Section 1231 property or as a capital asset. Section 1231 properties must be held for more than nine months, beginning in 1977, and for twelve months for properties purchased in 1978 and thereafter, and include real estate used in one's trade or business. Interestingly, many income-producing properties, such as apartment buildings, retail stores, and office buildings held by a noncorporate taxpayer also are classified as Section 1231 properties. Although the owner may consider these properties to be "investments" held for capital appreciation and for the production of income, the Internal Revenue Service and the courts have permitted Section 1231 to apply.[6]

The advantage of Section 1231 is full deductibility of any long-term capital loss against other ordinary income. The taxpayer aggregates all long-term gains and losses from the disposition of Section 1231 properties during the year. If a net gain results, it is added to any other long-term capital gains and taxed accordingly. If a net loss results, the net loss is fully deductible against other ordinary income.[7] Whether or not the property qualifies under Section 1231 becomes important at time of disposition of the real estate. Depreciation methods applicable to the property during the holding period are not affected by this classification.

---

[6] Income-producing properties may not be eligible for Section 1231 treatment if the investor is protected against loss of income or is guaranteed a rate of return on investment. For instance, a property leased on a net basis with the tenant paying all, or practically all, expenses would not qualify.

[7] The tax treatment of long- and short-term capital gains and long- and short-term capital losses, realized in various combinations by noncorporate and corporate taxpayers in a given taxable year are beyond the scope of this introduction to tax factors affecting real estate. The interested reader is referred to John O. McCoy, et al., *Federal Taxes Affecting Real Estate*, 3d ed. (Chicago: National Institute of Farm and Land Brokers, 1970).

Beginning in 1977, the noncorporate investor can deduct $2,000 of a net long-term capital loss on a non-Section 1231 investment property in a joint return.[8] The deduction increases to $3,000 in 1978. Any overage can be carried forward indefinitely. The long-term capital loss carried forward is first deducted from any capital gains and then from other income subject to the above limitation. Before 1977 the noncorporate investor was able to benefit only partially from any carry-over of a long-term capital loss. The taxpayer received a carry-over deduction of $1 toward the maximum capital loss write-off against ordinary income for each $2 of long-term capital loss carried forward. The investor with sufficient long-term capital gains in subsequent years could fully offset any carry-over long-term capital loss. The $1 deduction for each $2 of carry-over loss applied only against other ordinary taxable income.

Recapture of excess depreciation. The ability to depreciate certain types of real estate using rapid write-off or modified rapid write-off methods produces excess depreciation, which is the difference between depreciation taken during the holding period and that which would have been taken using the straight-line depreciation method. Excess depreciation, of course, disappears if the real estate is held for its entire useful tax life. Investors in real estate enjoy a tax shelter if depreciation taken exceeds true economic depreciation of the property. The use of rapid write-off depreciation methods increases the probability of this circumstance's occurring. Indeed, some investors have found their properties appreciating in value over the holding period, rather than depreciating. The shelter afforded by rapid write-off depreciation would be even more beneficial if the investors could receive favorable treatment of their capital gains at time of sale. This shelter, however, has been moderated by provisions which are designed to "recapture" all or part of the excess depreciation at time of sale. The recaptured portion of the capital gain is taxed as ordinary income.

The provisions for recapture of excess depreciation tend to promote longer investment holding periods. Real estate operators who invest primarily for tax-sheltered income and who sell or exchange whenever their real estate begins to produce a taxable income are dealt with more severely than investors who buy and hold for the long term.

Residential and nonresidential real estate

1. If the residential real estate[9] is held less than one year, all depreciation taken is recaptured and taxed as ordinary income to the extent of the

---

[8] A net long-term capital loss can occur when long-term capital losses exceed long-term capital gains. If only one capital gain transaction occurs during the year, and it produces a loss, the loss is carried forward under the above rule.

[9] The holding periods for residential real estate financed under a federal housing program or state and local programs for low- or moderate-income families remain

capital gain. Any portion of the gain attributable to appreciation in market value will be taxed as a long-term capital gain.

Example

Mr. and Mrs. A's building on leased land had an original tax basis of $100,000 at time of purchase on January 1, 1977. Mr. A sold his property on December 5, 1977, thereby qualifying for a long-term capital gain. (The property, purchased in 1977, was held for longer than nine months. Properties purchased in 1978 or thereafter must be held twelve months to obtain capital gains treatment.)

Net sale price (property had appreciated)	$110,000
Adjusted basis (original basis less approximate depreciation taken)	91,000
Capital gain	$ 19,000
Portion recaptured and taxed as ordinary income (depreciation taken)	9,000
Portion taxed as a long-term capital gain (appreciation in market value)	$ 10,000

2. If real estate is held for longer than one year, the excess of depreciation taken over what would have been taken using straight-line depreciation is recaptured and taxed as ordinary income.[10] Beginning in 1978, this holding period will be the only meaningful rule applicable to long-term capital gains for properties purchased or constructed in 1978. If these properties are not held for twelve months, any gain will be treated as short-term and taxed as ordinary income.

Example

Mr. and Mrs. A's original tax basis for a building on leased land was $100,000 on January 1, 1977. They sold their property on December 31, 1978.

---

under less stringent 1969 regulations. The capital gain for these properties is recaptured to the extent of depreciation taken if the property is not held twelve months. If the property is held for 12–100 months, all depreciation taken in excess of straight-line depreciation is recaptured to the extent of the capital gain. For each month held past 100 months, a one percent reduction is permitted in the excess depreciation taken after December 31, 1975. A project held for 16 years, 8 months (200 months) would have no portion of the capital gain recaptured as ordinary income.

[10] Excess depreciation attributable to periods after December 31, 1975 is to be recaptured fully, regardless of the date when the property was constructed. If the capital gain exceeds post-1975 excess depreciation, it is considered first attributable to excess depreciation taken after December 31, 1967 and before December 31, 1975, and then to excess depreciation taken after December 31, 1963 and before December 31, 1969.

Net sale price (property had appreciated)	$110,000
Adjusted basis (original basis less approximate depreciation taken)	81,000
Capital gain	$ 29,000
Less: Excess depreciation recaptured and taxed as ordinary income [depreciation taken ($19,000) less straight-line depreciation ($10,000)]	9,000
Taxed as long-term capital gain	$ 20,000

The rules for recapture, all else equal, tend to reduce the aftertax return on equity investment and are a factor promoting longer investment holding periods. Other factors in the investment decision, however, are never constant. Rising rents contributing to appreciation in market value can result in an advantageous sale within one year or within 100 months. Even without appreciation in market value, the recapture of a portion of the gain as ordinary income becomes less of a factor in the decision to sell as the investment holding period lengthens.

Tax preference items and the minimum tax

Real estate investors may experience certain "tax preference items" in the process of sheltering income from taxation. Tax preference items particularly related to real estate investments are excess depreciation and, for the noncorporate taxpayer, the deductible one-half of any net long-term capital gain.[11] A surtax of 15 percent is levied when these tax preference items total greater than $10,000 (an arbitrary sum permitted as a deduction) or one-half of any income taxes otherwise payable in that year.

Example

Mr. and Mrs. A had a net long-term capital gain in 1976 of $60,000. They elect to report one-half of the gain together with their other ordinary taxable income for the year ($50,000). Their total taxable income is $80,000. Their taxes are $33,340 before the surtax. They have other depreciable real estate that produced excess depreciation of $40,000 in 1976.

Mr. and Mrs. A's surtax is

---

[11] Long-term capital gains less any long-term capital losses.

Tax preference items:
Deductible one-half of long-term capital gain ....$ 30,000
Excess depreciation 40,000

Total ....$ 70,000
Less:
One-half of tax liability 16,670

Difference liable for surtax ....$ 53,330
Surtax rate ....× 0.15

Surtax ....$ 8,000
Taxes due before surtax 33,340

Total tax bill ....$ 41,340

The surtax, or minimum tax, attempts to prevent taxpayers from completely sheltering their income from taxation. The 1976 Tax Reform Act increased the surtax rate from ten to fifteen percent and significantly reduced allowable deductions in computing the income liable for surtax.

TAX DEFERRAL

Exchanges

Real estate held for investment purposes and meeting the "like kind" and "investment property" tests, can be exchanged for other real estate on a tax-free or partially tax-free basis. Only boot is taxed.

Boot. Boot is any asset or liability transferred as part of the realty exchange. The most typical forms of boot are cash, mortgages existing prior to the exchange, purchase money mortgages created within the exchange, and debt instruments transferred in lieu of cash.

Neither party in a tax-free exchange is permitted to recognize a loss at the time of exchange. The party receiving boot in any form will likely have a gain that is subject to taxation, but the party who gives up boot may only add the surrendered boot to the tax basis. The following rules apply to boot.

1. Cash received is subject to taxation; cash paid is added to basis.
2. Mortgages exchanged as a part of the property exchange are netted against one another. The party who ends up with a smaller mortgage must report taxable boot on the difference in mortgages. The party who accepts the larger mortgage adds the difference in mortgages to the tax basis.
3. Notes made in lieu of cash are treated as mortgages. The party making the notes adds the amount of the notes to the basis.

For each party in a tax-free exchange, the adjusted basis after the exchange is calculated as follows.

To original basis of original property:

    Add: Cash paid

            Notes issued

            Mortgage obligation accepted (assumed or taken subject to)

    Deduct: Mortgage obligation passed to other party(s)

                Cash received

                Notes accepted

This yields the new basis. If the exchange caused the party to achieve a taxable gain, any gain recognized (taxed) is added back to the basis. This permits one to avoid double taxation at the time the property is sold.

Example

Jane Dillon owns a hotel property that has a depreciated tax basis of $600,000 and a fair market value of $950,000. She has an outstanding $500,000 mortgage.

Mr. Cartwright would like to acquire Ms. Dillon's hotel by trading a vacant tract of land having a fair market value of $800,000 plus $200,000 cash. Mr. Cartwright will not assume Ms. Dillon's mortgage; it must be paid at the time of closing. Mr. Cartwright has a tax basis of $300,000 in his land and no mortgage.

If Ms. Dillon were to sell her property outright, she would report a $350,000 capital gain. Mr. Cartwright's gain would be $500,000 in the event of a sale.

This is not an even exchange. Ms. Dillon is giving up a $950,000 value for $1 million. Thus, Ms. Dillon's maximum gain is increased to $400,000 and Mr. Cartwright's drops to $450,000 after the exchange.

Ms. Dillon must report a gain of $200,000 in this exchange—the amount of cash boot she received. Mr. Cartwright incurs no gain and pays no tax. He adds $200,000 to his basis.

Apportionment of basis. In effecting the exchange, the relative values of land and depreciable improvements become very important. Both parties normally wish to achieve depreciable status on as much of their bases as possible, and increasing the building-to-land ratio is desirable in nearly any exchange of properties.

Example

	M	T
Fair market value of property	$100,000	$100,000
Building value	70,000	70,000
Land value	30,000	30,000
Tax basis at time of exchange	20,000	40,000

In this example, an exchange of equal value properties would affect future depreciation, thereby affecting future tax basis. Mr. M would take Ms. T's property, retaining the old basis of $20,000. M would split the $20,000 on a 70 percent building ($14,000), 30 percent land ($6,000) basis. T would allocate her $40,000 basis in the same way—$28,000 building and $12,000 land.

Assumption of a mortgage increases one's tax basis, as does paying cash. Also, payment of tax on gain recognized at the time of exchange is added back to basis. The total of these items is apportioned to buildings and land on the basis of relative appraisals.

Depreciation recapture. Depreciation recapture must be considered at the time a tax-free exchange occurs. Unpermitted excess depreciation must be reported as ordinary income in the tax year that the exchange is consummated.

Example

Miss W. purchased improved land on January 1, 1977, for $100,000—$80,000 building and $20,000 land. During 1977, 1978, and 1979, she deducted $10,321 at a 150 percent rate of a 33⅓-year life. Her adjusted basis on December 31, 1979, is $89,679 and she exchanges the property (without boot) for unimproved land valued at $93,800.

Straight-line depreciation during the three years was $7,200 at 3 percent per year. Miss W. is entitled to no excess depreciation (100 percent recapture), so she must report ordinary income of $3,121 ($10,321 − 7,200).

In this example, gain on property equals recaptured depreciation. Had the gain been less than the recaptured amount, only the amount of the gain would be recaptured. This rule recognizes the fact that actual incurred depreciation is certain at the time of disposal and sets the gain limit. In other words, recapture cannot of itself create a loss in which basis exceeds the value of property held after the exchange.

The tax-free exchange creates a substantial amount of flexibility for the real estate investor. Any type of real property can be exchanged for another, without regard to whether it is raw land or improved property. Thus, the investor who wants to acquire a particular parcel of property can find a substitute property that the desired property's owner would accept in trade, purchase it, arrange for financing that is identical in amount to that of the desired property, and exchange the two parcels on a tax-free basis.

The original owner transfers the old tax basis to the new property, and incurs no tax detriment in the exchange. Normally the owner hopes to secure a greater value in the new property than that of the old one.

The investor is able to secure the desired property, which usually is ready for immediate development. He or she may wish to use the exchange technique to upgrade the tax basis by assuming a larger debt in the exchange, or one might wish to transfer from a parcel of raw land to an income-producing property. Through careful planning, nearly any property acquisition or disposal can be worked out as a tax-free advantage.

Installment sale

The installment method of reporting permits the seller to defer taxable gain on each dollar of selling price until that dollar is collected. If the total gross profit is 25 percent of the contract price, then 25 cents per dollar collected is taxable in the year of collection. Any property eligible for long-term capital gain can retain its eligibility and be taxed accordingly.

The installment treatment helps the buyer avoid bringing together dollars needed to purchase the property, and it permits the seller to pay tax only when the money is received. Income averaging is accomplished easily in this manner.

Most installment sales are set with a 29 percent downpayment. This figure is below the 30 percent maximum established by the Internal Revenue Service, probably because it offers the opportunity to make a slight error without upsetting the installment treatment.

Qualifying for installment treatment. The seller must comply with two conditions to qualify for installment treatment:

1. Not more than 30 percent of the gross selling price can be received in the year of sale.
2. The seller must elect the installment method in a timely return.

Terms must be defined carefully in dealing with installment sales. Two objectives are to be accomplished, one of which is to verify that 30 percent or less of the selling price is received by the seller in the year of the sale. The other objective is to establish a system wherein 100 percent of the taxable gain is reported over the time that the selling price is received.

Gross selling price. The total gross sale price is used in determining whether or not 30 percent or less was realized in the year of sale. The seller may receive up to 30 percent of this amount in the year of sale, including downpayment and installment payments received (both principal and interest).

The total gross selling price includes the following:

1. Cash received by the seller.
2. Payments made on behalf of the seller such as liens, taxes, and so on.

3. Mortgage on the property to the extent that it exceeds the seller's tax basis.
4. Any property accepted in lieu of cash.
5. Option payments that apply toward purchase price, regardless of when received.

Mortgage assumed. Note that the assumed mortgage is not considered part of the selling price unless the seller is "mortgaged out" (for example, borrowed more than the tax basis in the property). The assumed mortgage involves money that will never be paid to the seller, and there is no reason to assume that the mortgage will be paid to the seller in the year of sale. The mortgage in excess of basis is actually income, and since the income was received prior to the date of sale (at the time of mortgage financing), then it must be reported as immediate income.

Marketable bonds are part of first-year collections. A bond or other evidence of indebtedness which is payable upon demand or which is tradeable in an established securities market is treated as cash rather than as evidence of indebtedness of the purchaser. This is also true of marketable obligations of a government or corporation. Thus, only relatively nonmarketable securities such as those that are unsecured, nonnegotiable, subjected to extended repayment terms, or containing contingencies are exempted from treatment as income in the year of sale.

Imputed interest. The code contains special provisions for users of the installment sale method regarding interest-free payment plans. The installment sale permits capital gain treatment, and most sellers would prefer to receive all proceeds as principal rather than interest, with the Internal Revenue Service being required to impute 6 percent interest unless at least 4 percent is charged by the seller. The imputed interest applicable to the year of sale is considered in calculating the 30 percent for installment sale qualification.

The benefits of an installment sale are obvious to a property seller. The buyers do not appear to achieve any personal benefits, yet they are usually able to accommodate the tax needs of the sellers while securing low-cost financing on more than 70 percent of the contract price. In practice, most installment sales involve much less than a 30 percent downpayment, and the sellers usually get a lower-than-market interest rate on the unpaid balance.

The major problem that can arise in an installment sale transaction is that the buyers must arrange for property title releases to match their development schedule. If partial releases are established according to a fixed payment schedule, then the buyers might be unable to gain clear title when needed. Solving this problem usually leads to an installment sale that benefits both parties.

Example

Mr. Lsmft desired to sell a parcel of property on the installment basis. This property was purchased five years ago for $10,000.

Mr. Kreosote offered to buy the property on the following basis: $5,000 down on January 1, 1979, and $5,000 per year for three years payable each January 1 starting January 1, 1980. Mr. Lsmft accepted this offer with no mention being made of interest costs.

Mr. Lsmft must separate his gain into capital gain and interest income. He must state in the contract at least 4 percent per annum interest to avoid an Internal Revenue Service assumption that 6 percent has been charged.

Answer

	Year				
	1	*2*	*3*	*4*	*Total*
Recapture of investment	$2,500	$2,500	$2,500	$2,500	$10,000
Interest: 4 percent on balance each year	600	400	200	0	1,200
Long-term capital gain	1,900	2,100	2,300	2,500	8,000
Total	$5,000	$5,000	$5,000	$5,000	$20,000

TAX FACTORS AFFECTING THE HOMEOWNER

Deduction of mortgage interest and the property tax. Homeowners who itemize their deductions in calculating their taxable income have their aftertax cost of homeownership reduced by being able to deduct interest on indebtedness used to finance the purchase of the home and any real property tax paid. Other housing expenses incurred by the homeowner are not deductible.

Example

Mr. and Mrs. A own a $50,000 home financed with a $40,000, 25-year, 9 percent mortgage. Their monthly mortgage payment is $335. Interest during the year on their monthly level-payment mortgage is about $3,400. Their property tax bill is $800 annually. Their other taxable income is $30,000.

Other taxable income: $30,000
Less: Mortgage interest   3,400
         Property taxes   800

Taxable income $25,800
Effective tax rate (joint return) ....× 0.244

Taxes ....$ 6,308

Taxable income without the above deductions $30,000
Effective tax rate ....× 0.263

Taxes ....$ 7,880

Taxes before ....$ 7,880
Taxes after ....− 6,308

Tax savings ....$ 1,572

The tax savings generated by homeownership tend to permit a greater expenditure for housing and the purchase of a larger, better quality unit. Also, these tax advantages are influential in attracting families to home-ownership, including condominiums and cooperatives, and thus increase the number of dwelling units demanded for owner occupancy.

Capital gain on disposition. A personal residence cannot be depreciated for tax purposes, but it can be sold for a capital gain. The capital gain is the difference between adjusted sale price of the home and its tax basis. The adjusted sale price is the sale price received, less the broker's commission, other sales expenses (legal fees, prepayment penalties on the mortgage), and "fix-up" expenses incurred within 90 days prior to the contract for sale and paid for within 30 days after sale. These expenses are perhaps for painting, decorating, or repairs; they are not capital expenditures. As their description indicates, fix-up expenses are made to ready the property for sale. The tax basis for a personal residence is its acquisition cost or the construction cost of the home plus the acquisition cost of the lot. This original tax basis may be increased by capital improvements made during the holding period.

Example

Mr. and Mrs. A bought a lot in 1973 for $5,000 and constructed a home costing $20,000. Their original tax basis is $25,000. In 1975, they added a family room costing $5,000, increasing their tax basis to $30,000. In January 1978, they painted the exterior of the house and made some minor repairs on the advice of their broker, who said that the house would sell more quickly and would realize its full value potential if these items were done. The cost of these fix-up expenses was $2,000. On March 1, 1978, Mr. and Mrs. A executed a contract for sale with Mr. and Mrs. B for $45,000. Mr.

and Mrs. A eventually paid a $3,150 commission to their broker and $100 to an attorney, netting $41,750 from the sale.

Mr. and Mrs. A's capital gain is

Sale price:		$45,000
Less: Commission	$ 3,150	
Legal fees	100	
Fix-up expenses	2,000	5,250
Adjusted sales price		$39,750
Less: Original tax basis	25,000	
Capital addition	5,000	
Adjusted tax basis		30,000
Capital gain		$ 9,750

Deferment of the capital gain. The taxpayer is able to defer payment of the tax on a capital gain realized from the sale of a personal residence, if he or she reinvests the proceeds in another personal residence within 18 months prior to or 18 months after the sale of the home. If the taxpayer is having a new home constructed, he or she has 18 months after the sale of the prior residence to provide evidence of reinvestment (securing a building permit will suffice) and 24 months in which to occupy the new home. However, only expenditures made on the new residence within the 36 month period (18 months before and 18 months after sale of the former residence) are counted in the tax basis of the new residence. Whether an existing home is purchased or a new or rehabilitated property is obtained, the taxpayer will be liable for taxes on any part of the adjusted sale price realized from the former residence that is not reinvested in the new property. In effect, the taxpayer is taxed to the extent that he or she disinvests.

Example

Mr. and Mrs. A from the preceding example buy a new home within the allotted time for $35,000. Their adjusted sales price for their former residence was $39,750. They have a taxable capital gain of $4,750. The tax basis of their new home is

Cost of home		$35,000
Less: Gain from sale of former residence	$9,750	
Gain taxed at time of sale	4,750	
Deferred gain		5,000
Tax basis of new residence		$30,000

These adjustments leave Mr. and Mrs. A in the same position after their reinvestment in a new residence as they were when they sold their former home. Mr. and Mrs. A, if they sell their new home for its purchase price of $35,000, will have a $5,000 capital gain, given the $30,000 tax basis. Since they were taxed on $4,750 of gain at the time of sale of their former residence, they pay taxes on a total capital gain of $9,750, the same gain they would have realized upon the sale of their former residence without reinvestment. The provision for deferring part or all of the capital gain is tax postponement, not tax avoidance. The same circumstances exist when the taxpayer moves up to a more expensive home.

Example

Mr. and Mrs. A buy a new home for $60,000. Their tax basis for their new home is

Cost of new home	$60,000
Less: Gain on sale of old home deferred	9,750
Adjusted tax basis of new residence	$50,250

In this instance, the $50,250 tax basis represents the $30,000 adjusted basis of their former home, plus a $20,250 additional investment in the more expensive home (cost of new home, $60,000, less adjusted sale price of former residence, $39,850). Mr. and Mrs. A have postponed the entire $9,750 gain, which would be realized if they sold their new home for an adjusted sale price of $60,000.

Avoidance of tax on the capital gain. A taxpayer 65 years of age or older is relieved of all or a portion of the taxable capital gain upon the sale or exchange of a personal residence. To qualify for this exemption, the following criteria must be met:

1. The residence must be owned and used by the person at least five of eight years prior to sale.
2. Either spouse, who is at least 65 years of age, can elect to take the exemption for a couple holding joint ownership. A taxpayer can benefit from the exemption only once in his or her lifetime. The capital gain realized is taxed only if the adjusted sale price exceeds $35,000. The proportion of gain taxed is determined by the ratio of $35,000 to the adjusted sale price of the residence.

Example

Our Mrs. A attains 65 years of age while residing in her latest residence, which she decides to sell in order to move into an apartment on Sanibel

Island, where she intends to hunt sea shells. She sells her home for an adjusted sale price of $65,000.

Her capital gain is

Adjusted sale price $65,000
Less: Tax basis 50,250
Capital gain $14,750
Portion of gain not taxed $\dfrac{\$35,000}{\$65,000} \times \$14,750$ ....$ 7,942

Tax credit for the purchase of a new principal residence.   The tax credit recently instituted for the purchase of a new principal residence is another example of federal tax policy designed to achieve economic goals. The general business recession of 1974–75 was magnified in the housing industry, which was suffering not only from the scarcity and high cost of credit, but also from a large oversupply of housing units available for sale. New construction was unlikely until these existing units were absorbed. To stimulate the purchase of these homes, Conress provided a tax credit of 5 percent of the adjusted basis of the new residence, up to a maximum of $2,000. Units eligible for this credit were required to be under construction before May 26, 1975 and must have been acquired and occupied after May 12, 1975 and before January 1, 1976. The tax credit was a deduction from taxes owed, rather than a deduction determining taxable income.

The 5 percent tax credit was applied to the adjusted tax basis of the new home. When the homebuyer had a deferred capital gain from the sale of a previous residence, the adjusted tax basis for a new home was less than its sale price.

Example

Mr. and Mrs. A sold their home for a net sale price of $39,750; their adjusted tax basis was $30,000, resulting in a $9,750 capital gain. Mr. and Mrs. A reinvest in a new home that is eligible for the five percent tax credit. Mr. and Mrs. A's new home was purchased for $45,000. Their adjusted tax basis for this property is

Cost of new home ....$ 45,000
Less: Gain on sale of old home deferred 9,750
Adjusted basis of new residence ....$ 35,250
Their tax credit is
Adjusted basis 35,250
Tax credit rate ....× 0.05
Tax credit $1,762.50

Whether the tax credit stimulated the sale of eligible residences, or whether new construction not eligible for the tax credit was at a competitive disadvantage with eligible units, continues to be debated. However, equity considerations among taxpayers suffered. Homebuyers who purchased before or after the statutory time period, or who bought a home on which construction began after May 26, 1975, were not benefitted. Also, the high-income taxpayer who was able to buy the more expensive home received full advantage of the $2,000 maximum credit; lower-income families, who could not afford new homes with a tax basis of $40,000, received less benefit. To prevent the tax credit from being absorbed by developers' marking up the sale price of eligible units, the seller was required to provide a statement affirming that the sale price was the lowest price at which the property had been offered prior to the act.

SUMMARY

The real estate investor and the homeowner remain beneficiaries of favorable treatment under the federal income tax statutes. Investors can depreciate certain improvements using rapid write-off depreciation schedules and have the potential of sheltering part or all of the cash flow from taxation. Tax losses generated by an investment property can be used to reduce other ordinary taxable income. Investment property can be sold for a capital gain, and the gain may be at least partially deferred by exchange of like-kind properties or by the installment sale. In response to economic conditions and a perceived reordering of national priorities from housing to other needs, and in the desire to attain greater equity in the tax structure, Congress reduced real estate tax shelters in 1976. Although tax reform undoubtedly will again reduce the advantages enjoyed by the real estate investor, opportunities for tax planning to maximize aftertax income are expected to remain. The complexity of tax planning has only been suggested in this chapter; the assistance of a tax.expert is important in this aspect of real estate.

Homeowners may take interest expense and the property tax in itemizing deductions to determine taxable income. A personal residence can be sold for a capital gain and the gain may be deferred by reinvesting in another personal residence. The homeowner 65 years of age may avoid all or part of the gain upon sale of his or her residence. Home-ownership has been promoted by these tax advantages; it is unlikely that Congress will remove them.

QUESTIONS FOR REVIEW

1. Describe how tax factors affect investment value and market value.
2. What criteria must be met for real estate to be a depreciable asset and to be eligible for capital gains treatment upon sale?

3. How does allowable depreciation differ for new and used residential and nonresidential properties?

4. Why is part of the cash throw-off "tax free" as long as tax depreciation expense exceeds the principal repayment portion of the annual debt service?

5. What is meant by the term *depreciation recapture*?

6. Describe the two methods for computing the amount of capital gains tax owed.

7. What is the advantage of having a Section 1231 asset?

8. What is the intent of the surtax levied on tax preference items?

9. What are the potential advantages of an exchange of like-kind properties?

10. What conditions must be met to qualify as an installment sale?

11. What are the tax advantages of homeownership?

REFERENCES

Berman, Daniel S., and Schwartz, Sheldon. *Tax Saving Opportunities in Real Estate Deals.* Englewood Cliffs, N.J.: Prentice-Hall, 1971.

Boyd, Orton W. *Atlas' Tax Aspects of Real Estate Transactions.* Washington, D.C.: Bureau of National Affairs, 1971.

Casey, William J. *Tax Shelter in Real Estate.* New York: Institute for Business Planning, 1971.

J. K. Lasser Tax Institute. *J. K. Lasser's Successful Tax Planning for Real Estate.* Rev. ed. Edited by Bernard Greisman. Garden City, N.Y.: Doubleday & Company, 1972.

McCoy, John O.; Olsen, Harvey A.; Reed, Charles H.; Sandison, Robert W.; and Wright, Robert F. *Federal Taxes Affecting Real Estate.* 2d ed. Chicago: National Institute of Farm and Land Brokers, 1970.

Weiss, Robert M. *How to Maximize Tax Savings in Buying, Operating, and Selling Real Property.* Englewood Cliffs, N.J.: Prentice-Hall, 1971.

Wendt, Paul F., and Cerf, Alan R. *Real Estate Investment Analysis and Taxation.* New York: McGraw-Hill, 1969. This book does not contain the Tax Reform Acts of 1969 or 1976.

Tax, legal, and financial reporting services

American Institute of CPAs, 666 5th Avenue, New York, N.Y. 10017.

Commerce Clearing House, Inc., 4025 West Peterson, Chicago, Ill. 60645.

Federal Tax Press, 19 Roosevelt Avenue, West Haven, Connecticut 06516.

Prentice-Hall, Englewood Cliffs, N.J. 07632.

PART III
Real estate functions

chapter **11**

REAL ESTATE
MARKETING

MARKETING IS ONE of the essential functions that must be performed by every business firm. A useful good or service may be produced and financed, but if it is not distributed to the proper people or firms who will pay a fair price, the cycle of business activity has not been completed. One view (propounded mostly by marketing people) is that marketing is the most important business function of all. Marketing, this view holds, is the drive wheel of every economic enterprise. If a firm cannot identify and serve a particular demand in the economy, the other functions of producing and financing will be to no avail; the firm is doomed to failure. Of course, the same observation could be made with regard to producing and financing.

Consistent with the view of marketing as a broad, important business function is the following definition of marketing. "Marketing is the process by which the demand structure for economic goods and services is anticipated or enlarged and satisfied through the conception, promotion, exchange, and physical distribution of such goods and services."[1]

This definition implies or assumes several characteristics about markets and how to serve them. First, it suggests that demand cannot be created by a marketer. It can be magnified or pushed forward in time, but every demand function exists prior to a marketer's exploitation of it. Therefore, it is crucially important to a marketer to be able to "read" the demand structure. The marketer must collect relevant data and analyze the data to determine what products and services can be marketed successfully.

---

[1] Marketing faculty of Ohio State University, *Statement of the Philosophy of Marketing* (Columbus: College of Commerce and Administration, Ohio State University, May 1964).

The marketing mix

After identifying markets with specific needs that can be satisfied, enlarged, or pushed forward in time, the marketer must decide how best to accomplish the marketing job. The marketing mix in most cases is determined by the market and its needs.

Usually, the marketer will have several alternative products and services to offer. Deciding what these products and services are and in what proportions to be offered is the objective of this step in developing a marketing strategy. Builders may offer homes of standard design in various styles and interior decoration. Or custom design and architecture may be offered in the higher-priced homes. They may offer some combination—say 75 percent standard and 25 percent custom—depending upon their analysis of market needs. If real estate marketers find a low medium-income market in dire need of modern, safe, sanitary housing, they may find that the only way of attempting to serve this market economically would be through a government program, such as the Section 8 subsidized occupancy program.

The activities of marketing are extremely broad in nature. They include the formulation of ideas of new goods and services that will meet the expected demand. Ways in which the availability of these products can be made known to the public and methods by which the public can be convinced of their desirability are all part of the marketing function. Finally, the marketer is concerned with the legal and physical arrangements for the transfer of title and possession to a purchaser.

The marketing of real estate is a major function of real estate brokerage firms, land developers, and builders. Brokerage firms specialize in bringing together buyers and sellers of existing properties; land developers convert unused or agricultural land to residential or business uses, usually holding title to the land and selling parcels from their own account; and builders construct residences or business structures for sale to ultimate purchasers. Variations in the activities of these types of firms may occur. Builders may construct buildings which they do not own but for which they are paid a builder's fee. A brokerage firm may have a building constructed for speculative resale from its own account. And a land development company may also do construction work and have a brokerage division. Nevertheless, they all engage in the marketing of real properties.

Other types of real estate firms—management, appraisal, counseling, and financing companies—also have a marketing function to perform. They must market the services provided by their firms. They differ from brokerage, development, and construction firms, however, in that they do not create or maintain an inventory of real properties for sale. Our analysis of the marketing function is oriented primarily to those firms maintaining an inventory of properties, although marketing principles are applicable to other types of firms as well. Brokerage firms are a focus of analysis because marketing is the principal business function of these firms; it is their reason for existence.

The term *marketing* carries a much broader connotation than does the term *brokerage*. Brokerage usually refers to the legal relationships —rights and obligations—among the parties to a real estate transaction.[2] While a knowledge of these relationships may be regarded as prerequisite to a viable marketing effort, they are not the whole story—or even most of it. Marketing, as we said before, deals with the entire process of enlarging and satisfying needs in society. It is the process by which resources are allocated in the economy.

The brokerage firm may specialize in the type, location, or price range of homes it lists and attempts to sell. Or it may offer a variety in each category. The decision as to the combination, however, should be made only after and in consideration of an analysis of market needs.

In addition to the types of properties to offer and sell, the brokerage firm has a choice among services to offer. It may offer only selling services for its own listings. Or it may participate in a multiple listing service and attempt to sell the listings of other firms as well. A firm may offer insurance along with its marketing service. It may also offer other real estate services, such as appraisal, management, or counseling. Its marketing service could include financial analyses for income properties, inspection and appraisal services for prospective purchasers, or a trade-in program for sellers wishing to purchase another property. Other possible services may come to mind. Whether they are provided or not should be a conscious decision of the firm's marketing strategy.

MARKETING STRATEGY

Since marketers cannot hope to fulfill all the needs in society, they must limit the market they hope to serve. They must decide which needs they will try to meet, who the people are who have those needs, where they are, and when they will likely experience the need. Note that the decisions focus upon the needs and people having the needs—not upon a particular service or product.

Failure to focus upon needs has been termed marketing myopia.[3] Many examples could be cited of businesses that failed because of marketing myopia. Automobile companies such as Studebaker Corporation

---

[2] These relationships are covered in depth in Chapter 9.

[3] Theodore Levitt, "Marketing Myopia," *Harvard Business Review* 38, no. 4 (July–August 1960): 45–56.

that did not provide those types of styling, design, engine performance, or other features the market desired have gone out of business. Ford Motor Company lost its market dominance in the 1930s because it failed to modify its styles, designs, and colors to meet market desires. *Esquire* magazine lost its dominance of the would-be sophisticate male readership market to *Playboy* by not providing the desired mix of features, interviews, stories (and photographs). Railroad companies have experienced great difficulties because they did not realize they should be in the general transportation business.

In the world of real estate, many builders have failed because the properties they constructed did not have the desired features. Many apartment buildings have lost tenants to other properties because the owners or managers did not regard themselves as purveyors of housing services. They did not provide the features and services desired by the market. Brokerage firms have failed because they did not project the image of security, trustworthiness, or adequate service desired by homebuyers.

Our purpose is not to emphasize the negative—to dwell on how or why firms fail. We do want to point out that failures can occur without proper attention to the marketing concept. Failures can occur from other sources as well, of course. Improper management of the production, financing, organization, or personnel functions are just as likely to produce unfavorable results. Nevertheless, marketing myopia leads to a high proportion of failures and may be difficult to diagnose.

The best defense against marketing myopia is a marketing strategy. A strategy identifies long-range objectives and the general means for achieving those objectives. In marketing, the development of a strategy requires the identification and delineation of the market or submarket that exhibits needs or desires the firm believes it can serve and the types, quantities, and prices of products or services to fulfill those needs.

Real estate is a field composed primarily of marketers whose strategy is to seek out buyers or renters for products within specialized categories. The most basic product differentiation is a delineation of the type of land marketed by the firm. Few firms are capable of providing competent marketing services for the various types of land, including agricultural land, predeveloped (planned, zoned, and so on) suburban land, developed building sites, and land which has been improved with buildings for commercial, industrial, residential or other usages. Varied skills are needed, and firms which attempt to acquire all of these skills tend to expand beyond the top executives' ability to manage.

Each firm must identify its most efficient level of activity and devise a marketing strategy that is specialized to fit the talents of its members. As the firm's scale changes, its capabilities to extend into new areas of specialization also change, and therefore its marketing strategy must be reevaluated frequently.

In developing a marketing strategy, a firm usually selects a type of property, identifies the strengths of this product, and highlights these strengths for target purchasers. Examples of this process follow.

Unimproved acreage sales

Most sales of unimproved acreage are made to purchasers who seek appreciation from future reuse demand. Reuse potential factors such as the following are typically highlighted by the marketer.

1. Proposed highways, proposed utility extensions, or redevelopment.
2. Residential and commercial growth in the direction of the subject property.
3. The subject property's superior forestation, topography, water amenities, and other amenities.
4. The subject property's price and terms relative to competitors.
5. A projection of timing of expansion into the area with an identification of the subject property's best prospects.

The purchasers of this type of project are typically speculators who seek land of many investment types. They depend heavily upon the reputation and performance record of a marketing specialist.

This specialty has been a popular one among marketers who have been highly aggressive and optimistic about development timing. Many states now require that formal prospectuses be prepared which provide facts, both positive and negative, about the subject property. Land syndications for investors have been both popular and profitable, but many syndicators have been overly optimistic and have generated projects at prices and on financing terms that require substantial appreciation for profit to occur. The market downturn of the mid 1970s caused many defaults and losses by investors, thereby leading to greater regulation of syndicators and a poor reputation for this marketing specialty.

Predeveloped land sales

The marketer of predeveloped land converts land from unimproved acreage to buildable sites without performing the physical site development. The steps usually taken to enhance the value of sites are to:

1. Prepare a land-use plan.
2. Secure rezoning of the site to higher density uses.

3. Secure agreements from the county or city to bring utilities to the site.
4. Secure agreements from the highway department to improve roads as needed.
5. Prepare engineering analyses:
   a. Two-foot interval topographic analysis.
   b. Soils studies.
   c. Hydrological studies.
   d. Forestation analyses.
   e. Final land plan and stake out lots/sites.
6. File plat.

The purchasers of predeveloped land are usually land developers. The predevelopment process minimizes the time required to commence physical development, and it renders the property ready for immediate consideration for a land development loan. The development loan will normally fund the land at a "retail price," causing the services of the predeveloper to be recognized as value added.

Developed land sales

The land developer divides tracts into sites that are ready for immediate use by builders. The land price paid by the user includes all utilities, streets, curbs, gutters, sidewalks, street lights, and other improvements desired by the builder-purchaser. If the developer is efficient, a sufficient profit is gained through the development process to pay retail price for raw land and convert it to building sites worth more to builders than their cost of preparation.

Improved land sales

The constructor of buildings for sale seeks a profit by creating user-ready structures primarily for nonreal estate entities. Manufacturers, retailers, wholesalers, and others are not in the business of constructing buildings. They either purchase or rent existing buildings or commission new ones to be built. At times, the marketer creates an investment group to own a building created for rental and use by another party.

Resale property sales

Marketers of resale properties normally promote the virtues of owner occupancy or those of a seasoned, stable income. These properties are priced as a function of location, physical amenities, or capitalized income. The marketing specialist concentrates on reasons why the formerly owned property is superior to new space or alternative properties.

Leasing as a marketing specialty

The leasing agent's primary market is tenants who for one reason or another choose to rent rather than own. Such marketers sell freedom from making a downpayment and the absence of a permanent user commitment to the property.

Marketing specialized services

The most sophisticated type of product to sell is the many service specialties in real estate. Research, management, and appraisal firms must develop strong reputations for performance and then support these reputations with each client. Direct solicitation is not permitted in those areas where professional associations are prominent, so performance and reputation are critical to success. The product specializations discussed here tend to occur in geographically separated market areas as shown on Figure 11–1. The relationships between stages and location

FIGURE 11–1

Real estate development stages

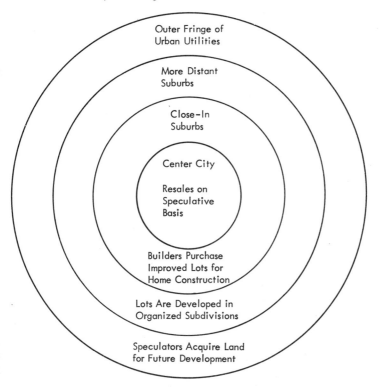

are simplified in an effort to separate strategy types, showing the maximum extent of specialization that is typically found in the market. Obviously, many variations and combinations of product mix occur.

Land speculation is shown to exist primarily in the outer fringe of urban utilities. Large tracts of rural land are frequently purchased on long-range financial terms. Lot development occurs primarily in the more distant suburbs, and homebuilders are drawn from close-in suburbs to the slightly further out areas as they seek lower land prices and more desirable lots. The center city rarely contains large tracts for new development, so resales and redevelopment represent the principal forms of activity.

Buyer market segmentation

Identifying and delineating the market to be served involves the process of market segmentation—carving out submarkets from larger, more general markets. This process recognizes that needs and desires of consumers are not homogeneous. In the extreme, individuals would have their own private preferences for any type of want-satisfying product or service. Fortunately, however, preferences can usually be grouped into market segments, or submarkets. For example, some groups of consumers prefer tooth-decay preventing toothpaste, some consumers prefer a breath sweetening product, and still others prefer a tooth whitening product. Crest, Close-up, and Ultra Brite toothpastes attempt to serve each of these segments or submarkets of the larger market for toothpaste.

Similarly, real estate marketers should segment their markets. A builder cannot realistically expect to construct houses of every architectural style, size, and design in every price range for every type of purchaser in every section of the country, region, or community. A real estate broker cannot effectively serve every category of seller or purchaser. Apartment developer-owners cannot expect their buildings to appeal to all groups of prospective tenants.

Identification of potential submarkets should be undertaken in a systematic way. One of the best ways of undertaking this process is to construct a marketing grid.[4] Ideally, such a grid contains characteristics of one dimension on one axis and characteristics of another dimension along another axis. For example, a construction firm seeking to identify potential markets for office buildings might construct the grid in Figure 11–2 showing desired features among several types of owners or occupants. Marketers would emphasize those features which meet the specific needs of each user type interviewed.

---

[4] For a more thorough treatment of the development and construction of marketing grids, see E. Jerome McCarthy, *Basic Marketing: A Managerial Approach*, 5th ed. (Homewood, Ill.: Richard D. Irwin, 1975).

FIGURE 11–2
Market grid for new office needs

Savings and loans and banks	Real estate and insurance officers	Attorneys	Physicians	Accounting firms	Finance companies	
	X	X		X	X	Variable space patterns
X			X			Special plumbing and fixtures
	X	X		X		View
	X			X	X	Informational service
X					X	Special security arrangements
X	X			X	X	Central location
	X	X	X	X	X	Climate conditioning
X	X	X	X		X	Customer parking
X		X		X		Prestige building
	X				X	Low rental rate
		X		X		Expansion potential

Such a grid focuses upon the needs of potential customers, not upon specific ways of fulfilling those needs. For example, the need for variable space patterns in offices might be met with movable partitions, removable walls, or added units in modular construction. The desirability of a pleasant view might be met with an interior courtyard, a site with a natural view, or height. And climate conditioning would require a different mix of heating, cooling, and purification in New York, Miami, and Fairbanks.

A grid identifying possible submarkets for a residential brokerage firm might appear as shown in Figure 11–3. A firm wishing to provide marketing services to purveyors and consumers of real estate services would find that it could serve the market for single-family residences, most of which are occupied by their owners, in all sections of the city except the center and northeast areas. Single-family units are available in all sections of the city except the center and northeast areas. Multi-family units are available in all sections except the center, north, and northwest areas. High-income buyers and properties are located in the north, east, and northwest areas of the city. And the low-income market is concentrated in the south, east, center city, and west sections. Thus, brokers wishing to serve the high-income, single-family residence market could operate in the north, east, and northwest sections of the city. They might further wish to specialize by limiting their operations to one of those areas. Given, for example, a conscious decision to concen-

FIGURE 11–3

Market grid for real property marketing services

Center city	North	South	East	West	NW	NE	SW	SE	
	X	X	X	X	X		X	X	Detached single-family residences (owner market)
		X	X	X		X	X	X	Multifamily units (rental market)
	X		X		X				High income
	X	X	X	X			X	X	Medium income
X		X	X	X					Low income
X	X		X					X	Condominium
X			X						Cooperative

trate the firm's efforts on marketing detached single-family homes in the north, east, and northwest sectors of the city, the marketer must select a target segment of the buying public which can be defined at the outset of the marketing effort.

Homes in these areas are large and expensive, and purchasers tend to have the following characteristics:

1. *Age:* Head of household between 35 and 50.
2. *Income:* Household income above $25,000 per year.
3. *Employment:* Head of household holds professional position near perimeter highway or downtown.
4. *Family size:* Four persons.
5. *Locational requirements:* Must be near private schools and major shopping center.
6. *Qualitative factor:* Neighborhood must have significant "snob appeal."

If these characteristics are stated accurately, the firm can concentrate its time and advertising budget on locating these purchasers and meeting their home purchase needs.

A similar process is used when the firm specializes in commercial property marketing. Location is less important, but purchaser requirements can be cataloged, and purchaser characteristics can be defined.

THE BUYING PROCESS

The goal of the marketing effort is to produce a consummated transaction with a satisfied buyer. After developing a viable, consistent marketing strategy in both the market for properties and the market for marketing services, the marketing executive hopes the sales force will be able to convince individual members of the market that the services and properties offered by the firm are worthy of purchase. The analysis to this point helps to identify these individuals and their needs; it does not help in developing an approach to consummating a transaction. This step results from completion of the stages in the buying process.

Stages in the buying process

All buyers experience several phases during the time that they are considering a major purchase. Each phase may be short lived or extended over weeks or even months. Nevertheless, the successful completion of each stage is prerequisite to a successful transaction.[5]

Felt need. The buying process begins when consumers experience a need. They realize for one reason or another that they may require a new home, office, or commercial facility. The need for a different home may be felt because of an impending family addition, a job transfer to another city, or the desire to upgrade or change location. Whatever the source, experiencing the need produces a state of tension in the potential buyer—a feeling that a problem requires resolution.

Prepurchase activity. Individuals, as a result of a felt need, become sensitive to advertising, bits of news, educational programs, experiences of others, and other cues in their environment which may bring them closer to satisfying the need. During the stage of prepurchase activity, the potential buyer's perception becomes tuned in to differences in sizes, styles, designs, location, price, and other characteristics; they learn and accumulate experience.

This is the stage during which the real estate marketer should provide information—not only about available properties, but about the entire purchase process. For most new buyers, and many older buyers as well, the purchase of a home is a traumatic experience. The more they can learn about the process, the greater will be the possibility of overcoming their fears and consummating the sale.

Prepurchase activity can be used to create a sequence of changes in the buyer's state of mind that bring the buyer closer to the act of purchase. Buyers proceed from a state of awareness of their needs and the necessity to satisfy them to knowledge about various alternative properties that could fulfill the need. They then begin to like one or several properties and develop a preference for one over the alternatives. The preference ripens into a conviction that one property can best satisfy the need and relieve their state of tension. Conviction leads to purchase.

---

[5] For a thorough analysis of buyer behavior, see Philip Kotler, *Marketing Management: Analysis, Planning, and Control* (Englewood Cliffs, N.J.: Prentice-Hall, 1967), chap. 4.

Purchase decision. The decision to purchase is made in relation to the amount of risk perceived by consumers. This depends on the degree of subjective certainty that they will do well by making the purchase. Consumers try to reduce this risk by gathering information and making comparative judgments as to the amount of risk involved among various alternatives. The purchase decision is in effect the manifestation of favorable prepurchase activity.

Use behavior. The buying process is not completed by the purchase decision. In some respects the consumers' "buying" has just begun. They must study and learn how to use the property just purchased; they must learn various aspects of its use, such as how the dishwasher works, when to pay taxes, how to get the porch fixed, and so on. The broker can be very helpful during this stage by anticipating the types of questions buyers will have and taking the initiative in providing that type of information. The property purchased should be viewed as part of the consumption system; it is the means by which the purchasers of the property attempt to meet their needs.

Postpurchase feelings. A buyer usually sees the purchase as both a reward and a punishment. It is a reward because it helps to satisfy a felt need. Buying the property is a lengthy process, and the new home is the end result of all the time, effort, and money expended. But it is also punishment because the purchaser continues to have doubts as to the wisdom of the purchase. Nearly all purchasers wonder whether they should have gone so far into debt, whether the house will be adequate for a growing family, whether the family should have gotten along a little longer in an apartment and gotten into better financial shape before purchasing a home. Opportunity costs—the passing up of alternative uses of their resources—become apparent during the postpurchase stage.

The anxiety experienced during this stage has been termed *cognitive dissonance.* The dissident feelings that occur following a purchase can be allayed by an effective real estate broker and will produce a satisfied customer—and a potential client for the future. The broker should reassure buyers by visiting them, introducing them to the neighbors, pointing out the favorable aspects of the property, and perhaps giving them a housewarming gift. This should be regarded as one of the most effective ways of building a satisfied clientele—people who will recommend the broker to others and who will call the broker when they wish to sell.

Buying process roles

Different roles may be assumed by the various parties concerned with a real estate purchase. In a home-buying situation, one member of the family may dominate and be the principal decider. Yet, if one member dominates in that decision (say, the wife), another member (the husband) may dominate in another decision—for example, the city where the family will live.[6] In the purchase of business real estate, the company president may be the final decider but only after receiving advice from others in the firm. Other functions in the process may be undertaken by different persons. Kotler groups these activities into the roles of influencers, deciders, buyers, and users.[7]

Influencers are those who provide information, persuade, or stimulate a buyer during any stage of the buying process. Sales representatives, advertising media, and friends are examples of some influencers. Some part of the real estate advertising budget should be aimed at those who will influence buyers. Children are often important influencers of parents who are deciding whether or which home to purchase. Yet, how often do real estate sales representatives discourage children from speaking up or expressing their opinions? Sometimes they are encouraged to remain outdoors while the parents tour the property. The sales representative may be passing up an opportunity to direct some marketing effort toward important influencers!

Deciders make the actual decision. It may be the wife who decides she likes one house better than another. It may be the husband's decision; or it may be a democratically formed family decision. The real estate marketer would do well to try to identify the decision-maker(s) in every buying situation and address a great deal of effort to that person or persons.

Those who make the actual purchase are termed the *buyers*. The buyer may be a different person than the decider, for example, a child sent to the store to buy a carton of milk for her mother. For most real estate transactions both husband and wife are the buyers, since both usually sign the contract and/or deed. If, however, the buyers are different from the deciders, more attention should be directed to the deciders.

Those individuals who use or consume a product or service are the *users*. As with the buyer, the user may be someone different from the decider. The person who receives a gift or the employee who uses the facilities provided by an employer is a user but not a decider. The user, however, may be a strong influencer, and marketing effort directed to the user who is also an influencer may pay off handsomely. Apartment dwellers who complain to the landlords about the noise level between apartments will induce the landlords to desire better soundproofing in

[6] James F. Engel, Hugh G. Wales, and Martin R. Warsaw, *Promotional Strategy*, 3d ed. (Homewood, Ill.: Richard D. Irwin, 1975), pp. 141–43.

[7] Kotler, *Marketing Management*, pp. 79–80.

their next apartment building investment. Workers who experience difficulty in performing tasks in a building with inadequate lighting will likely influence their employer to modify the lighting system. Supportive communication should be addressed to such users-influencers to make them aware of the availability of more adequate facilities.

Benefits of buying process analysis

Analysis of the stages in the buying process through which buyers progress and the roles played by various parties to a real estate purchase can be quite rewarding. Perceptive insight can tell the sales representative who the decider is, who the influencers are, and who the users are likely to be. The appropriate sales message can then be directed to each person.

By attempting to understand which stage of the buying process prospective buyers are in, the sales representative will be better able to direct the appropriate type of information to the prospect. If the prospect is still in the prepurchase activity stage, the prospect will likely be offended if the sales representative attempts to close the sale; the buyer has not yet completed the information gathering and analysis necessary to make a decision.

Similarly, sales representatives may gain many new clients by understanding the significance of postpurchase feelings. By allaying fears and concerns after a purchase, a sales representative makes a satisfied, convinced buyer who will use that sales representative the next time a need arises to buy or sell and who will recommend the sales representative and firm to friends. It should be realized that a postpurchase gift by itself does not perform the function of allaying cognitive dissonance.

MARKETING PROPERTIES OR SERVICE?

The discussion relating to the development of a marketing strategy suggests that there is more involved to the marketing of real estate than simply listing properties for sale and making the list available for public perusal. Indeed, with multiple listing services, all brokerage firms in a community have essentially the same list of properties for sale as does one's favorite firm. Within a given market, every firm has the same function—to help expedite and consummate transactions of real properties. For fulfilling this function a commission is paid.

Since a number of firms within a market attempt to achieve the same objective, the degree of success of any individual firm will be dependent largely upon how it goes about its pursuit of the objective, first, in terms of internal management of the firm and, second, in ability to attract buyers and sellers. The first type of activity involves recruitment and training of personnel, cost accounting, control procedures, and so forth. A firm may be able to consummate a high volume of sales and yet receive a small return for its services because of unwise expenditures of time and money in the running of the business. The second type of activity, attracting buyers and sellers, is crucial to the survival (or maintenance) of the business and is the focus of this chapter. The nature of the competition suggests that the firm itself must be marketed. The firm must convince potential customers through deed and word that it provides a better service—or at least a different service—than other firms serving the same market.

Thus, two markets are relevant to the real estate business—the market for the product and the market for the services of real estate intermediaries. Real estate markets and the marketing function presumably would exist even without broker-intermediaries. The broker-intermediary's role should be viewed as a facilitating, expediting, convenience-rendering function which causes the market to work *better*, but which in itself does not "make the market."

Firms as monopolistic competitors

The economic analysis of the product in Chapter 7 developed the contention that the real estate market, in which the product is land and its improvements, best fits the model of monopolistic competition. Many parcels of real estate are sold and purchased each day, and each parcel is different from every other parcel. Each parcel is imperfectly substitutable for others, but each parcel usually is in competition with other parcels that are to some degree substitutable for it. Since there is effective competition among various parcels, the demand curve for one parcel may shift left as other substitutable parcels are brought onto the market. True monopoly prices will not be available in a well-functioning market, but purchasers will pay for perceived differential advantages of one property over another.

The model of monopolistic competition would seem also to fit many of the markets for the services of real estate firms. Particularly in the field of residential brokerage, this model realistically describes the market structure: many small firms in a community, each seeking to differentiate its service, vie for a share of the market. To a limited extent a firm may build up a loyal clientele; but as other firms enter the market, an individual firm's demand curve will shift to the left.

Firms as oligopolists

Some real estate markets, particularly those involving large, special purpose properties, are served by fewer, larger, more specialized firms. Commercial and industrial brokerage firms typically are more specialized, larger, and fewer in number than are residential brokerage firms. These markets and some residential markets, both for the product and for the services of the firms, may more appropriately be described by the model of differentiated oligopoly.

Differentiated oligopoly may be regarded as a special case of monopolistic competition. The difference is that there is even greater interdependence among the larger firms. This interdependence leads to the belief by a firm that if it lowers its price, other firms will follow suit. If, however, it raises its price, other firms will not. Whether in fact other firms behave according to these beliefs is irrelevant to the way in which a firm perceives its demand function. Its pricing policy and determination of level of operation will be decided on the basis of its assumptions about the actions other firms will take in response to its own pricing policy and level of operation.

Price-fixing

To avoid the traumatic results of price competition, many real estate firms formerly adhered to a schedule of suggested commission rates promulgated by a local trade or professional group—usually a board of Realtors. In the early 1970s the practice of requiring or even suggesting a standard structure of commission rates was attacked by the U.S. Department of Justice and by private individuals. Suits to require an end to such practices were filed under both the Sherman Anti-Trust Act and the Clayton Act against boards of Realtors and groups of brokers in a number of cities.

One important example of such actions was the suit against the Atlanta Real Estate Board filed by the U.S. Department of Justice.[8] It was settled in early 1972 by agreement of the Atlanta Real Estate Board to accept a consent judgment which prohibits the fixing or recommending of commission rates or fees. It further requires the board not to take any punitive action against anyone for failing or refusing to charge any particular commission or fee in connection with the sale, lease, or management of real estate.[9]

DEVELOPING MONOPOLISTIC ADVANTAGE

The theories of monopolistic competition and differentiated oligopoly, as well as the need for a marketing strategy, suggest that a real estate

---

[8] United States of America v. Atlanta Real Estate Board, Civil Action No. 14744, Feb. 17, 1971.

[9] *Realtor's Headlines* "Atlanta Board Signs Agreement" (Washington, D.C.: National Association of Real Estate Boards, January 10, 1972).

marketing firm should attempt to carve out an area of operation that it can serve as well or better than any other firm. Realization that the firm must market its own services and not just a list of properties also suggests the need for specialization and differentiation of its services. In other words, the firm needs to offer that combination of products and services that will be most useful to its target submarket.

The purpose of specializing and differentiating markets and services is, of course, to develop a monopoly advantage in one area of operation. A monopoly advantage will produce a profit above the minimum wage level as long as the firm is able to maintain its market position. As one real estate analyst has stated: "The ultimate objective of the firm within a free enterprise system is to create a monopoly to some extent either in fact or in the mind of the consumer."[10] Or as a marketing expert has put it: "The real dough is in what economists call monopoly profits. I don't mean in a restrictive sense. I mean being first, the guy who skims the cream."[11]

As demonstrated in the previous section, the firm engaged in real estate marketing competes in a market for services, as well as in a market for real properties. Therefore, marketing strategy should be formulated with respect to the functions involved in the firm's entire operation. Through advertising, public relations, quality of personnel, management efficiency, and selling techniques (as well as by segmenting markets), the firm can be different or more efficient than other firms performing the same economic function. The job of top management, including marketing management, in a real estate firm is to perform the long-range planning necessary to identify target submarkets of properties and services, and to determine the appropriate mix of properties and services for these markets.

Advertising. This activity is one which every business executive must engage in to some extent or another. Good advertising practices and techniques can often mean the difference between a successful firm and one that is less than successful. In the advertising function, as we will maintain for the remaining four areas, the marketer of real estate products and services should keep in mind that the objective is to establish a monopolistic advantage. That is, the advertising program and the content and nature of the advertising should be formulated in such a way that prospective clients will tend to prefer the subject firm over others.

In carrying out that advertising function, the principal purposes of the advertising will be to gain attention for the firm and to present

---

[10] Graaskamp, *A Guide to Feasibility Analysis*, p. 35.

[11] Theodore Levitt, "Innovation and the Art of Thinking Small," *Sales Management*, October 1, 1965, p. 32.

specific properties which the firm has listed for sale to the public. These two types of advertising are called firm advertising and specific advertising. Another type of advertising, institutional advertising, has as its purpose the popularizing of real estate in general. It is usually carried on by a trade or professional group. For example, the National Association of Realtors® carries on a fairly extensive advertising campaign to promote real estate and the term *Realtor.* Similarly, local real estate boards often promote real estate activity and encourage buyers and sellers to deal with members of the local board.

In seeking to establish a monopolistic advantage in this area of activity, the broker-manager should consider how to use the various advertising media available. Most real estate firms rely heavily upon newspapers and signs for their advertising efforts. However, other media such as radio, television, posters, direct mail, streetcar and bus cards, calendars, office displays, letterheads, pencils, and matchbooks are additional possible media that can be used. Newspaper advertising is most appropriate for specific advertising, where the broker-manager wishes to present various properties for sale. This type of advertising, however, also provides an important opportunity for the broker to engage in name advertising. A unique name or initials can be used for effective public identification. For example, through successful advertising and promotion, the Harley E. Rouda Company in Columbus, Ohio, has become known as HER. This symbol has become identified with a fast-growing, progressive firm. The initials appear in bold print on all advertising media used by this firm.

The choice of advertising media will also depend upon the market segment that the firm wishes to exploit. For example, brokers dealing in very expensive residential properties may want to advertise in the *Wall Street Journal,* where executives with high incomes may be likely to notice the advertisement. Firms catering to particular ethnic groups may advertise in newspapers serving those groups. Some firms in university cities seek to serve university-related personnel and may advertise heavily in the campus newspaper. In all of these kinds of advertising efforts, an effective analysis of the objectives and the media to accomplish those objectives will often mean the difference between a favorable public image and a lack of public identification.

Public relations. Public relations can be defined as constituting all of those activities in which business executives and firms come in contact with the public. Real estate marketers need to realize that a public image of the individual and the firm is built up over a period of time in the public mind. All external activities of the firm, such as advertising, attendance at public meetings, statements made on public issues, how the firm deals with clients, quality of the sales force, attractiveness and neatness of the office facilities, and manner of dress and personal appearance, blend together to create a public image of the individual and the firm. Business executives should consider all of these activities and whether they are helping to create the type of public image desired. Is the image desired, for example, that of a dynamic, progressive, fast-growing firm, or is the desired image one of stability—an old line, conservative firm?

In attempting to establish a public image, the use of a theme, as well as a unique name or initials, may be helpful. Such a theme might emphasize the friendliness or courteousness of the firm's staff. Or it might emphasize the high volume of sales created by the firm. In a subtle way, a theme can quickly and efficiently help establish the public image desired.

Quality of personnel. The real estate broker-manager needs to consider the capacity and efficiency of the sales force. How well educated and trained are the sales associates who meet with and deal with the public? This question needs to be considered in relation to the market being served. For example, an extremely high level of education may not be required to perform the sales function efficiently. Advanced degree training typically is not oriented to the persuasive techniques which lead to sales, and the years of advanced degree training frequently lead to an overemphasis upon details rather than concentration upon issues associated with buyer motivation.

Too often sales personnel are chosen on the basis of the number of people they presumably know. Little thought or attention is traditionally given to a prospective sales representative's education level, knowledge of art and music, level of success in other fields, or even aptitude for saleswork. With the growing sophistication of real estate investors, however, a background that includes a good education and the ability to converse intelligently on a variety of subjects is becoming more important than the number of people that a particular sales representative can call by their first names. It is often possible, we contend, to train and develop a good sales representative from a well-educated, personable background; the reverse process is much more difficult.

The objective of personnel policies in a real estate marketing office should be to attract, train, and retain competent people who will take a *professional* approach to the sales function. This approach requires that sales personnel analyze prospective buyers, as well as the properties that they have listed for sale. It means that they should be aware of and should use the steps in the buying process as described later in this chapter. It means that they must be aware of investment principles and what constitutes good investment and bad investment practice. It requires a desire to study continually to upgrade one's competence in helping clients solve their real estate problems. This approach takes a longer-run viewpoint than many sales representatives seem to have. It should emphasize the buildup of a clientele over a period of time, rather than maximizing the number of sales in any one month. If the sales representative develops an attitude of trying to help people solve real estate problems, he or she will indeed be successful over the long run.

Management efficiency. Few firms can be successfully and profitably operated for long without fairly good reporting and control. A sizable portion of the broker-manager's time should be spent in analyzing the performance of the firm as it relates to forecasted performance levels. Thus, budgeting and meaningful reports are essential.

Sales performances by individual sales personnel should be analyzed regularly. Such items as the number of hours spent by each sales representative in the office, the time spent in transportation, the time spent in open houses, the time spent in analyzing potential customers, the geographic locations served by the sales representative, the length of time that the sales representative has been with the firm, and the educational level are all important items that should be correlated to the sales performance being rendered.

This type of analysis should be undertaken with the view of helping the sales force to do a better, more professional job of marketing real estate. Reports and control devices should not be used with the objective of checking up on or taking punitive action. A sales representative who has been employed by a firm for more than a probationary period should be considered a permanent part of the firm and should not be subject to dismissal except in very unusual circumstances. Thus, the objective of management efficiency should be positive rather than negative; it should seek to develop ways in which greater service and more productivity can be attained but should not be a tool for penalizing members of the sales force.

Selling techniques. The development of selling techniques can be overemphasized. A book answer to every possible objection, or a canned pitch to every prospect will lead to an unthinking, unprofessional approach to real estate marketing. Rather, selling techniques should be related to the roles played by various parties in a real estate transaction, as described above in this chapter. The sales representative needs to understand these roles and seek to analyze potential buyers in terms of whether they are actual buyers, influencers, users, or a combination of several. Furthermore, the sales representative needs to analyze potential buyers in terms of the stage in the buying process in which they happen to be. Some buyers will be going through the stage of prepurchase activity. It would be a mistake to ask such a person to close a sale when he or she has not completed this stage of activity and is not yet ready to make a purchase decision. Furthermore, the professional sales representative needs to consider the long-run needs of the client relative to the properties available for sale and also relative to what the potential buyer says that his or her needs are. It may be, for example, that a family says that it needs a three-bedroom house. And such a house might be adequate for one or two years. If the sales representative has reason to believe that the family may have need for a larger house within a couple of years, he or she should point this out and attempt to have the family upgrade the size of house they consider for purchase. Similarly, if he or she believes that a client needs a smaller or less expensive property than he or she is considering, the sales representative should encourage the prospective buyer to scale down his or her desires.

Books have been written about the ways that sales personnel can overcome objections of buyers. Such an approach has little to commend it for two reasons: first, a buyer may have legitimate reasons why he or she does not consider any particular property appropriate. The design, the architecture, or the interior arrangement of the property might not be acceptable. To try to overcome such an objection when it is real and legitimate does not serve the buyer in a professional manner. Second, such an approach assumes that a stock answer to an objection will be satisfactory to everyone. Obviously, no stock answer will satisfy all potential buyers, and a great injustice is done to the art of selling by trying to get by on stock answers. Again, if the philosophy of trying to help people solve real estate problems prevails, the sales representative will attempt to discuss the disadvantages as well as the advantages of a property with a potential buyer. By gaining the confidence of the buyer, the sales representative will ultimately be able to consummate a transaction with a happy, satisfied client. To high pressure a buyer into a purchase which he or she is regretful about afterwards is to win a battle but lose the war.

The actual techniques of selling are as varied as individual sales representatives. Sales representatives must develop a selling approach based upon their own personality, philosophy, and training. Nevertheless, we can identify the steps that a real estate sales representative should go through. They include these ten items:

1. Find and meet prospective buyers and sellers of properties.
2. Orient selling techniques to concerns of the individual buyer or seller.
3. Provide information and advice—help the seller list or the buyer buy.
4. Answer questions and objections.
5. Provide assurance about doubts.
6. Show several acceptable properties to buyers—help them compare.
7. Help indecisive buyers make up their minds.
8. Close the sale—ask the buyer to sign a contract.
9. Suggest steps the buyer should take before closing the transaction.

Include the purchase of complementary items, such as insurance, that the buyer may purchase from the brokerage firm.
10. Assure the buyer's satisfaction: allay cognitive dissonance after the purchase.

These steps may seem obvious; but how many purchases can you recall in which the sales representative did not follow them? Unfortunately, they are all too often ignored or misapplied. Some sales personnel have never been exposed to them or have not been instructed in how to implement them. These responsibilities must also be borne by marketing management.

LEGAL FRAMEWORK OF REAL ESTATE MARKETING

Most real estate transactions are effected by intermediaries, licensed by the state, whose relationship to their principals is that governed by the law of agency. The law of agency requires that an agent, such as a real estate broker, in effect stand in the shoes of his or her employing principal. Thus, a real estate agent must be careful to protect the interests of a client and do nothing that would compromise the probability of consummating a transaction. An agent must exercise the restraint of a "prudent man" in protecting the interests of his client. He or she cannot, for example, purchase the property from the client and then resell the property at a higher price, pocketing both the commission and the profit on the transaction.

A real estate agent's principal to whom the agent owes legal fealty is normally the owner of the property. The owner hires a real estate broker to attempt to sell the property. And it is the owner who agrees to pay a commission to the broker if the broker is successful in finding a buyer who is "ready, willing, and able" to buy the property on the terms specified by or acceptable to the seller. In most cases a transaction is not actually required to take place before the seller is liable for the commission.

The terms of the sale that the seller is willing to accept and other aspects of the relationship between the seller and agent are usually spelled out in a written listing contract. The listing is the legal document that gives the broker the right to attempt to sell the property. Upon agreement by a seller and purchaser, each signs a contract verifying and legalizing the agreement. The contract must be in writing to be enforceable and should cover all the important concerns to both buyer and seller.[12]

---

[12] Listings and contracts, as well as other important documents and legal requirements are discussed thoroughly in Chapter 9.

SUMMARY

Intelligent marketing is crucial to the success of every business firm. For those firms operating in a market characterized by effective competition, intelligent marketing requires the development of a marketing strategy. Identifying markets or submarkets having needs and devising the proper services or products to meet those needs are the components of strategy development.

Although the real estate market, including the market for properties and the market for the services of marketing firms, often fits the model of monopolistic competition, the marketing of larger, more specialized types of properties may better fit the model of differentiated oligopoly. Price leadership and inflexibility are characteristic of these firms. To avoid the ravages of price competition, oligopolists often attempt to adhere to previously agreed upon price schedules. Such practices in the real estate business have been under attack by the federal government.

The job of marketing real estate can be analyzed in terms of buyer behavior and the roles that individuals play during the buying process. The stages of felt need, prepurchase activity, purchase decision, use behavior, and postpurchase feelings are sequential steps through which a purchaser of a major item progresses. It is helpful to a real estate marketer to know which stage a buyer may be in and to know what roles are played in a group purchase. In addition to the final decision-maker, there may be influencers, a buyer (as distinguished from the decision-maker), and users.

A marketing strategy and analyses of buying stages and roles are useful, often indispensable, components of the marketing function. They do not guarantee success, however. Only effective implementation of them by each member of the sales force can produce the desired results. To implement strategy and analysis, the real estate sales representative should carry through several basic steps, tailoring them to the individual customer. Selling techniques should be determined by the individual's own personality and the firm's policies and training procedures.

Real estate marketers operate within the legal framework of the law of agency and use several types of legal documents and procedures.

QUESTIONS FOR REVIEW

1. What is the difference between *real estate marketing* and *brokerage?*
2. What is a general definition or concept of strategy? Are other types of strategy relevant to real estate firms? If yes, what are they?
3. What kinds of information would be required to identify appropriate submarkets for a new construction firm? For a new brokerage firm? For a new appraisal-investment analysis firm? For a new property management firm?

4. What would be some potential different marketing mixes for a residential construction firm? A residential brokerage firm? An industrial brokerage firm?

5. How would a sales representative's approach differ between a buyer who is believed to be in the prepurchase activity stage and the same buyer who is in the felt need stage?

6. How would a sales representative's approach differ between a decider and a buyer (assuming they are different individuals)?

7. What do you believe should be the role of a "sales manager" in a real estate marketing firm?

8. What types of analyses might sales managers want to make and what types of information would they need to make such analyses? What types of reports from the sales personnel would be required for these analyses?

9. Comment upon problems of the selling job that appear to be unique to the real estate sales representative.

10. Identify the actions of real estate boards that have led recently to charges of price-fixing.

REFERENCES

Case, Fred E. *Real Estate Brokerage.* Englewood Cliffs, N.J.: Prentice-Hall, 1965.

Engel, James F.; Kollat, David T.; and Blackwell, Roger D. *Consumer Behavior.* New York: Holt, Rinehart & Winston, 1968.

Engel, James F.; Wales, Hugh G.; and Warshaw, Martin R. *Promotional Strategy.* 3d ed. Homewood, Ill.: Richard D. Irwin, 1975.

Hadar, Josef. *Elementary Theory of Economic Behavior,* Chaps. 5, 6, 7 and 8. Reading, Mass.: Addison-Wesley Publishing Co., 1966, pp. 53–158.

Kotler, Philip. *Marketing Management: Analysis, Planning, and Control,* chaps. 3–5. Englewood Cliffs, N.J.: Prentice-Hall, 1967, pp. 43–123.

McCarthy, E. Jerome. *Basic Marketing: A Managerial Approach.* 5th ed. Homewood, Ill.: Richard D. Irwin, 1975.

$$\text{chapter } 12$$

REAL ESTATE
PRODUCTION

REAL ESTATE INVESTORS usually can choose among properties that already are in existence or properties that can be created to their specifications. The principles and procedures governing any type of real estate investment, along with the legal and market framework, discussed previously, are now brought to bear upon the production of new properties.

Real estate production can conveniently be classified into two principal phases—land development and construction. Land development concerns all those steps taken to prepare raw land for building or improvement. Included in this phase are land procurement, land planning, land preparation, installation of utilities, and installation of streets and curbs. Construction of buildings can then follow. Included in the construction phase are planning the building, contracting for its construction, and managing the construction process. In most production operations both phases must be financed; typically each phase is financed separately.[1]

Economic significance

Real estate production is one of the most important segments of the national economy. New construction in the United States (including land development) was 10.6 percent of gross national product (GNP) in 1965 9.4 percent in 1970, and 8.7 percent in 1975 (see Table 12–1). The year 1975 was a recession year for new construction, so no downward trend should be implied from these figures. In addition to new construction, maintenance and repair on existing structures serves to raise the value

---

[1] Administration of the financing function is discussed in Chapter 13.

TABLE 12-1

Value of construction and gross national product (in billions)

	1965	1970	1975
GNP	681.9	974.1	1,498.8*
Total new construction	72.3	91.3	131.8
Percent of GNP	10.6	9.4	8.7
New private construction	50.3	63.1	90.8
Percent of GNP	6.9	6.5	4.2

* Estimated.

Source: *Federal Reserve Bulletins,* October 1971, pp. A65, A71, and December 1975, p. A51; U.S. Bureau of the Census, *Statistical Abstract of the United States: 1971,* 92d ed. (Washington, D.C.: U.S. Government Printing Office, 1971), pp. 657, 660.

of total construction to about 15 percent of GNP. Investment in new residential and nonresidential structures is the principal component of gross private domestic investment in the GNP accounts (see Table 12–2). Also, a measure of the importance of the construction industry is

TABLE 12-2

Value of new construction put in place in the United States: 1965–1974

Type of construction	Value in millions of dollars		
	1965	1970	1974
Total new construction	72,319	91,266	131,815
Private construction	50,253	63,079	96,389
Percent of total	(69.5)	(69.1)	(71.5)
Residential buildings (nonfarm)	26,268	29,273	46,769†
Nonresidential buildings	16,592	22,292	29,726
Farm construction	189	—*	2,652
Public utilities	5,788	—*	16,243
All other private	416	946	999
Public construction	22,066	28,187	38,426
Percent of total	(30.5)	(30.9)	(28.5)
Buildings	7,875	10,657	14,990
Highways and streets	7,550	9,989	12,105
Military facilities	852	791	1,188
Conservation and development	2,019	1,919	2,286
Other public construction	3,770	4,831	7,256

* Not available.

† Includes farm homes.

Source: U.S. Bureau of the Census, *Statistical Abstract of the United States: 1971,* 92d ed. (Washington, D C.: U.S. Government Printing Office, 1971), p. 657, and *Construction Reports,* Series C 30, 1974.

the fact that roughly four million people are employed in the production of real estate resources and several million more are employed in related industries that manufacture products that become components of new properties.

Implications of theory

Elasticity of supply. Chapter 7 is concerned with the interaction of demand and supply forces in the market. It was pointed out that the supply of real estate is inelastic relative to price increases in the short run. In other words, because of the length of time required in the marshaling of resources to produce new real estate resources, an upward shift in the demand curve will result in relatively greater increases in rents and prices than in the additional units of space supplied. As the time period of analysis lengthens, however, the supply curve becomes relatively more elastic.

The clear implication for those in the construction industry is that forecasting is of paramount importance to successful business operations. Because of cyclical fluctuations in demand conditions, it will often be too late to take full advantage of an increased demand situation after it has arrived. By the time builders get tooled up, their resources organized, and construction well along, a period of six months to one year may have elapsed and either demand conditions may have slackened or another builder will have provided the needed units. Furthermore, by the time builders get their workers laid off and their construction activities diminished, cyclical variations are apt to produce another upturn, with builders being once again out of phase. Unfortunately, this description is not atypical of average builders today.

We must realize, however, the difficulties and uncertainties with which the construction demand forecaster is faced. Unfortunately, the federal government's housing policies are more in the nature of short-run expedient tactics rather than long-run strategies for significantly upgrading American housing. Shifts from tight money to loose money and back again are promulgated periodically by the Federal Reserve Board. Sometimes such shifts are reinforced and sometimes mitigated by actions of the Federal Home Loan Bank Board, the Federal Home Loan Mortgage Corporation, the Federal National Mortgage Association, and the Government National Mortgage Association. In addition, fiscal policy and actions by the Federal Housing Administration and the Veterans Administration serve at times to run the forecasting art into little more than a guessing game. Myrdal points out the need for longer range planning in the United States.

... the main thing (needed) in long-range planning is all the separate pieces of the jigsaw should be integrated into a single comprehensive plan for the development of the economy as a whole. Such a plan, specifying not only the speed but also the main direction of economic growth, is vital for the framing of government policy. It is equally vital as a basis for planning in private business, which must otherwise operate with a complex of important parameters in the form of mere guesses, based on no real knowledge.[2]

Certainly, however, within the limits of forecasting ability, a six-months to one-year forecast is crucial to construction firms.

Filtering.   Filtering is the movement of people of one income group into homes that have recently dropped in price and which were previously occupied by those in the next higher income group. The implication of the filtering phenomenon is that for the continual improvement of housing standards, even in a static economy or community, new construction must occur to maintain a surplus of supply at each family income level. To stand still in the production of housing even when economic conditions are static means to regress. Urban development and community progress require a continuing supply of new housing above and beyond that level needed to house an increasing population. However, it is doubtful whether such a condition can be sustained by the market.[3]

A critical problem in community development is that old, in-town properties often cannot be economically upgraded. Lenders and appraisers have found that older neighborhoods sometimes tend to reflect values which are lower than those in neighborhoods which are newer and more modern. The Department of Housing and Urban Development (HUD) has responded to this need through community development grants, and some cities have experienced efforts by major lenders to revitalize older neighborhoods. A lawsuit was filed in April 1976, by the U.S. Department of Justice against the American Institute of Real Estate Appraisers, the Society of Real Estate Appraisers, the United States League of Savings Associations, and the Mortgage Bankers Association for alleged discrimination against minority groups who typically purchase homes in older, in-town neighborhoods. The suit requests that practices which downgrade values in such areas be stopped, and the defendants are asked to create new ways to appraise and underwrite older homes in older neighborhoods. The outcome of the suit and its impact upon the filtering process have not been determined as of the date of this writing.

LAND DEVELOPMENT

Although land development is normally undertaken by private real estate developers and entrepreneurs, it is one of the most socially signifi-

---

[2] Gunnar Myrdal, *Challenge to Affluence* (New York: Pantheon Books, 1965), p. 84.

[3] See the discussion in Chapter 7.

cant types of business activity. The individual or firm that converts raw, agricultural land to urban usage establishes land-use patterns and other physical arrangements that often prevail into the future for 100 years or longer. Productivity of the real estate after development will depend upon the extent to which the developer has made wise decisions and has established land-use patterns that will protect and enhance long-run values.

Much criticism has been leveled at land developers in recent years. Too often land developer-builders have failed in other businesses and have then moved on to try their hands in the field of real estate production. Too often their motives have not been concerned with the long-run best interest of the community; instead, they have in many cases subdivided small acreages with inefficient layouts—small lots, narrow streets, insufficient services, unattractive designs—having little relation to previously established subdivisions, road systems, and utility services. Many times land developer-builders have had no education in real estate. They are unknowledgeable about economic analysis, social trends, legal influences, and administrative concepts and tools. In more cases than not real estate production has been performed by carpenters or other tradespeople who have attempted to go into business for themselves or to expand a limited operation. Clearly, with America's urban problems becoming increasingly crucial with each passing month and year, society cannot long tolerate the luxury of nonprofessional dominance in this field.

A specific indication of this state of affairs is realization that land developers tended to outwit themselves in the early 1970s. The activity of land development became separate from that of the builder; land developers produced lots, planned communities, office parks, and industrial parks at a scale beyond the capacity of builders to use them. Developers continued to expand beyond demand in an effort to secure loan draws.

To bring some control and efficiency to land development, many communities have established various regulations and agencies which govern new real estate development. Developers legally must comply with some of these controls and should coordinate their development planning with other community plans and agencies whether there is a legal obligation or not. The plans and limitations that may be involved are briefly discussed in this section.

Zoning. Zoning is an exercise of the community's police power in regulating land usage, including the height, width, bulk, and density of buildings.[4] Zoning laws are well established in most communities and compliance is mandatory, although not infrequently the laws have been subverted through political influence. Appointees to a planning com-

_____
[4] See the discussion in Chapters 1 and 14.

mission are sometimes pressured to repay political debts or favors by voting favorably on a requested zoning change. Still, a change in the law or a "variance" is required to defeat the purpose of a zoning ordinance. Misinterpretations of the law or blatant favoritism will be overturned by the courts. In a few cases of noncompliance developers and builders have been forced to tear down buildings and realign subdivisions. Obviously, the developer and builder should know and thoroughly understand the zoning laws applicable to their developments.

Master plan. Many communities have developed a master plan, often on a metropolitan area or regional basis. The Franklin County Regional Planning Commission, for example, has prepared a plan (known as the Blue Plan) for the entire Columbus, Ohio, metropolitan area. The plan concerns a number of municipalities and attempts to forecast and to plan for future land development. The plan itself is not legally enforceable; however, most of the communities encompassed by the plan have developed their own city plans and zoning ordinances in conformity with the regional plan. Certainly professional real estate developers should coordinate their developments with a master plan so as to promote sound, long-run growth.

Building and housing codes. These local codes regulate, respectively, construction standards and housing conditions and maintenance. Normally the latter would not be of concern to a developer except insofar as construction could influence future housing conditions. The builder obviously must be concerned with the building code and comply with it.

Transportation plans and facilities. Various governmental levels (city, county, and state) may have plans for street and highway development and expansion of other public transportation facilities. Many cities, for example, have airport expansion plans which could drastically influence land development plans in the area. The large amount of freeway construction in recent years has cut through many existing and planned real estate developments. Plans for extending city streets into newly developing areas in many cases will determine the basic street layout for a new subdivision.

Sewer extensions. As a community expands, both sanitary sewers and storm sewers should be extended to serve new areas. Developers must be aware of such plans. In some housing developments subdivisions have been established without storm sewers with disastrous results. In some other situations the facilities were inadequate or the land was too low for adequate drainage.

Activities in land development

Land development encompasses all those steps taken from the inception of the decision to undertake a development project to the construction phase. In other words, it involves all those activities necessary to procure and prepare land for construction of a building. Each of these activities is discussed in this section.

Land procurement. Although the necessity of this activity is obvious, the execution and problems associated with it can be quite complex. Furthermore, the considerations vary depending upon whether land acquisition is for the purpose of combining already improved parcels into a more intensive use or for the development of agricultural land into single-family residential lots. Land should be procured for either purpose only after an adequate market analysis has been performed to determine the feasibility of the proposed undertaking.

In procuring previously developed land within an urbanized area, complex problems often arise from two sources: (*a*) the existence of improvements on the individual parcels and (*b*) having to deal with multiple owners of the several parcels needed. For example, the acquisition of land in a downtown area for the purpose of constructing a new, larger building usually requires the developer to acquire a number of older, smaller parcels having structures of various ages and sizes. The owners of these parcels may for various reasons have inflated opinions of the value of their parcels or may even refuse to sell at any price—particularly when they realize that it is imperative for the developer to obtain a given parcel to complete the land procurement plan. This problem has been especially significant in large-scale, private redevelopment efforts. William Zeckendorf, Jr., has proposed that developers of such extensive projects be given the right of eminent domain.[5]

The early 1970s was a period of "land boom" which matched or exceeded that of the 1920s. The advent of real estate investment trusts, the attractiveness of real estate syndications, and the seemingly insatiable demand for lots, homes, commercial properties, and so on, attracted everyone from airline pilots to brain surgeons into land investment. Deals grew larger and larger, and "leverage," the nemesis of real estate, led a select small number of people to become millionaires overnight. The bubble burst in 1973–74, and both institutions and individuals lost substantial sums. Caution has become the watchword of the industry, and the need for sound market and financial feasibility analysis has gained substantial prominence.

Zoning. The parcel must be zoned properly for the proposed usage. If changes in zoning are needed, the developer must commence processing as quickly as possible. The rezoning procedure involves time delay that can be costly if land improvement and construction must be delayed.

Land preparation. Most tracts of land that are to be developed from

---

[5] "Large-Scale Urban Redevelopment—Some Problems and Issues," paper delivered to Annual Meeting of American Real Estate and Urban Economics Association in New York City, December 28, 1965.

agricultural to urban uses require the application of a considerable amount of labor and capital. Redevelopment projects in urbanized areas typically require much greater costs for land preparation. In either case the land must be cleared of unwanted debris, old buildings, and trees that hinder construction.

Subdividing. For residential developments, which typically involve the conversion of rural to urban land, the site must be further developed after the land has been cleared. This phase is known as subdividing and usually involves the plotting of lots; the grading of the cleared site; and the installing of utilities, drainage facilities, and roads. Many substeps involving various kinds of costs are of course involved in this process. Surveying charges; preparation of blueprints for the subdivision; installation of curbs, catch basins, and sewers; and providing for water lines are but a few of these steps and costs.

In addition to the above types of cash outlays, land developers must also consider the property taxes they will incur during the time they own the lots and also their equity cost that accrues because their capital is tied up. From an economic point of view, all of these costs plus the developer's profit must be considered the cost of society's obtaining the newly developed real estate.

Financing. Rarely can land developers pay cash for the land to be developed. Rather, they must usually finance the property by one of several methods. They might borrow from the seller (with a purchase money mortgage serving as security), obtain an option from the owner to purchase the lots one at a time as they sell previously developed lots (with or without a house constructed on the lot), form a syndicate or corporation to obtain equity capital from other individuals, or obtain a land development loan from a financial institution. In all such cases, the developers must usually convince the lenders (whether they be owners, investors, or financial institutions) of the feasibility of the project. Therefore, the developers need to have specific plans and budgets for the land development and construction that is to take place on the land. A market survey showing the demand expected for the completed units is usually necessary in convincing a seller or financial institution to advance the needed funds.

Significance to urban development

Our purpose is not to describe in detail the steps and processes involved in land development. Rather, we wish to identify and analyze some of the important considerations that should concern developers and society in the production of profitable and socially desirable real estate projects. Society has the responsibility of providing incentives to the developers who perform their function by creating the long-term utility that is to society's advantage; that is, developers who subdivide in accordance with future requirements and long-term values should be rewarded more than those who are in business to turn a quick dollar and get out. Developers, on the other hand, have a responsibility to understand their social responsibility as well as their financial reward. They should be educated in the area of long-run aesthetics and values. Too often they are not, and the zoning regulations are not intended or sufficient to preclude developments that may produce short-term profits, but long-term slums.

Integrated development. The modern approach to land development is to assure proper relationships among the various land uses. Martin defines an integrated development as "one in which many kinds of land improvements are planned in relation to each other and constructed as a unit, as a whole."[6] Subdivisions which provide for shopping facilities, entertainment and recreational areas, public parks, and churches are integrated developments. A shopping center, in which the various land uses are planned ahead of time and are related to each other, is another example of an integrated development. Integrated developments are related to existing and future land uses, utilities, and streets that now or in the future will border the development.

Integrated development contrasts with the so called add-on type, in which individual lots are developed and improved one at a time. Development of this type, however, usually results in too much consideration being given existing bordering uses which are probably obsolete. It also fails to provide for needed services and utilities. The ultimate result is unplanned, uncoordinated, nonhomogeneous land uses which do not retain their values as long as integrated developments.

Integrated development requires large-scale development and construction operations. The large firms that can engage in this type of development usually experience economies of scale in their business operations, making large-scale, integrated developments generally more profitable. Workers can be assigned to specialized functions, materials can be bought in large quantities, advertising is more rewarding, and managerial talent is equally applied to all phases of the job.

The benefits to planned, systematic urban development of the integrated approach are obvious. Compliance with a master plan and the implementing provisions of the zoning regulations have become crucial in the effort to stem unplanned, topsy-turvy urban sprawl.

One note of caution is needed in analyzing integrated developments. All major lending institutions are fearful that common area facilities such as parks, playgrounds, recreational amenities, parking garages, and

---

[6] Preston Martin, *Real Estate Principles and Practices* (New York: Macmillan Co., 1959), p. 96.

so on, will become a burden on property owners after the developer has sold out and gone. Care must be taken to scale phases of common elements in such projects at levels which permit sound maintenance at reasonable costs.

Land planning and control. Planning for the allocation and control of land uses within an integrated development requires an understanding of desirable and undesirable locational relationships. It is one thing to state simply that adequate shopping facilities should be provided in a residential development; it is quite another to decide the actual layout and thus the relationship between the residential properties and the shopping area. In general, the shopping area should be convenient enough so that residents can travel there within five or ten minutes, but it must be located so as not to spoil the view or access of the residences. Consideration must be given relationships between number, types, and sizes of various stores and the number of people and their income characteristics who are to be served.

The residential lots themselves must be developed so that the homes to be constructed will have adequate space and will be in pleasing relationships with neighboring properties and views, while being shielded from nuisances such as dumps, railroads, and highways. Street patterns should be planned to avoid monotony and high-speed traffic, yet should provide convenient access. The natural contours of the land and other natural advantages such as streams, trees, and views should be considered.

Once the subdivision has been planned and developed, steps should be taken to insure its continued existence as a planned, integrated development. The zoning laws may provide some control, but as discussed previously, these laws serve only to provide a broad framework within which many variations may occur. The developer of an integrated subdivision may well decide that more precise controls are needed. These usually take the form of deed restrictions.

Deed restrictions operate in addition to the zoning laws. The restrictions are placed on every parcel in the subdivision being developed, with provision for termination in 20 or 30 years unless extended by the property owners. Typically the restrictions should place minimum limitations on the size or ground area of the structures, restrict the land use and type of structure that can be constructed, provide adequate setback lines, and provide for architectural control through an architectural control committee of subdivision property owners. Formerly, restrictions limiting the cost of structures to those above a given dollar level were often placed in deeds, but they have become meaningless with the increasing price level over the years. Restrictions involving measures that are subject to change, such as prices and costs, should generally be avoided. Similarly, restrictions that run for indefinite periods should be avoided. Land uses change, and adequate flexibility (as well as the desired degree of control) should be provided.

Role of the developer-investor

Land developers are investors who commit their equity, equipment, labor force, and managerial talents to the conversion of land from one use to another. The developer's role is to conceptualize, plan, organize, and carry out the development of land resources. The developer's social responsibility must be regarded as of highest importance when one considers the vast amount of wealth represented by the land and the fact that society must usually live with developers' accomplishments many years. As such, then, the economic rationale for land development and redevelopment should be understood by developers so that they can carry out their function in the best interest of both society and themselves.

Most simply, land development or redevelopment is justified when the present value of the expected benefits are equal to or greater than the cost of obtaining those benefits. Developers should predict future income levels and patterns that are obtainable under various uses. They should then estimate the costs necessary to develop the land for those purposes and compare the results. The costs for redevelopment projects should, of course, include the costs of demolishing existing uses and the foregoing of income from the existing use. In either development or redevelopment projects, the developers' cost of capital should be the point below which they will not undertake the project. The returns afforded by alternative uses above the cost of capital should be ranked, and the use showing the highest overall return should be chosen.

This suggests that the developer-investor must be intimately familiar with costs, income estimation procedures, and capitalization concepts. Income estimation requires knowledge of market analysis techniques, and these require knowledge and understanding of data sources and research methodology. Certainly the development field should be no place for unsophisticated, nonanalytically oriented individuals. They should command the highest level of competency in business decision-making techniques.

The developer's role is also that of risk bearer. Developers' commitment of capital and labor subject them to interest rate risk, and the projects in which they have their capital and labor committed are subject to business risk (failure of the undertaking) and market risks (the possibility that the project will decline in value). In most cases the financial risk associated with borrowed funds will also be incurred. Developers must know and understand these risks and be prepared to accept some, avoid some, and pass some along to insurers. As risk managers, they must be aware of the alternative courses of action that are possible.

The land developer's role can be illustrated by the considerations involved in a decision by one large land development firm. The firm, Winter and Company, purchases land for subsequent resale—either developed or undeveloped. All of the land purchased by the company is located in or around a large metropolitan area in the Southwest. The area has a well-diversified economic base, with major categories of basic employment being heavy manufacturing, national defense, state government, and education. The area has a population of about 1 million persons and has been growing at a rate of about 10 percent per year. In short, the demand for well-located, high-quality raw acreage is expected to continue strong.

A tract of 55 acres of land has been offered for sale and is being considered for purchase by Winter and Company. The land is now zoned for agricultural and rural residential uses. Winter and Company believes the land can be rezoned for urban residential usage (single family), at a density of 3.5 homes per acre (9,000 to 12,000 square foot lots). The land is located about one-half mile outside a recently completed circumferential highway. The asking price for the land is $825,000 ($15,000 per acre). If the land is developed for single-family residences, Winter and Company estimate development costs will run approximately $5,000 per lot. It is believed that the lots can be sold within five years for an average price of $13,000, with about 3.5 lots per acre. A bank line of credit will finance 75 percent of the land acquisition and development costs at 10 percent. Real estate taxes are expected to amount to 1 percent of the unsold land value per year. The company's marginal tax bracket is 50 percent, and its return is calculated in Figure 12–1.

As can be seen in Figure 12–1, a discount rate of 16 percent comes close to equating the present value of the cash intake from the sale of lots with the present value of the cash outlays and expenses. The exact rate of return is somewhat more than 16.5 percent.

Several questions arise from this analysis. First, how reliable and accurate are the expected sale prices of lots? Second, are all the expenses that will actually be incurred included? Third, are the financing assumptions valid and realistic? Obviously, any variation of substantial proportion will cause the yield to be different from that calculated. There is always some probability that the lot prices will be lower than expected or that sales cannot be made at the expected prices at the time anticipated. Are these risks adequately compensated by a 16 percent aftertax rate of return?

To state the problem differently, the land should not be purchased and developed unless the expected rate of return is above the firm's cost of capital. Its cost of capital is a weighted average of the cost of debt

FIGURE 12-1

Winter and Company calculation of investment project profitability

Year	1	2	3	4	5	Total
Sales revenue (38 lots/year)	494,000	494,000	494,000	494,000	494,000	2,470,000
Less costs:						
Real estate commissions (5 percent)	24,700	24,700	24,700	24,700	24,700	123,500
Title matters	5,000					5,000
Surveys	3,000					3,000
Land acquisition cost	825,000					825,000
Land development cost ($5,000 per lot)	190,000	190,000	190,000	190,000	190,000	950,000
Real estate taxes	24,700	19,800	14,800	9,900	4,900	74,100
Total costs	1,072,400	234,500	229,500	224,600	219,600	1,980,600
Revenue minus costs	(578,400)	259,500	264,500	269,400	274,400	489,400
Deduct:						
Loan interest at 10 percent*	80,430	57,840	31,890	5,440	–0–	175,600
Income taxes at 50 percent	(329,415)	100,830	116,305	131,980	137,200	156,900
Net cash flow	(329,415)	100,830	116,305	131,980	137,200	156,900
Present value of 1 factor at 16 percent	.8621	.7432	.6406	.5523	.4761	
Present value of cash flow	(283,989)	74,937	74,505	72,893	65,321	3,667†

* Loan interest is based on the assumption that costs occur at the beginning of the year and revenues occur at the end of the year. The maximum loan is 75 percent of land acquisition and development cost. Thus, the loan balance at the end of year 1 is $1,072,400 times 75 percent equals $804,300. This loan is assumed to be reduced to $578,400 on January 1 of year 2; to $318,900 on January 1 of year 3; to $54,400 on January 1 of year 4, and to $0 on January 1 of year 5. All repayments are assumed to be made from project revenues.

† This figure represents value above a 16 percent (aftertax) rate of return. When discounted at a 17 percent rate, the ending balance is ($2,259), indicating that the project is capable of earning approximately 16.6 percent.

capital and equity. Since equity capital in land development will require a high rate of return to compensate for the risks, the weighted cost of capital will be relatively high—probably at least 15 percent. Winter and Company thus must consider its cost of capital in relation to the project's expected return. It should be confident that its predictions of sale prices, costs, and expenses are as complete and reliable as they can be. The company is then in a position to make a judgmental decision about whether to proceed with the project.

Role of the development lender

One of the major problems in forecasting by construction firms is that construction lenders have a tendency to overextend credit in times of "loose" money and overrestrict credit when money availability is limited. They serve to accelerate the cyclical swings of the market rather than stabilize them. Marginal loans made during expansion periods lead to substantial overbuilding, creating unsold or unrented inventory. When money is tight, the same lenders typically refuse to provide permanent loans on the products created through their loan efforts. This practice obviously places developers in financial jeopardy.

Good development lenders are moderately conservative, making only those loans which can be supervised effectively. They stand behind the borrower and develop a financing plan that does not end until the unit is financed permanently. Savings and loan associations performed unusually well in this regard during the 1974–75 recession; real estate investment trusts performed poorly.

Role of the secondary financing market

Residential markets are by far the largest in dollar volume, number of loans, and amount of necessary supervision. The housing market is cyclical in the same direction as the general economy, but it tends to lag the economy by several months. In recent years, the Federal National Mortgage Association (FNMA) and the Federal Home Loan Mortgage Corporation (FHLMC) have been geared to offer funding during tight money periods. These secondary markets also supervise subsidized emergency assistance home loans issued by the Government National Mortgage Association (GNMA), another program to encourage market stability. During 1975 the GNMA program injected $10 billion into the economy for new single-family homes. In 1976 an initial injection of $3 billion was placed in multifamily homes, while approximately $5 billion went into loans for detached homes. A total of $10 billion of emergency assistance money was allocated for the year.

When money is tight, interest rates rise, and yields commanded on home loans purchased by FNMA and FHLMC increase. However, FNMA sells forward standby commitments which permit knowledgeable developers to hedge against such increases. These commitments may be purchased at a price of 1 percent of the amount of loans to be delivered. They are at a fixed yield rate, and they can be exercised or allowed to expire at the purchaser's option. If exercised, 0.5 percent is refunded. Commitments of this type tend to stabilize the market, but they have not been used extensively to date.

A new secondary market vehicle that has been developed at the Chicago Board of Trade is the sale of forward commitments to buy FHA and VA home loans through the GNMA. The GNMA commits to purchase loans at fixed future dates and at fixed yields. Purchasers of the commitments bid on them in the same manner as they would on other types of futures commodities. This vehicle was developed in 1975, and its impact upon the stability of the mortgage market cannot be evaluated at the date of this writing.

CONSTRUCTION

The building or construction process is carried on by an industry which, when considered in total, is our largest single industry. Although the economic significance of the construction industry was discussed earlier, Table 12–3 shows total construction and its principal categories projected to 1980 and 2000. The projected figures represent an increase of roughly 300 percent in total construction, which is a faster rate of growth than that expected for GNP.

Size alone—present and future—however, is not the only consideration that is expected to enhance the place of the construction industry in the national economy. Increases in efficiency and productivity of the industry may well occur at a faster rate than formerly and at faster rates than increases in other productive segments of the economy. Heretofore, the construction industry has been regarded as the least progressive of our major industries. Although productivity has increased, the gains have been lower than productivity increases in other fields. As Weimer, Hoyt, and Bloom point out:

> The industry suffers from restrictive building codes, restrictive labor practices, and from its dependence on the development of regional supporting facilities by government to allow for new land development. Many builders, of course, continue to follow outmoded practices. Informal agreements sometimes result in price-fixing and the reduction of competition.[7]

To the extent that productivity gains in construction have not kept pace with other industries, the construction industry has contributed less

---

[7] Weimer, Hoyt, and Bloom, *Real Estate*, p. 367.

TABLE 12–3

Principal categories of construction, 1950, 1960, and medium projections for 1980, 2000 (billion 1960 dollars)

			Medium projection	
	1950	*1960*	*1980*	*2000*
Total construction	58.6	76.2	166.3	348.4
New construction	42.2	56.6	130.1	280.9
Maintenance and repair	16.4	19.6	36.2	67.5
for residential construction	6.2	7.2	10.8	14.7
Residential new construction including				
additions and alterations	19.6	22.6	54.7	126.4
Nonresidential new construction	22.7	31.1	75.4	151.5
Private new construction	32.8	40.6	90.2	196.8
Public new construction	9.4	16.0	39.9	84.1
Components of public new nonresidential				
construction:	9.1	15.3	37.2	77.8
Schools and hospitals	2.3	3.2	5.0	7.4
Highways	2.6	5.5	16.1	31.6
Military and industrial	.6	1.8	5.1	12.3
All other (water, sewerage, and so on)	3.6	4.8	11.0	23.5

Source: "Resources in America's Future," Appendix Table A4–3. Reprinted in Arthur Weimer and Homer Hoyt, *Real Estate,* 5th ed. (New York: Ronald Press, 1966), p. 370.

growth to our total national wealth than other segments of the economy. If productivity gains can be increased significantly, however, construction will contribute an even greater share of increase to our national resources. Weimer, Hoyt, and Bloom also point out that the building industry may be having its industrial revolution, which suggests that the industry may shortly take off in productivity relative to (*a*) its past performance and (*b*) other industries.[8]

Structure of the industry

Construction firms range in size all the way from very small to very large companies that engage in building operations in several countries. However, most of today's builders are small-time operators who are often dropouts from other small business failures. In home building even the large builders such as Levitt and Sons, Inc., Ryan Homes, Inc., and U.S. Home are small in relation to the total market; each of the largest builders accounts for less than 0.5 percent of total production.

Also characteristic of the industry are the small outlays on research and development expended by construction firms and industry groups. Little research and development effort is undertaken by private firms, with the result that little new knowledge is obtained or distributed about con-

---

[8] Ibid., p. 371.

struction materials and methodologies. Prefabrication techniques are considerably further advanced in European countries, and laborsaving techniques are employed more extensively. The conclusion is that profit squeezes will be felt increasingly by smaller firms and that increases can be expected in the number of large-scale regional and national builders.

The construction process

Many steps and operations are involved in the construction of any major improvement to the land—whether the improvement be a home, apartment building, commercial structure, factory, or hydroelectric dam. Construction concerns the conversion of prepared but vacant land to a usable, productive parcel of real estate. It represents the creation of economic resources by the combining of various components into new time, form, and place relationships—both among themselves and with the land.

Functions

Planning. As with every complex task, the management functions of planning, organizing, and controlling must be performed in the construction process. In the planning function, provisions must be made for designing the structure, specifying the materials and components that will make up the structure, arranging for the purchase and timely availability of materials and components, arranging for the labor force required to assemble the materials and components, and providing for financing adequate to support these activities. Typically, an architect and contractor are hired to perform all except the financing activity for the investor-builder.

The planning objective of the architect is to design a building that will serve most appropriately the functions or uses to which the building will be put. To do this the architect must thoroughly understand the requirements of the owner or user of the property, whether the property is to serve as a home or an industrial plant. As Ratcliff points out:

Design involves space planning, engineering design, and aesthetics. Space planning includes site planning—the disposition of the structure on the land —and interior planning—the distribution of the space within the building; engineering design relates to the structural features of the building, the floor and wall construction, roof framing, stairways, footings, and other features that determine the structural strength of the building. From an aesthetic standpoint, the architect endeavors to impart a pleasing appearance to the structure through the arrangement of masses and proportions and the selection of materials and architectural details.[9]

---

[9] Ratcliff, *Urban Land Economics,* p. 177.

Also, under the planning function, the architect specifies the quality, grade, brand name, or model number (hence, the term *specification* or *specs*) of the exact materials and component assemblies that are to go into the building. The architect must keep abreast of new materials, building techniques, and local building codes in writing the specifications. Every subsurface aspect as well as every surface aspect of the structure must be designed and integrated in the plans. The architect must be able to visualize the finished product and convert this visualization to a step-by-step plan for achieving it.

Organizing. Except for arranging for suitable financing, other activities involved in the organizing function are usually performed by the architect and/or contractor. In addition to designing and specifying the structure and its components, architects may be engaged to supervise the building process. They control the activities of the builder to insure conformance with the plans and specifications. They check the construction process to ascertain that the quality is acceptable.

Although architects are not ordinarily employed in the construction of single-family homes costing under $40,000, it seems likely that professional architectural services could profitably be used for the construction of many homes above the $50,000 level. The typical fee for full architectural service runs about 10 percent of the cost, and for this figure the advantages of architectural design and supervision may more than make up for the cost in higher-priced homes. Studying the functional requirements of the family that is to occupy the dwelling and incorporating a design and features into a structure that will best meet these needs is ordinarily not work for an amateur.

For their fee architects attempt to provide an aesthetically pleasing environment and building, yet one which conforms to the pocketbook constraints of their employers. Since each family's makeup, age structure, personalities, and interests are different from every other's, it stands to reason that individual attention to the design of a home would be desirable for most families that can afford a relatively high-priced structure.

The purchase of a house that has been built for speculative resale (although constituting the largest source of new home purchases) may not offer the best compromise between the desirable attributes of efficiency and beauty and the cost expended. Indeed, the disadvantages may extend even further to inferior quality of work, materials, and components. To their credit, many of the larger, more experienced speculative builders now offer reliable warranties on ready-built houses. Furthermore, some recent court decisions have enforced the concept of vendor (builder-seller) warranty and in some cases have even extended the concept to financial institutions that have significant control over the building process. Nevertheless, the larger issue between architectural cost and advantage will not be resolved by the courts—only by the service provided.

Financing of the construction process is ordinarily organized by owners or contractors. Owners may be speculative builders who are erecting a large number of houses for resale or individuals who have contracted for the building of a home for their own occupancy. In the construction of multifamily residential buildings, commercial buildings, or industrial structures, owners may be individual investors, partnership syndicates, corporations, or other types of organization. In almost all cases, however, the individual or organization doing the actual construction must obtain the financing. Because of the large and unusual risks involved in this type of financing, a number of special safeguards and arrangements have evolved for construction financing.

The need for construction financing arises because the individuals who have contracted to have a building constructed will not pay for the work until it is completed, and builders are not able or do not want to pay the bills for labor and materials out of their own pockets before receiving payment from their employer. The builder thus borrows by means of a short-term (usually two to nine months), secured loan from a financial institution. Security for the loan is the land and a nonexistent building. Because of the risk that the building will not be built or will not be completed according to plans and specifications in the time period forecasted, the financial institution will typically not pay out the loan before construction has begun. Rather, the loan is usually paid out in stages after specified portions of the building have been completed—for example, after the foundation is in, after the roof is on, after the plumbing and electrical work are completed, and when the building is finished. The financial institution will pay out portions of the loan, the total of which is smaller than the value of the security or the percentage of the job accomplished. For example, one-third of the loan might be paid out after the roof is on although the building would be approximately 50 percent complete. Also, the lender will require the builder to show proof of payment of bills and to provide lien waivers from contractors and subcontractors.

Controlling. The controlling function for the construction process is performed by the owner, architect, contractor, and sometimes the financier. As discussed above, an architect representing the owner may control the construction process by supervising the builder. Owners, of course, could perform this function if they are qualified, but usually they are not capable of adequate supervision. Typically for small, single-family home construction jobs, the owners employ contractors who are entrusted with the controlling function, as well as the actual building process. Owners periodically check major aspects of the job such as general layout, brand names of components, and general construction quality. It would be quite easy in most cases, however, for a dishonest contractor to get by with inferior materials and a poor quality of work.

For large-scale development and construction projects, a team of engineers and inspectors representing the general contractor maintain constant supervision of the actual work. Spot checks by the owners, their architects, or the financial institution could cause nonpayment to the contractor. In large residential developments the speculative builder's team of inspectors is charged with maintaining certain minimum standards of materials and a poor quality of work. If builders wish to be able to sell houses on a continuing basis, the buying public must have a favorable image of the builder's capability and product. Also, in order to sell the houses, builders may have to rely on government underwritten financing for buyers and must therefore meet the standards required by the FHA and VA.

Role of the builder

Although various aspects of the functions of planning, organizing, and controlling are performed by parties other than builders, they are the crucial element in the construction process. More of the construction process is performed by builders than anyone else. The builders' role consists of a number of activities. They must estimate construction costs, submit bids on building jobs that will allow them an acceptable rate of return, assemble and organize materials and labor, arrange for construction financing, disburse payments to workers and subcontractors, supervise actual construction, and work with the owner.

The key to success for builders is their ability to estimate costs realistically and accurately. A reliable cost estimate and breakdown will allow them to submit acceptable bids, obtain materials and labor, cover their overhead, and make a profit. Figure 12–2 is a builder's house for which there is a detailed description and a cost breakdown in Figures 12–3 and 12–4. As shown in Figure 12–4, the costs are usually categorized according to the labor and materials going into the main structure, with heating, plumbing, and electric systems considered separately from the main structure. If the builders have heating engineers, plumbers, and electricians on their workforce, they would do this work. Often, however, smaller builders subcontract the heating, plumbing, and electrical work to specialized firms in these fields. The heating, plumbing, and electrical installations make up significant components percentagewise in the total cost of the house. (Together, they total 18.16 percent.)

Another category is indirect costs. This type of cost is for items that pertain to the entire property but are not functionally identifiable. Costs

FIGURE 12–2

Builder's house plan

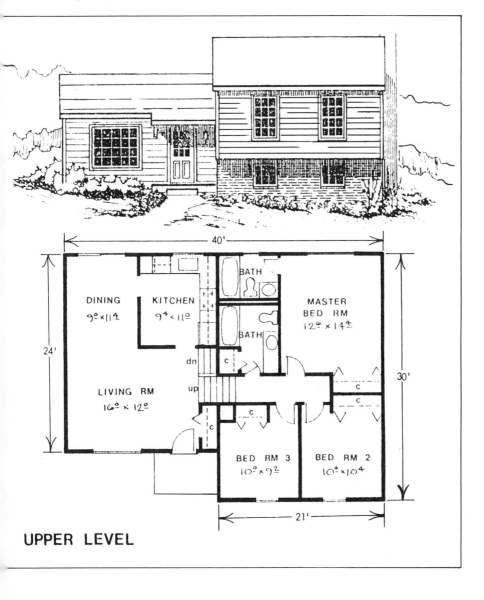

UPPER LEVEL

FIGURE 12–3

Builder's house (detailed description)

Description:

Three-bedroom, brick and stone, side split-level home.

Seven rooms, 2½ baths.

Built-ins in kitchen.

Partial basement under living area.

Brick fireplace in family room.

Two-car garage.

Structure:

Excavation and clay gravel: 11 courses, 8″ C.B., waterproofing; termite protection; metal windows.

Chimney: C.B. with brick facing fireplace flue size 12″ × 12″, gas vented into 8″ × 12″ flue; water heater vented.

Fireplace (in family room): Firebrick lining; stone hearth; ceiling high mantle.

Exterior walls: Sheathing Gyplap, ½″, 4′ × 8′, solid; face brick; frame backup, 2′ × 4′; door sills concrete; stone window sills; exterior painting lead and oil.

Floor framing: #1 fir, 2″ × 8″–16″ O.C.; 1″ × 3″ bridging; joist anchors concrete slab basement floor.

Fill under slab: 4″ gravel.

Subflooring: ⅜″ plywood.

Finish flooring: Nylon shag carpeting over 60 oz. foam pad.

Partition framing: #1 fir, 2″ × 4″–16″ O.C.

Ceiling framing: #1 fir, 2″ × 6″–16″ O.C.; bridging 1″ × 3″.

Roof framing: #1 fir, 2″ × 6″ O.C.; collar beams #1 fir, 2″ × 4″–24″ O.C.

Roofing: Asphalt shingle #210, size 12″ × 36″; tin flashing 26 ga.

Gutters: Galvanized iron, 26 ga., 5″ o.g.

Downspouts: Galvanized iron; 26 ga.; 3″ o.g.; number 4; connected to tile and to curb.

Drywall: Walls and ceiling; ½″ thick; tape and sanded; joints cemented.

Decorating: Kitchen and baths—3 coats I. & O. (1 flat—2 enamel); living room, hall, and bedrooms—flat oil base paint, 2 coats; recreation room—paneled.

Interior doors and trim: Doors—slab, flush; door trim—modern; finish—doors and trim. Stain shellac, varnish.

Windows: Aluminum sliding—glass, single strength. Trim—molding W.P., painted 3 coats; screens—full aluminum; basement windows—Truscon or equal steel.

Entrance and exterior detail: Main entrance door—3′ wide 1¾″ thick; other entrance doors—W.P., head flashing 26 ga.; screen doors 1¼″ thick; railings and louvers, exterior millwork, redwood-plywood under overhang painted 3 coats.

Cabinets and interior detail: Westinghouse kitchen; base units, birch; Formica counter top, stainless steel edging, 4″ back splash; medicine cabinet; all cabinets fruit wood stain—1 sealer, 1 filler, 1 finish shellac.

FIGURE 12-3 (continued)

> *Special floors and wainscot:* Kitchen & bath—Armstrong inlaid linoleum, rubber base ⅝" plywood underfloor; bath—ceramic tile recess 4½" high.
> *Plumbing:* 1 kitchen double bowl sink, Westinghouse disposer and dishwasher; 3 single bowl sinks in bathrooms (tinted fixtures); 3 water closets (3 white fixtures); 2 bathtubs (tinted fixture); 2 showers over tub (ceramic tile recess 4½'); 1 40-gallon glass-lined automatic water heater.
> *Heating:* Gas forced air (100,000 Btu input—80,000 output capacity); kitchen exhaust hood.
> *Electric wiring:* Circuit breaker—110–220 volts.
> *Hardware:* Chrome and brass.

of utilities are lumped together in this category, together with items such as the building permit, survey expense, and other similar costs.

A much larger category is overhead and profit. Overhead includes the builder's office and general expenses. The breakdown in Figure 12–4 also identifies loan-related costs, surveys and soil tests, architect and engineering fees, and real estate taxes during the construction period. A normal builder's profit of about 15 percent of total costs is included in this example. A marketing cost of 5 percent provides for brokerage commissions, on-site sales personnel, and advertising.

Site improvements and the garage are shown as structural costs in Figure 12–4. These items are frequently shown separately when a builder offers options such as concrete drives, one-car garage, and so on. When shown separately they can be deleted or modified without affecting the basic house analysis.

The total costs of construction, site preparation, land, overhead, profit, and sales costs comprise the anticipated sale price of the home. If estimated well, an appraisal of the finished home will support them and allow the purchaser to secure desirable financing while the builder earns the desired profit.

The possibility or, more accurately, the likelihood of being in error on the cost estimate, together with the vagaries inherent in the real estate market, should point up the hazards to small builders. A small underestimation of costs can easily wipe out most of their profit. Or, if the demand for the type of property they have produced is not strong, they may not be able to sell it at the desired prices or at the times of completion. The supply of mortgage money may become tighter, an industry may leave town, employment levels may drop, or the market just may not react favorably to the new property. Relative to the profit, the structure may be too large, too small, unattractive, poorly designed, or low in quality. Thus, we find that many small builders go bankrupt or leave the business each year.

FIGURE 12–4

Builder's house (cost estimate)

Cost Breakdown

Engr. stake. & mat. ....$	60	Vanity tops	—
Excavation	350	Bath accessories	57
Concrete	2,045	Stairs	85
Termite treatment	45	Rails and dividers	28
Carpentry labor	1,526	Hardware	—
Lumber and est. trim; floor		Sliding glass doors	116
trusses and roof trusses	3,050	Glass and mirrors, carpet,	
Windows and front door	453	vinyl flooring	1,131
Plumbing	2,080	Painting	1,275
Roofing material and labor	365	Ceramic tile	600
Metal gutters	—	Cleaning—unit final	65
HVAC	1,575	Mail boxes and number	—
Electric and electric fixtures	772	Prefab chimney	435
Insulation	286	Chimney surround	100
Sheet rock	1,490	Brick-stone	168
Trim wood interior	460	Nails and carpentry	150
Metal bifold doors	161	Garage	2,500
Metal closet shelves	55	Sitework (landscaping,	
Kitchen cabinet and vanity tops	451	seed, asphalt)	1,500
Kitchen equipment hood	405	Contingency	500
		Total ....$	24,370

Cost Analysis

	Dollar cost	Cost per square foot	Percentage of total cost
Construction ....$	24,370	$14.56	55.4
Overhead and general conditions	1,400	.84	3.2
Land (7,500 square feet)	7,500	4.48	17.0
Architect and engineering	200	.12	0.4
Survey	100	.06	0.2
Soil tests	50	.03	0.1
Taxes	100	.06	0.2
Interest (6 months)	760	.45	1.7
Construction loan closing costs,			
legal fees, title insurance	1,750	1.05	3.9
Contingency	350	.21	.7
Total	36,530	21.86	82.8
15%± builder's profit	5,480	3.27	12.4
Total before cost of sales	42,010	25.13	95.2
Cost of sales (5%±)	2,100	1.25	4.8
Sale price (value) ....$	44,110	$26.38	100.0

Administrative problems and considerations

Market analysis. Data available regarding demand are the same whether an existing or new structure is being contemplated, but changes in supply require consideration of possible adjustments in activity patterns that might result. A development of new retail shopping facilities might reroute traffic, causing great demand in the new shopping area and a deterioration of demand in the old area. Property values follow consumer demand, the problem being one of determining whether a new development can pull business from old ones. The investors in the older structures have a proven record, providing them with a sound base for holding their business.

A closely related problem is that of attempting to produce a product that offers a competitive advantage over existing land uses in the vicinity. An apartment builder might find a strong demand for three-bedroom apartments, the meeting of which might draw families out of two-bedroom units located in the area. A residential subdivider might choose to specialize in $40,000–$50,000 homes for a given tract, even though the surrounding area is improved with homes of substantially lesser value. In all such cases it is much easier to determine the demand experience of existing uses than the proposed new one. Market research studies under these circumstances thus must be of two types: (*a*) analyses of demand for the proposed use and (*b*) analyses of demand for existing uses in the area. The latter studies might indicate that a greater advantage could be gained by developing land in the same manner that surrounding properties are developed.

Once an initial program is tested by market research, an exploratory development effort should be made. Unit sizes, price ranges, and development densities can be tested empirically before large-scale development is undertaken. Major homebuilders, such as Fox and Jacobs in Dallas, follow this approach and construct model homes to sell from rather than building an inventory of homes for immediate sale. They limit their financial risk to the investment in the models.

Financing. The cost of money changes frequently, and new construction is subject only to current costs. When current money costs are high, new structures are at a cost disadvantage as compared with existing structures. Rents/sales prices must be increased to accommodate high-interest rates on construction loans, and an increase in permanent loan interest rates can cause a permanent realignment in developmental economics. A 9.5 percent interest rate requires $2,000 more net income per year than a 7.5 percent rate on a $100,000 loan for an apartment building, an amount that would require higher rental charges than those received by the older buildings. Of course, a low interest rate market has the opposite effect in terms of interest cost.

The complication of financing creates administrative problems for developers. They must develop substantial written information regarding the project, the owners, and other projects developed by themselves. This information is submitted to a permanent lender who is asked to issue a letter of commitment for a future loan. If this is successful, the letter and the data package flow to a construction lender who is asked to issue the first funds. The construction loan, when approved, is made in stages as the project is built and repaid by the permanent loan.

Each lender in this process has a set of conditions that forces the developer to get the project completed and rented/sold as quickly as possible. Most construction loans are issued for less than the full amount that the permanent lender has agreed to fund, so the developer must seek out a third lender for what is known as a "gap" loan. The interest rate on such financing is usually very high. As a further complication, most permanent loans require that the project achieve a predetermined level of rent/sales before the permanent loan can be closed. This forces the developer to pay high-interest rates on interim loans until occupancy reaches the required level.

Aside from the interest expense of money, the investor must consider the downpayment required and the terms of repayment possible in the present market. Real estate investments normally involve loans that comprise a high percentage of appraised value.

Leverage, that is, the use of borrowed money to earn a sum greater than the cost of that money, provides a higher percentage return on investment than would be possible with 100 percent equity financing. Financing terms requiring high downpayments and 10-year amortized repayments require a much higher net income than would be necessary with lower downpayments and 20-year amortization. This increased net income would not be forthcoming where competing investments have competitive financing advantages.

Taxation. A common practice in recent years has been for developers to establish rapid depreciation techniques that minimize taxes in the first few years of operations. Reported profits are low or nonexistent, yet the cash flow from the investment is substantial. After about ten years the annual write-off is reduced, thereby increasing the annual income tax, but the investor has withdrawn much of the capital. It has been invested elsewhere in a manner that has earned more than it would have using a more gradual depreciation form.

The important point regarding the use of the concept is that investors look toward sources other than reported income to justify new improvements. A tax advantage today is more beneficial than an advantage gained after several years, and past exchanges of investment properties have indicated a tendency for different types of investors to operate in the short-run construction arena and the long-run operational arena. The former look toward cash flow and capital gain through property sales for this return; the latter look toward net income.

A significant point to note in this regard is that Congress periodically changes those tax laws which offer the benefits desired by real estate developers. The 7 percent investment credit tax feature developed in 1962 offered a cash flow benefit to some industrial developers. Its termination in 1966 was a detriment to them. The 1966 moratorium on several of the commonly used rapid depreciation methods was a hindrance to apartment builders and commercial developers. In 1976 Congress reduced investment interest as a tax deductible expense. The investor who specializes in the production of improvements must examine depreciation alternatives and related tax provisions before attempting to compare an investment with those already existing in the area.

Zoning. New structures frequently do not fit the existing zoning plan. Zoning is nearly always a hindrance rather than a help to land developers. Existing structures operate under innumerable forms of former zoning regulations or variances. When a new use is contemplated that requires rezoning or granting of a variance, the potential competitors are able to fight it through the city council or zoning board. The competitors' position is more secure when new competition is thwarted.

Labor unions and productivity. Labor unions have frequently been attacked as a principal cause of the high costs and slow productivity advances in the construction industry. Certainly in an industry which requires large inputs of hand work, labor costs are bound to be high and the role of unions highly visible. In residential construction, for example, on-site labor costs typically run about 50 percent of the total. In prefabrication of buildings the input of hand labor is still relatively high—both in the assembling of components at the site and in the manufacturing process. Undoubtedly labor practices have added to the rocketing costs of construction; however, in the overall picture too much of the blame for the industry's problems probably has been attributed to unions.

One method by which unions impede productivity in the construction industry is the attempt to dictate supply terms to the market by placing limitations on the number of new workers admitted to a trade; the effect, of course, is to maintain high wage rates. High initiation fees and trade examinations are sometimes used to control entrance to a trade. The degree to which unions are able to manipulate the labor supply varies from community to community.

Restrictive entrance requirements have had as one objective and effect the exclusion of racial minority groups to union membership. Such practices came under strong attack in the late 1960s with the push for civil, social, and economic rights. Today requirements by federal and state governments for more than token employment has resulted in the increasing employment of blacks and women in the building trades; many business firms building large structures specify that a certain percentage of the workforce must belong to minority groups.

Another difficulty occurs because trade and craft unions are highly specialized, resulting in jurisdictional disputes and work stoppages where specific areas of work are unclear. Some unions demand jurisdiction in activities which do not involve specialized talent, such as the right to clean paint spots by the painters' union.

Perhaps the greatest negative effect in limiting production comes from unions' efforts, often violent, to fight the use of laborsaving devices and new materials that threaten the need for skilled labor. As one example, the use of plastic pipe was resisted forcefully in many communities with arguments that the new type of pipe is inferior to cast iron or copper, which is untrue. Plumbers' unions also argued that plastic pipe is a cheap substitute requiring no ability to install—arguments which are irrelevant to accomplishing the job. Some other examples are forbidding the use of paint spray guns, limiting the size of paint brush used, and forbidding the use of premixed concrete.

It should be pointed out that the real underlying motivation for unions to engage in restrictive practices is the concern for job security. The nature of the construction industry and the construction process has produced quite unstable employment. Neither social legislation nor approaches by employers have allowed unions to take a positive viewpoint toward laborsaving innovations.

It seems likely, however, that labor unions have been criticized too harshly and assigned too much of the responsibility for the construction industry's slow productivity advances. The basic culprit must be identified as the structure of the industry itself, since a structure of larger firms would allow more effective dealings with unions. A situation in which small, weak, unsophisticated firms must deal with larger, more powerful unions is not the ideal model for collective bargaining.[10]

The impact of OSHA.   The Occupational Safety and Health Act of 1973 established new construction safety standards which increased substantially the cost of constructing new buildings. Workers are required to wear protective clothing and equipment, guard rails and barriers are to be constructed during the building period, and openings or holes are to be covered. Contractors must comply with these requirements or financial penalties (fines) are imposed. The requirements have been controversial, and cost increases have been emphasized. However, after two years the compliance enforcement agency has gained considerable experience, and problems are becoming fewer. The law does produce improved safety conditions and hopefully will soon achieve a balance between costs and benefits.

---

[10] Halbert C. Smith, "Housing: Are We Paying More and Getting Less?" *Business Horizons,* Winter 1967, pp. 7–20.

SUMMARY

The production of new real estate resources is one of the country's most important economic functions, with new construction in the United States averaging about 10 percent of the GNP. The construction industry holds added significance for economic forecasters and related industries because of the difficulty of predicting future activity. Forecasting is difficult because supply lags demand, the industry is composed of primarily small, unsophisticated firms, and labor unions can interrupt work and increase costs after a project has been started.

Developers, builders, and lenders must coordinate their efforts to balance supply and demand relative to the final product of their efforts. The cost efficiencies of developing large land assemblages must be balanced against the potential cost of carrying improved land inventory for an extended period. The source of construction loans and permanent financing should be known before the improvement program begins.

Both land development and construction must operate in a framework of social controls such as zoning, building codes, community plans, and local regulations pertaining to streets, sewers, and utilities. Effective performance of the management functions of planning, organizing, and controlling are required in the construction field to minimize cost overruns which are often disastrous to small builders. Important roles may be played in some or all of these functions by the owner, architect, contractor, and financier.

At the microadministration level, business administrator-investors need to estimate accurately all costs to be incurred in evaluating the desirability of a land holding and development project or a construction project. They must then estimate gross and net proceeds to be obtained, placing all proceeds and costs on a present-value basis. A rate of return may then be calculated which can be compared with the firm's cost of capital.

QUESTIONS FOR REVIEW

1. How can zoning affect a land developer's rate of return?
2. Is the holding of land a useful economic function? Why? Can land holding be socially undesirable? How?
3. Do you believe that great increases in productivity in the construction industry are possible? Why or why not?
4. If you were to build a new home for your family, would you employ an architect? Why or why not?
5. Why does the structure of the construction industry contribute to an inefficient handling of labor disputes?

6. How could greater job security be provided for construction workers while taking full advantage of laborsaving machines?

7. How does the development of single-family residential areas favorably affect the already existing metropolitan area? What are the disadvantages or costs of such development?

8. What social controls over development and construction do you believe are necessary? Why?

9. Devise a critical path type of chart in which development process steps are shown in chronological order.

10. Diagram the relationship between housing market construction cycles and the general business cycle. Comment upon reasons why the two cycles are likely to be parallel but different.

REFERENCES

Beaton, William R. *Real Estate Investment.* Englewood Cliffs, N.J.: Prentice-Hall, 1971.

David, Philip. *Urban Land Development.* Homewood, Ill.: Richard D. Irwin, 1970.

Martin, Preston. *Real Estate Principles and Practices.* New York: Macmillan Co., 1959.

Ratcliff, Richard U. *Real Estate Analysis.* New York: McGraw-Hill, 1961, pp. 269–305.

Ring, Alfred A. *Real Estate Principles and Practice,* 7th ed. Englewood Cliffs, N.J.: Prentice-Hall, 1972, pp. 425–55.

Unger, Maurice A. *Real Estate,* 4th ed. Cincinnati: South-Western Publishing Co., 1969, pp. 649–70.

Weimer, Arthur M.; Hoyt, Homer; and Bloom, George F. *Real Estate,* 6th ed. New York: Ronald Press, 1972, pp. 335–73.

chapter 13

REAL ESTATE
FINANCING

EPIC HOMES CORPORATION, a medium-sized builder, began development of a 74-acre tract of land. Its objective was to create a well-planned subdivision of $50,000 to $60,000 homes at the edge of a medium-sized city. As preliminary work began at the site, an observer could not see and perhaps would not comprehend the importance of financing to this project. Neither James Randolph, president of Epic, nor Epic Homes Corporation had invested any cash in the project. The land was purchased, development was begun, and homes would be constructed entirely with funds borrowed from others.

While most development projects require some financial input by the investor-entrepreneur, almost all real estate developments rely on a preponderant proportion of borrowed funds. The complex structure of institutions that lend money, the legal instruments and arrangements, the methods of evaluating risk, and many specialized conventions and techniques of the mortgage market form a system that is essential to real estate development. It is a system that must be studied one part at a time and yet for effective understanding it also should be visualized in toto. The arrangements in any given real estate venture will constitute a unique combination; no two financing transactions are identical. However, the successful real estate entrepreneur understands thoroughly each component part of the system and is able to combine them in creative ways.

In the case of Epic Homes, the land was provided by the landowner in exchange for 25 percent of the profit to be derived from the project plus a 10 percent interest in the stock of Epic Homes Corporation. On the basis of the planned layout, engineering studies, and home designs, a local bank extended a loan for development and agreed to provide construction financing for up to one-third of the homes. The bank also agreed to make long-term mortgage loans on prevailing terms for up to one-third of the homes in the development to home purchasers who qualify under the bank's requirements. Other local lending institutions had expressed interest in financing both the construction and long-term purchases of the remaining two-thirds of the homes. Mr. Randolph was confident that with the successful completion and sale of one-eighth to one-fourth of the homes, public acceptance of the project would insure that the remaining financing could be obtained.

The financing pattern for the Epic Homes project could have been quite different. Epic might have owned or purchased the land with its own capital—all or part of which might have been equity. Epic might have purchased the land partially with its own capital and partially with a loan from the landowner. The land development loan might have been obtained from the landowner at market interest rates or the landowner might have been given a larger share of the profits to make the loan. Both the land development loan and the construction financing might have been obtained from a mortgage investment trust or a savings and loan association. Or one loan might have been obtained from one institution and the other loan from another institution. A permanent financing commitment might have been obtained for all of the new homes from a savings and loan, a mutual savings bank, a mortgage banker, or directly from a life insurance company. The terms—including interest rates, discounts and fees, maturities, privileges, and penalties—of the various loans could differ greatly among lenders. Thus, financing as an element in the real estate development process is subject to greater variation than almost any other factor.

In addition to making real estate development possible, financing often determines whether a project is profitable. If the interest rate on a major loan is too high or a discount too great, a project's profit may be eaten away. If a loan must be repaid before other funds are obtained, the entire project may be forfeited. If a lender exerts too much control over the project, unpopular designs and inefficient methods may be required or too much effort in paperwork may result. All of these considerations point up the great importance of financing to the production of new real estate resources and the significance of understanding the role of financing to every real estate investor.

FLOW OF FUNDS TO FINANCE REAL ESTATE

Funds may be defined as cash or any resource having value which is capable of being sold in order to buy some other asset. We may think of funds as being composed of deposits in banks and savings and loan associations, reserves built up in life insurance policies,[1] equity interests in investments such as stocks, bonds, or real estate, or other noninvestment assets such as homes, paintings, oriental rugs, automobiles, or any item of value. The great bulk of funds used for real estate originates from two sources: (*a*) equity buildup in real estate and (*b*) cash savings of individuals and businesses in financial institutions.

Equity buildup in real estate is a continuous source of financing for the owner of real estate. Equity buildup occurs because (*a*) the real estate may increase in value and/or (*b*) the mortgage debt is paid down gradually, leaving more value to the owner or equity interest. Equity value results from legal ownership rights—the right to use the real estate in any legal manner, the right to sell it, and the right to convey title upon death. The cost of equity funds, however, may be high. This cost must be measured primarily by the opportunity of investing in other assets which might be higher yielding. Also, an equity interest in real estate may be relatively illiquid and unmarketable—and there may not be enough equity funds to finance the real estate. Because of the disadvantages of having to rely totally on equity funds, then, real estate users, as well as other capital users, use borrowed funds extensively.

Figure 13–1 reflects that the principal sources of borrowed funds are the financial institutions, including banks, savings and loans, mutual savings banks, and life insurance companies. They are regarded as sources even though they depend on savings by individuals and companies. The institutions decide how the funds will be used and allocated among loan applicants. Of course, when individuals loan funds directly for real estate usage, they are also regarded as sources. Real estate mortgages constitute the single largest use of funds in the U.S. economy, with government securities (U.S., state, and local) being second. Although the importance of real estate credit in the employment of funds is great, the percentage of funds applied in this way declined from about 35 percent in the early 1960s to about 25 percent in the mid-1970s. This development reflects the increased demand for funds by large corporations and government agencies. Higher interest rates prevailing during the mid-1970s allowed securities other than mortgages to have relatively more attractive yields.

Table 13–1 is a summary of the sources and uses of funds in the U.S. economy from 1960 to 1974. Commercial banks are the most important source of funds shown in Table 13–1, accounting for nearly 30 percent of total funds sources. Individuals and others were the second largest source in 1974, but they have shown wide cycles of activity, ranging from

---

[1] Savings or reserves build up in nonterm life insurance policies because a purchaser pays a higher premium than would be required for pure protection. Part of the premium of an ordinary life, limited pay life, or endowment policy thus accumulates as "cash value" and is available to the policyowner.

FIGURE 13–1

Model of flow of funds into real estate

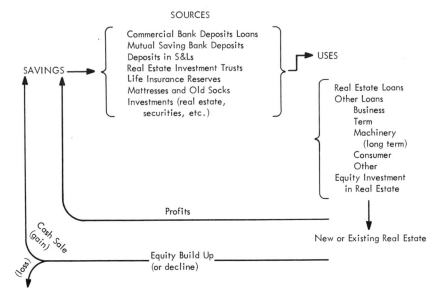

second largest source to one of the largest user categories. Savings and loans have been a stable major source, accounting for about 10 percent of total funds sources in 1974.

In essence, then, the problem of the real estate investor is to be able to tap into the flow of funds at the best time and source to obtain the needed amount of funds at the least expense. Mr. Randolph and Epic Homes were able to tap the funds flow, although we cannot say without further information (nor can we ever be certain—except with hindsight) whether the best mix of equity and debt funds was used, whether the least expense was incurred, and whether the time was correct in relation to beginning the project. Perhaps a different mix of types of funds, a different combination of sources, or different terms would have been more advantageous to Epic Homes. The problem of determining best mix, terms, and cost is a part of the return on investment calculus and is considered in depth later in this chapter.

It is often the explicit or implicit strategy on the part of a real estate investor to attempt to tap the funds flow on whatever terms fund suppliers will offer. Although not usually stated so bluntly, it is felt that no lender will grant a loan that is beyond the limit of reasonable risk. Furthermore, given a fairly high level of risk, which most real estate projects contain, the cost and terms among the various potential sources will not vary a great deal. Thus, for large, unique projects, the developer too often

TABLE 13–1

Uses and sources of funds—summary: 1960–1974 (in billions of dollars)

Item	1960	1965	1968	1969	1970	1971	1972	1973	1974
Uses, funds raised	39.1	65.9	89.2	87.0	92.3	138.3	177.8	178.3	187.4
Investment funds	27.4	44.4	54.3	60.2	66.4	101.1	114.7	113.3	111.5
Short-term funds	13.8	23.4	26.2	35.7	19.0	20.5	42.5	65.5	66.9
U.S. securities, privately held	-2.2	-1.9	8.7	-8.8	6.9	16.7	20.5	-.4	9.0
Sources, gross funds supplied	42.4	73.9	100.5	111.2	103.9	148.4	203.8	210.8	210.8
Insurance co. and pension funds	12.4	18.8	23.0	23.0	26.9	32.9	37.3	40.1	39.9
Insurance companies	6.5	9.7	11.2	11.0	13.0	18.1	20.2	21.7	19.6
Private noninsured pension funds	3.7	5.8	7.0	6.4	7.8	8.6	9.3	9.2	10.0
State and local govt. retirement funds	2.1	3.3	4.7	5.6	6.1	6.2	7.8	9.2	10.3
Thrift institutions	9.4	14.6	16.1	14.4	18.3	41.2	49.0	33.8	26.9
Savings and loan associations	7.3	9.6	10.2	9.5	12.5	28.9	35.8	25.4	20.8
Mutual savings banks	1.5	3.9	4.4	2.8	4.2	9.8	10.2	4.7	3.0
Credit unions	.6	1.1	1.6	2.0	1.6	2.5	3.0	3.7	3.1
Investment companies	1.1	1.9	2.4	3.5	1.7	.4	-.2	*	1.1
Other financial intermediaries	3.3	5.7	5.3	9.0	2.8	5.9	12.8	14.7	7.2
Finance companies	3.3	5.7	5.1	8.1	.7	3.4	7.9	10.2	5.8
Real estate investment trusts	(z)	(z)	.2	.9	2.1	2.5	4.9	4.5	1.4
Commercial banks	9.5	28.6	40.0	17.1	36.5	49.7	74.6	78.2	62.5
Business	-3.2	1.2	7.5	4.5	2.5	7.8	7.7	11.3	12.4
Government	2.4	4.0	4.5	9.4	10.9	1.8	11.4	13.1	16.4
Foreign investors	1.8	.3	1.5	.1	11.0	27.1	10.6	3.4	7.0
Residual: Individuals and others	5.8	-1.3	.1	30.2	-6.7	-18.3	.7	16.2	37.4
Less: Funds raised by financial intermediaries	3.3	8.0	11.2	24.1	11.6	10.1	26.0	32.5	23.4
Total net sources	39.1	65.9	89.2	87.0	92.3	138.3	177.8	178.3	187.4

* Less than $50 million.

Source: *Credit and Capital Markets* (New York: Bankers Trust Co., 1975).

simply tries to obtain financing at whatever cost or terms are required. Rather than accepting the terms that are offered by one or two lenders, the developer should shop around thoroughly and be prepared, if possible, to wait until better terms can be obtained.

The inability to be selective or to have bargaining power in the borrowing process is a resultant of weakness in the equity position and should be avoided with three exceptions: (*a*) when the investor has relatively little (in funds, reputation, or other commitments) to lose, while at the same time has a great profit potential, (*b*) in spite of a slim profit potential and costly financing, there is little risk of default, and (*c*) when the project is so large that a chunk of borrowed funds will be required even with a sizable chunk of equity.

Of course, the risks and profit potentials are difficult to assess. In periods of growth and/or inflation, risks are underestimated and profit potentials overestimated. During recessions the opposite assessments are likely to prevail. The real estate investor needs to look beyond the immediate period to the long-run future.

In any event—whether merely to try to obtain a loan on any terms available or to bargain for funds—investor-borrowers should understand the concept of the flow of funds. Where to go to tap the flow and what to expect after they get there are items of information equally important to real estate entrepreneurs as is the knowledge of construction technique. Thus, we now move to a brief analysis of the principal sources, their characteristics, and legal constraints in making real estate loans.

Savings and loan associations

A type of thrift institution which accumulates savings from individuals, savings and loan associations specialize in lending funds to purchasers of single-family homes. The lender obtains a personal note evidencing the debt and a first mortgage lien on the property. Savings and loans may also loan a portion of their funds on other types of properties such as commercial and industrial properties, mobile homes, and apartment buildings, but the greatest bulk of their loans must be in one- to four-family residences and government bonds. As shown in Tables 13–2 and 13–3, savings and loans hold twice as much of the outstanding mortgage debt as the next largest institutional holder and by far the largest percentage of mortgage debt to savings of these same institutions.

Savings and loan associations may be either state or federally chartered, and they may be either stock-owned companies or mutually owned by the savers. Federally chartered associations must belong to the Federal Home Loan Bank System and the Federal Savings and Loan Insurance Corporation (FSLIC). Many state-chartered associations also elect to belong. The FSLIC insures savings by investors and periodically examines

TABLE 13–2

Mortgage debt outstanding by type of holder, 1950–1975 (selected years)*

Year	Total	Mutual savings banks	Commercial banks	Savings and loans	Life insurance companies	Others†
1950............	72,800	7,054	10,431	13,657	16,102	25,536
	(100.00)	(9.6)	(11.0)	(18.8)	(22.1)	(38.5)
1955............	129,988	17,457	21,004	31,461	29,445	30,621
	(100.0)	(13.4)	(16.2)	(24.2)	(22.7)	(23.6)
1960............	206,800	26,935	28,806	60,070	41,771	49,218
	(100.0)	(13.0)	(13.9)	(29.0)	(20.2)	(23.8)
1965............	326,100	44,617	49,675	110,306	60,013	61,489
	(100.0)	(13.7)	(15.2)	(33.8)	(18.4)	(18.9)
1970............	450,400	57,948	72,882	150,562	74,345	94,686
	(100.0)	(12.8)	(16.2)	(33.4)	(16.5)	(21.0)
1971............	499,900	61,978	82,515	174,385	74,700	106,322
	(100.0)	(12.4)	(16.5)	(34.9)	(14.9)	(21.3)
1972............	564,825	67,556	99,314	206,182	76,948	114,825
	(100.0)	(12.0)	(17.6)	(36.5)	(13.6)	(20.3)
1973............	634,954	73,230	119,068	231,733	81,369	129,554
	(100.0)	(11.5)	(18.8)	(36.5)	(12.8)	(20.4)
1974............	688,546	74,920	132,105	249,293	86,234	145,994
	(100.0)	(10.9)	(19.2)	(36.2)	(12.5)	(21.2)
1975............	724,367	76,429	134,025	270,583	88,477	154,853
	(100.0)	(10.6)	(18.5)	(37.3)	(12.2)	(21.4)

* Amounts given in millions with percentages given in parentheses.

† Government agencies, individuals, and other institutions (pension funds, mortgage bankers, and so on).

Source: National Association of Mutual Savings Banks, *National Fact Book of Mutual Savings Banking* (New York, 1972), p. 52 and *Federal Reserve Bulletin,* December 1975, p. A42.

TABLE 13–3

Mortgage loans as a percentage of savings by institution, 1950–1974 (selected years)

Year	Mutual savings banks	Commercial banks	Savings and loans	Life insurance companies
1950	35.5	29.6	97.7	29.8
1955	62.0	45.4	97.8	39.0
1960	74.1	42.9	96.6	42.4
1965	85.0	37.0	99.9	47.0
1967	83.8	35.0	97.8	49.9
1969	83.8	39.9	103.4	45.4
1970	80.4	31.0	102.7	44.4
1971	75.6	—*	100.0	42.1
1972	73.3	30.8	99.7	40.0
1973	75.4	31.7	102.1	40.0
1974	75.4	30.3	102.7	40.0

* Not available.

Source: U.S. Bureau of the Census, *Statistical Abstract of the U.S.: 1975* (Washington, D.C.: U.S. Government Printing Office, 1975), Tables 752, 756, 760, and 791.

loans made by the associations to determine whether there is any excess risk. The Federal Home Loan Bank Board establishes liquidity requirements, enforces rules and regulations, and maintains a source of funds at district Federal Home Loan Banks which can be borrowed by member savings and loan associations.

Although the policies and operations of the individual savings and loans vary greatly, legal requirements and common practices direct savings and loan lending into patterns that are describable in general terms. Associations are limited as to the loan-to-value ratio and maturity period for mortgage loans they may grant. Since 1971 savings and loans have been empowered to make 95 percent loans with mortgage insurance or special reserves on amounts above 80 percent. These loans have replaced much of the FHA lending. Additionally, savings and loan limitations have been somewhat more liberal with respect to loan maturity than other types of institutions. FHA and VA regulations govern the limits on government underwritten loans, and prior to 1971, these were generally more liberal than terms for conventional loans.

Most (but not all) savings and loans prefer to make conventional loans. They have not been constrained by ceilings on interest rates or the extensive paperwork required by the FHA and VA. Savings and loans have obtained somewhat higher interest rates on their loans than have most other lenders but have given more liberal terms to borrowers.

Savings and loans have been limited to the direct making of loans within 100 miles of the main office and 100 miles of each branch office, provided the territory around a branch office does not cross a state boundary. Thus, savings and loans are considered to be localized lending institutions. This limitation often results in greater specialized knowledge of the local area by the savings and loans, enabling them to fulfill more effectively their role of making loans on residential properties. Savings and loans can participate in lending of wider geographic scope by purchasing portions of loans through the Federal Home Loan Mortgage Corporation.

Life insurance companies

Historically, the second largest source of funds for mortgages has been the approximately 1,500 life insurance companies. However, life insurance companies are no longer a large source of *new* mortgages. Most of the mortgage lending has been done by the large companies; many smaller life insurance companies do not make mortgage loans. Some life insurance companies, including the largest ones, until the late 1960s invested over one-half of their assets in mortgage loans, although just following World War II life insurance companies held less than 15 percent of their assets in such loans. The great increases in real estate lending by life insurance companies occurred principally because mortgages (especially FHA-insured mortgages) provided the right combination of safety and attractive yields, whereas prior to World War II less government underwriting of risk and lower yields made mortgages undesirable. In the early 1970s, however, mortgage yields (particularly on residential properties) were not as attractive to insurance companies as securities and equities. The 1974–75 recession caused life insurance companies to become even more conservative about real estate investments than they were previously. The newspaper article reproduced as Exhibit 13–1 reflects the attitudes of five investment executives who are concerned about the wisdom of maintaining a real estate portfolio. The general consensus in October 1975, was that bond portfolios were more attractive than real estate loans.

Large insurance companies have much greater flexibility in making loans over wide geographic areas than any other type of lender. Most of the large companies are qualified to do business in most or all states, and they utilize a network of mortgage bank correspondents to obtain and service loans.[2] Since the large insurance companies have vast amounts of funds to invest, they prefer to make large loans. The larger loans typically carry higher interest rates, and, as a result of fewer loans, less analysis and paperwork is involved. The correspondent typically continues to service the loan for the insurance company, usually receiving a fee of about 0.3 percent of the outstanding balance.

For these reasons, loans on large commercial, industrial, and apartment properties are the dominant type made by insurance companies. When mortgage interest rates are favorable, life insurance companies also lend on entire groups (or packages) of single-family homes that are assembled by mortgage bankers. Because of their unfamiliarity with local real estate markets, the large national lenders usually demand that single-family home loans be underwritten by the FHA or VA.

Commercial banks

Although primarily lenders of short-term business loans, commercial banks in recent years have expanded into the mortgage lending field. These institutions currently hold about 14 percent of the outstanding mortgages; their real estate loans average about 14 percent of their assets. While these percentages indicate that banks are not nearly as important in absolute or relative terms to the mortgage market as are savings and loans and insurance companies, their influence as a source of funds is keenly felt. The reasons for this influence are that (*a*) banks have attempted to expand their role in mortgage lending, (*b*) banks have fluctuated in the extent to which they have been active in the mortgage market, and (*c*) FHA and VA mortgages are not counted in the limits placed by law on the level of mortgages that banks may hold.

---

[2] See Halbert C. Smith, *Interregional Mortgage Placement: Lenders' Policies, Practices and Characteristics* (Storrs, Conn.: Center for Real Estate and Urban Economic Studies, 1969) for a critical analysis of life insurance companies' operations in this field.

EXHIBIT 13-1

Life Insurance Companies
Pulling Out of Real Estate

By GEORGE ADCOCK
Constitution Business Writer

Life insurance companies are pulling money out of real estate and putting it in high-yield, low-risk corporate bonds. The devastating beating taken by the real estate market has made it most unattractive for conservative insurance firms.

Over the years, insurance companies maintained about 35 per cent of their total assets in mortgages, and 3 per cent in real estate equities. Last year, the firms invested only 10 per cent of their new income in mortgages, and only 1 per cent in equities.

Purchases of corporate bonds on the other hand soared, accounting for 74 per cent of their new investments in 1974. Traditionally, corporate bonds have made up only 25 per cent of total assets.

"Insurance firms have considerably decreased their net purchases of equities," advises McKee Nunnelly Jr., security analyst with Reynolds Securities. They are adding bonds to their portfolios, and in fact increasing the quality of the bonds. Many firms that normally bought A- and Aa-rated bonds are moving up to Aaa-rated paper. Almost everyone has become extremely quality-conscious."

The movement into the corporate bond market has been almost lemming-like. Once some big insurance guns fired the first shot, everybody else had to jump in just to keep their earnings competitive.

Ernest Steele, president of Coastal States Insurance, headquartered here, acknowledges that his firm is moving strongly into corporate bonds.

"We were into commercial paper and certificates of deposit through last year," he says, "but we have moved out of these and into the bond market.

"We have to try to stay competitive," he admits.

Beyond the competition, the plunging real estate market has made such moves virtually a necessity.

"Insurance management has had to become much more stringent, Reynolds Securities Nunnelly observes.

Willliam T. Taylor, Life of Georgia president for investments, says his firm is "taking a hard look at its whole investment portfolio policy."

"Our investments this year have been quite different from previous years," Taylor reveals. "We've gone to the bond market more than ever before." Taylor adds that his firm was very active in real estate for years.

"But now the only thing we might look at is property occupied by the borrowing entity, or property leased to a large corporate entity."

He adds that investments in home loans are running light, and motels are strictly out of the picture.

Through August of this year, Life of Georgia had $18 million in corporate bonds, compared to $11 million last year. Mortgages held dropped to $19.5 million from $28.4 million. Common stock accounts for only 3 per cent of total assets.

"We are not heavy buyers of common stock at the moment," Taylor admits.

Interfinancial Inc., the Atlanta-based holding company that owns United Family Life Insurance Co. and American Security Insurance Co., has not included real estate in its portfolio for the past two years.

"Currently we are buying nothing but corporate bonds," says Forrest Hobbs, a vice president of the firm. "About 30 per cent of our assets are in mortgage loans, but we are not now in that market."

One significant exception to this exodus is Equitable Life Assurance Society, whose involvement in real estate has recently increased right here in Atlanta. The nation's third-largest insurance firm, Equitable became full

owner and developer of Rivermont, a residential community in north Fulton county, this summer. Equitable took on the development when Atlanta developer Roy D. Warren ran into financial difficulties.

Rivermont in fact is one of three such developments around the country that Equitable is involved in full-tilt. The others are in Birmingham and California.

"We look on these ventures as long-term investments," says Bill Rogers, vice president for mortgage and real estate investments. "We have done some development before, but to be this deep into it is new to us."

Equitable traditionally has maintained one of the strongest real estate positions in the industry. Currently, 50 per cent of its $19 billion investment portfolio is in real estate in one form or another, according to Rogers.

"Not many firms have maintained the position in real estate that we have over the past two years," Rogers notes. "I think we are probably the only company that is still this active."

Reynolds Securities' Nunnelly agrees that Equitable probably is stronger in real estate right now than most. "But the big insurance firms like Equitable can ride out the problems," he says, "because it takes four to seven years for any real percentage decline to show up in the asset mix.

"But I have to believe," he adds, "that if they could get out of real estate they would. The big firms like Equitable are still in it because over the years they have made such large purchases they have to stay in."

Equitable's Rogers acknowledges that "we are in the bond market and limiting our real estate funds." But he says he hopes the race away from real estate will not long continue. "If the major insurance firms cease putting money into the market, the construction industry is going to be hurt worse than ever."

Source: *Atlanta Constitution*, October 30, 1975.

In recent years the most progressive commercial banks have attempted to become the department stores of finance. Competitive pressures for savings by other institutions and the need for profitable investment outlets for funds have encouraged banks to offer a wide variety of financial services and to make other types of loans in addition to short-term commercial loans. Mortgage loans (as well as consumer loans, construction and development loans, and business term loans) are now made by most banks.

Mortgages have been attractive investment outlets for banks, particularly during periods of "easy money" and relatively low interest rates. During these periods the yield on mortgages has been high relative to yields on government and municipal bonds and business loans. While mortgage yields typically suffer in comparison with other yields during "tight money" times, the large commercial banks that have entered the mortgage loan business have continued to grant mortgage loans during these periods. Nevertheless, the level of all banks' activity in mortgage lending has decreased substantially during periods of monetary restraint.

Banks are limited in the volume of mortgage loans they may have. Current regulations limit holdings of mortgage loans to no more than 70 percent of savings or 100 percent of equity capital, whichever is greater. Since FHA and VA loans are insured and guaranteed by the government, the risk of loss to a bank is very low on these loans, and they do not fall under the mortgage loan limitation.

Because of their background of conservative lending policies and more stringent regulations, banks typically grant less liberal loans than savings and loans. However, the interest rate charged has often been lower. Mortgage terms usually involve lower loan-to-value ratios and shorter maturities than savings and loans.

Banks strive to please their good customers. Consequently they will often grant a mortgage loan to a good customer when they would not make such a loan to a noncustomer. They typically prefer loans in the middle- to upper-value range in housing or larger loans on commercial and industrial property. Sometimes commercial banks grant a loan in order to service a good customer but then sell the loan to another financial institution, continuing to service the loan. This practice allows the bank to maintain a desirable liquidity position while maintaining the goodwill of customers.

Commercial banks are also good sources of construction and development loans. The regulations for banks' lending in this area have been less stringent than those imposed on savings and loans. These loans are usually short-term and are not counted in the bank's portfolio of mortgage loans. Often a bank makes a construction loan when another institution has agreed to make the long-term mortgage loan.

Many banks indirectly make mortgage lending possible by "warehousing" loans for mortgage bankers. Mortgage bankers often need short-term financing while they accumulate a package of loans to sell to a life insurance company. The mortgage company obtains the funds from a commercial bank, pledging mortgages held in the firm's inventory as security for the loan.

Because of these activities and the volatility of banks' activity in the mortgage market, their influence is quite important. Additionally, however, the absolute amount of mortgage lending by banks is significant. The role of banks in providing funds for construction and development is crucial for the creation of new real estate resources.

Mutual savings banks

From their depression-era image as perhaps the most staid and conservative type of lending institution, mutual savings banks have become some of the most imaginative and aggressive lenders. Regarded as something of a cross between commercial banks and savings and loan associations, mutual savings banks have wider investment powers than savings and loans, but they do not have the capability of leveraging demand deposits, as do commercial banks. Their relatively wide investment power has enabled mutual savings banks to grant mortgage loans on all types of real estate as well as to purchase stocks and bonds of private corporations and all levels of government securities. In contrast, savings and loans have been limited primarily to granting first mortgage loans on one-to-four-family residential real estate and U.S. government securities.

As shown by Table 13–2, mutual savings banks as of December 31, 1975, held almost $77 billion in mortgage loans. This compares with the approximate amounts of $134 billion and $271 billion in mortgage loans held by commercial banks and savings and loans at the same date. Of the total assets held by mutual savings banks, mortgages are by far the most important. Mortgages are almost five times as large as the next largest investment—corporate securities.

Compared with the other major institutional lenders, the volume of mortgages held by mutual savings banks would not appear impressive. However, the concentration of these institutions in New York and New England emphasizes their importance as mortgage lenders in those states. In terms of savings held, New York is by far the largest state, while Massachusetts has the largest number of savings banks (see Table 13–4).

Real estate investment trusts

In 1960 the federal income tax law was amended to recognize the real estate investment trust (REIT) as a passive investment vehicle whose income that is passed on to beneficiaries is not taxed. Only retained income

TABLE 13–4
Number of institutions and amount of savings held in
mutual savings banks by states, December 31, 1972

State	Number of institutions	Savings ($000,000)
Massachusetts	167	$14,072
New York	121	51,718
Connecticut	68	6,880
Maine	32	1,201
New Hampshire	30	1,340
New Jersey	20	4,239
Washington	9	1,801
Pennsylvania	8	5,802
Rhode Island	7	1,420
Vermont	6	380
Maryland	4	1,047
Indiana	4	147
Wisconsin	3	45
Alaska	2	81
Delaware	2	493
Minnesota	1	782
Oregon	1	158
Puerto Rico	1	7
Total	486	$91,613

Source: National Association of Mutual Savings Banks, *National Fact Book of Mutual Savings Banking* (New York, 1973), pp. 12 and 46.

is subject to taxation. This provision gave investors in REITs the same tax advantage that investors in mutual funds have. Funds to purchase investment real estate are obtained from many investors (there must be at least 100 or more persons to qualify for the tax advantage) in the same way that a corporation obtains capital by selling stock. The REIT sells shares, which are really certificates of beneficial interest in the trust. The shares are freely transferable and are limited in liability to the amount paid. A board of trustees runs the investment trust for the benefit of the share owners.

The financial problems of REITs in the 1970s resulted in several provisions in the 1976 Tax Reform Act designed to provide relief for beleaguered trusts. A summary of these provisions follows:

1. The REIT must distribute at least 90 percent of its taxable income in dividends until 1980. Thereafter, a REIT must distribute 95 percent of its taxable income in dividends, and 75 percent of its income must be distributed by the end of its taxable year. The 1976 Tax Reform Act required these more stringent regulations in return for providing a procedure for issue of a "deficiency dividend" by a REIT which failed to meet the income distribution test and risks losing its special

tax status. The deficiency dividend, together with penalty and accrued interest, can be issued in subsequent years to bring the total distribution to the required 90 or 95 percent.

2. The provision that a trust cannot hold property primarily for sale to customers as a dealer was repealed. Now, the net income realized from such sales is subject to a 100 percent tax.

3. The REIT, until 1980, must receive 90 percent of its gross income from passive sources or 75 percent from real estate, first mortgages, cash or government securities. In 1980, the REIT must receive 95 percent of its gross income from passive sources. However, the REIT will not lose its tax status if it does not meet the 90 or 95 percent asset test, provided it lists the source and nature of gross income and has basically acted in good faith. Also, the definition of rent from realty was broadened, which permits the trust to meet these tests more easily.

4. A voluntary disqualification of REIT status now prevents requalification for five years. Circumstances by 1976 had resulted in some trusts converting to corporations to avoid meeting the various tests imposed upon the REIT. A corporation could accumulate earnings and deal in property, providing the flexibility needed to overcome potential dissolvency. A REIT which is disqualified for other reasons, such as failing to meet a required income or asset test, can requalify in the following year.

5. The REIT can now carry forward net operating losses for eight years (but cannot carryback an operating loss).

6. Ordinary losses can now be used to offset against capital gains, or the trust may elect to pay tax at a 30 percent rate on net capital gains not distributed to shareholders. This enables the trust with operating losses to reduce the taxable income subject to the 90 or 95 percent test.

REITs are a vehicle by which a relatively small investor can own a share of a much larger property. Actually share owners in a REIT own shares of many properties in most cases. Thus, there is a great amount of diversification through trust ownership of several properties. Share owners are usually paid a regular dividend on their shares coming from the income produced by the real estate and by the depreciation expense charged on the books. If the property accumulates in value at a rate greater than the depreciation rate, the share owners' equity capital may appreciate in value. An additional advantage to small investors is that they obtain the benefits of professional management which they would not have if they saved their funds and invested them in a property on their own. Also, they may benefit from the use of leverage by the investment trust. That is, the trust may borrow funds from a financial institution to help finance properties that it purchases.

Two major types of trusts have evolved, one investing primarily in equity ownership positions and the other concentrating in mortgage loans. The equity trusts fared reasonably well during the stormy 1974–75 market period. The mortgage trusts tended to seek out high-risk loans through which they could invest substantial amounts of money in short periods of time. They frequently invested in combination land acquisition, development, and construction loans which relied upon uncertain permanent loan commitments. Many of these loans were made to purchasers whose financial strength and experience levels were marginal at best. The trusts were able to charge high rates of interest on borrowed funds, and they usually were able to secure a substantial percentage of profits in exchange for permitting the borrower to fund all costs plus a handsome draw for overhead. Investors found the mortgage trusts' earnings to be high, and the equity shares they purchased generated a sizable base for the issuance of bonds by the trusts. Within a few years the mortgage trusts were able to multiply their assets significantly, with their entire net worths being based upon the earnings generated from loans. The equity trusts were much more conservative, concentrating their property purchases in stable income producing properties.

The excellent performance of the trusts in 1971–72 led to competition by commercial banks, and many formed their own trusts with remarkable results. The Chase Manhattan Realty Trust sold $100 million worth of shares on the first day of sales, and the Bank of America enjoyed a similar experience. At least half of the nation's 20 largest banks entered the market. Unfortunately, the number of good borrowers was limited, and nearly all of the mortgage trusts lowered their credit requirements to place their funds rapidly. Popular market areas such as Miami, Atlanta, and Houston became overbuilt with large-scale residential, commercial, and office developments, and borrowers began to default on interest and principal payments. The value of equity shares fell, and bonds began to mature before capital could be recovered from loans. The mortgage trusts incurred substantial losses.

A peculiarity of accounting practices aided in the downfall of several mortgage trusts. The trusts permitted loan draws made by borrowers to include interest on the loan, causing the trusts to pick up income in one account as they increased the loan amount out of another account. The income shown to stockholders was high, but it was funded by sales of new trust shares. The underlying asset had not shown an attractive earnings picture. This process worked until money became tight in 1973 and shares stopped selling. The trust managers then had to look to asset values for earnings, and many assets were illiquid and experiencing slow sales or rentals.

As loans fell into default, the trusts stopped funding and booking interest. They were forced to foreclose on projects so that they could take possession and protect the asset values from waste, and vandalism, and so on. When this occurred, they were obligated by their CPA auditors to place funds into special reserve accounts to provide for eventual losses that were expected to arise when the foreclosed assets were sold. They could not accumulate funds for this purpose out of profits generated by healthy projects, since the special income tax provisions under which they operated forced them to distribute profits to shareholders as received. Their shares were not selling, so they could not issue bonds. Their only vehicle for funding loss reserves was to sell their good loans and use the funds for loss reserves on the poor loans. A number of trusts gave up their special REIT tax status to become taxable entities, thereby permitting them to retain earnings for use as operating funds.

The future of the REIT concept is uncertain as of the date of this writing. Some will self-liquidate over time. Those REITs which have been managed well will seek out high-quality projects and supervise loans with care. Some will convert from mortgage trusts to equity trusts.

The idea of one entity's providing land acquisition, land development, and construction loan needs simultaneously has not been found successful in the case of REITs. The trusts, in the main, were not effective at supervising their loans, and they found difficulties associated with (*a*) finding good sites and evaluating them, (*b*) working out all contracts and subcontracts needed to create building sites (adding streets, curbs, gutters, sidewalks, utilities, and so on) and (*c*) understanding when value-adding factors exceed costs. A good loan supervisor must be a cost specialist, an attorney, an appraiser, and a marketing specialist. For this reason, the division of the loan business into specialized subareas seems to be necessary.

Mortgage bankers

Mortgage companies or bankers originate mortgage loans to individuals and firms, but they do not normally continue to hold the mortgage loans as assets. Rather, the mortgage banker usually sells the mortgage paper to a large lender, such as a savings and loan association, a life insurance company, or a mutual savings bank. (Savings and loans were the largest outlet for mortgage bankers in 1971–72.) As discussed under Life Insurance Companies, the mortgage banker typically continues to service the loan for the purchaser of the loan and is compensated for this service by the purchaser. Servicing is defined as taking all steps necessary to make certain the loan provisions are carried out; procedures include collecting the monthly payments from the borrowers and forwarding these to the investor-lenders, rendering accounting to investors and borrowers, and handling foreclosures. The servicing fee usually runs about 0.25 to 0.5 percent of the outstanding balance of the loan.

Mortgage companies sometimes have continuing arrangements with large institutional lenders to obtain loans for them. A large lender will sometimes commit itself to purchase a specified amount of mortgage-secured loans from a mortgage company during a certain time period. Or a lender may let a mortgage banker know what types of loans it would like to purchase. The mortgage banker is then invited to submit such loans to the lender to determine whether to purchase the loan. This procedure is usually followed for large loans. When a mortgage company has a continuing arrangement or commitment to sell loans to an institutional investor, the mortgage banker is known as a correspondent.

Summary of the flow of funds into real estate finance

In summary, Table 13–5 reflects the uses of credit funds supplied to real estate and the sources from which they came over a 24-year period. The largest amounts of funds were placed in conventional home mortgages, and the bulk of these loans was supplied in order of decreasing importance by savings and loans, commercial banks, and mutual savings banks. Mortgage companies do not appear in the table because most of the mortgages they originate are sold to other institutional lenders.

LENDING AND BORROWING DECISIONS

With an understanding of the roles that the various institutional lenders play in financing real estate, a real estate investor-entrepreneur can set about to tap into the flow of funds. The entrepreneur usually wants to obtain financing at the lowest cost and under the most reasonable terms possible. The lender wants to believe that the loan will be safe, that is, it will be repaid according to schedule by the borrower, and that the yield obtained from the loan is consistent with yields on investments of comparable risk. Additionally, in recent years lenders have increasingly demanded protection from the risk of inflation through participation in any increased profits generated by the real estate.

Lenders today must be extremely careful not to become overzealous in their efforts to achieve safety. The U.S. Department of Justice has filed a number of lawsuits against those who "redline," or discriminate against, a neighborhood in their lending practice. Also, efforts by lenders to obtain profit shares through unusual computations of loan interest must now be in accordance with recently enacted truth in lending laws. As lending practices become more sophisticated, federal involvement tends to increase.

Because of the objectives and requirements of lenders, real estate entrepreneurs must submit a total plan for any development to a lender for approval, modification, or rejection. The lender wants to examine such aspects as street layout, subdivision design, adequacy of utilities, lot sizes,

TABLE 13–5. Mortgage activity of banks, insurance companies, and savings and loan associations: 1950–1974*

Item	1950	1955	1960	1965	1970	1971	1972	1973	1974
Commercial banks:									
Loans outstanding†	13,664	21,004	28,806	49,675	73,275	82,515	99,314	119,068	131,047
Nonfarm residential	10,431	15,888	20,362	32,387	45,640	52,004	62,782	74,930	81,380
FHA-insured	(NA)	4,560	5,851	7,702	7,919	8,310	8,495	8,234	7,568
VA-guaranteed	(NA)	3,711	2,859	2,688	2,589	2,980	3,203	3,297	3,176
Conventional	(NA)	7,617	11,652	21,997	35,131	40,714	51,084	63,399	70,636
Other nonfarm	2,264	3,819	6,796	14,377	23,284	26,306	31,751	38,696	43,639
Farm	968	1,297	1,648	2,911	4,351	4,205	4,781	5,442	6,028
Mutual savings banks:									
Loans acquired	2,496	4,560	4,437	8,654	5,944	9,915	(NA)§	(NA)	(NA)
Loans outstanding	8,261	17,457	26,935	44,617	57,948	61,978	67,556	73,226	74,890
Nonfarm residential	7,053	15,568	24,306	40,096	49,936	53,027	57,140	61,090	62,181
FHA-insured	1,615	4,150	7,074	13,791	16,087	16,141	16,013	15,506	15,209
VA-guaranteed	1,457	5,773	8,986	11,408	12,008	12,074	12,622	12,946	12,921
Conventional	3,982	5,645	8,246	14,897	21,842	24,812	28,505	32,638	34,051
Other nonfarm	1,164	1,831	2,575	4,469	7,893	8,901	10,354	12,085	12,656
Farm	44	58	54	52	119	50	62	64	53
Life insurance companies:									
Loans acquired	4,894	6,623	6,086	11,137	7,181	7,573	8,696	11,463	11,389
Nonfarm	4,532	6,108	5,622	9,988	6,867	7,070	7,996	10,457	10,382
Farm	362	515	464	1,149	314	503	700	1,006	1,007
Loans outstanding	16,102	29,445	41,771	60,013	74,375	75,496	76,948	81,369	86,258
Nonfarm	14,775	27,172	38,789	55,190	68,726	69,895	71,270	75,373	79,937
FHA-insured	4,573	6,395	9,032	12,068	11,419	10,767	9,962	9,208	8,568
VA-guaranteed	2,026	6,074	6,901	6,286	5,394	5,004	4,660	4,402	4,176
Other	8,176	14,703	22,856	36,836	51,913	54,124	56,648	61,763	67,193
Farm	1,327	2,273	2,982	4,823	5,649	5,601	5,678	5,996	6,321
Savings and loan associations:									
Loans made	5,237	11,255	14,304	24,192	21,386	39,419	51,369	49,412	38,959
Loans outstanding‡	13,657	31,408	60,070	110,306	150,331	174,250	206,182	231,733	249,306
FHA-insured	848	1,404	3,524	5,145	10,178	13,675	15,400 }	29,738	29,820
VA-guaranteed	2,973	5,883	7,222	6,398	8,494	10,623	13,474		
Conventional	9,836	24,121	49,324	98,763	131,659	149,952	177,308	201,995	219,486

* In millions of dollars. Loans outstanding are as of end of year. Bank data include Puerto Rico; savings and loan data include Puerto Rico and Guam. See *Historical Statistics, Colonial Times to 1970*, series N 266–267, for nonfarm residential holdings. † Includes loans held by nondeposit trust companies; excludes holdings of trust departments of commercial banks. ‡ Beginning in 1960, includes shares pledged against mortgage loans, and, beginning in 1970, junior liens and real estate sold on contract. Beginning in 1970, reflects minor downward adjustment for change in universe. § NA = Not available.

location, architecture, and the attractiveness of buildings. Whether the local market will absorb a new building or development in terms of each of these aspects is the primary concern of the lender. Thus, cost to the developers and the prices they must sell or rent units to the public for must be related to a project's desirability. The entrepreneur must demonstrate that costs are reasonable and realistic, that materials, labor, land, and capital can be combined to produce a marketable project, and that the income from the project will allow the borrower to repay the loan with interest and do so with an adequate safety factor.

Types of real estate loans

During the early 1970s the real estate market incurred an aberration in which some lenders, most notably real estate investment trusts and commercial banks, expanded their lending practices to cover a variety of loan types within given projects. Many major failures occurred in the 1974–75 period and were caused partly by the inability of lenders to service the broad range of loan types they chose to make. These loan types include the following:

Land acquisition loans. The initial loan by which land is acquired by a developer is typically referred to as a land acquisition loan. Such loans historically were avoided by institutional lenders, and many have been made wherein the lender advances funds for downpayments and for small parcel releases, with the land seller providing most of the necessary financing.

Land acquisition loans rarely exceed three years in duration, and they typically bear interest at two to four percentage points above the prime rate of a given bank. This practice presented a major problem in the mid-1970s when interest rates increased, while the market demands needed for parcel releases diminished. The institutional lenders were forced to foreclose and continue making payments to the land seller in an attempt to protect the value of the equity position.

Acquisition and development loans. A parcel of land taken down for immediate improvement is financed by an acquisition and development loan. This loan releases the land from the seller, meaning that it must be paid for in full. The cost of streets, curbs, gutters, sidewalks, utilities, streetlights, entrance markers, and other improvements is included in the loan. Many of these loans have provided working capital and covered interest expense for the developer for a period of time.

Acquisition and development loans are funded in the same manner as land acquisition loans. They typically are larger loans which are based upon projections of repayment as building sites are sold.

Construction loans. Loans for the erection of buildings are construction loans. They rarely exceed one year for residential construction or three years for major commercial buildings. They often are made based upon a permanent loan commitment which provides for their payoff at a future date. They usually bear interest at two to four percentage points above the prime rate of the bank which funds them.

Permanent loans. Loans of 25 years or more are sought for improved residential and commercial properties. They typically bear lower interest rates, and they accommodate the user of the property—the person for whom all of the development steps were performed.

The problem of one lender's attempting to make all four types of loans on a single project is that loan draws for all types of activity must be supervised to ensure that all funds are committed properly to the job. Poor supervision has led to losses where borrowers "skimmed" the projects, usually by using cheaper materials than those called for in the specifications. A second problem is that developers sometimes build more product than they can sell, creating substantial inventory and large loan balances. Lenders could not make loans fast enough to absorb their available funds during the period of 1972–73, and they encouraged borrowers to expand the scope of their projects. When the market turned down, many lenders refused to fund the final stages of commitments, causing their borrowers to default.

Financial analysis

In applying for a loan from an institutional lender, the borrower-developer will be required to submit an estimation of expected costs and a projection of future income and expenses. Examples of such schedules are shown in Tables 13–6 and 13–7. The lender will analyze the financial plan

TABLE 13–6

Presidential Manor Apartment project estimated costs

Land:	
15.013 acres, or 655,263 sq. ft. at $.46/sq. ft.	$ 301,420
Improvements:	
29 apartment buildings, 252,000 sq. ft. at $14.50/sq. ft.	3,654,000
Blacktop, 191,000 sq. ft. at $.40/sq. ft.	76,400
Laundry and maintenance building, 1,350 sq. ft. at $11/sq. ft.	14,850
Estimated total cost	$4,046,670

to determine whether it is accurate and realistic. An appraisal will be made either by the lender's appraisal staff or an independent appraiser. The lender may accept the plans and projections, suggest modifications, or reject them. Of course, a lender may believe that a proposed development has merit, yet not grant a loan because of a current lack of loanable funds or because of the availability of other desirable projects.

One large apartment project recently proposed to a life insurance company, Presidential Manor, contained estimates of cost as shown in Table 13–6.

TABLE 13–7

Presidential Manor projected income and expenses

Unit type	Number of units	Monthly rental	Sq.ft./ unit	Mo.rent/ sq. ft.	Number of rooms	Rent/room/ month	Total
1-bedroom flat	80	$160	620	25.8¢	3	$53.33	$153,600
2-bedroom flat	152	185	812	22.8	4	46.25	337,440
2-bedroom townhome	76	200	928	21.6	4	50.00	182,400

Total Projected Annual Rental Income	$673,440
Other income: Laundry at $25/unit	7,700
Gross annual income	681,140
Less: Vacancy and collection allowance at 5%	34,072
Effective Gross Income	**$647,068**

Less expenses:
Operating:

Management at 4½%	$ 29,118	
Custodial	17,000	
Heat and air conditioning at $25/room	28,900	
Electric (common areas only)	6,000	
Maintenance at $12/room	13,872	
Painting and redecorating at $12/room	13,872	
Miscellaneous	5,000	
Total Operating Expenses	$113,762	

Fixed:

Real estate taxes at $200/unit	$ 60,160	
Insurance at $40/unit	12,320	
Reserve for replacements	30,150	
Total Fixed Expenses	$102,630	
Total Operating and Fixed Expenses		216,392
Net Operating Income		**$430,676**

The builder should have the building costs itemized for all materials, assemblies, parts, and labor. The costs should include the costs involved in drawing plans and blueprints, obtaining permits, paying city fees, the construction financing expense, legal fees, the marketing expense, and overhead and profit, as well as the direct materials and labor costs. If lenders are convinced that the buildings as planned, the land, and other improvements can be obtained for the estimated costs, they will proceed with an analysis of income and expense projections. The Presidential

Manor proposal contained the income and expense projections shown in Table 13–7.

If lenders agree with this projection of income and expense, they can capitalize the net income stream to estimate the property's value. If a capitalization rate of 10 percent is appropriate and an economic life of the improvements of 40 years is used, the level annuity factor of 9.8 produces an estimated value of 4,220,624, or approximately $4,220,600. To this is added the present value of the land reversion ($301,420 × .022) of $6,631 for a total value of $4,227,200. On the basis of this value, a life insurance company in this state legally can lend 80 percent, or $3,381,760. The borrower has requested this amount from the insurance company in the form of a 20-year, annually amortized mortgage loan, bearing a 9 percent interest rate.

Assuming that the insurance company is satisfied that the income and expense projections are as realistic and accurate as can be determined, the lender will still want to examine other factors and may propose an alternate financing arrangement to the developer. Important additional considerations are (*a*) the relation of the cash flow to be generated from the property to the financing payments and (*b*) the effect of the federal income tax on the stream of earnings.

The income projection of Table 13–7 can be extended as follows:

Net Operating Income (first year)		$430,676
Less annual depreciation (40 years straight-line on building only)	$ 91,350	
Less interest (first year)	304,358	395,708
Net Taxable Income		$ 34,968
Income tax (50%)		17,484
Net Income (after depreciation, interest expense, and income tax)		17,484
Add: Depreciation	$ 91,350	
Deduct: Mortgage principal payment (first year)°	66,100	25,250
Net Cash Flow (first year)		$ 42,734

° Calculation of principal payment

Total mortgage payment (9%)	$ 370,458
Interest (first year)	304,358
Principal payment (first year)	$ 66,100

By dipping into the funds earmarked for depreciation, it is evident that the borrowers would be able to meet their mortgage payments and have some cash ($42,734) left over. The margin is not great, however, and both borrowers and lender should consider the possibility that the rental estimates may be optimistic. If rents should turn out to be less than anticipated, the borrowers might not be able to meet their mortgage commitment. The lender, therefore, proposed a different financing arrangement.

The new arrangement proposed that the lender grant a loan of $3 million for 25 years at 10 percent interest (amortized annually) and purchase the land for $300,000. The borrowers would lease back the land for $30,000 per year (10 percent), this amount being deductible by the borrowers for income tax purposes. Additionally, to protect itself against the risk of inflation, the lender wanted a "kicker." The kicker took the form of additional rent on the ground tied to net operating income. The lender would be entitled to 25 percent of any additional operating income above that obtained in the current rental schedule. The kicker would continue for the length of the lease on the ground, although the mortgage would in all probability be paid off much sooner. Additionally, the lender stipulated that the property could not be sold or refinanced without its permission for 12 years.

The cash flow generated by the new financing arrangement was estimated as shown in Figure 13–2.

FIGURE 13–2
Estimated cash flow produced by bank-proposed financing arrangement (first year)*

Net Operating Income		$430,676
Less:		
Rent	$ 30,000	
Interest	300,000	
Depreciation	93,665	423,665
Taxable income		$ 7,011
Income tax (50%)		3,505
Net income after tax		$ 3,506
Add depreciation		93,665
		$ 97,171
Deduct mortgage principal payment (1st year)		30,504
Cash Flow (first year)		$ 66,667

* Loan terms: Amount—$3,000,000; Term—25 years; Amortization—Annual; Annual payment—$330,504; Constant—.110168; Interest rate—10%.

Although the interest rate on the lender's proposed loan is higher than for the loan requested by the developer, the cash flow is greater. The better cash position results because of two factors: (a) the term of the loan is longer, reducing the annual mortgage payment and (b) the ground rent is tax deductible, producing a lower income tax liability for the developer.

If rental income did not increase or if expenses increase as much as income, of course the lender would obtain no increased yield from the kicker. In its projections, however, the lender assumed that net operating income (gross income less vacancy and operating expenses) would increase 3 percent per year. The property's cash flow would increase each year under the assumption, and both the lender's and developer's yields would increase, as shown in Tables 13–8 and 13–9. Thus, for the second

TABLE 13–8

Lender's rate of return for 12-year locked-in period*

Year	Net operating income	Additional income over previous year	Kicker (25 percent of additional income)	Interest + Ground rent + Kicker	Lender's investment (mortgage balance + land)	Lender's rate of ROI†
1	...........$430,676	–0–	–0–	$330,000	$3,300,000	10.00%
2	 443,596	$12,920	$3,230	330,180	3,269,496	10.09
3	 456,896	13,308	3,327	326,921	3,235,942	10.10
4	 470,204	13,705	3,426	323,329	3,199,032	10.10
5	 484,310	14,106	3,527	319,370	3,158,431	10.11
6	 498,839	14,529	3,632	315,009	3,113,770	10.11
7	 513,804	14,965	3,741	310,205	3,064,643	10.12
8	 529,218	15,414	3,854	304,914	3,010,603	10.12
9	 545,095	15,877	3,969	299,085	2,951,159	10.13
10	 561,448	16,353	4,088	292,665	2,885,771	10.14
11	 578,291	16,843	4,211	285,585	2,813,744	10.14
12	 595,640	17,349	4,337	277,798	2,734,614	10.15

* Amount of loan—$3,000,000; Term—25 years; Interest rate—10 percent; Amortization—Annual; Mortgage constant—.110168; Annual payment—$330,504.

† Return on Investment = $\dfrac{\text{Total income}}{\text{Outstanding investment}}$

year $12,920 additional operating income would be generated, the lender receiving $3,230 and the developer receiving the remainder. The rates of return for each year are calculated by adding the total inflows to each party—the lender and developer—and dividing by the total investment of each. Income to the lender consists of mortgage interest, ground rent, and kicker income.

The developer's before-tax cash return to invested equity is calculated by deducting from net operating income ground rent and total debt service (mortgage interest plus principal payments) and adding the expected increases in net operating income, after subtracting the kicker paid to the lender. Although the mortgage principal payments serve to build up equity in the property, it can be assumed that depreciation equals the annual principal payments. The resulting rate of return is equal to increasing the developer's investment each year by the amounts of the principal payment and increasing the developer's cash by the same amount of depreciation.

TABLE 13–9

Developer's before-tax rate of return for 12-year locked-in period

Year	Developer's additional NOI	Total income to developer	Developer's ROI[*]
1	–0–	$ 70,172[†]	9.41%
2	$ 9,690	79,862	10.71
3	9,981	89,843	12.05
4	10,279	100,122	13.43
5	10,579	110,701	14.85
6	10,897	121,598	16.31
7	11,224	132,822	17.82
8	11,560	144,382	19.37
9	11,908	155,290	20.83
10	12,265	167,555	22.48
11	12,632	180,187	24.17
12	13,012	193,199	25.92

[*] Return on Investment $= \dfrac{\text{Total income}}{\text{Outstanding investment}}$

Developer's investment calculated as follows:

Cost of improvements:	$3,745,250
Less mortgage:	3,000,000
	$ 745,250

[†] Income to developer = 1st year's NOI − Ground rent and debt service
= $430,676 − ($30,000 + $330,504)
= $70,172

From the example it is clear that the developers of the apartment complex are able to obtain the financing necessary to produce the project and to realize an extremely attractive rate of return. The rate of return, however, is dependent upon the assumption of an annual, compounded growth rate of net income by 3 percent. The requirement that they pay a higher interest rate (10 percent versus 9 percent) and extend the maturity five years has worked to their advantage. Their annual mortgage payments are lower, thus giving them a greater cash flow. If the apartment project is successful, the higher interest rate and longer maturity will not be burdensome, whereas they will have gained a more secure financial position. On the other hand, the insurance company will have gained a higher rate of return, which to it is very important.

Obviously, any number of different financing schemes could be worked out. Interest rates, maturities, amortization schedules, and kickers could be changed to reflect the best combination for one or both parties. In recent years the field of income property financing has experienced almost every conceivable financing arrangement. There is no such thing as a "standard" or even "preferred" type of loan package.

The clear implication for real estate developers is that they need to understand the various instruments and techniques of real estate finance.

They need to realize that they can and should shop around for a lender who will put together a financing package suitable for their requirements. Even better, they need to be able to suggest financing arrangements to lenders that will meet the lender's requirements for legality and safety, yet which provide the required amount of funds at the proper place and time. The key to most successful real estate developments is financing.

INSTRUMENTS OF REAL ESTATE FINANCE

The principal instruments, or legal arrangements, used in financing real estate are the note, the mortgage, the deed of trust, the land contract, and the lease.[3] In a review of these instruments, these questions should be kept in mind: (*a*) What is their essential nature? (*b*) What legal responsibilities do they create? and (*c*) How are they used in real estate transactions?

If investors, as well as lenders, understand the implications of these questions, they should be able to structure creative financing arrangements for proposed investment opportunities. For example, investors may find that an advantageous method of financing an investment is to create a split ownership situation by selling the land and leasing it back. Another investor with little or no capital may be able to obtain control of a property by purchasing on a land contract. A homebuilder may increase sales by having obtained prior agreement from a lender to finance major appliances in a package mortgage. Investors may decrease their tax liability by making an installment purchase. And yet other investors may be able to finance properties by forming syndicates and selling limited partnership shares. These arrangements require the creation of legal rights and obligations appropriate for each party to a transaction. Such arrangements and combinations (as well as others) are created by the basic instruments of real estate finance, tailored to the individual situation and purpose.

SPECIALIZED TYPES OF REAL ESTATE FINANCE

Several types of ownership or purchase arrangements of parcels of real estate have developed in recent years. Several reasons can be hypothesized for the growth of these arrangements. First, demographic characteristics of the country have greatly increased the need for the services of real estate. The great population increase, the density of population in our cities, and the large numbers of population in the older and younger categories have all resulted in great demands being placed upon housing and commercial and industrial establishments that serve housing and

---

[3] These are described in Chapter 9.

related industries. The young and old age groups have been particularly significant in increasing the demand for apartments. Housing construction costs have risen in the last several years at a faster rate than have other costs in the economy. Thus, the necessity for financing these needs has shown that the traditional purchase of a single-family residence by means of a large downpayment mortgage loan has been inadequate.

Additionally, investors have not had the same kinds of opportunities to purchase small shares or interests in real estate as have investors in securities. In an effort to gain the capacity to attract the savings of small investors, interests in real estate have been divided up and sold in relatively small shares.

Condominiums

The condominium arrangement differs from traditional real estate ownership arrangements in that a single property is divided into several physical portions, usually apartments or office spaces, with each unit being owned by a different owner. Condominium purchasers can pay cash or finance their purchases in any of the traditional ways. As with any property ownership, owners must pay real estate taxes and all other costs and expenses associated with their property. Additionally, however, they must pay a monthly charge for the management and maintenance of the common areas of the property, such as hallways and the lawn. The advantage to this arrangement, as contrasted with some other possibilities, is that condominium owners have long-term possession and control of the property, and any value increases will be reflected in equity buildup for the owners. If they vacate rented property, of course, their rent receipts would not reflect any increased real estate value.

Condominiums are particularly attractive arrangements for large apartment buildings and are being used to a great extent in Florida, California, and large cities in some other states. Condominiums are also attractive to builders in that the builder is able to get out from under the responsibilities of owning and continuing to manage and maintain the property. These functions are usually turned over to professional managers by the condominium owners.

Cooperatives

In their practical effect, cooperatives are similar to condominiums. A building's space is divided up, and owners of partial interest occupy the space. Unlike condominiums, however, the cooperative owners do not own real estate; they own stock in a corporation which owns the real estate. The main result of this difference is that purchaser-owners must purchase stock and finance it by means other than a mortgage loan. Since they do not own the fee simple title, they cannot mortgage their real estate ownership. Their right to equity buildup and possession and control of the premises would be similar to that of condominiums.

Like the condominium owner, cooperative owners must also pay monthly charges for maintaining common areas and other common expenses such as janitorial service, management, and maintenance. Whereas condominium owners can sell their interest in real estate, cooperative owners can sell their stock and the occupancy rights which accompany their ownership.

Real estate syndicates

Syndicates are not a separate form of business organization.[4] Rather, the term refers to the fact that several investors in real estate accumulate their capital within one of the traditional forms of business organization for a particular purpose—such as the purchase of a parcel of real estate.

A syndicate is usually formed as a corporation or a limited partnership. If it is formed as a corporation, the investors receive shares as evidence of their interest in the venture. If the syndicate is formed as a limited partnership, the investors receive limited partnership interests. In the limited partnership arrangement there is at least one general partner with unlimited liability; however, most of the investors will have limited liability. There will be supplementary agreements among the members outlining the rights and responsibilities of various interest holders. Although the limited partners have no voice in the management of the syndicate or the property, they do have the right to a proportional share in the earnings of the syndicate as they are distributed. When the venture for which the syndicate is formed is completed, the syndicate is dissolved.

RISK IN REAL ESTATE FINANCING

Risk in using borrowed funds to help purchase and own real estate can be viewed from the standpoint of either the owner-investor or the lender. In the case of the investor, the principal risk associated with financing is that the monthly or annual cash flow will not be sufficient to meet the mortgage payments. In such a case, the owner must be prepared to obtain funds from other sources to pay the mortgage loan or to forfeit the property. The chart on page 25 shows the relationship between cash flow and mortgage payment on a month by month basis for a year. It is evident that during the months of April and June the owners must be prepared to obtain additional funds from other sources in order to meet their debt obligation. If they cannot do this, it is likely that they will not be able to retain the property.

---

[4] Syndicates are also discussed in Chapter 10.

It is evident therefore that an investor and a lender should carefully consider the factors that would cause the projected income and cash flow not to be realized and to try to evaluate the likelihood that external events would influence any projected income flows. Vacancies, deaths, illnesses, and external economic, political, and social considerations must be analyzed. Final determination as to safety of the loan will of necessity be subjective. Nevertheless, such an analysis is crucial to successful real estate lending and investment.

GOVERNMENT INFLUENCE ON REAL ESTATE FINANCE

Government influence on real estate finance is pervasive, although largely indirect. The influence is indirect in the sense that governmental agencies do not become directly involved in the financing operations of real estate transactions. Rather, they establish and operate a framework of interest rates, insurance, regulation of secondary markets, and special purpose assistance. The framework, however, is pervasive in that every real estate transaction is affected by government activity. Since it has hopefully been demonstrated earlier in this chapter that financing is a major determinant of the profitability of real estate investments, the significance of government influence on financing arrangements and terms can hardly be overemphasized.

One may analyze the structure and operations of government activity through the various agencies or through the functions they perform. The primary agencies affecting real estate finance are (*a*) the Federal Reserve System, (*b*) the Federal Home Loan Bank System, (*c*) the U.S. Treasury, (*d*) the Department of Housing and Urban Development, and (*e*) the Veterans Administration. Abbreviated organization charts are shown in Figures 13–3 to 13–5 of three of these agencies. As can be seen from these charts, several subagencies or organizations affiliated with these agencies are important components of the total picture. While it is not our purpose to describe in detail the nature of these agencies and subagencies, we do need to examine the ways in which they affect the financing of real estate. In order to do this we refer to Table 13–10, which identifies six major functions and the agencies and organizations that carry out each function. It is hoped that this manner of presentation will emphasize the complexity of the bureaucratic web which plays such an important role in determining the attractiveness of real estate transactions and investments.

Regulation of the supply of funds and interest rates

The supply of funds and the level of interest rates in the economy are influenced by several factors, including Federal Reserve policy, debt management policies of the U.S. Treasury, the financing of new plants

FIGURE 13-3

Federal Reserve System organization structure

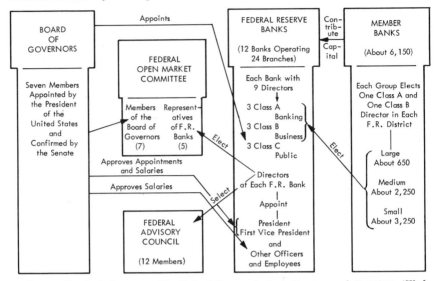

Source: Board of Governors, *The Federal Reserve System: Purposes and Functions* (Washington, D.C.; U.S. Government Printing Office, 1963), p. 23.

and equipment, purchases by large corporations, and the financing needs of individual investors and consumers. The Federal Reserve System is perhaps the most important one of these determinants. Its function is to establish, maintain, and supervise the monetary system for the country. It has direct control of the supply of money in the economy and of certain interest rates, which in turn influence all interest rates. This control is exercised through the instruments of monetary regulation—the discount rate, reserve requirements, and open market operations. Through the operation of these instruments, the board of governors of the Federal Reserve System can effectively increase or decrease the rate of growth of the money supply and can drive interest rates upward or downward.

The important point for our consideration in considering the Federal Reserve System is that the policies adopted by its board of governors influence real estate to a greater extent than any other economic good. If the board of governors decides to slow the rate of growth of the money supply and to drive interest rates upward, the effect is to make real estate financing for many would-be purchasers more difficult and costly. With the decreased availability of funds and higher interest rates, many persons will stay out of the market. On the other hand, during periods of monetary ease, when the money supply is growing at an ample rate and interest rates are relatively low, financing is more readily available to a greater

FIGURE 13-4

Federal Home Loan Bank System organization structure

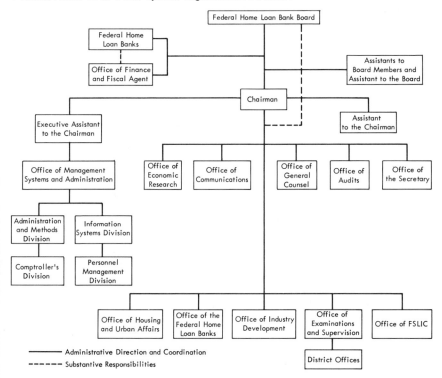

Source: *Federal Home Loan Bank Board Annual Report, 1969* (Washington, D.C.: U.S. Government Printing Office, 1969), p. 91.

number of people. Marginal buyers will be able to obtain financing, and real estate activity will tend to increase.

Obviously, this analysis is much oversimplified. Other factors may at times be equal in importance or perhaps even more important to real estate financing than Federal Reserve policy. For example, if there is general pessimism about the future of the economy, an increased rate of growth of the money supply and lower interest rates will not by themselves overcome this factor. Also, if the demand for funds increases greatly on the part of the government or by private industry for nonreal estate purposes, an increase in the total availability of funds would perhaps not benefit real estate interests. Nevertheless, the influence of Federal Reserve policies must be considered both in terms of their own effects on real estate finance and in relation to other considerations that we have just discussed. The importance of financing to almost every real estate transaction means that Federal Reserve policy will often mean the differ-

FIGURE 13–5

Department of Housing and Urban Development organization structure

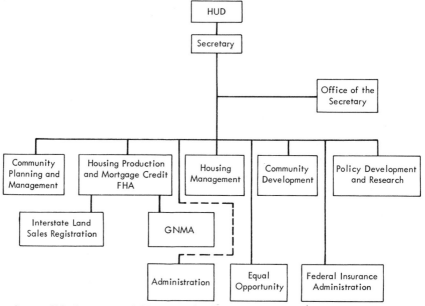

Source: *U.S. Department of Housing and Urban Development Annual Report, 1969* (Washington, D.C.: U.S. Government Printing Office, 1969).

ence between whether a buyer can or cannot afford to complete a transaction.

The financing of the national debt of the United States is also an important consideration to the financing of real estate. The amount which the U.S. government owes holders of short-term and long-term debt is well over $650 billion. Since the amount of the debt continues to grow and there is no thought that the debt will be paid off to any significant extent, the Treasury must continually refinance the debt. As this refinancing takes place, the amounts of funds drained from the capital market and the interest rates paid on the securities that are issued have a significant impact upon the amount of funds available and interest rate levels in the economy. In general, as interest rates rise and government bonds become relatively more attractive, funds are siphoned off from potential real estate usage. When funds become more readily available and interest rates on government securities are relatively low, mortgage investment is more attractive, and funds flow into real estate finance.

Secondary market activities

Two government-related agencies operate to provide a market for those wishing to sell previously originated mortgage loans. Such an operation

TABLE 13–10

Functions and government agencies associated with real estate finance

Function	Government agency
Regulation of the supply of funds and interest rates.	1. Federal Reserve System. 2. U.S. Treasury (debt management).
Secondary market activities.	1. Federal National Mortgage Association. 2. Federal Home Loan Mortgage Corporation. 3. Government National Mortgage Association—Department of Housing and Urban Development.
Supervision and insurance.	1. Federal Reserve System. 2. Federal Deposit Insurance Corporation. 3. Comptroller of the Currency. 4. Federal Home Loan Bank Board. 5. Federal Savings and Loan Insurance Corporation. 6. State Regulatory Agencies.
Special aid for low-income housing and community development.	1. Offices for Housing Production and Mortgage Credit, Housing Management, and Community Development—Department of Housing and Urban Development. 2. Government National Mortgage Association.
Mortgage loan insurance and guarantee.	1. Federal Housing Administration—Department of Housing and Urban Development. 2. Veterans Administration.
Taxation.	1. U.S. Internal Revenue Service. 2. Local Taxing Authorities (real estate tax).

provides liquidity for mortgage loans and thus stimulates a large flow of funds for financing real estate. The Federal National Mortgage Association (known as Fanny May) has specialized in buying and selling mortgages that are insured by the Federal Housing Administration or guaranteed by the Veterans Administration. Its intent is to develop secondary market operations in nongovernment underwritten (conventional) mortgages as well, however. The Federal National Mortgage Association (FNMA) tends to be a net buyer of mortgage loans, as it unpopularly tightens the mortgage market when it sells loans. It buys loans by periodically announcing a dollar amount of mortgages that it will purchase. Those who wish to sell mortgages to it, typically mortgage companies, then auction their mortgages to Fanny May on the basis of yield. Fanny May will buy those mortgages up to the indicated amount that are offered to it at the lowest prices offered. FNMA obtains its funds to buy mortgages by selling capital stock to those who sell mortgages to the association, by the sale of mortgage-backed debentures, short-term discount notes, and U.S. Treasury borrowing.

The second organization is the Federal Home Loan Mortgage Corporation (FHLMC). This is a relatively new organization, having been established by an act of Congress in 1970. Capital stock of FHLMC of $100 million was acquired by the 12 Federal Home Loan Banks. It is closely associated with the Federal Home Loan Bank System, since the three members of the Federal Home Loan Bank Board also serve as the directors of the FHLMC, and policy is coordinated with credit policies of the 12 regional Federal Home Loan Banks. The FHLMC will buy conventional, as well as FHA- and VA-backed mortgages.

Another organization, the Government National Mortgage Association (GNMA) also serves as a secondary market for mortgages granted under special purpose government programs. It will purchase mortgages made under sections of the National Housing Act designed to help particular needy groups. For example, it might purchase a mortgage loan made to a sponsor of an apartment project for low-income families who are under a government subsidy program.

During 1975 a program was developed wherein GNMA sold loan commitments in a form of futures market through the Chicago Board of Trade. Millions of dollars worth of loan commitments can now be purchased at fixed yield rates, offering assurance of both money availability and cost. As in other futures markets, these commitments can be allowed to expire if interest rates become more favorable in the future. Investors would lose only their commitment fees.

Supervision and insurance

The Federal Reserve Board, the Comptroller of the Currency, the Federal Home Loan Bank Board, state regulatory agencies, the Federal Deposit Insurance Corporation (FDIC), and the Federal Savings and Loan Insurance Corporation (FSLIC) all have a supervisory role over banking and thrift institutions under their jurisdictions. The Federal Reserve Board and the Comptroller of the Currency supervise commercial banks—all national banks and state banks which are members of the system. The Federal Home Loan Bank Board supervises savings and loan associations that are members—all federally chartered associations and state chartered member associations. State regulatory agencies for both banks and savings and loan associations that are chartered by the states and that are not members of the Federal Reserve System or the Federal Home Loan Bank System supervise the operations of these institutions. All of these institutions are required to abide by specific regulations and standards in regard to the loans that they make. The supervisory function is for the purpose of assuring that the standards and regulations are observed by the various institutions.

The FDIC and the FSLIC insure deposits or accounts in banks or savings and loans up to a maximum of $40,000 each. By so doing, the agencies provide real relief in the rare instances where a financial institution goes bankrupt, and they insure public confidence as to the safety of funds placed in financial institutions. They also regulate and supervise the institutions for which they provide insurance. Public confidence had been greatly shaken during the Great Depression of the 1930s, leading to the formation of the FDIC and the FSLIC.

Mortgage loan insurance and guarantee

The Federal Housing Administration is an agency under the Department of Housing and Urban Development. This agency, which was also born in the depth of the Great Depression, and the Veterans Administration insure and guarantee, respectively, loans that might otherwise be considered too risky by lending institutions. The terms on FHA-insured loans and VA-guaranteed loans are usually considerably more liberal than those allowed by conventional lenders. The U.S. government, however, backs the loans which qualify, thus giving added capacity for borrowing to veterans and others who could not otherwise purchase a home. In order to obtain government backing, both the borrowers and the properties which they intend to purchase must meet specified standards. Insurance premiums to pay for the backing are made in the monthly mortgage payment.

In recent years, a number of private mortgage insurance companies have been formed. These companies insure the top 15 to 20 percent of a mortgage for a fee of approximately 1 percent of the amount insured plus an annual premium of 0.25 percent. An example is a 95 percent loan with a 15 percent insurance coverage. If the insured lender forecloses the loan and sells the property for 85 percent of loan amount, the insurer pays the 10 percent loss (or buys the property for the full loan amount). This permits the primary lender or secondary lender to gain protection similar to that of FHA and VA with less difficult administrative procedures. The large private insurors such as Mortgage Guaranty Insurance Corporation (MGIC), Foremost Guaranty, and PMI, Inc., now underwrite a large portion of mortgages written in excess of 75 percent of appraised value.

Special aid for low-income housing and urban renewal

The Department of Housing and Urban Development's functional offices for Community Development, Housing Management, and Housing Production and Mortgage Credit—FHA are primarily responsible for the government effort in the fields of low-income housing and community development.[5]

Taxation

It should be recognized here that income, estate, and gift taxes exert a great influence on real estate decisions.[6] Tax rates applied to various types and amounts of income, and the rules promulgated to calculate the tax burden must be considered when analyzing an investment decision. Rules regarding allowable economic lives and rates of depreciation are particularly important in this regard. When the rules governing these matters are changed, the relative attractiveness of real estate investments may be altered drastically. For example, the Tax Reform Act of 1976 greatly altered such matters as construction period interest and taxes, long-term capital gain periods, depreciation recapture, and deductions for offices in homes and vacation homes. Investment in some types of real estate projects thus became considerably less desirable than had formerly been the case.

SUMMARY

Obtaining financing on favorable terms and at a reasonable cost is an important aspect of creating successful real estate projects. Although some amount of equity funds will normally be required in the production or purchase of real estate, the bulk of funds usually will be borrowed; these funds constitute the debt capital committed to a project.

In seeking debt capital, the real estate investor attempts to tap into the flow of funds available for such financing. The principal sources of debt capital are savings and loan associations, commercial banks, life insurance companies, and mutual savings banks. Mortgage bankers play a facilitat-

---

[5] The various government programs are summarized in Chapter 17.

[6] The manner in which income taxes influence a particular real estate investment is described and analyzed in Chapter 10.

ing role by granting loans for real estate use and then selling the loans to institutional lenders. When shopping for loans, real estate investors need to understand the legal framework, characteristics, and practices of the institutional lenders. In bargaining with lenders, they can often be prepared to concede a point of relatively small importance to them (such as a somewhat higher interest rate) in order to obtain a feature of great importance to them but of less importance to the lender (such as a higher loan-to-value ratio).

In analyzing a proposed real estate project, developers should compute their expected rate of return by relating forecasted net income to their required capital investment. Expenses, as well as rental income, should be evaluated carefully and projected as realistically as possible for the expected life of the investment. Vacancy rates, management expense, and replacement reserves must be included in the expense forecast.

Some basic legal documents used in real estate finance—the note, the mortgage, the deed of trust, the land contract, and the lease—are discussed in terms of their significance to the investor. By knowing the possible relationships that can be established by these documents, one can be creative in designing financing arrangements that meet the needs of both the providers of equity capital and the providers of debt capital.

In recent years several specialized types of real estate finance have gained prominence. Condominiums and cooperatives have made it possible for occupants of apartments and offices to obtain the advantages of ownership (and for condominium owners to obtain the advantages of mortgage financing) over the leasing arrangement. In both the condominium and cooperative arrangement, any increases in value of the properties accrue to the owners. Real estate investment trusts and syndicates are designed to allow investment in real estate by relatively small investors and offer the potential advantages of expert analysis and professional management.

Lastly, the chapter deals with the pervasive influence of government on real estate finance. While government agencies normally do not become directly involved in private financing transactions and arrangements, their influence plays a prominent role in determining the quantity and types of financing available. The Federal Reserve System, the Federal Home Loan Bank System, the U.S. Treasury, the Comptroller of the Currency, the Federal Home Loan Mortgage Corporation, the Federal National Mortgage Association, the U.S. Department of Housing and Urban Development, and the Veterans Administration establish and operate a framework for real estate finance of interest rate determination, institutional supervision and regulation, secondary mortgage market activity, loan insurance, and special purpose assistance.

QUESTIONS FOR REVIEW

1. In what ways is financing real estate different from financing corporate securities? Why?
2. Why are mortgage bankers not shown as an important source of mortgage funds in the U.S. flow of funds accounting system?
3. What are the advantages and dangers of purchasing and selling by land contract? How would you protect yourself against the dangers?
4. How do you explain the fact that savings and loan associations dropped in the percentage of funds supplied in the U.S. economy from an average of about 16 percent per year in the early 1960s to less than 10 percent in the late 1960s?
5. Why do savings and loans and mutual savings banks lend a much higher percentage of their savings on mortgages than do commercial banks?
6. What is a *kicker*? Do you believe kickers will continue to exist during periods of lower interest rates?
7. How does financing influence a developer's expected return on investment? How is cash flow influenced by financing? What role is played by principal repayments?
8. Look up an annual report of the U.S. Department of Housing and Urban Development. What are the principal kinds of programs carried on by this agency?
9. What are the advantages of condominium ownership of an apartment over leasing the same apartment? What are the advantages of leasing over ownership? Which do you prefer?
10. Why are the effects of monetary policies of the board of governors of the Federal Reserve System so keenly felt in the field of real estate finance?

PROBLEMS

1. Indicate the cash flow and taxable income associated with the following facts:

Gross income	$500,000
Vacancy allowance	5 percent of gross
Variable expenses	27 percent of gross
Fixed expenses	$50,000
Mortgage (new)	$1,800,000
Debt service constant	.0967
Interest rate on mortgage	8.5 percent
Depreciation—1st year	$100,000

2. Prepare a numerical example that shows an after-income tax advantage of owning a condominium apartment over renting the same apartment. Incorporate the following data into your example:

Rental level if rented	$300 per month
Purchase price	$35,000

Mortgage ....90 percent of price
Marginal income tax rate ....40 percent
Utilities and maintenance ....$800 per year
Real estate taxes ....$700 per year

REFERENCES

Beaton, William R. *Real Estate Finance*. Englewood Cliffs, N.J.: Prentice-Hall, 1975.

Hoagland, Henry E., and Stone, Leo D. *Real Estate Finance*, 5th ed. Homewood, Ill.: Richard D. Irwin, 1973.

Ricks, R. Bruce, and McElhone, Josephine T. "A Five-year Plan of Asset-Liability Restructuring for S&L's" *Federal Home Loan Bank Board Journal*, March 1971, pp. 3–8 and 27.

Smith, Halbert C. "Institutional Aspects of Interregional Mortgage Investment," *Journal of Finance* 23, no. 2 (May 1968): 349–58.

_____. *Interregional Mortgage Placement: Lenders' Policies, Practices and Characteristics*. Storrs, Conn.: University of Connecticut, Center for Real Estate and Urban Economic Studies, 1969.

_____. "Regional Placement of Mortgage Funds by Life Insurance Companies and Mutual Savings Banks," *Journal of Risk and Insurance* 31, no. 3 (September 1964): 429–36.

Smith, Halbert C., and Tschappat, Carl J. "Monetary Policy and Real Estate Values," *Appraisal Journal* 34, no. 1 (January 1966): 18–26.

Wiedemer, John P. *Real Estate Finance*. Reston, Va.: Reston Publishing Co., 1974.

—

chapter 14

REAL ESTATE PLANNING

PLANNING IS one of the principal functions of management in the execution stage of microadministration (along with organizing, directing, and controlling).[1] Planning is especially important to real estate development and urban growth because of the long-term commitment to which most land uses subject a community. Once the characteristics of real estate development are determined, they establish a community's economic and social pattern. This pattern,[2] in turn, helps determine the nature of further development and growth. Thus, careful planning is necessary to achieve the desired type of land-use pattern through the guidance of future growth.

Although there are many areas of overlap, real estate planning can generally be divided between public planning and private planning. Public planning is often termed *city (or urban) planning*, while private planning is usually termed *land planning*. Generally, either type of planning involves an attempt to guide development so as to achieve maximum efficiency, utility, and attractiveness for a community or a neighborhood. In this sense, planning is a problem-solving process and requires a step-by-step approach in order to formulate a good plan.

PUBLIC PLANNING

Comprehensive planning

The formulation of a plan for a city, county, or region requires a planning agency to take an overall approach to the planning problem. Planning

---

[1] Planning is also discussed in Chapter 1.

[2] The land-use patterns are discussed in Chapter 2 under the concentric circle, multiple nuclei, axial, and sector theories.

involves much more than merely the physical aspects; social, economic, and governmental-political-legal matters must all be considered. Kent has emphasized that the proper role of the public planner is usually that of land-use adviser to an elected public body—typically a city council or county commission.[3] The planner must forecast the jurisdiction's future needs for utilities, streets, roads, public service buildings, parks and recreational facilities, police and fire protection, and public welfare. And, in the most general view, the public planner must forecast tax and other revenues for the jurisdiction and recommend ways to balance revenues against needed expenditures. Although the extent of the planner's role in these matters is a continuous issue of debate, any general, or broad, approach to public planning is termed *comprehensive planning*. There are five basic steps in the continuing process of urban planning.

Define fundamental land-use goals for the constituency to be served. Fundamental land-use goals are determined in a public forum, through the making of key decisions by elected public officials. Clearly defined community goals are often obscured by a plethora of conflicting interests and individual concerns. Examples can be cited for several cities.

The city councils of Boca Raton, Florida, and Petaluma, California, have reflected the wishes of their citizens in establishing the goal of a maximum future population. They are planning for a fixed number of citizens, and they consider the impact of every requested rezoning or new building permit in light of this overriding goal. Private developers have challenged these actions in courts of law, but to date the policies have been found to be constitutional.

Palm Beach, Florida, has adopted a zoning ordinance which limits density of residential development to a level that prohibits development of high-rise condominiums along beach frontage. The town's goal is to avoid the problems involved in rebuilding its street network, utility systems, pollution control system, and public service base to accommodate the congestion inherent in such high density. It seeks to retain a quality of environment deemed desirable by its present residents. The goal has been challenged in court by property owners who contend they are being denied the right to develop their landholdings to maximum values, thereby causing a public taking without just compensation. The issue has not been resolved as of the date of this writing.

The cities of Atlanta, Washington, D.C., and San Francisco have established a goal of promoting rapid transit systems by limiting the development of new parking structures in congested downtown areas. New office buildings are not designed to accommodate employees' and customers' total parking needs. One important implication of such a goal

---

[3] T. J. Kent, Jr., *The Urban General Plan* (San Francisco: Chandler Publishing Co., 1964).

for the private sector is that decisions must be based upon judgments regarding the success of yet unbuilt rapid transit facilities. While New York, Chicago, and Montreal have had rapid transit facilities for many years, the experience of newer systems, such as BART in San Francisco and Metro in Washington, D.C., is insufficient to allow an unequivocal forecast of success for this goal.

Formulate alternative plans to accomplish the goals. In formulating a comprehensive plan, many needs and desires must be considered. Priorities must be determined, and the political implications weighed. Any proposed plan must reflect a balancing of diverse concerns and interests in the community. For example, the need for an adequate road system must be balanced by the desire of residents of existing neighborhoods not to have streets widened to accommodate additional traffic. Additionally the planner's research must establish the need for funding and create the understanding of its importance. Ruth Mack has commented upon the frustration felt by planners as they encounter this bartering process.[4] However, it is a political fact of life which planners cannot avoid.

In formulating a comprehensive plan, the following steps are usually necessary.

Inventory existing conditions. The planner must evaluate the location of utilities (sewerage, gas, water, telephone, and power) and who provides service; the status of street, highway, and expressway improvements; the provision of services such as medical, police and fire protection, transit, sanitation, and welfare; the age and condition of structures; the availability of unimproved or underdeveloped land; property ownership patterns; and community facilities for both business and recreation. Inventory maps must be developed which reflect what the jurisdiction contains and the condition of private and public improvements. Both air and water pollution must be considered in this process. Goals for improvement can then be established, followed by formal policy statements and priorities for use of scarce monetary resources.

Prepare an assessment of trends in population, employment, and business growth. Identify clearly the direction and magnitude of growth.

Prepare independent plans for municipal utilities (sewer and water), community facilities, streets and roads, and public housing. Estimate costs for each plan.

Analyze potential funding sources. The capacity of the property tax and other local sources of revenue must be analyzed to determine their potential for financing the plan. Additionally, support may be available

---

[4] Ruth Prince Mack, *Planning on Uncertainty* (New York: Wiley-Interscience, 1971).

from state and federal agencies. Funding programs have a major impact upon the ability of a local planner to forecast future revenues. The planner must catalog the requirements of federal- and state-aid programs and prepare drafts of application for such aid. The potential use of special taxing districts, new bond issues, general tax increases, and new taxes must be assessed.

Assemble data from earlier steps and overlay them on a single set of base maps for use in developing alternative comprehensive plans. Given that costs have been estimated for subelements, overall cost estimates can be made for each alternative plan. Align such costs with potential funding sources and devise strategies regarding sources of specific revenues and timing of expenditure. Keep the plan reasonably general; allow urban design alternatives to be considered within the plan.

Select the plan that best meets the goals, within political and funding constraints. Selection of the plan that best meets goals and constraints is made by the political governing body, for example, the city council or county commission. However, the plan selected can be influenced by the advantages and disadvantages identified by the planners. Additionally, public reactions to alternative plans can be influential (and often determinative) about which plan is chosen.

When a new plan is formulated, or an existing plan substantially revised, public hearings are usually required. At such hearings citizen opinions and inputs to the plan are obtained. Based upon these reactions and suggestions the plan may be selected, rejected, or modified to include components of alternative plans. Needless to say, public approval of a plan usually requires citizen input during its formulation, "selling" of the plan to elected officials, and commitment to and selling of the plan by the officials to their constituents.

Implement the plan. Implementation of the comprehensive plan is accomplished through zoning. Zoning may be defined as the regulation of land use, population density, and building size by district. The overall zoning pattern and rezoning decisions should be made in conformance with the comprehensive plan.

Monitor the operation of the plan and modify it as required. Plans must be modified as conditions change or as the plan is found to be deficient. One of the key tests of the plan's success is the extent to which it is accepted by the area's residents. A substantial outpouring of criticism or court challenges to the plan will likely cause the plan to be modified. A successful plan normally contains both a strong element of rigidity and provisions for flexibility. Once the plan has been adopted, capricious changes should be precluded. At the same time, however, changes of a more general nature should be allowed, if they are based upon well-founded reasoning and research. The comprehensive plan should be regarded as a document subject to continual review, analysis, and modification.

Zoning

Zoning may be regarded as a phase of comprehensive planning. As noted previously, zoning is the process by which a plan is implemented. This process involves the delineation of zones or districts, within which certain land uses are permitted and others are prohibited. The broadest categorization of zones is residential, commercial, and industrial. The category of residential would be indicated by R; commercial by C; and industrial by I. These categories are further divided into many subcategories. For example, R1a may designate that only detached single-family residences may be built on lots of a specified minimum size and shape, R1b may allow smaller lots, R2 may allow duplexes, and R3 may allow high-density apartments. The zoning code for a moderate-sized city may contain several hundred pages of small print to identify and explain the various zones.

Objective. The objective of the zoning process is to bring order to the otherwise uncontrolled market of private competition for land. Without zoning, many diverse opinions as to the most profitable use of land would undoubtedly result in widely differing uses of adjacent parcels. Offices, apartments, and even factories could be constructed in a neighborhood of single-family homes. Or homes could be constructed in an area subject to pollution, poor drainage, or industrial usage. The ultimate result of these types of practices is a reduction of all land values (compared with land values under zoning control). Thus, the main advantage claimed for zoning is that land values are preserved and enhanced.

Legal basis. The legal basis for zoning is the police power of the government. The police power is the inherent right of government to protect the general welfare by the regulation of public health, morals, and safety. Legislative enabling acts confer the specific zoning authority upon local governments.

Since zoning limits the right of property owners to develop and use property as they may desire, zoning has been attacked in the courts as a method of taking property *without* compensation. Many such attacks have been unsuccessful; the courts have upheld the concept of zoning as a legitimate exercise of police power. However, a recent California U.S. District Court case, *Arastra Limited Partnership* v. *City of Palo Alto*, suggests that there are definite limits to zoning powers. The court ruled that Palo Alto's open-space zoning regulations precluded private development of land that the city had intended to buy and thus constituted "inverse condemnation"—illegal taking of land. The implications of the case will likely be quite significant. Local governments or agencies who downzone property that they had intended to buy, will find that they have gone beyond the limits of zoning authority.[5]

Additionally, zoning must be applied fairly, impartially, and in conformance with a community's comprehensive plan. Many specific applications of zoning have been overturned when these criteria were not met. For example, the Georgia Supreme Court ruled in 1975 that the Commissioners of Cobb County were arbitrary and capricious in failing to rezone a developer's property.[6] Further, the court warned that the state courts would be looking over the shoulder of all zoning bodies to see that all future decisions are made in consideration of the public health, safety, morals, and general welfare. Within six months after this decision, more than 100 zoning cases in several states were placed on court dockets.

The increasing use of private planners who present expert testimony in various public forums has led to a new category of planners—the *advocacy planner*. Altshuler, Bolan, and others have developed the viewpoint that the public hearing mechanism for making land-use decisions requires greater involvement by professional planners.[7] Although such professionals are advocates, it is believed that they can present pertinent facts and develop solutions that will meet the required criteria.

Administration. Appendix B describes the administrative structure for planning and zoning in Gainesville, Florida, a city of approximately 100,000 population. The structure is typical, in that a planning commission of appointed, nonprofessional planners comprises the planning agency for the city. The planning commission hires a staff of professional planners, who carry out the day-to-day planning and zoning activities. The planning commission either approves, rejects, or modifies its staff's recommendations. In planning and zoning matters, the commission's decisions then become recommendations to the city commission, which has the final decision-making authority. The planning commission holds final authority for the approval of site plans, subdivision plats, and commercial signs and billboards.

Requests for rezoning are typically made to the chief staff planner, or zoning administrator. The property owner must submit an application for rezoning, accompanied by a plan for the property which reflects the proposed use. Larger rezoning requests must also be reviewed by state and federal agencies, school officials, and utility companies that will be affected by the proposed plan.

---

[5] "The Limits on Zoning," *Business Week*, May 3, 1976, p. 74.

[6] Earnest W. Barrett et al., *Commissioners v. Doyle Hamby*, Exr. 30 Ga. 015, decided September 16, 1975.

[7] Alan A. Altshuler, *The City Planning Process: A Political Analysis* (Ithaca, N.Y.: Cornell University Press, 1965), and Richard S. Bolan, "Emerging Views of Planning," *Journal of the American Institute of Planners*, July 1967, pp. 233–45.

Following these reviews, a notice of the rezoning request is posted on the property, and surrounding property owners are notified of the proposed rezoning. The request is then scheduled for public hearing, where the petitioner presents the proposal; affected property owners are asked to testify, and the zoning administrator is asked to recommend for or against the proposal. The commission then makes a recommendation to the elected governing body who in turn holds a hearing and renders a final approval or denial.

The political power of the zoning administrator should be analyzed by anyone seeking a rezoning. In some jurisdictions the governing body rarely votes in opposition to the administrator, while in others the recommendations have little or no effect on the final decision. The hearings in this process are tending to become more formal in most jurisdictions, and the administrator's ideas are typically given more attention than in the past. Thus, the administrator's political power over land-use decisions appears to be increasing.

Social and economic issues

Because of the pervasive impact of planning and zoning decisions, they have been subject to many controversies. The legal issue regarding whether zoning results in confiscation without compensation has been noted. Although the general authority to zone is well established, legal battles will continue to be waged over the question of whether specific planning and zoning decisions meet the criteria of reasonableness, fairness, and necessity to the general welfare. It has been shown that the courts will not hesitate to intervene in zoning decisions to uphold the fundamental tests.

In addition to the legal issues, economic and social concerns have been expressed regarding the effects of zoning on the private enterprise system and upon groups of citizens. These issues are discussed in the following paragraphs.

Zoning interferes with the efficient operation of the private market. Zoning seeks to guide and direct market decisions in ways that enhance all land values. To accomplish this goal, however, zoning must anticipate market needs. In effect, land must be zoned so as to reflect decisions that the private market might well have made without the zoning. Land zoned for single-family residences should be generally recognized as appropriate for that use, and land zoned for commercial uses should be amenable to that type of use.

Planning and zoning decisions may not, however, accurately forecast market activity. Too much land may be zoned for one purpose and not enough for another. Or, land zoned for one use may not fit in with the trends of development and other uses. These inaccurate market interpretations lead to imbalances in supply and demand relationships. Market inefficiency is the result, with the price of some land being too high and other land too low.

Siegan has attacked the basic premise of zoning by contending that zoning does not improve upon the private market's ability to produce a desirable structure of land uses.[8] In his study of Houston, the only major U.S. city without zoning, he concluded that the private market produced a structure of land uses equally desirable to the structure produced under zoning in other cities. Although Siegan's research and value judgments can be (and have been) questioned, the basic issue of the relationship between planning, zoning, and the private market will continue to be debated. Perhaps the most satisfactory resolution of the issue is to assure sufficient flexibility in the comprehensive plan and in the planning and zoning processes so that changes can be made to reflect market realities.

The administration of planning and zoning is inherently subject to favoritism and political manipulation. Given the administrative structure of planning and zoning, perhaps favoritism and political influence are unavoidable and should be recognized as a definitional aspect of these activities. Nevertheless, when these types of considerations affect zoning or rezoning decisions, they defeat the fundamental criteria which form zoning's legal justification. The economic effect of manipulative influences is, as with any antimarket force, to subvert the operation of the market and to produce prices that are too high or too low. Some land may be developed too soon, while other land is delayed. And, of course, some property owners or developers profit at the expense of the general public. As Audrey Moore, a member of the Board of Supervisors of Fairfax County, Virginia, has expressed: "Every time they meet, the local zoning boards create wealth for some to the detriment of others."[9]

The increasing use of professional planners in the planning and zoning process is perhaps the most important way of preventing or limiting favoritism and political influence. The lay members of the planning and zoning commission can serve to insulate the professional staff. After the staff's recommendations have been made, the commission may endorse or reject them, but their decisions are subject to careful public scrutiny. Rejection of professional advice focuses attention upon the personalities, the process, and influencing factors.

The appointment of well-qualified, highly regarded, ethical, and moral members of planning and zoning commissions is always a desirable form

---

[8] Bernard H. Siegan, *Land Use without Zoning* (Lexington, Mass.: D. C. Heath & Co., 1972).

[9] Audrey Moore, "The Case against Zoning," *Central Atlantic Environment News* 3, no. 1 (January 1973): 2.

of protection from favoritism and political influence. Given the economic and social importance and the pervasiveness of planning and zoning decisions, appointments to the commission should be of the highest caliber. Even so, however, political cronies and underqualified candidates cannot always be identified and their appointments prevented. Probably the only answer to this issue is to be aware of the problem and to obtain the greatest possible public scrutiny of planning and zoning activities.

Zoning is used to discriminate against low-income and minority groups. With the attainment of open-housing laws and court decisions,[10] minority groups undoubtedly expected housing in middle- and upper-class suburbs to be more easily attainable. Very few inroads have been made, however. Minority and low-income families have found their attempts to obtain such housing thwarted by high prices and costs. Provision of lower-priced housing in such areas has been made impossible by zoning ordinances which impose strict limits upon density. Minimum lot sizes (in some cases of one to three acres), building sizes, height and setback restrictions, utilities, and street requirements have limited access to the more desirable living areas.

The issue of exclusionary zoning practices has been taken to several courts. To date the court decisions have not settled the question of exclusionary zoning; however, the net effect seems to have upheld communities' authority to impose such zoning.

Another important factor in the issue of exclusionary zoning is the role of the federal government. When the government supplies vast sums of money for the construction of public housing or the subsidization of other housing, it may have the obligation to assure that this housing does not perpetuate racial segregation. Indeed, the U.S. Supreme Court ruled unanimously in 1976 that federal courts can order low-cost public housing for minorities to be built in suburban areas as an effort to relieve racial segregation in housing in the inner city. The U.S. Department of Housing and Urban Development was found to be guilty of fostering segregation in public housing programs it has supported. Even so, however, the court indicated that the decision would not mean that public housing projects could be forced automatically on suburban communities that do not request them.[11]

PRIVATE PLANNING

The private planning process parallels the public planning process. Private planners inventory a site's physical features and the utilities and roads available to the site. They study the markets for all proposed uses

---

[10] See Appendix A.

[11] Hills v. Gautreaux, No. 74–1047, April 20, 1976, (___ U.S. ___, 47 L. Ed. 2d 792, 96 SCt ___).

and study the legal, social, and economic constraints to the site's use. Several alternative use plans are prepared, and one is selected that appears to balance costs and revenues over a reasonable planning period. Within design and pollution control parameters, the use mix is devised. The plan is then promoted to the developer and lenders, with implementation leading to continuous monitoring.

An example of a land plan for Kimball Knoll prepared by a prominent planner in Atlanta, Dr. Terrance L. Love[12] is presented in Figure 14–1. This plan reflects the development of a new access road connecting Kimball Bridge Road and Haynes Bridge Road (see inset map), offering ready access to Georgia Highway 400. Georgia Highway 400 is a four-lane, limited access highway which connects north Atlanta to Lake Lanier. It carries 5,000 to 7,000 automobiles per day past the site, and its volume of traffic is expected to grow steadily. The highway has been a popular road for apartment and office park development. The subject site is sewered and has water, gas, and electric utilities available at its border. It has a moderately steep slope that varies in altitude from a low of 1,005 feet above mean sea level in the southwest corner of the tract to a high of 1,140 feet at the crown near the northeast corner and is thus highly visible from Georgia 400. The property lies less than 15 minutes driving time from more than 50 office parks and three regional shopping centers. It is a prestige location.

The plan is overlaid on a topographic base map having five foot intervals of elevation. The development plan calls for 90 apartment units on 7.5 acres, 7 office building sites on 8 acres, and 2 commercial tracts totaling 4 acres. The site is 19.5 acres in size.

The commercial usage lies on Kimball Bridge Road, anchoring the subject tract's end to the new access road. All of the office sites lie above Highway 400, providing excellent commercial visibility, coupled with ease of access via Haynes Bridge Road. The apartments terrace a gentle hillside, providing excellent separation of tiers of units to render a feeling of spaciousness even though a density of 12 units per acre is maintained.

The wide band which bisects the property from east to west is a power company easement. The power lines lie in a swail, or depressed area, so they are not visually prominent. The easement area is grassed, and it provides substantial open space within the apartment area. It is not felt to be a development hindrance by the planner.

The use program shown for Kimball Knoll is felt to bring the 19.5 acre property to its highest and best use. The land plan is schematic only— it is not precise enough to permit specific building siting. An engineer will next overlay the plan on a two foot interval topographic map and

---

[12] Dr. Love is a member of the American Institute of Architects (AIA) and the American Institute of Planners (AIP).

FIGURE 14–1

Site plan for Kimball Knoll

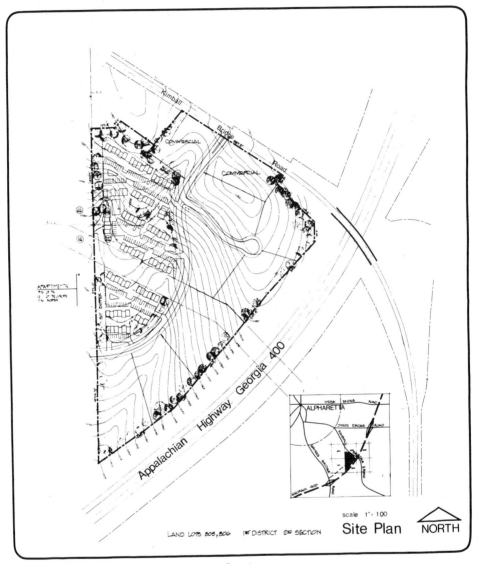

Source: Land Development Analysts, Atlanta, Georgia.

prepare plans for specific building siting, water runoff, and utility line placements.

Most land planners work first at the concept level, relying on market analyses of the amount and types of space that will be demanded. Then they prepare a rough schematic plan as shown here, followed by a final engineered plan suitable for courthouse recording as a final use program. The last step involves a sewer plan, a water plan, an underground electric/ telephone line plan, and a gas line plan, coupled with a new topographic survey. This final plan is quite expensive compared with the preliminary efforts, and it is normally completed immediately prior to the start of development.

This example identifies the process involved in land planning for a relatively simple project. High-density projects with several subterranean levels and interconnecting buildings, joint parking garages, and sophisticated fire fighting systems require extremely complex development plans. These plans must then be integrated into architectural efforts. For low-density work, the planner is typically trained as a pure planner or as a landscape architect. As density increases, so must the planner's knowledge of architecture.

TRENDS AND THE FUTURE

The planning process is characterized by conflict and compromise. It has been implemented poorly in many past efforts, and it has developed a poor public image because of seemingly arbitrary decisions on the part of political decision-makers. However, the authors are finding that developers have begun to prepare better justification for their proposed projects. Prior to rezoning they are now often required to prepare "A–95" review documents in which every impacted state, federal, and local agency must identify problems that the proposed development might cause if implemented according to plan. These problems must be worked out prior to rezoning. Many development lenders, sensitive to criticism of poorly planned projects are requiring that residential projects be approved by FHA and/or VA prior to development. Many local jurisdictions have retained trained planners to aid developers in eliminating future problems at the planning stage.

This is not to say that cities will be able to plan themselves out of blight and into vitality. Funds are limited, and many causes of blight are related to people who will not, or cannot, improve their properties to meet code standards. Planners have developed few tools with which to solve social problems, and there seems to be no economically practical vehicle to provide quality housing for low-income families. Environmental analysis techniques are crude, and few programs exist to aid in keeping our air and water pure while cities go through the inevitable process of change.

Planning has come a long way in the past 50 years, but only recently has it reached the point at which private and public planners work together to prevent the "fast buck" developer from stripping a site and building substandard structures for quick resale. The American Institute of Planners, an association designed to serve as a forum for discussing the planning process, is focusing attention on solving the public/private equation. Developers should be aware of these efforts and seek to incorporate the long-range planning perspective into the profit equation.

SUMMARY

Real estate planning occurs in two spheres—the public sector and the private sector. Public planning agencies plan for the logical and orderly development of a community, while private planning involves the formulation of a plan that will maximize the utility and efficiency of a site or tract of land. Whether public or private, the planning process requires a definition of land-use goals, preparation of possible alternative plans, selection of one plan, promotion and implementation of the plan, and monitoring and modification of the plan as necessary. The planning process must consider the physical characteristics of the site or community, its social aspects, its economic aspects, and urban design principles.

Public planning is usually carried on by a planning commission that is assisted by a professional staff. The commission normally is in charge of implementing the approved comprehensive plan by the process of zoning. Zoning involves the delineation of districts that allow and prohibit specified uses. Nevertheless, in most matters, the commission is advisory to the governing council of the jurisdiction.

Private planning is undertaken to design for an owner or developer a property's use to serve a specific market. The plan seeks to attract workers, residents, or customers having specified socioeconomic characteristics. The plan is formulated in recognition of existing public facilities, such as sewers, water, schools, churches, and libraries. The plan may call for additional public facilities to be provided in the project, or it may contemplate public construction of additional facilities. The private planner must cooperate closely with public planners and service agencies in seeking rezoning, utility services, building permits, public transportation, and other required approvals.

The zoning process is based upon the police power. It must be administered fairly, impartially, and in conformance with the comprehensive plan. Even more fundamentally, zoning should not go so far as to confiscate property without compensation. The goal of zoning is to guide the market in its ultimate determination of land uses and values.

Several socioeconomic issues regarding planning and zoning are discussed in the chapter. Whether zoning interferes with efficient operation of the private market, is inherently subject to favoritism and political manipulation, and is used as a tool for racial and class discrimination are overriding questions of continuing concern. While there are undoubtedly significant elements of truth in a positive response to all of these questions, the solution to date has been to try to improve the existing system and to limit its abuses. Abandonment of the system seems very unlikely.

QUESTIONS FOR REVIEW

1. What is *land planning?* Distinguish between "private" land planning and "public" city or county planning.
2. What are the goals of a private land planner? How do they differ from the basic goals of a public planner?
3. Can a planner assume the role of an advocate in public proceedings? Why is the planner's role different from that of a real estate appraiser?
4. Is it proper for the planner to be a key person in carrying out the implementation of a goal adopted by a county commission?
5. Identify several potential conflicts among public agencies that tend to arise as the planner establishes priorities in preparing a comprehensive plan.
6. How often should a comprehensive plan be redone? What steps can be taken to extend the life of the plan?
7. Do you feel that the planner is the proper person to serve as zoning administrator? Who else could logically do the job?
8. Is the political power of the public planner increasing or decreasing? Comment upon the positive and negative considerations involved in your answer.

REFERENCES

Altshuler, Alan A. *The City Planning Process: A Political Analysis.* Ithaca, N.Y.: Cornell University Press, 1965.

Black, Alan. *The Comprehensive Plan: Principles and Practice of Urban Planning.* Washington, D.C.: International City Managers Association, 1968, pp. 349–78.

Bolan, Richard S. "Emerging Views of Planning," *Journal of the American Institute of Planners,* July 1967, pp. 233–45.

Cartwright, Timothy J. "Problems, Solutions and Strategies: A Contribution to the Theory and Practice of Planning," *Journal of the American Institute of Planners,* May 1973, pp. 179–87.

Friedmann, John. "Notes on Societal Action." *Journal of the American Institute of Planners,* September 1969, pp. 311–18.

Kent, T. J., Jr. *The Urban General Plan.* San Francisco: Chandler Publishing Co., 1964.

Williams, Charles W., Jr. "Inventing a Future Civilization," in *The Futurist.* Bethesda, Md.: World Future Society, August 1972, pp. 137–41.

PART IV
Real estate administration in the public sector

————————————————— chapter 15

GOVERNMENT INVOLVEMENT
IN REAL ESTATE DECISIONS

REAL ESTATE DECISION-MAKING and implementation of decisions have been analyzed in previous chapters as processes within the private sector of the economy. The thesis of the book is that the decision-maker as an individual, household, or firm collects relevant information, engages in rational problem-solving behavior, and reaches decisions based upon objectives and priorities. The term microadministration is used to describe this individual decision-making process and its implementation. As discussed in the immediately preceding section [Part III], the activities of real estate marketing, production, financing, and private planning are the principal business functions involved in the creation and exchange of real estate resources.

This chapter provides an overview of the process of decision-making in the public sector. It is concerned with identification of decision-makers, their decision-making processes, and the manner in which alternatives are generated.

Subsequent chapters focus on decision-making and implementation of decisions by the public sector in the areas of taxation, housing and community development, environmental preservation, and transportation. With the exception of Chapter 16, attention is deliberately focused on the expenditure decision in the public sector. It must be recognized that all actions taken by the public sector (including regulatory activities, such as the formulation of a master plan and its implementation through zoning) require expenditures. The funds for these expenditures must, of course, be obtained by taxation, profit-making ventures, (such as utility operations) or debt financing.

Decisions made by the federal government can affect cities and communities throughout the nation or within an entire region, such as the Tennessee Valley or Appalachia. Federal programs and policies in areas such as housing, transportation, financing, and environmental preservation have a pervasive impact on all urban development. It should also be recognized that decisions made at the local government level may have a macroeffect within the community. For example, a decision to improve an urban arterial route sets in motion repercussions throughout the community. Travel patterns may be affected, the demand for transit altered, and the linkages among land uses changed drastically. The final result often is a restructuring of values among individual parcels of real estate in the community.

Macroadministration of urban real estate resources may also produce a widespread impact because of the relatively large-scale investment undertaken. Investors in the private sector continually demolish existing structures and construct new improvements, but rarely, if ever, is reconstruction undertaken in the magnitude of an urban renewal project. Public investment, such as an urban renewal project or subsidized housing, often produces a macroeffect in the community and becomes an input to the microadministration of other private real estate projects. For example, the construction of a Section 8 or Section 235 housing project may make construction of additional unsubsidized housing for moderate-income families impracticable.

THE ROLE OF GOVERNMENT

When economists debate the relative magnitudes of expenditure and investment to be made by the public sector of our economy, their opinions are based upon the value judgments that influence any individual in the selection of goals and the means for meeting them. Economists differ in their goals and selection of means, as do other citizens. As a nation, we have been committed by tradition and philosophy to the tenets of capitalism, individual freedom, and equality of opportunity. We advocate a competitive market, free enterprise, and the sovereign consumer. Different individuals define these goals differently, or they may repudiate one or more of them entirely. Indeed, our collective goal of individual freedom sanctions this right to disagree.

Regardless of the personal philosophy of the citizen, economic principles in their most abstract form are universal and apply in any culture. Two economic principles are relevant for any nation. *First, a country's resources and production should be distributed between the public sector and private sector in such a manner that the marginal satisfaction from the last dollar spent (invested by) the public sector just equals the marginal satisfaction from the last dollar spent (invested by) the private sector. The second principle is that total welfare is maximized when the resources controlled by each sector of the economy are utilized in the most efficient manner.* Application of these principles could produce government budgets of different magnitude in nations equal in total resources and technology. Our nation might obtain a lesser quantum of satisfaction from a dollar spent by the public sector than another country which embraces goals of government ownership of the means of production and a high degree of income equality among its citizens.

Additionally, as Hendon points out, we must be concerned with who gains in the attempt to maximize the present value of benefits over the present value of costs. He suggests that the decision-maker can see these results by developing a table that shows who receives the benefits of government activities classified by age, race, and income. "The maximizing statement relates to efficiency, but the distribution of benefits relates to equity."[1]

Our society accepts public expenditures for the purchase of goods and services, investment in social overhead capital, and transfer payments. The provision of public services requires that persons be paid as administrators, legislators, civil servants, and judges and that materials and consumer goods be purchased (primarily from the private sector) for programs of national defense, space exploration, housing, and other government activities. Bridges, schools, public buildings, housing projects, highways, and parks are constructed and become public investments in social capital. Social Security payments, unemployment compensation, and partial payments of rent or mortgage payments are examples of transfer payments that redistribute income in the attempt to achieve equity. In considering the role and size that are best for the federal government, the three major types of involvement by the government can be identified, and the amount of government activity in each area can then be debated.

Transfer payments. Some government expenditures result from perceived needs, with the perceptions being determined by our values and attitudes. Transfer programs such as old age assistance, veterans' cash bonuses, housing subsidies, unemployment compensation, and farm subsidies belong in this category. These programs transfer income among groups in our society, but they do not necessarily cause resources to bypass the market. Rather, the income provided by these programs is likely spent upon a different array of products and services than it would have been otherwise.

A different approach has been taken in the attempt to provide safe and sanitary housing for some low-income families. The approach has provided standard housing, rather than cash income, to qualifying house-

---

[1] William S. Hendon, *Economics for Urban Social Planning* (Salt Lake City: University of Utah Press, 1975), p. 84.

holds. The value judgment was made by our elected representatives that the national welfare would be maximized by providing safe, sanitary, and adequate housing to needy families. Nevertheless these families might have obtained a higher level of total satisfaction, if they had been given money income and allowed to vote dollars in the marketplace for housing, automobiles, food, and other goods and services.

Technical monopolies. Other public expenditures for social overhead capital and for purchase of goods and services from the private sector may be justified because of the existence of a "technical monopoly."[2] A technical monopoly results when only one firm or entity can economically afford to serve a particular function in a given market. Efficient operation of power generating or public transit facilities, for example, may result in losses, requiring a subsidy for such operations to stay in business. If the public, through its elected representatives, decides that the power generating facility or the public transportation system is worth retaining, a subsidy is required. In these situations, government may intervene as a regulator of a private monopoly, or as the provider of a public-owned enterprise. For example, many private power companies are regulated by state regulatory commissions; airlines have been subsidized and are regulated by the federal government; and many cities own public transit systems. Note that in some cases a private industry may be both regulated and subsidized.

Public goods. A public good is the extreme case in which the marginal cost of additional use of the good or service is zero. Once produced, the goods or service can be divided among innumerable users, and the benefits received by each user do not detract from the benefits received by others. The national defense is close to being a pure public good. All citizens benefit equally, and the benefit obtained by one of us does not reduce the benefits available to all. Many goods and services qualify to a greater or lesser extent as public goods. Schools, parks, highways, street lighting, police protection, sanitation facilities, public health programs, and urban renewal are examples. When such goods or services are provided, their benefits are available to everyone, and it is not feasible to charge any users for benefits that differ among citizens.

Public goods have "neighborhood" or spillover effects. It is usually not possible to identify the magnitude of effects on users and nonusers in order to assign a differential charge. Friedman points out that neighborhood effects can either penalize or benefit an individual in the market.[3] The penalty side occurs when property owners believe they

---

[2] A technical monopoly occurs in a strongly decreasing cost industry having a high original fixed cost and very low variable unit cost. Electric power and public transit companies are among these industries.

[3] Milton Friedman, "The Role of Government in a Free Society," in *Private Wants and Public Needs*. Edited by Edmund S. Phelps. (New York: W. W. Norton & Co., 1965), pp. 104–17. Also see Milton Friedman, *Capitalism and Freedom* (Chicago: University of Chicago Press, 1962).

cannot economically maintain or improve their properties. Net income after improvement is not sufficient to generate the additional value necessary to cover the costs of the improvement. A neighborhood effect results when the individual inaction on the part of separate owners produces a blighted condition for the entire area. Individuals have then become prisoners of the inaction of their neighbors. Residents elsewhere in the community may also suffer because of higher costs of police protection, fire protection, schooling, and other public services provided residents in the blighted area.

The beneficial type of neighborhood effect may be obtained when urban renewal is undertaken to remove the blight. Renewal may have a positive neighborhood effect because it benefits many groups that do not necessarily bear the cost of the public action in proportion to their respective net benefits. The renewal action itself produces a pattern of benefits and costs among groups in the community that makes it very difficult to identify the beneficiaries of the action and to charge them according to the benefits received. Thus, urban renewal exhibits the elements of a public good.

Friedman points out in such a case that the social costs of the neighborhood effects prior to and following public intervention must be carefully weighed. Although the blighted area exhibits many social costs such as unsanitary and unhealthful housing, higher crime rates, lower education levels of inhabitants, and higher requirements for police and fire protection, the costs of urban renewal are also huge. These costs must be borne by all taxpayers, whose aftertax incomes are thereby reduced. And after the costs are incurred and urban renewal is carried out, it may be that the blighted area is relocated in another section of the community. This would be the anticipated result, if increases were not achieved in residents' incomes, educational levels, and social adaptability.

Once again, our values and goals influence our decisions concerning the propriety of public action and the magnitude of action needed. If one felt as Friedman, that any government intervention in the free operation of the market reduces the sphere of individual freedom, then a large increment might be added to social costs for the government's intrusion into the private market.

How much government?

The question of "how much government" will undoubtedly be debated as long as our republic continues to exist. Some citizens believe as J. K. Galbraith that our national affluence permits more government activity than is presently undertaken in our society. This viewpoint would support more and larger programs in education, housing, job training, health insurance, and so on. In contrast, Prof. Friedman would restrict government activity when the persons benefited can be identified and charged. He would classify a city park and a city street as public goods that justify government expenditures. The national park and the limited access freeway, however, would not be public goods, because their users could be identified and charged directly for construction and maintenance of the facilities.

Public sector decision-makers

The atomistic decision-maker in the public sector is the public servant—perhaps a government executive, an elected or appointed administrator, a judge, or a legislator. These elected or appointed officials can be classified into four branches in both the federal and state governments: the legislature, the executive branch, the judiciary, and the bureaucracy. The legislative, executive, and judicial branches are commonly recognized as the primary sources of power and decision-making in our government. The bureaucracy, comprised of regulatory or administrative agencies such as the Federal Trade Commission, the Federal Communications Commission, the Federal Aviation Administration, and the Federal Home Loan Bank Board, is sometimes regarded as politically neutral and subordinate to the other three branches, each of which exercises some control over agency policy and operations. The bureaucracy, however, is better viewed as an active participant in decision-making in the public sector.[4] For example, the rules promulgated by the Federal Home Loan Bank Board, under authority of a basic law, may largely determine whether a builder or developer is able to obtain a loan to finance a proposed project.

At times, an administrative agency acts in an advisory capacity to other decision-making units. Congressional committees and government executives call upon the professional expertise of administrators when proposing legislation pertaining to the area of policy administered by, say, the Department of Housing and Urban Development, the Environmental Protection Agency, or the Federal Energy Administration. The administrative agency also formulates and implements policy at the operational level, where it functions in its own right, within limits, as a decision-making unit.

THE DECISION-MAKING PROCESS IN THE PUBLIC SECTOR

Behavioral aspects. Microadministration of real estate in the private sector assumes that the decision-making unit behaves in ways that are

---

[4] The concept of the administrative agency as an active participant in government decision-making, rather than simply an extension of the executive branch, has been developed by Millett. See John D. Millett, *Organization for the Public Service* (New York: D. Van Nostrand Co., 1966), p. 159.

believed to maximize personal profit, satisfaction, or utility. Utility maximization by individuals also can explain how decisions are reached in the public sector.[5] Public servants array the benefits and costs associated with each decision as they perceive them, assess the subjective probabilities of their realization, and make the trade-offs necessary to reach their preferred positions, that is, the decision and course of action that maximizes their net satisfaction. The concept of benefit can be defined broadly enough to include all alternatives that produce satisfaction for the individual. A decision made "for the public good" (as the individual legislator perceives it) may result in enough personal satisfaction to overcome a result which may be considered distasteful or damaging in some way (a cost to that legislator). For instance, legislators who own developable real estate may vote in favor of environmental legislation because they believe it is for the public good.

Another explanation of the decision-making process in government has been termed by Downs as the "economic theory of democracy." The central premise in this theory is that each political party designs its budget, both revenues and expenditures, to maximize its candidates' chances of winning the next election.[6] The budget is a mix of expenditure programs and taxation or borrowing proposals to finance these programs. Voters act to maximize their own positions by deciding which budget produces the greatest net benefit for the candidates who, in their estimation, will maximize their personal satisfaction. The victorious candidates have until next election to demonstrate their ability to perform as expected.

The ultimate decision or policy made in the public sector represents the end result of a complex bargaining process. Compromises and trade-offs are arranged among individuals and various interest groups. For example, within a regulatory agency, a senior staff member may propose a rule change to alleviate an undesirable restriction upon the industry that is regulated. Other staff members will voice their opinions, and the commission or board will decide according to majority vote whether to issue a proposed rule. If a rule is proposed, it is published, but it cannot go into effect until public comments are obtained and considered. Comments will likely be received from industry members, public interest groups, and other interested parties. For example, envi-

---

[5] Roland N. McKean, *Public Spending* (New York: McGraw-Hill, 1968), p. 13, and "The Unseen Hand in Government," *American Economic Review* 40, no. 3 (June 1965): 496–506.

[6] Anthony Downs, *An Economic Theory of Democracy* (New York: Harper & Row, 1957). Our respected mentor, Prof. Robert O. Harvey, was fond of asking his real estate classes: "Which has the longer-run planning horizon, private enterprise or the government?" The temptation is to reply, "the government," since the public sector establishes national parks, builds dams, and sponsors other programs having an impact for generations. The answer sought, however, was private enterprise, on the premise that the time horizon of government is constrained by the next election.

ronmental groups would undoubtedly protest a rule that would allow the industry more lenient pollution standards. Industry groups would likely support such a rule change. There would also likely be some disagreement among staff members.

In any regulatory, administrative, legislative, or judicial action, a decision is reached, and the regulatory or administrative agency speaks with a single voice. In the case of a legislative or judicial action, however, a disparate opinion may be expressed openly by a minority of legislators or justices. The bargaining process preceding a decision in the public sector performs the function of the marketplace in the private sector. As McKean explains: "Both mechanisms tend to substitute voluntary exchange for direct coercion and induce decision makers to take into account many of the indirect or external impacts of their decisions." [7]

Power and influence. Decisions made at the community level reflect basic characteristics of the community and its leadership and decision-making structure.[8] Sociologists attempt to relate these decisions to the demographic, economic, legal-political, and cultural characteristics of the community. The integrating functions performed by local political and voluntary organizations (such as the Democratic and Republican Parties, the League of Women Voters, or Common Cause) also are important in deriving the final decision. The activities of these organizations permit groups of individuals in the community to have a voice in the decision process.

Power and influence are involved in the analysis of leadership and the structure of decision-making. Power is defined as the "potential ability of an actor or actors to select, to change, and to attain the goals of a social system." Influence is defined as the "exercise of power that brings about change in a social system."[9] Power can be regarded as a static distribution of resources at a point in time. Clark identifies resources providing power as money and credit, control over jobs, control of mass media, high social status, knowledge and specialized technical skills, popularity and esteemed personal qualities, legality, subsystem solidarity, the right to vote, social access to community leaders, commitments of followers, manpower and control of organization, and control over the interpretation of values. The exercise of influence is a dynamic process which relates the existing distribution of power to the final decision.

Nuttall, Scheuch, and Gordon report an example of power and influence culminating in the final decision on an urban renewal project

---

[7] McKean, *Public Spending,* p. 19.

[8] Terry N. Clark, ed., *Community Structure and Decision-Making: Comparative Analysis* (San Francisco: Chandler Publishing Co., 1968), pp. 15–24 and 57–58.

[9] Ibid., pp. 46–47.

in Cambridge, Massachusetts.[10] The authors identify four separate decision processes occurring over time. The first decision process was the planning stage, begun in 1957, involving the Cambridge Redevelopment Authority, the Housing and Home Finance Agency (HHFA),[11] the mayor and city manager, major local business people and bankers, and the CIO union, which was to be the eventual owner and operator of the new buildings. Following the lengthy administrative planning process, the first public hearing was held in 1961. At this point, new actors, including families and small business people in the renewal area, a church in the area, and low-income groups residing outside the area, were able to exercise their influence. The person speaking for the church emphasized that persons in the renewal area would pay more for the new low-income housing than they presently paid for rent. Blacks and low-income families elsewhere in the community were fearful of future displacement if renewal was begun in Cambridge.

The second decision process occurred in the political arena when the city council had to ratify the proposed project. The dissident groups possessed power and the ability to exercise influence in this arena. On the other hand, the HHFA, the local redevelopment authority, the CIO union, and the large business people and bankers found their influence limited in the political debate. The second decision process resulted in defeat of the proposed renewal plan.

The third decision process involved reformulation of the plan. This time, the administrative process included a citizens advisory committee representing residents, small business people in the renewal area, and the church. The reformulated plan received the greatest opposition in public hearings from large business people who held property in the area, two city council representatives whose constituents were black, and low-income persons from other parts of the city. A threat of legal action by the large business people resulted in the mayor's effecting a compromise in their behalf before the city council finally approved the plan. This approval was the fourth decision process.

The case study of the Cambridge, Massachusetts, urban renewal project demonstrates the bargaining and compromise occurring in all public decision-making that is not routine and institutionalized. The influence of certain individuals and groups was brought to bear on the issue over time. Although some groups were not appeased by the final decision (the black and low-income elements outside the renewal area), they were able to exercise whatever influence their power base permitted.

---

[10] Ronald L. Nuttall, Erwin K. Scheuch, and Chad Gordon, "In the Structure of Influence," in Clark, *Community Structure and Decision-Making*, pp. 349–80.

[11] This agency was later superseded by HUD.

Institutional aspects. Decisions made in the public sector and their implementation depend in large part upon the institutional structure of government. Power, influence, and political factors are channeled through these institutions in the bargaining process that culminates in final decisions. As discussed earlier in this chapter, the primary institutions in government are the executive, legislative, and judicial branches. The regulatory and administrative agencies comprising the bureaucracy are an extension of both the executive and legislative branches. While they have extensive regulatory responsibilities, their ultimate authority is derived from the legislature. Our system of government incorporates this separation of power among institutions, but it also involves a sharing of power among the federal, state, and local governments. The U.S. Constitution enumerates the power of our federal government, while the states retain all other residual powers, including the police power.

Today, state and local governments can best be described as exercising concurrent power with the federal government.[12] The exercise of concurrent powers necessitates a system of shared administrative responsibilities. Federal, state, and local administrative agencies are concerned with a particular activity but are not formally subordinate to each other. For example, the U.S. Department of Housing and Urban Development administers housing subsidy programs, but a state also may have a housing agency to oversee the activities of communities participating in the federal programs. Additionally, each community or county may have its own local housing authority that owns and operates the public housing and administers other housing programs. The interagency problems are to define their respective spheres of influence and to resolve conflicts of authority.

It is through administrative agencies (such as HUD, a state department of housing, or a city planning commission) that public policy is translated into highways and streets, subsidized housing, the city plan, zoning enforcement, and other public sector activities. The operating policies and regulations established by the agencies in carrying out the legal mandate of Congress or the legislature have the force of law and control the character of the public good or service provided. Control over operations of the agency to insure that it continues to fulfill its policy objectives is exercised by congressional oversight committees, budgetary review, and, in extreme instances, congressional or legislative investigation. At the federal level, the department, agency, commission, or board head must submit requests for operating funds to the president, who reviews the requests in context with all other needs and sources of funds for operation of the government. Broad national goals

---

[12] Millett, *Organization for the Public Service,* pp. 19–20.

must be considered, including the need for economic growth, full employment, and price stability. The budget is then sent to Congress where it is reviewed once again. The administrator may be called upon to inform congressional committees of programs and policies. The authorization of funds and their ultimate appropriation for administrative activity will depend at least partly upon the ability of the administrator and other expert witnesses to convince Congress or the legislature that a public need will be met. The size of the government budget determines the extent to which the government participates in the total economy. The administrative agencies play an important role in determining both the size of the total budget and the proportion devoted to each area of concern, such as housing, national defense, education, and other public needs.

ECONOMIC ANALYSIS IN THE DECISION-MAKING PROCESS

The broadest goal our government could attain would be to maximize the welfare of all citizens collectively by assuming control only over functions delegated by the citizens and by organizing to carry out its assigned roles efficiently. McKean points out that several levels of decision-making are involved in this process.[13] First, there is the problem of how much control over national resources should be given to the government. Second, resources available to the government must be allocated among perceived needs. Third, after it has been decided to support various public needs in varying proportions, the policy-maker is faced with almost infinite alternatives for carrying out each program. A choice must be made among these alternative courses of action. Fourth, given a course of action for each program, the most efficient organization for producing the desired results must be developed.

These decisions are not independent of each other. For example, the case for giving more control over our resources to government may rest upon an argument that a centralized entity will be more efficient in producing desired results. The demonstrated or expected ability of one government agency to get more utility than other agencies from its appropriations can influence the division of the total budget. The ability of administrators to select the most appropriate program for translating policy into action and the organizational efficiency of their agencies can enhance their image with the chief executive and can influence the share of the budget devoted to its programs.

Political factors, judgment, and personal bias influence decision-making at all levels. These factors are particularly important in determining

---

[13] Roland N. McKean, *Efficiency in Government through Systems Analysis* (New York: John Wiley & Sons, 1958). The following problems in the economic analysis of public expenditures are among those discussed by McKean.

the extent of government control over resources and the allocation of these resources among perceived needs. Analytical tools are useful at the third and fourth levels of decision-making, where the problems involve selection of an alternative course of action for carrying out the policy decision and the most efficient form of organization to achieve the goal.

Economic analysis at the third level of decision-making, where alternative programs are considered, may demonstrate efficiency in the form of benefits minus costs, a ratio of benefits to cost, cost minimization given a specified goal, or benefit maximization given cost. A continual difficulty in the economic analysis of government programs is the inability to quantify all costs and benefits. Not only are spillover effects too numerous to identify completely, but social costs and benefits often defy measurement in dollars and cents. What is the dollar value of the human lives saved by improvement of a city street or control of pollution?

Another inescapable problem arises from the fact that a public program can affect different groups in our society. Higher-income groups may experience a net disbenefit to provide subsidized housing for a lower-income group, who experience a net benefit. A value judgment must be made that society will experience a net benefit before the program is undertaken. Still another problem in the economic analysis of public programs is that alternative programs available to meet a perceived need are too numerous to consider each of them separately. Consequently, the analysis of an expenditure decision usually involves suboptimal or partial analysis.

Analysis also should be made of the impact of the financing required to make the expenditure possible. This analysis should include the incidence of the tax, the effect of borrowing to finance the expenditure, and the economic effect of expanding the money supply. In many instances, the financing side of government decisions is not explicitly considered in the analysis of program alternatives. Often the budget for the program is considered as given, with the problem being how to spend the money most efficiently. Viewed in this manner, the problem of scale is not adequately considered. Significant cost savings or net benefits could perhaps be achieved either by expanding or decreasing the scale of expenditures in a given program. Furthermore, government programs are interrelated, and expenditures for one program may affect the costs and benefits of another. Spending for public housing or other subsidized housing, for instance, may enhance worker productivity and affect the costs and benefits of the welfare program. Tracing and quantifying these side effects usually is beyond the capability of the analysts.

Economic analysis whether it is cost-benefit analysis, systems analysis, or simulation admittedly will not replace the public decision-maker. The analysis of alternative programs, however, does provide the decision-maker with better knowledge and understanding, and it permits more consistent and logical choices to be made. Subsequent chapters deal with various areas for public decisions and the types of economic considerations involved in determining the levels of taxation, public expenditures, and types of programs.

SUMMARY

Decisions in the private sector are not made in a vacuum. Factors considered in the microadministration of our real estate resources include the results of public sector decision-making, such as the nature of our financial system, transportation policy, urban renewal, subsidized housing, tax policy, and planning and zoning. If such factors are taken as given, microadministration in the private sector is based upon partial analysis, where the problem typically is to maximize profit and satisfaction within the constraints imposed by government regulation and the programs. The private decision-maker must also usually work with the existing social overhead capital in the form of streets, schools, sewers, and utility system. The role of government in our economy is to provide the optimal level of regulation and social overhead capital, while preserving the greatest possible degree of individual freedom and responsibility.

A general analysis of the production and use of our urban real estate resources would consider decisions, actions, and results in both the private and public sectors, and their interrelationships. To borrow two current "buzz" words, the interfaces between systems would be examined. A circular system would be conceptualized in which the decisions, actions, and results of the private sector are recognized as inputs to the public sector. The public sector, in turn, generates outputs affecting microadministration in the private sector.

This chapter examines some of the characteristics of administration in the public sector. The extent of government involvement in the economy is constrained by our values. Any government regulation or expenditure reflects this value system, as well as our framework of government, in which behavioral aspects, power and influence, and institutional aspects play important roles. Our values and perceptions of need influence the selection of programs involving transfer payments that redistribute income among segments of our society. Government actions in dealing with technical monopolies and in the provision of public goods are influenced importantly by these factors. Economic analyses of government programs and expenditure decisions are useful in generating alternative courses of action for implementation of policy and in quantifying at least some of the costs and benefits. Economic analysis may contribute to the formulation of consistent and logical choices by public sector decision-makers, but it is usually, by necessity, partial and suboptimal analysis.

QUESTIONS FOR REVIEW

1. How does *microadministration* differ from *macroadministration?*
2. How can you justify government spending for transfer payments?
3. What are the roles of power and influence in the decision-making process of government?
4. What is the role of economic analysis in the government decision-making process?
5. What is meant by *cost-benefit analysis?* Is it comparable to investment analysis discussed in preceding chapters?
6. What is the *bureaucracy?* What types of decisions are made in a federal regulatory agency?
7. What is the economic theory of democracy?
8. What types of considerations influence a public decision-maker, such as a member of the Securities and Exchange Commission or the secretary of HUD?

REFERENCES

Clark, Terry N., ed.   *Community Structure and Decision-Making: Comparative Analyses.* San Francisco: Chandler Publishing Co., 1968.

Due, John F. and Friedlaender, Ann F.   *Government Finance: Economics of the Public Sector.* 5th ed. Homewood, Ill.: Richard D. Irwin, 1973.

Hendon, William S.   *Economics for Urban Social Planning.* Salt Lake City: University of Utah Press, 1975.

McKean, Roland N.   *Efficiency in Government Through Systems Analysis.* New York: John Wiley & Sons, 1958.

_____.   *Public Spending.* New York: McGraw-Hill, 1968.

Margolis, Julius, ed.   *The Analysis of Public Output.* New York: National Bureau of Economic Research, 1970.

Millett, John D.   *Organization for the Public Service.* New York: D. Van Nostrand Co., 1966.

Phelps, Edmund S., ed.   *Private Wants and Public Needs.* New York: W. W. Norton & Co., 1965.

chapter 16

REAL ESTATE TAXATION

SINCE REAL ESTATE, unlike most economic goods and products, is physically immobile, it is particularly vulnerable to taxation. All that a government must do to levy and collect taxes is to identify the parcel of real estate and its owner. The property cannot be moved to another taxing district; and, if the owner cannot or will not pay the tax, the property can be confiscated and sold to satisfy the government's claim.

The constitutional requirement that effectively prohibits a property tax to be levied by the federal government provides little solace to a property owner who must usually pay 2 to 4 percent of the property's value each year to local taxing authorities.[1] The property tax burden can be especially onerous to the moderate- or low-income family struggling to obtain the benefits of homeownership. And, even for more affluent property owners, the tax liability may be a negative inducement to development of a site to its most efficient use, maintenance and rehabilitation of existing properties, or the conversion of older uses into new or combined uses.

Yet the property tax is probably the most pervasive of all taxes. In spite of heated criticism of both the theoretical basis for the tax and its practical effect and administration, the tax survives, just as important as ever to local governments and taxing districts—and perhaps more firmly entrenched than ever. Undoubtedly, its persistence stems from the several substantial advantages it carries over possible alternative ·

---

[1] The U.S. Constitution (Section 9) states that: "No capitation, or other direct, tax shall be laid, unless in proportion to the census or enumeration herein before directed to be taken." The Sixteenth Amendment, ratified in 1913, specifically exempted taxes on incomes from this requirement.

taxes—its ability to raise large sums of revenue, its amenability to small incremental changes in tax rates, the immobility of the tax object, and its historic tie to local governments and local needs. Despite its many defects and possible inequities, the property tax seems likely to remain the most important revenue source for local governments and taxing districts during the foreseeable future.

Nature of the property tax

The property tax is calculated as a percentage (or millage rate) of a property's value, or some equally applied portion thereof. Therefore, it is called an *ad valorem* tax. For example, a property appraised for taxation at $50,000 (in a jurisdiction where the tax rate is applied to 100 percent of market value), and located in a taxing area in which the total tax rate is 2.5 percent, or 25 mills, would be taxed $1,250 for the year.

Obviously, the tax liability of the property can be increased either by raising its appraised value or by increasing the tax rate. And, in jurisdictions where the rate is applied to some percentage of market value (say 50 percent), the tax liability can be increased by increasing the applicable percentage (to say 55 percent). It should be apparent that unless restrictions are placed on tax rates, percentages of market value that may be taxed, and appraisal procedures, a property's tax burden can be set at any required or desired level.

Many states have attempted to mitigate some of the inequities of the property tax by requiring professional appraisal procedures, limiting tax rates, requiring standardized value ratios for taxation, and exempting certain classes of owners from a portion of the tax. For example, Florida requires that all property must be taxed at 100 percent of its market value and that tax rates cannot exceed 28 mills (10 mills per taxing authority of city and county and 8 mills per school district). Exempted from the rate limitation, however, is a rate for interest and capital retirement of bonds approved by voters in the jurisdiction. Florida also provides a $5,000 homestead exemption, a $500 exemption for disabled veterans, and a $5,000 exemption for homeowners over 65 who have lived in the state for at least five years. However, the maximum exemption, unless the homeowner is disabled and immobile, is $10,000. Totally disabled and immobile homeowners are given complete exemption from the tax.

Thus, a homeowner over 65, who has lived in the state more than five years and who qualifies for homestead, living in a community where the tax rates are 10 mills for the county, 8 mills for the city, and 8 mills for the school district would have to pay $1,040 on property appraised at $50,000.

```
County: ............. 0.01 × $40,000 = $  400
City: .................... 0.008 × $40,000 =   320
School district: .... 0.008 × $40,000 =   320
                                         $1,040
```

If the homeowner qualified for none of the exemptions, the total tax bill would be $1,300.

$$0.026 \times \$50,000 = \$1,300.00$$

Additional exemptions extend to certain corporate classes of property owners. Property owned by governments—federal, state, county, or city —is exempted. And property owned by nonprofit organizations, such as churches, schools, and public authorities, is usually exempted. Sometimes a public authority, such as a local housing authority or a port authority, will agree to make payments to the local community in lieu of property taxes.

Establishing the tax rate

The tax rate for a jurisdiction (such as a city, a county, or a school district) is calculated by dividing the budgeted expenditures less nonproperty tax income by the jurdisdiction's total assessed valuation minus exemptions:

$$R = \frac{E - I}{V - X}$$

where

R = Tax rate.
E = Budgeted expenditures.
I = Expected income from sources other than the property tax.
V = Total assessed valuation.
X = Value of exemptions.

For example, if a community's budget calls for expenditures of $5 million, nonproperty tax income is expected to be $1 million, there is $450 million of assessed value in the community, and the value of all exemptions is estimated to be $50 million, the tax rate would be calculated as follows:

$$R = \frac{\$5,000,000 - \$1,000,000}{\$450,000,000 - \$50,000,000} = 0.01$$

Converted to mills (dollars per thousand), the tax rate would be 10 mills.

Special assessments

A community may require that public improvements adjacent to private property be paid for by the private property owners. These taxes are termed special assessments and are used to finance such improvements as streets, gutters, sewers, and sidewalks. The rationale for special assessments is that they increase the property's value and therefore the property owner should pay at least the cost of the improvements. Most cities share the cost of the improvements with the property owners, charging them only a percentage (say 75 percent) of the total cost or only for the materials used.

Most cities will not make specific improvements and assess property owners, unless owners of more than 50 percent of the street frontage request the improvements. The total cost assigned the property owners is usually allocated on a front foot basis and charged to each owner (on both sides of a street) according to the number of front feet owned.

Special assessments result in a lien on the property, equal in priority to regular property taxes. Unpaid assessments can result in foreclosure and sale of the property at public auction. Thus, a buyer should not purchase a property without knowing whether or not there are special assessments, and the dollar amount, if they exist.

ECONOMIC AND SOCIAL ISSUES

As mentioned earlier in the chapter, the property tax has been severely criticized for several reasons. Controversy continues to rage over the property tax. Occasionally modifications in the tax are made to lessen the impact of some criticism or to lessen its impact on a particular segment. However, nowhere has the property tax been radically changed or repealed. Its important advantages seem to outweigh its disadvantages. For complete evaluation of the tax it is necessary to consider some 'of the criticisms and issues surrounding the tax.

The property tax is regressive. When a tax falls more heavily on lower-income than on higher-income taxpayers, the tax is termed *regressive.* The property tax has been accused of this malady. The principal reasoning for this contention is that the value of housing does not increase proportionately to increases in income. People having incomes of $200,000 per year typically do not live in homes ten times as valuable as people having incomes of $20,000 per year. The Keynesian consumption function applies to housing, as well as other consumer goods. Since the property tax is based upon property values (*ad valorem*), high-income taxpayers tend to pay less property tax *per dollar of income* than lower-income taxpayers. Thus, the tax is regressive.

Another, although secondary, reason for the contention that the property tax is regressive is that some studies have shown that owners of poor housing occupied by low-income tenants pay property taxes at a higher rate than owners of higher-value housing. For example, Peterson et al. found such a pattern in four major cities.[2] Presumably, however, such patterns result from poor appraisal practices and could be corrected.

Netzer, in his landmark study, agrees that the property tax *payments* are regressive. However, he realized that there may also be disparities in the benefits or services derived from the tax. Perhaps lower-income taxpayers require more police and fire protection, place more reliance on the court system, and utilize more heavily the public health, welfare, and school systems. Netzer's conclusion regarding this aspect is that the net result of the tax is *not* regressive, when the benefits are taken into account.[3] Thus, lower-income taxpayers utilize the services provided by the property tax to a greater degree than the additional cost to them.

The property tax inhibits construction of new housing. This criticism usually implies adoption of a single property tax on land only. Henry George denounced taxes on personal property, structures, and improvements to a site as inequitable and a deterrent to investment.[4] Certainly we would anticipate a much greater investment in all types of structures, including housing, if taxes were removed from them. A much greater burden would be shifted to landowners, and much earlier development of raw land would be encouraged. However, it is doubtful that a single tax on land could raise the revenue necessary to provide the existing level of municipal, county, and state services. Heilbrun has concluded: "These (disadvantages) are sufficiently important to make site value unacceptable as the sole basis of the contemporary real estate tax, but they do not rule out a compromise involving use of a relatively heavier land tax."[5] Also, econometric studies attempting to estimate land values, separately from improvements, have not been promising.[6] Netzer, however, has concluded that a combination of user

---

[2] George E. Peterson, Arthur P. Solomon, Hadi Madjid, and William C. Apgar, Jr., *Property Taxes, Housing, and the Cities* (Lexington, Mass.: Lexington Books, 1973).

[3] Dick Netzer, *Economics of the Property Tax* (Washington, D.C.: Brookings Institution, 1966), pp. 45–62.

[4] Henry George, *Progress and Poverty* (New York: Robert Schalkenbach Foundation, 1948), book 8, chap. 3.

[5] James Heilbrun, *Real Estate Taxes and Urban Housing* (New York: Columbia University Press, 1966), p. 169.

[6] See Eugene F. Brigham, "The Determinants of Residential Land Values," *Land Economics* 41 (November 1965): 325–34, and Paul B. Downing, "Estimating Residential Land Value by Multivariate Analysis," in *The Assessment of Land Value.* Edited by Daniel M. Holland for the Committee on Taxation, Resources, and Economic Development (Madison: University of Wisconsin Press, 1970), pp. 101–23.

charges, particularly for congestion and pollution, and land-value taxation would be the best system.[7]

The property tax inhibits maintenance and rehabilitation of existing housing. Again, the argument is advanced that the absence of annual property taxes would allow owners to maintain their properties in better condition. Such a contention, however, seems unlikely, since numerous properties today are maintained in superior condition. Most property owners probably could decrease their maintenance expenditures, if they so wished, but they realize such action would deplete their long-run income potential. Property tax forgiveness might have some beneficial impact on the maintenance of properties by lower-income owners, but it is highly doubtful that all, if any, such tax saving would be channeled into property maintenance.

The effect of the property tax on rehabilitation is another matter, however. The property owner who considers the cost of rehabilitation may well regard the increased property tax (resulting from the property's increased value) to be sufficiently burdensome to forego a modernization project. Undoubtedly, a substantial part of the housing "problem" could be alleviated, if the cost impediment to rehabilitation could be eliminated.

Heilbrun suggests that "tax abatement" might be applied to the *additional* values created by new construction or rehabilitation.[8] Such an abatement would (compared with the present system) encourage new construction and rehabilitation that create greater values through more efficient operation or better condition of properties. The original tax base would be maintained. And the revenue obtained from properties that are not allowed to deteriorate would offset the revenue lost by not taxing the increased values.

The property tax is not based on ability to pay. One of the prime criteria of an equitable tax is that it be related to the taxpayer's ability to pay. This criterion is often violated by the property tax, say its critics. Relatively high-income taxpayers may elect to live in modest homes, while other, lower-income taxpayers may, because of large families or personal desires, stretch to afford larger, more valuable homes. The higher-income taxpayers will undoubtedly hold their wealth in such assets as stocks, bonds, or savings accounts. Intangibles and other personal property are often taxed at lower rates than real estate. The property tax thus places a greater strain on the real estate owner than on the owners of other types of property.

[7] Dick Netzer, "Is There Too Much Reliance on the Local Property Tax?" in *Property Tax Reform.* Edited by George E. Peterson. (Washington, D.C.: John C. Lincoln Institute and the Urban Institute, 1973), p. 23.

[8] Heilbrun, *Real Estate Taxes and Urban Housing*, p. 171.

It must be pointed out, of course, that the earnings of most assets are taxed by the federal and sometimes state and municipal governments. Homeowners gain the advantage of not having to pay income tax on rent saved. They also gain another substantial benefit from the mortgage interest deduction.

The property tax is inherently subject to poor administration. This criticism, while admitting that administrative improvements may be possible, contends there will always be difficulties in administering the property tax. The large number of assessing jurisdictions and the popular election of assessors seem to guarantee that many assessors will be less than totally competent to handle the task of property appraisal. While important progress has been made in many counties to upgrade assessors' qualifications, many assessing officials (particularly in small counties) have little or no education or background in property appraisal. Inefficiencies, inequities, and errors are bound to occur in these areas.

Additionally, because of the political nature of assessors' offices, they are usually subject to great pressure for favorable appraisals. Most assessors have wisely insulated themselves from individual requests, but assessors undoubtedly hesitate to raise the assessments of large groups of voters or politically influential property holders beyond an acceptable level. It should be noted that assessment decisions can be appealed to a board of review and to the courts.

Assessors have attempted to improve their own competence through their organization, the International Association of Assessing Officials (IAAO), and by attendance at courses sponsored by the major appraisal organizations. Also, some state governments have established statewide agencies to audit the appraisal practices and valuations of county assessing officials, to insure that minimum standards are met.

The property tax varies widely among geographic areas. Even if the tax is applied uniformly within a county, it may be applied differently in the next county. And its variation among states may be even greater. Since each county employs a different appraisal staff, tax appraisals are almost certain to vary among counties for similar properties. And different states operate under differing legal requirements regarding the assessment function. In order to create greater uniformity among counties, some states, as noted above, have established agencies to audit assessments and appraisal practices of the counties. Their objective is usually to ascertain that laws mandating assessments at a specified percentage of market value (say 100 percent) are being carried out and that appraisal procedures are being uniformly applied. Undoubtedly such agencies contribute to a more equitable assessment of property taxes within a state.

Some critics, notably Benson, have suggested that the property tax be administered regionally.[9] Regional administration would reduce the number of assessors and facilitate uniformity in assessment practices. For the foreseeable future, however, local administration of the property tax appears to be firmly entrenched.

SUMMARY

Counties, cities, and taxing districts usually obtain most of their revenues from the property tax. The tax is levied within the geographic jurisdiction of the governmental unit. The amount of tax levied is determined by the unit's budgeted expenditures, less all nonproperty tax income. This amount is then divided by the assessed value of all taxable property in the jurisdiction less the value of all exemptions, to obtain a tax percentage. The millage rate can then be obtained by converting the tax percentage to dollars per $1,000 of value.

The property tax has received much criticism. The principal arguments against it are (a) the tax is regressive; (b) it inhibits new construction; (c) it inhibits maintenance and rehabilitation of existing housing; (d) it is not based on ability to pay; (e) it is inherently subject to poor administration; and (f) there are wide geographic variations in the tax. Even with such criticism, however, the property tax seems well entrenched.

The property tax's three big advantages are its ability to raise large amounts of revenue, its long history of usage in the United States, and its preference to other types of taxes that also produce problems and inequities. The advantages are so great that they counterbalance all of the criticisms and defects. Undoubtedly the property tax will continue to be the largest source of revenue for local governments. Owners of real property should not expect to be relieved of this burden in the forseeable future.

QUESTIONS FOR REVIEW

1. How is a community's property *tax base* established?
2. How is a community's *tax rate* established?
3. Identify other important sources of a community's revenue.
4. What is a *mill?* How is the millage tax rate derived?
5. What is the role of the community's budget in determining its property tax rate?

---

[9] George C. S. Benson, Sumner Benson, Harold McClelland, and Procter Thompson, *The American Property Tax: Its History, Administration, and Economic Impact* (Claremont, Calif.: Claremont Men's College, Institute for Studies in Federalism and the Lincoln School of Public Finance, 1965).

6. Why is the property tax often considered regressive?

7. What effect would the property tax likely have on maintenance and rehabilitation of housing?

8. Why is the property tax often considered to be poorly administered?

9. If the property tax were abolished, how could local governments raise needed revenues? Evaluate each method in comparison with the property tax?

10. A city's budget for the coming year calls for expenditures of $30 million. Nonproperty-tax income of $8 million is expected, and the city contains $1.4 billion of taxable property value. What tax rate is called for (a) in percentage terms? (b) In mills?

11. Calculate the amount of property tax you would be required to pay in the following situation. Your state allows a homestead exemption of $5,000; it also provides a $5,000 exemption for homeowners over 65 from school taxes only.

    a. You, a homeowner, are 68 years old.

    b. Your home, in the city, is assessed at $60,000.

    c. You qualify for homestead exemption.

    d. Millage tax rates are city—10 mills; county—8 mills; and school district—6 mills.

12. A street is to be paved and gutters installed in front of your property. The city assesses property owners 75 percent of the cost of such improvements, which are estimated to be $40 per running foot. Your property has 100 feet of frontage on one side of the street to be improved. How much will be your special assessment?

REFERENCES

Benson, George C. S.; Benson, Sumner; McClelland, Harold; and Thompson, Procter. *The American Property Tax: Its History, Administration, and Economic Impact.* Claremont, Calif.: Claremont Men's College, Institute for Studies in Federalism and the Lincoln School of Public Finance, 1965.

Curtis, Clayton C. *Real Estate for the New Practitioner.* 4th ed. Gainesville, Fla.: B. J. Publishing, 1975, chap. 8.

Heilbrun, James. *Real Estate Taxes and Urban Housing.* New York: Columbia University Press, 1966.

Holland, Daniel M., ed. *The Assessment of Land Value.* Madison: University of Wisconsin Press, 1970.

Lindholm, Richard W., ed. *Property Taxation and the Finance of Education.* Madison: University of Wisconsin Press, 1974.

Netzer, Dick. *Economics of the Property Tax.* Washington, D.C.: Brookings Institution, 1966.

Peterson, George E., ed. *Property Tax Reform.* Washington, D.C.: John C. Lincoln Institute and Urban Institute, 1973.

GOVERNMENT IN HOUSING AND COMMUNITY DEVELOPMENT

THE FEDERAL GOVERNMENT has played a significant role in providing subsidized housing for approximately 40 years. Until recently governmental activity expanded continually in this field. The history of federal involvement is replete with laws establishing numerous housing, urban renewal, and conservation programs that were later replaced or disbanded. In many instances the programs were very expensive, cumbersome, and inefficient. They were incapable of solving the complex problem of providing adequate housing for those in need of such housing.

Reasons for government involvement

Several reasons can be ascribed for the strong interest of the federal government in providing housing. Perhaps first in importance is the fact that a large segment of the population lives in substandard housing. Approximately 12 million, or about 14 percent of all housing units, were considered to be substandard in one or more aspects in 1973. Just as our elected representatives concern themselves with other aspects of our well being (such as work conditions, health and medical care, and education) so are they apt to detect and concern themselves with the general housing condition. Such concerns may be both altruistic and selfish.[1] Whatever the motivation, however, the need is perceived, and, through the decision-making process of government, programs to deal with the problem become conceived and adopted. Many voters will then hopefully be grateful for improved housing and reelect to office the wise incumbents.

---

[1] See Chapter 15.

A second reason for the government's concern is that increased housing and other urban construction is beneficial to the economy. As pointed out earlier, the construction industry is our largest single industry. Furthermore, many other industries depend upon construction (for example, appliance manufacturers, carpet manufacturers, heating and air conditioning manufacturers, and lumber companies). Therefore, the creation of jobs through stimulation of the housing market provides employment and enhances the chance for reelection of representatives and senators who provide such programs.

Third, housing is sometimes regarded as the key to unlocking the solutions to other social problems. At least it is regarded as a necessary, if by itself inadequate, ingredient in the search for improved levels of education, income, health (physical and mental), and employment potential among the disadvantaged portions of the population. People cannot, the theory goes, be given education, job training, medical services, and other community benefits and have their overall social condition permanently improve, if their housing is deteriorating or dilapidated. The motivation for additional and sustained improvement will be thwarted by a depressing and frustrating physical environment for everyday living.

To indicate its assessment of the desirability of good housing, the U.S. Congress in 1949 declared its intention to pursue the goal of "a decent home and suitable living environment for every American family." In the late 1960s the president established a Committee on Urban Housing to estimate the country's housing needs and the steps that would be required to meet the needs. The report of this committee in 1969 estimated the need for new and rehabilitated housing units at about 26 million in the period 1968–78.[2] Of this total, 6 million units would need to be subsidized. Housing construction and rehabilitation of this magnitude were expected to permit low-income families to occupy physically standard units, although overcrowding could persist.

HOUSING

Unsubsidized

As indicated in Table 17–1, we can regard the National Housing Act of 1934 as the government's initiation into the housing field. It has also proven to be the most successful housing program undertaken by the government. Perhaps the reason for its success is that the Federal Housing Administration and the Federal Savings and Loan Insurance Corporation, established by the 1934 law, are insurance agencies, rather than direct providers of housing. The FHA was authorized to insure lenders

---

[2] Report of the President's Committee on Urban Housing (Kaiser Report), *A Decent Home* (Washington, D.C.: U.S. Government Printing Office, 1969), p. 39.

TABLE 17-1

Historical summary of federal housing programs

Year	Type of program	Principal provisions	Current status
1934	*a.* Mortgage insurance	Established FHA and insurance programs	Operative
	b. Insurance of accounts in thrift institutions	Established FSLIC	Operative
1937	Public housing	Capital grants and loans plus annual contribution to local housing authorities to provide low-rent housing for low-income families.	Dormant
1949	*a.* Subsidized housing	Established principle of governmental assistance to privately constructed housing.	Principle and goal are still being pursued
	b. National housing goal	Established national housing goal of a "decent home and suitable living environment for every American family."	Principle and goal are still being pursued
	c. Slum clearance and urban redevelopment	Intiated slump clearance and urban redevlopment.	Replaced
1954	Conservation and rehabilitation	Broadened scope of Housing Act of 1949 by adding conservation and rehabilitation programs for housing in renewal areas. Also, required a "workable program" for funds to be provided for renewal or subsidized housing.	Replaced
1961	Section 221 (d)(3) BMIR	Subsidized the interest rate on subsidized housing for moderate-income families sponsored by limited dividend and nonprofit organizations.	Dormant

TABLE 17-1 (continued)

Year	Type of program	Principal provisions	Current status
1965	a. Rent supplements	Paid subsidies to landlords for difference between 25 percent of tenants' income and fair market rent.	Dormant
	b. Leased public housing	Also permitted public housing units to be leased from private owners.	Dormant
1966	a. Blighted area FHA loans	Allowed standard FHA-insured loans (Section 203) to be made in blighted areas.	Replaced
	b. Model cities	Provided grants and technical assistance to cities which had an acceptable comprehensive plan for dealing with the social, economic, and physical problems of selected neighborhoods.	Replaced
1967	Home counseling service	Prospective homeowners could obtain information about opportunities under various FHA programs and could have FHA procedures explained.	Operative
1968	a. Subsidized housing (Sections 235 and 236)	Subsidized homebuyers (235) and multi-family rental housing (236).	Section 235 revived, but modified Section 236 Dormant
	b. Special credit risk mortgage insurance (Section 237)	Provided mortgage insurance for families who could not meet credit requirements under other sections of the act.	Dormant
	c. National housing partnership	Profit-making organization was to produce subsidized housing.	Dormant

TABLE 17-1 (continued)

Year	Type of program	Principal provisions	Current status
	d. Rehabilitation	Permitted nonprofit organizations to rehabilitate housing for resale to low-income families.	Dormant
	e. Mortgage insurance for displaced families	Provided mortgage insurance for families displaced by government actions.	Dormant
	f. Multifamily FHA financing	Provided favorable financing for new or rehabilitated units for low- and moderate-income families.	Dormant
	g. Subsidies for nonprofit sponsors of subsidized housing	Provided subsidies for nonprofit sponsors of subsidized housing.	Replaced
1974	Housing and community development act		Operative
	a. Title I: community development	Consolidates several existing programs into a single program providing block grants.	
	b. Title II: assisted housing	Authorizes the leasing of new and rehabilitated private housing, not in ghetto areas, to low-income families. Families must contribute not less than 15 percent but no more than 25 percent of family income to rent.	
	c. Title III: mortgage credit assistance	Raises FHA single-family home mortgage limits.	Basic applicable housing law
	d. Title IV: comprehensive planning	Provides funds for comprehensive planning by communities to determine housing needs.	

TABLE 17-1 (concluded)

Year	Type of program	Principal provisions	Current status
	e. Title V: rural housing	Existing rural housing law is liberalized.	
	f. Title VI: mobile home construction	Establishes construction safeguards and enforcement of safety standards for mobile home manufacturers.	
	g. Title VII: consumer home mortgage assistance	Raises loan limits for federal savings and loans and revises the real estate lending authority of national banks.	
	h. Title VIII: miscellaneous	Authorizes urban homesteading; authorizes a demonstration program for solar heating and cooling; authorizes an experimental housing allowance program; raises FNMA and GNMA mortgage purchase limits; makes communities eligible for national flood insurance at subsidized rates; outlaws discrimination on basis of sex; encourages formation of state housing and development agencies.	

Source: Authors' summary, 1976.

that borrowers would repay long-term, amortized mortgage loans. Previously, lenders had been reluctant to make loans having maturities of longer than 10 or 15 years. They were also skeptical of periodic amortization and often insisted upon full repayment at the end of a relatively short-term mortgage loan.

As discussed in Chapter 13, the FSLIC (Federal Savings and Loan Insurance Corporation) is a government agency under the Federal Home Loan Bank Board. It insures deposits in thrift institutions up to $40,000.

FHA programs were concentrated in Sections 203 and 207 of the National Housing Act. Section 203 provided for the insurance of privately granted, long-term, fully amortized loans to borrowers who met established credit standards. The loans had to be for the purchase of properties that met minimum standards of construction and size. The loans allowed low downpayments by borrowers. This program is still operative and can be credited with having revolutionized mortgage lending practices. At the writing of this book, the minimum downpayment schedule is as follows:

> First $25,000 of appraised value: 3 percent
> Next $10,000 of appraised value: 10 percent
> $35,000 to $45,000 (maximum): 20 percent

Thus a house appraised for $42,000 would require a downpayment of

$$\$750 + \$1,000 + \$1,400 = \$3,150.$$

Under a typical conventional (nongovernment underwritten) loan, a 5 percent downpayment would require the borrowers to have $2,100 of their own funds. Private mortgage insurance on loan amounts in excess of 80 percent of a property's value has made conventional lending more desirable than FHA, and FHA presently accounts for less than 10 percent of the nation's home loan volume.

The FHA was authorized under Section 207 to insure mortgages for the construction of rental apartments, and Title I of the act provided insurance for loans to repair or improve existing homes. These basic programs have been modified through the years, but they continue in existence to this date. They involve no government subsidy because borrowers pay an insurance premium in their monthly mortgage payment. The premiums establish a fund from which losses are paid.

Many housing and community development programs operate through the FHA by authorizing insurance on mortgage loans for specific purposes. For example, Section 220 provides insurance for loans on housing units in urban renewal areas, Section 221(d)(2) provides insurance for loans on low- and moderate-income housing, Section 231 provides insurance for multifamily projects to serve the elderly or handicapped, Section 232 provides insurance for nursing home loans, and Section 234 provides insurance for condominiums. All of these lending programs are unsubsidized and are seldom used.

Subsidized

Through the years Congress has further sought to encourage the construction of housing for specific purposes by providing subsidies in FHA programs. Also, many of the urban renewal and community development subsidy programs are administered by the FHA. For example, Section

101 provides rent supplement payments to owners of private housing projects that serve eligible low-income tenants. Section 202 provides below market interest rate (BMIR) loans for construction of multifamily rental projects for the elderly or handicapped. Section 221(d)(3) provides insurance for below market rate or market rate loans for low- and moderate-income multifamily projects. And Sections 235 and 236 provide insurance for single-family and multifamily projects serving low- and moderate-income families, who also obtain interest and rent subsidies. As shown in Table 17–1, many of the programs have been replaced or are dormant.

The primary subsidized housing program currently in effect is contained in Section 8 of Title II of the Housing and Community Development Act of 1974. As described in Table 17–1, this program authorizes the leasing of new and rehabilitated private housing units, not in ghetto areas, to low-income families. Families must contribute at least 15 percent, but no more than 25 percent, of family income to rent. The government subsidizes the difference between a family's contribution to rent and the fair market rental of the unit, as determined by the FHA.

Also operative at the present time is a modified Section 235 program. This program provides insurance on loans whose interest rates are subsidized down to 5 percent. The loans are made to purchase single-family houses. The developer, in the case of new construction, obtains FHA approval for inclusion of the homes in the Section 235 program. Builders obtain their profits from an overhead and profit allowance of 12–13 percent of total replacement cost. The FHA-determined value for mortgage lending purposes considers lot value, closing costs, sale expense (broker's commission), structure cost, and on-site improvements. The builder's profit and overhead allowance is included in the value, which can be adjusted up or down within limits to reflect the quality of construction. The final value estimated by FHA usually is very close to sale price.

COMMUNITY DEVELOPMENT

The owners of property in a blighted or slum area are subject to the external diseconomies imposed by the surrounding neighborhood.[3] They cannot afford to rehabilitate their properties because their values will be constrained by adjacent properties. Each property owner is faced with a "prisoner's dilemma."[4] Also, property values in a community may be negatively affected by inadequate public facilities and services. Unpaved streets, an absence of sanitary and storm sewers, inadequate police and fire protection, and poor garbage pickup, and other municipal services

---

[3] This is discussed in depth in Chapter 15.

[4] Otto A. Davis and Andrew B. Whinston, "Economics of Urban Renewal," *Law and Contemporary Problems* 26, no. 1 (Winter 1961): 105–17.

inhibit the desire and feasibility of property owners to improve existing property or construct new ones. Therefore, the federal government has provided programs for communities to upgrade or construct new community facilities, to renew blighted sections of cities, and to encourage property owners to conserve and rehabilitate deteriorating properties. From the beginning of various types of community development programs, the concepts of subsidization have changed dramatically. In 25 years the major type of financial assistance to communities has evolved from slum clearance administered under federal aegis to one of block grants to communities for uses that are locally determined.

Urban renewal

As shown in Table 17–1, The National Housing Act of 1949 initiated slum clearance and urban redevelopment that evolved into large urban renewal projects. Urban renewal was accomplished in cities by a local renewal agency. It purchased or condemned (if necessary) properties in the blighted area, demolishing existing improvements, and providing or improving streets, utilities, schools, and municipal buildings as planned in the reuse of the area. Sites in the renewal area were sold to private developers who agreed to build improvements suggested by the renewal plan. The site was sold at a price sufficient to induce the desired development.

The subsidy in urban renewal was the difference between (a) proceeds realized from resale of sites and (b) the costs of purchasing the blighted properties, razing them, and supplying the required municipal improvements. The federal government supplied two-thirds of this subsidy, and the local government provided one-third, which could be in the form of labor and municipal improvements.

Rationale. The rationale for urban renewal includes the contention that removal of neighborhood externalities permits improvement of an area that could not occur in normal operation of the market. Only by removing the blighted condition of the neighborhood can families be attracted who are willing and able to pay the necessary rents. Other reasons given for urban renewal include the attraction of the middle-class family back to the central city; increasing the city's property tax base and tax revenues; removal of aesthetically unattractive structures; and reduction of the cost of police and fire protection, health services, and education by eliminating the slum conditions making provision of these services necessary and costly.

Problems. Urban renewal was beset by problems. Blighted areas had to be identified, and concerned citizens protested neighborhoods' being classified as "blighted" and, therefore, eligible for renewal. At what point does an area contain sufficient substandard properties to be blighted? The relocation of families displaced from the renewal areas presented continual complications. Before an urban renewal program was authorized, the local agency had to demonstrate that sufficient standard housing was available in the community within the financial means of families to be displaced and reasonably close to their place of work. At times, public housing had to be provided before renewal was begun. The local public agency was required to provide counseling and relocation assistance to displaced families. Families forced to move, however, did not have to take advantage of this service. Urban renewal was further accused of shifting slum conditions from the renewal area to other low-income neighborhoods. The broad generalization that renewal merely shifts slum conditions to other neighborhoods in all instances is not supported by empirical evidence, although in some communities displaced families did concentrate in other neighborhoods.[5] Each local public agency was required to trace the displaced families and assess their new housing condition and housing expense. A summary of several of these relocation studies concludes that relocated families generally were better housed, but they were paying more in housing expenses.[6]

The reuse of urban renewal sites for offices, commercial, and other nonhousing purposes has been severely criticized. Similarly, replacement of low-rent housing with units priced for higher-income families has been questioned. A decrease in the supply of units within the financial means of low-income families is a disbenefit for all such families in the community.

If the "benefits" view of filtering is accepted, reuse of a renewal area for higher-priced residential units can be viewed as less of a problem than reuse for nonresidential purposes. The higher-rent units could result in vacancies elsewhere in the market as families move to the new housing, precipitating the filtering process. Ultimately, better quality units than they are occupying may be available to low-income families at the same or lower housing expense.

It is our contention, however, that filtering is a slow and uncertain process, which can be impeded by net in-migration, undoubling of households, and new household formations that absorb vacancies.[7] The cost of moving, unwillingness to move because of neighborhood ties, lack of knowledge about the availability of better housing, and prejudice that restricts freedom of choice in the housing market further hamper the process. Rents and prices in the market can be slow to fall as landlords tolerate marginal increases in vacancy rate and property owners accept longer waiting periods for sale of their properties. If blight exists because people are poor, filtering down of better quality housing will

---

[5] Chester Hartman, "The Housing of Relocated Families," *Journal of the American Institute of Planners* 30, no. 4 (November 1964): 266–86.

[6] Ibid.

[7] See Chapter 7 for additional discussion of the filtering concept.

not prevent blight from reoccurring.[8] Properties which filter down may have maintenance and repair foregone over time because of insufficient rental income to induce normal upkeep. Eventually, the property will become physically substandard.

Urban renewal has the potential of increasing land values in the renewal area and increasing the property tax base of the central city. Land values in the vicinity of the renewal area also may appreciate. When the metropolitan area is considered as a whole, however, the net long-term effect on land values may be minimal.[9] If aggregate land value is some multiple of aggregate rent, the total value of land following urban renewal increases to the extent that households pay more in total rent after renewal. This increase in aggregate rent may be very small. Land values increase in the renewal area because new residents can afford to pay more rent than the displaced families. However, the increased rental income realized in the renewal area may be lost by owners of other competitive properties in the market, who are experiencing a higher vacancy loss. Displaced families moving elsewhere in the market may be faced with higher rents and may choose to buy less housing. Certainly, they are limited in the amount of additional housing expense they can tolerate. The renewal project may alter the pattern of land values in the metropolitan area without appreciably affecting the aggregate value.

Increases in land value resulting from commercial and other land uses locating in the renewal area can be counted as a net increase in aggregate land value only if these establishments would not have located elsewhere in the community. Renewal may increase the community's aggregate income and the demand for goods and services, since the federal subsidy dollars can be, in part, a net gain to the community. These dollars are acted upon by the local income multiplier to produce a greater regional or community income. This amount would be small, and the additional derived demand for commercial and other nonresidential improvements generated by this increased local purchasing power should not be expected to call forth construction of any magnitude.

Empirical studies of the costs and benefits of urban renewal have been attempted by Messner and Mao.[10] Rothenberg, however, notes that the most important benefits from urban renewal may be the reduction in the social costs of slum living.[11] Fire hazards and crime may be lessened;

---

[8] Hugh O. Nourse, "The Economics of Urban Renewal," *Land Economics* 42, no. 1 (February 1966): 67.

[9] Ibid., pp. 68–69.

[10] J. C. T. Mao, *Efficiency in Public Urban Renewal Expenditures through Capital Budgeting*, research report no. 27 (Berkeley: University of California, Center for Real Estate and Urban Economics, 1965); and Stephen D. Messner, "Urban Redevelopment in Indianapolis: A Benefit-Cost Analysis." *Journal of Regional Science* 8, no. 2 (Winter 1968): 149–58.

[11] Jerome Rothenberg, *Economic Evaluation of Urban Renewal* (Washington, D.C.: Brookings Institution, 1967), p. 175.

health hazards are reduced; and the conditions fostering personality problems are removed. These items are difficult to quantify in rigorous cost-benefit analysis.

Rehabilitation and conservation

Disenchantment with urban renewal resulted in programs designed to rehabilitate deteriorating properties and to conserve "gray" areas that might further deteriorate. The model cities program initiated in 1966 provided grants and technical assistance to municipalities or other government bodies which proposed an acceptable comprehensive plan for dealing with the social, economic, and physical problems of selected neighborhoods. Proposals for grants to assist in carrying out a model cities program were required to show that several social and economic criteria would be met.

Rehabilitation of deteriorating properties in urban renewal areas and in neighborhoods designated for conservation had to be facilitated by strict code enforcement. However, landlords decide to make necessary improvements only if the cost is no greater than the loss of value experienced by abandoning their property. And some landlords seem capable of inordinately extending the period of compliance. Furthermore, declaring units unfit for human habitation and boarding the windows does not solve the housing problem of the occupants who must seek housing elsewhere. Nor does an increase in rent following improvement of the property aid low-income families to achieve adequate housing within their financial means. If strict code enforcement is effectively to encourage rehabilitation, the availability of credit and other incentives must make rehabilitation the viable alternative to abandonment without unduly increasing the rent of the units.

The federal government has helped provide credit for rehabilitation, both directly as grants and loans and indirectly in the form of mortgage insurance or rehabilitation loans. Further incentive to provide rehabilitated units for low- and moderate-income families was incorporated in the 1969 Tax Reform Act and extended by the 1976 Tax Reform Act until 1978. The act permitted a maximum of $15,000 of rehabilitation expenditures per unit to be written off using straight-line depreciation over five years.

Direct block grants

Title I of the Housing and Community Development Act of 1974 consolidated several programs (such as urban renewal, public facility loans, model cities supplemental grants, and rehabilitation loans) into a single program of direct block grants. Eighty percent of the funds ($2.5 to $2.95 billion per year) are allocated to urban cities and counties; 20

percent are allocated for nonurban areas. The formula which determines the amount each community obtains is complex; it considers such factors as (*a*) population of the community, (*b*) extent of poverty in the community, and (*c*) the extent of overcrowded housing.[12] The grants are to be used by the community in terms of its priorities for eliminating slums and blight, increased public services, improved land use, and preservation of property values.

IMPACT OF FEDERAL HOUSING PROGRAMS

Federal housing programs are available to families that vary not only in size, income, and assets, but also in tastes and preferences, stage in the family cycle, and other characteristics. Some families have more than one wage earner, others have none. Moreover, their places of employment can be widely distributed over the urban area. These characteristics determine the location and type of unit occupied in the private housing market by families eligible for subsidized housing. Since the subsidized programs admit families having different income distributions (and different distributions of other characteristics), it can be expected that each program would admit families from units in the housing market that vary in type (single-family residence or apartment), size, physical condition, location, rent, and value. One study showed that in Columbus, Ohio, for instance, families moving into federal housing generally came from the inner city, from apartments, from deteriorating and dilapidated units, and from low-rent units. Various programs differed with respect to the proportion of occupants coming from the inner city or from various types of housing units.[13]

New housing developed under the federal programs has conceptualized as a factor contributing to the filtering process when it provides a net increase in the number of units available in the market. The vacancy rate in the nonsubsidized portion of the local housing market would rise, in this instance, contributing to the potential for a decline in the level of rents in submarkets affected and permitting low-income families to better their housing condition at the same or less expense. In reality, separation of the net impact of units provided by the federal programs from other forces operating in the market to influence the demand for and supply of housing would, indeed, be very difficult. The net increase in total housing units represented by these programs and the rise in the level of vacancies in the housing submarkets affected can only be

---

[12] Wallace B. Agnew, "The Housing and Community Development Act of 1974: An Interpretation," *Real Estate Appraiser* 41, no. 1 (January–February 1975): 9–11.

[13] Ronald L. Racster, Halbert C. Smith, and William B. Bruggeman, "Federal Housing Programs in the Local Housing Market," *Appraisal Journal* 39, no. 3 (July 1971): 402–6.

viewed as a marginal change that may be swamped by in-migration of households, undoubling of existing households, new household formations, and loss of units from demolition and conversion, all of which simultaneously affect this part of the local housing market. Further, as we have seen, supply-oriented housing programs, over the longer run, probably result in little or no overall improvement in the housing condition of families in the market.[14]

Rehabilitated units supplied by the federal programs improve the quality of the housing stock, but they do not increase the number of units available in the market. Large-scale rehabilitation could increase prices of properties in lower quality submarkets as investors and public agencies bid for suitable units to be placed in the federal programs. This increase in market prices could give incentive to owners of better quality units to allow their properties to filter down into the lower quality housing stock by foregoing maintenance and repair.[15] Better quality submarkets lose units to the lower quality submarkets that are experiencing relatively higher prices. Prices, in turn, rise in these better quality submarkets, attracting units from still higher value submarkets. The process repeats itself until it reaches those submarkets which are competitive with new properties and calls forth new construction.

Policy for the provision of adequate housing

The decision to improve the housing condition of the ill-housed is a high-level government decision, where the problem is to allocate the national budget among broad categories of perceived needs. At a lower level of decision-making, methods of meeting the need must be determined. Our present federal housing programs are the result of past decisions at this level. However, there are unresolved problems that deserve consideration and further analysis. For example, should income supplements be provided to low-income families rather than subsidizing the development and operation of their housing? Our national housing policy, to date, has provided housing developed specifically for disadvantaged families. An alternative solution would be to give income to these families which they could spend for housing if they choose, or for other goods and services. The negative income tax is one proposal for this purpose. Another variation on income supplements is the housing allowance program presently being tried experimentally in selected cities. The housing allowance is tied to expenditure for housing, but it may be spent on any standard unit in the private market. The final form which the housing

---

[14] See Chapter 7.

[15] Edgar O. Olsen, "A Competitive Theory of the Housing Market," *American Economic Review* 59, no. 4 (September 1969): 612–22.

allowance program will take is not yet known, but the concept seems to have the capabilities of replacing present federal housing programs that provide new and rehabilitated housing for low- and moderate-income families.

If the decision is to subsidize low-income families by providing housing directly, what form of subsidized program should be used? Should housing be subsidized for only low-income families, or should moderate-income families also be provided housing? What mix of subsidized housing should be provided? Public housing directly admits low-income families, improving their housing condition and at the same time reducing their housing expense. However, the subsidy cost per public housing unit is relatively large. Units available to moderate-income families in Section 235, Section 8, and other programs can be supplied at a lower subsidy cost per unit. Federal appropriations for housing subsidies are limited. Therefore, should a greater number of moderate-income program units be supplied from a given appropriation or should fewer low-income program units be supplied?

Income redistribution effects

The economic analysis of subsidized housing can involve examination of broader income redistribution effects. In one analysis of income redistribution, Nourse uses the example of development and operation of conventional public housing.[16] A schematic presentation of the potential shifts in income from this housing program is depicted in Figure 17–1. His analysis notes a potential increase in national income, if construction workers otherwise were unemployed, or a shift from the development of other types of real estate to public housing (with no change in national income) if workers would have been employed elsewhere. If the program places additional demand upon the construction industry during full employment, wage and construction cost increases are to be expected, with income shifting to favor persons in the building industry. Otherwise, it is noted that raising funds by issuing bonds to finance public housing shifts income from other investments. A local government may get more or less tax revenue from the housing project (which pays 10 percent of rent collected in lieu of the property tax) than from the properties condemned for project construction, depending upon the relative intensity of use of the site before and after project development. Whether or not slum landlords whose property is taken for the project experience a net benefit or disbenefit will depend upon their condemnation award. If they are paid more than fair market value of their property, they benefit at the

---

[16] Hugh O. Nourse, "Redistribution of Income from Public Housing," *National Tax Journal* 19, no. 1 (March 1966): 27–37.

FIGURE 17–1

Channels of potential income redistribution in the development and operation of public housing

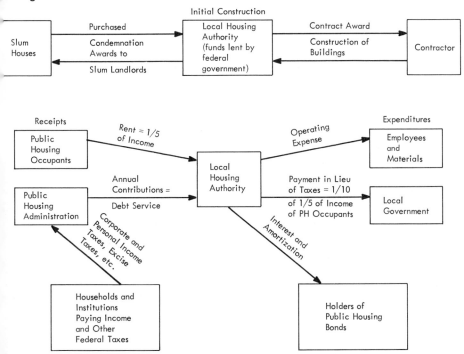

expense of the taxpayer. The most important shift of income is from the taxpayer to the public housing tenants. The following point made by Nourse should be kept in mind: the economist can trace potential income redistribution effects, but it is not possible to state objectively that the total national welfare has been increased following redistribution. The decision to provide public housing or any form of subsidized housing remains a value judgment.[17]

SUMMARY

Our national housing policy is to provide "a decent home and suitable living environment for every American family." In pursuit of this goal, several federal housing programs have been initiated. Public housing was a depression-born program designed to provide adequate housing for

---

[17] Ibid.

low-income families. Over time, public housing has evolved from high-rise projects to less intensive developments and to lease or purchase programs and the public housing homeownership program. The rent supplement program enables low-income families to occupy adequate housing without paying a disproportionate share of their income for rent. Housing for families of moderate income has been made available through the Section 221(d)(3) BMIR, Section 236, Section 235, and Section 8 programs. Both new and rehabilitated housing are included in these programs. Other federal programs have provided grants and loans for renovation and rehabilitation of housing in renewal and conservation districts.

The emerging intent of these programs has been to encourage private enterprise to construct, own, and operate the needed housing. Federal subsidy is provided when necessary to encourage development. The subsidy permits below-market rents and housing expense to be charged and, at the same time, gives the developer and investor satisfactory profits. With the exception of the rent supplements, federal programs have focused upon the provision of housing units for the underhoused. Other alternatives are possible, such as the housing allowance program, which can supplement the income of poor families, although the subsidy still will be earmarked for housing expense. Proposals for unrestricted income supplements have not been well received.

Currently, the emphasis in the federal subsidization of housing is through the direct subsidization of rents in apartment units and the subsidization of the interest rate in single-family homes. The latter type is a "shallow" subsidy, permitting marginal purchasers to afford standard housing. The same number of subsidy dollars are thus spread among more beneficiaries. Large-scale community development programs, such as urban renewal and model cities, have been disbanded in favor of block grants to communities. This approach seems to be part of the trend to shift more decisions from the federal level back to the states and communities. Whether it will be more effective and efficient in solving urban problems than more direct federal involvement can only be determined with the passage of time.

Employment, education, and equality of opportunity will, in the longer run, alleviate the socioeconomic problems besetting our minority groups and low-income families. In the interim, provision of decent housing directly for some disadvantaged families can only be a partial solution.

QUESTIONS FOR REVIEW

1. How does the developer-investor profit from a Section 235 project?
2. Discuss the effects on the local housing market of the simultaneous provision of housing units in two or more subsidy programs.

3. Not every low- or moderate-income family can be provided with a sub-sidized housing unit. Given a total allocation for subsidy, what factors are involved in an analysis of the alternatives of providing fewer units requiring a higher subsidy cost per unit directly to low-income families versus pro-viding a larger number of units to moderate-income families?

4. What prevents the economist from stating that federal housing programs increase the total national welfare?

5. Explain the rationale for urban renewal.

6. Do you agree with the statement: "Blight exists because people are poor"? Is this contention a complete analysis of the problem?

7. What potential advantages and disadvantages do you see in the housing allowance program?

8. Do you prefer to have the government make block grants to communities or to have specific programs for community development, such as urban renewal? Why?

REFERENCES

Agnew, Wallace B. "The Housing and Community Development Act of 1974: An Interpretation," *Real Estate Appraiser* 41, no. 1 (January–February 1975): 9–11.

Brueggeman, William B.; Racster, Ronald L.; and Smith, Halbert C. "Research Report: Multiple Housing Programs and Urban Housing Policy," *Journal of the American Institute of Planners* 38, no. 3 (1972): 161–67.

Grigsby, William G. *Housing Markets and Public Policy*. Philadelphia: University of Pennsylvania Press, 1963.

Lansing, J. B.; Clifton, C. W.; and Morgan, J. N. *New Homes and Poor People: A Study of Chains of Moves*. Ann Arbor: University of Michigan, Institute for Social Research, 1969.

O'Block, Robert P., and Kuehn, Robert H., Jr. *An Economic Analysis of the Housing and Urban Development Act of 1968*. Boston: Harvard University, Graduate School of Business Administration, Division of Research, 1970.

Racster, Ronald L.; Smith, Halbert C.; and Brueggeman, William B. "Federal Housing Programs in the Local Housing Market." *Appraisal Journal* 39, no. 3 (July 1971): 402–6.

Report of the President's Committee on Urban Housing. *A Decent Home*. Washington, D.C.: U.S. Government Printing Office, 1969.

Rothenberg, Jerome. *Economic Evaluation of Urban Renewal*. Washington, D.C.: Brookings Institution, 1967.

Smith, Wallace F. *Housing: The Social and Economic Elements*. Berkeley: University of California Press, 1970.

U.S. Department of Housing and Urban Development, *Digest of Insurable Loans and Summaries of Other Federal Housing Administration Programs*. Washington, D.C.: U.S. Government Printing Office, March 1970.

chapter 18

ENVIRONMENTAL ISSUES AND REAL ESTATE DEVELOPMENT

Two ALTERNATIVES available to our society—the preservation of the environment or the development of real estate—often appear to be mutually exclusive. Real estate developers are sometimes regarded as rapists of the countryside, while defenders of the environment are viewed as naive do-gooders who would sabotage economic growth in order to preserve some wildlife and vegetation. Laws have been passed at all levels of government to help preserve the environment. Many of these laws have imposed restrictions and additional costs upon both the developers and users of real estate. The purpose of this chapter is to examine the nature and background of environmental issues, the responses to the issues, and impact of these responses upon real estate investors.

RISE OF ENVIRONMENTAL CONCERN

Deterioration of the environment is a relatively recent issue in national affairs. Agitation for legal means of environmental protection began to occur in the mid-1960s and early 1970s. During this period significant and far-reaching legislation was imposed at the federal level. Additionally, a number of states enacted restrictive laws which more directly affect real estate development and investment.

This period also saw efforts at the local level to increase standards in land-use controls, to impose more comprehensive planning, and to limit population growth. Candidates for political office at all levels became known as proponents or opponents of environmental preservation or of further growth and development. The traditional form of land-use control —zoning—was both attacked and defended in regard to its impact upon environmental issues. Urban environmentalists saw zoning as the principal tool by which suburban and high-income groups keep inner-city (usually black) low-income people from escaping the congested, polluted, deteriorated central portions of cities. Middle- and high-income groups saw zoning as a device to prevent congestion, maintain property values, exclude low-income residents, and discourage development of all but single-family housing.

Underlying factors of environmental concern

Attempting to assign sources to the rise in environmental concern is, as always in attempting to analyze motivations, hypothetical and hazardous. Nevertheless, we can note other social trends and their close relationship to environmental issues. Some substantial degree of cause and effect can reasonably be assigned to factors such as population trends, industrialization and urbanization, economic prosperity, the extension of civil rights, and the energy crisis.

Population trends. An increase in the U.S. population from approximately 140 million in 1940 to approximately 215 million in 1976 has required a substantially large drain upon our natural resources. More food and fiber have been required for food and clothing. The increased need for housing, transportation, education, employment, and other goods and services has added to the complexity of society. Our public and private institutions have multiplied and changed to accommodate this growth perhaps more than during any comparable period in our country's history. The growth has contributed to congestion in our urban areas and to urbanization in formerly rural and isolated regions.

Coupled with net natural increases in population, migratory growth patterns have contributed to fast growth rates in some areas. Population growth rates have been above average in states having climatic and scenic advantages, such as Florida, California, Arizona, Texas, Colorado, and Oregon. For these states and regions, the impact upon natural resources, social complexity, public and private institutions, and the need for all goods and services has been even greater.

With population increases emanating from net natural increase and net migration, many urban centers have experienced more concentrated living patterns. High-rise apartments and condominiums have added to the demands for urban services and resources in cities such as New York, Chicago, Washington, D.C., Atlanta, St. Louis, Seattle, and Toronto. Additionally, other areas such as the lower southeast and southwest coasts of Florida, southern California, and the mid-Atlantic coast have been developed with hotels and resort accommodations, as well as high-rise residential buildings. These concentrations of population have inevitably contributed to pressures and frictions in everyday living and have placed heavy demands upon resources and environmental systems.

Industrialization and urbanization. The industrial revolution of the late 19th and early 20th centuries led to the development of industrial centers and the consequent urbanization of society. Early manufacturing centers, such as New York, Chicago, Detroit, Pittsburgh, and Cleveland attracted large numbers of rural residents with the promise of relatively high-paying jobs and the hope of prosperity. Further advances in transportation and communication, particularly jet airplanes, television, and the interstate highway system, extended the ideas and values of urban America to rural areas. Leisure time, planned obsolescence, throwaway containers, conspicuous consumption, and "buy now—pay later" credit plans became the distinguishing characteristics of American society. Until the mid-1960s, little concern was shown that continued adherence to these tenets would place intolerable strains upon the land resources of the nation.

Economic prosperity. The continued industrialization and urbanization of the United States, particularly after World War II, produced an economic prosperity greater than any country had previously known. Along with population growth, technology, and mass markets, purchasing power became characteristic of large segments of the urbanized society. Increasing numbers of people, the pent-up demand from World War II, and the large amounts of savings from the war period initiated a cycle of production and consumption that was to last over 25 years. Furthermore, the cycle was self-sustaining through the economic processes of employment, investment, and consumption. If the economy hit an occasional hitch, the government was prepared to prime the pump with stimulative monetary and fiscal policies. America was enjoying prosperity which seemingly could not be deterred, even by the simultaneous waging of the Vietnam War.

Civil rights. Also during the 1960s, the major push by minority groups to attain their full civil rights and a proportionate share of the American economic pie brought into question some of the traditional values and theories of American capitalism. Could the system operate without exploiting people? If the system had relied to any extent upon the exploitation of people, had it also relied upon the exploitation of resources and the environment? Do firms that discriminate in hiring and advancement policies also exploit the majority by dumping wastes into lakes and streams? Do firms that manufacture throwaway containers transfer part of their costs of cleanup and disposal to the taxpayers? And are firms that discriminate against certain groups in hiring and promotion capable or trustworthy to make decisions affecting the general welfare through the environment? Certainly it seems plausible that an increased awareness of discrimination and exploitation carried over to increased concern for the environment.

Additionally, minority groups became vocal and even violent about the quality of the center-city environments into which many of their members were drawn and contained by overt and economic discrimination. Dissatisfaction and frustration of center-city residents led to skyrocketing crime rates and to the suburban migration of white residents. The downtown areas of major cities became no-man's-land at night. Urban decay, crime, pollution, and fear began to spread like cancer from the inner city to outlying areas of the city, and even to suburban enclaves of the privileged classes. The urban environment had become truly repressive and disheartening to many members of the vast majority of Americans who lived in cities.

The energy crisis. The Arab oil embargo of 1973, followed by dramatic cost increases for all forms of energy, painfully accentuated our dependence upon the world's limited supply of raw materials and resources. The American public realized for the first time that the United States did not have unlimited access to basic resources. Furthermore, U.S. technology was incapable of replacing oil with a substitute energy source, except at huge cost, long-time delays, and great risk. The necessity to conserve energy suggested the desirability of conserving other resources, including the environment.

RESPONSES TO ENVIRONMENTAL CONCERN

Legislation has been enacted at all governmental levels to preserve the environment. Generally, legislation enacted at the state and local levels has more directly affected land use and control than federal laws. Federal laws generally have dealt with pollution standards and control and with the organization of administrative agencies to enforce pollution legislation. In 1974 when the U.S. Congress considered land planning and control legislation, strong elements of opposition were successful in preventing its passage. This proposed legislation would have established standards and criteria for land planning and control for areas as small as counties and municipalities. If planning and control did not meet the federal standards, federal funds could be withheld from the jurisdiction. It seems doubtful that the country has seen the end of efforts to enact this type of legislation.

Federal response

The federal response to environmental concern consists of several significant laws and an administrative structure to carry out many aspects of environmental preservation. While the legislative effort in this field is not new—examples of pioneering legislation are the Public Health Service Act of 1912, the Oil Pollution Act of 1924, and the Water Pollution Control Act of 1948—our attention will be focused upon legislation and executive activity from the mid-1960s to the present time. Several of these laws were enacted as amendments to existing laws that had been passed earlier. For example, the Water Pollution Control Act Amendments of 1972 represented only the latest in a series of amendments to the 1948 act.

Federal Water Pollution Control Act Amendments of 1972. This act represented a complete rewrite of all existing water pollution control laws on the federal statute books. The 1972 act sets as a national goal the elimination of all pollution from America's waters by 1985. The law requires secondary treatment for all municipal wastes by mid-1977, and the application of more advanced disposal methods by mid-1983. For industry, the law establishes a two-phase cleanup program, with increasingly tight restrictions on industrial pollution, backed up by penalties of fines and imprisonment for violators.

President's reorganization plan no. 3 of 1970. This executive order by President Nixon established the Environmental Protection Agency and transferred numerous functions and personnel from other departments and agencies to the new EPA. For example, the functions formerly vested in the Federal Water Quality Administration of the Department of the Interior and functions of the National Air Pollution Control Administration, the Environmental Control Administration, the Bureau of Solid Waste Management, the Bureau of Water Hygiene, and the Bureau of Radiological Health of the Department of Health, Education, and Welfare were mandated to the EPA.

The purpose of the EPA is to protect the health and welfare of Americans by controlling environmental pollution hazards. The agency establishes and enforces air and water pollution standards, establishes drinking water standards, regulates the sale and use of pesticides, sets standards for noise and ambient radiation, develops techniques and procedures for solid waste management, studies toxic substances, conducts research, and demonstrates new pollution control methods and technology. Major federal laws administered by the agency include the Clean Air Act; the Federal Water Pollution Control Act; the Safe Drinking Water Act; the Solid Waste Disposal Act; the Federal Insecticide, Fungicide, and Rodenticide Act; and the Noise Control Act.

Clean Air Act of 1963. This act and its amendments[1] established comprehensive and specific requirements for the maintenance and improvement of air quality. Some of the act's more significant aspects were the following:

---

[1] Amendments to this act were made in the Motor Vehicle Air Pollution Control Act of 1965, the Clean Air Act Amendments of 1966, the Air Quality Act of 1967, and the Clean Air Amendments of 1970, 1971, and 1973.

1. Establishment of various types of research programs relating to air pollution and pollutants.
2. Establishment of air quality control regions.
3. Requirement for the EPA Administrator to establish ambient air quality standards.
4. Implementation plans and schedules.
5. Establishment of standards of performance of new stationary sources emitting air pollutants.
6. Establishment of emission standards for moving sources (such as automobiles and airplanes) of air pollutants.
7. Establishment of national emission standards for hazardous air pollutants.
8. Establishment of the president's Air Quality Advisory Board.

Noise Control Act of 1972. This legislation requires the EPA administrator to identify major sources of noise, noise criteria, and control technology. The administrator is charged with developing noise emission standards for products distributed in commerce, railroads, and motor carriers; and assessing the adequacy of noise emission standards for new and existing aircraft and airports. Included in this charge is provision for the control of aircraft noise and sonic boom.

Solid Waste Disposal Act of 1965. This act seeks to promote the demonstration, construction, and application of solid waste management and resource recovery systems which preserve and enhance the quality of air, water, and land resources; to provide technical and financial assistance to states and local governments and interstate agencies in the planning and development of resource recovery and solid waste disposal programs; and to promote research and development in solid waste disposal and recycling.

National Materials Policy Act of 1970. This act established the National Commission on Materials Policy. It was the commission's task to develop a comprehensive policy regarding the priorities, use, disposition, recycling, and environmental impact of various materials. The commission terminated after submission of its report to the president.

National Environmental Policy Act of 1969. It established the Council on Environmental Quality within the executive office of the president and directed the president to submit an annual report to Congress on environmental quality. It also stated that

. . . It is the continuing policy of the federal government, in cooperation with state and local governments, and other concerned public and private organizations, to use all practicable means and measures, including financial and technical assistance, in a manner calculated to foster and promote the general welfare, to create and maintain conditions under which man and nature can exist in productive harmony, and fulfill the social, economic, and other requirements of present and future generations of Americans.

Among other provisions to implement the policy, this act requires all agencies of the federal government in every recommendation or report on proposals for legislation and other major federal actions significantly affecting the quality of the human environment, to include a detailed statement on its environmental impact, unavoidable adverse environmental effects, short-run versus long-run considerations, commitments of resources involved, and alternatives to the proposed action.

Coastal Zone Management Act of 1972.   This law provides grants for any coastal state to develop a coastal zone management plan and program for the land and water resources of its coastal zones. The plans must identify permissible land and water uses and indicate how the state will enforce compatibility among land uses. It must identify areas of particular concern and describe the planning and regulatory provisions for effectively managing the coastal zone. This act is administered by the National Oceanic and Atmospheric Administration of the U.S. Department of Commerce. The goal of this act is to avoid adverse impacts upon the coastal waters, which include the Great Lakes, Atlantic, Pacific, and Arctic Oceans, Gulf of Mexico, and Long Island Sound.

Safe Drinking Water Act of 1974.   Finally, this act empowered the EPA to develop standards to safeguard public drinking water supplies from contaminants such as bacteria, inorganic chemicals, and organic pesticides. The standards apply to more than 240,000 public water supplies after June 1977.

U.S. Army Corps of Engineers

In addition to the EPA, the U.S. Army Corps of Engineers has important regulatory authority over the nation's waterways. The corps' authority in this area derives from the Constitution through several laws and court decisions. The Constitution empowers Congress to "regulate commerce with foreign nations and among the several states," and it has been held that the power to regulate commerce includes the power to regulate navigation. The following laws and court decisions provide the authority for U.S. Army Corps of Engineers' regulatory activities.

River and Harbor Act of 1899.   Sections 9 through 20 of this act form the original basis for the corps' authority. Most important are Sections 9 and 10, which prohibit unauthorized construction in navigable waters of the United States.

Fish and Wildlife Act of 1958.   This act requires that consideration be given to fish and wildlife resources, and that federal and state fish and wildlife agencies coordinate their activities.

Zabel v. Tabb (*1968*). This court decision established the precedent that all "public interest factors" must be considered in permit applications for dredge and fill operations.

National Environmental Policy Act of 1969. As described previously, this act states the national policy of encouraging productive and enjoyable harmony between people and their environment.

Federal Water Pollution Control Act of 1972. As described previously, this law governs the disposal of dredged or fill material in waterways.

Marine Protection Research and Sanctuaries Act of 1972. This law regulates the transportation of dredged material for the purpose of dumping in ocean waters.

Coastal Zone Management Act of 1972. As described previously, this act requires coordination with a state's coastal zone management plan.

In 1975 the corps was directed by a U.S. District Court ruling to expand its regulatory authority to include *all waters* of the United States. This decision is estimated to extend the corps' jurisdiction over navigable waters from 50,000 to 5.5 million miles. Additionally, tributaries of navigable waters, marshlands, wetlands adjacent to navigable waters, interstate waters, and intrastate waters used for interstate purposes are included.

Revised regulations expanded the corps' responsibilities in three phases, as shown in Figure 18–1. These regulations require permits for activities such as construction of dams or dikes; obstruction or alteration of navigable water; construction of piers, wharves, bulkheads, pilings, marinas, or docks; dredging; and filling of waters or wetlands. No permit is granted unless its issuance is found to be in the public interest.

State response

A number of states have enacted legislation that more directly affects many types of real estate developments than do federal laws. Additionally, regional and local planning councils have become more concerned with environmental effects of proposed developments. Consequently, the planning councils and local governing bodies they advise have become more demanding in specifying characteristics and features of developments to preserve the environment. Such requirements often add substantially to the costs of new developments or encourage developers to plan smaller and perhaps less efficient projects. In many cases, the concern of regional and local planning agencies results from state laws mandating their supervision. State legislation generally can be classified as to requirements for environmental impact statements, preservation of environmentally endangered zones, and planning and zoning.

Environmental impact statements. A number of states require that developers of projects of certain size or having certain characteristics

FIGURE 18–1

Regulatory authority of U.S. Army Corps of Engineers

PRIOR TO 25 JULY 1975

Regulatory authority under River and Harbor
Act of 1899. (Includes all "navigable waters"
and coastal areas)

Typical River Basin

Coastal Area

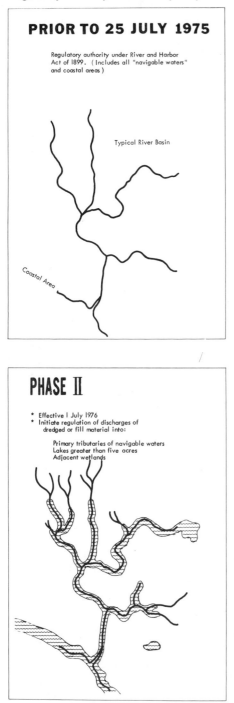

PHASE I

* Effective 25 July 1975
* Extends existing permit procedures to
  include adjacent wetlands
* Wetlands – – Endangered and valuable
  resource

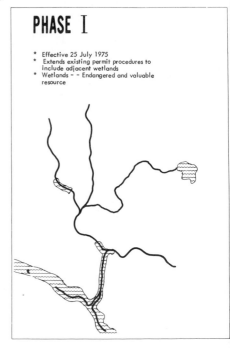

PHASE II

* Effective 1 July 1976
* Initiate regulation of discharges of
  dredged or fill material into:

  Primary tributaries of navigable waters
  Lakes greater than five acres
  Adjacent wetlands

PHASE III

* Effective 1 July 1977
* Regulate discharges of dredged or fill
  material into other waters up to their
  headwaters of 5 cubic feet per second
  or less (Includes all tributaries)

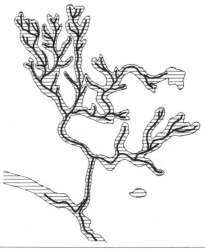

prepare a detailed analysis of the project's impact upon the environment, or subsystems, such as water, sewers, and transportation. In California, for example, the Environmental Quality Act of 1970 is modeled after the National Environmental Policy Act of 1969 and requires the preparation of environmental impact reports (EIR) on all state and local projects which are permitted or funded by state or local agencies. Any EIR must contain the following information:

1. Environmental impact of the proposed action.
2. Adverse environmental effects which cannot be avoided if the proposal is implemented.
3. Measures proposed to minimize the impact.
4. Alternatives to the proposed action.
5. Relationship between short-term and long-term considerations.
6. Irreversible environmental changes which the proposed action might cause.
7. Growth-inducing impact of the proposed action.

The Florida Environmental Land and Water Management Act of 1972 requires approval for any proposed development which, because of its character, magnitude, or location, would have a substantial effect on the health, safety, or welfare of citizens of more than one county. The application must contain a detailed analysis of these items:

1. Environment and natural resources.
2. Regional economy.
3. Public facilities.
4. Public transportation.
5. Housing.
6. Other relevant areas.

Such projects are termed "developments of regional impact" (DRIs), and are defined for various types of uses. For example, a *residential* development is deemed to be a DRI, if it is planned to contain more than the following numbers of units:

1. 250 units—in counties of less than 25,000 population.
2. 500 units—in counties with population between 25,000 and 50,000.
3. 750 units—in counties with population between 50,000 and 100,000.
4. 1,000 units—in counties with population between 100,000 and 250,000.
5. 2,000 units—in counties with population between 250,000 and 500,000.
6. 3,000 units—in counties with population over 500,000.

Estimates of cost for the preparation of an environmental impact statement or a DRI application range from $20,000 to $40,000 for a straightforward residential project to $150,000 for a large, fairly complex residential project. Statements for commercial projects range from

$50,000 for a small shopping center to $250,000 for a regional shopping center. And, of course, these costs do not include additional charges or requirements which may be imposed for approval of the project. Frequently, developers must add or upgrade sewer treatment plants, water systems, water drainage retention ponds, and transportation systems. Needless to say, environmentally motivated requirements have greatly increased the "front-end costs" of developments. If the demand for these developments is inelastic, the costs can be transferred to consumers through increased rents and prices, while an elastic demand structure will result in the project's inability to cover costs. Investment decisions resulting from a consideration of total costs should thus reflect more accurately the environmentally related costs and social priorities.

Preservation of environmentally endangered lands. Some states have passed laws that stringently regulate environmentally endangered zones or provide for outright purchase by the state of such areas. Again, Florida and California are leaders in this type of legislation. Some states, such as Oregon, Maryland, and Nevada, require state government review of local zoning decisions that would have broader, regional impact. California's Coastal Zone Conservation Act of 1972 gives a state commission and six regional commissions the task of developing a comprehensive, enforceable plan for the conservation and management of the entire California coastal zone. The zone is defined as an area extending from three miles offshore to the highest elevation of the mountain range closest to shore, or five miles from the mean high tide line. Additionally, the Commissions are empowered to regulate all construction up to 1,000 yards inland from the mean high tide line by denial of permits for development within their territorial jurisdictions. These permits are required in addition to other, customary required approvals such as zoning, subdivision, and building permits.

The Florida legislation allows the governor and cabinet to designate areas of critical state concern. Once so designated, the local governments within the area must adopt land development regulations that are satisfactory to the state land planning agency, the governor, and cabinet. If such regulations are not adopted and implemented, the state may impose its own regulations. The threat of such a state imposition of development regulations created a great deal of controversy when it was applied to the Florida Keys. As reported by *Business Week,* some local business people were afraid that the regulations would discourage development and would disrupt the local tax base. Robert Matthews of the Council of State Governments stated that "It is the first time a state government has stepped in to take over the local planning function."[2]

---

[2] "A State Crackdown Scares the Developers," *Business Week,* August 11, 1975, pp. 22–24.

Planning and zoning. As noted above, several states encourage or require adequate planning to preserve and protect the environment. States review local planning and zoning regulations and decisions that affect larger areas or environmentally endangered areas. And states have established regional planning agencies and commissions, as well as state agencies, to review and approve large-scale developments, or developments in environmentally threatened areas. Linowes and Allensworth, have reported upon land-use programs by state as of January 1974 (see Table 18–1). They have included a "report card" for each state (see Table 18–2), indicating the degree of influence wielded by the state planning agency in the various programs of land-use control.[3] Hawaii, Vermont, Florida, Maine, Minnesota, and Oregon currently have the greatest influence in statewide land-use planning and control. Still, many predominantly rural counties and communities in almost all states have weak local land-use controls. Additional state intervention in local areas where minimal planning and zoning exist seems inevitable.

ECONOMIC ASPECTS OF ENVIRONMENTAL ISSUES

A major shift in public attitudes toward the environment suggests a national reordering of priorities, costs, and economic advantage. The need for such reordering reflects an inappropriate structure of charges applied to the production and delivery of many goods and services. This structure has not recognized the full costs of both private and public products. It has encouraged greater, not lesser, consumption and destruction, rather than conservation, of the environment. In attempting to steer a changed course of direction through the murky waters of environmental concern, policy-makers at all levels need to be cognizant of the economic effects of externalities, marginal cost pricing, efficiencies of scale, and cost-benefit analysis.

Externalities

Economies or diseconomies result from goods that have a positive or negative effect upon people other than those who produce or own the good. For example, an external economy occurs when one class of ticket purchasers for a concert pay a price higher than the cost of their seats so that others may attend at a subsidized price. Or, another example is when property owners landscape the front of their properties so that others may enjoy the beauty. When external economies are applicable on a wide scale, the product or service is a good candidate for gov-

---

[3] R. Robert Linowes and Don T. Allensworth, *The States and Land-Use Control* (New York: Frederick A. Praeger, 1975), pp. 30–35.

TABLE 18-1

State land-use programs (January 30, 1974)

	Statewide land-use planning and control[1]	Coastal zone management[2]	Wetlands management[3]	Power plant siting[4]	Surface mining[5]	Designation of critical areas[6]	Land-use tax incentives[7]	Flood plain management[8]
Alabama	P	—	—	—	yes	—	—	—
Alaska	—	NA	—	—	—	—	yes	—
Arizona	P	NA	—	yes	—	—	—	yes
Arkansas	—	NA	—	yes	yes	—	yes	yes
California	P	yes	—	yes	—	—	yes	yes
Colorado	P	NA	—	—	yes	yes	yes	yes
Connecticut	P	—	yes	yes	—	—	yes	yes
Delaware	P	yes	yes	—	—	yes	yes	—
Florida	P and R	yes	yes	yes	—	yes	—	—
Georgia	P	—	yes	—	yes	—	—	—
Hawaii	P and R	yes	—	yes	—	yes	yes	yes
Idaho	—	NA	—	—	—	—	—	—
Illinois	—	—	—	yes	yes	—	yes	—
Indiana	—	—	—	—	yes	—	yes	—
Iowa	—	NA	—	—	yes	—	yes	—
Kansas	—	NA	—	—	yes	—	—	—
Kentucky	—	NA	—	—	yes	—	yes	—
Louisiana	P and R	—	yes	—	—	—	—	yes
Maine	P and R	yes	—	yes	yes	—	yes	yes
Maryland	R (limited)	—	yes	yes	yes	—	yes	—
Massachusetts	—	—	yes	—	—	—	—	—
Michigan	P	yes	—	—	yes	—	—	yes
Minnesota	P and R	yes	—	yes	yes	yes	yes	yes
Mississippi	—	yes	—	—	—	—	—	—
Missouri	—	NA	—	—	yes	—	—	—
Montana	—	NA	—	yes	yes	—	yes	yes
Nebraska	—	NA	—	yes	—	—	—	yes
Nevada	—	NA	—	yes	—	—	—	—

State	[1]	[2]	[3]	[4]	[5]	[6]	[7]	[8]
New Hampshire	—	—	yes	yes	—	—	yes	—
New Jersey	—	—	yes	yes (cz)	—	—	yes	yes
New Mexico	—	NA	—	yes	yes	—	yes	—
New York	P	—	yes	yes	—	yes	yes	—
North Carolina	—	NA	yes	—	yes	—	yes	—
North Dakota	—	NA	—	—	yes	—	—	—
Ohio	—	—	—	—	yes	—	—	—
Oklahoma	—	NA	—	—	yes	—	—	yes
Oregon	P and R	yes (partial)	—	yes	yes	yes	yes	—
Pennsylvania	P	—	—	yes	yes	yes	yes	—
Rhode Island	—	yes	yes	yes	—	yes	yes	—
South Carolina	—	—	—	yes	—	—	—	—
South Dakota	—	NA	—	—	yes	—	yes	—
Tennessee	—	NA	—	—	yes	—	—	—
Texas	—	yes	—	—	—	yes	yes	—
Utah	—	NA	—	—	—	—	yes	—
Vermont	P and R	NA	yes	yes	—	yes	yes	yes
Virginia	—	yes	yes	—	yes	—	yes	—
Washington	—	yes	yes	yes	yes	—	yes	yes
West Virginia	—	NA	—	—	yes	—	—	—
Wisconsin	P	yes	yes	—	—	yes	—	yes
Wyoming	—	NA	—	—	—	—	yes	—
Guam	P and R	yes	—	yes	yes	yes	—	yes
Puerto Rico	P and R	—	—	yes	yes	—	—	yes

[1] P indicates the state has a land-use planning program under way. R indicates the state has authority to review local plans or has direct control.

[2] State has authority to plan or review local plans or the ability to control land use in the coastal zone. NA indicates not applicable.

[3] State has authority to plan or review local plans or the ability to control land use in the wetlands.

[4] State has authority to determine the siting of power plants and related facilities.

[5] State has authority to regulate surface mining.

[6] State has established rules or is in the process of establishing rules, regulations, and guidelines for the identification and designation of areas of critical state concern (for example, environmentally fragile areas, areas of historical significance).

[7] State has adopted tax inducements to withhold or delay development of open space (for example, tax on present use, rollback penalty, contract between the state and landholders to provide preferential tax for commitment to open-space usage).

[8] State has authority to regulate the use of flood plains.

Note: Indications that a state has a program in one of the above categories does not constitute an evaluation of the effectiveness of the program.

Source: H. Milton Patton et al., The Land-Use Puzzle (Lexington, Ky.: Council of State Governments, 1974), pp. 34–35.

TABLE 18–2

Report card on emerging model in official state planning agencies, 1967–1972[1]

	Develop-ment plan	Functional planning coordi-nation	Regional coordi-nation and allocation	Technical assistance	Infor-mation system	Budget coordi-nation	Develop-ment controls	Applied research	Stimu-lation and support
Alabama	Lim	Lim	Lim	Lim	Lim	Lim	Lim	Lim	Mod
Alaska	Mod	Mod	Lim	Lim	Lim	Lim	Lim	Mod	Mod
Arizona	Lim	Mod	Mod	Sig	Mod	Mod	Lim	Lim	Mod
Arkansas	Lim	Lim	Lim	Mod	Lim	Lim	Lim	Mod	Mod
California	Mod	Mod	Mod	Mod	Sig	Mod	Mod	Mod	Mod
Colorado	Mod	Lim	Mod	Mod	Lim	Lim	Sig	Lim	Lim
Connecticut	Mod	Mod	Mod	Mod	Lim	Lim	Mod	Lim	Sig
Delaware	Sig	Mod	Sig	Sig	Mod	Mod	Mod	Mod	Mod
Florida	Mod	Mod	Mod	Lim	Lim	Mod	Sig	Lim	Mod
Georgia	Mod	Sig	Sig	Sig	Lim	Sig	Mod	Mod	Sig
Hawaii	Sig	Sig	Sig	Sig	Sig	Sig	Sig	Sig	Sig
Idaho	Lim	Lim	Mod	Mod	Lim	Lim	Lim	Mod	Mod
Illinois	Lim	Mod	Lim	Sig	Lim	Mod	Lim	Sig	Lim
Indiana	Lim	Mod	Lim	Lim	Mod	Lim	Lim	Lim	Lim
Iowa	Lim	Mod	Lim	Sig	Mod	Lim	Mod	Mod	Lim
Kansas	Mod	Mod	Mod	Sig	Mod	Lim	Lim	Lim	Sig
Kentucky	Lim	Lim	Lim	Mod	Lim	Lim	Lim	Lim	Mod
Louisiana	Lim	Mod	Mod	Mod	Lim	Lim	Mod	Mod	Mod
Maine	Sig	Mod	Mod	Lim	Lim	Mod	Sig	Mod	Mod
Maryland	Lim	Sig	Mod	Sig	Lim	Sig	Sig	Lim	Mod
Massachusetts	Mod	Mod	Mod	Mod	Mod	Mod	Mod	Mod	Mod
Michigan	Lim	Mod	Lim	Sig	Lim	Mod	Lim	Mod	Lim
Minnesota	Lim	Mod	Mod	Sig	Lim	Lim	Lim	Mod	Mod
Mississippi	Lim	Lim	Lim	Lim	Lim	Lim	Lim	Lim	Lim
Missouri	Lim	Mod	Lim	Mod	Lim	Lim	Lim	Lim	Mod
Montana	Lim	Mod	Lim	Lim		Lim	Lim	Mod	Mod

					Effectiveness evaluation	Interest of officials	Opinion survey	Content analysis
Nevada	Lim	Lim	Lim	Lim	Lim	Mod	Lim	Lim
New Hampshire	Mod	Mod	Sig	Mod	Mod	Sig	Mod	Lim
New Jersey	Sig	Lim	Mod	Lim	Lim	Sig	Mod	Sig
New Mexico	Sig	Sig	Lim	Mod	Mod	Mod	Lim	Mod
New York	Mod	Sig	Mod	Mod	Sig	Mod	Mod	Mod
North Carolina	Mod	Lim	Lim	Lim	Mod	Mod	Mod	Mod
North Dakota	Lim	Mod	Lim	Lim	Lim	Mod	Mod	Mod
Ohio	Sig	Mod	Lim	Lim	Lim	Mod	Mod	Lim
Oklahoma	Sig	Lim	Lim	Mod	Mod	Sig	Mod	Mod
Oregon	Mod	Lim	Sig	Mod	Mod	Sig	Mod	Mod
Pennsylvania	Sig	Sig	Mod	Mod	Mod	Mod	Mod	Mod
Rhode Island	Lim	Lim	Lim	Lim	Mod	Lim	Sig	Sig
South Carolina	Mod	Mod	Mod	Mod	Lim	Mod	Mod	Mod
South Dakota	Lim	Lim	Lim	Lim	Lim	Lim	Mod	Lim
Tennessee	Mod	Lim	Lim	Lim	Lim	Mod	Mod	Mod
Texas	Mod	Lim	Lim	Mod	Mod	Mod	Sig	Sig
Utah	Mod	Mod	Mod	Lim	Lim	Lim	Mod	Lim
Vermont	Mod	Lim	Sig	Sig	Lim	Mod	Mod	Sig
Virginia	Sig	Mod	Lim	Lim	Lim	Sig	Sig	Mod
Washington	Sig	Lim	Mod	Mod	Mod	Sig	Mod	Mod
West Virginia	Mod	Lim	Lim	Lim	Lim	Mod	Mod	Mod
Wisconsin	Mod	Mod	Sig	Sig	Sig	Sig	Mod	Sig
Wyoming	Mod	Mod	Lim	Lim	Lim	Mod	Lim	Lim

[1] Grades were awarded by using the criteria presented in the Table Key.

Key:

Grade	Content analysis	Opinion survey	Interest of officials	Effectiveness evaluation
Sig = Significant	Sophisticated development stage	Generally accepted and desirable	High	Strong
Mod = Moderate	Being developed or modest stage	Some acceptance but varying desirability	Modest	Medium
Lim = Limited	Initial development stage or none	Little acceptance or desirability	Little	Little

Source: Anthony James Catanese, "Reflections on State Planning Evaluation," in *State Planning Issues 1973* (Lexington, Ky.: Council of State Governments, 1973), p. 27.

ernmental provision. Bridges, highways, police and fire protection, and other commonly provided services are provided more cheaply per customer through common purchase by the government than by separate purchase by each individual. Perhaps national defense is the most conspicuous example of achievement of external economies by governmental activity. It would be prohibitively expensive for citizens to provide their own systems of national defense.

External diseconomies occur when costs or inconveniences are imposed by an individual or firm upon other people. For example, the person who litters imposes the costs of cleanup upon other people. The business firm that erects an unattractive sign imposes the cost of offensive visual sensations upon all who must pass the sign. Similarly, the factory that spews forth smoke, soot, and fumes imposes serious costs upon all who happen to be in the path of the pollutants. The costs imposed by the radioactive fallout from the testing of thermonuclear weapons constitute perhaps the most dramatic external diseconomies of wide geographic scope.

Exploitation of the environment typically produces external diseconomies. When an individual or a business firm pollutes water or air, despoils the countryside, or allows property to deteriorate, the resulting costs, inconveniences, and offenses must be borne by many people. When a manufacturer does not include such costs in the price of the products, purchasers of the factory's products pay a price that is too low. If the prices had to be set to cover all costs (including those to prevent or clean up pollution), fewer items would be sold. Thus, a redistribution of costs would produce a shift in the priorities among various products and services that would more accurately reflect economic preferences. Conversely, subsidized costs tend to establish inappropriate preference patterns that fail to reflect the true priorities of social needs. Some goods cost too much; others cost too little. Inefficiency is the result.

Federal and state laws that require standards to be met in such areas as air pollution, water pollution, or oil spills raise the cost of certain products. For example, automobiles must be equipped with antipollution devices. Such costs are then usually transmitted to the products' purchasers in increased prices. Depending upon the price elasticity for the products, manufacturers may be able to cover the additional cost fully, or they may have to absorb part of the increased cost. Some manufacturers may be forced out of business, or they may have to drop or modify some product lines.

In the real estate field, state and local regulations often require developers and builders to design and construct projects in a more costly manner than would otherwise be done. Zoning ordinances and building codes have long imposed certain kinds of additional costs upon builders that they might otherwise choose not to incur. More recently, however, additional laws and regulations that require developers of large projects to consider the project's impact upon regional systems and environmental concerns have greatly added to development costs. Such considerations often require developers to widen public roads, construct pedestrian walkways and overpasses, construct water holding basins, preserve natural features of the terrain, construct sewage treatment systems, install traffic lights, and take any other steps to conform to local, regional, or state planning agencies' recommendations.

As mentioned previously, the result of laws and regulations that impose additional costs upon real estate developers, as well as manufacturers and other business firms, is to shift the burden of many external diseconomies to the consumers of the products. Such shifts represent an attempt to internalize previously external costs or diseconomies.

Marginal cost pricing

The U.S. economy has tended to reward larger numbers and size over small numbers and size. For example, manufacturers of automobiles tend to produce additional cars as long as marginal revenue exceeds marginal costs. Profit margins are greater in standard size automobiles than for compacts; for luxury cars rather than more modest models. Utility companies have been classic examples of a decreasing cost industry in which unit costs are lowered by higher levels of output. Thus the tendency has been to encourage greater use of utility services by pricing marginal amounts lower than the average costs. Such pricing breaks have typically given large customers lower per unit prices and have encouraged greater, rather than lesser, use of utility services. Rapidly increasing energy costs have shifted the relationship between fixed and variable costs. With variable fuel costs taking a much larger share of total costs, the old decreasing rate pricing policies may no longer be reflective of the marginal costs incurred.

On the other side of marginal price influences has been the tendency of some city services, such as water and garbage removal, to be priced at average cost when marginal costs are actually increasing. In other words, new outlying areas of communities are sometimes provided such services at prices lower than the costs incurred to provide the services. The effect of such pricing, of course, is to subsidize and encourage new development at the periphery of cities. In its extreme form, such subsidization helps produce urban sprawl. And urban sprawl produces added social costs of its own, in terms of transportation costs, increased burdens on community services, and various forms of pollution.

As demonstrated by Guntermann, the economically correct and efficient solution to the problem of pricing products and services whose production contributes to environmental degradation is to internalize all environmental costs, as well as other production costs, and to charge prices reflecting total marginal costs.[4] Such a solution however, is extremely difficult and costly to impose. After all, how do we know when all costs are truly internalized? The costs of air pollution or urban sprawl, for example, are virtually impossible to measure.

Additionally, there are costs associated with identifying, measuring, and enforcing antipollution requirements. One recently reported example illustrates a situation in which the control of pollution from one source may generate even more pollution from another source:

Coming clean, or maybe not. Armco Steel Corp. says special pollution-control equipment it had to install at one plant cleans up 21.2 pounds of visible iron oxide dust every hour. But the equipment is run by a 1,020-horsepower electric motor, Armco notes. "Producing that power at the electric utility's plant spews out 23 pounds an hour of sulphur and nitrogen oxides and other gaseous pollution," the company claims.[5]

Thus, another economic principle should be recognized with respect to pollution control: the marginal cost associated with identifying, measuring, and enforcing environmental protection efforts should not exceed the value of the marginal benefit to be derived.

The goal of marginal cost pricing is to reflect accurately in consumer prices the full cost of producing the unit to be consumed. If the costs of environmental preservation are included in these costs, the total stock of wealth in the economy is not diminished. As Boulding has expressed this view:

The essential measure of the success of the economy is not production and consumption at all, but the nature, extent, quality and complexity of the total capital stock. . . . And any technological change which results in the maintenance of a given total stock with a lessened throughput (that is, less production and consumption) is clearly a gain.[6]

Economies of scale

The basic economic phenomenon of increasing returns to scale is indirectly responsible for a large part of our environmental difficulties. It explains why many of our goods and products are produced by large companies in large factories. The principle states that when all input factors are increased at the same time in the same proportion, output

[4] Karl L. Guntermann, "Cost-Benefit Analysis and the Economics of Air Pollution" in *Real Estate and Urban Land Analysis.* Edited by James R. Cooper and Karl L. Guntermann. (Lexington, Mass.: D. C. Heath & Company, 1974), pp. 151–63.

[5] *Wall Street Journal* 187, no. 59 (March 25, 1976), p. 1.

[6] Kenneth E. Boulding, "The Economics of the Coming Spaceship Earth," in *Environmental Quality in a Growing Economy.* Edited by Henry Jarrett. (Baltimore: Johns Hopkins Press for Resources for the Future, 1966), pp. 9–10.

may be increased by an even greater proportionate amount. The key is, as those readers who have been students of economics may remember, that *all* inputs are increased. Decreasing returns may occur when some inputs are increased, while others are held constant or increased by a smaller proportionate amount.

Since many production processes go through a stage of increasing returns to scale, there is a natural tendency for firms to expand the size of their manufacturing facilities to take advantage of the increased output. And, of course, the number of managers and other support personnel and facilities must also be expanded. Along with the greater output of goods and products, however, is also produced a proportionately greater quantity of pollutants. In other words, the undesirable output obtains the scalar effects, just as do the desirable outputs. Thus, the smoke, soot, and chemical pollutants *may* be increased more than two times with a doubling of factory size (if technological improvements to control pollution are not incorporated into the new factory).

On the other side, it should be noted that the higher productivity and profit levels emanating from larger-scale operations may enable firms to expend larger amounts to curtail or limit environmental pollutants. Whether firms voluntarily incur such costs often determines what net effect the increased size of operations has on the environment.

The steel industry in Pittsburgh provides a good example of the stages of physical growth, environmental pollution, and subsequent cleanup. The industry's plants expanded through the 1940s, emitting ever-increasing amounts of pollutants. During the 1950s, however, a concerted, largely voluntary, community-industry program resulted in substantial cleanup efforts by the industry, removal of dilapidated business structures from downtown, and construction of many new, modern buildings in Pittsburgh's "golden triangle." Industry leaders saw curtailment of pollution as an absolute necessity for the continued viability, and even survival, of the city. And many external costs were internalized through the expenditure of retained profits, obtained from operations based upon efficiencies of scale.

Other types of developments and projects may also have potential environmental advantages, as well as disadvantages, resulting from scalar size. Although large shopping centers create environmental problems (such as traffic, water and waste disposal, and inharmonious relationships with neighboring residential areas) one large shopping center may be less environmentally damaging than several smaller ones. And one large, well-planned residential area may contain more adequate environmental safeguards than several smaller developments. For example, the larger development can utilize one water system, one sewage disposal system, and one system of other municipal services. Smaller, less well-planned areas may place proportionately larger burdens upon the community and the environment. Thus, some current environmental legislation may have the effect of defeating the potential benefits from economies of scale.

Cost-benefit analysis

We have already noted the principle that the marginal costs of identifying, measuring and enforcing environmental protection measures should not exceed the value of the marginal benefit to be derived. While the principle is a valid proposition of economic theory, it is often a hazardous and tenuous basis upon which to make many types of decisions.

Hazards stem from the difficulties of quantifying both sides of the equation. First, the costs associated with environmental preservation or cleanup may be extremely high. The direct costs of installing special equipment, water and sewage treatment systems, water runoff retaining ponds, special landscaping, traffic facilitation and control devices, and so on, may easily double the cost of a project. Additionally, however, indirect costs may be even higher and virtually impossible to measure. The costs of preserving or restoring the environment may involve extending or enlarging the area's transportation system (for example, the Disney World development in Central Florida which required an expansion of the highway system for many miles in all directions), the provision of additional water and sewage facilities and other municipal services, or the curtailment of some private rights and privileges (perhaps limiting the use of private automobiles in smog-susceptible areas such as Los Angeles, Phoenix, or Washington, D.C.).

The benefits obtained by incurring such costs are usually even more difficult to measure. What is the value of the prevention of disease and early death from smoke and chemical pollution for an undeterminable number of residents of an area? What is the value of preventing consumers from being poisoned by the mercury found in fish products from Lake Erie? And what is the value of wildlife preservation, clear streams, and aesthetic appeal of residential, commercial, or even industrial developments?

Cost-benefit analysis is used to attempt the measurement of such costs and benefits. Costs are conceptually easier to measure because they involve capital outlays, capitalized expenditures, or outflows. Benefits, however, often involve nonfinancial matters. The cost of preventing mercury contamination of Lake Erie may be quantifiable; the benefits are more subjective.

To utilize cost-benefit analysis, some measurement of the benefits, as well as the costs, must be undertaken. The income to the Lake Erie fishing industry would be one of the benefits in the example. The average earning power of the people who would otherwise die from mercury poisoning, for the average length of life curtailed, might be the measure of another major benefit. This average benefit would be applied to the estimated number of people so benefited, and the total earning power saved would be discounted at the appropriate rate for human life. Other, less major benefits such as the preservation of safe swimming and plant life in the lake would be included.

Although the task may be difficult, values can be estimated for the various benefits. As can be seen, the benefits are usually measured by the value of damages avoided. Such values will often require large amounts of judgment and informed guesses. As Guntermann concludes, however: ". . . even rough estimates of damages are better than none at all and may allow those in a policy position to make more rational control decisions."[7] Nevertheless, the nature of the estimates and the types of judgments entering into them should be clearly understood by policy-makers in deciding the types and amounts of environmental preservation efforts to be undertaken.

TRENDS AND THE FUTURE

The previous sections hopefully provide some idea of the outpouring of legislation designed to counteract specific aspects of environmental degradation. Although the various federal laws do not directly address the problems and issues of land-use control, several of them contain general references or inferences to land-use regulation. For example, the Water Pollution Control Act of 1972 refers to land-use control as one means of achieving the goals of reduced pollution of rivers and lakes. And the Clean Air Act of 1970 specifies that land-use controls and state review of new sources of air pollution be utilized to achieve and maintain national air quality standards.

Even more directly, however, the additional front-end costs imposed both by federal and state environmental legislation forebode a restructuring of costs and priorities. Whether the marginal benefits will prove to equal the marginal costs to alleviate the perceived difficulties can only be ascertained over the long-term future. Even whether the laws and regulations come close to accomplishing their stated objectives, no matter what level of cost is incurred, is perhaps a more realistic question to pose. Given the numerous federal and state programs that have failed totally or partially, the issue seems a fair one to pose.

Another observation is apparent: the state and federal legislative response to environmental concerns has resulted in a hodgepodge of requirements and regulations to cover the concerns of the moment. Pamela C. Mack terms this the "ad hoc approach" and demonstrates that such an approach to other types of concerns has often produced unintended

---

[7] Guntermann, "Cost-Benefit Analysis," p. 162.

results which turned out to be worse than the original problems.[8] Her principal concern, however, is that although the various environmental laws contain important land-use implications, they are not coordinated in any comprehensive land-use policy. Such laws may even be counter-productive. "For example, implementation of the water act could mean sewer moratoriums in prime suburban areas. The developer would then seek land further out where sewer permits are available. Thus, leapfrog development occurs and results in more urban sprawl."[9]

Finally, it seems clear that environmental concerns and legislation have been spawned by growth—demographic and economic. People generate pollution, and more people generate more pollution. And when combined with continually increasing levels of production of every conceivable type of consumer good, pollution has reached unacceptable magnitudes. As Ralph R. Widner has stated: "Most of our concerns with the problems of growth now center upon the undesired consequences that flow from the development of a metropolitanized, land-hungry, high-energy, high-consumption society."[10] These consequences have taxed the capacity of the air, the lakes, the oceans, and natural resources —all of which seemed to have infinite capacity only a few years ago. Thus, growth control policies and laws will inevitably be intertwined with environmental policies and laws. The combined impact upon land use and development can only involve more government involvement and control. Such government control must attempt to balance the often conflicting demands of private property rights, environmental preservation, and economic advancement.

It seems likely that the future role of land-use determination and real estate development will be regarded as a matter for public concern. Private property rights will be increasingly constrained by laws and regulations expressing the public's concern for the environment, growth control, and efficiency in land utilization. Land seems destined to be increasingly regarded as a public resource; developers will find their alternatives limited and buffeted by often costly, sometimes capricious, but almost always serious and searching public review.

SUMMARY

Increasing concern about preservation of the environment has produced additional factors that must be considered in real estate develop-

---

[8] Pamela C. Mack, "Piecemeal Approach Dilutes Federal Environmental Laws," *Mortgage Banker* 34, no. 12 (September 1974), pp. 6–10.

[9] Ibid., p. 7.

[10] Ralph R. Widner, "State Growth and Federal Policies: A Reassessment of Responsibilities," in *Management and Control of Growth*, vol. 3 (Washington, D.C.: Urban Land Institute, 1975), p. 404.

ment and investment. These factors often result in increased costs of development for projects to meet various requirements imposed by federal, state, and local governments. Criteria for maintenance of water and air quality, disposal of solid waste, control of noise, protection of drinking water supplies, and preservation of coastal zones have been mandated by federal legislation. Requirements for environmental impact reports, the purchase or control of environmentally endangered lands, and regulation of local planning and zoning procedures have been undertaken by some states.

The dramatic rise of environmental concern during the last ten years undoubtedly stems from such phenomena as the increasing population and population shifts, industrialization and urbanization of society, unprecedented economic prosperity, the struggle for full civil rights by minority groups, and the realization that energy supplies and other natural resources are not unlimited. Although the resulting legislation and administrative structures have expressed the country's desire to preserve the environment, severe burdens have sometimes been placed upon real estate development. In addition to the added direct costs, developers may also incur indirect costs through changed traffic patterns, shifts in migratory patterns, encouragement of developments that may be less efficient, and imposition of requirements that do not accomplish their stated objectives. The justification for the added costs must be the internalization of a development's total costs, including environmental charges.

In determining whether environmental costs should be imposed, the economic principle that the additional benefits should at least equal the added costs should prevail. In attempting to implement the principle, policy-makers should consider such economic concepts as externalities, marginal cost pricing, efficiencies of scale, and cost-benefit ratios. Their proper use and measurement would produce costing and pricing policies that reflect the value placed by society upon a clean, healthful environment.

QUESTIONS FOR REVIEW

1. What environmental legislation has been enacted by your state's legislature within the past ten years? In what ways does it affect real estate development?
2. How could air pollution affect real estate values? Do you believe it is in the best interest of real estate developers to allow pollution to increase? Why or why not?
3. What is the role of the Environmental Protection Agency? Identify some of the laws administered by the agency.
4. Explain the economic principle that should determine the level of costs

that should be imposed upon developers and consumers for environmental preservation.

5. What is the nature of cost-benefit analysis, and how does it relate to the analysis of environmental legislation and programs?
6. How may some types of environmental requirements encourage less efficient developments?
7. How does marginal cost pricing relate to internalization of the costs of environmental preservation?

REFERENCES

Beaton, William R., and Bond, Robert J. *Real Estate.* Pacific Palisades, Calif.: Goodyear Publishing Co., 1976, chap. 25.

Boulding, Kenneth E. "The Economics of the Coming Spaceship Earth," in *Environmental Quality in a Growing Economy.* Edited by Henry Jarrett. Baltimore: Johns Hopkins Press for Resources for the Future, 1966, pp. 9–10.

Guntermann, Karl L. "Cost-Benefit Analysis and the Economics of Air Pollution," in *Real Estate and Urban Land Analysis.* Edited by James R. Cooper and Karl L. Guntermann. Lexington, Mass.: D. C. Heath & Co., 1974, pp. 151–63.

Hodges, Allan A. "California Environmental Laws Challenge Real Estate and Finance Industries." *Mortgage Banker* 36, no. 1 (October 1975): 42–48.

Mortgage Banker 34, no. 12 (September 1974). (Entire issue is devoted to articles on environmental matters.)

Pearson, Karl G. *Real Estate Principles and Practices.* Columbus, Ohio: Grid Publishing Co., 1973, chap. 26.

Urban Land Institute. *Management and Control of Growth,* vols. 1, 2, and 3. Washington, D.C.: Urban Land Institute, 1975.

chapter 19

URBAN TRANSPORTATION AND REAL ESTATE DEVELOPMENT

CITIES BEGAN when there was sufficient surplus agricultural production to support an urban population, when sanitary facilities permitted a dense aggregation of persons to survive, and when transportation had progressed sufficiently to provide the urban population with a market for its goods and services. As transportation became more efficient and less costly, the market increased in size and the city grew in population and area. At the same time, the internal structure of the urban area was reflecting changes in transportation technology. The city and transportation evolved simultaneously to their present state. Our urban transportation problem today stems, in large part, from the necessity to adapt improved transportation methods to cities developed in response to yesterday's technology.

Each of us can recount the major symptoms of our urban transportation problem: traffic jams, insufficient parking, mass transit that is deficient in both quality and quantity of service, air pollution, and so on. The problem has instigated legislation, experimentation, and considerable analysis, some of which is summarized in this chapter.

URBAN TRANSPORTATION SYSTEM

Urban transportation should be viewed as an integrated system. The physical components of the system are streets, highways, railways, airways, and ancillary structures such as parking facilities, airports, and transit terminals. These facilities are used by automobiles, mass transit, and aircraft in moving persons and goods within and among cities.

Analysis of urban transportation in an integrated system involves considering all modes of transportation used to move goods and persons from their origin to final destination in the urban area. The system is a "market" in which the supply of transportation service and the demand for its use could conceptually reach equilibrium. In the short run, the equilibrium is constrained by a fixed transportation network. In the long run, the equilibrium would be attained when the overall level of service generated by the system is balanced by the willingness to pay by all beneficiaries. Users, property owners, and other taxpayers would be willing to pay the cost entailed by this system, but would not be willing to pay for further improvements.

Manheim points out that the transportation system is not an end in itself.[1] The system exists to fulfill policy decisions made in both the private and public sectors of our economy. Policy decisions typically relate to only one subsystem or component of the system, such as rapid rail transit or improvement of a single arterial highway route. These policy decisions must be made after considering the repercussions throughout the system, including traffic diversion and traffic generation. In making these decisions, the direct and indirect impacts of transportation on both users and nonusers of the system should be recognized.

User benefits

Improvement in highways provides user benefits such as increased safety, lower vehicle operating costs, time saving, and reduced strain and annoyance of driving. Viewed in another manner, accidents, vehicle operating expenses, time spent in travel, and the discomforts associated with travel are user disbenefits in that they represent real costs to the private motorist and to the commercial user. The social costs of accidents, loss of time, and discomfort defy exact valuation in dollars. Accidents involving personal injury or property damage, however, result in loss to society of productive capacity which otherwise would be available. Medical expenses and payments for property damage express the quantifiable cost of accidents to the individuals and concerns involved.

The value of time losses is another intangible cost. Estimates of time saving involve consideration of these factors: (a) the actual total amount of time lost by various classes of vehicles because of traffic conditions and (b) the value of the unit of time. The mobility of the motor vehicle and the ability to vary its speed and path of movement in accordance with the whims and objectives of certain classes of drivers makes measurement of time loss difficult. There is also the problem, especially for the noncommercial driver, of assigning a dollar value to the loss of time.

---

[1] Marvin L. Manheim, "Principles of Transport Systems Analysis," *Papers—Seventh Annual Meeting: Transportation Reseach Forum, 1966* (Oxford, Ind.: Richard B. Cross Co., 1966), p. 11.

Certain measurable costs which enter into the operation of the vehicle, such as fuel and the wages of drivers in commercial vehicles, are directly affected by loss of time.

Even greater difficulties have blocked attempts to assign a dollar value to the intangible benefits of reduced discomfort and strain experienced by the motorist traveling a freeway or other highway-type facility. Although quantification is impractical, limited-access highways and other highway improvements theoretically increase the comfort and pleasure of the motorist in some proportion to increases in average speed and to decreases in the frequency and magnitude of necessary changes in speed resulting from stops, turns, and slow traffic.

Vehicle operating costs are the most directly and easily measured user costs. Vehicle operating costs can be separated into fixed costs (such as interest, depreciation, license fees and taxes, insurance, driver's wages, and supervision) and variable costs (such as gasoline, oil, tires, and maintenance). Only the costs that vary directly with distance and speed of travel, such as gasoline, oil, and maintenance expenses, are typically used to indicate vehicle operating costs. Fairly dependable estimates can be made of these costs.

Other user benefits are attained by diversion of traffic from alternate routes. Diversion of traffic and consequent relief of congestion on alternative routes give benefits to users of the latter routes that otherwise would not have been obtained.

Benefit-cost ratios have been developed and used by engineers to determine the feasibility of construction of highways and the order of priority of construction. These ratios are concerned mostly with the user (or direct) benefits discussed above. Benefit-cost ratios provide part of the information needed for policy decisions in community planning, but additional information must be obtained, such as the value which the community attaches to savings in travel time and reduced accident risk, the capital costs of the improvement, and the opportunity costs foregone by investment in a highway facility instead of some other form of community improvement. Wingo has pointed out that social income from the project must be matched with social costs, and these may not be identical to money savings or money costs.[2]

Transportation and the value of urban sites

The value of an urban site depends upon the type and intensity of use of urban sites; accessibility, in turn, is inversely related to the sum of transport costs from other sites in the urban area. These transport costs reflect user benefits that depend upon the urban transport system.

---

[2] Lowdon Wingo, Jr., *Transportation and Urban Land* (Washington, D.C.: Resources for the Future, 1960), p. 112.

The value of an urban site is determined by the amount that must be paid to hire it from its next best use. Its value, then, is an opportunity cost. And when a site's use changes to a more profitable use such as a retail store, a warehouse, or residence, it may earn a surplus above the price paid for its original use. A retail store in an area served by a new traffic artery may receive this surplus or abnormal profit because of its increased accessibility.

Whether the value of the urban site increases because of its greater accessibility will depend upon the monopoly position enjoyed by that site. If landlords have strong bargaining positions by virtue of an inelastic supply of sites of that type and the need for the service of the site increases, then they can raise the rent, and site value will increase. Apartment owners may be able to raise the rent of a tenant who has experienced reduced transportation costs. Owners of a single-family residence may find that their homes have increased in value for the same reason.

In a dynamic world, these abnormal profits continually arise as relative accessibility changes for particular sites. However, these profits can vanish as more firms enter the market or as the character of the neighborhood or trade area changes. An improvement in transportation can make alternative sites available and, thus, destroy the "monopoly" position of certain areas of the community, such as the central business district. The intensity of use of such areas and the values of sites would be reduced in response to the changing supply conditions.

Empirical studies. The conception and implementation of the national system of interstate and defense highways by the federal-aid highway acts of 1944 and 1956 greatly accelerated interest in the economic influence of motor transportation on urban communities. A large number of empirical studies of the impact of highway improvements have been completed since the inception of the interstate system.[3] These empirical studies differed in objective, type of highway improvement studied, geographic area analyzed, data used to measure the changes attributed to the highway improvement, methodology used in the process of measurement, and their findings. Consequently, no definitive statement can be made concerning the effect of a particular type of highway improvement on property values in its vicinity. However, there is evidence to support a generalization that increased urban land values are associated with a highway improvement.

One synopsis of several studies involving 183 properties encom-

---

[3] Research on highway impact has been summarized in Massachusetts Department of Public Works, *Social and Economic Aspects of Highways,* publication no. 2: "Review of Important Studies and Selected Bibliography" (Boston, 1961), and Warren A. Pillsbury, *The Economic and Social Effects of Highway Improvement: An Annotated Bibliography* (Charlottesville: Virginia Council of Highway Investigation and Research, 1961).

passing all types of land uses showed that only 20 properties exhibited a decline in annual percentage change of property value (in constant dollars) following a highway improvement.[4] The studies varied in methodology and type of highway facility analyzed. Some were only "before and after" analyses, which makes it difficult to separate the effect of the highway on land values from other factors in the local economy. Other investigations used study and control areas or correlation and regression analysis to isolate the effect of the highway. Some of the studies dealt with the location of an intraurban freeway or expressway, while other studies examined the impact of bypasses.

One of the better empirical studies examined the economic impact of Massachusetts Route 128, a 55-mile limited-access highway around Boston.[5] Surveys were made of industrial and commercial developments in an area one mile wide on either side of the highway. As "controls," industries which were located in the area before the new highway was opened were studied to determine benefits they might receive from the highway. A second control group was comprised of plants built after the highway had opened in areas not influenced by Route 128.

The industrial survey disclosed that of the new plants on Route 128, 22 percent were either new companies or new branches, and 78 percent were relocated from other areas. The relocated plants came predominately from in-town areas. The industrial expansion along the route was significant and strengthened the tax base of the communities; there was an increase in the value of land for industrial uses from $1,000–$1,500 per acre prior to the highway to $8,000–$26,000 per acre afterwards.

Companies gave a number of reasons for locating on Route 128, in-

---

[4] U.S. Department of Commerce, *Final Report of the Highway Cost Allocation Study,* part 6: *Data Concerning the Economic and Social Effects of Highway Improvement* (Washington, D.C.: U.S. Government Printing Office, 1961), Table 6–1, p. 7. Nineteen of the 20 observations experienced a decline of 1 to 5 percent, while only one observation experienced a fall of 5 percent; 137 of the observations fell between a zero increase in value and an increase of 20 percent. When the 183 observations are classified as to type of land use and a median annual percentage change of property value is determined in constant dollars, the ranking of median change shows (*a*) a median annual percentage increase in value of about 18 percent for industrial land use (11 observations); (*b*) a median increase of almost 13 percent for unimproved land (22 observations); (*c*) a median increase of over 10 percent for commercial land (33 observations); and (*d*) a median increase of over 8 percent for residential land (85 observations). The total of all classified uses had a median annual percentage increase of slightly less than 10 percent (151 observations), and unspecified types of land use had a median increase of less than 6 percent (32 observations). The type of land use evidently is a determinant of the amount of value change experienced. Speculation could account for the large value change experienced by unimproved land. Conversion of land to industrial and commercial uses could account for the greater median percentage changes in value experienced by the industrial and commercial land.

[5] A. J. Bone, *Economic Impact Study of Massachusetts Route 128* (Cambridge: Massachusetts Institute of Technology, 1958).

cluding the need for land for expansion, accessibility for commercial purposes, an attractive site, labor market considerations, accessibility for employees, advertising value of the site, and adequate parking facilities. A factor that was very important in motivating these industries was the desire for ease of regional access, implying desire for freedom from traffic and parking congestion prevalent in downtown areas. The urge to decentralize was evident. Companies representing more than half of the total investment on Route 128 considered only suburban locations as being feasible.

The effect which Route 128 had upon residential development was examined, particularly in the towns of Lexington and Needham. The study method considered residential development in an area close to the highway both before and after the highway had been built, and trends before and after in a control area having similar characteristics. This study area divided Lexington into two parts. An area one-half mile from Route 128, and running parallel to it, was the study area; the remainder of the town was the control area.

Access distance zones were established to determine the effects of access to Route 128 upon residential growth. These zones contain privately owned land within 250 feet of a street which could be reached by driving less than one and one-half miles from the nearest Route 128 interchange. The control zone included all privately owned and public land within 250 feet of streets more than one and one-half miles from the interchanges. Three access zones were studied in the belief that highway influence is related to ease of access to the highway. Zone 1 was up to one-half mile from the interchange, zone 2 was from one-half to one mile, and zone 3 from one to one and one-half miles.

In Lexington, a bedroom city for Boston, assessed valuation increased 180 percent in the land area adjacent to the Route 128, compared to only 83 percent in the rest of the town. The cumulative number of occupancy permits issued in the adjacent band increased 538 percent, and house density increased 112 percent, compared with 383 percent and 58 percent respectively in the control area. The number of residential real estate sales also showed a greater increase in the adjacent band than in the control area. However, the average prices of the houses sold were less along Route 128. In comparing access distance and control zones, a somewhat similar, but less marked difference between Route 128 and the other areas was observed. Activity was especially spirited in the zero to one-half mile zone around the interchange.

In the city of Needham, more building occurred in the area adjacent to the highway than in the control area. The rate of increase in building permits in residential sales also exceeded that of the control area. In both Lexington and Needham, some part of the residential development took place because of the convenience offered by Route 128.

The methodology used in the Route 128 study is typical of a large number of empirical studies completed after construction of the interstate system. The findings of these several studies, however, vary significantly. Furthermore, many of the impact investigations using study and control areas mention that changes in land or property values in the study area can only be considered as net benefits if the economic activity producing the change, such as industry moving to the area, would not have located elsewhere in the community in the absence of the highway improvement.

Regional effects

Transportation innovations and improvements free resources needed to overcome the cost of movement and permit these resources to be used otherwise for production. The changes in national product following a highway improvement between regions have been examined by Tinbergen[6] and Bos and Koyck.[7] Their analyses emphasize direct and indirect increases in productivity following the improved transport route and suggest that user benefits are only one form of the total benefit to the regional economy. Further investment in productive capacity may be made following a reduction in transportation costs.

Empirical studies. · Studies that assess the intraregional influence of new, improved, or relocated transportation routes on relatively large areas, such as a county, state, or larger region, typically find net benefits accruing to the area. In one study of the Sunshine State Parkway in Florida, the potential impact on the basic determinants of the economic growth in the state were studied.[8] The geographic area affected by the highway was delineated and divided into five districts, each composed of several counties. The authors concluded the following facts: (*a*) Tourism will benefit most from the highway. The volume of tourists will increase and there will be greater dispersion of tourists throughout the state. Seasonal fluctuations in the tourist industry should be reduced. (*b*) The highway is not expected to increase population migration to Florida, but the dispersion of population within the state may be affected. (*c*) The market structure of the state will become more integrated and the spatial arrangement of wholesaling and industry will be affected. (*d*) The volume of agricultural output will not be appreciably

[6] J. Tinbergen, "The Appraisal of Road Construction: Two Calculation Schemes," *Review of Economics and Statistics* (August 1957), pp. 241–49.

[7] H. C. Bos and L. M. Koyck, "The Appraisal of Road Construction Projects: A Practical Example," *Review of Economics and Statistics* (February 1961), pp. 13–26.

[8] First Research Corporation, *An Economic Study on the Proposed Florida Sunshine State Parkway* (New York, 1956).

increased, but truck transportation will experience a competitive advantage over rail. The new route was expected to affect volume not only where tourists were concerned, but it was expected to alter the pattern of organization of economic activities within the state.

Another regional study analyzing the economic benefits of two possible locations of an interstate highway between Phoenix and Brenda, Arizona, considered gains and losses in business volume, agricultural production, gasoline and sales tax revenues, real estate taxes, and highway user costs savings.[9] The net gain for the new route to be constructed 35 miles south of the alternate, existing route was estimated to exceed $39 million. The principal contribution to this gain would be additional agricultural production resulting from increased accessibility to relatively uncultivated land.

Once again, empirical studies measuring the net benefits accruing to a region may fail to reflect losses of population and industry from places outside the chosen area of influence. In this respect, the size of the area analyzed can influence the extent of net benefits realized. When the size of the area is enlarged, net benefits attributed to a smaller area could disappear. For benefits to exist, the increase in regional economic activity must be the result of an investment that otherwise would not occur using resources that otherwise would be unemployed.[10] A transportation route that makes previously unused resources or agricultural land available could produce significant benefits. Even if increased volumes of business activity or population in the region are not forthcoming, however, rearrangement of existing economic activity would be expected.

Transportation and urban land use

Generalized explanations of the spatial dimensions of urban activities include the concentric circle hypothesis and the sector hypothesis.[11] Transportation is a factor in these descriptive schemes of urban land use, together with other economic, social, and physical factors.

Concentric circle hypothesis. Transportation is a central force in the concentric circle hypothesis. The central business district, for instance, is near the center of the zones of land uses because it is the area of optimum accessibility, where transportation facilities tend to converge. The "zone of workers' homes" is located near their place of work, in part, to minimize transport costs. Zones of more expensive apartments

---

[9] Stanley Womer Associates, *Economic Study of Alternate Proposals for the Construction of Route I–10 between Phoenix and Brenda, Arizona* (Phoenix: Arizona Highway Department, 1958).

[10] Herbert Mohring and Mitchell Harwitz, *Highway Benefits: An Analytical Framework* (Chicago: Northwestern University Press, 1962), p. 143.

[11] See the discussion in Chapter 2 for further descriptions.

and single-family residences appear further from the center, in part, because of the lower sensitivity of their occupants to transport costs. Expansion of the city occurs from the inner zones and depends primarily upon the mobility of the population. Land values are indexes of mobility, with the highest land values found at the point of greatest mobility. The urban transportation system permits and channels mobility and, therefore, is a major determinant of land values.

Sector theory. The sector theory of urban land use is primarily concerned with the pattern and determinants of residential land use. The reasonably homogeneous sectors typically grow outward to the periphery of the city. Automobile transportation can cause the outward movement to skip over undeveloped land. Generally, high-quality residential areas follow lines of most rapid transportation and are pulled to areas of natural beauty or other advantageous residential sites. Intermediate and some low-quality residential areas are drawn along. Other low-price residential areas develop around places of work to minimize commuting costs.

Systems of activities. Another descriptive scheme of urban land patterns views urban land uses as systems of activities.[12] In this explanation, the physical structure of cities reflects the institutionalized activities of groups and individuals, each of whom is engaged in routine actions and random movements. Once institutions evolve, they interact in numerous cross-relationships. The repetitive activities of individuals in groups create establishments, which use specific locations for carrying on that activity. Establishments occupy the physical structure and give concrete evidence of institutionalized activities and their cross-relationships. Establishments are linked together by the movement of persons, goods, and information that are, in turn, reflections of the linkages between firms and individuals. The "pulls" exerted by the multitude of linkages with other establishments determine the spatial arrangement of urban land uses.

Transportation is an establishment of the systems-of-activity explanation of urban land-use patterns. Transportation is connected with the activities of all urban establishments and provides the means of movement between locations. Transportation facilities develop in response to the need for them, but the new patterns of land use which evolve require yet additional needs.

The system-of-activities scheme shows that the relationship between land use and transportation is reciprocal and that the cause and effect between increased differentiation of urban activity systems and accompanying developments in transportation cannot be ascertained. Market

---

[12] John Rannells, *The Core of the City: A Pilot Study of Changing Land Uses in the Central Business District* (New York: Columbia University Press, 1956), and Robert B. Mitchell and Chester Rapkin, *Urban Traffic: A Function of Land Use* (New York: Columbia University Press, 1954).

imperfections, together with the relatively fixed transport system and physical structures, cause establishments to adapt to the existing physical arrangement, even though the internal activities and relationships among these establishments might be better served by some other arrangement.

Hypothesis of median location. The hypothesis of median location has been advanced as an explanation of the tendency for nonprofit urban land uses, retail stores, office buildings, wholesaling outlets, financial institutions, industrial uses, and residences to locate at the geographical median in a time-cost sense with respect to (*a*) the resources utilized by a particular urban activity; (*b*) the people or businesses to which the activity is related; and (*c*) the customers that it serves.[13] For each particular land use, the median responds to different factors. The type of clientele, their incomes, the goods and services produced or sold, the market area served, the type of workers employed, and the shopping areas and work places of homeowners determine the median applicable to each particular urban land use. The concept of median location has been used to describe the tendency of natural areas to form within the urban community as land uses of the same general type respond to similar sets of locational determinants.[14] Median location involves the concept of minimization of costs or maximization of profit or net satisfaction, which, in turn, lies behind location theory and other explanations of urban land-use structure.

Empirical studies. The value of an urban site is determined by its most profitable use. An improvement in the transportation system can result in a site's becoming more valuable because it becomes capable of generating higher net income or greater amenities. The site may be utilized more intensively for its original purpose, or it may have become suitable for a different use. The greatest change in value typically results from a change in land use, perhaps from residential to commercial or from rural to urban use. Since conversion of use often is impeded by zoning and other factors, the change in site value may precede actual redevelopment.

Generalizations from empirical studies of the effects of transportation on urban land use suffer because of the diversity of route improvements and urban areas affected. Improvements may be a bypass, an outerbelt, an arterial route through the city, a limited-access freeway, an expressway without limited access, or a one-way street. Each of these improvements may have its effects on land use determined in part by existing development and zoning in the area traversed.

Several studies indicate that if other circumstances are favorable,

---

[13] James A. Quinn, "The Hypothesis of Median Location," *American Sociological Review,* April 1943, pp. 148–56.

[14] Paul Hatt, "The Concept of Natural Area," *American Sociological Review,* August 1946, pp. 423–27.

there will be a conversion of existing uses and development of vacant land to commercial use following a highway improvement.[15] Studies have found commercial and business uses developing more rapidly near downtown and along the highway improvements. Another study found these land uses developing most rapidly along the major access routes and feeder streets to a limited-access freeway. In many studies, the time needed for conversion was believed to be too long to allow the full impact of the highway improvement to be felt.

Surveys of business people indicate that highways are important in the location decisions of commercial and business land uses. One survey of 52 establishments engaged in retailing or wholesaling and distribution activities showed that 19 of the respondents considered factors of highway access and highway exposure to be the dominant criteria in the selection of a location.[16] Fourteen other respondents indicated factors related to the highway network were important. A Dallas study found that advantages for businesses located along the expressway included accessibility, freedom from congestion, expansion potential, and advertising and parking advantages.[17]

The location of industry along or near a highway improvement is often observed in highway impact studies.[18] All types of highway improvements seem to attract industrial development, but circumferential

---

[15] The following studies are indicative of the research in this area, but are not inclusive: William G. Adkins, *Effects of the Dallas Central Expressway on Land Values and Land Use,* bulletin 6 (College Station, Tex.: Transportation Institute, 1957); Bone, *Economic Impact Study of Massachusetts Route 128;* Donald D. Carroll et al., *The Economic Impact of Highway Development upon Land Use and Values: Development of Methodology and Analysis of Selected Highway Segments in Minnesota* (Minneapolis: University of Minnesota, 1958); George W. Childs, *The Influence of Limited Access Highways on Land Value and Land Use: The Lexington, Virginia, By-pass* (Charlottesville: Virginia Council of Highway Investigation and Research, 1958); Richard Duke, "The Effects of a Depressed Expressway—A Detroit Case Study," *Appraisal Journal,* October 1958; John C. Frey et al., *The Economic and Social Impact of Highways: A Process Summary of the Monroeville Case Study* (University Park: Pennsylvania State University, Agricultural Experiment Station, 1960); James H. Lemly, *Expressway Influence on Land Use and Value, Atlanta, 1941–1956,* paper no. 10 (Atlanta: Georgia State College of Business Administration, Bureau of Business and Economic Research); David R. Levin, "Land Use Development and the Highway Interchange," mimeographed (Washington, D.C.: Bureau of Public Roads, 1960).

[16] Real Estate Research Corporation, *Highway Network as a Factor in the Selection of Commercial and Industrial Locations* (Chicago, 1958), p. 18.

[17] Adkins, *Effects of the Dallas Central Expressway.*

[18] The following references are suggestive of the many studies reporting this type of highway impact: Donald Bowersox, *Influence of Highways on Selection of Six Industrial Locations,* bulletin 268 (Washington, D.C.: Highway Research Board, 1960); Bureau of Business Research, *The Effect of the Louisville-Watterson Expressway on Land Use and Land Values and Lexington Northern Belt Line* (Lexington: University of Kentucky, 1960); John R. Bochert, *Beltline Commercial-Industrial Development: A Case Study in the Minneapolis–St. Paul Metropolitan Area* (St. Paul: University of Minnesota, 1960).

or beltline highways and interchanges may be particularly attractive. Beltlines allow access to the highway net, while making space available for one-story plants, parking, and expansion. Determination of the relative importance of highways in interregional and intraregional plant location decisions is hampered by the complexity of the decision and the variation among industries with respect to labor needs, market and material orientation, plant requirements, and need to maintain contact with other businesses. A survey of 68 manufacturing and processing firms found that a single highway was rarely the foremost consideration in the location and success of an industrial enterprise.[19] A more important factor is the entire network of highways, of which the particular road is but a part. The transportation network determines access to markets, to the labor force, and to needed materials.

Highway improvements can make land available for residential use, and several studies indicate that residential development occurred along the highway or within its area of influence.[20] Other studies, however, did not find residential development stimulated by the highway.[21] Zoning, the degree of development of the area prior to the highway improvement, business uses along the facility, traffic volume, and noise have been advanced as reasons for lack of residential development. Opinion surveys were used in several studies to determine whether the highway was an important influence on the residential land use.[22] Considerable diversity of opinion existed with respect to whether or not the highway was a material consideration when buying; whether the noise was bothersome; and whether the facility depressed or enhanced the value of their property. In general, a majority felt that the facility had little or no adverse effect on property values. Opinions of homeowners were found to be conditioned by factors such as proximity to the highway, with more residents approving as their distance from the facility increased; by the type of facility, with a parkway preferred to a

[19] Real Estate Research Corporation, *Highway Network as a Factor.*

[20] The following studies are indicative of research in this area, but are not inclusive: *Traffic Impact: A Study of the Effects of Selected Roads on Residential Living in Southern Westchester* (White Plains, N.Y.; Westchester County Department of Planning, 1954); Bone, *Economic Impact Study of Massachusetts Route 128;* William Adkins and Alton Tieken, *Economic Impacts of Expressways in San Antonio* (College Station, Tex.: Transportation Institute, 1958); Bayard O. Wheeler, "The Effect of Freeway Access upon Suburban Real Property Values," part 5, *Allocation of Road and Street Costs* (Seattle: University of Washington, 1956).

[21] Duke, "The Effects of a Depressed Expressway"; Dale Gustafson and Everett G. Smith, Jr., *A Highway Change in Changing Fairbault* (Minneapolis: University of Minnesota, 1959); Norris & Elder, consulting engineers, *A 15-Year Study of Land Values and Land Use along the Gulf Freeway in the City of Houston, Texas* (Houston, 1956).

[22] Adkins, *Effects of the Dallas Central Expressway;* Adkins and Tieken, *Economic Impacts of Expressways in San Antonio;* Bone, *Economic Impact Study of Massachusetts Route 128;* Maryland State Roads Commission, *Three Economic Impact Studies on a Portion of the Baltimore Beltway* (Annapolis, 1960).

freeway and a depressed highway preferred to an elevated highway; and by the presence of children in the household. The question can be asked, of course, as to whether the opinions of people who bought or owned homes in an affected area are representative of the attitudes of the entire population.

The traffic artery as an urban land use

The location of urban streets and highways ideally is based in large part upon the criterion of greatest efficiency in movement of people and goods, although the exercise of political and various environmental factors may have significant roles in site selection. The preservation of historical landmarks and cemeteries, for instance, may affect route location. The relatively high cost of a route in areas already developed with valuable residential, commercial, or industrial property may result in the facility's traversing blighted or vacant tracts. Urban arterial routes in many American cities have served to accomplish at least the demolition aspect of urban renewal.

Several alternate locations for an arterial route usually are considered. Origin and destination surveys indicate major desire lines of the urban traffic pattern and the corridors in which arterial routes should be located. Assignment of traffic to the route determines whether a major street, expressway, freeway, or parkway is required. Prediction of the volume and type of traffic involves estimating these items: (a) normal growth of traffic; (b) additional traffic generated by the new or improved facility; (c) traffic resulting from land uses which will locate near the facility; (d) number of zone-to-zone trips that each type of expected land development will produce; and (e) comparative advantage of the route for zone-to-zone traffic considering travel distance, travel times, economies and ease of operation of vehicles, and safety of operation on alternate routes. Estimates of the cost of right-of-way and construction, user benefits, the feasibility of construction of the facility in stages, and the ease of handling traffic during construction also are considered in choosing among alternate locations.

The reciprocal nature of urban land uses and street and highway location is evident. The land-use pattern creates a demand for routes by generating traffic. The predicted volume and character of future traffic influences the type of facility to be constructed, and the present and prospective land-use pattern typically dominates the choice of location.

URBAN TRANSPORTATION PROBLEM

The most vexing urban transportation problem is moving people to and from areas of high population and work place density, that is, the twice-a-day "rush hour," which in many American cities should be "hours."[23] The increasing number of cross-haul and reverse commuter trip patterns has aggravated the rush hour problem. Cross-haul trips arise from dispersion of places of origin and destination, resulting in people's wishing to traverse the central city during periods of peak load on the system.

The problem has been aggravated by declining use of mass transit, which is caught in the vicious cycle of lower patronage, rising operating costs, declining service, and still lower levels of patronage. The decentralization of American cities has rendered mass transit relatively uneconomical in many cities or subareas. Decentralization has at least been permitted by the advent of the automobile, but it cannot solely be attributed to the changing transportation technology. Some dispersion would be expected, given our increasing urban population. Certainly many families have been attracted by the provision of relatively inexpensive, good quality, single-family housing in the outskirts of the city and the tax concessions promoting homeownership.

Mass transit also has suffered from the changing character of downtown, which has become the location for offices and other activities of a professional nature requiring face-to-face contact. Office workers and professional persons comprise one group of demanders wishing access to the central city. At the other extreme are the low-income service workers employed in the supporting retail and service establishments remaining in the central city. It may be difficult for these contrasting groups to accept the same quality of transportation service or even to travel together. Social stratification may hinder joint use of transit, as it alters the spatial pattern of demand.

The automobile has made parking a part of the urban transportation problem. Inadequacy of parking is believed to be associated with decentralization of the central business district and, consequently, with the level of central business district land values. Shopping centers, office buildings, and industrial plants have located in suburban areas to accommodate, in part, customers and workers seeking adequate parking. Dispersion of retail stores has slowed the rate of growth in central business district retail sales and land values.

While it is too early to determine the extent to which the trend toward urban decentralization has been altered, undoubtedly the Arab oil embargo of 1973 and the subsequent increases in energy costs will have a significant impact upon cities' future development. Although many people seem to have adjusted to an approximate doubling of gasoline prices between 1973 and 1976, some urban residents are likely

---

[23] John Meyer, John Kain, and Martin Wohl, *The Urban Transportation Problem* (Cambridge, Mass.: Harvard University Press, 1966), pp. 360–67.

to elect housing closer to their city's core to save the added transport costs. And if gasoline prices should again double as widely expected, the impact upon urban development could be dramatic. The efficiencies of mass transit, coupled with newer, better vehicles, could produce a reversal of attitudes toward mass transit.

Fragmentation of government in our metropolitan areas also contributes to the urban transportation problem. Historically, there has been an inability to plan for the urban region or to coordinate municipal efforts in providing an integrated transportation system. The fact that investment in the urban transportation system is made by federal, state, and local governments is a further complication. The interstate system is administered by the Federal Highway Administration, and the federal government provides 90 percent of the cost of constructing these facilities. Other arterial routes in the urban area include state or federal highways, with part of the cost of construction and maintenance being shared between these governments and the municipalities. Mass transit often is privately owned, but it is regulated by the state. Once again, there is a problem of shared administrative authority, with federal, state, and local agencies struggling to define their respective spheres of influence in providing an adequate transportation system.

Alleviation of the urban transportation problem

Technological development. The urban transportation problem may be alleviated in the long run by technological advances that permit a greater level of service at the same cost. Several promising transportation innovations are presently in various stages of development and experimentation. These improvements center around making mass transit more attractive to the user and improving the efficiency of the urban transportation system.

The limited-stop express bus, complete with stewardess, perhaps traveling on its own restricted highway, is an effort to improve both attractiveness and efficiency. High-speed rail transportation traveling up to 150 miles per hour is now in limited use. V/STOL (vertical and short takeoff and landing craft) are in use in a few cities.[24] V/STOL permits connection between major air terminals and the central city or suburb and can serve short-haul traffic between central cities within the urban region. V/STOL will be less costly and less complex than the helicopter presently used to provide the link between air terminal and destination. The major requirements for a workable V/STOL system are slow-flying dependable aircraft capable of a short approach and

[24] P. Y. Davoud and W. T. Heaslip, "The Prospect of V/STOL Aircraft in Future Airline Operations," *Papers of the Transportation Research Forum* (Oxford, Ind.: Richard B. Cross Co., 1967), pp. 55–56.

takeoff and V/STOL ports in or near the central city, perhaps on parking structures, docks, or over rail yards. Other innovations are TACV (tracked air-cushion vehicle), a magnetic suspension vehicle in the 400-mile per hour class, and tube vehicles employing electric power or using a gravity vacuum tube.[25] All of these very rapid facilities are in the theoretical-experimental stage.

In addition to equipment innovations, techniques for improving the flow of traffic within the system are being explored. CARS (computer aided routing system), for instance, is an attempt to provide economical mass transit to low-density population areas such as the suburb.[26] Both the distribution and collection problems are aided by dynamic routing and scheduling of the evening and morning rush hours. In the evening, persons arriving on a train must be dispersed to available vehicles, which follow an optimal route to distribute the commuters to their homes. In the morning rush hour, the commuter must be picked up at different times and places and brought to the transit station.

Project CARS also is known as Dial-A-Ride, a personalized door-to-door public transportation service.[27] The Dial-A-Ride experiment used a fleet of small vehicles to serve customer requests as they were received. There were no fixed routes and schedules. Customers called the local Dial-A-Ride number and informed the operator that they wanted to make a trip, giving such information as their origin, desired destination, and number of passengers. A computer used this information to develop the optimum routes, as well as sequencing the stops, for the vehicles. Dial-A-Ride is adaptable both for the "many-to-one" situation, where travelers come from a variety of points of origin to a single destination, and the more complex "many-to-many" situation.

Intergovernmental cooperation. The manifest inability of local governments to coordinate their planning and actions resulted in federal legislation promoting a coordinated urban transportation system. The U.S. Department of Transportation was established in 1966 for the purpose of developing national transportation policies and programs conducive to the provision of expedient, safe, efficient, and convenient transportation service at reasonable cost.[28] The department has the responsibility of coordinating federal transportation programs and proj-

---

[25] Edward J. Ward, "A Progress Report on High Speed Ground Transportation (R & D)," *Papers of the Transportation Research Forum* (Oxford, Ind.: Richard B. Cross Co., 1967), pp. 297–309.

[26] Nigel H. M. Wilson and Daniel Roos, "CARS: Computer Aided Routing System," *Papers of the Transportation Research Forum* (Oxford, Ind.: Richard B. Cross Co., 1966), pp. 129–40.

[27] Daniel Roos et al., *The Dial-A-Ride Transportation System: Summary Report* (Cambridge: Massachusetts Institute of Technology, 1971).

[28] Grant M. Davis, *The Department of Transportation* (Lexington, Mass.: Heath Lexington Books, 1970), pp. 152–58.

ects involving federal, state, and local governmental agencies. Federal agencies engaged in various aspects of transportation prior to 1966 either were transferred to the department or had their functions placed under the jurisdiction of the department. The Department of Transportation presently has six operating agencies: U.S. Coast Guard, Federal Aviation Administration, Federal Highway Administration, Federal Railroad Administration, Urban Mass Transportation Administration, and St. Lawrence Development Corporation. Although the Federal Highway Administration, primarily through the Bureau of Public Roads, and the Federal Railroad Administration, through its Office of High Speed Ground Transportation, are active in research and development affecting the urban transportation system, it is the Urban Mass Transportation Administration which has the principal impact on our urban transportation problem.

The Urban Mass Transportation Administration administers the Urban Mass Transportation Act of 1964 and the Urban Mass Transportation Assistance Act of 1970. The Urban Mass Transportation Act of 1964 provided federal assistance for acquisition or improvement of facilities or equipment associated with mass transportation; for research, development, and demonstration projects related to urban mass transportation; engineering, planning, and designing mass transportation systems; and training personnel in managerial, technical, and professional positions related to urban mass transportation.[29]

The 1964 act authorized federal grants for up to two-thirds of the "net project cost" of a coordinated urban mass transit system that otherwise could not be financed. Net project cost is gross cost less the amount that could be financed from operating revenues. The applicant must be a public body with areawide responsibility for an urban system.

The Urban Mass Transportation Act of 1970 furthers federal assistance to urban mass transit.[30] The secretary of transportation was authorized to incur additional obligations up to $5 billion to finance grants and loans to state and local agencies for acquisition, construction, reconstruction, and improvement of mass transit. Loans can be made for advance acquisition of facilities, right-of-way, station sites, and related items, including payments for relocating families and businesses and the net cost of property management to cover the holding period. Facilities purchased must be used within a reasonable time (no longer than ten years), and the original loan may be repaid using part of a federal grant made at that time for construction of the system. The local share (one-third) of the net project cost of construction can come from public sources or from a local private transit system.

---

[29] U.S., Congress, Public Law 88–365, 88th Congress, 2d session, 1964.

[30] U.S., Congress, Public Law 91–453, 91st Congress, 2d session, 1970.

Congress has recognized that the nation's mass transportation needs will require a federal commitment of at least $10 billion over a 12-year period. The 1970 act is the first major step toward making this commitment. The funds, however, are for acquisition and construction of plant and equipment; mass transit operating deficits are not federally subsidized. Applicants for federal assistance under the 1970 act are to have a comprehensive transportation planning agency, encouraging a coordinated transport system for the urban region.

Planning for transportation. More rational use of land would promote a more efficient, less costly transportation system. Proper planning and zoning, by controlling the density of development and preventing urban sprawl, contribute to alleviation of the transportation problem. Planning for an efficient structure of urban land uses for the sole purpose of minimizing transportation costs, however, misplaces priorities. The transportation system exists to serve urban areas, which grow and change in response to a great number of determinants, only one of which is transportation.

Regional transportation planning. Comprehensive planning for the transportation system in the urban region copes with a critical aspect of the transportation problem. Areawide transportation planning exists in most metropolitan areas, although the experts' recommendations may not be implemented. The availability of federal funds for urban areas having a comprehensive plan, however, provides the coordinating agency with considerable power in debates over arterial route locations, mass transit programs, and other improvements.

The Northeast Corridor project is an example of large-scale coordinated transportation planning for a region. The Northeast Corridor project was initiated by the Northeast Corridor Act of 1964 and is presently administered by the Department of Transportation. The project involves planning a transportation system for the megalopolis stretching from southern New Hampshire to Virginia and from the East Coast to Appalachia. All modes of transportation are considered, with the planning horizon extending to 1980 and 1990.

The number of alternate transportation systems available for this region and the number and variety of impacts precluded using a single model for predictive purposes. Consequently, a "PSP" (problem-solving process) model was developed, which structured the analysis in seven levels (see Figure 19-1).[31] Analysis proceeds from policy decisions at Level I through successive levels to the design and operation of the transportation system. At each level of analysis, a number of alternatives are considered, and the results of their implementation are determined.

---

[31] H. W. Bruck, Marvin L. Manheim, and Paul W. Shuldiner, "Transportation Systems Planning as a Process: The Northeast Corridor Example," *Annals of the Transportation Research Forum* (Oxford, Ind.: Richard B. Cross Co., 1967), pp. 67–98.

FIGURE 19–1

Multilevel structure of the problem-solving process

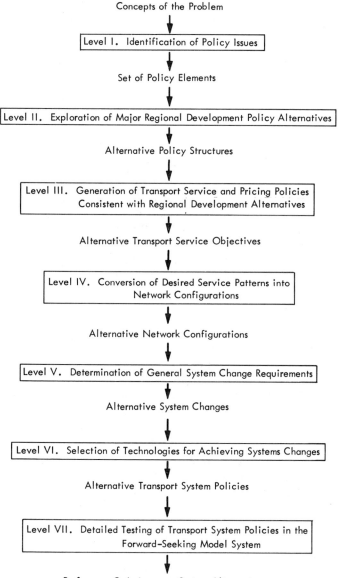

Source: H. W. Bruck, Marvin L. Manheim, and Paul W. Shuldiner, "Transportation Systems Planning as a Process: The Northeast Corridor Example," *Annals of the Transportation Research Forum* (1967), p. 82.

These consequences are evaluated and the preferred results serve as the beginning point for analysis at the next level. Detailed analysis is performed at the seventh level, which uses a "forward-seeking model system" to test a relatively small number of alternative transportation systems (see Figure 19–2). The forward-seeking model predicts outcomes, which are ranked according to preference. The methodology of the Northeast Corridor project reflects the enormous complexity of a planning process that must consider all modes of transportation, route configurations, levels of service, pricing policies, and the impact of alternative actions on users and nonusers.

Pricing alternative modes. The urban transportation problem may require pricing alternative modes of transportation to discourage the use of the automobile and to utilize mass transit more effectively. Vickrey suggests a two-pronged approach: (*a*) increase the cost of automobile usage in urban areas and (*b*) use differential fares for mass transit, with a lower fare during off-peak travel periods.[32] Differential fares for peak and off-peak periods should permit transit to operate more efficiently, with less over-capacity in nonrush hours and a higher quality of service during rush hours. Pricing street use sufficiently high would reduce automobile congestion, allowing rapid transit to provide a better level of service.

SUMMARY

The urban transportation system encompasses all modes of transportation, the network of streets and highways, parking facilities, railways, airways and terminal facilities, and the vehicles that move over the transportation network. The system is in continuous evolution, but it fails to adapt as rapidly as changing needs. Budgetary constraints permit only certain components of the system to be altered at any one time. A rapid transit route is initiated or extended, new vehicles are placed in service, a revised timetable for transit is developed, a new highway is located, streets are widened or converted to one-way traffic, additional parking facilities are provided in the central business district—the list of improvements to the system is endless.

Each change in a component of the system can affect other parts and can have an impact upon users and nonusers, and upon urban property values and land use. User benefits often are expressed in benefit-cost analyses employed to determine the feasibility and priority of transportation improvements, although benefit-cost ratios represent only partial analysis of the problem. Empirical studies have been made on the effects

---

[32] William S. Vickrey, "Pricing in Urban and Suburban Transport," *American Economic Review, Papers and Proceedings*, 53, no. 2 (May 1963): 452–65.

FIGURE 19–2

Northeast Corridor Project (sequence of operations in a run of the forward-seeking model system)

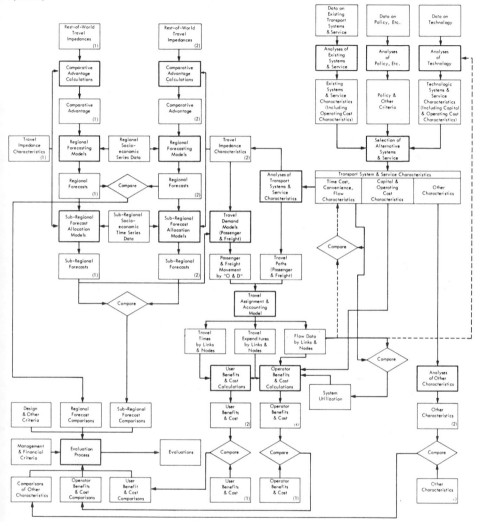

Source: H. W. Bruck, Marvin L. Manheim, and Paul W. Shuldiner, "Transportation Systems Planning as a Process: The Northeast Corridor Example," *Annals of the Transportation Research Forum* (1967), p. 86.

of highways and parking on urban land values, retail sales, and urban land use. Unfortunately, the results of these studies provide only broad generalizations of the expected direction of impact.

The complexity of the urban transportation system and its slowness to adapt to changing needs are reflected in our multifaceted urban transportation problem. Dimensions of the problem include rush hour demands upon the system, the mass transit dilemma, inadequacy of parking facilities in congested areas, interagency cooperation in coping with areawide transportation problems and, of course, the means of financing an acceptable level of service.

Public agencies and private organizations are involved with all aspects of the problem. Technological developments in equipment and the transportation network are being explored. Governmental cooperation is encouraged by formation of regional transportation planning agencies and by centralization of federal activities in the Department of Transportation. Methodologies for analyzing complex systems are being developed, such as the Northeast Corridor project discussed in this chapter. Consideration is being given to pricing policies that would promote the use of transit relative to the private automobile. The urban transportation problem is persistent, but abatement of the more critical aspects is on the foreseeable horizon. Ultimately, the condition of our urban transportation will depend upon the willingness of beneficiaries to finance it.

QUESTIONS FOR REVIEW

1. Discuss the following statement: the urban transportation system should be designed solely to minimize the costs of movement of persons and goods.
2. What are *user benefits?* Why is consideration of user benefits only partial analysis of the feasibility of a highway improvement?
3. How is an improvement in transportation related in theory to the value of an urban site?
4. What highway-related factors are considered important in industrial location?
5. Why is it impossible to generalize from empirical studies of highway benefits?
6. Itemize the components of the urban transportation problem in a particular urban area. What are the current programs for alleviation of these local problems? What will be the effects of these programs on the entire system? On urban land values? On urban land use?

REFERENCES

Alonso, William. *Location and Land Use: Toward a General Theory of Land Rent.* Cambridge, Mass.: Harvard University Press, 1965.

Meyer, John et al. *The Urban Transportation Problem.* Cambridge, Mass.: Harvard University Press, 1966.

Mills, Edwin S. *Urban Economics.* Glenview, Ill.: Scott, Foresman and Co., 1972, pp. 192–217.

Mohring, Herbert, and Harwitz, Mitchell. *Highway Benefits: An Analytical Framework.* Chicago: Northwestern University Press, 1962.

Thompson, Wilbur R. *A Preface to Urban Economics.* Baltimore: Johns Hopkins Press for Resources for the Future, 1965, pp. 333–79.

Vickrey, William S. "Pricing in Urban and Suburban Transport," *American Economic Review, Papers and Proceedings* 53, no. 2 (1963): 452–65.

Wingo, Lowdon, Jr. *Transportation and Urban Land.* Washington, D.C.: Resources for the Future, 1960.

OVERVIEW

READERS WHO HAVE PERUSED this volume from the beginning may have become very impatient with the authors. "When," they may ask, "are they going to discuss the important aspects of real estate?" Most of our readers, we suspect, became acquainted with our book as the result of curiosity about the real estate business or because they heard that real estate might be a profitable investment. The successful ventures of real estate investors and operators appear daily in the popular press. Syndication, joint ventures, tax-free income, and other terms have become part of our vocabulary. Books such as Nickerson's, *How I Turned $1,000 into a Million in Real Estate in My Spare Time,*[1] are not uncommon. Readers, whose eagerness has been whetted by this material, may wonder when the authors will explain the secrets of how to make a killing in real estate.

The authors believe that they have discussed the attributes which cause real estate to be a profitable and satisfying investment for many persons and a successful occupation for others. There would be no real estate success stories without the basic want-satisfying power of the economic good. Consequently, a portion of this treatise has been devoted to the characteristics of real estate that yield productivity and value.

Analytical approach. An analytical approach to real estate investment is proposed in which market value and investment value are central concepts. Appraisal methodologies provide techniques for estimating market value, which can be adapted to computations of investment value or justified investment price. Other return on investment calculations were examined as additional criteria for ranking investment alternatives.

---

[1] William Nickerson, *How I Turned $1,000 into a Million in Real Estate in My Spare Time* (New York: Simon and Schuster, 1959).

These measurements of the relative value or worth of a real estate investment in Chapters 4 and 5 are only the mathematical end product of the many factors affecting the future productivity and risk of the investment. These physical, locational, economic, and social determinants are too numerous to recount in detail in this brief overview. However, among major factors affecting real estate value are the physical characteristics of land and improvements; the character of the neighborhood or district in which the property is located; the market conditions in which the property is competing; the economic strength and stability of the local, regional, and national economies; property rights transferred and other legal aspects; form of ownership; financing; tax factors; and the public actions, controls, and regulations affecting the property and its future productivity.

Real estate business. Several sections of this book are concerned with various types of real estate businesses. In the minds of most people, the real estate business is most closely associated with real estate brokerage. Brokers and their sales staffs are the most visible occupation in the real estate business. Most of us have or will utilize their services in buying or selling our homes and other properties. The real estate business, however, encompasses a variety of occupations in the private and public sectors related to land development and construction, financing, management, law, appraisal, consulting, and brokerage. Each of these occupations has its specialties. Real estate brokerage, for instance, includes persons who specialize in one type of real estate (such as single-family residences or industrial properties), in negotiating leases, in arranging exchanges, and in effecting transactions.

The real estate business utilizes the economic and institutional aspects of real estate in organizing for the planning, production, financing, and marketing of the product. When persons in the business are creative in combining the various determinants of value, a profit should materialize. The real estate business has always offered great potential for creativity and resultant imitation as others attempt to duplicate successful ventures. We can all recount the history of several recent "innovations," such as 95 percent conventional loans, condominiums and quadraminiums, planned unit developments, new towns, resort communities and ranchettes for $10 down and $10 a month, wraparound mortgages, equity participations, joint ventures and syndications, and prefabrication and modular units; the list continually lengthens. These newsworthy developments in the real estate business obtain the most publicity. Many of these developments have been mentioned in this text, although the authors believe that detailed treatment should be reserved for advanced courses.

Administrative processes. Another major emphasis of this text has been on the decision-making process. In this regard, the authors have chosen to differentiate between microadministration and macroadministration of our real estate resources. Microadministration occurs in both the private and public sectors of our economy. Individuals and firms in the private sector combine land and improvements to create useful properties and valuable assets that are attractive to investors. The functions of production, financing, marketing, and management in the real estate business are manifestations of microadministration. Microadministration in the public sector by the executive branch, the legislature, the judicial branch, and the bureaucracy result in laws, regulations, and programs which have macroeffects. Zoning regulations, building codes, federal housing, community development, the property tax, and transportation policies and subsidies are examples of publicly enacted rules and programs which become inputs to the microadministration of our real estate resources. They comprise part of the list of determinants of real estate productivity and value. We have chosen to call these results of public sector decision-making macroadministration, to reflect their far-reaching and pervasive effects.

PROGNOSIS

The excitement of real estate as an academic field of study comes from two principal sources. First, there is the challenge of adapting the theory, concepts, and analytical methods from several disciplines in the process of analyzing the production of real estate and its investment qualities. Then, there is the need to impose ever-changing institutional factors upon the analytical framework.

Theory and concepts. Real estate "principles," removed of their institutional wrappings, are economic principles. Economic models are used to analyze urban economies and local housing markets. Recent developments in regional and urban economics blend with materials often included in real estate courses, particularly in the analyses of urban economies and the location of firms and households. The analysis of real estate investments claims kinship with the financial analysis of the firm, capital budgeting, and security analysis. General marketing and management theories and concepts are applicable to the real estate business. City planning, sociology, psychology, and geography make their contributions. Advancements in the state of the art in real estate investment analysis and appraisal; in housing market research; in understanding the motivations of investors, homebuyers, and renters; in the organization for efficient production and marketing of the product; and in other aspects of the field of real estate undoubtedly will come from continued adaptation of work in related fields to real estate problems.

Institutional factors. The study of real estate is differentiated from other academic fields by the institutional aspects of the subject. Legal aspects, for instance, are a large part of these institutional characteristics.

The law mirrors the attitudes and mores of our society. In recent years, statutory law and court interpretations have combined in a manner that affects real estate investment and the actions of persons involved in the real estate business. Civil rights legislation, open housing, and court decisions in antitrust cases are in the forefront of the evolution of the law.

The provision of new housing in our cities is primarily dependent upon the economic and demographic factors underlying the demand for shelter. However, enabling legislation permitting ownership of condominium units has created a new housing submarket. Legislation permitting the formation of real estate investment trusts has enabled the small investor to obtain the benefits and risks of real estate investments. Enactment of each new federal tax bill has repercussions on the profitability of real estate investment. The so-called tax shelters available to real estate investors were created initially to stimulate investment in needed social capital. However, in the Tax Reform Acts of 1969 and 1976, Congress pared away some of the shelters it previously created.

The real estate cycle is wasteful of our precious human and natural resources and has been ruinous to many individuals and firms in the real estate business. To a large extent, the fluctuations in real estate construction have been attributable to monetary conditions. New channels for the flow of funds into the mortgage market are opening through innovations under the auspices of the Federal Home Loan Bank Board, the Federal Home Loan Mortgage Corporation, the Federal National Mortgage Association, and the Government National Mortgage Association. Federal housing (Section 235, Section 8, and so on) has continued in quantity even in periods of tight monetary policy. The combined impact of these actions has the potential of containing fluctuations in housing starts within tolerable limits. Further efforts to stabilize the availability of credit and construction are to be expected.

The physical character of the housing unit is progressing to modular components and modular units, and further innovations in construction techniques and materials are being encouraged by government programs. Concomitant with new construction techniques is the industrialization of housing, applying the concept of mass production to the housing industry. Large-scale developments worthy of being called "new towns" have been fairly common. The profitability of real estate developments has attracted insurance companies into joint ventures with developers who obtain the needed long-term commitments of equity capital for very large-scale developments. American industry has also experimented with large-scale real estate development as potentially profitable activity and, in some instances, as a market for their products. The scale of developments in general has become larger. Real estate development firms are often merged or controlled by industrial corporations, providing them with the capital necessary to undertake larger projects. The scale of development is reflected in the diversification of the firms in the real estate business. A single firm and its subsidiaries may include a mortgage company, a brokerage company, a construction company, an investment company to buy and hold land and other properties, and a property management company.

Government involvement with real estate is increasing. Our nation is experiencing changes in social attitudes as we become more wealthy and urbanized. Acquisition of the means to obtain a better quality of life and increased interdependency in an urban environment reduce our tolerance for nuisances, for inequities in the distribution of opportunities, and for self-seeking actions considered to be detrimental to the social welfare. At the same time, our falling level of tolerance has been met by the rising intensity of certain nuisances, such as congestion and pollution. Government regulation, subsidies, and other actions are invoked by these conditions. Hopefully, our democratic form of government will continue to permit the will of the majority of our citizens to be reflected in these actions. The authors of this basic text find that, over time, a larger part of their courses in real estate principles is devoted to what we have called "macroadministration" of our real estate resources. This trend is expected to continue.

Appendixes

Laws prohibiting discrimination in housing

FEDERAL FAIR HOUSING LAW—APRIL 11, 1968

Title VIII of the Civil Rights Act of 1968, which is better known as the Federal Fair Housing Law, bans discrimination in the sale, rental, and leasing of housing in the United States because of race, color, religion, or national origin.

Under this law the following are typical discriminatory acts which are declared illegal:

1. Refusing to sell, rent, or deal with any person.
2. Making different terms and conditions for buying or renting housing.
3. Advertising housing as available to only certain buyers.
4. Denial of availability of housing for inspection for sale or rental when it actually is available.
5. Persuading someone to sell housing by telling him minority groups are moving in—commonly called blockbusting.
6. Denying or making different home loan terms by lender.
7. Denying or limiting the use of real estate services to anyone.
8. Coercing, intimidating, or interfering with any person in the exercise or enjoyment of these federal rights.

Enforcement procedures and penalties are as follows:

1. An aggrieved person may file a complaint with HUD which can attempt to conciliate after investigation.
2. A civil suit may be filed by an individual in federal or state court.
3. The U.S. Department of Justice can investigate and bring suit if the Attorney General has reasonable cause to believe there is a pattern or

practice of resistance to the act, or if the Attorney General believes that the case is one of general public importance.

4. The court may issue an injunction requiring or preventing the home or apartment sale or rental.

5. *Damages may be assessed against the defendant.*

Properties and people covered by this law include all housing in the United States except the rental of apartments up to four families if the owner occupies one, religious organizations and private clubs, and home owners who do not use the services of a real estate broker or advertise discriminatorily in the sale of a single-family home.

These exemptions are negated by the Ohio Fair Housing Act of 1969 and a provision of the Federal Civil Rights Act of 1866 as interpreted by the U.S. Supreme Court in a case known as *Jones* v. *Mayer Co.,* decided in 1968.

U.S. SUPREME COURT DECISION

Jones v. Mayer Co. (June 17, 1968)

In a case charging racial discrimination in the sale of housing emanating from St. Louis known as *Jones* v. *Mayer Co.,* the U.S. Supreme Court ruled that a law, enacted at the close of the Civil War in 1866 and reenacted in 1870 to protect the freed slaves and assure them equal citizenship, was applicable today in housing.

The law "bars all racial discrimination, private as well as public, in the sale or rental of property."

This law and its present-day application make it clear that racial discrimination by anyone in the sale or rental of property is illegal.

Under this mandate, no exemptions such as are permitted under the 1968 Federal Fair Housing Act can exist. No discrimination on a racial basis in housing can exist.

This ruling is enforceable by the federal district court or an appropriate state court.

STATE OF OHIO FAIR HOUSING LAW (HOUSE BILL 432)

As of November 12, 1969, when sections 4112.01 and 4112.99 of the Ohio Revised Code became effective, discrimination in the sale, rental, or leasing of housing on the basis of race, color, religion, national origin, or ancestry became illegal.

This law prohibits the following actions or activities in housing in Ohio by property owners or their agents.

1. Falsely denying availability.
2. Refusing to show.

3. Refusing to sell, rent, etc., because of race, religion, or ethnic background of any actual or prospective owner, occupant, or user of the property.
4. Inquiring into the keeping of records relating to property sales or rentals concerning race, religion, or ethnic origin.
5. Advertising or circulating any statement indicating a preference or limitation based on race, religion, or ethnic origin in connection with sales or rentals.
6. Aiding or abetting the commitment of any unlawfully discriminatory act or obstructing another person from complying with the law.
7. Induce or solicit real estate activity by representing that the presence or anticipated presence of persons of any race, religion, etc., will have any of the following effects:
   a) Lowering of property value.
   b) Change the race, religious, or ethnic composition of the area.
   c) An increase in criminal or antisocial behavior.

Real estate agents, following the mandates of this law, are protected from harassment and intimidation. Threats by neighbors for retaliation against real estate brokers in the event a home is sold to unwanted neighbors are not allowed and are violations of the law.

All real property in the State of Ohio is covered by this law. There are no exceptions! From single-family homes to vacant lots—from hotel rooms to graveyards.

Courses of action open to aggrieved persons:

1. The court may order affirmative action.
2. The court may issue an injunction if it finds a discriminatory practice has occurred or is about to occur.
3. Temporary or permanent injunctions may be granted by the court.
4. Actual damages and court costs may be assessed against the guilty party.
5. A penalty fine of not less than $100 nor more than $500 may be assessed.

Other provisions of the Ohio law are:

1. The accused may not be compelled to testify against himself.
2. Attorneys will be provided for plaintiffs if they don't have the money to hire one.
3. A bond must be posted by the plaintiff before temporary relief or a restraining order will be issued.

Administrative structure
for planning and zoning
in Gainesville, Florida

The top level in the administrative decision-making structure of Gainesville is the City Commission. The Commission is composed of five members elected by the citizens of the city at large. It is the legislative body of the city and thus must approve any changes in the zoning ordinance.

Directly below the City Commission is the City Planning Commission, or Plan Board, which is the main advisory body to the City Commission. Its function is to provide advice to the City Commission in the areas of current and future planning. The Plan Board is composed of seven lay members appointed by the City Commission. The appointive system presumably minimizes political pressure to which elected officials might be subject from constituent groups, thus allowing them to act more independently in reviewing controversial issues. In appointing these members, the legislative body is required to select a cross-section of citizens in order to prevent minority interest from being suppressed.

To assist it in carrying out its functions, the Planning Commission hires a full-time, paid Plan Board staff. At present the staff is composed of nine professionally trained urban planners, most of whom hold masters degrees in urban planning. The staff performs the research and analysis required in the formulation of planning concepts and developments. Its two main functions are (1) to plan for current needs and (2) to develop and continually update the city's Comprehensive Development Plan.

Current planning primarily involves zoning and ordinance changes. This phase is subdivided into three functions: A. Small area land use plans; B. Zoning; C. Site plan approval.

Small area land use plans

These are land use plans for small areas which the Comprehensive Plan does not include. When adopted by the City Commission, the plans are used for determining land uses in the area in the immediate future. Small area land use plans were used extensively before the city adopted a Comprehensive Plan several years ago. Since that time, these plans have generally not been needed.

Zoning

In this function, a request is filed by a property owner or his representative to change a zoning classification. The filing fee is $112. The professional staff analyzes requests in light of the city's Comprehensive Plan and small area land use plans. The Planning Commission then establishes a time and place for a public hearing on the zoning request. For this hearing, the public must be notified at least 16 days prior to the hearing. Notification is given by three methods. The first method involves publishing in a newspaper an agenda of items to be covered at the hearing and stating the change in zoning (e.g., "RI-A to Mobile Home Park"). The second method is to place a sign on the subject property stating the agenda and zoning change request. Third, all property owners within 300 feet of the site to be rezoned must be notified by mail. If more than 20 percent of these owners object to the rezoning, the vote of the City Commission must be 4 out of 5 to accomplish the zoning change.

Then comes the public hearing. The Plan Board listens to the advice of the staff, arguments of the property owner, and anyone who is against the zoning change. The request is then voted upon by the Board. If the decision confirms the zoning change, it is passed on to the City Commission for final consideration.

Site plan approval

The approval of site planning and development by the Plan Board is required for multiunit residential developments of four or more units and for shopping centers. The Board's decision about a site plan is final; if there is any appeal, it must be made directly to the courts. Site planning includes all the physical aspects of the development. It involves matters such as architectural style, layout of the land, location of buildings on the site, access to parking areas, landscaping, etc.

PLANNING FOR THE FUTURE

The second major function of the planning staff is to develop a future planning guide. This guide is better known as the Comprehensive Plan.

It is a land use plan for the growth of an area figured usually 10 years ahead of the present. It includes present and proposed land uses such as the type and number of recreational areas to be located in the city, proposed highways, police and fire stations, schools, and areas designated for residential, commercial, and industrial use.

Six background studies support the Comprehensive Plan. First and most important is the population study, designed to provide present population data and future growth statistics. Second is the economic base study, which analyzes the city's economy. These two studies attempt to predict the size and economic needs of the city 10 years hence. Third is the land use study, providing a physical inventory of all land in the area at the present time. Fourth is a recreation study, which provides an inventory of the recreational areas and attempts to relate the city's recreational needs to its future size and geographic distribution. Fifth is a physiographic study showing all soil conditions and qualities. Last is the land use and transportation study.

Another important agency in the zoning process is the Board of Adjustment. It is a semijudicial body appointed by the City Commission for the purpose of providing flexibility in the zoning ordinances. Its decisions are final; the only appeal is to the courts. It provides flexibility in two ways. First, the Board of Adjustment has the power to vary the strict letter of the zoning ordinance, i.e., to grant a variance. Although a variance does not involve changing the zoning law, it does involve changing the use requirements. To obtain a variance, the owner must show that he has a hardship (not caused by himself) which prevents him from following the normal zoning requirements. The Board will consider the request for a variance in accordance with criteria established by the Board.

The second method used in providing flexibility is through special exceptions to the zoning law. Under this method, the Board has the power to allow a use that is not a matter of right in a given area. By applying criteria established by the Plan Board, the Board of Adjustment can change the zoning limitations to allow a prohibited type of use for a given parcel.

Case situation: Queensworth Apartments

Mr. Queensworth recently purchased an obsolete, deteriorating factory building on 14.5 acres of land near the central business district. He hoped to use the building, a 160,000 sq. ft., three-story building, as a boutique-oriented shopping center.

A market analysis showed a lack of demand for the shopping center, but it suggested that the salvage market would accept the building's materials at high prices. The land was shown to be ideal for apartment usage in a strong apartment market.

Mr. Queensworth paid $175,000 for the property. Within two months thereafter, he sold two small commercial frontage sites for $60,000 and netted $120,000 from the sale of scrap metal, hard pine, water tank, air-conditioner, etc. Thus, he more than recaptured his initial cash investment, and he owned an excellent apartment site of 9.5 acres (net of internal streets) plus commercial frontage sites of approximately 2.5 acres.

The financial analysis indicated as Projection I shows the return that would result for apartment investors under market-based financing, rental, and expense projections. A net after-tax return of approximately 16 percent per year is shown for year 1, a return that is low for apartment investors.

Not shown in the projection are the following case facts:

1. The land is sold to the partnership at a substantial profit to Mr. Queensworth.
2. Mr. Queensworth absorbs all risks of construction cost overrun and slow rent-up. His $180,000 land sales income funds this risk.
3. Mr. Queensworth retains 80 percent of any funds remaining in the con-

Proposed Queensworth Apartments economics of apartment offering, Projection I (October 1976)

Gross annual rental income:

25 1-BR @ 700 sq. ft. @ $135/mo.	....	$　40,620
75 2-BR @ 950 sq. ft. @ $175/mo.	....	157,500
		$　198,120
Vacancy and collection loss allowance—5%	....	9,906
		$　188,214
Operating expenses @ 33% (tenants pay elec., gas)	....	62,738
Net Operating Income	....	$　125,476
Value (net income capitalized at 10.5%)	....	1,195,010
	say	$1,200,000
Loan—75%	....	$　900,000
Loan constant, 8.5% interest, 25 years	....	.0967

Cash throw-off analysis:

Net operating income	....	$　125,476
Debt service (.0967 × $900,000)	....	87,030
Cash Throw-off	....	$　38,446

Cash equity required:

Improvement cost (90,000 sq. ft. @ $11.00)	....	$　990,000
Land at cost	....	175,000
Total Cost	....	$1,165,000
Deduct loan proceeds	....	900,000
Cash Equity Required	....	$　265,000

Aftertax cash flow:

Interest at 8.5%	....	$　76,500
Depreciation—double-declining balance, 33 years	....	59,400
Total	....	$　135,900
Net operating income	....	$　125,476
First-Year Aftertax Cash Flow	....	($　10,424)

Investment position: Total equity

Sell 80% of total project for cash—20 shares at $13,250 each	....	$　265,000
Distribute first-year cash throw-off pro rata 80% of $38,446	....	$　30,957

Distribute first-year tax loss pro rata 80% of $10,424 = $8,340

Benefit for 40% taxpayer	....	3,336
Benefit for 50% taxpayer	....	4,170

Distribute first-year mortgage equity payments pro rata

80% of $10,530 = $8,424	....	8,424

Return on investment:

40% bracket taxpayers:

$$\frac{\$30,957 + 3,336 + 8,424}{\$265,000} = 16.1\% \text{ after tax}$$

50% bracket taxpayers:

$$\frac{\$30,957 + 4,170 + 8,424}{\$265,000} = 16.4\% \text{ after tax}$$

struction loan accounts at the time the permanent loan is closed. He draws no developer's fee.

4. Mr. Queensworth sells 80 percent of the equity for cash and retains 20 percent of the equity for his services.
5. The project is structured as a limited partnership.
6. All profits, losses, refinancing, and sales proceeds are distributed on a pro rata basis to investors and Mr. Queensworth based upon ownership share.

Mr. Queensworth did not think that his partnership shares would sell well based upon a 16 percent after-tax total earning and a cash flow of less than 12 percent. Thus, he worked out Projection II to improve the earnings picture.

Projection II utilizes the same market-based revenue and expense data, but it is premised upon a gross cost per sq. ft. of buildings of $10.50 as compared with $11.00 in Projection I. It also assumes an 80 percent mortgage rather than a 75 percent mortgage. This situation leads to an after-tax earning of approximately 24 percent, but it requires a higher-than-market mortgage amount and it reduces the project cost to a level that offers little or no protection from cost overruns.

Realizing the difficulties associated with Projection II, Mr. Queensworth reduced the loan amount to 75 percent and increased the cost of construction to $10.75. In reviewing market conditions, he also increased the loan interest rate from 8.5% to 9% and reduced the capitalization rate from 10.5% to 10%. This led to Projection III, which he decided was a sound structure for his project. He then prepared his pro forma financial statements upon this basis.

Throughout the three sets of calculations, Mr. Queensworth consistently retained a price of $175,000 for his land input. This was a profit to him, and it provided the financial assets needed to underwrite the risk of cost overruns.

The amount of equity money needed in the project varied from a high in Projection I of $265,000 to a low in Projection II of $165,000. The latter amount was insufficient to pay the full land price, thereby requiring that Mr. Queensworth draw $15,000 from loan proceeds at the end of the construction period. In Projection III, the equity cash of $187,000 appeared to be adequate to make the project work.

Proposed Queensworth Apartments economics of apartment offering, Projection II (October 1976)

Gross annual rental income:

25 1-BR @ 700 sq. ft. @ $135/mo.	$ 40,620
75 2-BR @ 950 sq. ft. @ $175/mo.	157,500
	$ 198,120
Vacancy and collection loss allowance—5%	9,906
	$ 188,214
Operating expenses @ 33% (tenants pay elec., gas)	62,738
Net Operating Income	$ 125,476
Value (net income capitalized at 10.5%)	1,195,010
	say $1,200,000
Loan—80%	$ 960,000
Loan constant, 8.5% interest, 25 years	.0967

Cash throw-off analysis:

Net operating income...	$ 125,476
Debt service (.0967 × $900,000)	92,732
Cash Throw-off	$ 32,744

Cash equity required:

Improvement cost (90,000 sq. ft. @ $10.50)	$ 945,000
Land at cost	175,000
Total Cost	$1,120,000
Deduct loan proceeds	960,000
Cash Equity Required	$ 160,000

Aftertax cash flow:

Interest at 8.5%	$ 81,600
Depreciation—Double-declining balance, 33 yr.	56,700
Total	$ 138,300
Net operating income	$ 125,476
First-Year Aftertax Cash Flow...................................	($ 12,824)

Investment position: Total equity

Sell 80% of total project for cash—20 shares at $8,000 each	$ 160,000
Distribute first-year cash **throw-off pro rata 80% of $38,446**	$ 25,995

Distribute first-year tax loss pro rata 80% of $12,824 = $10,259

Benefit for 40% taxpayer	4,104
Benefit for 50% taxpayer	5,130

Distribute first-year mortgage equity payments pro rata

80% of $11,132 = $8,906	8,906

Return on investment:

40% bracket taxpayers:

$$\frac{\$25,995 + 4,104 + 8,926}{\$160,000} = 24.4\% \text{ after tax}$$

50% bracket taxpayers:

$$\frac{\$25,995 + 5,130 + 8,926}{\$160,000} = 25.0\% \text{ after tax}$$

Proposed Queensworth Apartments first-year return on investment, Projection III (October 1976)

Gross annual rental income:

25 1-BR @ 700 sq. ft. @ $135/mo.	$ 40,620
75 2-BR @ 950 sq. ft. @ $175/mo.	157,500
Laundry, telephone, misc. income	2,500
	$ 200,620
Vacancy and collection loss allowance—5%	10,031
	$ 190,589
Operating expenses (tenants pay elec., gas)	63,300
Net Operating Income	$ 127,289
Value (net income capitalized at 10%)	$1,272,890
Loan—75%	$ 955,000
Loan constant, 9% interest, 25 years	.1018

Cash throw-off analysis:

Net operating income	$ 127,289
Debt service ($955,000 × .1018)	97,219
Cash Throw-off	$ 30,070

Cash equity required:

Improvement cost (90,000 sq. ft. @ $10.75)	$ 967,500
Land at cost	175,000
Total Cost	$1,142,500
Deduct loan proceeds	955,000
Cash Equity Required	$ 187,500

Aftertax cash flow:

Interest at 9%	$ 85,950
Depreciation—double-declining balance, 33 years	58,050
Total	$ 144,000
Net operating income	127,289
First-Year Aftertax Cash Flow	($ 16,711)

Investment position: Total equity

Sell 80% of total project for cash—20 shares at $9,375 each	$ 187,500
Distribute first-year cash throw-off pro rata 80% of $38,446	$ 24,056

Distribute first-year tax loss pro rata 80% of $16,711 = $13,369

Benefit for 40% taxpayer	5,347
Benefit for 50% taxpayer	6,684
Distribute first-year mortgage equity payments pro rata 80% of $11,269	9,015

Return on investment:

40% bracket taxpayers:

$$\frac{\$24,056 + 5,347 + 9,015}{\$187,500} = 20.5\% \text{ after tax}$$

50% bracket taxpayers:

$$\frac{\$24,056 + 6,684 + 9,015}{\$187,500} = 21.2\% \text{ after tax}$$

Proposed Queensworth Apartments pro forma statement of revenue and expenses

	Year 1	Year 2	Year 3	Year 4	Year 5	Year 6	Year 7	Year 8	Year 9	Year 10
Gross Annual Rental Income:										
25 1-BR @ 700 sq. ft.	$ 40,620	$ 40,620	$ 40,620	$ 41,850	$ 41,850	$ 41,850	$ 43,100	$ 43,100	$ 43,100	$ 43,100
75 2-BR @ 950 sq. ft.	157,500	157,500	157,500	162,289	162,289	162,289	167,238	167,238	167,238	167,238
Laundry, telephone, misc.	2,500	2,500	2,500	2,500	2,500	2,500	2,500	2,500	2,500	2,500
Total	$200,620	$200,620	$200,620	$200,639	$206,639	$206,639	$212,838	$212,838	$212,838	$212,838
Vacancy and collection loss allowance—5%	10,031	10,031	10,031	10,332	10,332	10,332	10,642	10,642	10,642	10,642
Effective Gross Income	$190,589	$190,589	$190,589	$196,037	$196,307	$196,307	$202,196	$202,196	$202,196	$202,196
Operating Expenses:										
Water and sewer	$ 7,000	$ 7,000	$ 7,000	$ 7,158	$ 7,150	$ 7,150	$ 7,300	$ 7,300	$ 7,300	$ 7,300
Trash service	2,500	2,500	2,500	2,650	2,650	2,650	2,800	2,800	2,800	2,800
Janitor/yard man	4,500	4,500	4,500	4,650	4,650	4,650	4,800	4,800	4,800	4,800
Painting and decorating	5,000	5,000	5,000	5,150	5,150	5,150	5,300	5,300	5,300	5,300
General repairs	2,500	2,500	2,500	2,650	2,650	2,650	2,800	2,800	2,800	2,800
Reserve for replacements	4,000	4,000	4,000	4,150	4,150	4,150	4,300	4,300	4,300	4,300
Supplies	1,000	1,000	1,000	1,150	1,150	1,150	1,300	1,300	1,300	1,300
Resident manager	8,000	8,000	8,000	8,150	8,150	8,150	8,300	8,300	8,300	8,300
Cable TV	1,300	1,300	1,300	1,450	1,450	1,450	1,600	1,600	1,600	1,600
Insurance	7,500	7,500	7,500	7,650	7,650	7,650	7,800	7,800	7,800	7,800
Property taxes	10,000	10,000	10,000	10,250	10,250	10,250	10,553	10,553	10,553	10,553
Management fee	10,000	10,000	10,000	10,150	10,150	10,150	10,300	10,300	10,300	10,300
Total Expenses	$ 63,300	$ 63,300	$ 63,300	$ 65,200	$ 65,200	$ 65,200	$ 67,153	$ 67,153	$ 67,153	$ 67,153
Net Operating Income	$127,289	$127,289	$127,289	$131,107	$131,107	$131,107	$135,043	$135,043	$135,043	$135,043

Proposed Queensworth Apartments 10-year return on investment

	Year 1	Year 2	Year 3	Year 4	Year 5	Year 6	Year 7	Year 8	Year 9	Year 10
Total Return on Investment:										
Gross revenue	$200,620	$200,620	$200,620	$206,639	$206,639	$206,639	$212,838	$212,838	$212,838	$212,838
Less vacancy and collection loss allowance—5%	10,031	10,031	10,031	10,332	10,332	10,332	10,642	10,642	10,642	10,642
Effective Gross Income	$190,589	$190,589	$190,589	$196,307	$196,307	$196,307	$202,196	$202,196	$202,196	$202,196
Less operating expenses	63,300	63,300	63,300	65,200	65,200	65,200	67,153	67,153	67,153	67,153
Net Operating Income	$127,289	$127,289	$127,289	$131,107	$131,107	$131,107	$135,043	$135,043	$135,043	$135,043
A. Deduct:										
Interest	85,950	84,936	83,830	82,625	81,312	79,880	78,320	76,619	74,765	72,744
Depreciation	58,050	54,567	51,293	48,215	45,323	42,603	40,047	37,644	35,385	33,262
Net Taxable Income	$(16,711)	$(12,214)	$ (7,834)	$ 267	$ 4,472	$ 8,624	$ 16,676	$ 20,780	$ 24,893	$ 29,037
B. Deduct:										
Debt service	$ 97,219	$ 97,219	$ 97,219	$ 97,219	$ 97,219	$ 97,219	$ 97,219	$ 97,219	$ 97,219	$ 97,219
Cash Throw-off	$ 30,070	$ 30,070	$ 30,070	$ 33,888	$ 33,888	$ 33,888	$ 37,824	$ 37,824	$ 37,824	$ 37,824
Principal Payments on Mortgage	$ 11,269	$ 12,283	$ 13,389	$ 14,594	$ 15,907	$ 17,339	$ 18,899	$ 20,600	$ 22,454	$ 24,475
Return on 80% Investors' Shares:										
Cash throw-off return on investment	12.8%	12.8%	12.8%	14.5%	14.5%	14.5%	16.1%	16.1%	16.1%	16.1%
Adjust for tax benefit (detriment) for 40% bracket taxpayer	2.9	2.1	1.3	(0.1)	(0.8)	(1.5)	(2.8)	(3.5)	(4.2)	(5.0)
Add mortgage payment value (assumes constant property value)	4.8	5.3	5.7	6.2	6.8	7.4	8.1	8.8	9.6	10.5
Total Aftertax Effective Return on Investment (property value does not change)	20.5%	20.2%	19.8%	20.6%	20.5%	20.4%	21.4%	21.4%	21.5%	21.6%

Thus a single 5% share costing $9,375 would receive $1,203 cash plus a tax refund of $267 plus a mortgage equity value of $450 in Year 1 if the above projections are correct. Note that these are only projections, even though they are based upon current market information.

FHA housing market
analysis outline

The following outline is indicative of the scope and sequence of subject matter to be considered in an overall market analysis. It does not reflect geographic submarket considerations; these can be incorporated by the analyst at appropriate points wherever feasible and to the extent required by each analysis. An abbreviated form of analytical treatment is adaptable from these components.

Preface

If a brief statement of the purpose of the analysis, i.e., the specific problem which occasioned the need for the market study, is desired, it could be included as a preface. Alternatively, it may be omitted or incorporated into a letter or memorandum of transmittal as a substitute for the preface.

Summary and conclusions

Generally, a summary is desired to provide a quick, overall perspective on the principal findings and conclusions of the analysis, preferably at the beginning rather than at the end of the report. The summary is not intended to be a résumé of the entire analysis. To achieve its purpose most effectively it should be limited to the salient statistical findings and major conclusions and presented concisely in a series of brief paragraphs in the same sequence of subject matter followed in the text. Specific page references to parallel subject matter in the text may be utilized to facilitate ready access to pertinent details.

Housing market area

1. Definition (delineation), including identification of entire area encompassed and principal cities; geographic submarkets discussed and defined.
2. Description, including:
   a. Size (total population)
   b. Major topographical features
   c. Principal transportation arteries (highway, rail, water) and distance to other urban areas
   d. General urban structure and direction of growth
   e. Special features, characteristics, or considerations
   f. Major community developments in process or planned which are germane to the present analysis
   g. Net (in or out) commutation; significance
3. Map of area.

Economy of the housing market area

1. Economic character and history
   a. General description
   b. Principal economic activities and developments—past and present
2. Employment—total, wage and salary, other
   a. Current estimate
   b. Past trend (last 8–10 years)
   c. Distribution by major industry
      (1) Current
      (2) Comparison with previous years
   d. Female employment participation rate
   e. Trend of employment participation rate
3. Discussion of principal employers
   a. Manufacturing
   b. Nonmanufacturing
   c. Military, if any (history and mission)
   d. Other
4. Unemployment
   a. Current level and composition
   b. Past trend
5. Estimated future employment
   a. Total and annual increments
   b. Analytical exposition
6. Income
   a. Average weekly wages of manufacturing workers

(1) Current level
(2) Trend since last census
b. Other data from state estimates for counties, if available
c. Estimates of current family income distribution after tax) for all families, for renter households, and for other segmental groups, if necessary

Demographic analysis

1. Population
   a. Current estimate
   b. Past trend
   c. Estimated future population—total and annual increments
   d. Net natural increase and imputed migration
   e. Distribution by age
   f. Trend of military and military-connected civilian strength, if applicable
   g. Trend of college enrollment, if applicable
2. Households
   a. Current estimate
   b. Past trend
   c. Estimated future households—total and annual increments
   d. Household size trends
   e. Military and military-connected civilian households, if applicable
      (1) Present—on-base and off-base with distribution by minor civil divisions
      (2) Projected
   f. College-oriented households, faculty and student, present and projected

Housing stock and market conditions

1. Housing supply
   a. Current estimate
   b. Past trends, including last census date
   c. Principal characteristics: last census and current estimates
      (1) Type of structure
      (2) Year built
      (3) Condition
      (4) Plumbing facilities
2. Residential building activity, by type
   a. Annually, last 10 years
   b. Monthly, January to latest month for current and previous year

    c. Units under construction
    d. Demolition and conversion trends and projections
3. Tenure of occupancy
    a. Current estimate
    b. Past trends
4. Vacancy
    a. Last census—net available
        (1) Overall, home owner, and rental
        (2) Number of units lacking one or more plumbing facilities
    b. Postal vacancy surveys—current and previous, if any, and conversion and adjustment to census concepts of owner and renter unit vacancy
    c. Other occupancy-vacancy indicators and surveys, including surveys of FHA-insured projects
    d. Current estimates—net available (qualified for units lacking one or more plumbing facilities)
        (1) Owner
        (2) Renter
        (3) Quality differentials
        (4) Evaluation
5. Mortgage market
    a. Sources and availability of funds
    b. FHA participation
    c. Interest rates and terms of mortgages
    d. Mortgage and deed recordings
6. Sales market
    a. General market conditions—strong and weak points
    b. Major subdivision activity
    c. Speculative versus contract building
    d. Marketing experience—new and existing
    e. Price trends—new and existing
    f. Unsold inventory of new houses
        (1) Price
        (2) Months unsold
        (3) Comparison with previous period, if available
    g. Houses under construction—volume and quality
    h. Foreclosures
        (1) Overall trend
        (2) FHA and other
        (3) Sales versus acquisitions
    i. Outlook
7. Rental market
    a. General market conditions—strong and weak points
    b. New rental housing, FHA and other, by years, type, and rents

      (1) General marketing experience
      (2) Competitive status with existing rental housing
    c. Rental housing under construction
      (1) Volume, type, and quality
      (2) Probable marketing schedule
    d. Rental housing committed but not started—volume, type, and quality
    e. Foreclosures—FHA and other
8. Urban renewal activity, if applicable (federal, state, and local)
    a. Summation: Overall renewal plan and progress
    b. Urban renewal areas
      (1) Identification and location (street boundaries)
      (2) Description and renewal plans of areas
      (3) Environment (surrounding area)
      (4) Housing unit demolitions and replacements
      (5) Present status and time schedule
9. Military housing, if applicable
    a. Housing available to military (including military-connected civilians, i.e., civil service and contractor employees)
      (1) Number of units by type and construction status, on- and off-base
      (2) Physical adequacy
      (3) Occupancy status
    b. Current and projected housing requirements and deficits
      (1) Eligible military personnel
      (2) Ineligible military personnel
      (3) Civilians, including contractor employees
10. Subsidized housing, Section 221(d)(3), rent-supplement, Section 235, Section 236; quantity, (existing, under construction, and planned), rents, income limits, vacancy

Demand for housing

1. Quantitative demand (annual basis)
    a. Projected increase in households
    b. Adjustments
    c. Net quantitative demand (privately financed), by tenure
    d. Net quantitative demand by geographic submarkets
    e. Occupancy potentials for subsidized types, with submarket proportions
2. Qualitative demand
    a. Demand for single-family housing (nonsubsidized)
    b. Demand for multi-family housing (nonsubsidized)

  c. General locations favorable to market absorption
  d. Qualitative occupancy potential for subsidized housing: Section 221(d)(3), rent-supplement, Section 235, Section 236, public housing.
  e. Geographic demand distribution for nonsubsidized housing and subsidized potential
3. Submarkets of demand—At times, the purpose of the housing market analysis may require an estimate of demand for one or more submarkets identified in chapter 7. Subject matter pertinent to a particular submarket may be integrated with the discussion of the broader scope of the respective subject matter in the comprehensive analysis; or it may be consolidated and presented as a supplement following the over-all estimates of qualitative demand for housing.

Statistical appendix

The statistical appendix is intended to contain the detailed tables of only the key data used in the analysis. It should not be used as a catchall for extensive statistical material of less than primary importance in the analysis.

Much of the data used in the analysis can be included in text tables or the narrative in the body of the report Text tables, maps, and charts, serve a helpful purpose when used effectively. They provide sharp focus on important facts, relationships, and trends which require special emphasis otherwise achievable only by lengthy narration. Text tables, however, must be carefully selected and strategically integrated with the discussion; they must be simple and highly condensed; and they must be minimized rather than maximized in usage. The accompanying text must be analytical and interpretative to reveal the significance of the data shown in the tables rather than a mere repetition of these data in narrative form. Caution must be exercised, of course, to avoid overloading the text with statistics—thus rendering the report difficult to read and distracting from the salient facts and findings.

The Columbus Area economy Structure and growth, 1950 to 1985*

By James C. Yocum

This article presents some highlights of an intensive, 3-volume economic base study of the Columbus Area, with detailed projections to 1985. The study was undertaken by the Bureau of Business Research for The Comprehensive Regional Plan of Columbus and Franklin County, Ohio, and required the assembly of a special research staff,[1] including members of the Bureau Staff and other faculty from the College of Commerce and Administration.

The long-term economic and demographic projections developed by this study are primarily for use in the preparation of a comprehensive, long-range Master Plan for Franklin County. The projections, and the historical and structural analysis of the economy of the Area, are useful as well in gaining a better understanding of the workings of the Area's economy as it has been in the recent past and as it is likely to be in the future, and provide a basis for assessing the viability of the Area's industrial location factors in the light of changing technology and U.S. regional trends in the location of population and industry

Volume I, Employment, and Value Added by Manufacture, analyzes the economic structure of the Columbus Area, its historic and recent

---

* Reprinted from *Bulletin of Business Research*, College of Commerce and Administration, The Ohio State University, vol. 41, no. 11 (November 1966), pp. 1, 6–9.

[1] Members of the staff were: James C. Yocum, Professor of Business Research and Director, Bureau of Business Research; Richard A. Tybout, Professor of Economics; Henry L. Hunker, Professor of Geography; Gilbert Nestel, Assistant Professor of Business Research and Economics; and Wilford L'Esperance, Associate Professor of Economics and Business Research. Kent P. Schwirian, Associate Professor of Sociology, was also a member of the staff as Principal Investigator for the population segment of the study.

growth, and its interrelationships both internally and with the rest of the world, and makes projections to 1985 of number employed, by 33 major industry classifications, and of dollar value added by manufacture, by 17 SIC 2-digit manufacturing industry classifications and for manufacturing industry classifications not now in the Columbus Area.

Volume II, Income, Trade, Housing, provides projections to 1985 of other economic parameters for the Columbus Area, including personal income, income distribution, retail sales, household automobile population, number of households by household type, and housing demand by housing unit tenure.

Volume III, Population and Labor Force, develops projections to 1985 of population and labor force of the Columbus Area and of some principal population characteristics.

Volume I is the basic work (comprising 466 pages) since it deals with the recent growth and industry distribution of employment and output, and their projection to 1985 in the light of changes in technology and productivity likely for the Columbus Area economy. The employment projections underlie and are the principal determinants of the projected levels of population, labor force, households, income, and other economic variables developed in the other volumes.

For this reason, and because of space limitations, the highlights presented here, and the summary of the projection methodologies employed, are chiefly from Volume I, and relate to number employed.

The Columbus area—location and growth

Although Ohio for decades has been one of the nation's leading manufacturing states, Columbus, despite its location, for many years was principally a capital city, education, transportation, and finance-and-trading center.

By 1940, when the population of Ohio was 6,908,000, the Franklin County population was 388,700; Franklin County had 138,662 employed, of which only 23.6 percent were employed in Manufacturing. World War II, however, brought new industrial activity to the Area and was the catalyst to an industrial expansion that continues to the present and that has changed the character of the Area's economy. With the war's end, the Columbus Area had the labor, space, facilities and the recognized location to attract new manufacturing firms. The dynamic growth of the Columbus Area's economy in the 1940s continued in the 1950s. By 1960, the population of Franklin County had risen to 683,000 and resident employment to 256,684.

The Area's growth in these two decades was the result of two main forces: the surging industrial expansion, especially in durables manufacture, that stemmed from a somewhat belated recognition of the locational advantages of the Area for many kinds of manufacturing; and the continuing growth of elements related to the strong and long-established orientation of the Columbus Area as a political, educational, and financial-and-trading center.

Present economic structure

By 1960 the industrial growth of the Columbus Area had proceeded to the point where Manufacturing accounted for 27.2 percent of total resident employment (adjusted), compared to 25.6 percent in 1950 and approximately 23.6 percent in 1940. The general pattern of industry composition of the Columbus Area in 1960 more closely resembled that of the United States than that of Ohio—e.g. Manufacturing accounted for 28.3 percent of total employment in the United States, 38.3 percent in Ohio. The principal departures of the Columbus Area from the United States pattern are the substantially lower proportions of Agricultural employment, and higher percentages of employment in Professional Services (including Education), in Services generally, in Government, and in Insurance.

The makeup of Columbus Area Manufacturing, however, is less diversified than the United States or than Ohio but more nearly resembles Ohio than the United States.

The growth of Manufacturing in the Columbus Area since 1940 was primarily in durable goods, with five durable goods industry classifications accounting for almost 90 percent of the total increase in Manufacturing employment. Increasingly, therefore, Franklin County has become oriented to durable goods production, so that in 1960 durable goods manufacturing represented 67 percent of its total Manufacturing employment.

By 1965, although Manufacturing employment had increased 7.2 percent from 1960, larger increases in other industry classifications resulted in a decline to 26.0 percent in the Area's ratio of Manufacturing-to-all employment. In economic base terms, in which "Basic Industries" and "Local Industries" are defined on the basis of an external (exogenous)-internal (endogenous) dichotomy with respect to the source of their demands (with Basic Industries selling primarily to buyers outside the Area and generating activity whose multiplicative and cumulative effects are conceived as determining the demands (internal) of the Local Industries), the Columbus Area economy, despite the industrial expansion of the previous 25 years, still retains the advantage of a relatively large reliance on Local Supporting Industries, as the following table shows:

Classification	Percent of total employment, 1965
Basic Industries—Total	46.0
Products (Manufacturing, Construction, Quarrying, Agriculture)..	(31.8)
Services (Exogenous)	(14.2)
Local Supporting & Services Industries	54.0
Total	100.0

Employment in the Local Industries and Basic Services is notably more stable, much less cyclically sensitive, than in Manufacturing and Construction.

Projections

The central concern of the study was with the rate of growth at which the Area's economy can be expected to proceed in the future, the probable nature and dimensions of the changes among the principal divisions of the economy, and the structure of the economic base, at five-year intervals, 1970 through 1985.

The projections of number employed by industry classifications were critical to the projections of all the other variables, and special pains were taken, therefore, in their preparation. Rather than relying on a *single* methodology and accompanying assumptions, a pluralistic research design was employed. As a safeguard, to minimize the deviations of the projected values from true future values, it might be said that redundancy was deliberately incorporated in the research design.

Thus, projections of employment for each industry classification were made by several methods. For the (existing) Manufacturing industry classifications these methods were:

a. Franklin County Share of U.S. Total

For each industry classification, ratios of Franklin County/U.S. value added by manufacture, and of Franklin County/U.S. value added per employee, were developed from historical data; subjective determinations of the possible range ("High," "Intermediate," and "Low") of these two ratios in the projection period were made; and projected High, Intermediate, and Low Franklin County industry employment was derived from the projected ratios using the National Planning Association's projections of U.S. value added and number employed, by industry.

b. Manufacturers' Markets

Empirical data were obtained by questionnaire from Franklin County manufacturers showing the distribution of their 1963 sales by industry (industrial goods) and/or by U.S. region (consumer goods). Sales were then projected to 1985, using NPA's projections of U.S. gross output by manufacturing industry classifications, and of personal income by U.S. regions; projected employment of each industry classification was then obtained by dividing the projected sales by the respective projected sales/employee ratios.

c. Input-Output

A table of Franklin County 1958 inter-industry transactions and external sales was specially constructed, which, for each industry expresses its total output (sales) as the sum of the purchases of its output by every other category of local business, plus its output exported outside Franklin County. A matrix of technical coefficients, representing for each industry, for each dollar of its output, the value of its inputs from each other Franklin County industry, was computed. The matrix was inverted, and projected total sales of each Franklin County industry were computed by multiplying the inverse matrix by the matrix of projected exports. Projected sales were then converted to projected employment as in (b.) above.

The projections from these separate methods were then compared (as illustrated in Chart 1, reproduced from Chart C.4, Volume I of the study)

CHART 1

Manufacturing industries (SIC 33 and 34) establishment employment: Projections by three methods, and final projections (high, judgment intermediate, and low), Franklin County, 1963, and projected 1965–1985

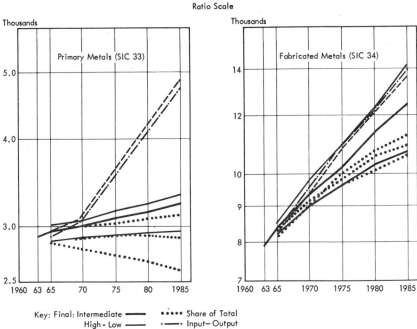

Ratio Scale

Key: Final: Intermediate —— •••• Share of Total
High - Low —— •——• Input—Output
——— Manufacturers' Markets

CHART 2

Major industry classifications: Franklin County resident employment, 1950, 1960, and 1965, and projected (judgment intermediate), 1970–1985

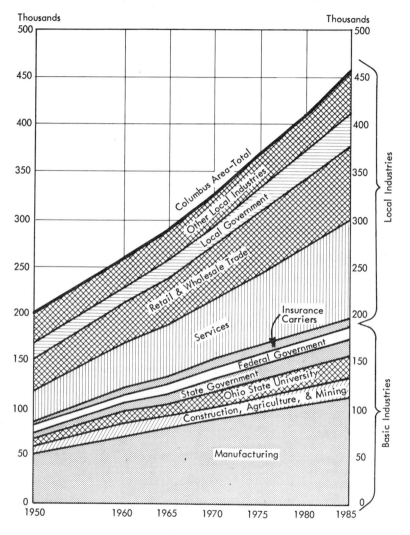

and used to develop a "Judgment Intermediate" (or implicitly a "most likely") level, and upper and lower bounds, which may be taken as "possible high" and "possible low." Where the projections by the various methods were closely confirming, the range between the upper and lower bounds is relatively small (as in the case of the Fabricated Metals industry in Chart 1). In a few industries in which the projections showed substantial dispersion (as in the case of the Primary Metals industry in Chart

1) the assumptions underlying the projection methods and subjective evaluations of the future prospects of the industry were restudied, and if a firm basis for decision among the alternatives was available, judgmental determinations were made; or if not, the range between the upper and lower bounds was left commensurately larger.

Historical and projected employment for all major industry classifications is shown in Chart 2 (reproduced from Chart 9.1, Volume I).

In summary it may be noted that on the basis of these projections no major structural changes in the employment of the Columbus Area are anticipated. Continuing large gains in manufacturing per-employee productivity, however, will limit the employment growth in this principal segment of the Basic Industries, so that by 1985 it will account for 23.6 percent of the total Area employment compared to 26.1 percent in 1965.

The rate of growth of employment projected for the Columbus Area, 1965–1985, compared with its recent historic rate, and with the United States as projected by NPA, is summarized in the following table:

	Average annual percent increase	
Area	*1950–1965*	*1965–1985*
Columbus Area total civilian resident employment		
High	—	2.7
Judgment Intermediate	2.5	2.3
Low	—	1.7
U.S. civilian employment	1.2	1.8

Projections of other selected economic variables are summarized in the accompanying table.

Columbus Area population, employment, and selected other economic and demographic measures, 1950 and 1960, and projected, 1965–1985

Item	1950	1960	1965	1970	1975	1980	1985
Total population (civilian) (thousands)*							
High			777.8	906.6	1,015.1	1,137.5	1,290.0
Intermediate	503.4	683.0	775.7	881.8	974.9	1,063.1	1,193.7
Low			774.2	849.5	922.6	978.8	1,068.3
Total labor force (civilian) (intermediate) (thousands)†	210.6	269.0	298.6	346.7	380.0	418.7	468.7
Total employment (civilian) (resident, adjusted) (thousands)‡							
High			288.4	339.3	383.1	432.2	488.9
Judgment Intermediate	200.0	256.7	288.2	327.0	367.9	408.8	453.6
Low			288.0	318.5	349.5	378.9	406.9
Total households (thousands)§							
High			218.0	263.3	286.7	316.4	364.1
Intermediate	145.7	200.8	217.9	254.9	277.7	299.1	345.5
Low			217.6	238.4	263.8	284.4	309.7
Total personal income (billion 1960 $s)‖							
High			$2.089	$2.664	$3.347	$4.193	$5.269
Judgment Intermediate	$1.030	$1.699	2.088	2.564	3.199	3.944	4.838
Low			2.086	2.492	3.026	3.633	4.310
Retail sales (intermediate) (billion 1960 $s) #	$ .610	$ .904	$1.097	$1.309	$1.591	$1.923	$2.321
Automobile ownership (households) (thousands)**							
High			255.8	307.7	354.2	403.5	483.5
Intermediate	n.a.	217.4(e)	254.2	305.7	351.6	400.3	479.5
Low			249.3	299.7	344.0	390.7	467.4

Source:
* *The Columbus Area Economy: Structure and Growth, 1950 to 1985*—Vol. III—*Population and Labor Force*, Bureau of Business Research, The Ohio State University, 1966, Tables 7 and 23.
† Ibid., Vol. III, Tables 13 and 23.
‡ Ibid., Vol. I—*Employment and Value Added by Manufacture*, Table 9.1.
§ Ibid., Vol. II—*Income, Trade, Housing*, Table 2.1 and Appendix Table B.13.
‖ Ibid., Vol. II, Appendix Table A.8.
Ibid., Vol. II, Table 5.1.
** Ibid., Vol. II, Table 4.1.

Use of compound
interest tables

Tables in Appendix G are provided for selected rates of return from 3 percent to 25 percent (shown at the top of each table). These rates of return represent what is sometimes called the "effective rate," the "risk rate of interest," the "discount rate," the "speculative rate," or the "return needed *on*" the amount invested. This rate of return shown at the top of each table is an interest rate, not a capitalization rate. A capitalization rate or factor includes both the return *on* investment and return *of* investment.

Two sets of tables are provided in Appendix G for each rate of return. The *Annual Compound Interest Table* assumes that interest is compounded annually and that the successive increments of income will come at equal annual intervals; the *Monthly Compound Interest Table* assumes monthly compounding of income coming at equal monthly intervals. Tables are also available for quarterly, semiannual, and other periodic payments. Compound interest factors in the annual tables extend to the 50th year and in the monthly tables to the 40th year. Tables are available for factors for 100 years, and factors in the 50- and 40-year tables can be extended in the absence of a more complete table.

The following discussion of the six columns in the compound interest tables uses the 8 percent annual table for illustration.

Column 1

Column 1 is headed "Amount of $1 at Compound Interest." The factors in Column 1 indicate the magnitude reached after a given number of years by a *single sum* (a one-time event) deposited *at the beginning* of year 1, if interest is compounded at the rate of 8 percent annually. The deposit today of $100 (a single sum) at 8 percent compound interest will accumulate to $125.97 (rounded) by the end of three years.

Example

To find future value of any single sum given that interest is to be compounded at 8 percent for three years, the procedure is

Factor × Single Sum = Future Value of the Single Sum
1.259712 × $100 = $125.97

Demonstration of what is assumed to occur during the three years:

Year	Outlay	*Interest during year*	*Balance at end of year*
1	$100	$8.00	$108.00
2	—	8.64	116.64
3	—	9.3312	125.9712
			(answer)

Interest each year is calculated on the outstanding balance at the end of the preceding year. The original balance plus accumulated interest total $125.97 by the end of the third year.

Note

The compound interest formula for calculating factors in Column 1 is

substituting
$$(1 + r)^n$$
$$(1 + 0.08)^3 = 1.259712.$$

Column 2

Column 2 in the table is headed "Accumulation of $1 per Period." The factors in Column 2 indicate the magnitude reached after a given number of years by *a series of equal annual amounts* deposited *at the end* of each successive year, if interest is compounded at the rate of 8 percent annually. The deposit of $100 each year at 8 percent compound interest will accumulate to $324.64 at the end of three years.

Example

To find the future value of any series of equal annual outlays for three years, given that interest is to be compounded at 8 percent, the procedure is

Factor × Annual Amount Deposited = Future Value of the Annual Deposits
3.246400 × $100 = $324.64

Demonstration of what is assumed to occur during the three years:

Year	End of year outlay	Interest during year	Balance at end of year
1	.... $100	$ 0.00	$100.00
2	.... $100	8.00	208.00
3	.... $100	16.64	324.64
			(answer)

Interest each year is calculated on the outstanding balance at the end of the preceding year. The series of three equal annual payments plus accumulated interest total $324.64 by the end of the third year.

Note

The compound interest formula for calculating factors in Column 2 is

$$\frac{(1 + r)^n - 1}{r}$$

substituting

$$\frac{(1 + 0.08)^3 - 1}{0.08} = 3.2464.$$

Column 3

Column 3 is headed "Sinking Fund Factor." In other books, the percentages in this column may be found in a table headed, "Amortization Rates" or "Deposits Needed to Accumulate $1.00." The percentages in Column 3 indicate the equal annual amounts necessary to set aside at the end of each year at 8 percent compound interest in order to accumulate to a certain sum at the end of a given number of years. The equal annual amount necessary to set aside in an 8 percent sinking fund to accumulate to $100 at the end of three years is $30.80 (rounded); that is, $30.80 each year will amortize the investment, assuming that the annual amortization payment is put at compound interest of 8 percent.

Example

To find the annual payment into the sinking fund, given that the fund earns 8 percent and that the $100 investment is amortized over three years, the procedure is

Percentage × Sum to Be Amortized = Sinking Fund Payment

or

0.308034 × $100 = $30.80

Demonstration of what is assumed to occur during the three years:

Year	End-of-year deposit in fund	Interest on fund during year	Balance at the end of year
1	$30.80	$0.00	$30.80
2	30.80	2.46	64.06
3	30.80	5.12	99.98*

    * Discrepancy from $100 caused by rounding.

Interest each year is calculated on the outstanding balance at the end of the preceding year. The series of three equal annual payments into the fund plus accumulated interest total $100 by the end of the third year.

Note

The compound interest formula for calculating the percentages in Column 3 is

$$\frac{r}{(1 + r)^n - 1}$$

substituting

$$\frac{0.08}{(1 + 0.08)^3 - 1} = 0.308034.$$

Column 4

Column 4 is headed "Present Value of Reversion of $1." The factors in Column 4 indicate the value today of a *single sum* (a one-time event) to be received at the end of a given number of years, discounted at 8 percent annual compound interest. The discounting phenomenon (or the process of capitalization) arises because of the fact that a dollar today is more valuable to us than a dollar that we expect to receive at some future time. If we had the dollar in hand today, we could invest it and earn a return; we would be liquid; and we would avoid risk of loss of capital. In this case, we need 8 percent to induce us to wait three years for the receipt of $100. The $100 (a single sum) to be received at the end of three years from today, discounted at 8 percent compound interest, is worth $79.38 (rounded) today.

Example

To find the present value of a single payment to be received at the end of three years, given that the rate of discount is 8 percent, the procedure is

Factor × Amount to Be Received = Present Value of the Single Sum

or

$$0.793832 \times \$100 = \$79.38 \text{ (rounded)}$$

Demonstration of what is assumed to occur during the three years.

Year	Original outlay	Interest during year	Balance at end of year
1	$79.38	$6.35	$ 85.73
2	—	6.86	92.59
3	—	7.41	100.00
			(single sum to be received at end of year three)

The receipt of $100 at the end of year three has permitted earning 8 percent interest compounded annually on the original investment of $79.38.

Note

The compound interest formula for calculating factors in Column 4 is

$$\frac{1}{(1 + r)^n}$$

substituting

$$\frac{1}{(1 + 0.08)^3} = 0.793832.$$

Column 5

Column 5 is headed "Present Value of Ordinary Annuity of $1 per Period." The factors in Column 5 indicate the value today of a series of equal annual payments (a series of payments; an income stream) to be received *at the end* of each successive year for a given number of years, discounted at 8 percent annual compound interest. Income of $100 to be received at the end of each of three years, discounted at 8 percent compound interest, is worth $257.71 (rounded) today.

Example

To find the present value of a series of equal annual payments to be received at the end of each year for three years, given that the rate of discount is 8 percent, the procedure is

Factor × Equal Annual Payment = Present Value of Series of Equal Annual
Payments

or

$$2.577097 \times \$100 = \$257.71 \text{ (rounded)}$$

Demonstration of what is assumed to occur during the three years.

Year	Payment to be received at end of year	Interest on outstanding balance of investment	Recapture of principal	End-of-year outstanding balance of investment
1	$100	$20.62*	$ 79.38	$178.33†
2	100	14.27	85.73	92.60
3	100	7.41	92.59	—
Totals	$300	$42.30	$257.70	

* 8% × original investment of $257.71 made at beginning of year.
† $257.71 less $79.38.

The original investment of $257.71 is fully recaptured out of the annual
receipts of $100 over the three years and the investor has earned 8 percent
on the outstanding balance of the original investment each year. (Note that
the portion of each annual receipt of $100 designated as recapture of
principal increases each year as the interest earned on the reducing balance
decreases.)

Note

The compound interest formula for calculating factors in Column 5 is

$$\frac{1 - (1 + r)^{-n}}{r}$$

substituting

$$\frac{1 - (1 + 0.08)^{-3}}{0.08} = 2.577097.$$

Column 6

Column 6 is headed "Installment to Amortize $1." In other books, the
percentages in this column may be found in a table headed "Partial
Payment of $1.00 of Loan." This table is often called a mortgage amorti-
zation table. The percentages in Column 6 indicate the equal annual
payment necessary to amortize fully the principal balance of a mortgage
over its term and to provide the lender a given rate of return on the
outstanding balance of unamortized principal each year. Payments are
assumed to be made at the end of each successive year. A loan of $100
with a term of three years and bearing a face rate of interest of 8 percent
(compound interest) requires an equal annual payment of $38.80.

Example

To find the equal annual installment necessary to amortize the 8 percent, three-year loan, the procedure is

Percentage × Original Amount of the Loan = Annual Payment

or

$$0.388034 \times \$100 = \$38.80 \text{ (rounded)}$$

Demonstration of what is assumed to occur during the three years.

Year	Payment to be made at end of year	Interest on outstanding balance of loan	Repayment of principal	End-of-year outstanding balance of loan
1	$ 38.80	$ 8.00°	$30.80	$69.20
2	38.80	5.54	33.26	35.94
3	38.80	2.88	35.92	—
Totals	$116.40	$16.42	$99.98†	

° 0.08 × original balance of $100.
† Discrepancy from $100 total caused by rounding.

The original loan of $100 is repaid from the three equal installments of $38.80, and the lender receives 8 percent interest calculated annually on the outstanding balance of the loan.

Note

The compound interest formula for calculating the percentages in Column 6 is

$$\left[\frac{1}{1 - (1 + r)^{-n}} \right] r$$

substituting

$$\left[\frac{1}{1 - (1 + 0.08)^{-3}} \right] 0.08 = 0.388034$$

Interrelation of Columns 1–6

The factors and percentages in Columns 1 through 6 are all based upon the compound interest premise and therefore are all related as discussed below.

1. Factors in Column 4 (present value of reversion of $1) are the reciprocals of factors in Column 1 (amount of $1 at compound interest), and vice versa.

Example

$$\frac{1}{1.259712 \text{ (Column 1, 8\%, 3 years)}} = 0.793832 \text{ (Column 4, 8\%, 3 years)}$$

2. If the Column 2 factors (accumulation of $1 per period) were calculated as though the equal annual increment of income were deposited at the beginning of each year, as is the case with Column 1 factors, then a Column 2 factor for any given year can be shown to be the sum of successive Column 1 factors. Column 2 factors can be converted to beginning-of-year payments by subtracting 1.0 from the next year's factor.

Example

$100 deposited at the beginning of each year for three years at 8 percent compound interest has a future worth of $350.61.

$100 × (4.506112 (Col. 2, 4 yrs. 8%) − 1.0) =

$$\$100 \times 3.506112 = \$350.611$$

The Column 2 factor for beginning of year payments (3.506112) equals the sum of each Column 1 factor for years 1–3.

$$
\begin{aligned}
&1.080000 \text{ (Column 1, 8 percent, 1 year)}\\
&1.166400 \text{ (Column 1, 8 percent, 2 years)}\\
&\underline{1.259712} \text{ (Column 1, 8 percent, 3 years)}\\
&3.506112 \text{ Total}
\end{aligned}
$$

3. In similar fashion, a Column 5 factor is the sum of successive Column 4 factors.

Example

$$
\begin{aligned}
&.925926 \text{ (Column 4, 8 percent, 1 year)}\\
&.857339 \text{ (Column 4, 8 percent, 2 years)}\\
&\underline{.793832} \text{ (Column 4, 8 percent, 3 years)}\\
&2.577097 \text{ (Column 5, 8 percent, 3 years)}
\end{aligned}
$$

4. Column 6 factors are reciprocals of Column 5 factors.

Example

$$\frac{1}{2.57709 \text{ (Col. 5, 8 percent, 3 yrs.)}} = .388034 \text{ (Col. 6, 8 percent, 3 yrs.)}$$

5. Column 5 factors are the reciprocals of Column 3 factors plus the rate of discount.

Example

$$\frac{1}{.08 \text{ (rate of discount)} + .308034 \text{ (Column 3, 8\%, 3 years.)}}$$
$$= 2.577097 \text{ (Column 5, 8\%, 3 years)}$$

Note

The Column 3 factor is a sinking fund factor that tells us what percentage of the total investment must be deposited each year in a sinking fund assumed to draw 8 percent compound interest over three years in order to accumulate to the total investment at the end of those three years. Appraisers often call this assumption the "Inwood Premise" for amortization of the investment. It might be pointed out that Column 4 factors also are based upon the Inwood Premise regarding recapture of investment.

Additional capitalization assumptions

Capitalization to perpetuity. An assumed perpetual level income stream (land income) is capitalized into present value by dividing the annual income by the rate of return *on* investment.

Example

Given that the rate of discount is 8 percent and the annual payments are $100 each, the procedure is

$$\frac{\text{Annual Income}}{\text{Rate of Interest}} = \text{Present Value of Perpetuity}$$

or

$$\frac{\$100}{0.08} = \$1,250.$$

You would pay $1,250 today for the right to receive $100 a year to perpetuity if you need 8 percent to induce you to wait to receive the income over time.

Demonstration of what is assumed to occur.

Year	Payment to be received at end of year	Interest on outstanding balance of investment	Recapture of investment	Outstanding balance at end of year
1	$100	$100*	0	$1,250
2	$100	$100	0	1,250
99	$100	$100	0	1,250
to infinity				

* (0.08 × outstanding balance at beginning of year, or $1,250)

The original investment of $1,250 is never recaptured from future income, the total of which represents interest at the rate of 8 percent on the full investment year after year. The original investment is recaptured only by selling the asset.

The 8 percent return on investment in the above example is treated as a capitalization rate and, when used to discount land income to present value, is sometimes called the "land capitalization rate." Rather than view this land capitalization rate as an exception to the rule that every capitalization rate has two components, the return *on* investment (8 percent in this instance) and the return *of* investment, it is contended that the return of investment component is present, but it has fallen to zero.

Straight-line capitalization. Other columns could be provided in addition to the six which have been discussed. A column of capitalization rates or capitalization factors (reciprocals of the rates) could be included for straight-line capitalization of future income into present value.

A straight-line capitalization rate is composed of (*a*) the speculative rate of discount (8 percent), and (*b*) a rate of amortization that permits recapture of the investment over the duration of the income stream (25-year income stream = 4 percent rate of recapture; 50-year stream = 2 percent rate of recapture; three-year stream = 33.3 percent rate of recapture; the rate of recapture can be found by dividing the number of years in the income stream into 1.0). A straight-line capitalization factor is the reciprocal of the straight-line capitalization rate.

Example

A three-year income stream beginning at $100 in the first year discounted at 8 percent using straight-line capitalization has a present value of $241.94 (rounded). To find the present value of a three-year income stream beginning at $100 given that the rate of discount is 8 percent, the procedure is

$$\frac{\text{Income in First Year}}{\text{Rate}} = \text{Present Value}$$

$$\frac{\$100}{(0.08 \text{ rate of discount} + 0.333 \text{ rate of recapture})} = \$241.94$$

Alternatively

$$\text{Factor} \times \text{Income in First Year} = \text{Present Value}$$

$$\left[\frac{1}{.08 + 0.333}\right] \times \$100 = \$241.94$$

Demonstration of what is assumed to occur during the three years.

Year	Income to be received at end of year	Interest on outstanding balance of investment	Recapture of principal	End-of-year outstanding balance of investment
1	$100.00	$19.36°	$ 80.64†	$161.30
2	93.54	12.90	80.64	80.66
3	87.09	6.45	80.64	—
	$280.63	$38.71	$241.92‡	

° (0.08 × $241.94)

† The most widely accepted assumption regarding straight-line capitalization is that the annual recapture of the original amount of the investment is in equal annual amounts (in this case, $80.64 each year). Since interest each year is calculated on the remaining outstanding balance of the investment at the beginning of that year, the portion of each annual increment of income designated as interest declines year by year (from $19.36 in year 1 to $6.45 in year 3). Income received each year from the investment is the sum of the annual recapture plus interest in that year, resulting in an income stream beginning at $100 in year 1 and declining to $87.09 in year 3.

‡ Discrepancy from $241.94 caused by rounding.

If the annual income stream projected by use of direct, straight-line capitalization is graphed, the stream is seen to decline in a straight-line from year 1 to year 3. The total stream can be divided into two parts: recapture of investment and return on investment.

Income stream: Straight-line capitalization

The above graph can be compared with a diagram demonstrating the income stream projected by use of a Column 5 present value of an annuity of one factor for three years at 8 percent.

Income stream: Level annuity

The assumption with regard to how the original investment is recaptured determines the shape of the projected income stream.

Other assumptions. Capitalization rates and factors can be calculated for discounting level income streams to present value assuming that the annual recapture of investment is reinvested at an interest rate less than the speculative rate of discount. Appraisers have called this recapture assumption the "Hoskold Premise." An Hoskold capitalization rate for a three-year level income stream of $100 each year, discounted at 8 percent and assuming that the annual recapture will be reinvested at 6 percent is obtained by adding the 8 percent return *on* investment to the Column 3 sinking fund factor for three years at 6 percent. This rate is converted to a factor by taking its reciprocal (1/rate).

Example

0.08 return *on* investment + 0.314110 return *of* investment* = 0.394110 Hoskold capitalization rate

$$\frac{\text{Income}}{\text{Rate}} = \text{Value}$$

$$\frac{\$100}{0.394110} = \$253.74$$

* Column 3, 6 percent, three years.

Still other capitalization rates and factors have been calculated for income streams assumed to take different flow patterns. For instance, Frederick Babcock developed tables for income streams assumed to decline in a curvilinear fashion over their duration.[1]

[1] Frederick Babcock, *Valuation of Real Estate* (New York: McGraw-Hill, 1932), pp. 543–99.

_____ appendix G

Interest tables

3.00%   MONTHLY COMPOUND INTEREST TABLES*   3.00%
                                      EFFECTIVE RATE 0.250

	1 AMOUNT OF $1 AT COMPOUND INTEREST	2 ACCUMULATION OF $1 PER PERIOD	3 SINKING FUND FACTOR	4 PRESENT VALUE REVERSION OF $1	5 PRESENT VALUE ORD. ANNUITY $1 PER PERIOD	6 INSTALMENT TO AMORTIZE $1	
MONTHS							
1	1.002500	1.000000	1.000000	0.997506	0.997506	1.002500	
2	1.005006	2.002500	0.499376	0.995019	1.992525	0.501876	
3	1.007519	3.007506	0.332501	0.992537	2.985062	0.335001	
4	1.010038	4.015025	0.249064	0.990062	3.975124	0.251564	
5	1.012563	5.025063	0.199002	0.987593	4.962718	0.201502	
6	1.015094	6.037625	0.165628	0.985130	5.947848	0.168128	
7	1.017632	7.052719	0.141789	0.982674	6.930522	0.144289	
8	1.020176	8.070351	0.123910	0.980223	7.910745	0.126410	
9	1.022726	9.090527	0.110005	0.977779	8.888524	0.112505	
10	1.025283	10.113253	0.098880	0.975340	9.863864	0.101380	
11	1.027846	11.138536	0.089778	0.972908	10.836772	0.092278	
12	1.030416	12.166383	0.082194	0.970482	11.807254	0.084694	
YEARS							**MONTHS**
1	1.030416	12.166383	0.082194	0.970482	11.807254	0.084694	12
2	1.061757	24.702818	0.040481	0.941835	23.265980	0.042981	24
3	1.094051	37.620560	0.026581	0.914034	34.386465	0.029081	36
4	1.127328	50.931208	0.019634	0.887053	45.178695	0.022134	48
5	1.161617	64.646713	0.015469	0.860869	55.652358	0.017969	60
6	1.196948	78.779387	0.012694	0.835458	65.816858	0.015194	72
7	1.233355	93.341920	0.010713	0.810797	75.681321	0.013213	84
8	1.270868	108.347387	0.009230	0.786863	85.254603	0.011730	96
9	1.309523	123.809259	0.008077	0.763637	94.545300	0.010577	108
10	1.349354	139.741419	0.007156	0.741096	103.561753	0.009656	120
11	1.390395	156.158171	0.006404	0.719220	112.312057	0.008904	132
12	1.432686	173.074254	0.005778	0.697990	120.804069	0.008278	144
13	1.476262	190.504855	0.005249	0.677386	129.045412	0.007749	156
14	1.521164	208.465626	0.004797	0.657391	137.043486	0.007297	168
15	1.567432	226.972690	0.004406	0.637986	144.805471	0.006906	180
16	1.615107	246.042664	0.004064	0.619154	152.338338	0.006564	192
17	1.664232	265.692670	0.003764	0.600878	159.648848	0.006264	204
18	1.714851	285.940350	0.003497	0.583141	166.743566	0.005997	216
19	1.767010	306.803882	0.003259	0.565928	173.628861	0.005759	228
20	1.820755	328.301998	0.003046	0.549223	180.310914	0.005546	240
21	1.876135	350.454000	0.002853	0.533011	186.795726	0.005353	252
22	1.933199	373.279777	0.002679	0.517277	193.089119	0.005179	264
23	1.992000	396.799821	0.002520	0.502008	199.196742	0.005020	276
24	2.052588	421.035250	0.002375	0.487190	205.124080	0.004875	288
25	2.115020	446.007823	0.002242	0.472809	210.876453	0.004742	300
26	2.179350	471.739961	0.002120	0.458852	216.459028	0.004620	312
27	2.245637	498.254766	0.002007	0.445308	221.876815	0.004507	324
28	2.313940	525.576044	0.001903	0.432163	227.134679	0.004403	336
29	2.384321	553.728325	0.001806	0.419407	232.237341	0.004306	348
30	2.456842	582.736885	0.001716	0.407027	237.189382	0.004216	360
31	2.531569	612.627767	0.001632	0.395012	241.995247	0.004132	372
32	2.608570	643.427810	0.001554	0.383352	246.659253	0.004054	384
33	2.687912	675.164665	0.001481	0.372036	251.185586	0.003981	396
34	2.769667	707.866827	0.001413	0.361054	255.578310	0.003913	408
35	2.853909	741.563657	0.001349	0.350397	259.841368	0.003849	420
36	2.940714	776.285408	0.001288	0.340054	263.978590	0.003788	432
37	3.030158	812.063254	0.001231	0.330016	267.993688	0.003731	444
38	3.122323	848.929318	0.001178	0.320274	271.890268	0.003678	456
39	3.217292	886.916698	0.001128	0.310820	275.671828	0.003628	468
40	3.315149	926.059501	0.001080	0.301646	279.341764	0.003580	480

*Tables on pages 430–59 are taken from Paul Wendt and Alan R. Cerf, *Tables for Investment Analysis* (Berkeley, Calif.: The Center for Real Estate and Urban Economics, Institute of Urban and Regional Development, the University of California), © 1966, The Regents of the University of California, Pages 22, 25, 54, 57, 70, 73, 78, 81, 86, 89, 94, 97, 102, 105–6, 109–10, 113–14, 117–18, 121, 126, 129, 138, 141, 158, 161, 178, and 181.

3.00%   ANNUAL COMPOUND INTEREST TABLES   3.00%
                                    EFFECTIVE RATE   3.00

---

	1 AMOUNT OF $1 AT COMPOUND INTEREST	2 ACCUMULATION OF $1 PER PERIOD	3 SINKING FUND FACTOR	4 PRESENT VALUE REVERSION OF $1	5 PRESENT VALUE ORD. ANNUITY $1 PER PERIOD	6 INSTALMENT TO AMORTIZE $1
YEARS						
1	1.030000	1.000000	1.000000	0.970874	0.970874	1.030000
2	1.060900	2.030000	0.492611	0.942596	1.913470	0.522611
3	1.092727	3.090900	0.323530	0.915142	2.828611	0.353530
4	1.125509	4.183627	0.239027	0.888487	3.717098	0.269027
5	1.159274	5.309136	0.188355	0.862609	4.579707	0.218355
6	1.194052	6.468410	0.154598	0.837484	5.417191	0.184598
7	1.229874	7.662462	0.130506	0.813092	6.230283	0.160506
8	1.266770	8.892336	0.112456	0.789409	7.019692	0.142456
9	1.304773	10.159106	0.098434	0.766417	7.786109	0.128434
10	1.343916	11.463879	0.087231	0.744094	8.530203	0.117231
11	1.384234	12.807796	0.078077	0.722421	9.252624	0.108077
12	1.425761	14.192030	0.070462	0.701380	9.954004	0.100462
13	1.468534	15.617790	0.064030	0.680951	10.634955	0.094030
14	1.512590	17.086324	0.058526	0.661118	11.296073	0.088526
15	1.557967	18.598914	0.053767	0.641862	11.937935	0.083767
16	1.604706	20.156881	0.049611	0.623167	12.561102	0.079611
17	1.652848	21.761588	0.045953	0.605016	13.166118	0.075953
18	1.702433	23.414435	0.042709	0.587395	13.753513	0.072709
19	1.753506	25.116868	0.039814	0.570286	14.323799	0.069814
20	1.806111	26.870374	0.037216	0.553676	14.877475	0.067216
21	1.860295	28.676486	0.034872	0.537549	15.415024	0.064872
22	1.916103	30.536780	0.032747	0.521893	15.936917	0.062747
23	1.973587	32.452884	0.030814	0.506692	16.443608	0.060814
24	2.032794	34.426470	0.029047	0.491934	16.935542	0.059047
25	2.093778	36.459264	0.027428	0.477606	17.413148	0.057428
26	2.156591	38.553042	0.025938	0.463695	17.876842	0.055938
27	2.221289	40.709634	0.024564	0.450189	18.327031	0.054564
28	2.287928	42.930923	0.023293	0.437077	18.764108	0.053293
29	2.356566	45.218850	0.022115	0.424346	19.188455	0.052115
30	2.427262	47.575416	0.021019	0.411987	19.600441	0.051019
31	2.500080	50.002678	0.019999	0.399987	20.000428	0.049999
32	2.575083	52.502759	0.019047	0.388337	20.388766	0.049047
33	2.652335	55.077841	0.018156	0.377026	20.765792	0.048156
34	2.731905	57.730177	0.017322	0.366045	21.131837	0.047322
35	2.813862	60.462082	0.016539	0.355383	21.487220	0.046539
36	2.898278	63.275944	0.015804	0.345032	21.832252	0.045804
37	2.985227	66.174223	0.015112	0.334983	22.167235	0.045112
38	3.074783	69.159449	0.014459	0.325226	22.492462	0.044459
39	3.167027	72.234233	0.013844	0.315754	22.808215	0.043844
40	3.262038	75.401260	0.013262	0.306557	23.114772	0.043262
41	3.359899	78.663298	0.012712	0.297628	23.412400	0.042712
42	3.460696	82.023196	0.012192	0.288959	23.701359	0.042192
43	3.564517	85.483892	0.011698	0.280543	23.981902	0.041698
44	3.671452	89.048409	0.011230	0.272372	24.254274	0.041230
45	3.781596	92.719861	0.010785	0.264439	24.518713	0.040785
46	3.895044	96.501457	0.010363	0.256737	24.775449	0.040363
47	4.011895	100.396501	0.009961	0.249259	25.024708	0.039961
48	4.132252	104.408396	0.009578	0.241999	25.266707	0.039578
49	4.256219	108.540648	0.009213	0.234950	25.501657	0.039213
50	4.383906	112.796867	0.008865	0.228107	25.729764	0.038865

5.00% MONTHLY COMPOUND INTEREST TABLES 5.00%
EFFECTIVE RATE 0.417

	1 AMOUNT OF $1 AT COMPOUND INTEREST	2 ACCUMULATION OF $1 PER PERIOD	3 SINKING FUND FACTOR	4 PRESENT VALUE REVERSION OF $1	5 PRESENT VALUE ORD. ANNUITY $1 PER PERIOD	6 INSTALMENT TO AMORTIZE $1	
MONTHS							
1	1.004167	1.000000	1.000000	0.995851	0.995851	1.004167	
2	1.008351	2.004167	0.498960	0.991718	1.987569	0.503127	
3	1.012552	3.012517	0.331948	0.987603	2.975173	0.336115	
4	1.016771	4.025070	0.248443	0.983506	3.958678	0.252610	
5	1.021008	5.041841	0.198340	0.979425	4.938103	0.202507	
6	1.025262	6.062848	0.164939	0.975361	5.913463	0.169106	
7	1.029534	7.088110	0.141081	0.971313	6.884777	0.145248	
8	1.033824	8.117644	0.123188	0.967283	7.852060	0.127355	
9	1.038131	9.151467	0.109272	0.963269	8.815329	0.113439	
10	1.042457	10.189599	0.098139	0.959272	9.774602	0.102306	
11	1.046800	11.232055	0.089031	0.955292	10.729894	0.093198	
12	1.051162	12.278855	0.081441	0.951328	11.681222	0.085607	
YEARS							MONTHS
1	1.051162	12.278855	0.081441	0.951328	11.681222	0.085607	12
2	1.104941	25.185921	0.039705	0.905025	22.793898	0.043871	24
3	1.161472	38.753336	0.025804	0.860976	33.365701	0.029971	36
4	1.220895	53.014885	0.018863	0.819071	43.422956	0.023029	48
5	1.283359	68.006083	0.014705	0.779205	52.990706	0.018871	60
6	1.349018	83.764259	0.011938	0.741280	62.092777	0.016105	72
7	1.418036	100.328653	0.009967	0.705201	70.751835	0.014134	84
8	1.490585	117.740512	0.008493	0.670877	78.989441	0.012660	96
9	1.566847	136.043196	0.007351	0.638225	86.826108	0.011517	108
10	1.647009	155.282279	0.006440	0.607161	94.281350	0.010607	120
11	1.731274	175.505671	0.005698	0.577609	101.373733	0.009864	132
12	1.819849	196.763730	0.005082	0.549496	108.120917	0.009249	144
13	1.912956	219.109391	0.004564	0.522751	114.539704	0.008731	156
14	2.010826	242.598299	0.004122	0.497308	120.646077	0.008289	168
15	2.113704	267.288944	0.003741	0.473103	126.455243	0.007908	180
16	2.221845	293.242809	0.003410	0.450076	131.981666	0.007577	192
17	2.335519	320.524523	0.003120	0.428170	137.239108	0.007287	204
18	2.455008	349.202022	0.002864	0.407331	142.240661	0.007030	216
19	2.580611	379.346715	0.002636	0.387505	146.998780	0.006803	228
20	2.712640	411.033669	0.002433	0.368645	151.525313	0.006600	240
21	2.851424	444.341787	0.002251	0.350702	155.831532	0.006417	252
22	2.997308	479.354011	0.002086	0.333633	159.928159	0.006253	264
23	3.150656	516.157528	0.001937	0.317394	163.825396	0.006104	276
24	3.311850	554.843982	0.001802	0.301946	167.532948	0.005969	288
25	3.481290	595.509709	0.001679	0.287250	171.060047	0.005846	300
26	3.659400	638.255971	0.001567	0.273269	174.415476	0.005733	312
27	3.846622	683.189213	0.001464	0.259968	177.607590	0.005630	324
28	4.043422	730.421325	0.001369	0.247315	180.644338	0.005536	336
29	4.250291	780.069922	0.001282	0.235278	183.533283	0.005449	348
30	4.467744	832.258635	0.001202	0.223827	186.281617	0.005368	360
31	4.696323	887.117422	0.001127	0.212933	188.896185	0.005294	372
32	4.936595	944.782889	0.001058	0.202569	191.383498	0.005225	384
33	5.189161	1005.398630	0.000995	0.192709	193.749748	0.005161	396
34	5.454648	1069.115587	0.000935	0.183330	196.000829	0.005102	408
35	5.733716	1136.092425	0.000880	0.174407	198.142346	0.005047	420
36	6.027066	1206.495925	0.000829	0.165918	200.179632	0.004996	432
37	6.335423	1280.501402	0.000781	0.157843	202.117759	0.004948	444
38	6.659555	1358.293140	0.000736	0.150160	203.961555	0.004903	456
39	7.000270	1440.064850	0.000694	0.142852	205.715609	0.004861	468
40	7.358417	1526.020157	0.000655	0.135899	207.384291	0.004822	480

ANNUAL COMPOUND INTEREST TABLES
                                          EFFECTIVE RATE   5.00

	1 AMOUNT OF $1 AT COMPOUND INTEREST	2 ACCUMULATION OF $1 PER PERIOD	3 SINKING FUND FACTOR	4 PRESENT VALUE REVERSION OF $1	5 PRESENT VALUE ORD. ANNUITY $1 PER PERIOD	6 INSTALMENT TO AMORTIZE $1
YEARS						
1	1.050000	1.000000	1.000000	0.952381	0.952381	1.050000
2	1.102500	2.050000	0.487805	0.907029	1.859410	0.537805
3	1.157625	3.152500	0.317209	0.863838	2.723248	0.367209
4	1.215506	4.310125	0.232012	0.822702	3.545951	0.282012
5	1.276282	5.525631	0.180975	0.783526	4.329477	0.230975
6	1.340096	6.801913	0.147017	0.746215	5.075692	0.197017
7	1.407100	8.142008	0.122820	0.710681	5.786373	0.172820
8	1.477455	9.549109	0.104722	0.676839	6.463213	0.154722
9	1.551328	11.026564	0.090690	0.644609	7.107822	0.140690
10	1.628895	12.577893	0.079505	0.613913	7.721735	0.129505
11	1.710339	14.206787	0.070389	0.584679	8.306414	0.120389
12	1.795856	15.917127	0.062825	0.556837	8.863252	0.112825
13	1.885649	17.712983	0.056456	0.530321	9.393573	0.106456
14	1.979932	19.598632	0.051024	0.505068	9.898641	0.101024
15	2.078928	21.578564	0.046342	0.481017	10.379658	0.096342
16	2.182875	23.657492	0.042270	0.458112	10.837770	0.092270
17	2.292018	25.840366	0.038699	0.436297	11.274066	0.088699
18	2.406619	28.132385	0.035546	0.415521	11.689587	0.085546
19	2.526950	30.539004	0.032745	0.395734	12.085321	0.082745
20	2.653298	33.065954	0.030243	0.376889	12.462210	0.080243
21	2.785963	35.719252	0.027996	0.358942	12.821153	0.077996
22	2.925261	38.505214	0.025971	0.341850	13.163003	0.075971
23	3.071524	41.430475	0.024137	0.325571	13.488574	0.074137
24	3.225100	44.501999	0.022471	0.310068	13.798642	0.072471
25	3.386355	47.727099	0.020952	0.295303	14.093945	0.070952
26	3.555673	51.113454	0.019564	0.281241	14.375185	0.069564
27	3.733456	54.669126	0.018292	0.267848	14.643034	0.068292
28	3.920129	58.402583	0.017123	0.255094	14.898127	0.067123
29	4.116136	62.322712	0.016046	0.242946	15.141074	0.066046
30	4.321942	66.438848	0.015051	0.231377	15.372451	0.065051
31	4.538039	70.760790	0.014132	0.220359	15.592811	0.064132
32	4.764941	75.298829	0.013280	0.209866	15.802677	0.063280
33	5.003189	80.063771	0.012490	0.199873	16.002549	0.062490
34	5.253348	85.066959	0.011755	0.190355	16.192904	0.061755
35	5.516015	90.320307	0.011072	0.181290	16.374194	0.061072
36	5.791816	95.836323	0.010434	0.172657	16.546852	0.060434
37	6.081407	101.628139	0.009840	0.164436	16.711287	0.059840
38	6.385477	107.709546	0.009284	0.156605	16.867893	0.059284
39	6.704751	114.095023	0.008765	0.149148	17.017041	0.058765
40	7.039989	120.799774	0.008278	0.142046	17.159086	0.058278
41	7.391988	127.839763	0.007822	0.135282	17.294368	0.057822
42	7.761588	135.231751	0.007395	0.128840	17.423208	0.057395
43	8.149667	142.993339	0.006993	0.122704	17.545912	0.056993
44	8.557150	151.143006	0.006616	0.116861	17.662773	0.056616
45	8.985008	159.700156	0.006262	0.111297	17.774070	0.056262
46	9.434258	168.685164	0.005928	0.105997	17.880066	0.055928
47	9.905971	178.119422	0.005614	0.100949	17.981016	0.055614
48	10.401269	188.025393	0.005318	0.096142	18.077158	0.055318
49	10.921333	198.426663	0.005040	0.091564	18.168722	0.055040
50	11.467400	209.347996	0.004777	0.087204	18.255925	0.054777

6.00% MONTHLY COMPOUND INTEREST TABLES 6.00%
EFFECTIVE RATE 0.500

	1 AMOUNT OF $1 AT COMPOUND INTEREST	2 ACCUMULATION OF $1 PER PERIOD	3 SINKING FUND FACTOR	4 PRESENT VALUE REVERSION OF $1	5 PRESENT VALUE ORD. ANNUITY $1 PER PERIOD	6 INSTALMENT TO AMORTIZE $1	
MONTHS							
1	1.005000	1.000000	1.000000	0.995025	0.995025	1.005000	
2	1.010025	2.005000	0.498753	0.990075	1.985099	0.503753	
3	1.015075	3.015025	0.331672	0.985149	2.970248	0.336672	
4	1.020151	4.030100	0.248133	0.980248	3.950496	0.253133	
5	1.025251	5.050251	0.198010	0.975371	4.925866	0.203010	
6	1.030378	6.075502	0.164595	0.970518	5.896384	0.169595	
7	1.035529	7.105879	0.140729	0.965690	6.862074	0.145729	
8	1.040707	8.141409	0.122829	0.960885	7.822959	0.127829	
9	1.045911	9.182116	0.108907	0.956105	8.779064	0.113907	
10	1.051140	10.228026	0.097771	0.951348	9.730412	0.102771	
11	1.056396	11.279167	0.088659	0.946615	10.677027	0.093659	
12	1.061678	12.335562	0.081066	0.941905	11.618932	0.086066	
YEARS							MONTHS
1	1.061678	12.335562	0.081066	0.941905	11.618932	0.086066	12
2	1.127160	25.431955	0.039321	0.887186	22.562866	0.044321	24
3	1.196681	39.336105	0.025422	0.835645	32.871016	0.030422	36
4	1.270489	54.097832	0.018485	0.787098	42.580318	0.023485	48
5	1.348850	69.770031	0.014333	0.741372	51.725561	0.019333	60
6	1.432044	86.408856	0.011573	0.698302	60.339514	0.016573	72
7	1.520370	104.073927	0.009609	0.657735	68.453042	0.014609	84
8	1.614143	122.828542	0.008141	0.619524	76.095218	0.013141	96
9	1.713699	142.739900	0.007006	0.583533	83.293424	0.012006	108
10	1.819397	163.879347	0.006102	0.549633	90.073453	0.011102	120
11	1.931613	186.322629	0.005367	0.517702	96.459599	0.010367	132
12	2.050751	210.150163	0.004759	0.487626	102.474743	0.009759	144
13	2.177237	235.447328	0.004247	0.459298	108.140440	0.009247	156
14	2.311524	262.304766	0.003812	0.432615	113.476990	0.008812	168
15	2.454094	290.818712	0.003439	0.407482	118.503515	0.008439	180
16	2.605457	321.091337	0.003114	0.383810	123.238025	0.008114	192
17	2.766156	353.231110	0.002831	0.361513	127.697486	0.007831	204
18	2.936766	387.353194	0.002582	0.340511	131.897876	0.007582	216
19	3.117899	423.579854	0.002361	0.320729	135.854246	0.007361	228
20	3.310204	462.040895	0.002164	0.302096	139.580772	0.007164	240
21	3.514371	502.874129	0.001989	0.284546	143.090806	0.006989	252
22	3.731129	546.225867	0.001831	0.268015	146.396927	0.006831	264
23	3.961257	592.251446	0.001688	0.252445	149.510979	0.006688	276
24	4.205579	641.115782	0.001560	0.237779	152.444121	0.006560	288
25	4.464970	692.993962	0.001443	0.223966	155.206864	0.006443	300
26	4.740359	748.071876	0.001337	0.210954	157.809106	0.006337	312
27	5.032734	806.546875	0.001240	0.198699	160.260172	0.006240	324
28	5.343142	868.628484	0.001151	0.187156	162.568844	0.006151	336
29	5.672696	934.539150	0.001070	0.176283	164.743394	0.006070	348
30	6.022575	1004.515043	0.000996	0.166042	166.791614	0.005996	360
31	6.394034	1078.806895	0.000927	0.156396	168.720864	0.005927	372
32	6.788405	1157.680906	0.000864	0.147310	170.537996	0.005864	384
33	7.207098	1241.419693	0.000806	0.138752	172.249581	0.005806	396
34	7.651617	1330.323306	0.000752	0.130691	173.861732	0.005752	408
35	8.123551	1424.710299	0.000702	0.123099	175.380226	0.005702	420
36	8.624594	1524.918875	0.000656	0.115947	176.810504	0.005656	432
37	9.156540	1631.308097	0.000613	0.109212	178.157690	0.005613	444
38	9.721296	1744.259173	0.000573	0.102867	179.426611	0.005573	456
39	10.320884	1864.176825	0.000536	0.096891	180.621815	0.005536	468
40	10.957454	1991.490734	0.000502	0.091262	181.747594	0.005502	480

ANNUAL COMPOUND INTEREST TABLES
EFFECTIVE RATE 6.00

	1 AMOUNT OF $1 AT COMPOUND INTEREST	2 ACCUMULATION OF $1 PER PERIOD	3 SINKING FUND FACTOR	4 PRESENT VALUE REVERSION OF $1	5 PRESENT VALUE ORD. ANNUITY $1 PER PERIOD	6 INSTALMENT TO AMORTIZE $1
YEARS						
1	1.060000	1.000000	1.000000	0.943396	0.943396	1.060000
2	1.123600	2.060000	0.485437	0.889996	1.833393	0.545437
3	1.191016	3.183600	0.314110	0.839619	2.673012	0.374110
4	1.262477	4.374616	0.228591	0.792094	3.465106	0.288591
5	1.338226	5.637093	0.177396	0.747258	4.212364	0.237396
6	1.418519	6.975319	0.143363	0.704961	4.917324	0.203363
7	1.503630	8.393838	0.119135	0.665057	5.582381	0.179135
8	1.593848	9.897468	0.101036	0.627412	6.209794	0.161036
9	1.689479	11.491316	0.087022	0.591898	6.801692	0.147022
10	1.790848	13.180795	0.075868	0.558395	7.360087	0.135868
11	1.898299	14.971643	0.066793	0.526788	7.886875	0.126793
12	2.012196	16.869941	0.059277	0.496969	8.383844	0.119277
13	2.132928	18.882138	0.052960	0.468839	8.852683	0.112960
14	2.260904	21.015066	0.047585	0.442301	9.294984	0.107585
15	2.396558	23.275970	0.042963	0.417265	9.712249	0.102963
16	2.540352	25.672528	0.038952	0.393646	10.105895	0.098952
17	2.692773	28.212880	0.035445	0.371364	10.477260	0.095445
18	2.854339	30.905653	0.032357	0.350344	10.827603	0.092357
19	3.025600	33.759992	0.029621	0.330513	11.158116	0.089621
20	3.207135	36.785591	0.027185	0.311805	11.469921	0.087185
21	3.399564	39.992727	0.025005	0.294155	11.764077	0.085005
22	3.603537	43.392290	0.023046	0.277505	12.041582	0.083046
23	3.819750	46.995828	0.021278	0.261797	12.303379	0.081278
24	4.048935	50.815577	0.019679	0.246979	12.550358	0.079679
25	4.291871	54.864512	0.018227	0.232999	12.783356	0.078227
26	4.549383	59.156383	0.016904	0.219810	13.003166	0.076904
27	4.822346	63.705766	0.015697	0.207368	13.210534	0.075697
28	5.111687	68.528112	0.014593	0.195630	13.406164	0.074593
29	5.418388	73.639798	0.013580	0.184557	13.590721	0.073580
30	5.743491	79.058186	0.012649	0.174110	13.764831	0.072649
31	6.088101	84.801677	0.011792	0.164255	13.929086	0.071792
32	6.453387	90.889778	0.011002	0.154957	14.084043	0.071002
33	6.840590	97.343165	0.010273	0.146186	14.230230	0.070273
34	7.251025	104.183755	0.009598	0.137912	14.368141	0.069598
35	7.686087	111.434780	0.008974	0.130105	14.498246	0.068974
36	8.147252	119.120867	0.008395	0.122741	14.620987	0.068395
37	8.636087	127.268119	0.007857	0.115793	14.736780	0.067857
38	9.154252	135.904206	0.007358	0.109239	14.846019	0.067358
39	9.703507	145.058458	0.006894	0.103056	14.949075	0.066894
40	10.285718	154.761966	0.006462	0.097222	15.046297	0.066462
41	10.902861	165.047684	0.006059	0.091719	15.138016	0.066059
42	11.557033	175.950545	0.005683	0.086527	15.224543	0.065683
43	12.250455	187.507577	0.005333	0.081630	15.306173	0.065333
44	12.985482	199.758032	0.005006	0.077009	15.383182	0.065006
45	13.764611	212.743514	0.004700	0.072650	15.455832	0.064700
46	14.590487	226.508125	0.004415	0.068538	15.524370	0.064415
47	15.465917	241.098612	0.004148	0.064658	15.589028	0.064148
48	16.393872	256.564529	0.003898	0.060998	15.650027	0.063898
49	17.377504	272.958401	0.003664	0.057546	15.707572	0.063664
50	18.420154	290.335905	0.003444	0.054288	15.761861	0.063444

6.50%   MONTHLY COMPOUND INTEREST TABLES   6.50%
                              EFFECTIVE RATE 0.542

	1 AMOUNT OF $1 AT COMPOUND INTEREST	2 ACCUMULATION OF $1 PER PERIOD	3 SINKING FUND FACTOR	4 PRESENT VALUE REVERSION OF $1	5 PRESENT VALUE ORD. ANNUITY $1 PER PERIOD	6 INSTALMENT TO AMORTIZE $1	
MONTHS							
1	1.005417	1.000000	1.000000	0.994613	0.994613	1.005417	
2	1.010863	2.005417	0.498649	0.989254	1.983867	0.504066	
3	1.016338	3.016279	0.331534	0.983924	2.967791	0.336951	
4	1.021843	4.032618	0.247978	0.978624	3.946415	0.253395	
5	1.027378	5.054461	0.197845	0.973351	4.919766	0.203262	
6	1.032943	6.081839	0.164424	0.968107	5.887873	0.169841	
7	1.038538	7.114782	0.140552	0.962892	6.850765	0.145969	
8	1.044164	8.153321	0.122649	0.957704	7.808469	0.128066	
9	1.049820	9.197485	0.108725	0.952545	8.761014	0.114142	
10	1.055506	10.247304	0.097587	0.947413	9.708426	0.103003	
11	1.061224	11.302811	0.088474	0.942309	10.650735	0.093890	
12	1.066972	12.364034	0.080880	0.937232	11.587967	0.086296	
YEARS							MONTHS
1	1.066972	12.364034	0.080880	0.937232	11.587967	0.086296	12
2	1.138429	25.556111	0.039130	0.878404	22.448578	0.044546	24
3	1.214672	39.631685	0.025232	0.823268	32.627489	0.030649	36
4	1.296020	54.649927	0.018298	0.771593	42.167488	0.023715	48
5	1.382817	70.673968	0.014149	0.723161	51.108680	0.019566	60
6	1.475427	87.771168	0.011393	0.677770	59.488649	0.016810	72
7	1.574239	106.013400	0.009433	0.635227	67.342623	0.014849	84
8	1.679669	125.477348	0.007970	0.595355	74.703617	0.013386	96
9	1.792160	146.244833	0.006838	0.557986	81.602576	0.012255	108
10	1.912184	168.403154	0.005938	0.522962	88.068500	0.011355	120
11	2.040246	192.045460	0.005207	0.490137	94.128569	0.010624	132
12	2.176885	217.271134	0.004603	0.459372	99.808260	0.010019	144
13	2.322675	244.186218	0.004095	0.430538	105.131446	0.009512	156
14	2.478229	272.903856	0.003664	0.403514	110.120506	0.009081	168
15	2.644201	303.544767	0.003294	0.378186	114.796412	0.008711	180
16	2.821288	336.237756	0.002974	0.354448	119.178820	0.008391	192
17	3.010235	371.120256	0.002695	0.332200	123.286152	0.008111	204
18	3.211836	408.338901	0.002449	0.311348	127.135675	0.007866	216
19	3.426938	448.050147	0.002232	0.291806	130.743570	0.007649	228
20	3.656447	490.420930	0.002039	0.273490	134.125004	0.007456	240
21	3.901326	535.629362	0.001867	0.256323	137.294192	0.007284	252
22	4.162605	583.865486	0.001713	0.240234	140.264456	0.007129	264
23	4.441382	635.332073	0.001574	0.225155	143.048282	0.006991	276
24	4.738830	690.245473	0.001449	0.211023	145.657372	0.006865	288
25	5.056198	748.836525	0.001335	0.197777	148.102695	0.006752	300
26	5.394821	811.351528	0.001233	0.185363	150.394529	0.006649	312
27	5.756122	878.053277	0.001139	0.173728	152.542509	0.006556	324
28	6.141620	949.222165	0.001053	0.162823	154.555664	0.006470	336
29	6.552936	1025.157366	0.000975	0.152603	156.442457	0.006392	348
30	6.991798	1106.178087	0.000904	0.143025	158.210820	0.006321	360
31	7.460052	1192.624917	0.000838	0.134047	159.868185	0.006255	372
32	7.959665	1284.861250	0.000778	0.125633	161.421521	0.006195	384
33	8.492739	1383.274822	0.000723	0.117748	162.877357	0.006140	396
34	9.061513	1488.279333	0.000672	0.110357	164.241813	0.006089	408
35	9.668379	1600.316190	0.000625	0.103430	165.520625	0.006042	420
36	10.315889	1719.856364	0.000581	0.096938	166.719167	0.005998	432
37	11.006763	1847.402364	0.000541	0.090853	167.842480	0.005958	444
38	11.743906	1983.490356	0.000504	0.085151	168.895284	0.005921	456
39	12.530417	2128.692413	0.000470	0.079806	169.882006	0.005886	468
40	13.369602	2283.618920	0.000438	0.074797	170.806793	0.005855	480

ANNUAL COMPOUND INTEREST TABLES   6.50%
                                      EFFECTIVE RATE 6.50

	1 AMOUNT OF $1 AT COMPOUND INTEREST	2 ACCUMULATION OF $1 PER PERIOD	3 SINKING FUND FACTOR	4 PRESENT VALUE REVERSION OF $1	5 PRESENT VALUE ORD. ANNUITY $1 PER PERIOD	6 INSTALMENT TO AMORTIZE $1
YEARS						
1	1.065000	1.000000	1.000000	0.938967	0.938967	1.065000
2	1.134225	2.065000	0.484262	0.881659	1.820626	0.549262
3	1.207950	3.199225	0.312576	0.827849	2.648476	0.377576
4	1.286466	4.407175	0.226903	0.777323	3.425799	0.291903
5	1.370087	5.693641	0.175635	0.729881	4.155679	0.240635
6	1.459142	7.063728	0.141568	0.685334	4.841014	0.206568
7	1.553987	8.522870	0.117331	0.643506	5.484520	0.182331
8	1.654996	10.076856	0.099237	0.604231	6.088751	0.164237
9	1.762570	11.731852	0.085238	0.567353	6.656104	0.150238
10	1.877137	13.494423	0.074105	0.532726	7.188830	0.139105
11	1.999151	15.371560	0.065055	0.500212	7.689042	0.130055
12	2.129096	17.370711	0.057568	0.469683	8.158725	0.122568
13	2.267487	19.499808	0.051283	0.441017	8.599742	0.116283
14	2.414874	21.767295	0.045940	0.414100	9.013842	0.110940
15	2.571841	24.182169	0.041353	0.388827	9.402669	0.106353
16	2.739011	26.754010	0.037378	0.365095	9.767764	0.102378
17	2.917046	29.493021	0.033906	0.342813	10.110577	0.098906
18	3.106654	32.410067	0.030855	0.321890	10.432466	0.095855
19	3.308587	35.516722	0.028156	0.302244	10.734710	0.093156
20	3.523645	38.825309	0.025756	0.283797	11.018507	0.090756
21	3.752682	42.348954	0.023613	0.266476	11.284983	0.088613
22	3.996606	46.101636	0.021691	0.250212	11.535196	0.086691
23	4.256386	50.098242	0.019961	0.234941	11.770137	0.084961
24	4.533051	54.354628	0.018398	0.220602	11.990739	0.083398
25	4.827699	58.887679	0.016981	0.207138	12.197877	0.081981
26	5.141500	63.715378	0.015695	0.194496	12.392373	0.080695
27	5.475697	68.856877	0.014523	0.182625	12.574998	0.079523
28	5.831617	74.332574	0.013453	0.171479	12.746477	0.078453
29	6.210672	80.164192	0.012474	0.161013	12.907490	0.077474
30	6.614366	86.374864	0.011577	0.151186	13.058676	0.076577
31	7.044300	92.989230	0.010754	0.141959	13.200635	0.075754
32	7.502179	100.033530	0.009997	0.133295	13.333929	0.074997
33	7.989821	107.535710	0.009299	0.125159	13.459088	0.074299
34	8.509159	115.525531	0.008656	0.117520	13.576609	0.073656
35	9.062255	124.034690	0.008062	0.110348	13.686957	0.073062
36	9.651301	133.096945	0.007513	0.103613	13.790570	0.072513
37	10.278636	142.748247	0.007005	0.097289	13.887859	0.072005
38	10.946747	153.026883	0.006535	0.091351	13.979210	0.071535
39	11.658286	163.973630	0.006099	0.085776	14.064986	0.071099
40	12.416075	175.631916	0.005694	0.080541	14.145527	0.070694
41	13.223119	188.047990	0.005318	0.075625	14.221152	0.070318
42	14.082622	201.271110	0.004968	0.071010	14.292161	0.069968
43	14.997993	215.353732	0.004644	0.066676	14.358837	0.069644
44	15.972862	230.351725	0.004341	0.062606	14.421443	0.069341
45	17.011098	246.324587	0.004060	0.058785	14.480228	0.069060
46	18.116820	263.335685	0.003797	0.055197	14.535426	0.068797
47	19.294413	281.452504	0.003553	0.051828	14.587254	0.068553
48	20.548550	300.746917	0.003325	0.048665	14.635919	0.068325
49	21.884205	321.295467	0.003112	0.045695	14.681615	0.068112
50	23.306679	343.179672	0.002914	0.042906	14.724521	0.067914

7.00%   MONTHLY COMPOUND INTEREST TABLES   7.00%
                              EFFECTIVE RATE 0.583

	1	2	3	4	5	6
	AMOUNT OF $1 AT COMPOUND INTEREST	ACCUMULATION OF $1 PER PERIOD	SINKING FUND FACTOR	PRESENT VALUE REVERSION OF $1	PRESENT VALUE ORD. ANNUITY $1 PER PERIOD	INSTALMENT TO AMORTIZE $1
MONTHS						
1	1.005833	1.000000	1.000000	0.994200	0.994200	1.005833
2	1.011701	2.005833	0.498546	0.988435	1.982635	0.504379
3	1.017602	3.017534	0.331396	0.982702	2.965337	0.337230
4	1.023538	4.035136	0.247823	0.977003	3.942340	0.253656
5	1.029509	5.058675	0.197680	0.971337	4.913677	0.203514
6	1.035514	6.088184	0.164253	0.965704	5.879381	0.170086
7	1.041555	7.123698	0.140377	0.960103	6.839484	0.146210
8	1.047631	8.165253	0.122470	0.954535	7.794019	0.128304
9	1.053742	9.212883	0.108544	0.948999	8.743018	0.114377
10	1.059889	10.266625	0.097403	0.943495	9.686513	0.103236
11	1.066071	11.326514	0.088288	0.938024	10.624537	0.094122
12	1.072290	12.392585	0.080693	0.932583	11.557120	0.086527

YEARS							MONTHS
1	1.072290	12.392585	0.080693	0.932583	11.557120	0.086527	12
2	1.149806	25.681032	0.038939	0.869712	22.335099	0.044773	24
3	1.232926	39.930101	0.025044	0.811079	32.386464	0.030877	36
4	1.322054	55.209236	0.018113	0.756399	41.760201	0.023946	48
5	1.417625	71.592902	0.013968	0.705405	50.501993	0.019801	60
6	1.520106	89.160944	0.011216	0.657849	58.654444	0.017049	72
7	1.629994	107.998981	0.009259	0.613499	66.257285	0.015093	84
8	1.747826	128.198821	0.007800	0.572139	73.347569	0.013634	96
9	1.874177	149.858909	0.006673	0.533568	79.959850	0.012506	108
10	2.009661	173.084807	0.005778	0.497596	86.126354	0.011611	120
11	2.154940	197.989707	0.005051	0.464050	91.877134	0.010884	132
12	2.310721	224.694985	0.004450	0.432765	97.240216	0.010284	144
13	2.477763	253.330789	0.003947	0.403590	102.241738	0.009781	156
14	2.656881	284.036677	0.003521	0.376381	106.906074	0.009354	168
15	2.848947	316.962297	0.003155	0.351007	111.255958	0.008988	180
16	3.054897	352.268112	0.002839	0.327343	115.312587	0.008672	192
17	3.275736	390.126188	0.002563	0.305275	119.095732	0.008397	204
18	3.512539	430.721027	0.002322	0.284694	122.623831	0.008155	216
19	3.766461	474.250470	0.002109	0.265501	125.914077	0.007942	228
20	4.038739	520.926660	0.001920	0.247602	128.982506	0.007753	240
21	4.330700	570.977075	0.001751	0.230910	131.844073	0.007585	252
22	4.643766	624.645640	0.001601	0.215342	134.512723	0.007434	264
23	4.979464	682.193909	0.001466	0.200825	137.001461	0.007299	276
24	5.339430	743.902347	0.001344	0.187286	139.322418	0.007178	288
25	5.725418	810.071693	0.001234	0.174660	141.486903	0.007068	300
26	6.139309	881.024426	0.001135	0.162885	143.505467	0.006968	312
27	6.583120	957.106339	0.001045	0.151904	145.387946	0.006878	324
28	7.059015	1038.688219	0.000963	0.141663	147.143515	0.006796	336
29	7.569311	1126.167659	0.000888	0.132112	148.780729	0.006721	348
30	8.116497	1219.970996	0.000820	0.123206	150.307568	0.006653	360
31	8.703240	1320.555383	0.000757	0.114900	151.731473	0.006591	372
32	9.332398	1428.411024	0.000700	0.107154	153.059383	0.006533	384
33	10.007037	1544.063557	0.000648	0.099930	154.297770	0.006481	396
34	10.730447	1668.076622	0.000599	0.093193	155.452669	0.006433	408
35	11.506152	1801.054601	0.000555	0.086910	156.529709	0.006389	420
36	12.337932	1943.645569	0.000514	0.081051	157.534139	0.006348	432
37	13.229843	2096.544450	0.000477	0.075587	158.470853	0.006310	444
38	14.186229	2260.496403	0.000442	0.070491	159.344418	0.006276	456
39	15.211753	2436.300456	0.000410	0.065739	160.159090	0.006244	468
40	16.311411	2624.813398	0.000381	0.061307	160.918839	0.006214	480

	1	2	3	4	5	6
	AMOUNT OF $1 AT COMPOUND INTEREST	ACCUMULATION OF $1 PER PERIOD	SINKING FUND FACTOR	PRESENT VALUE REVERSION OF $1	PRESENT VALUE ORD. ANNUITY $1 PER PERIOD	INSTALMENT TO AMORTIZE $1
YEARS						
1	1.070000	1.000000	1.000000	0.934579	0.934579	1.070000
2	1.144900	2.070000	0.483092	0.873439	1.808018	0.553092
3	1.225043	3.214900	0.311052	0.816298	2.624316	0.381052
4	1.310796	4.439943	0.225228	0.762895	3.387211	0.295228
5	1.402552	5.750739	0.173891	0.712986	4.100197	0.243891
6	1.500730	7.153291	0.139796	0.666342	4.766540	0.209796
7	1.605781	8.654021	0.115553	0.622750	5.389289	0.185553
8	1.718186	10.259803	0.097468	0.582009	5.971299	0.167468
9	1.838459	11.977989	0.083486	0.543934	6.515232	0.153486
10	1.967151	13.816448	0.072378	0.508349	7.023582	0.142378
11	2.104852	15.783599	0.063357	0.475093	7.498674	0.133357
12	2.252192	17.888451	0.055902	0.444012	7.942686	0.125902
13	2.409845	20.140643	0.049651	0.414964	8.357651	0.119651
14	2.578534	22.550488	0.044345	0.387817	8.745468	0.114345
15	2.759032	25.129022	0.039795	0.362446	9.107914	0.109795
16	2.952164	27.888054	0.035858	0.338735	9.446649	0.105858
17	3.158815	30.840217	0.032425	0.316574	9.763223	0.102425
18	3.379932	33.999033	0.029413	0.295864	10.059087	0.099413
19	3.616528	37.378965	0.026753	0.276508	10.335595	0.096753
20	3.869684	40.995492	0.024393	0.258419	10.594014	0.094393
21	4.140562	44.865177	0.022289	0.241513	10.835527	0.092289
22	4.430402	49.005739	0.020406	0.225713	11.061240	0.090406
23	4.740530	53.436141	0.018714	0.210947	11.272187	0.088714
24	5.072367	58.176671	0.017189	0.197147	11.469334	0.087189
25	5.427433	63.249038	0.015811	0.184249	11.653583	0.085811
26	5.807353	68.676470	0.014561	0.172195	11.825779	0.084561
27	6.213868	74.483823	0.013426	0.160930	11.986709	0.083426
28	6.648838	80.697691	0.012392	0.150402	12.137111	0.082392
29	7.114257	87.346529	0.011449	0.140563	12.277674	0.081449
30	7.612255	94.460786	0.010586	0.131367	12.409041	0.080586
31	8.145113	102.073041	0.009797	0.122773	12.531814	0.079797
32	8.715271	110.218154	0.009073	0.114741	12.646555	0.079073
33	9.325340	118.933425	0.008408	0.107235	12.753790	0.078408
34	9.978114	128.258765	0.007797	0.100219	12.854009	0.077797
35	10.676581	138.236878	0.007234	0.093663	12.947672	0.077234
36	11.423942	148.913460	0.006715	0.087535	13.035208	0.076715
37	12.223618	160.337402	0.006237	0.081809	13.117017	0.076237
38	13.079271	172.561020	0.005795	0.076457	13.193473	0.075795
39	13.994820	185.640292	0.005387	0.071455	13.264928	0.075387
40	14.974458	199.635112	0.005009	0.066780	13.331709	0.075009
41	16.022670	214.609570	0.004660	0.062412	13.394120	0.074660
42	17.144257	230.632240	0.004336	0.058329	13.452449	0.074336
43	18.344355	247.776496	0.004036	0.054513	13.506962	0.074036
44	19.628460	266.120851	0.003758	0.050946	13.557908	0.073758
45	21.002452	285.749311	0.003500	0.047613	13.605522	0.073500
46	22.472623	306.751763	0.003260	0.044499	13.650020	0.073260
47	24.045707	329.224386	0.003037	0.041587	13.691608	0.073037
48	25.728907	353.270093	0.002831	0.038867	13.730474	0.072831
49	27.529930	378.999000	0.002639	0.036324	13.766799	0.072639
50	29.457025	406.528929	0.002460	0.033948	13.800746	0.072460

7.50%　　　　　　　　MONTHLY COMPOUND INTEREST TABLES　　　　　　7.50%
EFFECTIVE RATE 0.625

	1 AMOUNT OF $1 AT COMPOUND INTEREST	2 ACCUMULATION OF $1 PER PERIOD	3 SINKING FUND FACTOR	4 PRESENT VALUE REVERSION OF $1	5 PRESENT VALUE ORD. ANNUITY $1 PER PERIOD	6 INSTALMENT TO AMORTIZE $1
MONTHS						
1	1.006250	1.000000	1.000000	0.993789	0.993789	1.006250
2	1.012539	2.006250	0.498442	0.987616	1.981405	0.504692
3	1.018867	3.018789	0.331259	0.981482	2.962887	0.337509
4	1.025235	4.037656	0.247668	0.975386	3.938273	0.253918
5	1.031643	5.062892	0.197516	0.969327	4.907600	0.203766
6	1.038091	6.094535	0.164081	0.963307	5.870907	0.170331
7	1.044579	7.132626	0.140201	0.957324	6.828231	0.146451
8	1.051108	8.177205	0.122291	0.951377	7.779608	0.128541
9	1.057677	9.228312	0.108362	0.945468	8.725076	0.114612
10	1.064287	10.285989	0.097220	0.939596	9.664672	0.103470
11	1.070939	11.350277	0.088104	0.933760	10.598432	0.094354
12	1.077633	12.421216	0.080507	0.927960	11.526392	0.086757

YEARS							MONTHS
1	1.077633	12.421216	0.080507	0.927960	11.526392	0.086757	12
2	1.161292	25.806723	0.038750	0.861110	22.222423	0.045000	24
3	1.251446	40.231382	0.024856	0.799076	32.147913	0.031106	36
4	1.348599	55.775864	0.017929	0.741510	41.358371	0.024179	48
5	1.453294	72.527105	0.013788	0.688092	49.905308	0.020038	60
6	1.566117	90.578789	0.011040	0.638522	57.836524	0.017290	72
7	1.687699	110.031871	0.009088	0.592523	65.196376	0.015338	84
8	1.818720	130.995147	0.007634	0.549837	72.026024	0.013884	96
9	1.959912	153.585857	0.006511	0.510227	78.363665	0.012761	108
10	2.112065	177.930342	0.005620	0.473470	84.244743	0.011870	120
11	2.276030	204.164753	0.004898	0.439362	89.702148	0.011148	132
12	2.452724	232.435809	0.004302	0.407710	94.766401	0.010552	144
13	2.643135	262.901620	0.003804	0.378339	99.465827	0.010054	156
14	2.848329	295.732572	0.003381	0.351083	103.826705	0.009631	168
15	3.069452	331.112276	0.003020	0.325791	107.873427	0.009270	180
16	3.307741	369.238599	0.002708	0.302321	111.628623	0.008958	192
17	3.564530	410.324766	0.002437	0.280542	115.113294	0.008687	204
18	3.841254	454.600560	0.002200	0.260332	118.346930	0.008450	216
19	4.139460	502.313599	0.001991	0.241577	121.347615	0.008241	228
20	4.460817	553.730725	0.001806	0.224174	124.132131	0.008056	240
21	4.807122	609.139496	0.001642	0.208025	126.716051	0.007892	252
22	5.180311	668.849794	0.001495	0.193039	129.113825	0.007745	264
23	5.582472	733.195558	0.001364	0.179132	131.338863	0.007614	276
24	6.015854	802.536650	0.001246	0.166227	133.403610	0.007496	288
25	6.482880	877.260872	0.001140	0.154252	135.319613	0.007390	300
26	6.986163	957.786129	0.001044	0.143140	137.097587	0.007294	312
27	7.528517	1044.562771	0.000957	0.132828	138.747475	0.007207	324
28	8.112976	1138.076109	0.000879	0.123259	140.278506	0.007129	336
29	8.742807	1238.849131	0.000807	0.114380	141.699242	0.007057	348
30	9.421534	1347.445425	0.000742	0.106140	143.017627	0.006992	360
31	10.152952	1464.472331	0.000683	0.098494	144.241037	0.006933	372
32	10.941152	1590.584339	0.000629	0.091398	145.376312	0.006879	384
33	11.790542	1726.486751	0.000579	0.084814	146.429801	0.006829	396
34	12.705873	1872.939621	0.000534	0.078704	147.407398	0.006784	408
35	13.692263	2030.762007	0.000492	0.073034	148.314568	0.006742	420
36	14.755228	2200.836555	0.000454	0.067773	149.156386	0.006704	432
37	15.900715	2384.114432	0.000419	0.062890	149.937560	0.006669	444
38	17.135129	2581.620647	0.000387	0.058360	150.662457	0.006637	456
39	18.465374	2794.459783	0.000358	0.054155	151.335133	0.006608	468
40	19.898889	3023.822174	0.000331	0.050254	151.959350	0.006581	480

ANNUAL COMPOUND INTEREST TABLES
                                   EFFECTIVE RATE 7.50

	1	2	3	4	5	6
	AMOUNT OF $1 AT COMPOUND INTEREST	ACCUMULATION OF $1 PER PERIOD	SINKING FUND FACTOR	PRESENT VALUE REVERSION OF $1	PRESENT VALUE ORD. ANNUITY $1 PER PERIOD	INSTALMENT TO AMORTIZE $1
YEARS						
1	1.075000	1.000000	1.000000	0.930233	0.930233	1.075000
2	1.155625	2.075000	0.481928	0.865333	1.795565	0.556928
3	1.242297	3.230625	0.309538	0.804961	2.600526	0.384538
4	1.335469	4.472922	0.223568	0.748801	3.349326	0.298568
5	1.435629	5.808391	0.172165	0.696559	4.045885	0.247165
6	1.543302	7.244020	0.138045	0.647962	4.693846	0.213045
7	1.659049	8.787322	0.113800	0.602755	5.296601	0.188800
8	1.783478	10.446371	0.095727	0.560702	5.857304	0.170727
9	1.917239	12.229849	0.081767	0.521583	6.378887	0.156767
10	2.061032	14.147087	0.070686	0.485194	6.864081	0.145686
11	2.215609	16.208119	0.061697	0.451343	7.315424	0.136697
12	2.381780	18.423728	0.054278	0.419854	7.735278	0.129278
13	2.560413	20.805508	0.048064	0.390562	8.125840	0.123064
14	2.752444	23.365921	0.042797	0.363313	8.489154	0.117797
15	2.958877	26.118365	0.038287	0.337966	8.827120	0.113287
16	3.180793	29.077242	0.034391	0.314387	9.141507	0.109391
17	3.419353	32.258035	0.031000	0.292453	9.433960	0.106000
18	3.675804	35.677388	0.028029	0.272049	9.706009	0.103029
19	3.951489	39.353192	0.025411	0.253069	9.959078	0.100411
20	4.247851	43.304681	0.023092	0.235413	10.194491	0.098092
21	4.566440	47.552532	0.021029	0.218989	10.413480	0.096029
22	4.908923	52.118972	0.019187	0.203711	10.617191	0.094187
23	5.277092	57.027895	0.017535	0.189498	10.806689	0.092535
24	5.672874	62.304987	0.016050	0.176277	10.982967	0.091050
25	6.098340	67.977862	0.014711	0.163979	11.146946	0.089711
26	6.555715	74.076201	0.013500	0.152539	11.299485	0.088500
27	7.047394	80.631916	0.012402	0.141896	11.441381	0.087402
28	7.575948	87.679310	0.011405	0.131997	11.573378	0.086405
29	8.144144	95.255258	0.010498	0.122788	11.696165	0.085498
30	8.754955	103.399403	0.009671	0.114221	11.810386	0.084671
31	9.411577	112.154358	0.008916	0.106252	11.916638	0.083916
32	10.117445	121.565935	0.008226	0.098839	12.015478	0.083226
33	10.876253	131.683380	0.007594	0.091943	12.107421	0.082594
34	11.691972	142.559633	0.007015	0.085529	12.192950	0.082015
35	12.568870	154.251606	0.006483	0.079562	12.272511	0.081483
36	13.511536	166.820476	0.005994	0.074011	12.346522	0.080994
37	14.524901	180.332012	0.005545	0.068847	12.415370	0.080545
38	15.614268	194.856913	0.005132	0.064044	12.479414	0.080132
39	16.785339	210.471181	0.004751	0.059576	12.538989	0.079751
40	18.044239	227.256520	0.004400	0.055419	12.594409	0.079400
41	19.397557	245.300759	0.004077	0.051553	12.645962	0.079077
42	20.852374	264.698315	0.003778	0.047956	12.693918	0.078778
43	22.416302	285.550689	0.003502	0.044610	12.738528	0.078502
44	24.097524	307.966991	0.003247	0.041498	12.780026	0.078247
45	25.904839	332.064515	0.003011	0.038603	12.818629	0.078011
46	27.847702	357.969354	0.002794	0.035910	12.854539	0.077794
47	29.936279	385.817055	0.002592	0.033404	12.887943	0.077592
48	32.181500	415.753334	0.002405	0.031074	12.919017	0.077405
49	34.595113	447.934835	0.002232	0.028906	12.947922	0.077232
50	37.189746	482.529947	0.002072	0.026889	12.974812	0.077072

8.00%   MONTHLY COMPOUND INTEREST TABLES   8.00%
                                    EFFECTIVE RATE 0.667

	1 AMOUNT OF $1 AT COMPOUND INTEREST	2 ACCUMULATION OF $1 PER PERIOD	3 SINKING FUND FACTOR	4 PRESENT VALUE REVERSION OF $1	5 PRESENT VALUE ORD. ANNUITY $1 PER PERIOD	6 INSTALMENT TO AMORTIZE $1	
MONTHS							
1	1.006667	1.000000	1.000000	0.993377	0.993377	1.006667	
2	1.013378	2.006667	0.498339	0.986799	1.980176	0.505006	
3	1.020134	3.020044	0.331121	0.980264	2.960440	0.337788	
4	1.026935	4.040178	0.247514	0.973772	3.934212	0.254181	
5	1.033781	5.067113	0.197351	0.967323	4.901535	0.204018	
6	1.040673	6.100893	0.163910	0.960917	5.862452	0.170577	
7	1.047610	7.141566	0.140025	0.954553	6.817005	0.146692	
8	1.054595	8.189176	0.122112	0.948232	7.765237	0.128779	
9	1.061625	9.243771	0.108181	0.941952	8.707189	0.114848	
10	1.068703	10.305396	0.097037	0.935714	9.642903	0.103703	
11	1.075827	11.374099	0.087919	0.929517	10.572420	0.094586	
12	1.083000	12.449926	0.080322	0.923361	11.495782	0.086988	
YEARS							**MONTHS**
1	1.083000	12.449926	0.080322	0.923361	11.495782	0.086988	12
2	1.172888	25.933190	0.038561	0.852596	22.110544	0.045227	24
3	1.270237	40.535558	0.024670	0.787255	31.911806	0.031336	36
4	1.375666	56.349915	0.017746	0.726921	40.961913	0.024413	48
5	1.489846	73.476856	0.013610	0.671210	49.318433	0.020276	60
6	1.613502	92.025325	0.010867	0.619770	57.034522	0.017533	72
7	1.747422	112.113308	0.008920	0.572272	64.159261	0.015586	84
8	1.892457	133.868583	0.007470	0.528414	70.737970	0.014137	96
9	2.049530	157.429535	0.006352	0.487917	76.812497	0.013019	108
10	2.219640	182.946035	0.005466	0.450523	82.421481	0.012133	120
11	2.403869	210.580392	0.004749	0.415996	87.600600	0.011415	132
12	2.603389	240.508387	0.004158	0.384115	92.382800	0.010825	144
13	2.819469	272.920390	0.003664	0.354677	96.798498	0.010331	156
14	3.053484	308.022574	0.003247	0.327495	100.875784	0.009913	168
15	3.306921	346.038222	0.002890	0.302396	104.640592	0.009557	180
16	3.581394	387.209149	0.002583	0.279221	108.116871	0.009249	192
17	3.878648	431.797244	0.002316	0.257822	111.326733	0.008983	204
18	4.200574	480.086128	0.002083	0.238063	114.290596	0.008750	216
19	4.549220	532.382966	0.001878	0.219818	117.027313	0.008545	228
20	4.926803	589.020416	0.001698	0.202971	119.554292	0.008364	240
21	5.335725	650.358746	0.001538	0.187416	121.887606	0.008204	252
22	5.778588	716.788127	0.001395	0.173053	124.042099	0.008062	264
23	6.258207	788.731114	0.001268	0.159790	126.031475	0.007935	276
24	6.777636	866.645333	0.001154	0.147544	127.868388	0.007821	288
25	7.340176	951.026395	0.001051	0.136237	129.564523	0.007718	300
26	7.949407	1042.411042	0.000959	0.125796	131.130668	0.007626	312
27	8.609204	1141.380571	0.000876	0.116155	132.576786	0.007543	324
28	9.323763	1248.564521	0.000801	0.107253	133.912076	0.007468	336
29	10.097631	1364.644687	0.000733	0.099033	135.145031	0.007399	348
30	10.935730	1490.359449	0.000671	0.091443	136.283494	0.007338	360
31	11.843390	1626.508474	0.000615	0.084435	137.334707	0.007281	372
32	12.826385	1773.957801	0.000564	0.077964	138.305357	0.007230	384
33	13.890969	1933.645350	0.000517	0.071989	139.201617	0.007184	396
34	15.043913	2106.586886	0.000475	0.066672	140.029190	0.007141	408
35	16.292550	2293.882485	0.000436	0.061378	140.793338	0.007103	420
36	17.644824	2496.723526	0.000401	0.056674	141.498923	0.007067	432
37	19.109335	2716.400273	0.000368	0.052330	142.150433	0.007035	444
38	20.695401	2954.310082	0.000338	0.048320	142.752013	0.007005	456
39	22.413109	3211.966288	0.000311	0.044617	143.307488	0.006978	468
40	24.273386	3491.007831	0.000286	0.041197	143.820392	0.006953	480

ANNUAL COMPOUND INTEREST TABLES
                                      EFFECTIVE RATE   8.00

	1 AMOUNT OF $1 AT COMPOUND INTEREST	2 ACCUMULATION OF $1 PER PERIOD	3 SINKING FUND FACTOR	4 PRESENT VALUE REVERSION OF $1	5 PRESENT VALUE ORD. ANNUITY $1 PER PERIOD	6 INSTALMENT TO AMORTIZE $1
YEARS						
1	1.080000	1.000000	1.000000	0.925926	0.925926	1.080000
2	1.166400	2.080000	0.480769	0.857339	1.783265	0.560769
3	1.259712	3.246400	0.308034	0.793832	2.577097	0.388034
4	1.360489	4.506112	0.221921	0.735030	3.312127	0.301921
5	1.469328	5.866601	0.170456	0.680583	3.992710	0.250456
6	1.586874	7.335929	0.136315	0.630170	4.622880	0.216315
7	1.713824	8.922803	0.112072	0.583490	5.206370	0.192072
8	1.850930	10.636628	0.094015	0.540269	5.746639	0.174015
9	1.999005	12.487558	0.080080	0.500249	6.246888	0.160080
10	2.158925	14.486562	0.069029	0.463193	6.710081	0.149029
11	2.331639	16.645487	0.060076	0.428883	7.138964	0.140076
12	2.518170	18.977126	0.052695	0.397114	7.536078	0.132695
13	2.719624	21.495297	0.046522	0.367698	7.903776	0.126522
14	2.937194	24.214920	0.041297	0.340461	8.244237	0.121297
15	3.172169	27.152114	0.036830	0.315242	8.559479	0.116830
16	3.425943	30.324283	0.032977	0.291890	8.851369	0.112977
17	3.700018	33.750226	0.029629	0.270269	9.121638	0.109629
18	3.996019	37.450244	0.026702	0.250249	9.371887	0.106702
19	4.315701	41.446263	0.024128	0.231712	9.603599	0.104128
20	4.660957	45.761964	0.021852	0.214548	9.818147	0.101852
21	5.033834	50.422921	0.019832	0.198656	10.016803	0.099832
22	5.436540	55.456755	0.018032	0.183941	10.200744	0.098032
23	5.871464	60.893296	0.016422	0.170315	10.371059	0.096422
24	6.341181	66.764759	0.014978	0.157699	10.528758	0.094978
25	6.848475	73.105940	0.013679	0.146018	10.674776	0.093679
26	7.396353	79.954415	0.012507	0.135202	10.809978	0.092507
27	7.988061	87.350768	0.011448	0.125187	10.935165	0.091448
28	8.627106	95.338830	0.010489	0.115914	11.051078	0.090489
29	9.317275	103.965936	0.009619	0.107328	11.158406	0.089619
30	10.062657	113.283211	0.008827	0.099377	11.257783	0.088827
31	10.867669	123.345868	0.008107	0.092016	11.349799	0.088107
32	11.737083	134.213537	0.007451	0.085200	11.434999	0.087451
33	12.676050	145.950620	0.006852	0.078889	11.513888	0.086852
34	13.690134	158.526670	0.006304	0.073045	11.586934	0.086304
35	14.785344	172.316804	0.005803	0.067635	11.654568	0.085803
36	15.968172	187.102148	0.005345	0.062625	11.717193	0.085345
37	17.245626	203.070320	0.004924	0.057986	11.775179	0.084924
38	18.625276	220.315945	0.004539	0.053690	11.828869	0.084539
39	20.115298	238.941221	0.004185	0.049713	11.878582	0.084185
40	21.724521	259.056519	0.003860	0.046031	11.924613	0.083860
41	23.462483	280.781040	0.003561	0.042621	11.967235	0.083561
42	25.339482	304.243523	0.003287	0.039464	12.006699	0.083287
43	27.366640	329.583005	0.003034	0.036541	12.043240	0.083034
44	29.555972	356.949646	0.002802	0.033834	12.077074	0.082802
45	31.920449	386.505617	0.002587	0.031328	12.108402	0.082587
46	34.474085	418.426067	0.002390	0.029007	12.137409	0.082390
47	37.232012	452.900152	0.002208	0.026859	12.164267	0.082208
48	40.210573	490.132164	0.002040	0.024869	12.189136	0.082040
49	43.427419	530.342737	0.001886	0.023027	12.212163	0.081886
50	46.901613	573.770156	0.001743	0.021321	12.233485	0.081743

8.50%   MONTHLY COMPOUND INTEREST TABLES   8.50%
                      EFFECTIVE RATE 0.708

	1 AMOUNT OF $1 AT COMPOUND INTEREST	2 ACCUMULATION OF $1 PER PERIOD	3 SINKING FUND FACTOR	4 PRESENT VALUE REVERSION OF $1	5 PRESENT VALUE ORD. ANNUITY $1 PER PERIOD	6 INSTALMENT TO AMORTIZE $1	
MONTHS							
1	1.007083	1.000000	1.000000	0.992966	0.992966	1.007083	
2	1.014217	2.007083	0.498235	0.985982	1.978949	0.505319	
3	1.021401	3.021300	0.330983	0.979048	2.957996	0.338067	
4	1.028636	4.042701	0.247359	0.972161	3.930158	0.254443	
5	1.035922	5.071337	0.197187	0.965324	4.895482	0.204270	
6	1.043260	6.107259	0.163740	0.958534	5.854016	0.170823	
7	1.050650	7.150519	0.139850	0.951792	6.805808	0.146933	
8	1.058092	8.201168	0.121934	0.945098	7.750906	0.129017	
9	1.065586	9.259260	0.108000	0.938450	8.689356	0.115083	
10	1.073134	10.324846	0.096854	0.931850	9.621206	0.103937	
11	1.080736	11.397980	0.087735	0.925296	10.546501	0.094818	
12	1.088391	12.478716	0.080136	0.918788	11.465289	0.087220	
YEARS							**MONTHS**
1	1.088391	12.478716	0.080136	0.918788	11.465289	0.087220	12
2	1.184595	26.060437	0.038372	0.844171	21.999453	0.045456	24
3	1.289302	40.842659	0.024484	0.775613	31.678112	0.031568	36
4	1.403265	56.931495	0.017565	0.712624	40.570744	0.024648	48
5	1.527301	74.442437	0.013433	0.654750	48.741183	0.020517	60
6	1.662300	93.501188	0.010695	0.601576	56.248080	0.017778	72
7	1.809232	114.244559	0.008753	0.552721	63.145324	0.015836	84
8	1.969152	136.821455	0.007309	0.507833	69.482425	0.014392	96
9	2.143207	161.393943	0.006196	0.466590	75.304875	0.013279	108
10	2.332647	188.138416	0.005315	0.428698	80.654470	0.012399	120
11	2.538832	217.246858	0.004603	0.393882	85.569611	0.011686	132
12	2.763242	248.928220	0.004017	0.361894	90.085581	0.011101	144
13	3.007487	283.409927	0.003528	0.332504	94.234798	0.010612	156
14	3.273321	320.939504	0.003116	0.305500	98.047046	0.010199	168
15	3.562653	361.786353	0.002764	0.280690	101.549693	0.009847	180
16	3.877559	406.243693	0.002462	0.257894	104.767881	0.009545	192
17	4.220300	454.630657	0.002200	0.236950	107.724713	0.009283	204
18	4.593337	507.294589	0.001971	0.217707	110.441412	0.009055	216
19	4.999346	564.613533	0.001771	0.200026	112.937482	0.008854	228
20	5.441243	626.998951	0.001595	0.183782	115.230840	0.008678	240
21	5.922199	694.898672	0.001439	0.168856	117.337948	0.008522	252
22	6.445667	768.800112	0.001301	0.155143	119.273933	0.008384	264
23	7.015406	849.233766	0.001178	0.142543	121.052692	0.008261	276
24	7.635504	936.777024	0.001067	0.130967	122.686994	0.008151	288
25	8.310413	1032.058310	0.000969	0.120331	124.188570	0.008052	300
26	9.044978	1135.761595	0.000880	0.110559	125.568199	0.007964	312
27	9.844472	1248.631307	0.000801	0.101580	126.835785	0.007884	324
28	10.714634	1371.477676	0.000729	0.093330	128.000428	0.007812	336
29	11.661710	1505.182546	0.000664	0.085751	129.070487	0.007748	348
30	12.692499	1650.705711	0.000606	0.078787	130.053643	0.007689	360
31	13.814400	1809.091800	0.000553	0.072388	130.956956	0.007636	372
32	15.035468	1981.477780	0.000505	0.066509	131.786908	0.007588	384
33	16.364466	2169.101112	0.000461	0.061108	132.549457	0.007544	396
34	17.810936	2373.308640	0.000421	0.056145	133.250078	0.007505	408
35	19.385261	2595.566257	0.000385	0.051586	133.893800	0.007469	420
36	21.098742	2837.469426	0.000352	0.047396	134.485244	0.007436	432
37	22.963679	3100.754635	0.000323	0.043547	135.028655	0.007406	444
38	24.993459	3387.311862	0.000295	0.040010	135.527934	0.007379	456
39	27.202654	3699.198142	0.000270	0.036761	135.986665	0.007354	468
40	29.607121	4038.652333	0.000248	0.033776	136.408142	0.007331	480

ANNUAL COMPOUND INTEREST TABLES
EFFECTIVE RATE 8.50

	1 AMOUNT OF $1 AT COMPOUND INTEREST	2 ACCUMULATION OF $1 PER PERIOD	3 SINKING FUND FACTOR	4 PRESENT VALUE REVERSION OF $1	5 PRESENT VALUE ORD. ANNUITY $1 PER PERIOD	6 INSTALMENT TO AMORTIZE $1
YEARS						
1	1.085000	1.000000	1.000000	0.921659	0.921659	1.085000
2	1.177225	2.085000	0.479616	0.849455	1.771114	0.564616
3	1.277289	3.262225	0.306539	0.782908	2.554022	0.391539
4	1.385859	4.539514	0.220288	0.721574	3.275597	0.305288
5	1.503657	5.925373	0.168766	0.665045	3.940642	0.253766
6	1.631468	7.429030	0.134607	0.612945	4.553587	0.219607
7	1.770142	9.060497	0.110369	0.564926	5.118514	0.195369
8	1.920604	10.830639	0.092331	0.520669	5.639183	0.177331
9	2.083856	12.751244	0.078424	0.479880	6.119063	0.163424
10	2.260983	14.835099	0.067408	0.442285	6.561348	0.152408
11	2.453167	17.096083	0.058493	0.407636	6.968984	0.143493
12	2.661686	19.549250	0.051153	0.375702	7.344686	0.136153
13	2.887930	22.210936	0.045023	0.346269	7.690955	0.130023
14	3.133404	25.098866	0.039842	0.319142	8.010097	0.124842
15	3.399743	28.232269	0.035420	0.294140	8.304237	0.120420
16	3.688721	31.632012	0.031614	0.271097	8.575333	0.116614
17	4.002262	35.320733	0.028312	0.249859	8.825192	0.113312
18	4.342455	39.322995	0.025430	0.230285	9.055476	0.110430
19	4.711563	43.665450	0.022901	0.212244	9.267720	0.107901
20	5.112046	48.377013	0.020671	0.195616	9.463337	0.105671
21	5.546570	53.489059	0.018695	0.180292	9.643628	0.103695
22	6.018028	59.035629	0.016939	0.166167	9.809796	0.101939
23	6.529561	65.053658	0.015372	0.153150	9.962945	0.100372
24	7.084574	71.583219	0.013970	0.141152	10.104097	0.098970
25	7.686762	78.667792	0.012712	0.130094	10.234191	0.097712
26	8.340137	86.354555	0.011580	0.119902	10.354093	0.096580
27	9.049049	94.694692	0.010560	0.110509	10.464602	0.095560
28	9.818218	103.743741	0.009639	0.101851	10.566453	0.094639
29	10.652766	113.561959	0.008806	0.093872	10.660326	0.093806
30	11.558252	124.214725	0.008051	0.086518	10.746844	0.093051
31	12.540703	135.772977	0.007365	0.079740	10.826584	0.092365
32	13.606663	148.313680	0.006742	0.073493	10.900078	0.091742
33	14.763229	161.920343	0.006176	0.067736	10.967813	0.091176
34	16.018104	176.683572	0.005660	0.062429	11.030243	0.090660
35	17.379642	192.701675	0.005189	0.057539	11.087781	0.090189
36	18.856912	210.081318	0.004760	0.053031	11.140812	0.089760
37	20.459750	228.938230	0.004368	0.048876	11.189689	0.089368
38	22.198828	249.397979	0.004010	0.045047	11.234736	0.089010
39	24.085729	271.596808	0.003682	0.041518	11.276255	0.088682
40	26.133016	295.682536	0.003382	0.038266	11.314520	0.088382
41	28.354322	321.815552	0.003107	0.035268	11.349788	0.088107
42	30.764439	350.169874	0.002856	0.032505	11.382293	0.087856
43	33.379417	380.934313	0.002625	0.029959	11.412252	0.087625
44	36.216667	414.313730	0.002414	0.027612	11.439864	0.087414
45	39.295084	450.530397	0.002220	0.025448	11.465312	0.087220
46	42.635166	489.825480	0.002042	0.023455	11.488767	0.087042
47	46.259155	532.460646	0.001878	0.021617	11.510384	0.086878
48	50.191183	578.719801	0.001728	0.019924	11.530308	0.086728
49	54.457434	628.910984	0.001590	0.018363	11.548671	0.086590
50	59.086316	683.368418	0.001463	0.016924	11.565595	0.086463

9.00%   MONTHLY COMPOUND INTEREST TABLES   9.00%
                                      EFFECTIVE RATE 0.750

	1 AMOUNT OF $1 AT COMPOUND INTEREST	2 ACCUMULATION OF $1 PER PERIOD	3 SINKING FUND FACTOR	4 PRESENT VALUE REVERSION OF $1	5 PRESENT VALUE ORD. ANNUITY $1 PER PERIOD	6 INSTALMENT TO AMORTIZE $1	
MONTHS							
1	1.007500	1.000000	1.000000	0.992556	0.992556	1.007500	
2	1.015056	2.007500	0.498132	0.985167	1.977723	0.505632	
3	1.022669	3.022556	0.330846	0.977833	2.955556	0.338346	
4	1.030339	4.045225	0.247205	0.970554	3.926110	0.254705	
5	1.038067	5.075565	0.197022	0.963329	4.889440	0.204522	
6	1.045852	6.113631	0.163569	0.956158	5.845598	0.171069	
7	1.053696	7.159484	0.139675	0.949040	6.794638	0.147175	
8	1.061599	8.213180	0.121756	0.941975	7.736613	0.129256	
9	1.069561	9.274779	0.107819	0.934963	8.671576	0.115319	
10	1.077583	10.344339	0.096671	0.928003	9.599580	0.104171	
11	1.085664	11.421922	0.087551	0.921095	10.520675	0.095051	
12	1.093807	12.507586	0.079951	0.914238	11.434913	0.087451	
YEARS							**MONTHS**
1	1.093807	12.507586	0.079951	0.914238	11.434913	0.087451	12
2	1.196414	26.188471	0.038185	0.835831	21.889146	0.045685	24
3	1.308645	41.152716	0.024300	0.764149	31.446805	0.031800	36
4	1.431405	57.520711	0.017385	0.698614	40.184782	0.024885	48
5	1.565681	75.424137	0.013258	0.638700	48.173374	0.020758	60
6	1.712553	95.007028	0.010526	0.583924	55.476849	0.018026	72
7	1.873202	116.426928	0.008589	0.533845	62.153965	0.016089	84
8	2.048921	139.856164	0.007150	0.488062	68.258439	0.014650	96
9	2.241124	165.483223	0.006043	0.446205	73.839382	0.013543	108
10	2.451357	193.514277	0.005168	0.407937	78.941693	0.012668	120
11	2.681311	224.174837	0.004461	0.372952	83.606420	0.011961	132
12	2.932837	257.711570	0.003880	0.340967	87.871092	0.011380	144
13	3.207957	294.394279	0.003397	0.311725	91.770018	0.010897	156
14	3.508886	334.518079	0.002989	0.284991	95.334564	0.010489	168
15	3.838043	378.405769	0.002643	0.260549	98.593409	0.010143	180
16	4.198078	426.410427	0.002345	0.238204	101.572769	0.009845	192
17	4.591887	478.918252	0.002088	0.217775	104.296613	0.009588	204
18	5.022638	536.351674	0.001864	0.199099	106.786856	0.009364	216
19	5.493796	599.172747	0.001669	0.182024	109.063531	0.009169	228
20	6.009152	667.886870	0.001497	0.166413	111.144954	0.008997	240
21	6.572851	743.046852	0.001346	0.152141	113.047870	0.008846	252
22	7.189430	825.257358	0.001212	0.139093	114.787589	0.008712	264
23	7.863848	915.179777	0.001093	0.127164	116.378106	0.008593	276
24	8.601532	1013.537539	0.000987	0.116258	117.832218	0.008487	288
25	9.408415	1121.121937	0.000892	0.106288	119.161622	0.008392	300
26	10.290989	1238.798494	0.000807	0.097172	120.377014	0.008307	312
27	11.256354	1367.513924	0.000731	0.088839	121.488172	0.008231	324
28	12.312278	1508.303750	0.000663	0.081220	122.504035	0.008163	336
29	13.467255	1662.300631	0.000602	0.074254	123.432776	0.008102	348
30	14.730576	1830.743483	0.000546	0.067886	124.281866	0.008046	360
31	16.112406	2014.987436	0.000496	0.062064	125.058136	0.007996	372
32	17.623861	2216.514743	0.000451	0.056741	125.767832	0.007951	384
33	19.277100	2436.946701	0.000410	0.051875	126.416664	0.007910	396
34	21.085425	2678.056697	0.000373	0.047426	127.009850	0.007873	408
35	23.063384	2941.784473	0.000340	0.043359	127.552164	0.007840	420
36	25.226888	3230.251735	0.000310	0.039640	128.047967	0.007810	432
37	27.593344	3545.779215	0.000282	0.036241	128.501250	0.007782	444
38	30.181790	3890.905350	0.000257	0.033133	128.915659	0.007757	456
39	33.013050	4268.406696	0.000234	0.030291	129.294526	0.007734	468
40	36.109902	4681.320272	0.000214	0.027693	129.640902	0.007714	480

9.00%   ANNUAL COMPOUND INTEREST TABLES   9.00%
                                    EFFECTIVE RATE   9.00

---

	1 AMOUNT OF $1 AT COMPOUND INTEREST	2 ACCUMULATION OF $1 PER PERIOD	3 SINKING FUND FACTOR	4 PRESENT VALUE REVERSION OF $1	5 PRESENT VALUE ORD. ANNUITY $1 PER PERIOD	6 INSTALMENT TO AMORTIZE $1
YEARS						
1	1.090000	1.000000	1.000000	0.917431	0.917431	1.090000
2	1.188100	2.090000	0.478469	0.841680	1.759111	0.568469
3	1.295029	3.278100	0.305055	0.772183	2.531295	0.395055
4	1.411582	4.573129	0.218669	0.708425	3.239720	0.308669
5	1.538624	5.984711	0.167092	0.649931	3.889651	0.257092
6	1.677100	7.523335	0.132920	0.596267	4.485919	0.222920
7	1.828039	9.200435	0.108691	0.547034	5.032953	0.198691
8	1.992563	11.028474	0.090674	0.501866	5.534819	0.180674
9	2.171893	13.021036	0.076799	0.460428	5.995247	0.166799
10	2.367364	15.192930	0.065820	0.422411	6.417658	0.155820
11	2.580426	17.560293	0.056947	0.387533	6.805191	0.146947
12	2.812665	20.140720	0.049651	0.355535	7.160725	0.139651
13	3.065805	22.953385	0.043567	0.326179	7.486904	0.133567
14	3.341727	26.019189	0.038433	0.299246	7.786150	0.128433
15	3.642482	29.360916	0.034059	0.274538	8.060688	0.124059
16	3.970306	33.003399	0.030300	0.251870	8.312558	0.120300
17	4.327633	36.973705	0.027046	0.231073	8.543631	0.117046
18	4.717120	41.301338	0.024212	0.211994	8.755625	0.114212
19	5.141661	46.018458	0.021730	0.194490	8.950115	0.111730
20	5.604411	51.160120	0.019546	0.178431	9.128546	0.109546
21	6.108808	56.764530	0.017617	0.163698	9.292244	0.107617
22	6.658600	62.873338	0.015905	0.150182	9.442425	0.105905
23	7.257874	69.531939	0.014382	0.137781	9.580207	0.104382
24	7.911083	76.789813	0.013023	0.126405	9.706612	0.103023
25	8.623081	84.700896	0.011806	0.115968	9.822580	0.101806
26	9.399158	93.323977	0.010715	0.106393	9.928972	0.100715
27	10.245082	102.723135	0.009735	0.097608	10.026580	0.099735
28	11.167140	112.968217	0.008852	0.089548	10.116128	0.098852
29	12.172182	124.135356	0.008056	0.082155	10.198283	0.098056
30	13.267678	136.307539	0.007336	0.075371	10.273654	0.097336
31	14.461770	149.575217	0.006686	0.069148	10.342802	0.096686
32	15.763329	164.036987	0.006096	0.063438	10.406240	0.096096
33	17.182028	179.800315	0.005562	0.058200	10.464441	0.095562
34	18.728411	196.982344	0.005077	0.053395	10.517835	0.095077
35	20.413968	215.710755	0.004636	0.048986	10.566821	0.094636
36	22.251225	236.124723	0.004235	0.044941	10.611763	0.094235
37	24.253835	258.375948	0.003870	0.041231	10.652993	0.093870
38	26.436680	282.629783	0.003538	0.037826	10.690820	0.093538
39	28.815982	309.066463	0.003236	0.034703	10.725523	0.093236
40	31.409420	337.882445	0.002960	0.031838	10.757360	0.092960
41	34.236268	369.291865	0.002708	0.029209	10.786569	0.092708
42	37.317532	403.528133	0.002478	0.026797	10.813366	0.092478
43	40.676110	440.845665	0.002268	0.024584	10.837950	0.092268
44	44.336960	481.521775	0.002077	0.022555	10.860505	0.092077
45	48.327286	525.858734	0.001902	0.020692	10.881197	0.091902
46	52.676742	574.186021	0.001742	0.018984	10.900181	0.091742
47	57.417649	626.862762	0.001595	0.017416	10.917597	0.091595
48	62.585237	684.280411	0.001461	0.015978	10.933575	0.091461
49	68.217908	746.865648	0.001339	0.014659	10.948234	0.091339
50	74.357520	815.083556	0.001227	0.013449	10.961683	0.091227

9.50%   MONTHLY COMPOUND INTEREST TABLES   9.50%
                              EFFECTIVE RATE 0.792

	1 AMOUNT OF $1 AT COMPOUND INTEREST	2 ACCUMULATION OF $1 PER PERIOD	3 SINKING FUND FACTOR	4 PRESENT VALUE REVERSION OF $1	5 PRESENT VALUE ORD. ANNUITY $1 PER PERIOD	6 INSTALMENT TO AMORTIZE $1	
MONTHS							
1	1.007917	1.000000	1.000000	0.992146	0.992146	1.007917	
2	1.015896	2.007917	0.498029	0.984353	1.976498	0.505945	
3	1.023939	3.023813	0.330708	0.976621	2.953119	0.338625	
4	1.032045	4.047751	0.247051	0.968950	3.922070	0.254967	
5	1.040215	5.079796	0.196858	0.961340	4.883409	0.204775	
6	1.048450	6.120011	0.163398	0.953789	5.837198	0.171315	
7	1.056750	7.168461	0.139500	0.946297	6.783496	0.147417	
8	1.065116	8.225211	0.121577	0.938865	7.722360	0.129494	
9	1.073548	9.290328	0.107639	0.931490	8.653851	0.115555	
10	1.082047	10.363876	0.096489	0.924174	9.578024	0.104406	
11	1.090614	11.445923	0.087367	0.916915	10.494940	0.095284	
12	1.099248	12.536537	0.079767	0.909713	11.404653	0.087684	
YEARS							MONTHS
1	1.099248	12.536537	0.079767	0.909713	11.404653	0.087684	12
2	1.208345	26.317295	0.037998	0.827578	21.779615	0.045914	24
3	1.328271	41.465760	0.024116	0.752859	31.217856	0.032033	36
4	1.460098	58.117673	0.017206	0.684885	39.803947	0.025123	48
5	1.605009	76.422249	0.013085	0.623049	47.614827	0.021002	60
6	1.764303	96.543509	0.010358	0.566796	54.720488	0.018275	72
7	1.939406	118.661756	0.008427	0.515622	61.184601	0.016344	84
8	2.131887	142.975186	0.006994	0.469068	67.065090	0.014911	96
9	2.343472	169.701665	0.005893	0.426717	72.414648	0.013809	108
10	2.576055	199.080682	0.005023	0.388190	77.281211	0.012940	120
11	2.831723	231.375495	0.004322	0.353142	81.708388	0.012239	132
12	3.112764	266.875491	0.003747	0.321258	85.735849	0.011664	144
13	3.421699	305.898776	0.003269	0.292253	89.399684	0.011186	156
14	3.761294	348.795027	0.002867	0.265866	92.732722	0.010784	168
15	4.134593	395.948628	0.002526	0.241862	95.764831	0.010442	180
16	4.544942	447.782110	0.002233	0.220025	98.523180	0.010150	192
17	4.996016	504.759939	0.001981	0.200159	101.032487	0.009898	204
18	5.491859	567.392681	0.001762	0.182088	103.315236	0.009679	216
19	6.036912	636.241570	0.001572	0.165648	105.391883	0.009488	228
20	6.636061	711.923546	0.001405	0.150692	107.281037	0.009321	240
21	7.294674	795.116775	0.001258	0.137086	108.999624	0.009174	252
22	8.018653	886.566731	0.001128	0.124709	110.563046	0.009045	264
23	8.814485	987.092874	0.001013	0.113450	111.985311	0.008930	276
24	9.689302	1097.595994	0.000911	0.103207	113.279165	0.008828	288
25	10.650941	1219.066282	0.000820	0.093888	114.456200	0.008737	300
26	11.708022	1352.592202	0.000739	0.085412	115.526965	0.008656	312
27	12.870014	1499.370247	0.000667	0.077700	116.501054	0.008584	324
28	14.147332	1660.715658	0.000602	0.070685	117.387195	0.008519	336
29	15.551421	1838.074212	0.000544	0.064303	118.193330	0.008461	348
30	17.094862	2033.035174	0.000492	0.058497	118.926681	0.008409	360
31	18.791486	2247.345541	0.000445	0.053216	119.593820	0.008362	372
32	20.656495	2482.925693	0.000403	0.048411	120.200725	0.008319	384
33	22.706602	2741.886606	0.000365	0.044040	120.752835	0.008281	396
34	24.960178	3026.548765	0.000330	0.040064	121.255097	0.008247	408
35	27.437415	3339.462955	0.000299	0.036447	121.712011	0.008216	420
36	30.160512	3683.433122	0.000271	0.033156	122.127671	0.008188	432
37	33.153870	4061.541498	0.000246	0.030162	122.505803	0.008163	444
38	36.444312	4477.176216	0.000223	0.027439	122.849795	0.008140	456
39	40.061322	4934.061676	0.000203	0.024962	123.162729	0.008119	468
40	44.037311	5436.291914	0.000184	0.022708	123.447408	0.008101	480

ANNUAL COMPOUND INTEREST TABLES
                                       EFFECTIVE RATE   9.50

	1 AMOUNT OF $1 AT COMPOUND INTEREST	2 ACCUMULATION OF $1 PER PERIOD	3 SINKING FUND FACTOR	4 PRESENT VALUE REVERSION OF $1	5 PRESENT VALUE ORD. ANNUITY $1 PER PERIOD	6 INSTALMENT TO AMORTIZE $1
YEARS						
1	1.095000	1.000000	1.000000	0.913242	0.913242	1.095000
2	1.199025	2.095000	0.477327	0.834011	1.747253	0.572327
3	1.312932	3.294025	0.303580	0.761654	2.508907	0.398580
4	1.437661	4.606957	0.217063	0.695574	3.204481	0.312063
5	1.574239	6.044618	0.165436	0.635228	3.839709	0.260436
6	1.723791	7.618857	0.131253	0.580117	4.419825	0.226253
7	1.887552	9.342648	0.107036	0.529787	4.949612	0.202036
8	2.066869	11.230200	0.089046	0.483824	5.433436	0.184046
9	2.263222	13.297069	0.075205	0.441848	5.875284	0.170205
10	2.478228	15.560291	0.064266	0.403514	6.278798	0.159266
11	2.713659	18.038518	0.055437	0.368506	6.647304	0.150437
12	2.971457	20.752178	0.048188	0.336535	6.983839	0.143188
13	3.253745	23.723634	0.042152	0.307338	7.291178	0.137152
14	3.562851	26.977380	0.037068	0.280674	7.571852	0.132068
15	3.901322	30.540231	0.032744	0.256323	7.828175	0.127744
16	4.271948	34.441553	0.029035	0.234085	8.062260	0.124035
17	4.677783	38.713500	0.025831	0.213777	8.276037	0.120831
18	5.122172	43.391283	0.023046	0.195230	8.471266	0.118046
19	5.608778	48.513454	0.020613	0.178292	8.649558	0.115613
20	6.141612	54.122233	0.018477	0.162824	8.812382	0.113477
21	6.725065	60.263845	0.016594	0.148697	8.961080	0.111594
22	7.363946	66.988910	0.014928	0.135797	9.096876	0.109928
23	8.063521	74.352856	0.013449	0.124015	9.220892	0.108449
24	8.829556	82.416378	0.012134	0.113256	9.334148	0.107134
25	9.668364	91.245934	0.010959	0.103430	9.437578	0.105959
26	10.586858	100.914297	0.009909	0.094457	9.532034	0.104909
27	11.592610	111.501156	0.008969	0.086262	9.618296	0.103969
28	12.693908	123.093766	0.008124	0.078778	9.697074	0.103124
29	13.899829	135.787673	0.007364	0.071943	9.769018	0.102364
30	15.220313	149.687502	0.006681	0.065702	9.834719	0.101681
31	16.666242	164.907815	0.006064	0.060002	9.894721	0.101064
32	18.249535	181.574057	0.005507	0.054796	9.949517	0.100507
33	19.983241	199.823593	0.005004	0.050042	9.999559	0.100004
34	21.881649	219.806834	0.004549	0.045700	10.045259	0.099549
35	23.960406	241.688483	0.004138	0.041736	10.086995	0.099138
36	26.236644	265.648889	0.003764	0.038115	10.125109	0.098764
37	28.729126	291.885534	0.003426	0.034808	10.159917	0.098426
38	31.458393	320.614659	0.003119	0.031788	10.191705	0.098119
39	34.446940	352.073052	0.002840	0.029030	10.220735	0.097840
40	37.719399	386.519992	0.002587	0.026512	10.247247	0.097587
41	41.302742	424.239391	0.002357	0.024211	10.271458	0.097357
42	45.226503	465.542133	0.002148	0.022111	10.293569	0.097148
43	49.523020	510.768636	0.001958	0.020193	10.313762	0.096958
44	54.227707	560.291656	0.001785	0.018441	10.332203	0.096785
45	59.379340	614.519364	0.001627	0.016841	10.349043	0.096627
46	65.020377	673.898703	0.001484	0.015380	10.364423	0.096484
47	71.197313	738.919080	0.001353	0.014045	10.378469	0.096353
48	77.961057	810.116393	0.001234	0.012827	10.391296	0.096234
49	85.367358	888.077450	0.001126	0.011714	10.403010	0.096126
50	93.477257	973.444808	0.001027	0.010698	10.413707	0.096027

10.00%   MONTHLY COMPOUND INTEREST TABLES   10.00%
                                     EFFECTIVE RATE 0.833

	1 AMOUNT OF $1 AT COMPOUND INTEREST	2 ACCUMULATION OF $1 PER PERIOD	3 SINKING FUND FACTOR	4 PRESENT VALUE REVERSION OF $1	5 PRESENT VALUE ORD. ANNUITY $1 PER PERIOD	6 INSTALMENT TO AMORTIZE $1	
MONTHS							
1	1.008333	1.000000	1.000000	0.991736	0.991736	1.008333	
2	1.016736	2.008333	0.497925	0.983539	1.975275	0.506259	
3	1.025209	3.025069	0.330571	0.975411	2.950686	0.338904	
4	1.033752	4.050278	0.246897	0.967350	3.918036	0.255230	
5	1.042367	5.084031	0.196694	0.959355	4.877391	0.205028	
6	1.051053	6.126398	0.163228	0.951427	5.828817	0.171561	
7	1.059812	7.177451	0.139325	0.943563	6.772381	0.147659	
8	1.068644	8.237263	0.121400	0.935765	7.708146	0.129733	
9	1.077549	9.305907	0.107459	0.928032	8.636178	0.115792	
10	1.086529	10.383456	0.096307	0.920362	9.556540	0.104640	
11	1.095583	11.469985	0.087184	0.912756	10.469296	0.095517	
12	1.104713	12.565568	0.079583	0.905212	11.374508	0.087916	
YEARS							**MONTHS**
1	1.104713	12.565568	0.079583	0.905212	11.374508	0.087916	12
2	1.220391	26.446915	0.037812	0.819410	21.670855	0.046145	24
3	1.348182	41.781821	0.023934	0.741740	30.991236	0.032267	36
4	1.489354	58.722492	0.017029	0.671432	39.428160	0.025363	48
5	1.645309	77.437072	0.012914	0.607789	47.065369	0.021247	60
6	1.817594	98.111314	0.010193	0.550178	53.978665	0.018526	72
7	2.007920	120.950418	0.008268	0.498028	60.236667	0.016601	84
8	2.218176	146.181076	0.006841	0.450821	65.901488	0.015174	96
9	2.450448	174.053713	0.005745	0.408089	71.029355	0.014079	108
10	2.707041	204.844979	0.004882	0.369407	75.671163	0.013215	120
11	2.990504	238.860493	0.004187	0.334392	79.872986	0.012520	132
12	3.303649	276.437876	0.003617	0.302696	83.676528	0.011951	144
13	3.649584	317.950102	0.003145	0.274004	87.119542	0.011478	156
14	4.031743	363.809201	0.002749	0.248032	90.236201	0.011082	168
15	4.453920	414.470346	0.002413	0.224521	93.057439	0.010746	180
16	4.920303	470.436376	0.002126	0.203240	95.611259	0.010459	192
17	5.435523	532.262780	0.001879	0.183975	97.923008	0.010212	204
18	6.004693	600.563216	0.001665	0.166536	100.015633	0.009998	216
19	6.633463	676.015601	0.001479	0.150751	101.909902	0.009813	228
20	7.328074	759.368836	0.001317	0.136462	103.624619	0.009650	240
21	8.095419	851.450244	0.001174	0.123527	105.176801	0.009508	252
22	8.943115	953.173779	0.001049	0.111818	106.581856	0.009382	264
23	9.879576	1065.549097	0.000938	0.101219	107.853730	0.009272	276
24	10.914097	1189.691580	0.000841	0.091625	109.005045	0.009174	288
25	12.056945	1326.833403	0.000754	0.082940	110.047230	0.009087	300
26	13.319465	1478.335767	0.000676	0.075078	110.990629	0.009010	312
27	14.714187	1645.702407	0.000608	0.067962	111.844605	0.008941	324
28	16.254954	1830.594523	0.000546	0.061520	112.617635	0.008880	336
29	17.957060	2034.847259	0.000491	0.055688	113.317392	0.008825	348
30	19.837399	2260.487925	0.000442	0.050410	113.950820	0.008776	360
31	21.914634	2509.756117	0.000398	0.045632	114.524207	0.008732	372
32	24.209383	2785.125947	0.000359	0.041306	115.043244	0.008692	384
33	26.744422	3089.330596	0.000324	0.037391	115.513083	0.008657	396
34	29.544912	3425.389448	0.000292	0.033847	115.938387	0.008625	408
35	32.638650	3796.638052	0.000263	0.030639	116.323377	0.008597	420
36	36.056344	4206.761236	0.000238	0.027734	116.671876	0.008571	432
37	39.831914	4659.829677	0.000215	0.025105	116.987340	0.008548	444
38	44.002836	5160.340305	0.000194	0.022726	117.272903	0.008527	456
39	48.610508	5713.260935	0.000175	0.020572	117.531398	0.008508	468
40	53.700663	6324.079581	0.000158	0.018622	117.765391	0.008491	480

10.00%   ANNUAL COMPOUND INTEREST TABLES   10.00%
                                    EFFECTIVE RATE 10.00

	1 AMOUNT OF $1 AT COMPOUND INTEREST	2 ACCUMULATION OF $1 PER PERIOD	3 SINKING FUND FACTOR	4 PRESENT VALUE REVERSION OF $1	5 PRESENT VALUE ORD. ANNUITY $1 PER PERIOD	6 INSTALMENT TO AMORTIZE $1
YEARS						
1	1.100000	1.000000	1.000000	0.909091	0.909091	1.100000
2	1.210000	2.100000	0.476190	0.826446	1.735537	0.576190
3	1.331000	3.310000	0.302115	0.751315	2.486852	0.402115
4	1.464100	4.641000	0.215471	0.683013	3.169865	0.315471
5	1.610510	6.105100	0.163797	0.620921	3.790787	0.263797
6	1.771561	7.715610	0.129607	0.564474	4.355261	0.229607
7	1.948717	9.487171	0.105405	0.513158	4.868419	0.205405
8	2.143589	11.435888	0.087444	0.466507	5.334926	0.187444
9	2.357948	13.579477	0.073641	0.424098	5.759024	0.173641
10	2.593742	15.937425	0.062745	0.385543	6.144567	0.162745
11	2.853117	18.531167	0.053963	0.350494	6.495061	0.153963
12	3.138428	21.384284	0.046763	0.318631	6.813692	0.146763
13	3.452271	24.522712	0.040779	0.289664	7.103356	0.140779
14	3.797498	27.974983	0.035746	0.263331	7.366687	0.135746
15	4.177248	31.772482	0.031474	0.239392	7.606080	0.131474
16	4.594973	35.949730	0.027817	0.217629	7.823709	0.127817
17	5.054470	40.544703	0.024664	0.197845	8.021553	0.124664
18	5.559917	45.599173	0.021930	0.179859	8.201412	0.121930
19	6.115909	51.159090	0.019547	0.163508	8.364920	0.119547
20	6.727500	57.274999	0.017460	0.148644	8.513564	0.117460
21	7.400250	64.002499	0.015624	0.135131	8.648694	0.115624
22	8.140275	71.402749	0.014005	0.122846	8.771540	0.114005
23	8.954302	79.543024	0.012572	0.111678	8.883218	0.112572
24	9.849733	88.497327	0.011300	0.101526	8.984744	0.111300
25	10.834706	98.347059	0.010168	0.092296	9.077040	0.110168
26	11.918177	109.181765	0.009159	0.083905	9.160945	0.109159
27	13.109994	121.099942	0.008258	0.076278	9.237223	0.108258
28	14.420994	134.209936	0.007451	0.069343	9.306567	0.107451
29	15.863093	148.630930	0.006728	0.063039	9.369606	0.106728
30	17.449402	164.494023	0.006079	0.057309	9.426914	0.106079
31	19.194342	181.943425	0.005496	0.052099	9.479013	0.105496
32	21.113777	201.137767	0.004972	0.047362	9.526376	0.104972
33	23.225154	222.251544	0.004499	0.043057	9.569432	0.104499
34	25.547670	245.476699	0.004074	0.039143	9.608575	0.104074
35	28.102437	271.024368	0.003690	0.035584	9.644159	0.103690
36	30.912681	299.126805	0.003343	0.032349	9.676508	0.103343
37	34.003949	330.039486	0.003030	0.029408	9.705917	0.103030
38	37.404343	364.043434	0.002747	0.026735	9.732651	0.102747
39	41.144778	401.447778	0.002491	0.024304	9.756956	0.102491
40	45.259256	442.592556	0.002259	0.022095	9.779051	0.102259
41	49.785181	487.851811	0.002050	0.020086	9.799137	0.102050
42	54.763699	537.636992	0.001860	0.018260	9.817397	0.101860
43	60.240069	592.400692	0.001688	0.016600	9.833998	0.101688
44	66.264076	652.640761	0.001532	0.015091	9.849089	0.101532
45	72.890484	718.904837	0.001391	0.013719	9.862808	0.101391
46	80.179532	791.795321	0.001263	0.012472	9.875280	0.101263
47	88.197485	871.974853	0.001147	0.011338	9.886618	0.101147
48	97.017234	960.172338	0.001041	0.010307	9.896926	0.101041
49	106.718957	1057.189572	0.000946	0.009370	9.906296	0.100946
50	117.390853	1163.908529	0.000859	0.008519	9.914814	0.100859

12.00%   MONTHLY COMPOUND INTEREST TABLES   12.00%
EFFECTIVE RATE 1.000

	1 AMOUNT OF $1 AT COMPOUND INTEREST	2 ACCUMULATION OF $1 PER PERIOD	3 SINKING FUND FACTOR	4 PRESENT VALUE REVERSION OF $1	5 PRESENT VALUE ORD. ANNUITY $1 PER PERIOD	6 INSTALMENT TO AMORTIZE $1	
MONTHS							
1	1.010000	1.000000	1.000000	0.990099	0.990099	1.010000	
2	1.020100	2.010000	0.497512	0.980296	1.970395	0.507512	
3	1.030301	3.030100	0.330022	0.970590	2.940985	0.340022	
4	1.040604	4.060401	0.246281	0.960980	3.901966	0.256281	
5	1.051010	5.101005	0.196040	0.951466	4.853431	0.206040	
6	1.061520	6.152015	0.162548	0.942045	5.795476	0.172548	
7	1.072135	7.213535	0.138628	0.932718	6.728195	0.148628	
8	1.082857	8.285671	0.120690	0.923483	7.651678	0.130690	
9	1.093685	9.368527	0.106740	0.914340	8.566018	0.116740	
10	1.104622	10.462213	0.095582	0.905287	9.471305	0.105582	
11	1.115668	11.566835	0.086454	0.896324	10.367628	0.096454	
12	1.126825	12.682503	0.078849	0.887449	11.255077	0.088849	
YEARS							MONTHS
1	1.126825	12.682503	0.078849	0.887449	11.255077	0.088849	12
2	1.269735	26.973465	0.037073	0.787566	21.243387	0.047073	24
3	1.430769	43.076878	0.023214	0.698925	30.107505	0.033214	36
4	1.612226	61.222608	0.016334	0.620260	37.973959	0.026334	48
5	1.816697	81.669670	0.012244	0.550450	44.955038	0.022244	60
6	2.047099	104.709931	0.009550	0.488496	51.150391	0.019550	72
7	2.306723	130.672274	0.007653	0.433515	56.648453	0.017653	84
8	2.599273	159.927293	0.006253	0.384723	61.527703	0.016253	96
9	2.928926	192.892579	0.005184	0.341422	65.857790	0.015184	108
10	3.300387	230.038689	0.004347	0.302995	69.700522	0.014347	120
11	3.718959	271.895856	0.003678	0.268892	73.110752	0.013678	132
12	4.190616	319.061559	0.003134	0.238628	76.137157	0.013134	144
13	4.722091	372.209054	0.002687	0.211771	78.822939	0.012687	156
14	5.320970	432.096982	0.002314	0.187936	81.206434	0.012314	168
15	5.995802	499.580198	0.002002	0.166783	83.321664	0.012002	180
16	6.756220	575.621974	0.001737	0.148012	85.198824	0.011737	192
17	7.613078	661.307751	0.001512	0.131353	86.864707	0.011512	204
18	8.578606	757.860630	0.001320	0.116569	88.343095	0.011320	216
19	9.666588	866.658830	0.001154	0.103449	89.655089	0.011154	228
20	10.892554	989.255365	0.001011	0.091806	90.819416	0.011011	240
21	12.274002	1127.400210	0.000887	0.081473	91.852698	0.010887	252
22	13.830653	1283.065278	0.000779	0.072303	92.769683	0.010779	264
23	15.584726	1458.472574	0.000686	0.064165	93.583461	0.010686	276
24	17.561259	1656.125905	0.000604	0.056944	94.305647	0.010604	288
25	19.788466	1878.846626	0.000532	0.050534	94.946551	0.010532	300
26	22.298139	2129.813909	0.000470	0.044847	95.515321	0.010470	312
27	25.126101	2412.610125	0.000414	0.039799	96.020075	0.010414	324
28	28.312720	2731.271980	0.000366	0.035320	96.468019	0.010366	336
29	31.903481	3090.348134	0.000324	0.031345	96.865546	0.010324	348
30	35.949641	3494.964133	0.000286	0.027817	97.218331	0.010286	360
31	40.508956	3950.895567	0.000253	0.024686	97.531410	0.010253	372
32	45.646505	4464.650519	0.000224	0.021907	97.809252	0.010224	384
33	51.435625	5043.562459	0.000198	0.019442	98.055822	0.010198	396
34	57.958949	5695.894923	0.000176	0.017254	98.274641	0.010176	408
35	65.309595	6430.959471	0.000155	0.015312	98.468831	0.010155	420
36	73.592486	7259.248603	0.000138	0.013588	98.641166	0.010138	432
37	82.925855	8192.585529	0.000122	0.012059	98.794103	0.010122	444
38	93.442929	9244.292938	0.000108	0.010702	98.929828	0.010108	456
39	105.293832	10429.383172	0.000096	0.009497	99.050277	0.010096	468
40	118.647725	11764.772510	0.000085	0.008428	99.157169	0.010085	480

ANNUAL COMPOUND INTEREST TABLES
EFFECTIVE RATE 12.00

	1 AMOUNT OF $1 AT COMPOUND INTEREST	2 ACCUMULATION OF $1 PER PERIOD	3 SINKING FUND FACTOR	4 PRESENT VALUE REVERSION OF $1	5 PRESENT VALUE ORD. ANNUITY $1 PER PERIOD	6 INSTALMENT TO AMORTIZE $1
YEARS						
1	1.120000	1.000000	1.000000	0.892857	0.892857	1.120000
2	1.254400	2.120000	0.471698	0.797194	1.690051	0.591698
3	1.404928	3.374400	0.296349	0.711780	2.401831	0.416349
4	1.573519	4.779328	0.209234	0.635518	3.037349	0.329234
5	1.762342	6.352847	0.157410	0.567427	3.604776	0.277410
6	1.973823	8.115189	0.123226	0.506631	4.111407	0.243226
7	2.210681	10.089012	0.099118	0.452349	4.563757	0.219118
8	2.475963	12.299693	0.081303	0.403883	4.967640	0.201303
9	2.773079	14.775656	0.067679	0.360610	5.328250	0.187679
10	3.105848	17.548735	0.056984	0.321973	5.650223	0.176984
11	3.478550	20.654583	0.048415	0.287476	5.937699	0.168415
12	3.895976	24.133133	0.041437	0.256675	6.194374	0.161437
13	4.363493	28.029109	0.035677	0.229174	6.423548	0.155677
14	4.887112	32.392602	0.030871	0.204620	6.628168	0.150871
15	5.473566	37.279715	0.026824	0.182696	6.810864	0.146824
16	6.130394	42.753280	0.023390	0.163122	6.973986	0.143390
17	6.866041	48.883674	0.020457	0.145644	7.119630	0.140457
18	7.689966	55.749715	0.017937	0.130040	7.249670	0.137937
19	8.612762	63.439681	0.015763	0.116107	7.365777	0.135763
20	9.646293	72.052442	0.013879	0.103667	7.469444	0.133879
21	10.803848	81.698736	0.012240	0.092560	7.562003	0.132240
22	12.100310	92.502584	0.010811	0.082643	7.644646	0.130811
23	13.552347	104.602894	0.009560	0.073788	7.718434	0.129560
24	15.178629	118.155241	0.008463	0.065882	7.784316	0.128463
25	17.000064	133.333870	0.007500	0.058823	7.843139	0.127500
26	19.040072	150.333934	0.006652	0.052521	7.895660	0.126652
27	21.324881	169.374007	0.005904	0.046894	7.942554	0.125904
28	23.883866	190.698887	0.005244	0.041869	7.984423	0.125244
29	26.749930	214.582754	0.004660	0.037383	8.021806	0.124660
30	29.959922	241.332684	0.004144	0.033378	8.055184	0.124144
31	33.555113	271.292606	0.003686	0.029802	8.084986	0.123686
32	37.581726	304.847719	0.003280	0.026609	8.111594	0.123280
33	42.091533	342.429446	0.002920	0.023758	8.135352	0.122920
34	47.142517	384.520979	0.002601	0.021212	8.156564	0.122601
35	52.799620	431.663496	0.002317	0.018940	8.175504	0.122317
36	59.135574	484.463116	0.002064	0.016910	8.192414	0.122064
37	66.231843	543.598690	0.001840	0.015098	8.207513	0.121840
38	74.179664	609.830533	0.001640	0.013481	8.220993	0.121640
39	83.081224	684.010197	0.001462	0.012036	8.233030	0.121462
40	93.050970	767.091420	0.001304	0.010747	8.243777	0.121304
41	104.217087	860.142391	0.001163	0.009595	8.253372	0.121163
42	116.723137	964.359478	0.001037	0.008567	8.261939	0.121037
43	130.729914	1081.082615	0.000925	0.007649	8.269589	0.120925
44	146.417503	1211.812529	0.000825	0.006830	8.276418	0.120825
45	163.987604	1358.230032	0.000736	0.006098	8.282516	0.120736
46	183.666116	1522.217636	0.000657	0.005445	8.287961	0.120657
47	205.706050	1705.883752	0.000586	0.004861	8.292822	0.120586
48	230.390776	1911.589803	0.000523	0.004340	8.297163	0.120523
49	258.037669	2141.980579	0.000467	0.003875	8.301038	0.120467
50	289.002190	2400.018249	0.000417	0.003460	8.304498	0.120417

15.00%

MONTHLY COMPOUND INTEREST TABLES
EFFECTIVE RATE 1.250

15.00%

	1 AMOUNT OF $1 AT COMPOUND INTEREST	2 ACCUMULATION OF $1 PER PERIOD	3 SINKING FUND FACTOR	4 PRESENT VALUE REVERSION OF $1	5 PRESENT VALUE ORD. ANNUITY $1 PER PERIOD	6 INSTALMENT TO AMORTIZE $1
MONTHS						
1	1.012500	1.000000	1.000000	0.987654	0.987654	1.012500
2	1.025156	2.012500	0.496894	0.975461	1.963115	0.509394
3	1.037971	3.037656	0.329201	0.963418	2.926534	0.341701
4	1.050945	4.075627	0.245361	0.951524	3.878058	0.257861
5	1.064082	5.126572	0.195062	0.939777	4.817835	0.207562
6	1.077383	6.190654	0.161534	0.928175	5.746010	0.174034
7	1.090850	7.268038	0.137589	0.916716	6.662726	0.150089
8	1.104486	8.358888	0.119633	0.905398	7.568124	0.132133
9	1.118292	9.463374	0.105671	0.894221	8.462345	0.118171
10	1.132271	10.581666	0.094503	0.883181	9.345526	0.107003
11	1.146424	11.713937	0.085368	0.872277	10.217803	0.097868
12	1.160755	12.860361	0.077758	0.861509	11.079312	0.090258

YEARS						**MONTHS**
1	1.160755	12.860361	0.077758	0.861509	11.079312	0.090258	12
2	1.347351	27.788084	0.035987	0.742197	20.624235	0.048487	24
3	1.563944	45.115506	0.022155	0.639409	28.847267	0.034665	36
4	1.815355	65.228388	0.015331	0.550856	35.931481	0.027831	48
5	2.107181	88.574508	0.011290	0.474568	42.034592	0.023790	60
6	2.445920	115.673621	0.008645	0.408844	47.292474	0.021145	72
7	2.839113	147.129040	0.006797	0.352223	51.822185	0.019297	84
8	3.295513	183.641059	0.005445	0.303443	55.724570	0.017945	96
9	3.825282	226.022551	0.004424	0.261419	59.086509	0.016924	108
10	4.440213	275.217058	0.003633	0.225214	61.982847	0.016133	120
11	5.153998	332.319805	0.003009	0.194024	64.478068	0.015509	132
12	5.982526	398.602077	0.002509	0.167153	66.627722	0.015009	144
13	6.944244	475.539523	0.002103	0.144004	68.479668	0.014603	156
14	8.060563	564.845011	0.001770	0.124061	70.075134	0.014270	168
15	9.356334	668.506759	0.001496	0.106879	71.449643	0.013996	180
16	10.860408	788.832603	0.001268	0.092078	72.633794	0.013768	192
17	12.606267	928.501369	0.001077	0.079326	73.653950	0.013577	204
18	14.632781	1090.622520	0.000917	0.068340	74.532823	0.013417	216
19	16.985067	1278.805378	0.000782	0.058875	75.289980	0.013282	228
20	19.715494	1497.239481	0.000668	0.050722	75.942278	0.013168	240
21	22.884848	1750.787854	0.000571	0.043697	76.504237	0.013071	252
22	26.563691	2045.095272	0.000489	0.037645	76.988370	0.012989	264
23	30.833924	2386.713938	0.000419	0.032432	77.405455	0.012919	276
24	35.790617	2783.249347	0.000359	0.027940	77.764777	0.012859	288
25	41.544120	3243.529615	0.000308	0.024071	78.074336	0.012808	300
26	48.222525	3777.802015	0.000265	0.020737	78.341024	0.012765	312
27	55.974514	4397.961118	0.000227	0.017865	78.570778	0.012727	324
28	64.972670	5117.813598	0.000195	0.015391	78.768713	0.012695	336
29	75.417320	5953.385616	0.000168	0.013260	78.939236	0.012668	348
30	87.540995	6923.279611	0.000144	0.011423	79.086142	0.012644	360
31	101.613606	8049.088447	0.000124	0.009841	79.212704	0.012624	372
32	117.948452	9355.876140	0.000107	0.008478	79.321738	0.012607	384
33	136.909198	10872.735858	0.000092	0.007304	79.415671	0.012592	396
34	158.917970	12633.437629	0.000079	0.006293	79.496906	0.012579	408
35	184.464752	14677.180163	0.000068	0.005421	79.566313	0.012568	420
36	214.118294	17049.463544	0.000059	0.004670	79.626375	0.012559	432
37	248.538777	19803.102194	0.000050	0.004024	79.678119	0.012550	444
38	288.492509	22999.400698	0.000043	0.003466	79.722696	0.012543	456
39	334.868983	26709.518627	0.000037	0.002986	79.761101	0.012537	468
40	388.700685	31016.054774	0.000032	0.002573	79.794186	0.012532	480

15.00%   ANNUAL COMPOUND INTEREST TABLES   15.00%
                           EFFECTIVE RATE 15.00

	1 AMOUNT OF $1 AT COMPOUND INTEREST	2 ACCUMULATION OF $1 PER PERIOD	3 SINKING FUND FACTOR	4 PRESENT VALUE REVERSION OF $1	5 PRESENT VALUE ORD. ANNUITY $1 PER PERIOD	6 INSTALMENT TO AMORTIZE $1
YEARS						
1	1.150000	1.000000	1.000000	0.869565	0.869565	1.150000
2	1.322500	2.150000	0.465116	0.756144	1.625709	0.615116
3	1.520875	3.472500	0.287977	0.657516	2.283225	0.437977
4	1.749006	4.993375	0.200265	0.571753	2.854978	0.350265
5	2.011357	6.742381	0.148316	0.497177	3.352155	0.298316
6	2.313061	8.753738	0.114237	0.432328	3.784483	0.264237
7	2.660020	11.066799	0.090360	0.375937	4.160420	0.240360
8	3.059023	13.726819	0.072850	0.326902	4.487322	0.222850
9	3.517876	16.785842	0.059574	0.284262	4.771584	0.209574
10	4.045558	20.303718	0.049252	0.247185	5.018769	0.199252
11	4.652391	24.349276	0.041069	0.214943	5.233712	0.191069
12	5.350250	29.001667	0.034481	0.186907	5.420619	0.184481
13	6.152788	34.351917	0.029110	0.162528	5.583147	0.179110
14	7.075706	40.504705	0.024688	0.141329	5.724476	0.174688
15	8.137062	47.580411	0.021017	0.122894	5.847370	0.171017
16	9.357621	55.717472	0.017948	0.106865	5.954235	0.167948
17	10.761264	65.075093	0.015367	0.092926	6.047161	0.165367
18	12.375454	75.836357	0.013186	0.080805	6.127966	0.163186
19	14.231772	88.211811	0.011336	0.070265	6.198231	0.161336
20	16.366537	102.443583	0.009761	0.061100	6.259331	0.159761
21	18.821518	118.810120	0.008417	0.053131	6.312462	0.158417
22	21.644746	137.631638	0.007266	0.046201	6.358663	0.157266
23	24.891458	159.276384	0.006278	0.040174	6.398837	0.156278
24	28.625176	184.167841	0.005430	0.034934	6.433771	0.155430
25	32.918953	212.793017	0.004699	0.030378	6.464149	0.154699
26	37.856796	245.711970	0.004070	0.026415	6.490564	0.154070
27	43.535315	283.568766	0.003526	0.022970	6.513534	0.153526
28	50.065612	327.104080	0.003057	0.019974	6.533508	0.153057
29	57.575454	377.169693	0.002651	0.017369	6.550877	0.152651
30	66.211772	434.745146	0.002300	0.015103	6.565980	0.152300
31	76.143538	500.956918	0.001996	0.013133	6.579113	0.151996
32	87.565068	577.100456	0.001733	0.011420	6.590533	0.151733
33	100.699829	664.665525	0.001505	0.009931	6.600463	0.151505
34	115.804803	765.365353	0.001307	0.008635	6.609099	0.151307
35	133.175523	881.170156	0.001135	0.007509	6.616607	0.151135
36	153.151852	1014.345680	0.000986	0.006529	6.623137	0.150986
37	176.124630	1167.497532	0.000857	0.005678	6.628815	0.150857
38	202.543324	1343.622161	0.000744	0.004937	6.633752	0.150744
39	232.924823	1546.165485	0.000647	0.004293	6.638045	0.150647
40	267.863546	1779.090308	0.000562	0.003733	6.641778	0.150562
41	308.043078	2046.953854	0.000489	0.003246	6.645025	0.150489
42	354.249540	2354.996933	0.000425	0.002823	6.647848	0.150425
43	407.386971	2709.246473	0.000369	0.002455	6.650302	0.150369
44	468.495017	3116.633443	0.000321	0.002134	6.652437	0.150321
45	538.769269	3585.128460	0.000279	0.001856	6.654293	0.150279
46	619.584659	4123.897729	0.000242	0.001614	6.655907	0.150242
47	712.522358	4743.482388	0.000211	0.001403	6.657310	0.150211
48	819.400712	5456.004746	0.000183	0.001220	6.658531	0.150183
49	942.310819	6275.405458	0.000159	0.001061	6.659592	0.150159
50	1083.657442	7217.716277	0.000139	0.000923	6.660515	0.150139

20.00%   MONTHLY COMPOUND INTEREST TABLES   20.00%
                     EFFECTIVE RATE 1.667

	1 AMOUNT OF $1 AT COMPOUND INTEREST	2 ACCUMULATION OF $1 PER PERIOD	3 SINKING FUND FACTOR	4 PRESENT VALUE REVERSION OF $1	5 PRESENT VALUE ORD. ANNUITY $1 PER PERIOD	6 INSTALMENT TO AMORTIZE $1	
MONTHS							
1	1.016667	1.000000	1.000000	0.983607	0.983607	1.016667	
2	1.033611	2.016667	0.495868	0.967482	1.951088	0.512534	
3	1.050838	3.050278	0.327839	0.951622	2.902710	0.344506	
4	1.068352	4.101116	0.243836	0.936021	3.838731	0.260503	
5	1.086158	5.169468	0.193444	0.920677	4.759408	0.210110	
6	1.104260	6.255625	0.159856	0.905583	5.664991	0.176523	
7	1.122665	7.359886	0.135872	0.890738	6.555729	0.152538	
8	1.141376	8.482551	0.117889	0.876136	7.431865	0.134556	
9	1.160399	9.623926	0.103908	0.861773	8.293637	0.120574	
10	1.179739	10.784325	0.092727	0.847645	9.141283	0.109394	
11	1.199401	11.964064	0.083584	0.833749	9.975032	0.100250	
12	1.219391	13.163465	0.075968	0.820081	10.795113	0.092635	
YEARS							**MONTHS**
1	1.219391	13.163465	0.075968	0.820081	10.795113	0.092635	12
2	1.486915	29.214877	0.034229	0.672534	19.647986	0.050896	24
3	1.813130	48.787826	0.020497	0.551532	26.908062	0.037164	36
4	2.210915	72.654905	0.013764	0.452301	32.861916	0.030430	48
5	2.695970	101.758208	0.009827	0.370924	37.744561	0.026494	60
6	3.287442	137.246517	0.007286	0.304188	41.748727	0.023953	72
7	4.008677	180.520645	0.005540	0.249459	45.032470	0.022206	84
8	4.888145	233.288730	0.004287	0.204577	47.725406	0.020953	96
9	5.960561	297.633662	0.003360	0.167769	49.933833	0.020027	108
10	7.268255	376.095300	0.002659	0.137585	51.744924	0.019326	120
11	8.862845	471.770720	0.002120	0.112831	53.230165	0.018786	132
12	10.807275	588.436476	0.001699	0.092530	54.448184	0.018366	144
13	13.178294	730.697658	0.001369	0.075882	55.447059	0.018035	156
14	16.069495	904.169675	0.001106	0.062230	56.266217	0.017773	168
15	19.594998	1115.699905	0.000896	0.051033	56.937994	0.017563	180
16	23.893966	1373.637983	0.000728	0.041852	57.488906	0.017395	192
17	29.136090	1688.165376	0.000592	0.034322	57.940698	0.017259	204
18	35.528288	2071.697274	0.000483	0.028147	58.311205	0.017149	216
19	43.322878	2539.372652	0.000394	0.023082	58.615050	0.017060	228
20	52.827531	3109.651838	0.000322	0.018930	58.864229	0.016988	240
21	64.417420	3805.045193	0.000263	0.015524	59.068575	0.016929	252
22	78.550028	4653.001652	0.000215	0.012731	59.236156	0.016882	264
23	95.783203	5686.992197	0.000176	0.010440	59.373585	0.016843	276
24	116.797184	6947.831050	0.000144	0.008562	59.486289	0.016811	288
25	142.421445	8485.286707	0.000118	0.007021	59.578715	0.016785	300
26	173.667440	10360.046428	0.000097	0.005758	59.654512	0.016763	312
27	211.768529	12646.111719	0.000079	0.004722	59.716672	0.016746	324
28	258.228656	15433.719354	0.000065	0.003873	59.767648	0.016731	336
29	314.881721	18832.903252	0.000053	0.003176	59.809452	0.016720	348
30	383.963963	22977.837794	0.000044	0.002604	59.843735	0.016710	360
31	468.202234	28032.134021	0.000036	0.002136	59.871850	0.016702	372
32	570.921630	34195.297781	0.000029	0.001752	59.894907	0.016696	384
33	696.176745	41710.604725	0.000024	0.001436	59.913815	0.016691	396
34	848.911717	50874.703013	0.000020	0.001178	59.929321	0.016686	408
35	1035.155379	62049.322767	0.000016	0.000966	59.942038	0.016683	420
36	1262.259241	75675.554472	0.000013	0.000792	59.952466	0.016680	432
37	1539.187666	92291.259934	0.000011	0.000650	59.961018	0.016678	444
38	1876.871717	112552.303044	0.000009	0.000533	59.968032	0.016676	456
39	2288.640640	137258.438382	0.000007	0.000437	59.973784	0.016674	468
40	2790.747993	167384.879554	0.000006	0.000358	59.978500	0.016673	480

20.00%   ANNUAL COMPOUND INTEREST TABLES   20.00%
                                         EFFECTIVE RATE 20.00

---

	1 AMOUNT OF $1 AT COMPOUND INTEREST	2 ACCUMULATION OF $1 PER PERIOD	3 SINKING FUND FACTOR	4 PRESENT VALUE REVERSION OF $1	5 PRESENT VALUE ORD. ANNUITY $1 PER PERIOD	6 INSTALMENT TO AMORTIZE $1
YEARS						
1	1.200000	1.000000	1.000000	0.833333	0.833333	1.200000
2	1.440000	2.200000	0.454545	0.694444	1.527778	0.654545
3	1.728000	3.640000	0.274725	0.578704	2.106481	0.474725
4	2.073600	5.368000	0.186289	0.482253	2.588735	0.386289
5	2.488320	7.441600	0.134380	0.401878	2.990612	0.334380
6	2.985984	9.929920	0.100706	0.334898	3.325510	0.300706
7	3.583181	12.915904	0.077424	0.279082	3.604592	0.277424
8	4.299817	16.499085	0.060609	0.232568	3.837160	0.260609
9	5.159780	20.798902	0.048079	0.193807	4.030967	0.248079
10	6.191736	25.958682	0.038523	0.161506	4.192472	0.238523
11	7.430084	32.150419	0.031104	0.134588	4.327060	0.231104
12	8.916100	39.580502	0.025265	0.112157	4.439217	0.225265
13	10.699321	48.496603	0.020620	0.093464	4.532681	0.220620
14	12.839185	59.195923	0.016893	0.077887	4.610567	0.216893
15	15.407022	72.035108	0.013882	0.064905	4.675473	0.213882
16	18.488426	87.442129	0.011436	0.054088	4.729561	0.211436
17	22.186111	105.930555	0.009440	0.045073	4.774634	0.209440
18	26.623333	128.116666	0.007805	0.037561	4.812195	0.207805
19	31.948000	154.740000	0.006462	0.031301	4.843496	0.206462
20	38.337600	186.688000	0.005357	0.026084	4.869580	0.205357
21	46.005120	225.025600	0.004444	0.021737	4.891316	0.204444
22	55.206144	271.030719	0.003690	0.018114	4.909430	0.203690
23	66.247373	326.236863	0.003065	0.015095	4.924525	0.203065
24	79.496847	392.484236	0.002548	0.012579	4.937104	0.202548
25	95.396217	471.981083	0.002119	0.010483	4.947587	0.202119
26	114.475460	567.377300	0.001762	0.008735	4.956323	0.201762
27	137.370552	681.852760	0.001467	0.007280	4.963602	0.201467
28	164.844662	819.223312	0.001221	0.006066	4.969668	0.201221
29	197.813595	984.067974	0.001016	0.005055	4.974724	0.201016
30	237.376314	1181.881569	0.000846	0.004213	4.978936	0.200846
31	284.851577	1419.257883	0.000705	0.003511	4.982447	0.200705
32	341.821892	1704.109459	0.000587	0.002926	4.985372	0.200587
33	410.186270	2045.931351	0.000489	0.002438	4.987810	0.200489
34	492.223524	2456.117621	0.000407	0.002032	4.989842	0.200407
35	590.668229	2948.341146	0.000339	0.001693	4.991535	0.200339
36	708.801875	3539.009375	0.000283	0.001411	4.992946	0.200283
37	850.562250	4247.811250	0.000235	0.001176	4.994122	0.200235
38	1020.674700	5098.373500	0.000196	0.000980	4.995101	0.200196
39	1224.809640	6119.048200	0.000163	0.000816	4.995918	0.200163
40	1469.771568	7343.857840	0.000136	0.000680	4.996598	0.200136
41	1763.725882	8813.629408	0.000113	0.000567	4.997165	0.200113
42	2116.471058	10577.355290	0.000095	0.000472	4.997638	0.200095
43	2539.765269	12693.826348	0.000079	0.000394	4.998031	0.200079
44	3047.718323	15233.591617	0.000066	0.000328	4.998359	0.200066
45	3657.261988	18281.309940	0.000055	0.000273	4.998633	0.200055
46	4388.714386	21938.571928	0.000046	0.000228	4.998861	0.200046
47	5266.457263	26327.286314	0.000038	0.000190	4.999051	0.200038
48	6319.748715	31593.743577	0.000032	0.000158	4.999209	0.200032
49	7583.698458	37913.492292	0.000026	0.000132	4.999341	0.200026
50	9100.438150	45497.190751	0.000022	0.000110	4.999451	0.200022

25.00%   MONTHLY COMPOUND INTEREST TABLES   25.00%
                                   EFFECTIVE RATE 2.083

	1 AMOUNT OF $1 AT COMPOUND INTEREST	2 ACCUMULATION OF $1 PER PERIOD	3 SINKING FUND FACTOR	4 PRESENT VALUE REVERSION OF $1	5 PRESENT VALUE ORD. ANNUITY $1 PER PERIOD	6 INSTALMENT TO AMORTIZE $1	
MONTHS							
1	1.020833	1.000000	1.000000	0.979592	0.979592	1.020833	
2	1.042101	2.020833	0.494845	0.959600	1.939192	0.515679	
3	1.063811	3.062934	0.326484	0.940016	2.879208	0.347318	
4	1.085974	4.126745	0.242322	0.920832	3.800041	0.263155	
5	1.108598	5.212719	0.191838	0.902040	4.702081	0.212672	
6	1.131694	6.321317	0.158035	0.883631	5.585712	0.179028	
7	1.155271	7.453011	0.134174	0.865598	6.451310	0.155007	
8	1.179339	8.608283	0.116167	0.847932	7.299242	0.137001	
9	1.203909	9.787622	0.102170	0.830628	8.129870	0.123003	
10	1.228990	10.991531	0.090979	0.813676	8.943546	0.111812	
11	1.254594	12.220521	0.081830	0.797070	9.740616	0.102663	
12	1.280732	13.475115	0.074211	0.780804	10.521420	0.095044	
YEARS							MONTHS
1	1.280732	13.475115	0.074211	0.780804	10.521420	0.095044	12
2	1.640273	30.733120	0.032538	0.609654	18.736585	0.053372	24
3	2.100750	52.835991	0.018926	0.476021	25.151016	0.039760	36
4	2.690497	81.143837	0.012324	0.371679	30.159427	0.033157	48
5	3.445804	117.398588	0.008518	0.290208	34.070014	0.029351	60
6	4.413150	163.831191	0.006104	0.226596	37.123415	0.026937	72
7	5.652060	223.298892	0.004478	0.176927	39.507522	0.025312	84
8	7.238772	299.461053	0.003339	0.138145	41.369041	0.024173	96
9	9.270924	397.004337	0.002519	0.107864	42.822522	0.023352	108
10	11.873565	521.931099	0.001916	0.084221	43.957406	0.022749	120
11	15.206849	681.928746	0.001466	0.065760	44.843528	0.022300	132
12	19.475891	886.842782	0.001128	0.051346	45.535414	0.021961	144
13	24.943389	1149.282656	0.000870	0.040091	46.075642	0.021703	156
14	31.945785	1485.397684	0.000673	0.031303	46.497454	0.021507	168
15	40.913975	1915.870809	0.000522	0.024442	46.826807	0.021355	180
16	52.399819	2467.191326	0.000405	0.019084	47.083966	0.021239	192
17	67.110102	3173.284913	0.000315	0.014901	47.284757	0.021148	204
18	85.950026	4077.601254	0.000245	0.011635	47.441536	0.021079	216
19	110.078911	5235.787733	0.000191	0.009084	47.563949	0.021024	228
20	140.981536	6719.113709	0.000149	0.007093	47.659530	0.020982	240
21	180.559502	8618.856102	0.000116	0.005538	47.734160	0.020949	252
22	231.248253	11051.916141	0.000090	0.004324	47.792431	0.020924	264
23	296.166936	14168.012922	0.000071	0.003376	47.837929	0.020904	276
24	379.310342	18158.896417	0.000055	0.002636	47.873455	0.020888	288
25	485.794726	23270.146862	0.000043	0.002058	47.901193	0.020876	300
26	622.172638	29816.286623	0.000034	0.001607	47.922851	0.020867	312
27	796.836134	38200.134414	0.000026	0.001255	47.939762	0.020860	324
28	1020.533185	48937.592880	0.000020	0.000980	47.952966	0.020854	336
29	1307.029059	62689.394819	0.000016	0.000765	47.963275	0.020849	348
30	1673.953366	80301.761578	0.000012	0.000597	47.971325	0.020846	360
31	2143.884907	102858.475544	0.000010	0.000466	47.977611	0.020843	372
32	2745.741063	131747.571026	0.000008	0.000364	47.982518	0.020841	384
33	3516.557237	168746.747367	0.000006	0.000284	47.986350	0.020839	396
34	4503.765838	216132.760226	0.000005	0.000222	47.989342	0.020838	408
35	5768.115051	276821.522428	0.000004	0.000173	47.991678	0.020837	420
36	7387.406991	354547.535558	0.000003	0.000135	47.993502	0.020836	432
37	9461.285285	454093.693657	0.000002	0.000106	47.994927	0.020836	444
38	12117.366668	581585.600079	0.000002	0.000083	47.996039	0.020835	456
39	15519.093924	744868.508353	0.000001	0.000064	47.996907	0.020835	468
40	19875.793381	953990.082294	0.000001	0.000050	47.997585	0.020834	480

	1 AMOUNT OF $1 AT COMPOUND INTEREST	2 ACCUMULATION OF $1 PER PERIOD	3 SINKING FUND FACTOR	4 PRESENT VALUE REVERSION OF $1	5 PRESENT VALUE ORD. ANNUITY $1 PER PERIOD	6 INSTALMENT TO AMORTIZE $1
YEARS						
1	1.250000	1.000000	1.000000	0.800000	0.800000	1.250000
2	1.562500	2.250000	0.444444	0.640000	1.440000	0.694444
3	1.953125	3.812500	0.262295	0.512000	1.952000	0.512295
4	2.441406	5.765625	0.173442	0.409600	2.361600	0.423442
5	3.051758	8.207031	0.121847	0.327680	2.689280	0.371847
6	3.814697	11.258789	0.088819	0.262144	2.951424	0.338819
7	4.768372	15.073486	0.066342	0.209715	3.161139	0.316342
8	5.960464	19.841858	0.050399	0.167772	3.328911	0.300399
9	7.450581	25.802322	0.038756	0.134218	3.463129	0.288756
10	9.313226	33.252903	0.030073	0.107374	3.570503	0.280073
11	11.641532	42.566129	0.023493	0.085899	3.656403	0.273493
12	14.551915	54.207661	0.018448	0.068719	3.725122	0.268448
13	18.189894	68.759576	0.014543	0.054976	3.780098	0.264543
14	22.737368	86.949470	0.011501	0.043980	3.824078	0.261501
15	28.421709	109.686838	0.009117	0.035184	3.859263	0.259117
16	35.527137	138.108547	0.007241	0.028147	3.887410	0.257241
17	44.408921	173.635684	0.005759	0.022518	3.909928	0.255759
18	55.511151	218.044605	0.004586	0.018014	3.927942	0.254586
19	69.388939	273.555756	0.003656	0.014412	3.942354	0.253656
20	86.736174	342.944695	0.002916	0.011529	3.953883	0.252916
21	108.420217	429.680869	0.002327	0.009223	3.963107	0.252327
22	135.525272	538.101086	0.001858	0.007379	3.970485	0.251858
23	169.406589	673.626358	0.001485	0.005903	3.976388	0.251485
24	211.758237	843.032947	0.001186	0.004722	3.981111	0.251186
25	264.697796	1054.791184	0.000948	0.003778	3.984888	0.250948
26	330.872245	1319.488980	0.000758	0.003022	3.987911	0.250758
27	413.590306	1650.361225	0.000606	0.002418	3.990329	0.250606
28	516.987883	2063.951531	0.000485	0.001934	3.992263	0.250485
29	646.234854	2580.939414	0.000387	0.001547	3.993810	0.250387
30	807.793567	3227.174268	0.000310	0.001238	3.995048	0.250310
31	1009.741959	4034.967835	0.000248	0.000990	3.996039	0.250248
32	1262.177448	5044.709793	0.000198	0.000792	3.996831	0.250198
33	1577.721810	6306.887242	0.000159	0.000634	3.997465	0.250159
34	1972.152263	7884.609052	0.000127	0.000507	3.997972	0.250127
35	2465.190329	9856.761315	0.000101	0.000406	3.998377	0.250101
36	3081.487911	12321.951644	0.000081	0.000325	3.998702	0.250081
37	3851.859889	15403.439555	0.000065	0.000260	3.998962	0.250065
38	4814.824861	19255.299444	0.000052	0.000208	3.999169	0.250052
39	6018.531076	24070.124305	0.000042	0.000166	3.999335	0.250042
40	7523.163845	30088.655381	0.000033	0.000133	3.999468	0.250033

GLOSSARY OF TERMS

A–95 review. Comprehensive analysis of a proposed project by all affected governmental, environmental, citizens', or other groups.

Abstract of title. History of documents affecting title to real property.

Ad valorem. Latin for "according to value."

Acceleration clause. Mortgage contract clause that makes all payments due immediately if a scheduled payment is missed.

Accretion. Growth in size, especially by addition or accumulation; the addition of soil to land by gradual, natural deposits.

Accrued depreciation. Loss of value from any cause.

Adjusted tax basis. Original tax basis plus any capital improvements, less depreciation taken.

Adverse possession. Acquisition of title to real property by action of law through fulfilling certain statutory requirements.

Advocacy planner. One who defends the role of a client, usually in a public hearing.

Agency. Law governing the relationship between employers and their agents.

Amenities. The pleasant satisfactions, other than money, which are obtained in using real property.

Amortization. Systematic apportionment of costs, loan principal, or other input to discrete periods of time such as months, years, and so on.

Apportionment of basis. Division of income tax basis (or investment in asset) between depreciable improvements and nondepreciable land. This division must be acceptable to the Internal Revenue Service.

Assessed value. The dollar amount assigned to taxable property for tax purposes by the assessor or county property appraiser. It is usually a statutory percentage of market value.

537

Avulsion. The sudden transference of a piece of land from one person's property to another's without change of ownership, as by a change in the course of a stream.

Balloon payment. Amount of principal of loan remaining unamortized and outstanding at the end of the mortgage term.

Base line. An east/west line in the rectangular survey system from which land lying north or south is described in rows of townships.

Blanket mortgage. Mortgage lien secured by several land parcels.

BMIR (below-market interest rate). Subsidy by FHA to private lending institutions which lowers the amount of interest paid by low-income families on mortgage loans while giving lenders their market interest rate via the subsidy.

Boot. Cash or other nonreal estate assets exchanged for real property.

Break-even cash throwoff. Operating expenses plus mortgage payment divided by gross income.

Broker. In real estate, a person licensed to buy, sell, lease, rent, exchange, auction, or appraise real property as an agent for another, for compensation.

Building residual technique. An income capitalization methodology in which site value is known and net operating income is divided into site income and building income. Building income is discounted to present value and added to site value (given) to estimate the market value of the property.

Business risk. Possibility of losses caused by internal operating inefficiencies and external factors.

Capital gain. Net sale price less the adjusted base.

Capital improvement. A modification which adds to value of real estate, extends its useful life, or adapts the property to a different use.

Capital recapture. Expression of the manner in which the dollars of investment in a property are to be returned to investors. Stated as a rate or dollar amount per unit of time.

Capitalization. Process of converting a net operating income into value. Usually shown by the formula $V = I \div R$ where R is a predetermined return rate.

Capitalization rate. Percentage of return required from an investment which provides for investor income, principal and interest on debts, and loss in value from depreciation.

CARS (computer aided routing system). Personalized door-to-door public transportation service.

Cash flow aftertax. Cash throwoff minus income taxes paid or plus income tax deduction benefits.

Cash throwoff. Net operating income minus annual debt service on a mortgage loan.

Certificates of beneficial interest. Ownership shares of a trust or mutual fund.

Closing. Event at which title to real estate is transferred.

Closing costs. Expenses resulting from the purchase of real property.

Cognovit clause. Borrower confesses judgment or authorizes lender to secure a judgment that can be attached to borrower's property as a lien.

Collateral. Assets that are pledged to secure or guarantee the discharge of an obligation.

Comprehensive planning. The formulation of a land-use program for a city, county, or other region in terms of social, economic, governmental, political, and legal criteria.

Condemnation. A declaration that property is legally appropriated for public use; also, a declaration that something is unfit for use or service (example: the condemnation of a slum tenement).

Condominium. An arrangement under which tenants in an apartment building or in a complex of multiunit dwellings hold full title to their own units and joint ownership in the common grounds.

Conduit. A channel for conveying income from one entity to another wherein only the final recipient incurs the income tax consequences of the income.

Confiscation. Private property which is seized for the public treasury, usually as a penalty.

Conspicuous consumption. Purchasing and displaying a good primarily for its prestige value. An example is parking a Cadillac in front while keeping a Volkswagen in the garage.

Contract for sale. Legal document between buyer and seller which states the manner in which ownership rights are to be transferred and the purchase price.

Contract rent. Rental fixed by agreement among parties which may or may not be comparable to rentals of similar properties.

Conventional mortgage. Mortgage not insured by a public or private agency.

Conveyancing. Passage of title or ownership to real estate.

Cooperative. Ownership form in which a single property is divided into several use portions, with each user owning stock in a corporation that owns the property.

Corporeal. Ownership estates in real property that give the right to use and to occupy.

Cost of capital. Charge that must be paid to attract money into an investment project.

CPM. Certified Property Manager.

Cross-elasticity of demand. The effect of a change in the price of a good on the quantity supplied of another good.

Curable deterioration or obsolescence. The cost to correct the item of physical deterioration or functional obsolescence is matched by the value added to the property.

Dealer. Person or entity who cannot depreciate real estate held or take capital gains on real estate sold because the properties are his or her stock in trade.

Debt capital. Borrowed long-term money.

Debt service. Annual mortgage payment.

Debt service coverage. Requirement imposed by lender that earnings be a percentage or dollar sum higher than debt service.

Deed. Document transferring title to real property.

Deed covenants. Warranties made by a seller of property to protect the buyer against items such a liens, encumbrances, or title defects.

Deed of trust. Transfer of ownership interest to a trustee acting on behalf of a money lender. The trustee is usually instructed to supervise collection of the debt and return the trust deed to the borrower upon retirement of the debt.

Deed restrictions. Land-use constraints imposed in the deed passed from seller to buyer. These constraints then pass with the property in future transfers.

Defeasance clause. Prevents the mortgagee from foreclosing so long as the debtor fulfills the conditions of the mortgage.

Demographic. Characteristics of population, size, age, density, and economic distribution.

Depreciable basis. Portion of original tax basis representing value or cost of improvements.

Depreciation. (1) Loss in value from all causes; (2) apportionment of improvement cost to time periods.

Descent. Transfer of ownership upon death by action of law as stated in the state's Statute of Descent.

Development of regional impact (DRI). In Florida, any proposed development which is large enough to have a measurable effect upon the economy, environment, or public services of more than one county.

Devise. Transfer of ownership by means of a will.

Direct capitalization. Processing net operating income into value by dividing by an overall capitalization rate.

Direct sales comparison. A value estimation methodology utilizing the sales prices of comparable properties to which adjustments are made to reflect value-creating 'differences between the property under appraisal and the comparables.

Discount. Additional interest taken by a lender by lending less actual cash than the mortgage loan principal.

Discount rate. Relationship between dollars transmitted from a lender to a borrower and dollars that must be repaid by the borrower. If a lender advances $960 and the borrower must repay $1,000, the discount rate is $40/$1,000 = 4 percent.

Discounting. Process of converting any cash flow into present value at a selected rate of return. Based upon the idea that one would pay less than $1 today for the right to receive $1 at a future date.

Dower. That part of man's property which his widow inherits for life.

Earnest money. Money paid to evidence good faith when a contract of purchase is submitted to a property owner by a prospective purchaser.

Easement. A right or privilege that a person may have in another's land, as the right-of-way.

Economic base analysis. Study of a community's employment and income to forecast population changes and to plan for future expansion of basic and service employment.

Economic life. The length of time improvements (usually buildings) will produce a competitive return; land may have an infinite economic life.

Economic good. Any material or immaterial thing which satisfies human desire and which is relatively scarce, such that it commands a price in market exchange.

Economies of scale. The situation in which costs of production per unit are less for large firms than for smaller firms.

EDUCARE. Educational Foundation for Computer Applications in Real Estate.

Egress. A way out; exit.

Elastic demand. The phenomenon of a large response in quantity demanded to a small change in price.

Elasticity. Ability of supply of real estate to respond to price increases over a short period of time.

Ellwood technique. A mortgage-equity income capitalization methodology for estimating market value or determining investment value.

Embargo. An action by one government prohibiting trade with another country.

Encumbrance. A claim against title, such as a mortgage, tax lien, or mechanic's lien.

Environmental impact report (EIR). A detailed analysis of a project's potential effect upon environmental subsystems, such as air, water, sewer, and transportation of the area.

Environmental Protection Agency (EPA). Federal agency set up to protect the health and welfare of Americans by controlling environmental pollution hazards.

Equity. Share of property possessed by residual owners after allowing for borrowed funds.

Equity-dividend rate. Cash throwoff divided by the initial equity investment. May be before or after taxes.

Escalator clause. Permits a lender to vary the mortgage interest rate unilaterally, usually upward. Variance is not tied to an index.

Escheat. Reversion of real property to the government when the owner dies without a will or heirs.

Escrow. Real estate transactions are accomplished in escrow when the deed is delivered to a third party (escrow agent) for delivery to the buyer upon performance of a condition. The condition may be that title shows clear in the buyer. Escrow also refers to earmarked bank accounts in which are kept earnest money or other funds designated for a particular use.

Escrow agreement. Establishment of a fiduciary who holds documents, cash, or both until all elements of a transaction can be completed.

Estate. The quantity, duration, or extent of interest in real property.

Excess depreciation. Accelerated depreciation taken less depreciation that would have been taken using straight-line.

Exchange. Ownership of like-kind properties are transferred between two or more owners; can result in postponement of part or all of the capital gain tax for one or more of the parties to the exchange.

Exclusive listing. Agreement between seller of property and broker in which broker is assured a commission if the seller's property is sold by anyone other than the seller.

Exclusive right to sell listing. Agreement between seller of property and broker in which broker is assured a commission if the property is sold, no matter how or by whom it is sold.

FDIC. Federal Deposit Insurance Corporation.

Feasibility analysis. Study of the cash flow, profitability potential, and overall desirability of a project.

Fee simple absolute. The entire bundle of rights to use and control of real property.

FHA (Federal Housing Administration). Agency of the Department of Housing and Urban Development (HUD) which insures private lending institutions against loss on loans under various housing programs established by Congress.

FHLMC. Federal Home Loan Mortgage Association.

Filtering. Movement of people of one income group into homes that have recently dropped in price and that were previously occupied by persons in the next higher-income group.

Financial risk. Possibility of losses caused by the amount of and legal provisions concerning borrowed funds.

Firm advertising. Advertising intended to call attention to the firm and its specific offerings.

First user. First owner of the real estate to take tax depreciation on improvement value.

Fixture. Fittings or furniture of a property attached to a building and ordinarily, and legally, considered to be a part of the real estate.

Flat lease. Equal rental payments are made over the term of the lease.

Flow of funds accounts. Governmental system of accounting for movement of money throughout the economy.

Foreclosure. The act of depriving a borrower of the right to redeem a mortgage when regular payments have not been kept up.

Forfeiture. Anything lost or given up because of some crime, fault, or neglect of duty; specifically, a fine or penalty.

FNMA (Fanny Mae). Federal National Mortgage Association.

Freehold estate. An estate in land held for life or with the right to pass it on through inheritance.

Friction of space. The effort required to move persons and goods between geographically separate sites and to communicate between establishments; results in transfer costs.

FSLIC. Federal Savings and Loan Insurance Corporation.

Functional capability. The capacity of the structure to perform its intended use.

Functional obsolescence. Decline in value of property caused by changes in technology or by defects in design, layout, or size of building. Loss of a building's ability to perform its function.

Funds. Cash or any resource having value which is capable of being sold in order to buy some other asset.

GNMA (Ginny Mae). Government National Mortgage Association, a buyer in the secondary mortgage market for some programs of federally-sponsored loans.

Government (rectangular) survey. A method of providing a legal description for land involving the use of principal meridians, base lines, ranges, and townships.

Graduated (graded, step-up) lease. Rental payments are changed over term of lease as stipulated by contract.

Grantee. Purchaser of rights to real property.

Grantor. Person selling rights to real property.

Guaranteed mortgage. The Veteran's Administration idemnifies the lender for a portion of the mortgage debt in the event sale at foreclosure does not satisfy the entire obligation.

Gross income. Total dollars of revenue generated by an investment property.

Gross income multiplier (GIM). Expression of value based upon a multiple of project gross income.

Gross national product (GNP). Governmental system of accounting for annual output or production of the economy.

Gross equity yield. Aftertax cash flow plus mortgage principal repayment divided by equity investment.

Ground lease. A long-term lease of the site.

HHFA. Housing and Home Finance Agency.

Highest and best use. Vacant site—that use of the site which results in maximum productivity and return on investment. Improved property—existing improvements remain the highest and best use until a new use of the site generates sufficient value for the site to permit acquisition and demolition of the existing improvements.

Homestead.   Primary domicile, as declared by the head of a family and filed with county clerk of courts. Purpose is to exempt homestead from claims of creditors.

Homestead exemption.   A deduction from assessed value for purposes of real estate tax calculation, granted by state laws to the head of a family on property designated as his or her homestead.

IAAO.   International Association of Assessing Officials.

Imputed interest.   In an installment sale, the Internal Revenue Service establishes an interest payment schedule even when the principals to a transaction mention no interest. This causes part of the seller's capital gain to be treated as ordinary interest income.

Incorporeal.   The right to use the land of another or to remove minerals (profit) without having title and ownership.

Incurable deterioration or obsolescence.   The cost to correct the item of physical deterioration or functional obsolescence exceeds the value added to the property.

Inelastic demand.   The situation in which a change in price produces a proportionately smaller change in quantity demanded.

Ingress.   A place or means of entering; entrance.

Input-output accounts.   Measurement of products exported from a community and goods and services imported into the same community.

Installment sale.   Disposition of a property that permits deferral of capital gain over time provided certain rules are observed.

Institutional advertising.   Advertising intended to popularize an industry such as real estate.

Insured loan.   A loan for which an insurance premium is part of the monthly payments. If the loan is defaulted by the borrower, FHA (or the private insuror) will reimburse the lender from these premiums.

Insured mortgage.   Mortgage insured by the Federal Housing Administration or a private insurance agency such as Mortgage Guaranty Insurance Corporation, or Foremost Guaranty Corporation.

Intermediate title theory.   With respect to the rights conferred to the mortgagee, an intermediate title theory state lies between a title theory and lien theory state.

Internal rate of return.   The interest rate which discounts future cash flows and cash reversion from a project equal to the initial investment.

Investment holding period.   Length of time that the investor is assumed to hold the property before sale or exchange.

Investment property.   An asset owned for the purpose of earning an investment return as opposed to one held as stock in trade or one held for operation in the ordinary course of business.

Investment value.   Value to investors based upon their particular requirements.

Investor. One who holds real estate for the production of income; may take depreciation and capital gains.

Joint tenancy. Special ownership situation in which two or more owners hold equal shares, acquire shares concurrently, and have equal rights of possession. The rights of one owner pass to the other owner upon the one's death.

Kicker. Surcharge payment on a loan; any loan payment in excess of ordinary principal and interest.

Land contract. A method of conveying title to real property in which legal title does not pass to the buyer until the contract for deed is fulfilled. The contract for deed usually requires the purchase price to be paid in installments.

Lease. Contract providing for the transfer of a right to use real estate.

Leaseholds. Less than freehold estates that are usually considered to be personal property.

License. A formal permission to do some specified thing, especially some activity authorized by law; also, a document, permit, and so on, indicating such permission has been granted.

Level annuity. Equal amounts of income over time; discounting a level annuity assumes the annual recapture of investment in improvements is reinvested at the rate of discount.

Leverage. Use of money borrowed at a fixed rate of interest in an investment project, with the expectation of obtaining a higher rate of return on the equity investment as a result.

Lien. A claim against property whereby the property is security for a debt. The holder of the lien is entitled to sell the property to satisfy the debt.

Lien theory. State law permitting lenders to secure a lien against property as collateral for a loan.

Limited partnership. Ownership form in which a general partner performs all management functions and assumes all operating liabilities on behalf of passive investors known as limited partners.

Linkage. Time and distance relationship between a subject site and an important location such as a school, a shopping area, or a place of employment.

Liquidity. Relationship between a speedy sale price and the total number of dollars invested in a property.

Locational obsolescence. Decline in value of property caused by deterioration in the quality of its neighborhood; also known as economic obsolescence.

Locked-in period. Time period in which a mortgage loan borrower is not permitted by contract to prepay any of the loan principal.

Marginal. Increment of change.

Marginal cost. Increment of cost resulting from a given business decision.

Marginal revenue.   Increment of revenue resulting from a given business decision.

Market analysis.   Study of the market in which a developer might supply new real estate resources; study of the reasons why current prices are being paid.

Market rent.   Rental level ascertained by seeking out similar properties in a selected market area.

Market segmentation.   Identification and delineation of the submarket to be served.

Market value.   The price which a property will bring in a competitive market when there has been a normal offering time, no coercion, an arms-length transaction, typical financing, and informed buyers and sellers; exchange value.

Marketability.   Relationship between a speedy sale price and the current market value of a property.

Marketer.   Person engaged in marketing of a product or service; deals with the satisfaction of human needs on a broad scale.

Marketing myopia.   Failure to focus upon needs and people who have needs.

Metes and bounds.   A mete is a unit of measure (foot, mile); a bound is a boundary marker. A method of legally describing real estate.

Millage rate.   Expressed as tax dollars payable per $1,000 assessed value of property; for example, 15 mills implies $15 tax on each $1,000 of assessed property value.

Model city.   A comprehensive plan dealing with the social, economic, and physical problems of selected neighborhoods.

Monopolistic competition.   Control of a market by a number of parties who differentiate their services effectively.

Monopoly.   Control of a market by one party.

Monument.   A permanent marker indicating a corner of a parcel of land. A method of legally describing real estate.

Mortgage.   Written evidence of the right of a creditor to have property of a debtor sold upon default of the debt.

Mortgage bank correspondents.   Mortgage bankers in local communities who serve as agents of lenders in placing and servicing loans.

Mortgage constant.   Percentage of original loan balance represented by constant periodic mortgage payment. A payment of $100,000 per year on $1 million mortgage converts to a 10 percent constant.

Multiple listing.   Sharing of property sales listings by several real estate brokers.

Mutual ownership.   Used in Chapter 13 to mean a financial institution that is owned by its depositors.

NAR (National Association of Realtors).   An organization of real estate brokers which sponsors educational and research activities in all areas of the real estate industry.

Net listing. The seller specifies the amount which he or she will accept from the sale of his or her property, with the broker keeping all proceeds in excess of that amount.

Net income multiplier. Expression of value based upon a multiple of project net income.

Net operating income (NOI). Gross possible revenue minus an allowance for vacancies and for operating expenses.

Nonmarketable securities. Usually notes taken in an installment or deferred payment sale that contain restrictive clauses that hinder their marketability. This hindrance may be designed to reduce the seller's income tax liability.

Note (promissory). Document evidencing a debt and describing the terms by which the debt is to be paid.

Occupancy. The period during which a house or other real estate is kept in possession; in law, the taking possession of a previously unowned object, thus establishing ownership.

Oligopoly. Control of a market by a small number of participants.

100 percent site. Location past which the largest number of customers or space users pass (within a given market area).

Open-end mortgage. Permits additional sums to be borrowed on a single mortgage.

Open listing. Agreement between seller of property and broker which permits broker to receive a commission if he or she sells the seller's property. No exclusive protection is provided the broker.

Operating expense ratio. Relationship between operating expenses and project gross income.

Option. Contract given by a landowner to another person, giving the latter the right to buy (lease) the property at a certain price within a specified time.

Original tax basis. Cost of acquisition of the real estate or cost of construction of improvements new plus the acquisition cost of the site.

OSHA. Occupational Safety and Health Act of 1973.

Package mortgage. A debt secured by pledge of both real property and personalty (range, refrigerator, and so on).

Participation mortgage. Lender participates in profits or ownership as well as receiving contract interest.

Payback period. Length of time required for cash throwoff from project to equal amount of money invested.

Personal property (personalty). A chattel; an item of property that is neither the land nor is permanently attached to the land.

Physical characteristics. The nonlocational attributes of a property and its immediate surroundings.

Physical deterioration. Loss of utility resulting from impairment in physical condition.

Planned obsolescence. Attempting to increase sales by purposefully manufacturing goods or products to wear out or lose utility more quickly than would be necessary.

Plat. Drawing that shows boundaries, shape, and size of a parcel of land.

Plottage value. Value added to land by assembling small parcels into large tracts.

Points. Additional interest charged by the lender; one point equals 1 percent of the mortgage loan principal.

Police power. The constitutional authority of government to limit the exercise of private property rights as necessary to protect the health, safety, and welfare of all citizens. It constitutes the legal basis for zoning.

Predeveloped land. Land which has been zoned, planned, and made ready for immediate development.

Prepaid interest. Payment in advance of a portion of the total interest due over term of the loan.

Prepayment privilege. Mortgage contract clause permitting borrower to pay loan payments in advance of their due dates.

Prescription. One who uses the land of another for a period of time stated by law obtains the right of easement to the subject land.

Present value. Today's value derived by measuring all future benefits of an investment and converting those benefits into terms of today's dollars.

Prisoner's dilemma. The situation in which an individual owner's desire for action is restrained by surrounding owners' inaction, as in the case of neighborhood deterioration.

Private planning. Employed by landowner, developer, builder, or other non-government entity to prepare comprehensive plan for a parcel of land. Private planning frequently relies upon governmental agencies for provision of utilities, schools, garbage collection, highways, and other urban services.

Productivity. The relationship between output in the production process and the total of all inputs.

Property residual technique. An income capitalization methodology which discounts net operating income and the site reversion value to present value without separating NOI into income attributable to the building and to the site.

Proration. Allocation of costs or revenues between buyer and seller of real property.

Public planning. Process followed by a public agency to prepare community-wide comprehensive plans.

Purchase money mortgage. Mortgage taken by the seller of property as part of the purchase price.

Qualified fee. An estate in real property which terminates with the occurrence of a specified event.

Quantity survey. Method of estimating building replacement cost in which all elements of labor, materials, and overhead are priced and totaled to obtain building cost.

Quitclaim deed. Deed passing title with no warranties regarding quality and quantity of ownership passed by seller to buyer.

Range. A north/south line from which land lying east or west is described in columns of ranges.

Rapid write-off (accelerated) depreciation. All tax depreciation methods that permit taking depreciation expense greater than that which would have been taken using straight-line depreciation.

Real estate. Land, including the buildings or improvements, and its natural assets, as minerals, water, and so forth.

Real estate investment trust (REIT). A passive investment vehicle whose distributed earnings are taxed only to investors who receive them. Similar to a corporation in every way except for the permitted avoidance of double taxation of dividends.

Realtor. Registered trademark reserved for members of the National Association of Realtors; Realtors subscribe to an idealistic code of ethics which sets standards for conduct and integrity in all business dealings.

Real property. The legal rights to possession, use, and disposition of real estate.

Reappraisal lease. Lease having a clause calling for periodic reevaluation of rental levels.

Recapture (depreciation). The disallowance of a portion of rapid depreciation income tax deductions caused by disposing of the depreciable asset at a time when accumulative rapid depreciation exceeds the amount of depreciation that would have been taken during the holding period if straight-line depreciation had been used. Only the amount by which accumulative depreciation exceeds straight-line depreciation is disallowed.

Redlining. Delineation of geographical areas in which a lender does not make real property loans or in which loans are made on terms less favorable than those found in preferred areas.

RESPA. Real Estate Settlement Procedures Act of 1973.

Regressive tax. A tax which requires a proportionately higher percentage of lower-income taxpayers' incomes than higher-income taxpayers' incomes.

Rehabilitation. Restoration of a property to satisfactory condition without changing the plan, form, or style of a structure.

Reliction. Boundary of owned land extended by water receding and leaving dry land.

Remainder. The right held by someone other than the grantor to receive title to the property after an intervening estate, such as a life estate.

Reproduction cost. The cost at current prices of constructing a duplicate of the improvements.

Reserve for replacements. An operating expense account by which the prorated cost of replacing short-lived items is deducted from effective gross income.

Residual techniques. Assignment of a portion of income to part of an asset, with the remainder (or residual) flowing automatically to the rest of the asset. Also, the assignment of part of the income to cover debt payments with the balance accruing to the equity.

Return on investment (ROI). A percentage relationship between the price paid by an investor and the stream of income dollars obtained from the investment.

Reversion. The return of an estate to the grantor and his or her heirs by operation of law after the period of grant is over.

Reversion value. Worth of the site at a time when improvements value is zero (end of their economic life); worth of the property (improvements and site) at the end of an investment holding period.

Right-of-way. Right to passage, as over another's property; also, land over which a public road, an electric power line, and so forth, passes.

Risk-adjusted rate of return. A return on investment from which the premium for business risk has been removed.

Salvage value. Estimated market value of improvements or other depreciable assets at the end of their useful life.

Secondary financing market. A market composed of purchasers of mortgages from institutions that originate mortgage loans to individual users. The principal entities in the secondary home loan market are the Federal National Mortgage Association (FNMA), the Federal Home Loan Mortgage Corporation (FHLMC), and the Government National Mortgage Association (GNMA).

Section 8 subsidized occupancy program. A program of rent supplements established in 1975 by HUD and allocated to local governments.

Section 1231 property. Includes property used in one's trade or business and many income properties held by investors; property must be held more than six months.

Settlement. Final accounting in a real estate transaction which shows amounts owed by seller and buyer and to whom payable; closing.

Site residual technique. An income capitalization methodology in which building cost is assumed to equal building value. Net operating income is divided into building income and site income, which is capitalized into site value and added to building value (cost) to obtain market value of the property.

Social class. Group of people delineated by selected social characteristics.

Special assessment. A charge made by government against properties to defray costs of public improvements which especially benefit the properties assessed.

Specifications. Restrictions imposed on the quantity and quality of materials and labor to be used in a construction project.

Statement of consideration. Statement in a deed that affirms the fact that the purchaser actually paid something for the property.

Statute of frauds. Legal requirement that all matters affecting title to real estate must be in writing if they are to be enforced by a court of law.

Statutory redemption period. Time permitted delinquent borrowers to cure their deficiencies before their property is taken permanently from them.

Straight-line capitalization. Process of discounting future income into present value given the assumption that the investment in improvements is recaptured in equal annual amounts that are not reinvested.

Straight-term loan. No repayment of the principal of the loan until the due date.

Subdividing. Separation of a parcel of land into smaller parcels. Selling more than five parcels in a single year can cause investors to become dealers in real property.

Submarket (housing). A collection of housing units considered to be close substitutes by a relatively homogeneous group of households; similar housing units that provide equal utility or satisfaction.

Surcharge. An additional amount added to the usual charge.

Syndicate. Group of individuals, corporations, or trusts who pool money to undertake economic ventures. The syndicate can take the form of a corporation, a trust, a partnership, a tenancy in common, or any other legal ownership form.

Syndication. The formation of an association of individuals or corporations to carry out a financial venture.

TACV. Tracked air-cushion vehicle.

Tax abatement. The reduction, forgiveness, or cancellation of a tax.

Tax credit. Allowable reduction in the amount of income tax owed.

Tax deferral (postponement). The payment of the tax bill is deferred to a later date (but not avoided).

Tax preference items. Include excess depreciation and the deductible one-half of any net long-term capital gain; under federal income tax rules, tax preference items greater than a certain amount are liable for a surtax.

Tax shelter. Net loss that can be deducted from other income for income tax purposes.

Tax shelters. Legally permissible methods of reducing or postponing the burden of the federal income tax, including accelerated depreciation, capital gains, exchanges, and so on.

Taxable income. Gross possible revenue minus an allowance for vacancies, operating expenses, depreciation, and interest paid on borrowed funds.

Title. Right of ownership, especially of real estate.

Title insurance. Insurance paying monetary damages for loss of property from superior legal claims not expected in the policy.

Title theory.   State law permitting lenders to secure title to property as collateral for a loan.

Transfer characteristics.   The movement of goods, persons, and messages among geographically separated sites and establishments that result in transfer costs.

Transfer costs.   Costs of overcoming the friction of space.

Torren's certificate.   Method of providing evidence of ownership to real property.

Transfer payments.   A redistribution of private sector income via the government to citizens or groups, in an attempt to achieve equity.

Trust deed.   Conveyance of contingent title to a trustee who holds it as security for the lender; used in some states in lieu of a mortgage.

Trustee.   One who administers property held in trust for another.

Unit-in-place costs.   Method of estimating building replacement cost in which quantities of materials are costed on an in-place basis and summarized to obtain building cost.

Urban decay.   Falling of urban centers to a condition of disrepair.

Urban renewal.   Process of renovation or rehabilitation of deteriorated areas within a city.

Useful life.   Period of time permitted by the Internal Revenue Service for computing annual depreciation expense.

VA.   Veterans Administration.

Value.   A ratio at which goods exchange; the relative worth of an object, usually measured in money terms.

Value in exchange.   Price an investment asset is expected to bring based upon comparable market transactions.

Value in use.   Price an investor would pay based upon his or her personal assessment of the investment asset's merit.

V/STOL.   Vertical and short takeoff and landing aircraft.

Warehousing (loans).   Provision of funds to a mortgage banker so that he or she may increase the inventory of mortgage loans. Typically a commercial bank does the warehousing of loans.

Yield.   Relationship between income or cash received from an investment and the value of the capital producing the income or cash.

Zoning.   The regulation of land use, population density, and building size by district. May be viewed as a phase of comprehensive planning in which the plan's implementation is enforced through police power.

INDEX

A

Abstract, 207–8
Acceleration clause, 209
Ad valorem tax, 386
Administration
  functional activities for, 9–11
  macro, 8
  micro, 6–8
Advertising, 277–78
Aftertax equity dividend rate, 100–102
Agency, law of, 282
Amenities, 35
American Institute of Planners, 365
American Institute of Real Estate Appraisers, 10
American Society of Real Estate Counselors, 11
Amortizatzion of $1 table, 507–36
Amortized loan, 209
Annuity method, 64–66
Appraisal Institute of Canada, 10
Appraising, 10, 57–90
Average aftertax return on equity, 100–102

B

Benefit-cost ratios, 404–5, 439
Block grants, 405–6
Break-even cash throw-off ratio, 99
Brokerage, 190–227
Brokers
  economic justification for, 136
  licensing of, 14

Building codes, 13–14
Building residual technique, 69–71
Bureau of Public Roads, 453
Bureaucracy, 376
Business risk, 23–24
Buying process, 270–74
  analysis, 274
  nature of, 270–71
  roles, 272–74
  stages
    felt need, 271
    postpurchase feelings, 272
    prepurchase activity, 271
    purchase decision, 272
    use behavior, 272

C

Capital gains and losses, 240–46
Capitalization; see Income capitalization
Capitalization rates, 66, 72
  components of, 59
  estimation of, 66
Cash flow, 93
Cash throw-off, 93
Certified Property Manager (CPM), 11
Clean Air Act, 416
Closing costs, 196–200
Coastal Zone Management Act, 418–20
Cognovit clause, 211
Commercial banks, 323–26
Commission (fee), 224–25
Community development, 401–6
  direct block grants, 405–6
  rehabilitation and conservation, 405

Community development—*Cont.*
  urban renewal, 402–5
    problems, 402–5
    rationale, 402
Community property, 184
Comparison method, 81–82
Compound interest tables, use of, 494–505
Computer aided routing system (CARS), 452
Computers, 104–7
Condominiums, 184, 341
Constraints upon real estate decisions, 12–16
  eminent domain, 16
  escheat, 16
  police power, 12–15
    building codes, 13–14
    licensing of brokers, 14
    open housing laws, 14–15
    zoning, 12–13
  taxation, 15
Construction, 299–312
  administrative problems and considerations, 308–12
    financing, 309–10
    labor unions and productivity, 311–12
    market analysis, 308–9
    OSHA, 312
    taxation, 310–11
    zoning, 311
  economic role, 299–300
  functions, 301–4
    controlling, 303–4
    organizing, 302–3
    planning, 301–2
  industry structure, 300–301
  process, 301
  role of the builder, 304–8
Construction period interest, 239
Consulting, 10–11
Conveyancing functions, 195–225
  closing the sale, 196–200
  making an offer, 191–93
  reaching agreement, 193–96
  searching title, 207–8
  securing funds, 209–18
  transferring ownership, 200–207
Cooperatives, 341–42
Corporation, 185
Cost, 50
  of capital, 24
Cost analysis, 80–86
  accrued depreciation, 82–84
    obsolescence
      functional, 82–83
      locational, 83–84

Cost analysis—*Cont.*
    physical deterioration, 82
  estimation of, 81–82
  example, 84–86
  penalty
    curable, 83
    incurable, 83
  relation to value, 50, 80–81
  reproduction cost, 81–82
Cost benefit analysis, 432–33
Counseling, 10–11
Curable penalty, 83
Curtesy, 179

D

Debt service, 95–96, 336–40
  coverage ratio, 99
Deeds, 204
  essentials, 207
  requirements, 204–7
  types, 204–6
    bargain and sale, 206
    officer's, 206
    quitclaim, 204–6
    warranty
      general, 204
      special, 206
Defeasance clause, 214
Demand determinants, 137–51
  income
    community, 148–50
    national, 145–46
    regional, 147–48
  need, 137–38
  price structure, 150–51
  societal trends, 142–43
  values and attitudes, 143–45
Depreciation, 82–84
  recapture of excess, 243–44
  tax, 230–37
Dial-A-Ride, 452
Direct sales comparison, 77–78
  adjustments, 78
  grid analysis, 78
Discounting, 494–505
Dower, 178–79
Downs, Anthony, 377

E

Easements, 181–82
Economic base analysis, 148–50, 486–92
Economic life, 62–63
Economic theory of democracy, 377
Economies of scale, 431

Elasticity, 132–33
Eminent domain, 16
Energy crisis, 415
Environmental impact statements, 419, 421
Environmental Protection Agency, 8, 416
Environmentally endangered lands, 422
Escheat, 16
Equity
    build-up, 317
    dividend rate, 100–102
Escalator clause, 211
Escrow agent, 225–26
Estate, 200
Evidence of title, 206–8
Exchanging properties, 226
Externalities, 423, 428–29

F

Fair housing laws, 14–15, 467–69
Feasibility analysis, 162–65
Federal Aviation Administration, 453
Federal Highway Administration, 451
Federal Home Loan Bank Board, 8, 321, 399
Federal Home Loan Bank System, 322, 343
Federal Home Loan Mortgage Corporation, 298–99, 347–48
Federal Housing Administration (FHA), 217, 343, 349, 395–401
Federal housing programs, impact of, 408–9
    income redistribution effects, 408–9
    provision of adequate housing, 407–8
Federal National Mortgage Association, 8, 298–99, 347–48
Federal Railroad Administration, 453
Federal Reserve Board, 8, 343–46, 349
Federal Reserve System, 343–46
Federal Savings and Loan Insurance Corporation (FSLIC), 320, 349 395, 399
Fee simple estate, 175–76
Fee tail estate, 176
FHA Housing Market Analysis, 480–85
Filtering, 157–58, 288, 403–6
Financial ratios, 99
    break-even cash throw-off, 99
    debt service coverage, 99
    loan to value, 99
    operating, 99
Financial risk, 24
Financing, 10, 209–18, 315–53
    adjustment, 77–79
    expense, 94–7, 99

Financing—*Cont.*
    flow of funds, 316–31
    government influence on, 342–50
        low-income housing, 350, 394–411
        mortgage insurance and guarantee, 349–50
        secondary market activities, 346–48
        supervision and insurance, 348–49
        supply of funds and interest rates, 343–46
        taxation, 350
    institutional lenders, 320–31
    instruments, 340
    lending and borrowing decisions, 331–40
    necessity for, 315–16
    risk, 342–43
    specialized arrangements, 340–42
        condominiums, 341
        cooperatives, 341–42
        need for, 340–41
        real estate investment trusts, 326–30
        syndicates, 342
    types of loans, 333–34
        acquisition and development, 333
        construction, 333–34
        land acquisition, 333
        permanent, 334
Fish and Wildlife Act, 418
Fixtures, 174–75
Flow of funds, 146
Foremost Guaranty Corp., 350
Forfeiture clause, 190
Friction of space, 122
Friedman, Milton, 374–76
Functional obsolescence, 82–83
Future worth of $1 per period table, 506–36
Future worth of $1 table, 506–36
Futures market for mortgages, 299

G

Galbraith, J. K., 375
Government involvement, 371–84
    economic principles, 372–73
    extent, 375–76
    role of government, 372–76
        public goods, 374–75
        technical monopolies, 374
        transfer payments, 373–74
Government National Mortgage Association, 8, 298–99, 347–48
Ground leases, 219
Gross income multiplier, 98
Gross national product, 145–46
Gross yield on equity, 100–102

H

Harvey, Robert O., 377
Highest and best use, 51–54
  improved sites, 53–54
  vacant site, 51–53
Home counseling service, 397
Homeowner tax factors, 251-56
Homestead, 179–80
Housing, 394–401
  subsidized, 400–401
  unsubsidized, 395–400
Housing allowance program, 407–8
Housing and Community Development
    Act of 1974, 398–99
Housing market, 153–58
  conceptualizing, 153–58
  filtering, 157–58
  submarkets, 154–58

I

Income, 68–69, 92–94
  flows, 92–94
  psychic, 34–36
  stability, 25
Income capitalization, 58–77
  building residual technique, 70–71
  direct capitalization, 72
  discounting, 494–505
  Ellwood method, 72–75
  expense estimation, 61–62
  highest and best use, 51–54
  inputs, 59–68
    capitalization rates, 66
    net operating income, 59–62, 68–69
    pattern of income, 64–66
    remaining economic life, 62–63
    reversion, 66–68
  mortgage-equity techniques, 72–74
  nature of approach, 58
  overall rate, 72
  process, 59
  property residual technique, 69–71
  relation to other approaches, 77–78
  revenue estimation, 60
  site residual technique, 71–72
Income flows, 92–94
  cash flow, 93
  cash throw-off, 93
  net operating income, 59–62, 68–69,
      92–93
Income tax, 228–57
  considerations in, 228–29
  nature of, 228–29
Incurable penalty, 83
Input-output analysis, 146–47
Institute of Real Estate Management, 11

Integrated development, 293–94
Internal rate of return, 102–3
Investment, 19–38, 91–111
  analysis case, 473–77
  applicability of approach, 34–36
    nonincome producing properties, 34–
        36
    social problems, 36
  approach, 19–37
  calculation, 91–111
    role of computers, 104–7
    varying assumptions, 103–4
  criteria, 23–25, 97–103
    business risk, 23–24
    cost of capital, 24
    financial risk, 24
    liquidity, 25
    return, 23
    stability of income, 25
  interest limitation, 238
  objectives
    profit, 21
    service, 21–22
    social, 22
  premises, 19–20
  price calculation, 91–97
  process, 11–12
  value, 47–49
    from aftertax cash flow, 94–95
    from appraisal methodologies, 94
    and profitability, 92

J–K

Joint tenancy, 183–84
Kicker, 337–40

L

Labor unions and productivity, 311–12
Land
  contract, 220
  development, 288–99
    activities, 290–92
      financing, 292
      preparation, 291–92
      procurement, 291
      subdividing, 292
      zoning, 291
    plans and limitations, 289–90
      building and housing codes, 290
      master plan, 290
      sewer extensions, 290
      transportation plans and facilities,
          290
      zoning, 289–90
    role
      of the developer-investor, 295–98

Land—*Cont.*
  role—*Cont.*
    of the development lender, 298
    of secondary financing market, 298–99
    significance to urban development, 292–95
    integrated development, 293–94
    land planning and control, 294–95
  sales, 265–66
    developed, 266
    improved, 266
    predeveloped, 265–66
    resale, 266
    unimproved acreage, 265
  value, 66–68
Land use patterns, 26–28
Leased public housing, 397
Leasehold estates, 180–81
Leases, 218–19
  contents, 218–19
  payment plans, 219
  specialized arrangements, 219
Leasing, 267
Legal descriptions, 169–74
  government or rectangular survey, 171–73
  metes and bounds, 170
  monuments, 170–71
  recorded plat, 173–74
  street and number, 169–70
Leverage, 310
License (privilege), 182
Licensing of brokers, 14
Liens, 211–16
  priority, 215–16
  theory, 211–14
  types, 214–15
Life estates, 178–80
Life insurance companies, 322–23
Linkages, 123–26
Liquidity, 25
Listings, 221–25
  exclusive agency, 221
  exclusive right to sell, 221
  multiple, 223–24
  net, 221–23
  open, 221
Loan to value ratio, 99
Location, 122–28
  analysis of, 123–27
Location adjustment, 77–79
Locational obsolescence, 83–84

M

Management, 11
Marginal cost pricing, 429–30

Marine Protection Research and Sanctuaries Act, 419
Market
  analysis, 159–62
  definition, 130
  functions, 132–34
  imperfections, 134–35
  models, 134–36
    monopolistic competition, 135, 275
    oligopoly, 275–76
    perfect competition, 40, 134
    pure monopoly, 135–36
Market conditions adjustment, 77–79
Marketing, 9–10, 261–84
  definition, 261
  leasing, 267
  legal framework, 282
  mix, 262
  relationship to brokerage, 263
  strategy, 263–70
    land sales, 265–66
      developed, 266
      improved, 266
      predeveloped, 265–66
      resale, 266
      unimproved acreage, 265
    properties versus service, 274–75
    segmentation, 252–70
    specialized services, 267–68
Mass transit, 450–51
Median location, hypothesis of, 446
Metes and bounds, 170
Model cities program, 397
Monopolistic advantage
  advertising, 277–78
  nature of, 276–77
  public relations, 278–79
  quality of personnel, 279–80
  selling technique, 280–82
Monopolistic competition, 135–36
Monopolists, 275
Monopoly, 134–35
Monuments, 170–71
Mortgage bankers, 330–31
Mortgage constant, 95–96, 336–40
Mortgage-equity techniques, 72–74
Mortgage Guaranty Insurance Corporation, 350
Mortgage lenders, 316–31
  commercial banks, 323–26
  life insurance companies, 322–23
  mortgage bankers, 330–31
  mutual savings banks, 326
  REITs, 326–30
  savings and loan associations, 320–22
Mortgages, 211–18
  blanket, 216
  conventional, 217–18

Mortgages—*Cont.*
  guaranteed, 217–18
  insured, 217–18
  open-end, 216
  package, 216
  participation, 216–17
Motivation of investors, 107–8
Multipliers, 98–99
  gross income, 98
  net income, 98
Mutual savings banks, 326

N

National Association of Realtors, 1, 10, 11
National Environmental Policy Act, 417, 419
National Housing Act, 395–402
National housing goal, 395–96
National housing partnership, 397
National Materials Policy Act, 417
Negative income tax, 407–8
Neighborhood effects, 374
Net income multiplier, 98
Net operating income, 59–62, 68–69
Noise Control Act, 417
Nonincome producing properties, 34–36
Northeast Corridor Act, 454
Note, 209–11

O

Objectives, 20–23
  profit, 21
  service, 21–22
  social, 22
Office of High Speed Ground Transportation, 453
Off-site improvements, 118, 120
Oligopolists, 275–76
Open housing laws, 14–15, 467–69
Operating and interest expenses (tax), 238–39
Operating ratio, 99
Option, 225
OSHA, 312
Overall capitalization rate, 72, 100–102
Ownership rights, 175–84
  freehold estates of inheritance, 175–78
    fee simple, 175–76
    fee tail, 176
    qualified fee, 176–78
  leasehold estates, 180–81
  life estates, 178–80

Ownership rights—*Cont.*
  life estates—*Cont.*
    conventional, 178
    legal, 178–80
      curtesy, 179
      dower, 178–79
      homestead, 179–80
Ownership strategy, 184–87

P

Partnership, 184–86
Payback period, 100–102
Personal property, 174
Personnel, quality, 279–80
Physical characteristics
  adjustments, 77–79
  analysis, 119–22
Physical deterioration, 82
Planning, 354–67, 419–23
  comprehensive, 354–58
  private, 362–65
  state land-use programs, 419–23
  trends, 365
Planning commission, 359, 470–72
PMI, Inc., 350
Points and discounts, 238–39
Police power, 12–15
Population, 137–42
  growth, 138
  shifts, 138–42
Prepaid interest, 239
Prepayment clause, 209–11
Present value of $1 per period table, 506–36
Present value of $1 table, 506–36
President's Committee on Urban Housing, 395
Price fixing, 276
Processing costs, 116–22
Production, 9, 285–314
  construction, 299–312
  economic significance, 285–87
  land development, 288–99
  nature of, 9, 285
Productivity, 115–27
  elements of
    nature of, 115
    physical characteristics, 115–22
    transfer characteristics (location), 115–17, 122–27
Profit, 21
Profit (property right), 182
Profitability ratios, 100–102
  aftertax equity dividend rate, 100–102
  average aftertax return on equity, 100–102

Profitability ratios—*Cont.*
  equity dividend rate, 100–102
  gross yield on equity, 100–102
  internal rate of return, 102–3
  overall capitalization rate, 100–102
  payback period, 100
Property residual technique, 69–71
Property tax, 385–93
  calculation, 386–87
  establishing rate for a jurisdiction, 387
  issues and problems, 388–92
  special assessments, 388
Proportionality, 32–34
  of land uses, 32
  in relation to markets, 33
  of structures, 33–34
Public housing, 396
Public relations, 278–79
Public sector, 371–84
  decision-makers, 376
  decision-making process, 376–81
    behavioral aspects, 376–78
    institutional aspects, 380–81
    power and influence, 378–79
  economic analysis in, 381–83
Pure competition, 40, 134

Q

Qualified fee estate, 176–78
Quantity survey method, 81

R

Ratcliff, Richard U., 91
Real estate
  administration, 6–11, 461–62
  analytical approach, 19–20, 460–61
  businesses, 9–11, 461
  conveyancing, 190–227
  definition of, 5, 168–69
  distinguished from real property, 5, 168–69
  economic importance of, 4
  market characteristics of, 41–46
    few buyers and sellers, 45
    large economic size, 43–45
    long economic life, 43
    physical immobility, 41–43
  nature of, 4–6
  prognosis for, 462–64
    institutional factors, 462–64
    theory and concepts, 462
Real estate investment trusts (REITs), 185–86, 326–30
Real Estate Settlement Procedures Act of 1974 (RESPA), 200
Real property, 169

Realtron Corporation, 104–7
Recorded plat, 173–74
Rectangular survey system, 171–73
Rehabilitation and conservation, 396, 405
Remainder, 179
Rent supplements, 397
Reproduction cost, 81–82
  comparison, 81–82
  quantity survey, 81
  unit-in-place costs, 81
Return on investment, 23
Reversion, 66–68, 177
Riparian rights, 203–4
River and Harbor Act, 418
Role of builder, 304–8

S

Safe Drinking Water Act, 418
Savings and loan association, 320–22
Section 8 program, 401
Section 101, 401
Section 202, 401
Section 207, 400
Section 220, 400
Section 221(d)(2), 400
Section 221(d)(3), 401
Section 231, 400
Section 232, 400
Section 234, 400
Section 235, 397, 401
Section 236, 397, 401
Section 237, 397
Selling, 280–82
Sinking fund, 65
  factor table, 506–36
Site plan, 362–65
Site residual technique, 71–72
Slum clearance, 396
Social class, 143–45
Social problems, 36
Society of Real Estate Appraisers, 10
Solid Waste Disposal Act, 417
Statutes of Frauds, 190
Statutory redemption, 211
St. Lawrence Development Corporation, 453
Subdividing, 292
Submarkets, 154–58
Sunshine State Parkway, 443
Supply determinants, 151–53
  anticipations of demand, 151
  availability
    and price of financing, 152
    and prices of land and utilities, 151–52
    and prices of materials and labor, 152–53

Supply determinants—*Cont.*
 taxes, 153
 utilization of existing resources, 151
Supply elasticity, 132–33

T

Tax
 deferral, 246–51
  exchanges, 246–49
   apportionment of basis, 247–48
   boot, 246–47
   depreciation recapture, 248
  installment sale, 249–51
   gross selling price, 249–50
   imputed interest, 250
   marketable bonds, 250
   mortgage assumed, 250
   qualifying, 249
 factors, 230–46
  affecting homeowner, 251–56
   avoidance of tax on capital gain,
    254–55
   capital gain on disposition, 252–53
   deferment of the capital gain,
    253–54
   mortgage interest and property
    tax, 251–52
   tax credit for purchase, 255–56
  capital gains, 240–46
   defined, 240
   long-term loss, 242–43
   recapture of excess depreciation,
    243–44
   tax bill, 241–42
   tax preference items, 245–46
  depreciation, 230–37
   basis, 231–32
   election of method, 236–37
   leasehold, 237
   methods, 232–35
   rapid write-off, 237
  operating and interest expenses, 238–
   39
   construction period interest and
    real estate taxes, 239
   investment interest limitation, 238
   points and discounts, 238–39
   prepaid interest, 239
  preference items, 245–46
  property, 385–93
  shelters, 93–94, 230
Taxation, 15, 228–57, 385–93
Tenancy in common, 183, 186
Tenancy by the entireties, 184
Terms of sale adjustment, 77–79
Title, 200–203, 206–8

Title insurance, 208
Torrens certificate, 208
Transfer of ownership, 200–204
 adverse possession, 203
 descent, 203
 devise, 203
 foreclosure, 203
 from nature (riparian rights), 203–4
 prescription, 203
 private grant, 203
Transportation, 437–59
 nature of system, 437–38
 regional effects, 443–44
 relation to land use, 444–49
  concentric circle hypothesis, 444–45
  empirical studies, 446–49
  hypothesis of median location, 446
  sector theory, 445
  systems of activities, 445–46
 relation to values, 439–43
 traffic artery as an urban land use, 449
 user benefits, 438–39
Transportation problem, 449–56
 alleviation of, 451–56
  intergovernmental cooperation, 452–
   54
  planning, 454
  pricing alternative modes, 456
  regional planning, 454–56
  technological development, 451–52
 nature of, 449–51
Trust, 184–86
Trust deed, 214

U

Unit-in-place method, 81–82
Urban growth, theories of, 28–32
 axial, 29
 concentric circle, 29
 multiple nuclei, 30
 sector, 29–30
Urban Mass Transportation Administra-
  tion, 453
Urban renewal, 402–5
U.S. Army Corps of Engineers, 418–20
U.S. Coast Guard, 453
U.S. Department of Housing and Urban
  Development, 8, 343, 347, 349
 Office for Community Development,
  350
 Office for Housing Management, 350
 Office for Housing Production and
  Mortgage Credit, 350
U.S. Department of Transportation, 452–
  53
U.S. Treasury, 343, 346–47

V

Value, 39–56
  central idea, 39
  definition of, 46
  as a market concept, 40–46
  measurement of, 57–90
    cost analysis, 80–86
    direct sales comparison, 77–79
    income capitalization, 58–77
  in a perfectly competitive market, 40
  relation
    to money, 45–46
    to price and cost, 50
  types of, 47
Variable rate mortgage, 211
Veterans Administration (VA), 217–18,
  299, 343
V/STOL, 451–52

W

Warehousing loans, 325–26
Water Pollution Control Act, 416, 419
Worth
  future, 494–97
  present, 497–500

Z

Zabel v. *Tabb*, 419
Zoning, 12–13, 289–90, 291, 358–62, 423
  administration, 359–61
  administrative structure for, 470–72
  issues and problems, 360–62
  legal basis, 358–59
  nature of, 12–13
  objective, 358

This book has been set in 10 and 9 point Caledonia, leaded 2 points. Part numbers and titles are in 24 point (small) Helvetica; chapter numbers are in 16 and 30 point Helvetica and chapter titles are in 18 point Helvetica. The size of the type page is 27 x 45½ picas.